Der Zweck dieses Le
Leser auf einen Blic
jedes verstorbenen Sc
onisten, Künstlers, P
kers oder anderer
einflußreicher Persön

Jeder Abschnitt – der ... ..
Nachschlagen einen Zeitraum von 25
Jahren umfaßt – ist:
(a) alphabetisch angeordnet,
(b) in zweckmäßige Rubriken unterteilt,
(c) mit einer Einleitung versehen, die
  wichtige Ereignisse, Staatsoberhäup-
  ter und Päpste dieses Zeitabschnitts
  sowie Persönlichkeiten, die den Lauf
  der Geschichte beeinflußten, ent-
  hält.

Ein Nachschlagewerk von beträcht-
lichem Wert für den Biographen, Histori-
ker, Studenten und jeden Leser, durch das
sich nicht nur die Zeitgenossen eines
Menschen und sein Geburts– und Todes-
jahr leicht feststellen lassen, sondern auch,
wer vor und nach ihm gelebt hat und
somit sein Denken und sein Werk beein-
flussen konnte oder von ihm beeinflußt
werden konnte.

Lo scopo di questo dizionario è di mostrare
al lettore, dando solo uno sguardo, i
contemporanei di qualsiasi scrittore, com-
positore, artista, filoso, storico od altra
autorevole personalità creativa o in-
fluenziale.

Ciascuna sezione (che per facilitare il
riferimento è stata suddivisa in periodi di
25 anni) è:
(a) Messa in ordine alfabetico
(b) Suddivisa sotto titoli adeguati
(c) Preceduta dagli avvenimenti più
  importanti, dai Capi di Stato al
  potere e Papi regnanti dell'epoca,
  da autorevoli personalità che sono
  state responsabili o che hanno influenzato il corso della Storia.

Una pubblicazione di riferimento di
grande assistenza sia al biografo, allo
storico, allo studente che al lettore
normale, e che permette un confronto
semplice, non solo con i contemporanei e
l'anno di nascita e di morte di una personalità, ma pure chi lo ha preceduto e
successo, e perciò, avrebbe potuto in-
fluenzare o essere influenzato dal proprio
lavoro e dalle proprie idee.

DICTIONARY OF CONTEMPORARIES

DICTIONARY
OF
CONTEMPORARIES

DICTIONNAIRE DES CONTEMPORAINS
LEXICON DER ZEITGENOSSEN
DIZIONARIO DI CONTEMPORANEI
DICCIONARIO DE CONTEMPORANEOS
СЛОВАРЬ СОВРЕМЕННИКОВ

COMPILED BY
A. J. LAUNAY

PHILOSOPHICAL LIBRARY

© CENTAUR PRESS LTD. 1967

Published, 1967, by Philosophical Library, Inc.,
15 East 40th Street, New York 16, N.Y.
All rights reserved.
Printed in Great Britain for Philosophical Library
by T. J. Winterson Company

PREFACE

THE aim of this dictionary is to show who were the contemporaries of any writer, artist, composer, philosopher or other influentially creative person of note, born at any time before 1900 A.D.

By alphabetical arrangement of names with dates, in sections of twenty-five years, a simple check can be made not only on a subject's contemporaries and his year of birth and death, but also on who preceded and followed him and so could have influenced, or been influenced by, his own work and ideas. This, indeed, is the book's major purpose.

In each section of twenty-five years, writers, artists and composers are given separate headings, and the sections are preceded throughout the book by a general list that includes major events, kings, presidents, heads of State, reigning popes, and notable persons.

Under the heading of Writers are included authors of novels, biographies and non-fiction, poets, historians, theologians and philosophers — in short, anyone who has written anything which can be said to have contributed significantly to the ethos of his own or a subsequent time. The same criterion has been applied to Artists (which heading includes painters, sculptors, architects and others who have created visually) and to Composers.

In the Index all writers, artists and composers are again listed with their dates to provide reference to the appropriate twenty-five-year section.

Up to 1501 Events and Prominent People were comparatively few. In order to simplify the periods prior to this, therefore, the twenty-five-year sections are preceded by Events and Prominent People listed in chronological order and in spans of 500 years up to the year 1001 A.D., and in spans of 100 years up to 1501, after which they are listed alphabetically every twenty five years.

While the attempt has been made to list the name of every creative person whose work has been recognised as contributory to the cultural climate of his or her era (the hard core of the internationally famous presenting no problems of selection), the vast number of lesser-known people has given rise to the question "Were

5

they influential enough to be included?" Clearly some limitation of numbers has had to be accepted, and it is likely that some readers will feel that notable persons have wrongly been omitted. The Editor can but hope that this dictionary will nevertheless serve its basic purpose in the eyes of that audience at whom it is primarily directed — students, biographers, historians, and indeed all serious readers who are concerned with assessing, through a realisation of the key figures in the creative field, the artistic and inspirational ethos of a given period.

Acknowledgements

I wish to express my grateful thanks to all those who assisted me in the compilation of this work, especially M. A. Henderson who checked through the whole dictionary for omissions, E. Launay who helped me search for and file the names, and C. Taylor-Whitehead and M. Melbourn who helped me read through the proofs.

A.J.L.

Publisher's Note

It has not been possible to refer to any one source in checking the orthography, accents and dates of certain subjects in this dictionary, surprising inconsistencies being found in even the most respectable sources. Existing authorities are also contradictory as to the first names of certain persons included.

While every reasonable effort has been made to avoid inconsistencies and errors, readers are advised to use the dictionary for its essential purpose in tracing contemporaries, and not as a final authority as to the spelling of names or the dates of births and deaths.

It has in fact been found that there are so many errors and contradictions in the accenting of names in the works of different authorities, that it is less misleading to omit accents altogether.

B.C. 3000	Early Minoan Age.
	Gold, Silver, Copper in use. Pictographical writing.
B.C. 2900	Great Pyramid Age begins.
B.C. 2850	Golden Age of China begins.
B.C. 2205	Hsai dynasty in China.
B.C. 2200	Linear writing with pen and ink. Copper in use.
B.C. 1766	Shang dynasty in China.
B.C. 1600	Bronze in use.
B.C. 1280	Iron in use.
B.C. 1220	Exodus of Israelites from Egypt.
B.C. 1190	Fall of Troy.
B.C. 1000	Jerusalem capital of Israel. King David.
B.C. 973	Solomon's Temple built in Jerusalem.
B.C. 846	Carthage founded.
B.C. 776	First Olympiad.
B.C. 753	Rome founded.
B.C. 675	Byzantium founded.
B.C. 660	Japanese history begins. First Mikado.
B.C. 597	Jerusalem destroyed.
B.C. 525	Persian conquest of Egypt.

PROMINENT PEOPLE

Pythagoras	582-500	Gautama (Buddah)	563-483

CHINESE DYNASTIES

The Five Sovereigns		Shang or Yin	1766-1122
(Legendary Epoch)	2697-2205	Chou	1122-255
Hsia	2205-1766		

WRITERS

Aeschylus	525-456	Heraclitus	540-475
Aesop	620-560	Hesiodus	c. 735
Alcaeus	c. 600	Hipponax	546-520
Alcmaeon	c. 520	Homer	c. 850
Alcman	c. 620	Laotse (Lao Tsu)	c. 500
Anacreon	c. 560	Parmenides of Elea	513-c. 430
Anaxagoras	500-428	Pindar	522-440
Anaximander	611-547	Sappho	c. 600
Anaximenes	c. 500	Simonides of Ceos	556-469
Archilochus	720-676	Stesichorus	c. 630-556
Bacchylides	c. 500	Thales	c. 580
Choerilus	c. 500	Theognis	fl. 544-541
Confucius	551-479	Tso Chiuming	c. 600
Cratinus	520-423	Tyrtaeus	fl. 685-668
Epicharmus	540-450	Xenophanes	576-480
Hecataeus of Miletus	550-476		

ARTISTS

Archermus	c. 500	Dipoenus	fl. 560
Bathycles	c. 600	Endoeus	c. 500
Chersiphron	c. 600		

B.C. 430   Great Plague in Egypt.
B.C. 390   Gauls sack Rome.
B.C. 331   Alexandria founded.
B.C. 264   First Punic war.
B.C. 221   Emperior Chi Huang Ti.   Great Wall of China.
B.C. 218   Second Punic war.
B.C. 205   Rosetta Stone.
B.C. 202   Punic war ends.
B.C. 166   Tartar invasion of China.
B.C. 146   Carthage destroyed.
B.C. 60   First Triumvirate.   Caesar, Pompey, Crassus.
B.C. 58   Caesar's victories in Gaul.
B.C. 55   Caesar's invasion of Britain.
B.C. 48   Defeat of Pompey in Egypt by Caesar.
B.C. 47   Cleopatra enthroned by Caesar.
B.C. 44   Caesar assassinated.
B.C. 30   Deaths of Anthony and Cleopatra.
B.C. 4   Birth of JESUS CHRIST.
B.C. 1   Christian era begins.

PROMINENT PEOPLE

Pericles	490-429	Julius Caesar	102-44
Alexander the Great	356-323	Herod the Great	73-4
Archimedes	287-212	Cleopatra	69-30
Euclid	died 282	Augustus	63-14
Hannibal	247-183	Jesus Christ	B.C. 4-33 A.D.

CHINESE DYNASTIES

Chou	1122-255	Han	B.C. 206-A.D. 220
Ch'in	255-206		

WRITERS

Aeschylus	525-456	Heraclitus	540-475
Choerilus	c. 500	Herodotus	484-425
Confucius	551-479	Pindar	522-440
Cratinus	520-423	Protagoras	481-411
Empedocles	490-430	Simonides of Ceos	556-469
Epicharmus	540-450	Sophocles	495-406
Euripides	484-407	Xenophanes	576-480
Gorgias	485-380		

ARTISTS

Antenor	fl. 500

WRITERS

Aeschylus	525-456	Herodotus	484-425
Cratinus	520-423	Magnes	fl. 460
Democritus	born 460	Pindar	522-440
Empedocles	490-430	Protagorus	481-411
Epicharmus	540-450	Simonides of Ceos	556-469
Euripedes	484-407	Socrates	470-399
Gorgias	485-380	Sophocles	495-406
Heraclitus	540-475	Thucydides	460-400

ARTISTS

Agatharcus	460-415	Polygnotus	470-440

WRITERS

Agathon	448-400	Herodotus	484-425
Antisthenes	444-365	Isocrates	436-338
Aristippus	435-356	Philoxenus	435-380
Aristophanes	448-385	Pindar	522-440
Cratinus	520-423	Plato	428-348
Democritus	born 460	Plato (Poet)	428-389
Empedocles	490-430	Protagoras	481-411
Epicharmus	540-450	Socrates	470-399
Euclid	450-374	Sophocles	495-406
Eupolis	446-411	Sophron	460-420
Euripedes	484-407	Thucycides	460-400
Gorgias	485-380	Xenophon	430-357

ARTISTS

Agatharcus	460-415	Polygnotus	470-440

WRITERS

Agathon	448-400	Iophon	fl. 405
Antisthenes	444-365	Isocrates	436-338
Aristippus	435-356	Philoxenus	435-380
Aristophanes	448-385	Plato	428-348
Cratinus	520-423	Plato (Poet)	428-389
Diogenes	412-323	Protagoras	481-411
Euclid	450-374	Socrates	470-399
Eupolis	446-411	Sophocles	495-406
Euripides	484-407	Sophron	460-420
Gorgias	485-380	Xenophon	430-357
Herodotus	484-425		

ARTISTS

Agatharcus	460-415	Hippodamus	fl. 420
Alcamenes	fl. 420		

WRITERS

Agathon	448-400	Isocrates	436-338
Antisthenes	444-365	Leucippus	fl. 400
Archelaus of Miletus	fl. 400	Phidias	c. 400
Aristippus	435-356	Philoxenus	435-380
Aristophanes	448-385	Plato	428-348
Aristotle	384-322	Plato (Poet)	428-389
Ctesias	fl. 400	Socrates	470-399
Diogenes	412-323	Theopompus	378-300
Ephorus	400-330	Xenocrates	396-314
Euclid	450-374	Xenophon	430-357
Gorgias	485-380	Zeno of Elea	fl. 400
Iophon	fl. 405		

ARTISTS

Ictinus	c. 400	Nicomachus	390-340

WRITERS

Antisthenes	444-365	Euclid	450-374
Aristippus	435-356	Isocrates	436-338
Aristotle	384-322	Plato	428-348
Callistheles	360-328	Theophrastus	372-286
Diogenes	412-323	Theopompus	378-300
Ephorus	400-330	Xenocrates	396-314
Eubulus	fl. 370	Xenophon	430-357

ARTISTS

Nicomachus	390-340

WRITERS

Aristotle	384-322	Plato	428-348
Callistheles	360-328	Pyrrho	360-270
Diogenes	412-323	Theopompus	378-300
Diphilus	342-291	Theophrastus	372-286
Ephorus	400-330	Timaeus	345-250
Epicurus	341-270	Xenocrates	396-314
Isocrates	436-338	Zeno of Citium	342-270
Menander	349-291		

ARTISTS

Leochares	fl. 350-338	Nicomachus	390-340

WRITERS

Aeneas, Tacticus	c. 300	Patrocles	312-261
Arcesilas	316-241	Pyrrho	360-270
Aristotle	384-322	Rhinthon	323-285
Cleanthes	301-232	Theopompus	378-300
Dicaerchus	c. 320	Theophrastus	372-286
Diogenes	412-323	Timaues	345-250
Diphilus	342-291	Timon	320-230
Epicurus	341-270	Xenocrates	396-314
Menander	349-291	Zeno of Citium	342-270

ARTISTS

Apelles	c. 325	Protogenes	fl. 332-300

WRITERS

Apollodorus of Carystus	300-260	Mencius	c. 300
Arcesilas	316-241	Patrocles	312-261
Chrysippus	280-207	Pyrrho	360-270
Cleanthes	301-232	Rhinton	323-285
Crantor	fl. 300	Sositheus	c. 284
Diphilus	342-291	Speusippus	c. 300
Epicurus	341-270	Theocritus	fl. 285
Eratosthenes of Alexandria	276-194	Theophrastus	372-286
Hecataeus of Abdera	c. 300	Timaeus	345-250
Livius Andronicus	284-204	Timon	320-230
Menander	349-291	Zeno of Citium	342-270

ARTISTS

Eutychides	c. 300	Protegenes	fl. 332-300

B

Apollodorus of Carystus	300-260	Naevius, Gnaeus	264-194
Arcesilas	316-241	Patrocles	312-261
Aratus of Soli	fl. 270	Plautus, Titus Maccius	250-184
Chrysippus	280-207	Pyrrho	360-270
Cleanthes	301-232	Rhianus	275-195
Epicurus	341-270	Timaeus	345-250
Eratosthenes of Alexandria	276-194	Timon	320-230
Fabius, Pictor Quintus	c. 254	Zeno of Citium	342-270
Livius Andronicus	284-204		

WRITERS

Antigonus of Carystus	241-197	Eratosthenes of Alexandria	276-194
Arcesilas	316-241	Livius Andronicus	284-204
Ariston	c. 250	Naevius, Gnaeus	264-194
Callimachus	c. 250	Plautus, Titus Maccius	250-184
Chrysippus	280-207	Rhianus	275-195
Cleanthes	301-232	Timaeus	345-250
Ennius, Quintus	239-170	Timon	320-230

ARTISTS

Aetion	fl. 250

Antigonus of Carystus	241-197	Livius Andronicus	284-204
Apollonius of Rhodes	fl222-181	Naevius, Gnaeus	264-194
Carneades	214-129	Pacuvius, Marcus	220-130
Chrysippus	280-207	Plautus, Titus Maccius	250-184
Ennius, Quintus	239-170	Polybius	201-120
Erastophones of Alexandria	276-194	Posidippus	fl. 225
Hostius	c. 225	Rhianus	275-195

Agatharchides	181-146	Naevius, Gnaeus	264-194
Antigonus of Carystus	241-197	Nicander	185-135
Apollonius of Rhodes	222-181	Pacuvius, Marcus	220-130
Carneades	214-129	Plautus, Titus Maccius	250-184
Critolaus	197-111	Polybius	200-120
Ennius, Quintus	239-170	Rhianus	275-195
Eratosthenes of Alexandria	276-194	Terence (Publius Terentius	
Lucilius, Gaius	180-103	Afer)	c. 190-159

Accius, Lucius	born 170	Lucilius, Gaius	180-103
Agatharchides	181-146	Nicander	185-135
Aristobulus	c. 160	Pacuvius, Marcus	220-130
Carneades	214-129	Polybius	200-120
Critolaus	197-111	Terence (Publius Terentius	
Ennius, Quintus	239-170	Afer)	c. 190-159

Agatharchides	181-146	Nicander	185-135
Aristeides	150-100	Pacuvius, Marcus	220-130
Carneades	214-129	Polybius	200-120
Critolaus	197-111	Posidonius	131-51
Lucilius, Gaius	180-103	Ssu-Ma Ch'ien	145-87

Archias, Aulus, Licinius	born 120	Laberius, Decimus	105-43
Aristeides	150-100	Lucilius, Gaius	180-103
Atticus, Titus Pomponius	109-32	Polybius	200-120
Bibaculus, Marcus Furius	born 103	Posidonius	131-51
Cicero, Marcus Tullius	106-43	Ssu-Ma Ch'ien	145-87
Critolaus	197-111	Varro, Marcus Terentius	116-27

Aenesidemus	c. 100	
Afranius, Lucius	fl. 100	
Aristeides	150-100	
Atta, Titus, Quintus	died 77	
Atticus, Titus Pomponius	109-32	
Cato, Marcus, Porcius	95-46	
Cato, Publius Valerius	fl. 100	
Catullus, Gaius Valerius	84-54	
Cicero, Marcus Tullius	106-43	
Dionysius of Halicarnasus	fl. 100	
Dionysius, Thrax	fl. 100	
Hirtius, Aulus	90-43	
Laberius, Decimus	105-43	
Licinius, Macer Valvus Gaius	82-47	
Lucretius	98-55	
Nepos, Cornelius	99-24	
Pollio, Gaius Asinius	B.C. 76-5 A.D.	
Posidonius	131-51	
Sallust	86-34	
Ssu-Ma Ch'ien	145-87	
Varro, Marcus, Terentius	116-27	

Andronicus	fl. 70-50	Livy	B.C. 59-17 A.D.
Athenodorus, Cananites		Messalla, Corvinus, Marcus	
	B.C. 74-7 A.D.	Valerius	B.C. 64-8 A.D.
Atticus, Titus Pomponius	109-32	Nepos, Cornelius	99-24
Cato, Marcus Porcius	95-46	Pollio, Gaius, Asinius	B.C. 76-5 A.D.
Catullus, Gaius Valerius	84-54	Posidonius	131-51
Cicero, Marcus Tullius	106-43	Rufus, Lucius, Varius	74-14
Diodorus, Siculus	fl. 60	Sallust	86-34
Fenestella	B.C. 52-19 A.D.	Seneca, Annaeus	B.C. 54-39 A.D.
Gallus, Cornelius	70-26	Strabo	B.C. 60-21 A.D.
Hirtius, Aulus	90-43	Tibullus, Albius	54-19
Horace	65-8	Varro, Marcus, Terentius	116-27
Laberius, Decimus	105-43	Virgil	70-19
Licinius, Macer Calvus Gaius	82-47		

WRITERS

Andronicus	fl. 70-50	Messalla, Corvinus Marcus	
Athenodorus, Cananites B.C. 74-7 A.D.		Valerius	B.C. 64-8 A.D.
Atticus, Titus Pomponis	109-32	Nepos, Cornelius	99-24
Cato, Marcus, Porcius	95-46	Ovid	B.C. 43-17 A.D.
Cicero, Marcus Tullius	106-43	Pollio, Gaius, Asinius	B.C. 76-5 A.D.
Cordus, Aulus Cremutius	fl. 43-18	Propertius, Sextus	48-15
Fenestella	B.C. 52-19 A.D.	Rufus, Lucius, Varius	74-14
Gallus, Cornelius	70-26	Sallust	86-34
Hirtius, Aulus	90-43	Seneca, Annaeus	B.C 54-39 A.D.
Horace	65-8	Strabo	B.C. 60-21 A.D.
Laberius, Decimus	105-43	Tibullus, Albius	54-19
Licinius, Macer, Calvus, Gaius	82-47	Varro, Marcus Terentius	116-27
Livy	B.C. 59-17 A.D.	Virgil	70-19

ARTISTS

Agesander	42-21

WRITERS

Asconius, Pedianus, Quintus	Pollio, Gaius, Asinius B.C. 76-5 A.D.
B.C. 9-A.D. 76	Propertius, Sextus 48-15
Athenodorus, Cananites B.C. 74-A.D. 7	Rufus, Lucius, Varius 74-14
Cordus, Aulus, Cremutius fl. 43-18	Seneca, Annaeus B.C. 54-39 A.D.
Fenestella B.C. 52-19 A.D.	Seneca, Lucius Annaneus
Horace 65-8	B.C. 4-65 A.D.
Livy B.C. 59-17 A.D.	Strabo B.C. 60-21 A.D.
Macer, Aemilius died 16	Tibullus, Albius 54-19
Mesalla, Corvinus Marcus	Velleius, Paterculus Marcus
Valerius B.C. 64-8 A.D.	B.C. 19-31 A.D.
Nepos, Cornelius 99-24	Virgil 70-19
Ovid B.C. 43-17 A.D.	

ARTISTS

Agesander   42-21

33	The Crucifixion.
43	Claudius invades Britain.
51	St. Paul begins missionary travels.
64	Nero burns Rome. Persecution of Christians.
78	Agricola governor of Britain.
79	Pompeii and Herculaneum destroyed.
80	Colosseum in Rome built.
105	Paper invented by Tsai Lun.
121	Hadrian in Britain. Hadrian's wall.
212	Roman citizenship accorded to all free subjects.
238	Goths invade Eastern Europe.
253	Franks invade Gaul.
259	Destruction of the Temple of Diana at Esphesus.
285	Division of Empire, East and West.
292	Quadruple partition of the Empire.
350	Huns invade Europe.
364	Empire divided again. Emperors in East and West.
365	Picts and Scots in Britain.
397	Confessions of St. Augustine of Hippo.
406	Franks overrun Gaul.
410	Rome sacked by Alaric.
432	St. Patrick missionary in Ireland.
449	Britain invaded by Angles, Saxons and Jutes.
484	First schism. Eastern and Western churches.

PROMINENT PEOPLE

Jesus Christ	B.C. 4-33 A.D.	**Boadicea**	died 62 A.D.
Hadrian	76-139	**St. Augustine**	353-430
St. Patrick	385-461		

Han   B.C. 206-220 A.D.

ROMAN EMPERORS

Tiberius   14-37

WRITERS

Asconius Pedianus,		**Pliny** the Elder	23-79
Quintus	B.C. 9-76 A.D.	**Pollio,** Gaius	
Athenodorus,		Asinius	B.C. 76-5 A.D.
Cananties	B.C. 74-7 A.D.	**Seneca,** Annaeus	B.C. 54-39 A.D.
Fenestella	B.C. 52-19 A.D.	**Seneca,** Lucius	
Horace	B.C. 65-8 A.D.	Annaeus	B.C. 4-65 A.D.
Livy	B.C. 59-17 A.D.	**Silius,** Italicus	25-101
Messalla Corvinus,		**Strabo**	c. B.C. 60-21 A.D.
Marcus Valerius	B.C. 64-8 A.D.	**Velleius,** Paterculus	
Ovid	B.C. 43-17 A.D.	Marcus	B.C. 19-31 A.D.

Han   B.C. 206-220 A.D.

ROMAN EMPERORS

Caligula   37-41   Claudius   41-54

WRITERS

Asconius, Pedianus		Plutarch	46-120
Quintus	B.C. 9-76 A.D.	Quintilian, Marcus Fabius	
Curtius, Quintus	fl.41-54	Quintilianus	c. 35-100
Frontinus, Sextus Iulius	40-103	Seneca, Annaeus	B.C. 54-39 A.D.
Josephus, Flavius	37-95	Seneca, Lucius	
Lucan	39-65	Annaeus	B.C. 4-65 A.D.
Martial, Marcus Valerius		Silius, Italicus	25-101
Martialis	40-104	Statius, Publius Papinus	c. 45-96
Mela, Pomponius	fl. 40	Velleius, Paterculus	
Pan Chao, Ts'as Ta Ku	45-114	Marcus	B.C. 19-31 A.D.
Pliny the Elder	23-79		

Han   B.C. 206-220 A.D.

ROMAN EMPERORS

Claudius	41-54	Otho	68
Nero	54-68	Vitellius	68
Galba	68	Vespasian	68-79

POPES

St. Peter	64-c. 67	St. Linus	67-c. 79

WRITERS

Asconius, Pedianus		Pliny the Elder	23-79
Quintus	B.C. 9-76 A.D.	Pliny the Younger	61-113
Bassus, Aufidius	d.60	Plutarch	46-120
Curtius, Quintus	fl. 41-54	Quintilian, Marcus Fabius	
Epictetus	fl. 60	Quintilianus	c. 35-100
Frontinus, Sestus Iulius	40-103	Seneca, Lucius	
Josephus, Flavius	37-95	Annaeus	B.C. 4-65 A.D.
Juvenal	60-140	Silius, Italicus	25-101
Lucan	39-65	Statius, Publius Papinius	c. 45-96
Martial, Marcus Valerius		Suetonius, Tranquillus Gaius	75-160
Martialis	40-104	Tacitus, Cornelius	55-120
Pan Chao, Ts'as Ta Ku	45-114		

Han   B.C. 206-220 A.D.

ROMAN EMPERORS

Vespasian	68-79	Nerva	96-98
Titus	79-81	Trajan	98-117
Domitian	81-96		

POPES

St. Linus	67-c. 79	St. Clement I	92-c. 101
St. Anacletus	79-c. 91	St. Evaristus	101-105

WRITERS

Apollonius of Tyana	fl. 76	Pan Chao, Ts'as Ta Ku	45-114
Arrianus, Flavius	90-c. 160	Pliny the Elder	23-79
Asconius Pedianus,		Pliny the younger	61-113
Quintus	B.C. 9-76 A.D.	Plutarch	46-120
Celsus	fl. 100	Quintilian, Marcus Fabius	
Frontinus, Sesxtus Iulius	40-103	Quintilianus	c. 35-100
Josephus, Flavius	37-95	Silius, Italicus	25-101
Juvenal	60-140	Statius, Publius Papinius	c. 45-96
Martial, Marcus Valerius		Suetonius, Tranquillus Gaius	75-160
Martialis	40-104	Tacitus, Cornelius	55-120

C

Han　　　　　　　B.C. 206-220 A.D.

ROMAN EMPERORS

Trajan　　　　　　　　　98-117　Hadrian　　　　　　　117-138

POPES

St. Clement I	92-101	St. Alexander	105-115
St. Evaristus	101-105	St. Sixtus I	115-125

WRITERS

Arrianus, Flavius	90-c. 160	Pan Chao, Ts'as Ta Ku	45-114
Basilides	fl. 125	Pliny the Younger	61-113
Frontinus, Sextus Iulius	40-103	Plutarch	46-120
Juvenal	60-140	Suetonius, Tranquilus Gaius	75-160
Lucian	125-190	Silius Italicus	25-101
Marcus Aurelius, Antoninus	121-180	Tacitus, Cornelius	55-120
Martial, Marcus Valerius			
Martialis	40-104		

ARTISTS

Apollorodus of Damascus　　104-129

Han   B.C. 206-220 A.D.

ROMAN EMPERORS

Hadrian	117-138	Antoninus Pius	138-161

POPES

St. Telesphorus	125-136	St. Pius I.	140-155
St. Hyginus	136-140		

WRITERS

Apuleius	fl. 150	Hegesippus	150-180
Arrianus, Flavius	90-c. 160	Juvenal	60-140
Cassius Dio, Cocceianus	150-235	Lucian	125-190
Clement of Alexandria	c. 150	Marcus Aurelius, Antoninus	121-180
Gellius Aulus	130-180		

ARTISTS

Appolodorus of Damascus	104-129

Han   B.C. 206-220 A.D.

ROMAN EMPERORS

Antoninus, Pius   138-161   Marcus Aurelius   161-180

POPES

St. Pius   140-155   St. Soter   166-175
St. Anicetus   155-166   St. Eleutherius   175-189

WRITERS

Africanus, Sextus Julius	170-240	Gellius, Aulus	130-180
Alciphron	fl. 180	Hegesippus	150-180
Ammonius	175-242	Lucian	125-190
Apuleius	fl. 150	Marcus Aurelius, Antoninus	121-180
Arrianus, Flavius	90-c. 160	Philostratus	170-245
Cassius Dio, Cocceianus	150-235	Tertullian	c. 160-230

Han   B.C. 206-220 A.D.

ROMAN EMPERORS

Marcus Aurelius	161-180	Pertinax	193
Commodus	180-193	Niger	193
Didius Julianus	193	Septimus Severus	193-211

POPES

St. Eleutherius	175-189	St. Zephyrinus	199-211
St. Victor I	189-199		

WRITERS

Africanus, Sextus Julius	170-240	Herodianus	180-c. 238
Ammonius	175-242	Lucian	125-190
Bhasa	fl. 200	Marcus Aurelius, Antoninus	121-180
Cassius Dio, Cocceianus	150-235	Origen	185-254
Gellius Aulus	130-180	Philostratus	170-245
Hegesippus	150-180	Tertullian	c. 160-230

| Han | B.C. 206-220 A.D. | San Kuo (Epoch of the three kingdoms) | 220-265 |

ROMAN EMPERORS

Septimus Severus	193-211	Macrinus	217-218
Caracalla }	211-217	Elegalabus	218-222
Geta		Alexander Severus	222-235

POPES

| St. Zephyrinus | 199-217 | St. Hyppolytus (anti-pope) | 217-235 |
| St. Calixtus I | 217-222 | St. Urban I | 222-230 |

WRITERS

Aelienus, Claudius	d. 222	Longinus, Dyonisius Cassius	213-273
Africanus, Sextus Julius	170-240	Origen	185-254
Ammonius	175-242	Philostratus	170-245
Cassius Dio, Cocceianus	150-235	Plotinus	205-270
Dexippus, Publius Herrenius	210-273	Tertullian	c. 160-230
Herodianus	180-238		

San Kuo (Epoch of
   the three kingdoms)   220-265   \

ROMAN EMPERORS

Alexander, Severus	222-265	Gordian III.	238-244
Maximus I	235-238	Philip	244-249
Gordian I		Decius	249-251
Gordian II			
Balbinus	238		
Pupienus			

POPES

St. Urban I	222-230	St. Anteros	235-236
St. Pontianus	230-235	St. Fabian	236-250

WRITERS

Africanus, Sextus Juilus	170-240	Origen	185-254
Ammonius	175-242	Philostratus	170-245
Cassius Dio, Cocceianus	150-235	Plotinus	205-270
Dexippus, Publius Herennius	210-273	Porphyry	233-304
Herodianus	180-c. 238	Tertullian	c. 160-230
Longinus, Dyonisius Cassius	213-273		

| San Kuo (Epoch of the three kingdoms) | 220-265 | Tsin | 265-420 |

ROMAN EMPERORS

Decius	249-251	Gallienus	260-268
Gallus	251-253	Claudius II	268-270
Aemilian		Aurelian	270-275
Valerian	253-260	Tacitus	275-276
Gallienus			

POPES

Novatian (anti-pope)	251-	St. Sixtus II	257-258
St. Cornelius	251-253	St. Dionysius	259-268
St. Lucius I	253-254	St. Felix I	269-274
St. Stephen I	254-257	St. Eutychianus	275-283

WRITERS

Dexippus, Publius Herennius	210-273	Origen	185-254
Eusebius of Caesarea	264-340	Plotinus	205-270
Lactantius, Firmianus	260-340	Porphyry	233-304
Longinus, Dyonisius Cassius	213-273		

Tsin   265-420

ROMAN EMPERORS

Tacitus	275-276	Maximian ⎫	284-286
Florian	276	Diocletian ⎭	
Probus	276-282	Diocletian	286-305
Carus	282-284		
Carinus ⎫	284		
Numerian ⎭			

POPES

St. Eutychianus	275- c.283	St. Marcellinus	296-304
St. Gaius	283-c. 296		

WRITERS

Agathangelus, Agathange	c. 300	Lactantius, Firmianus	260-340
Athanasius (St.)	c. 296-373	Nemesianus, Marcus Aurelius	
Cato, Dionysius	c. 300	Olympus	fl. 283
Crysanthius	c. 300	Quintus, Smyrnaeus	c. 300
Eusebius of Caesarea	264-340	Porphyry	233-304

Tsin   265-420

ROMAN EMPERORS

Diocletian	286-305	Constantine The Great ⎤	
Constantius ⎫	305-306	Licinius	
Galerius ⎭		Maximin	
Severus	306	Galerius ⎬	309-323
Constantine The Great	306-307	Maxentius	
Licinius	307-308	Maximian ⎦	
Maximin	308-309	Constantine The Great	323-337

POPES

St. Marcellinus	296-304	St. Miltiades	311314
St. Marcellus I.	308-309	St. Sylvester I.	314-335
St. Eusebius	309-310		

WRITERS

Athanasius (St.)	c. 296-373	Lactantius, Firmianus	260-340
Ausonius, Decimus Magnus	310-395	Porphyry	233-304
Eusebius of Caesarea	264-340		

Tsin   265-420

ROMAN EMPERORS

Constantine The Great	323-337
Constantine II ⎱	
Constantius II ⎰	337-353
Constans ⎰	

POPES

St. Sylvester I	314-335	St. Julius I	337-352
St. Marcus	336		

WRITERS

Ammianus, Marcellines	330-390	Lactantius, Firmianus	260-340
Athanasius (St.)	c. 296-373	Plutarch of Athens	350-430
Ausonius, Decimus Magnus	310-395	Prudentius, Marcus Aurelius	
Eusebius of Caesarea	264-340	Clemens	348-410
Iamblicus	d. 338	Victorinus, Gaius Marius	fl. 350
Jerome (St.)	c. 340-420		

Tsin 265-420

ROMAN EMPERORS

Constantine II ⎫		Valens ⎫	
Constantius II ⎬	337-353	Valentinian I. ⎬	364-367
Constans ⎭		Valentinian I ⎫	
Constantius II	353-361	Gratian ⎬	367-375
Julian	361-363	Gratian ⎫	
Jovian	363-364	Valentinian II ⎬	375-379

POPES

St. Julius I	337-352	St. Damasus I	366-384
St. Liberius	352-366	Ursinus (anti-pope)	366-367
Felix II. (anti-pope)	355-365		

WRITERS

Aedesius	d. 355	Jerome (St.)	c. 340-420
Ammianus, Marcellines	330-390	Pelagius	c. 360-c. 420
Athanasius (St.)	c. 296-373	Plutarch of Athens	350-430
Augustine of Hippo (St.)	353-430	Prudentius, Marcus Aurelius	
Ausonius, Decimus Magnus	310-395	Clemens	348-410
Ephraem, Syrus	d. 373	Severus, Sulpicius	363-425
Eutropius	364-c. 378	Synesius	375-413
Hypatia	370-c. 415		

| Tsin | 265-420 | Northern | 386-581 |

ROMAN EMPERORS

| Gratian }
Valentinian II } | 375-379 | Theodosius The Great
Honorius | 379-395
393-423 |

POPES

| St. Damasus I | 366-384 | St. Anastasius I | 399-401 |
| St. Siricius | 384-399 | | |

WRITERS

Ammianus, Marcellines	330-390	Nemesius	fl. 390
Ammonius	c. 400	Pelagius	c. 360-c. 420
Augustine of Hippo (St.)	353-430	Plutarch of Athens	350-430
Ausonius, Decimus Magnus	310-395	Prudentius, Marcus Aurelius	
Claudianus, Claudius	fl. 395	Clemens	348-410
Dracontius, Blossius Aemilius	c. 400	Rutilius, Claudius	
Eutropius	364-378	Namatianus	c. 400
Fa Hsien	fl. 399-414	Severus, Sulpicius	363-425
Hypatia	370-415	Synesius	375-413
Jerome (St.)	c. 340-420	Theodoret	c. 393-458
Macrobius, Ambrosius			
Theodosius	395-423		

Tsin	265-420	Southern	420-589
Northern	386-581		

ROMAN EMPERORS
(Western)

Honorius	393-423	John (Usurper)	423-425
Constantine III (Usurper)	407-411	Valentinian III	425-455
Constantius III	421		

POPES

St. Anastasius I	399-401	St. Boniface I	418-422
St. Innocent I	401-417	Eulalius (anti-pope)	418-419
St. Zosimus	417-418	St. Celestine I	422-432

WRITERS

Augustine of Hippo (St.)	353-430	Pelagius	c. 360-c. 420
Fa Hsien	fl. 399-414	Plutarch of Athens	350-430
Hypatia	370-415	Proclus	412-485
Isaac of Antioch	408-450	Prudentius, Marcus Aurelius	
Jerome (St.)	c. 340-420	Clemens	348-410
Macrobius, Ambrosius		Severus, Sulpicius	363-425
Theodosius	395-423	Synesius	375-413
Orosius, Paulus	c. 415	Theodoret	c. 393-458

Northern   386-581   Southern   420-589

ROMAN EMPERORS

Valentinian III   425-455

POPES

St. Celestine I	422-432	St. Leo I	440-461
St. Sixtus III	432-440		

WRITERS

Achilles Tatius	fl. 450	Plutarch of Athens	350-430
Asclepigenia	430-485	Proclus,	412-485
Augustine of Hippo (St.)	353-430	Theodoret	c. 393-458
Isaac of Antioch	408-450		

Northern 386-581 Southern 420-589

ROMAN EMPERORS
(Western)

Valentinian III	425-455	Anthemius	467-472
Maximus (Usurper)	455	Olybrius (Usurper)	472-473
Avitus	455-456	Glycerius (Usurper)	473
Majorian	457-461	Julius Nepos	473-480
Severus (Usurper)	461-465	Romulus (Usurper)	475-476

POPES

St. Leo I	440-461	St. Simplicius	468-483
St. Hilarius	461-468		

WRITERS

Asclepigenia	430-485	Jacob of Serugh	451-521
Ennodius, Magnus Felix	475-521	Kalidasa	fl. 450
Hesychius of Miletus	fl. 450	Proclus	412-485

Northern　　　　　　356-581　Southern　　　　　　420-589

ROMAN EMPERORS
Julius Nepos (Last emperor)　473-480

POPES

St. Simplicius	468-483	Anastasius II	496-498
St. Felix III	483-492	St. Symmachus	498-514
St. Gelasius I	492-496	Laurentius (anti-pope)	498-c. 505

FRANCE. HEADS OF STATE
Merovingian Dynasty　　　　481-751

WRITERS

Amru 'Ul Quais	c. 500	Gildas	493-570
Antarah Ibn Shaddad	c. 500	Jacob of Serugh	451-521
Asclepigenia	430-485	Lydus, Joannes Laurentius	490-565
Boethius, Ancius Manlius		Nabigha Dhubyani	c. 500
Severinus	480-524	Philolaus	fl. 480
Cristodorus	491-518	Proclus	412-485
Corippus, Flavius Cresconius	c. 500	Procopius	499-656
Ennodius, Magnus Felix	475-521		

D

529   Code of Justinian.
542   Great plague in the East.
568   Lombard Kingdom founded.
622   The First year of the Mohammedan era.
787   Danish attacks on English coasts.
857   Papacy disputes. Roman and Greek Empires.
888   France separated from Empire.
980   Viking attacks on English coasts.
991   Venice an independent kingdom.

PROMINENT PEOPLE

Mohammed   570-632   **St. Augustine**   d. 604
                                  (1st Archbishop of Canterbury)

Northern　　　　　　　386-581　Southern　　　　　　420-589

POPES

St. Symmachus	498-514	St. Hormisdas	514-523
Laurentius (anti-pope)	498-c. 505	St. John I	523-526

FRANCE. HEADS OF STATE

Merovingian Dynasty　　　481-751

WRITERS

Boethius, Ancius Manlius Severinus	480-524	Gildas	493-570
Christodorus	491-518	Jacob of Serugh	451-521
Ennodius, Magnus Felix	475-521	Lydus, Joannes Laurentius	490-565
		Procopius	499-565

| Northern | 386-581 | Southern | 420-589 |

POPES

St. John I	523-526	John II	533-535
St. Felix IV	526-530	St. Agapetus I	535-536
Dioscorus (anti-pope)	530	St. Silverius	536-537
Boniface II	530-532	Vigilius	537-555

FRANCE. HEADS OF STATE

| Merovingian Dynasty | 481-751 |

WRITERS

Agathias	536-582	Gildas	493-570
Alqama Al-Fahl	c. 550	Gregory, St. of Tours	538-594
Anaximenes of Miletus	c. 550	Jordanes	fl. 530
Columban	543-615	Lydus, Joannes Laurentius	490-565
Evagrius	536-600	Procopius	499-565

| Northern | 386-581 | Southern | 420-589 |

POPES

| Vigilius | 537-555 | John III | 561-574 |
| Pelagius I | 555-561 | Benedict I | 574-579 |

FRANCE. HEADS OF STATE

| Merovingian Dynasty | 481-751 |

WRITERS

Agathias	536-582	Gregory St. of Tours	538-594
Columban	543-615	Isidore of Seville	560-636
Evagrius	536-600	Lydus, Joannes Laurentius	490-565
Gildas	493-570	Procopius	499-565

Northern	386-581	Sui	581-618
Southern	420-589		

POPES

Benedict I	574-579	St. Gregory I	590-604
Palagius II	579-590		

FRANCE. HEADS OF STATE

Merovingian Dynasty	481-751

WRITERS

Agathias	536-582	Evagrius	536-600
Aneurin	fl. 600	George Pisida	c. 600
Bhartrihari	fl. 600	Gregory St. of Tours	538-594
Columban	543-615	Isidore of Seville	560-636

Sui	581-618	T'Ang	618-907

POPES

St. Gregory I	590-604	St. Deusdedit	615-618
St. Sabinian	604-606	Boniface V	619-625
Boniface III	607-608	Honorius I	625-638
St. Boniface IV	608-615		

FRANCE. HEADS OF STATE

Merovingian Dynasty	481-751

WRITERS

Adamnan St.	625-704	Isidore of Seville	560-636
Columban	543-615	Simocatta, Theophylact	610-640
Hsuan Tsung	c. 605		

T'Ang   618-907

POPES

Honorius I	625-638	Theodore I	642-649
Severinus	638-640	St. Martin I	649-655
John IV	640-642		

FRANCE. HEADS OF STATE

Merovingian Dynasty   481-751

WRITERS

Adamnan St.	625-704	Isidore of Seville	560-636
Aldhelm St.	c. 640-709	Simocatta, Theophylact	610-640
Farazdaq	641-728		

T'Ang   618-907

POPES

St. Martin I, d. in exile   649-655   St. Vitalian   657-672
St. Eugenius I   654-657   Adeodatus II   672-676

FRANCE. HEADS OF STATE

Merovingian Dynasty   481-751

WRITERS

Adamnan St.   625-704   Farazdaq   641-728
Aldhelm St.   c. 640-709   Hassan Ibn, Thabit   d. 674
Bede, The Venerable   673-735

T'Ang   618-907

POPES

Adeodatus II	672-676	John V	685-686
Donus	676-678	Conon	686-687
St. Agatho	678-681	Theodore and Paschal	
St. Leo II	681-683	(anti-popes)	687
St. Benedict II	683-685	St. Sergius I	687-701

FRANCE. HEADS OF STATE

Merovingian Dynasty   418-751

WRITERS

Adamnan St.	625-704	Caedmon	d. 680
Akahito, Yamobe	fl. 700	Farazdaq	641-728
Aldhelm St.	c.640-709	John of Damascus	c. 676-c. 754
Bede, The Venerable	673-735	Li-Po	700-762

ARTISTS

Wang-Wei   699-759

T'Ang   618-907

POPES

St. Sergius I	687-701	Sisinnius	708
John VI	701-705	Constantine	708-715
John VII	705-707	St. Gregory II	715-731

FRANCE. HEADS OF STATE

Merovingian Dynasty   418-751

WRITERS

Adamnan St.	625-704	John of Damascus	c. 676-c. 754
Aldhelm St.	c. 640-709	Li Po	700-762
Bede, The Venerable	673-735	Paulus Diaconus	720-800
Farazdaq	641-728		

ARTISTS

Wang Wei   699-759

T'Ang　　　　　　　　　　618-907

POPES

St. Gregory II	715-731	Stephen II	752-757
St. Gregory III	731-741	St. Paul I	757-767
St. Zacharias	741-752		

FRANCE. HEADS OF STATE

Merovingian Dynasty　　　　481-751

WRITERS

Abu-L-Atahiya	748-828	Farazdaq	641-728
Alcuin	735-804	Jarir Ibn Atiyya, Ul-Khaffi	d. 728
Bede, The Venerable	673-735	John of Damascus	c. 676-c. 754
Bhavabuti	fl. 730	Li Po	700-762
Cynewulf	737-780	Paulus Diaconus	720-800

ARTISTS

Wang Wei　　　　　　　　699-759

T'Ang   618-907

POPES

St. Stephen	752-757	Philip (anti-pope)	768
St. Paul I	757-767	Stephen III	768-772
Constantine (anti-pope)	767-768	Adrian I	772-795

FRANCE. HEADS OF STATE

Merovingian Dynasty	481-751	Carolingian Dynasty	751-987

WRITERS

Abu-L-Atahiya	748-828	Ibn Ishaq	d. 768
Abu Nuwas	756-810	John of Damascus	c. 676-c. 754
Alcuin	735-804	Li Po	700-762
Cynewulf	737-780	Paulus Diaconus	720-800
Einhard	770-840	Po Chu I	772-846

ARTISTS

Wang Wei	699-759

T'Ang   618-907

POPES
Adrian I   772-795   St. Leo III   795-816

FRANCE. HEADS OF STATE
Carolingian Dynasty   751-987

WRITERS
Abu-L-Atahiya	748-828	Einhard	770-840
Abu Nuwas	756-810	Nicephorus, Patriarcha	789-829
Alcuin	735-804	Paulus, Diaconus	720-800
Cynewulf	737-780	Po Chu I	772-846

T'Ang 618-907

POPES

St. Leo III	795-816	St. Paschal I	817-824
Stephen IV	816-817	Eugenius II	824-827

FRANCE. HEADS OF STATE

Carolingian Dynasty 751-987

HOLY ROMAN EMPERORS

Charles I (Charlemagne) 800-814 Louis I 814-840

ENGLISH SOVEREIGNS

Egbert 802-839

WRITERS

Abu-L-Atahiya	748-828	Einhard	770-840
Abu Nuwas	756-810	Erigena, Johannes Scotus	815-877
Abutamman, Habbib Ibn		Hisham Ibn Al-Kalbi	d. 819
Aus	807-c. 850	Nicephorus, Patriarcha	789-829
Alcuin	735-804	Po Chu I	772-846
Buaturi, Al Walid Ibn			
Ubaid-Allah	820-897		

T'Ang   618-907

POPES

Eugenius II	824-827	John (anti-pope)	844
Valentinus	827	Sergius II	844-847
Gregory IV	827-844	St. Leo IV	847-855

FRANCE. HEADS OF STATE

Carolingian Dynasty   751-987

HOLY ROMAN EMPERORS

Louis I   814-840   Lothar   840-855

ENGLAND. SOVEREIGNS

Egbert   802-839   Ethelwulf   839-858

SWEDEN. KINGS

Olaf and Edmund   850-882

WRITERS

Abu-L-Atahiya	748-828	Ibn, Duraid	837-934
Abutamman Habib Ibn		Ibn, Qutaiba	828-889
Aus	807-c. 850	Israeli, Isaac Ben Solomon	845-940
Alfred the Great	849-899	Nicephorus, Patriarcha	789-829
Buaturi, Al Walid Ibn		Po Chu I	772-846
Ubaid Allah	820-897	Tabari, Abu Jofar Mohammed	
Einhard	770-840	Ben Jarirol	839-923
Erigena, Johannes Scotus	815-877		

T'Ang   618-907

POPES

St. Leo IV	847-855	St. Nicholas I	858-867
Anastasius (anti-pope)	855	Adrian II	867-872
Benedict III	855-858	John VIII	872-882

FRANCE. HEADS OF STATE

Carolingian Dynasty   751-987

HOLY ROMAN EMPERORS

Lothar	840-855	Charles II	875-881
Louis II	855-875		

ENGLAND. SOVEREIGNS

Ethelwulf	839-858	Ethelred I	865-870
Ethelbald	858-860	Alfred the Great	870-899
Ethelbert	860-865		

SWEDEN. KINGS

Olaf and Edmund   850-882

WRITERS

Alfred the Great	849-899	Ibn, Duraid	837-934
Arethas	860-940	Ibn, Qutaiba	828-889
Buaturi, Ali-Walid Ibn		Israeli, Isaac Ben Solomon	845-940
Ubaid-Allah	820-897	Kindi, Abu Yusuf Ya Qubibn	
Erigena, Johannes Scotus	815-877	Ibn Ishaq Ul-Kindi	c. 873
Farabi	870-950	Tabari, Abu Jofar Mohammed	
Ibn'Abd Rabbihi	860-940	Ben Jarirol	839-923

E

T'Ang 618-907

POPES

John VIII	872-882	Boniface VI	c. 896
Marinus I	882-884	Stephen VI	896-897
St. Adrian III	884-885	Romanus	897
Stephen V	885-891	Theodore II	897
Formosus	891-896	John IX	898-900

FRANCE. HEADS OF STATE

Carolingian Dynasty 751-987

HOLY ROMAN EMPERORS

Charles II	875-881	Lambert	894-896
Charles III	882-887	Arnulf	896-899
Guido	887-894	Louis the child	899-901

ENGLAND. SOVEREIGNS

Alfred the Great 870-899 Edward the Elder 899-925

SWEDEN. KINGS

Olaf and Edmund 850-882 Eric Edmundsson 882-905

WRITERS

Abu'L Faraj Al-Isfahani	897-967	Ibn'Abd Rabbihi	860-940
Alfred the Great	849-899	Ibn, Duraid	837-934
Arethas	860-940	Ibn, Qutaiba	828-889
Buaturi, Al-Walid Ibn		Israeli, Isaac Ben Solomon	845-940
Ubaid-Allah	820-897	Tabari, Abu Jofar Mohammed	
Erigena, Johannes Scotus	815-877	Ben Jarirol	839-923
Farabi	870-950	Ya Qubi	d. 891

T'Ang	618-907	Wu Tai (Epoch of the five Dynasties)	907-960

POPES

John IX	898-900	Sergius III	904-911
Benedict IV	901-903	Anastasius III	911-913
Leo V	903	Lando	913-914
Christoph (anti-pope)	903-904	John X	914-928

FRANCE. HEADS OF STATE

Carolingian Dynasty	751-987

HOLY ROMAN EMPERORS

Louis the Child	899-901	Berengar	915-918
Louis III	901-911	Henry I	918-936
Conrad I	911-915		

ENGLAND. SOVEREIGNS

Edward the Elder	899-925	Athelstan	925-939

SWEDEN. KINGS

Eric Edmundsson	882-905	Bjorn Ericsson and Ring	905-950

WRITERS

Abu'L Faraj Al-Isfahani	897-967	Israeli, Isaac Ben Solomon	845-940
Arethas	860-940	Liudprand	922-972
Farabi	870-950	Tabari, Abu Jofar Mohammed	
Ibn'Abd Rabbihi	860-940	Ben Jarirol	839-923
Ibn Duraid	837-934		

Wu Tai (Epoch of
  the five Dynasties)   907-960

POPES

John X	914-928	Leo VII	936-939
Leo VI	928	Stephen VIII	939-942
Stephen VII	928-931	Marinus II	942-946
John XI	931-935	Agapetus II	946-955

FRANCE. HEADS OF STATE

Carolingian Dynasty   751-987

HOLY ROMAN EMPERORS

Henry I   918-936   Otto I   936-973

ENGLAND. SOVEREIGNS

Athelstan	925-939	Edred	946-955
Edmund I	939-946		

SWEDEN. KINGS

Bjorn Ericsson and Ring   905-950   Eric the Victorious   950-993

WRITERS

Abbon of Fleury	945-1004	Hrosvitha	935-1002
Abu'L Faraj Al-Isfahani	897-967	Ibn-Abd Rabbihi	860-940
Arathas	860-940	Ibn Duraid	837-934
Farabi	870-950	Israeli, Isaac Ben Solomon	845-940
Firdausi	c. 950-1020	Liudprand	922-972

Wu Tai (Epoch of the five Dynasties)	907-960	**Sung**	960-1279

POPES

Agapetus II	946-955	John XIII	965-972
John XII	955-964	Benedict VI	973-974
Leo VIII	963-965	Boniface VII (anti-pope)	974
Benedict V	966	Benedict VII	974-983

FRANCE. HEADS OF STATE

Carolingian Dynasty	751-987

HOLY ROMAN EMPERORS

Otto I	936-973	Otto II	973-983

ENGLAND. SOVEREIGNS

Edred	946-955	Edgar	959-975
Edwy	955-959	Edward the Younger	975-978

SWEDEN. KINGS

Eric the Victorious	950-993

WRITERS

Abbon of Fleury	945-1004	Hamadhani	967-1007
Abu'L Faraj Al-Isfahani	897-967	Hrosvitha	935-1002
Abu-L-UL-Maarri	973-1057	Ibn Faradi	962-1012
Aelfric	955-c. 1020	Liudprand	922-972
Aimoin	960-1010	Masudi, Abul-Hasan	d. 956
Firdausi	c. 950-1020		

Sung   960-1279

POPES

Benedict VII	974-983	Gregory V	996-999
John XIV	983-984	John XVI (anti-pope)	997-998
Boniface VII (anti-pope)	984-985	Sylvester II	999-1003
John XV	985-996		

FRANCE. HEADS OF STATE

Carolingian Dynasty	751-987	Robert	996-1031
Hugh Capet	987-996		

HOLY ROMAN EMPERORS

Otto II	973-983	Otto III	983-1002

ENGLAND. SOVEREIGNS

Edward the Younger	975-978	Ethelred II	979-1016

SWEDEN. KINGS

Eric the Victorious	950-993	Olaf Scatt-King	999-1022
Period of Confusion	933-999		

WRITERS

Abbon of Fleury	945-1004	Firdausi	c. 950-1020
Abu-L-Ala UL-Maarri	973-1057	Hamadhani	967-1007
Aelfric	955-c. 1020	Hrosvitha	935-1002
Aimoin	960-1010	Ibn Faradi	962-1012
Avicenna Ibn Sina	980-1037	Murasaki Shikibu	978-1031

COMPOSERS

Guido Aretinus of Arezzo	990-1050

1001   Norse discovery of Nova Scotia.
1009   Danes attack London.
1028   Canute conquers Norway.
1054   Separation of Latin and Greek churches.
1066   Battle of Hastings.
1086   Domesday book.
1099   Capture of Jerusalem.   Knights of St. John instituted.
1100   William II killed in New Forest.

PROMINENT PEOPLE

El Cid   1035-1099   **Lady Godiva**   1040-1080
Godfrey of Bouillon   1061-1100

Sung   960-1279

POPES

Sylvester II	999-1003	Gregory (anti-pope)	1012
John XVII	1003-1004	Benedict VIII	1012-1024
John XVIII	1004-1009	John XIX	1024-1032
Sergius IV	1009-1012		

FRANCE. HEADS OF STATE

Robert   996-1031

HOLY ROMAN EMPERORS

Otto III	983-1002	Conrad II	1024-1037
Henry II	1002-1024		

ENGLAND. SOVEREIGNS

Ethelred II	979-1016	Canute	1016-1035
Edmund II	1016		

SWEDEN. KINGS

Olaf Scatt-King	999-1022	Anund Jacob	1022-1050

WRITERS

Abbon of Fleury	945-1004	Hamadhani	967-1007
Abu-L-Ala Ul-Maarri	973-1057	Hrosvitha	935-1002
Adhemar De Chabannes	988-c. 1034	Ibn Faradi	962-1012
Aelfric	955-c. 1020	Ibn Gabirol	1021-1058
Aimoin	960-1010	Murasaki Shikibu	978-1031
Avicebron	fl. 1020-1070	Psellus, Michael	
Avicenna Ibn Sina	980-1037	Constantine	1018-1079
Firdausi	c. 950-1020		

COMPOSERS

Guido Aretinus of Arezzo   990-1050

Sung   960-1279

POPES

John XIX	1024-1032	Clement II	1046-1047
Benedict IX	1032-1044	Benedict IX (restored)	1047-1048
Sylvester III	1045	Damasus II	1048
Gregory VI	1045-1046	St. Leo IX	1049-1054

FRANCE. HEADS OF STATE

Robert	996-1031	Henry I	1031-1060

HOLY ROMAN EMPERORS

Conrad II	1024-1037	Henry III	1037-1056

ENGLAND. SOVEREIGNS

Canute	1016-1035	Harthacanute	1040-1042
Harold	1035-1040	Edward the Confessor	1042-1066

SWEDEN. KINGS

Anund Jacob	1022-1050	Edmund the Old	1050-1060

WRITERS

Abu-L-Ala Ul-Maarri	973-1057	Bahya, Ibn Pauda	c. 1040
Adalberon	d. 1030	Ibn Gabirol	1021-1058
Adhemar De Chabannes	c. 988-1034	Murasaki Shikibu	978-1031
Anselm St.	1033-1109	Omar Khayam	1050-1123
Avicebron	fl. 1020-1070	Psellus, Michael	
Avicenna Ibn Sina	980-1037	Constantine	1018-1079

COMPOSERS

Guido Aretinus of Arezzo	990-1050

Sung   960-1279

POPES

St. Leo IX	1049-1054	Nicholas II	1059-1061
Victor II	1055-1057	Honorius II (anti-pope)	1061-1072
Stephen IX	1057-1058	Alexander II	1061-1073
Benedict X (anti-pope)	1058-1059	St. Gregory VII	1073-1085

FRANCE. HEADS OF STATE

Henry I   1031-1060   Philip I   1060-1108

HOLY ROMAN EMPERORS

Henry III   1037-1056   Henry IV   1056-1106

ENGLAND. SOVEREIGNS

Edward the Confessor	1042-1066	William I	1066-1087
Harold II	1066		

SWEDEN. KINGS

Edmund the Old	1050-1060	Period of Confusion	1066-1080
Stenkil	1060-1066		

WRITERS

Abu-L-Ala Ul-Maarri	973-1057	Hariri, Abu Mohammed	1054-1122
Adam of Bremen	fl. 1075	Ibn Gabirol	1021-1058
Anselm St.	1033-1109	Omar Khayam	1050-1123
Avicebron	fl. 1020-1070	Orderic Vitalis	1075-1142
Bryennius, Nicephorus	1062-1137	Psellus, Michael	
Eadmer	1060-1124	Constantine	1018-1079
Ghazali	1058-1111		

Sung 960-1279

POPES

St. Gregory VII	1073-1085	Clement III (anti-pope)	1084-1100
Victor III	1086-1087	Theodoric (anti-pope)	1100
Urban II	1088-1099	Paschal II	1099-1118

FRANCE. HEADS OF STATE

Philip I   1060-1108

HOLY ROMAN EMPERORS

Henry IV   1056-1106

ENGLAND. SOVEREIGNS

William I	1066-1087	Henry I	1100-1135
William II	1087-1100		

SWEDEN. KINGS

Period of Confusion	1066-1080	Inge the Good	1090-1118
Halstan	1080-1093		

WRITERS

Abelard, Peter	1079-1142	Halevi, Judah Ben	
Abenezra	1093-1167	Samuel	c. 1085-1140
Albert of Aix	c. 1100	Hariri, Abu Mohammed	1054-112
Anna, Comnena	1083-1148	Heinrich Von Veldecke	c. 1100
Anselm St.	1033-1109	Omar Khayam	1050-1123
Bernard of Clairvaux, St.	1090-1153	Orderic Vitalis	1075-1142
Bryennius, Nicephorus	1062-1137	Psellus, Michael	
Chretien De Troyes	c. 1100	Constantine	1018-1079
Eadmer	1060-1124	Tzetzes, Johannes	1120-1183
Ghazali	1058-1111	William of Malmesbury	c. 1095-1143

1147   Second Crusade.
1170   Thomas a Becket assassinated.
1180   Carthusian monastries established in England.
1187   Third Crusade.

PROMINENT PEOPLE

Thomas A Becket	1118-1170	Jenghiz Khan	1162-1227
Saladin	1137-1193		

Sung   960-1279

POPES

Paschal II	1099-1118	Gregory VIII (anti-pope)	1118-1121
Albert (anti-pope)	1102	Calixtus II	1119-1124
Sylvester IV (anti-pope)	1105-1111	Honorius II	1124-1130
Gelasius II	1118-1119	Celestine II (anti-pope)	1124

FRANCE. HEADS OF STATE

Philip I   1060-1108   Louis VI   1108-1137

HOLY ROMAN EMPERORS

Henry IV	1056-1106	Lothar II	1125-1138
Henry V	1106-1125		

ENGLAND. SOVEREIGNS

Henry I   1100-1135

SWEDEN. KINGS

Inge the Good   1090-1118   Inge II Halstansson   1118-1130

WRITERS

Abelard, Peter	1079-1142	Geoffrey of Monmouth	c. 1100-1154
Abenezra	1093-1167	Ghazali	1058-1111
Abraham, Ibn Doud	1110-1180	Halevi, Judah Ben	
Ailred, Ethelred	1109-1166	Samuel	c. 1085-1140
Anna, Comnena	1083-1148	Hariri, Abu Mohammed	1054-1122
Anselm, St.	1033-1109	Hilarius	c. 1125
Benoit de St. Maure	fl. c. 1150	Omar Khayam	1050-1123
Bernard of Clairvaux, St.	1090-1153	Orderic Vitalis	1075-1142
Bryennius, Nicephorus	1062-1137	Tzestzes, Johannes	1120-1183
Eadmer	1060-1124	Wace, Robert	c. 1115-c. 1183
Farid Ud-Din Attar	1119-1229	William of Malmesbury	c. 1095-1143

Kao Tsung
  (Sung Dynasty)   1127-1162

POPES

Honorius II	1124-1130	Celestine II	1143-1144
Innocent II	1130-1143	Lucius II	1144-1145
Anacletus II (anti-pope)	1130-1138	Eugenius III	1145-1153
Victor IV (anti-pope)	1138		

FRANCE. HEADS OF STATE

Louis VI	1108-1137	Louis VII	1137-1180

HOLY ROMAN EMPERORS

Lothar II	1125-1138	Conrad III	1138-1152

ENGLAND. SOVEREIGNS

Henry I	1100-1135	Stephen	1135-1154

SWEDEN. KINGS

Inge II Halstansson	1118-1130	Sverker	1132-1155

PORTUGAL. KINGS

Alfonso I	1139-1185

WRITERS

Aagesen, Svend	fl. 1130	Geoffrey of Monmouth	c. 1100-1154
Abelard, Peter	1079-1142	Giraldus, Cambrensis	1146-1220
Abenezra	1093-1167	Halevi, Judah Ben	
Abraham, Ibn Doud	1110-1180	Samuel	1085-1140
Acominatus, Michael	1140-1220	Ibn Athir Majd Ud-Din	1149-1210
Ailred, Ethelred	1109-1166	Maimonides	1135-1204
Anna, Comnena	1083-1148	Map, Walter	1137-1209
Avempace, Ibn Bajjah	c. 1138	Orderic Vitalis	1075-1142
Averhoes, Ibn Ruoshd	1126-1198	Saxo Grammaticus	1150-1206
Bernard of Clairvaux, St.	1090-1153	Thomas	fl. 1150
Bryennius, Nicephorus	1062-1137	Tzestzes, Johannes	1120-1183
Chang Chun Kiu	1148-1227	Wace, Robert	c. 1115-c. 1183
Cinnamus, John	c. 1143-1180	William of Malmesbury	c. 1095-1143
Daniel, Arnaut	fl. 1150	William of Newburgh	1135-1200
Fakhr Ud Din Razi	1149-1209	William of Tyre	1137-1190
Farid Ud-Din Attar	1119-1229		

Kao Tsung (Sung Dynasty)	1127-1162	Hsaio Tsung (Sung Dynasty)	1162-1189

POPES

Eugenius III	1145-1153	Victor IV (anti-pope)	1159-1164
Anastasius IV	1153-1154	Paschal III (anti-pope)	1164-1168
Adrian IV	1154-1159	Calixtus III (anti-pope)	1168-1178
Alexander III	1159-1181		

FRANCE. HEADS OF STATE

Louis VII	1137-1180

HOLY ROMAN EMPERORS

Conrad III	1138-1152	Frederick I	1152-1190

ENGLAND. SOVEREIGNS

Stephen	1135-1154	Henry II	1154-1189

SWEDEN. KINGS

Sverker	1132-1155	Charles VII	1160-1167
Eric IX (Saint)	1150-1160	Knut Ericsson	1167-1196

PORTUGAL. KINGS

Alfonso I	1139-1185

WRITERS

Abd-Ul-Latif	1162-1231	Hartmann, Von Aue	1170-1215
Abenezra	1093-1167	Ibn Arabi	1165-1240
Abraham, Ibn Doud	1110-1180	Ibn Athir	1160-1234
Acominatus, Michael	1140-1220	Ibn Athir, Diya Ud-Din	1163-1239
Ailred, Ethelred	1109-1166	Ibn Athir, Majd, Ud-Din	1149-1210
Averhoes, Ibn Ruoshd	1126-1198	Maimonides	1135-1204
Bar-Salibi, Jacob	d. 1171	Map, Walter	1137-1209
Bernard of Clairvaux, St.	1090-1153	Marie De France	c. 1175-1190
Brakelond, Jocelyn De	1173-1202	Saxo Grammaticus	1150-1206
Chang Chun Kiu	1148-1227	Tzestzes, Johannes	1120-1183
Cinnamus, John	c. 1143-1180	Villehardouin, Geoffroy De	1160-1213
Fakhr Ud-Din Razi	1149-1209	Wace, Robert	c. 1115-c. 1183
Farid Ud-Din Attar	1119-1229	Walther, Von Der	
Geoffrey of Monmouth	c. 1100-1154	Vogelweide	1170-1230
Giraldus, Cambrensis	1146-1220	William of Newburgh	1135-1200
Grosseteste, Robert	c. 1175-1253	William of Tyre	1137-1190

Hsaio Tsung (Sung Dynasty)	1162-1189	Kuang Tsung (Sung Dynasty	1189-1194
Ning Tsung (Sung Dynasty)	1194-1224		

POPES

Calixtus III (anti-pope)	1168-1178	Gregory VIII	1187
Innocent III (anti-pope)	1179-1180	Clement III	1187-1191
Lucius III	1181-1185	Celestine III	1191-1198
Urban III	1185-1187	Innocent III	1198-1216

FRANCE. HEADS OF STATE

Louis VII	1137-1180	Philip II	1180-1223

HOLY ROMAN EMPERORS

Frederick I.	1152-1190	Philip } (Rivals)	1197-120:
Henry VI	1190-1197	Otto IV	

ENGLAND. SOVEREIGNS

Henry II	1154-1189	John	1199-1216
Richard I	1189-1199		

SWEDEN. KINGS

Knut Ericsson	1167-1196	Sverker Carlsson	1196-1205

PORTUGAL. KINGS

Alfonso I	1139-1185	Sancho I	1185-1211

Abd-Ul-Latif	1162-1231	Ibn Athir	1160-1234
Abraham, Ibn Doud	1110-1180	Ibn Athir, Diya Ud-Din	1163-1239
Acominatus, Michael	1140-1220	Ibn Athir, Majd Ud-Din	1149-1210
Adam, Scotus	c. 1180	Ibn Farid	1181-1235
Ambrose	c. 1190	Ibn Tufail	d. 1185
Andre Le Chapelain	1180-1223	Maimonides	1135-1204
Anwari	d. 1196	Map, Walter	1137-1209
Averhoes, Ibn Ruoshd	1126-1198	Marie De France	c. 1175-1190
Beha Ud-Din Zuhair	1186-1258	Montreuil, Gerbert De	c. 1200
Berceo, Gonsalo De	1180-1246	Paris, Matthew	1200-1259
Brakelond, Jocelyn de	1173-1202	Sa'Di	1184-1291
Chand Bardai	c. 1200	Saxo Grammaticus	1150-1206
Chang Chun Kiu	1148-1227	Snorri Sturluson	1179-1241
Cinnamus, John	c. 1143-1180	Tzestzes, Johannes	1120-1183
Fakhr, Ud-Din Razi	1149-1209	Villehardouin, Geoffroy De	1160-1213
Farid Ud-Din Attar	1119-1229	Wace, Robert	c. 1115-c. 1183
Garland, John	1195-1272	Walther, Von De	
Giraldus, Cambrensis	1146-1220	Vogelweide	1170-1200
Gottfried, Von Strassburg	fl. 1200	William of Newburgh	1135-1200
Grosseteste, Robert	c. 1175-1253	William of Tyre	1137-1190
Hartmann, Von Aue	1170-1215	Wolfar Von Eschenbach	fl. 1200
Ibn Arabi	1165-1240		

ARTISTS

Hsai Kuei	1180-1230

F

1202	Fourth Crusade. France and England at War.
1203	Crusaders conquer Constantinople.
1206	Mogul Empire founded.
1209	Franciscan order established.
1215	Magna Carta signed by King John.
1216	First Parliament in England.
1217	Fifth Crusade.
1228	Sixth Crusade.
1229	Jerusalem ceded to Christians.
1248	Seventh Crusade.
1253	Jews driven out of France.
1265	Battle of Evesham.
1282	Sicilian Vespers massacre.
1290	Jews driven out of England.
1297	Battle of Stirling.
1298	Battle of Falkirk.

PROMINENT PEOPLE

| Jenghiz Khan | 1162-1227 | Bruce, Robert | 1274-1329 |
| Marco Polo | 1256-1323 | | |

Ning Tsung (Sung Dynasty)	1194-1224	T'Ai Tsu (Jenghiz Kahn— Mongol Dynasty)	1206-1229
Li Tsung (Sung Dynasty)	1224-1264		

POPES

Innocent III	1198-1216	Honorius III	1216-1227

FRANCE. HEADS OF STATE

Philip II	1180-1223	Louis VIII	1223-1226

HOLY ROMAN EMPERORS

Philip Otto IV } (Rivals)	1197-1208	Otto IV Frederick II	1208-1212 1212-1250

ENGLAND. SOVEREIGNS

John	1199-1216	Henry III	1216-1272

SWEDEN. KINGS

Sverker Carlsson	1196-1205	Period of Confusion	1205-1250

PORTUGAL. KINGS

Sancho I	1185-1211	Sancho II	1223-1248
Alphonso II	1211-1223		

WRITERS

Abd-Ul-Latif	1162-1231	Ibn Athir	1160-1234
Acominatus, Michael	1140-1220	Ibn Athir, Diya Ud-Din	1163-1239
Albertus Magnus	1206-1280	Ibn Athir, Majd Ud-Din	1149-1210
Andre Le Chapelain	1180-1223	Ibn Farid	1181-1235
Aquinus, Thomas	1225-1275	Jalal Ad-Din Rumi	1207-1273
Bacon, Roger	1214-1294	Joinvile, Jean	1224-1319
Beha Ud-Din Zuhair	1186-1258	Latini, Brunetto	1210-1294
Berceo, Gonzalo De	1180-1246	Maimonides	1135-1204
Brakelond, Jocelyn De	1173-1202	Map, Walter	1137-1209
Busri	1211-1294	Paris, Matthew	c. 1200-1259
Chang Chun Kiu	1148-1227	Rumi	1207-1273
Elmacin, George	1223-1274	Sa'Di	1184-1291
Fakhr Ud-Din Razi	1149-1209	Saxo Grammaticus	1150-1206
Farid Ud-Din Attar	1119-1229	Snorri, Sturluson	1179-1241
Garland, John	1195-1272	Thomas the Rhymer	
Gervase of Tilbury	c. 1211	(of Ercelduone)	c. 1220-c. 1297
Giraldus Cambrensis	1146-1220	Villehardouin,	
Gottfried, Von Strassburg	c. 1210	Geoffrey De	1160-1213
Grosseteste, Robert	c. 1175-1253	Walther, Von Der	
Hartmann, Von Aue	1170-1215	Vogelsweide	1170-1230
Ibn Arabi	1165-1240		

ARTISTS

Hsia Kuei	1180-1230	Pisano, Niccola	1225-1278

Li Tsung (Sung Dynasty)	1224-1264	T'Ai Tsung (Ogotai Khan—	
T'Ai Tsu (Jenghiz Khan—		Mongol Dynasty)	1229-1246
Mongol Dynasty)	1206-1229	Ting Tsung (Kuyak Khan—	
		Mongol Dynasty)	1246-1251

POPES

Honorius III	1216-1227	Celestine IV	1241
Gregory IX	1227-1241	Innocent IV	1243-1254

FRANCE. HEADS OF STATE

Louis VIII	1223-1226	Louis IX	1226-1270

HOLY ROMAN EMPERORS

Frederick II	1212-1250	Conrad IV	1250-1254

ENGLAND. SOVEREIGNS

Henry III	1216-1272

SWEDEN. KINGS

Period of Confusion	1205-1250	Valdemar	1250-1275

PORTUGAL. KINGS

Sancho II	1223-1248	Alphonso III	1248-1279

WRITERS

Abano, Pietro D'	1250-1316	Ibn Athir, Diya Ud-Din	1163-1239
Abdul Latif	1162-1231	Ibn Farid	1181-1235
Abul Faraj	1226-1286	Jacopone, Da Todi	1230-1306
Albertus Magnus	1206-1280	Jalal Ad-Din Rumi	1207-1273
Aquinas, Thomas	1225-1275	Joinville, Jean	1224-1319
Bacon, Roger	1214-1294	Latini, Brunetto	1210-1294
Beha Ud-Din Zuhair	1186-1258	Lully, Raymond	c. 1232-1315
Berceo, Gonsalo De	1180-1246	Maerlant, Jacob Van	1235-1300
Busri	1211-1294	Meung, Jean De	1250-1305
Cavalcanti, Guido	1230-1300	Paris, Matthew	c. 1200-1259
Chang Chun Kiu	1148-1227	Rumi	1207-1273
Elmacin, George	1223-1274	Sa'Di	1184-1291
Farid Ud-Din Attar	1119-1229	Siger De Brabant	1235-1281
Garland, John	1195-1272	Snorri, Sturluson	1179-1241
Grosseteste, Robert	c. 1175-1253	Thomas the Rhymer	
Guillaume De Lorris	c. 1230	(of Ercelduone)	c. 1220-c. 1297
Guittone D'Arezzo	1230-1294	Walther, Von Der	
Ibn Arabi	1165-1240	Vogelweide	1170-1230
Ibn Athir	1160-1234		

Arnoflo Di Cambio	1232-1301	**Pisano, Giovanni**	1249-1320
Cimabué, Giovanni	1240-1302	**Pisano, Niccola**	1225-1278
Hsia Kuei	1180-1230		

COMPOSERS

Hallé, Adam de la	1235-1287

Li Tsung (Sung Dynasty)	1224-1264	Hsien Tsung (Mangu Khan—	
Tu Tsung (Sung Dynasty)	1264-1274	Mongol Dynasty)	1251-1260
Kung Ti (Sung Dynasty)	1274-1276	Shih Tsu (Kublai Khan—	
Ting Tsung (Kuyak Khan—		Mongol Dynasty)	1260-1294
Mongol Dynasty)	1246-1251		

POPES

Innocent IV	1243-1254	Clement IV	1265-1268
Alexander IV	1254-1261	St. Gregory X	1271-1276
Urban IV	1261-1264		

FRANCE. HEADS OF STATE

Louis IX	1226-1270	Philip III	1270-1285

HOLY ROMAN EMPERORS

Conrad IV	1250-1254	Rudolf I	1273-1291
Interregnum			

ENGLAND. SOVEREIGNS

Henry III	1216-1272	Edward I	1272-1307

SWEDEN. KINGS

Valdemar	1250-1275	Magnus I Ladulas	1275-1290

PORTUGAL. KINGS

Alphonso III	1248-1279

WRITERS

Abano, Pietro D'	1250-1316	Guittone D'Arezzo	1230-1294
Abul Faraj	1226-1286	Immanuel Ben Solomon	1265-1330
Abul Feda, Ismail Ibn Ali	1273-1331	Jacopone, Da Todi	1230-1306
Albertus, Magnus	1206-1280	Jalal Ad-Din Rumi	1207-1273
Aquinas, Thomas	1225-1275	Joinville, Jean	1224-1319
Angioleri, Cello	1260-1312	Latini, Brunetto	1210-1294
Bacon, Roger	1214-1294	Lully, Raymond	c. 1232-1315
Bedaresi, Yedaiah	1270-1340	Maerlant, Jacob Van	1235-1300
Beha Ud-Din Zuhair	1186-1258	Mannyng, Robert	1264-1340
Busri	1211-1294	Meung, Jean De	1250-1305
Cavalcanti, Guido	1230-1300	Paris, Matthew	c. 1200-1259
Cecco D'Ascoli	1257-1327	Philes, Manuel	1275-1345
Celano, Thomas de	c. 1255	Robert of Gloucester	fl. 1260-1300
Cino Da Pistoia	1270-1336	Rumi	1207-1273
Dante, Aligheiri	1265-1321	Sa'Di	1184-1291
Duns Scotus, Johannes	c. 1265-1308	Siger De Brabant	1235-1281
Eckhart, Johannes	1260-1327	Thomas the Rhymer	
Elmacin, George	1223-1274	(of Erceldoune)	c. 1220-c. 1297
Garland, John	1195-1272	Villani, Giovanni	1275-1348
Grosseteste, Robert	c. 1175-1253		

Arnoflo Di Cambio	1232-1301	Giotto	1267-1337
Cavallini, Pietro	1259-1344	Pisano, Andrea	1270-1348
Cimabué, Giovanni	1240-1302	Pisano, Giovanni	1249-1314
Duccio Di Buoninsegna	1255-1319	Pisano, Niccola	1225-1278
Gaddi, Gaddeo	1260-1332		

COMPOSERS

Hallé, Adam de la	1235-1287

Kung Ti (Sung Dynasty)	1274-1276	Shih Tsu (Kublai Khan—	
Tuan Tsung		Mongol Dynasty)	1260-1294
(Sung Dynasty)	1278-1279	Ch'Eng Tsung	
Ti-Ping		(Mongol Dynasty)	1294-1307
(Sung Dynasty	1278-1279		

POPES

St. Gregory X	1271-1276	Martin IV	1281-1285
Adrian V	1276	Honorius IV	1285-1287
St. Innocent V	1276	Nicholas IV	1288-1292
John XXI	1276-1277	St. Celestine V	1294
Nicholas III	1277-1280	Boniface VIII	1294-1303

FRANCE. HEADS OF STATE

Philip III	1270-1285	Philip IV	1285-1314

HOLY ROMAN EMPERORS

Rudolf I	1273-1291	Albert I	1298-1308
Adolf of Nassau	1292-1298		

ENGLAND. SOVEREIGNS

Edward I	1272-1307

SWEDEN. KINGS

Magnus I Ladulas	1275-1290	Birger	1290-1318

PORTUGAL. KINGS

Alphonso III	1248-1279	Diniz	1279-1325

WRITERS

Abano, Pietro D'	1250-1316	Guittone D'arezzo	1230-1294
Abul Faraj	1226-1286	Hampole, Richard	
Abul Feda, Ismail-Ibn-Ali	1273-1331	Rolle De	1290-1349
Albertus, Magnus	1206-1280	Immanuel Ben Solomon	1265-1330
Angiolieri, Cecco	1260-1312	Jacopone Da Todi	1230-1306
Aungervyle, Richard	1287-1345	Joinville, Jean	1224-1319
Bacon, Roger	1214-1294	Latini, Brunetto	1210-1294
Bedaresi, Yedaiah	1270-1340	Lully, Raymond	c. 1232-1315
Buridan, Jean	1295-1366	Machaut, Guillaume De	1300-1377
Busri	1211-1294	Maerlant, Jacob Van	1235-1300
Cavalcanti, Guido	1250-1300	Mannyng, Robert	1264-1340
Cecco D'Ascoli	1257-1327	Meung, Jean De	1250-1305
Cino Da Pistoia	1270-1336	Philes, Manuel	1275-1345
Clanvowe, Sir Thomas	c. 1300	Robert of Gloucester	fl. 1260-1300
Conrad of Wurzburg	d. 1287	Ruis, Juan	1283-1350
Dafydd Ab Gwylym	c. 1300	Sa'Di	1184-1291
Dante, Alighieri	1265-1321	Siger De Brabant	1235-1281
Duns Scotus, Johannes	1265-1308	Thomas the Rhymer	
Eckhart, Johannes	1260-1327	(of Erceldoune)	c. 1220-c. 1297
Gersonides, Levi	1288-1344	Villani, Giovanni	1275-1348
Gregoras, Nicephorus	1295-1360		

Agnolo	c. 1300	Giotto	1267-1337
Agostino	c. 1300	Lorenzetti, Ambrogio	1300-1348
Arnolfo Di Cambio	1232-1301	Lorenzetti, Pietro	1280-1348
Cavallini, Pietro	1259-1344	Martini, Simone	1284-1344
Cimabue	1240-1302	Pisano, Andrea	1270-1348
Daddi, Bernardo	1290-1350	Pisano, Giovanni	1249-1314
Duccio Di Buoninsegna	1255-1319	Pisano, Niccola	1225-1278
Gaddi, Gaddeo	1260-1332	Strode, Ralph	c. 1300
Gaddi, Taddeo	1300-1366		

COMPOSERS

Hallé, Adam de la	1235-1278

1302   Battle at Courtrai.
1314   Battle of Bannockburn.
1346   Battle of Crecy.
1347   English capture Calais.
1348   Black Death plague.
1350   Order of the Garter instituted.
1351   Statute of labourers passed in England.
1354   Rienzi killed.
1356   Battle of Poitiers.
1381   Poll Tax established in England.
        Wat Tyler and peasant uprising.
1388   Battle of Otterburn.
1397   Duke of Gloucestershire murdered.
1400   Owen Glendower leads Welsh revolt.

PROMINENT PEOPLE

Marco Polo   1256-1323   Rienzi, Cola di   1313-1354
Bruce, Robert   1274-1329

[MONGOL (Yuan) DYNASTY]

Ch'Eng Tsung	1294-1307	Ying Tsung	1320-1323
Wu Tsung	1307-1311	T'Ai Ting Ti	1323-1328
Jen Tsung	1311-1320		

POPES

Boniface VIII	1294-1303	Clement V	
St. Benedict XI	1303-1304	(Avignon 1309)	1305-1314
		John XXII (Avignon)	1316-1334

FRANCE. HEADS OF STATE

Philip IV	1285-1314	Philip V	1316-1322
Louis X	1314-1316	Charles IV	1322-1328
John I	1316		

HOLY ROMAN EMPERORS

Albert I	1298-1308	Louis IV of Bavaria	1314-1347
Henry VII of Luxemburg	1308-1313		

ENGLAND. SOVEREIGNS

Edward I	1272-1307	Edward II	1307-1327

SWEDEN. KINGS

Birger	1290-1318	Magnus II	1319-1365

PORTUGAL. KINGS

Diniz	1279-1325	Alphonso IV	1325-1357

SCOTLAND. KINGS

Robert I (The Bruce)	1306-1329

WRITERS

Abano, Pietro D'	1250-1316	Guittone D'Areezo	1230-1394
Abulfeda, Ismail-Ibn-Ali	1273-1331	Hampole, Richard	
Angliolieri, Cecco	1260-1312	Rolle De	1290-1349
Aungervyle, Richard	1287-1345	Immanuel Ben Solomon	1265-1330
Barbour, John	1316-1395	Jacopone, Da Todi	1230-1306
Bedaresi, Yedaiah	1270-1340	Joinville, Jean	1224-1319
Boccaccio, Giovanni	1313-1375	Lully, Raymond	c. 1232-1315
Boner, Ulrich	1324-1349	Machaut, Guillaume De	1300-1377
Buridan, Jean	1295-1366	Mannyng, Robert	1264-1340
Cecco D'Ascoli	1257-1327	Pegolotti, Francesco	
Cino Da Pistoia	1270-1336	Balducci	1315-1340
Dante, Alighieri	1265-1321	Petracht	1304-1374
Duns Scotus, Johannes	c. 1265-1308	Philes, Manuel	1275-1345
Eckhart, Johannes	1260-1327	Ruis, Juan	1283-1350
Gersonides, Levi	1288-1344	Villani, Giovanni	1275-1348
Gregoras, Nicephorus	1295-1360	Wycliffe, John	c. 1320-1384
Guiart, Guillaume	d. 1316		

Arnolfo Di Cambio	1232-1301	Giotto	1267-1337
Cavallini, Pietro	1259-1344	Lorenzetti, Ambrogio	1300-1348
Cimabue, Giovanni	1240-1302	Lorenzetti, Pietro	1250-1348
Daddi, Bernardo	1290-1350	Martini, Simone	1284-1344
Duccio Di Buoninsegna	1255-1319	Orcagna	1308-1368
Gaddi, Gaddeo	1260-1332	Pisano, Andrea	1270-1348
Gaddi, Taddeo	1300-1366	Pisano, Giovanni	1249-1314

T'Ai Ting Ti	1323-1328	Wen Tsung	1329-1332
Yu Chu	1328	Ning Tsung	1332-1333
Ming Tsung	1328-1329	Shun Ti	1333-1368

POPES

John XXII (Avignon)	1316-1334	Benedict XII (Avignon)	1334-1342
Nicholas V		Clement VI (Avignon)	1342-1352
(anti-pope in Italy)	1328-1330		

FRANCE. HEADS OF STATE

| Charles IV | 1322-1328 | John | 1350-1364 |
| Philip VI | 1328-1350 | | |

HOLY ROMAN EMPERORS

| Louis IV of Bavaria | 1314-1347 | Charles IV of Luxumberg | 1347-1378 |

ENGLAND. SOVEREIGNS

| Edward II | 1307-1327 | Edward III | 1327-1377 |

SWEDEN. KINGS

| Magnus II | 1319-1365 |

PORTUGAL. KINGS

| Alphonso IV | 1325-1357 |

SCOTLAND. KINGS

| Robert I (The Bruce) | 1306-1329 | David II | 1329-1371 |

WRITERS

Abulfeda, Ismail Ibn Ali	1273-1331	Johannes Von Saaz	1350-1415
Aungervyle, Richard	1287-1345	Langland, William	1332-1400
Barbour, John	1316-1395	Lopez De Ayala,	
Bedaresi, Yedaiah	1270-1340	Don Pedro	1332-1407
Boccaccio, Giovanni	1313-1375	Machaut, Guillaume De	1300-1377
Boner, Ulrich	fl. 1324-1349	Mannyng, Robert	1264-1340
Buridan, Jean	1295-1366	Mezieres, Phillipe De	1327-1405
Cecco D'Ascoli	1257-1327	Michel of Northgate,	
Chaucer, Geoffrey	1340-1400	Dan	c. 1340
Cino Da Pistoia	1270-1336	Minot, Laurence	1333-1352
Crescas, Hasdai		Niem, Dietrich of	1345-1418
Ben Abraham	1340-1410	Pegolotti, Francesco	
Deschamps, Eustache	1346-1406	Balducci	1315-1340
Eckhart, Johannes	1260-1327	Petracht	1304-1374
Froissart, Jean	1338-1410	Philes, Manuel	1275-1345
Gersonides, Levi	1288-1344	Ruis, Juan de	1283-1350
Gregoras, Nicephorus	1295-1360	Sachetti, Franco	1330-1400
Hampole, Richard		Villani, Giovanni	1275-1348
Rolle De	1290-1349	Wycliffe, John	c. 1320-1384
Ibn Khaldun	1332-1406	Wyntoun, Andrew of	c. 1350-1420
Immanuel Ben Solomon	1265-1330		

Altichiero Da Zevio	1320-1385	**Lorenzetti,** Ambrogio	1300-1348
Cavallini, Pietro	1259-1344	**Lorenzetti,** Pietro	1280-1348
Daddi, Bernardo	1290-1350	**Martini,** Simone	1284-1344
Gaddi, Aquolo	1333-1396	**Orcagna**	1308-1368
Gaddi, Gaddeo	1260-1332	**Pisano,** Andrea	1270-1348
Gaddi, Taddeo	1300-1366	**Sluter,** Claus	1350-1405
Giotto	1267-1337	**Spinelo,** Aretino	1330-1410

Shun Ti [Mongol   T'Ai Tsu (Ming Dynasty)   1368-1398
   (Yuan) Dynasty]   1333-1368

POPES

Clement VI (Avignon)	1342-1352	Urban V (Avignon)	1362-1370
Innocent VI (Avignon)	1352-1362	Gregory XI	1370-1378

FRANCE. HEADS OF STATE

John	1350-1364	Charles V	1364-1380

HOLY ROMAN EMPERORS

Charles IV of Luxemberg   1347-1378

ENGLAND. SOVEREIGNS

Edward III   1327-1377

SWEDEN. KINGS

Magnus	1319-1365	Albert of Mecklenburg	1365-1388

PORTUGAL. KINGS

Alphonso IV	1375-1357	Ferdinand	1367-1383
Pedro I	1357-1367		

SCOTLAND. KINGS

David II	1329-1371	Robert II	1371-1390

WRITERS

Barbour, John	1316-1395	Langland, William	1332-1400
Bartoli, Taddeo	1362-1422	Lopez De Ayala,	
Boccaccio, Giovanni	1313-1375	Don Pedro	1332-1407
Bruni, Leonardo	1369-1444	Lydgate, John	1373-1450
Buridan, Jean	1295-1366	Machaut, Guillaume De	1300-1377
Chaucer, Geoffrey	1340-1400	Mezieres, Phillippe De	1327-1405
Crescas, Hasdai, Ben		Minot, Laurence	1333-1352
Abraham	1340-1410	Niem, Dietrich of	1345-1418
Deschamps, Eustache	1346-1406	Petracht	1304-1374
Froissart, Jean	1338-1410	Pisan, Christine De	1364-1430
Gregoras, Nicephorus	1295-1360	Sachetti, Franco	1330-1400
Hoccleve, Thomas	1368-1450	Wycliffe, John	c. 1320-1384
Ibn, Khaldun	1332-1406	Wyntoun, Andrew of	1350-1420
Johannes Von Saaz	1350-1415		

ARTISTS

Altichiero Da Zevio	1320-1385	Gaddi, Taddeo	1300-1366
Campin, Robert	1375-1444	Lorenzo, Monaco	1370-1425
Della Quercia, Jacopo	1374-1438	Orcagna	1308-1368
Eyck Van, Hubert	1366-1426	Sluter, Claus	1350-1405
Fabriano, Gentile Da	1370-1427	Spinelo, Arenito	1330-1410
Gaddi, Aquolo	1333-1396		

T'Ai Tsu	1368-1398	Hui Ti	1398-1402

POPES

Gregory XI	1370-1378	Boniface IX	1389-1404
Urban VI	1378-1389	Benedict XIII (anti-pope)	1394-1423
Clement VII (anti-pope)	1378-1394		

FRANCE. HEADS OF STATE

Charles V	1364-1380	Charles VI	1380-1422

HOLY ROMAN EMPERORS

Charles IV of Luxemberg	1347-1378	Rupert of the Palatinate	1400-1410
Wenzel of Luxemberg	1378-1400		

ENGLAND. SOVEREIGNS

Edward III	1327-1377	Henry IV	1399-1413
Richard II	1377-1399		

SWEDEN. KINGS

Albert of Mecklenburf	1365-1388	Eric of Pomerania (XIII)	1397-1439
Margaret	1389-1397		

PORTUGAL. KINGS

Ferdinand	1367-1383	John I	1385-1433
Civil War	1383-1385		

KINGS OF SCOTLAND

Robert II	1371-1390	Robert III	1390-1406

Alphonsus, A Sancta		Ibn, Khaldun	1332-1406
Maria	1396-1456	Johannes, Von Saaz	1350-1415
Barbour, John	1316-1395	Langland, William	1332-1400
Bartoli, Taddeo	1362-1422	La Sale, Antoine De	c. 1398-1470
Basselin, Olivier	1400-1450	Lopez De Ayala	
Berners, Juliana	c. 1388	Don Pedro	1332-1407
Bruni, Leonardo	1369-1444	Lydgate, John	1373-1450
Capgrave, John	1393-1464	Machaut, Guillaume De	1300-1377
Chartier, Alain	1392-1430	Madhava, Acharya	1380-
Chaucer, Geoffrey	1340-1400	March, Auzias	1379-1459
Codinus, George	c. 1400	Mezieres, Phillippe De	1327-1405
Crescas, Hasdai Ben		Niem, Dietrich of	1345-1418
Abraham	1340-1410	d'Orleans, Charles	1391-1465
Deschamps, Eustache	1346-1406	Petracht	1304-1374
Flavius, Blondus	1388-1463	Pisan, Christine de	1364-1431
Froissart, Jean	1338-1410	Poggio (Bracciolini)	1380-1459
George of Trebizond	1395-1484	Sachetti, Franco	1330-1400
Hafiz	fl. 1388	Schiltberger, Johann	1381-1440
Hans Der Guheler	c. 1400	Thomas A Kempis	1380-1471
Hardyng, John	1378-1465	Villena, Enrique De	1384-1433
Hilton, Walter	d. 1396	Wycliffe, John	c. 1320-1384
Hoccleve, Thomas	1368-1450	Wyntoun, Andrew of	1350-1420

ARTISTS

Angelico, Fra	1387-1455	Gaddi, Aquolo	1333-1396
Altichiero, Da Zievo	1320-1385	Ghiberti, Lorenzo	1378-1455
Bonfigli, Benedetto	c. 1400	Limburg, Pol De	c. 1400
Bouts, Dierick	1400-1475	Limburg, Hennequin de	c. 1400
Brunelleschi, Filippo	1377-1446	Limburg, Hermann de	c. 1400
Campin, Robert	1375-1444	Lochner, Stephan	1400-1451
Carpi, Ugo Da	c. 1400	Lorenzo, Monaco	1370-1425
Castagno, Andrea del	1409-1480	Masolino Da Panicale	1383-1447
Christus, Peter	1400-1473	Michelozzo Di	
Della Quercia, Jacopo	1374-1438	Martolommeo	1396-1472
Della Robbia, Luca	1399-1482	Pisano, Vittore	1397-1455
Diamante, Fra	c. 1400	Sasseta, Stefano	
Donatello	1386-1466	Di Giovanni	1392-1450
Eyck, Van Hubert	1366-1426	Spinelo, Arenito	1330-1410
Eyck, Van Jan	1385-1441	Squarcione, Francesco	1394-1474
Fabriano, Gentile Da	1370-1427	Uccello, Paolo	1397-1475
Filarete, Antonio	1400-1470	Weyden, Rogier, Van Der	1400-1464
Francke, Meister	c. 1400		

COMPOSERS

Wilkinson, Robert	c. 1400

G

1403	Battle of Shrewsbury.
1414	Council of Constance.
1415	Battle of Agincourt.
1428	English seige of Orleans.
1431	Joan of Arc burnt at stake.
1437	James I of Scotland murdered.
1438	First printing at Haarlem.
1440	Eton College founded.
1455	The start of the Wars of the Roses. Battle of St. Albans.
1460	Battle of Northampton.
	Battle of Wakefield.
1461	Second Battle of St. Albans.
	Battle of Towton Field.
1464	Battle of Hexham.
1471	Battle of Barnet.
	Battle of Tewkesbury.
1476	Caxton begins printing.
1478	Spanish inquisition begins.
1483	Edward V. murdered.
1485	Battle of Bosworth Field.
1497	Newfoundland discovered by the Cabots.
	Cape of Good Hope rounded by Vasco de Gama.
1498	Columbus discovers America.

PROMINENT PEOPLE

Joan of Arc	1412-1431	Copernicus, Nicolaus	1473-1543
Caxton, William	1422-1491	Warbeck, Perkin	1474-1499
Columbus, Christopher	1446-1506	Cabot, Sebastian	1474-1557
Savonarola, Fra Giralamo	1452-1498	Borgia, Cesare	1476-1507
Vascoe De Gama	1460-1524	More, Sir Thomas	1478-1535
Pizarro, Francesco	1471-1541	Borgia, Lucrece	1480-1519
Wolsey, Thomas, Cardinal	1471-1530		

T'Ai Tsu	1368-1398	Jen Tsung	1424-1425
Hui Tui	1398-1402	Hsuan Tsung	1425-1435
Ch'Eng Tsu	1402-1424		

POPES

Boniface IX	1389-1404	Alexander V (anti-pope)	1409-1410
Benedict XIII (anti-pope)	1394-1423	Martin V	1417-1431
Innocent VII	1404-1406	Clement VIII (anti-pope)	1423-1429
Gregory XII	1406-1415	Benedict XIV (anti-pope)	1425-1430
John XXIII (anti-pope)	1410-1415		

FRANCE. HEADS OF STATE

Charles VI	1380-1422	Charles VII	1422-1461

HOLY ROMAN EMPERORS

Rupert of the Palatinate	1400-1410	Sigismund of Luxumberg	1410-1437

ENGLAND. SOVEREIGNS

Henry IV	1399-1413	Henry VI	1422-1461
Henry V	1413-1422		

SWEDEN. KINGS

Eric of Pomerania	1397-1439

PORTUGAL. KINGS

John I	1385-1433

KINGS OF SCOTLAND

Robert III	1309-1406	James I	1406-1437

ELECTORS OF BRANDENBURG

Frederick I	1415-1440

WRITERS

Alberti, Leon Battista	1404-1472	Hardyng, John	1378-1465
Alphonsus, A Sancta	1396-1456	Hoccleve, Thomas	1368-1450
Bartoli, Taddeo	1362-1422	Ibn, Khaldun	1332-1406
Basselin, Olivier	1400-1450	Jami	1414-1492
Bruni, Leonardo	1369-1444	Johannes Von Saaz	1350-1415
Capgrave, John	1393-1464	La Salle, Antoine De c. 1398-1470	
Chartier, Alain	1392-1430	Lopez De Ayala, Don Pedro	1332-1407
Chastellain, Georges	1415-1475	Lydgate, John	1373-1450
Conti, Niccolo De	1419-1444	March, Auziàs	1397-1459
Deschamps, Eustache	1346-1406	Mena, Juan De	1411-1456
Dlugosz, Jan	1415-1480	Mezieres, Phillipe De	1327-1405
Flavius, Blondus	1388-1463	Niem, Dietrich of	1345-1418
Froissart, Jean	1338-1410	d'Orleans, Charles	1391-1465
George of Trebizond	1395-1484	Pecock, Reginald	1395-1460
Gower, John	d. 1408	Pisan, Christine De	1364-1430

Poggio, (Bracciolini)	1380-1459	Villena, Enrique De	1384-1433
Schiltberger, Johann	1381-1440	Worcester, William	1415-1482
Thomas A Kempis	1379-1471	Wyntoun, Andrew of	1350-1420

ARTISTS

Angelico, Fra	1387-1455	Lochner, Stefan	1400-1451
Bouts, Dierick	1400-1475	Lorenzo, Monaco	1370-1425
Brunelleschi, Filippo	1377-1446	Marmion, Simon	1425-1489
Campin, Robert	1375-1444	Masaccio	1401-1428
Castagno, Andrea Del	1409-1480	Michelozzi, Michelozzo	
Della Quercia, Jacopo	1367-1438	Di Bartolommeo	1396-1472
Della Robbia, Luca	1399-1482	Piero Della Francesca	1420-1492
Donatello	1386-1466	Pisano, Vittore	1397-1455
Eyck, Hubert Van	1366-1426	Rossellino, Bernado	1409-1464
Eyck, Jan Van	1385-1441	Sasseta, Stefano	
Fabriano, Gentile Da	1370-1427	Di Giovanni	1392-1450
Filarete, Antonio	1400-1470	Sluter, Claus	1350-1405
Fra Filippo Lippi	1406-1469	Spinelo, Aretino	1330-1410
Fouquet, Jean	1415-1485	Squarcione, Francesco	1394-1474
Ghiberti, Lorenzo	1378-1455	Uccello, Paolo	1397-1475
Gozzoli, Benozzo	1420-1497	Weyden, Rogier, Van Der	1400-1464

Hsuan Tsung	1425-1435	Tai Tsung	1449-1457
Ying Tsung	1435-1449		

POPES

Martin V	1417-1431	Eugenius IV	1431-1447
Clement VIII (anti-pope)	1423-1429	Nicholas V	1447-1455
Benedict XIV (anti-pope)	1425-1430	Felix V (anti-pope)	1439-1449

FRANCE. HEADS OF STATE

Charles VII	1422-1461

HOLY ROMAN EMPERORS

Sigismund of Luxumberg	1410-1437	Frederick III	1440-1493
Albert II	1438-1440		

ENGLAND. SOVEREIGNS

Henry VI	1422-1461

SWEDEN. KINGS

Eric of Pomerania	1397-1439	Charles VIII	1448-1457
Christopher of Bavaria	1439-1448		

PORTUGAL. KINGS

John I	1385-1433	Alphonso V	1438-1481
Edward	1433-1438		

SCOTLAND. KINGS

James I	1401-1437	James II	1437-1460

ELECTORS OF BRANDENBURG

Frederick I	1415-1440	Frederick II	1440-1470

WRITERS

Abarbanel, Isaac Ben		Ficino, Marsilio	1433-1499
Jehudah	1437-1508	Flavius, Blondus	1388-1463
Alberti, Leon Battista	1404-1472	George of Trebizond	1395-1484
Alphonsus, A Sancta Maria	1396-1456	Hardyng, John	1378-1465
Alunno, Niccolo	1430-1502	Hay, Gilbert	1450
Auvergne, Martial de	1430-1508	Hoccleve, Thomas	1368-1450
Basselin, Olivier	1400-1450	Holland, Richard	1450
Boiardo, Matteo Maria	1434-1494	Jami	1414-1492
Bradshaw, Henry	1450-1513	Krantz, Albert	1450-1517
Bruni, Leonardo	1369-1444	La Salle, Antoine De	1398-1470
Capgrave, John	1393-1464	Lydgate, John	1373-1450
Chartier, Alain	1392-1430	Manrique, Gomez	1415-1490
Chastellain, Georges	1415-1475	Manrique, Jorge	1440-1479
Comines, Phillippe De	c. 1445-1509	March, Auziàs	1397-1459
Conti, Nicolo De	1419-1444	Mena, Juan De	1411-1456
Dlugosz, Jan	1415-1480	Molinet, Jean	1433-1507
Ducas	1450	d'Orleans, Charles	1391-1465

Pecock, Reginald	1395-1460	Schiltberger, Johann	1381-1440
Pisan, Christine De	1364-1430	Thomas A Kempis	1379-1471
Poggio, (Bracciolini)	1380-1459	Villena, Enrique De	1384-1433
Pontanus, Jovianus	1426-1503	Villon, Francois	1431-1463
Pulci, Luigi	1432-1484	Worcester, William	1415-1482
Ros, Sir Richard	1429-		

ARTISTS

Angelico, Fra	1387-1455	Gozzoli, Benozzo	1420-1497
Antonello Da Messina	1430-1479	Liberale, Antonio	1445-1526
Baldovinetti, Alessio	1427-1499	Lochner, Stefan	1400-1451
Bellini, Gentile	1429-1507	Mantegna, Andrea	1431-1506
Bellini, Giovanni	1430-1516	Marmion, Simon	1425-1489
Botticelli, Sandro	1444-1510	Masaccio	1401-1428
Bouts, Dierick	1400-1475	Melozzo, Da Forli	1438-1494
Bramante, Douato	1444-1514	Memlinc, Hans	1430-1494
Brunelleschi, Filippo	1377-1446	Michelozzi, Michelozzo	
Campin, Robert	1375-1444	Di Bartolommeo	1396-1472
Castagno, Andrea Del	1409-1480	Mino Da Fiesola	1430-1484
Christus, Peter	1400-1473	Montagna, Bartolomeo	1450-1523
Civitali, Matteo	1435-1501	Morone, Domenico	1442-1517
Cossa, Francesco Del	1435-1477	Perugino, Pietro	1450-1524
Costa, Lorenzo	1460-1535	Piero Della Francesca	1420-1492
Crivelli, Carlo	1433-1493	Pisano, Vittore	1397-1455
Della Quercia, Jacopo	1367-1438	Rossellino, Antonio	1427-1479
Della Robbia, Andrea	1435-1525	Rossellino, Bernado	1409-1464
Della Robbia, Luca	c. 1400-1482	Sasseta, Stefano	
Desiderio Da Settignano	1428-1464	Di Giovanni	1392-1450
Domenico, Veneziano	1438-1461	Schongauer, Martin	1445-1491
Donatello	1386-1466	Signorelli, Luca	1450-1523
Eyck, Hubert Van	1366-1426	Sluter, Claus	1350-1405
Eyck, Jan Van	1385-1441	Spinelo, Aretino	1330-1410
Fabriano, Gentile Da	1370-1427	Squarcione, Francesco	1394-1474
Filarete, Antonio	1400-1470	Stoss, Veit	1438-1533
Fouquet, Jean	1415-1485	Tura, Cosimo	1430-1498
Florenzo Di, Lorenzo	1445-1525	Uccello, Paolo	1397-1475
Foppa, Vincenzo	1427-1515	Van Der Goes, Hugo	1440-1482
Fra Filippo Lippi	1406-1469	Verrocchio, Andrea Del	1435-1488
Francia	1450-1517	Vivarini, Antonio	1440-1476
Ghiberti, Lorenzo	1378-1455	Vivarini, Bartolommeo fl.	1450-1499
Ghirlandajo, Domenico	1449-1494	Weyden, Rogier Van Der	1400-1464
Giocondo, Fra Giovanni	1433-1515	Wohlgemuth, Michael	1434-1519

COMPOSERS

Des Pres, Josquin	1450-1521	Obrecht, Jakob	1430-1500
Isaac, Heinrich	1450	Okheghem, Joannes	1430-1495

Ying Tsung (Restored)   1457-1464   Hsien Tsung   1464-1487

POPES

Nicholas V	1447-1455	Paul II	1464-1471
Calextus III	1455-1458	Sixtus IV	1471-1484
Pius II	1458-1464		

FRANCE. HEADS OF STATE

Charles VII   1422-1461   Louis XI   1461-1483

HOLY ROMAN EMPERORS

Frederick III   1440-1493

ENGLAND. SOVEREIGNS

Henry VI (deposed)	1422-1461	Henry VI (again)	1470-1471
Edward IV	1461-1470	Edward IV	1471-1483

SWEDEN. KINGS

Charles VIII	1448-1457	Regency under Sten Sture	
Christian I	1457-1464	the elder	1470-1497
Charles VIII (again)	1464-1465		
	1467-1470		

PORTUGAL. KINGS

Alphonso V   1438-1481

SCOTLAND. KINGS

James II   1437-1460   James III   1460-1488

ELECTORS OF BRANDENBURG

Frederick II   1440-1470   Albert Achilles   1470-1486

RUSSIA. TSARS

Ivan III, The Great   1462-1505

WRITERS

Abarbanel, Isaac Ben		Boyce, Hector	1465-1536
Jehudah	1437-1508	Bradshaw, Henry	1450-1513
Accolti, Bernardo	1465-1536	Brant, Sebastian	1457-1521
Achillini, Alessandro	1463-1512	Capgrave, John	1393-1464
Alberti, Leone Battista	1404-1472	Castellesi, Adriano	1460-1521
Alunno, Niccolo	1430-1502	Celtes, Konrad	1459-1508
Ariosto, Lodovico	1474-1533	Chastellain, Georges	1415-1475
Auvergne, Martial D'	1430-1508	Comines, Phillipe De	c. 1445-1509
Azurara, Gomez Eannes D'	d. 1474	Copernicus, Nicolas	1473-1543
Bembo, Pietro	1470-1547	Delmedigo, Elijah	1460-1497
Boiardo, Matteo Maria	1434-1494	Dlugosz, Jan	1415-1480

Douglas, Gavin	1474-1522	Murner, Thomas	1475-1537
Dunbar, William	1460-1520	Nifo, Agostino	1473-1538
Dunstable, John	d. 1453	d,Orleans, Charles	1391-1465
Encina, Juan Del	1468-1529	Pecock, Reginald	1395-1466
Erasmus, Desiderius	1466-1536	Peter, Martyr Anglerius	1459-1525
Ficino, Marsilio	1433-1499	Pico Della Mirandola,	
Flavius, Blondus	1388-1463	Giovanni	1463-1494
George of Trebizond	1395-1484	Poggio (Bracciolini)	1380-1459
Gringoire, Pierre	1475-1539	Politian, Angelo Ambrogini	1454-1494
Harry, The Minstrel	1470-1490	Pontanus, Jovianus	1426-1503
Henryson, Robert	fl. 1470-1500	Pulci, Bernardo	1438-1488
Jami	1414-1492	Pulci, Luigi	1432-1484
Kennedy, Walter	1460-1508	Rastell, John	1475-1536
Krantz, Henry	1450-1517	Resende, Garcia De	1470-1536
Hay, Gilbert	1450	Reuchlin, Johann	1455-1522
Holland, Richard	1450	Ros, Sir Richard	1429-
La Salle, Antoine de	1398-1470	Ruccelai, Giovanni	1475-1525
Le Maire De Belges, Jean	1473-1525	Sannazaro, Jacopo	1458-1530
Machiavelli, Niccolo	1469-1527	Sanuto, Marino	1466-1533
Major, John	1470-1550	Savonarola, Girolamo	1452-1498
Malory, Sir Thomas	-1471	Skelton, John	1460-1529
Manrique, Gomez	1415-1490	Thomas A Kempis	1379-1471
Manrique, Jorge	1440-1479	Villon, Francois	1431-1463
March, Auziàs	1397-1459	Vincente, Gil	1465-1536
Molinet, Jean	1433-1507	Virgil, Polydore	1470-1555
Medwall, Henry	1462-1505	Worcester, William	1415-1482
Mena, Juan De	1411-1456		

ARTISTS

Albertinelli, Mariotto	1474-1515	Cranach, Lucas	1472-1553
Angelico, Fra	1387-1455	Credi, Lorenzo Di	1457-1537
Antonello Da Messina	1430-1479	Crivelli, Carlo	1433-1493
Baccio D'Agnolo	1460-1543	Della Robbia, Andrea	1435-1525
Baldovinetti, Alessio	1427-1499	Della Robbia, Giovanni	1469-1529
Bartolommeo, Di Paghlo		Della Robbia, Luca	c. 1400-1482
Fra	1475-1517	Desiderio Da Settignano	1428-1464
Bellini, Gentile	1429-1507	Domenico, Veneziano	1438-1461
Bellini, Giovanni	1430-1516	Donatello	1386-1466
Bianchiferrari, Francesco		Durer, Albrecht	1471-1528
de	1460-1510	Filarete, Antonio	1400-1470
Boltraffio, Giovanni		Fiorenzo Di Lorenzo	1445-1525
Antonio	1467-1516	Foppa, Vincenzo	1427-1515
Borgdgnone, Ambrogio	1473-1524	Fouquet, Jean	1415-1485
Bosch, Hieronymus	1460-1516	Fra Fillipo Lippi	1406-1469
Botticelli, Sandro	1444-1510	Francia	1450-1517
Bouts, Dierick	1400-1475	Froment, Nicolas	1450-1490
Bramante, Donato	1444-1514	Geertgen, Van Haarlem	1465-1493
Briosco, Andrea	1470-1532	Ghiberti, Lorenzo	1378-1455
Burgkmair, Hans	1473-1531	Ghirlandajo, Domenico	1449-1494
Carpaccio, Vittorio	1465-1522	Giocondo, Fra Giovanni	1433-1515
Castagno, Andrea Del	1409-1480	Gozzoli, Benozzo	1420-1497
Catena, Vincenzo		Holbein, Hans	
Di Biagio	1470-1531	the elder	1460-1524
Christus, Peter	1400-1473	Krafft, Adam	1455-1509
Cima, Giambattista	1459-1517	Leonardo Da Vinci	1452-1519
Civitali, Matteo	1435-1501	Liberale Antonio	1445-1526
Cossa, Francesco Del	1435-1477	Lippi, Fillipino	1458-1504
Costa, Lorenzo	1460-1535	Lochner, Stephan	1400-1451

Luini, Barnardino	1475-1532	Pisano, Vitorre	1397-1455
Mabuse, Jan	1472-1534	Riemenschneider, Tilman	1460-1531
Mantegna, Andrea	1431-1506	Roberti, Ercole Di	1455-1496
Marmion, Simon	1425-1489	Rossellino, Antonio	1427-1479
Matsys, Quentin	1466-1530	Rossellino, Bernardo	1409-1464
Melozzo Da Forli	1438-1494	Sansovino, Andrea	1460-1529
Memlinc, Hans	1430-1494	Schongauer, Martin	1445-1491
Michelangelo	1475-1564	Signorelli, Luca	1450-1523
Michelozzi, Michelozzo		Solario, Andrea Da	1460-1520
Di Bartolomeo	1396-1472	Squarcione, Francesco	1394-1474
Mino Da Fiesola	1430-1484	Stoss, Veit	1438-1533
Montagna, Bartolomeo	1450-1523	Suardi, Bartolommeo	1455-1536
Morone, Domenico	1442-1517	Torrigiano, Pietro	1472-1522
Morone, Francesco	1471-1529	Tura, Cosimo	1430-1498
Moulins, Master of	1460-1529	Van Der Goes, Hugo	1440-1482
Pacher, Michael	1465-1498	Verrocchio, Andrea Del	1435-1488
Patinir, Joachim De	1475-1524	Vivarini, Antonio	1440-1476
Perugino, Pietro	1450-1524	Vivarini, Bartolommeo	1450-1499
Piero Della Francesca	1420-1492	Vivarini, Luigi	1457-1503
Piero Di Cosimo	1462-1521	Weyden, Rogier Van Der	1400-1464
Pinturicchio	1454-1513	Wohlgemuth, Michael	1434-1519

COMPOSERS

Binchois, Gilles	d. 1460	Obrecht, Jakob	1430-1500
Cornyshe, William	1465-1523	Okhegem, Joannes	1430-1495
Despres, Josquin	1450-1521		

EMPERORS OF CHINA (MING DYNASTY) 1476-1500

Hsien Tsung 1464-1487 Hsiao Tsung 1487-1505

POPES

Sixtus IV 1471-1484 Alexander VI 1492-1503
Innocent VIII 1484-1492

FRANCE. HEADS OF STATE

Louis XI 1461-1483 Louis XII 1498-1515
Charles VIII 1483-1498

HOLY ROMAN EMPERORS

Frederick III 1440-1493 Maximilian I 1493-1519

ENGLAND. SOVEREIGNS

Edward IV 1471-1483 Richard III 1483-1485
Edward V 1483 Henry VII 1485-1509

SWEDEN. KINGS

Regency under Sten Sture John II 1497-1501
the Elder 1470-1497

PORTUGAL. KINGS

Alphonso V 1438-1481 Manoel I 1495-1521
John II 1481-1495

SCOTLAND. KINGS

James III 1460-1488 James IV 1488-1513

ELECTORS OF BRANDENBURG

Albert Achilles 1486-1499 John Cicero 1499-1535

RUSSIA. TSARS

Ivan III the Great 1462-1505

Abarbanel, Isaac Ben	
Jehudah	1437-1508
Accolti, Bernardo	1465-1536
Accorso, Mariangelo	1490-1544
Achillini, Alessandro	1463-1512
Aconsio, Jacopo	1500-1566
Agrippa Von Nettesheim,	
Henry Cornelius	1486-1535
Agricola (Magister Islebius)	
Johann	1492-1566
Alamanni, Luigi	1495-1556
Alberus, Erasmus	1500-1553
Alunno, Niccolo	1430-1502
Arason, Jon	1484-1551
Aretino, Pietro	1492-1556
Ariosto, Lodovico	1474-1533
Auvergne, Martial D'	1430-1508
Aventius	1477-1534
Avila, Juan De	1500-1569
Avila Y Zuniga, Luis	1490-1560
Baldung, Grun Hans	1476-1545
Bale, John	1495-1563
Bandello, Matteo	1480-1562
Bandinelli, Baccio	1493-1560
Barclay, Alexander	1476-1552
Barros, Joao De	1496-1570
Bembo, Pietro	1470-1547
Berni, Francesco	1497-1536
Biel, Gabriel	-1495
Boiardo, Matteo, Maria	1434-1494
Boone, Andrew	1490-1549
Boscan-Almogauer, Juan	1490-1542
Boscanalmogaver, Juan	1490-1542
Boyce, Hector	1465-1536
Bradshaw, Henry	1450-1513
Brant, Sebastian	1457-1521
Castellesi, Adriano	1460-1521
Castiglioni, Baldassare	1478-1529
Castillejo, Cristobal De	1490-1550
Cavendish, George	1500-1562
Celtes, Konrad	1459-1508
Colonna, Vittoria	1490-1547
Comines, Philippe De	1445-c. 1509
Copernicus, Nicolas	1473-1543
Coverdale, Miles	
(trans bible)	1488-1569
Cranmer, Thomas	1489-1556
Delmedigo, Elijah	1460-1497
Des Periers, Bonaventure	1500-1544
Diaz Del Castillo, Bernal	1492-1581
Dlugosz, Jan	1415-1480
Douglas, Gavin	1474-1522
Dunbar, William	1460-1520
Elyot, Sir Thomas	1490-1546
Encina, Juan Del	1468-1529
Erasmus, Desiderius	1466-1536
Ficino, Marsilo	1433-1499
Firenzuola, Agnolo	1493-1545
Fleuranges, Robert De La	
Marck	1491-1537

Folengo, Theofilo	1491-1544
George of Trebizond	1395-1484
Giraldi, Giglio Gregorio	1479-1552
Gringoire, Pierre	1475-1539
Guevara, Antonio De	1490-1545
Guicciardini, Francesco	1483-1540
Guidiccioni, Giovanni	1480-1541
Hall, Edward	1499-1547
Harry The Minstrel	1470-1492
Hay, Gilbert	1450-
Henryson, Robert	fl. 1470-1500
Hessus, Helius, Eobanus	1488-1540
Heywood, John	1497-1580
Holland, Richard	1450-
Hughes, Thomas	1500-
Jami	1414-1492
Jovius, Paulus	1483-1552
Kennedy, Walter	1460-1508
Krantz, Albert	1450-1517
Latimer, Hugh	c. 1485-1555
Le Maine De Belges, Jean	1473-1525
Loyala, Ignatius de	1491-1556
Luther, Martin	1483-1546
Lyndsay, Sir David	1490-1555
Machiavelli, Niccolo	1469-1527
Magnus	1490-1558
Maitland, Sir Richard	1496-1586
Major, John	1470-1550
Manrique, Gomez	1415-1490
Manrique, Jorge	1440-1479
Marguerite of Navarre	1492-1549
Marot, Clement	1496-1544
Medwall, Henry	1462-1505
Melanchthon, Philip	1497-1560
Molinet, Jean	1433-1507
More, Sir Thomas	1478-1535
Murner, Thomas	1475-1537
Nardi, Jacopo	1476-
Nifo, Agostino	1473-1538
Oviedo Y Valdes, Gonzales	
Fernandez De	1478-1557
Paracelsus	1493-1541
Pedersen, Christiern	1480-1554
Peter, Martyr Anglerius	1459-1525
Picco Della Mirandola,	
Giovanni	1463-1494
Politian, Angelo	
Ambrogini	1454-1494
Pulci, Bernardo	1438-1488
Pulci, Luigi	1432-1484
Rabelais, Francois	1495-1553
Rastell, John	1475-1536
Resende, Garcia De	1470-1536
Reuchlin, Johann	1455-1522
Ribeiro, Bernardim	1482-1552
Ros, Sir Richard	1429-
Ruccelai, Giovanni	1475-1525
Sachs, Hans	1494-1576
Sa De Miranda,	
Francisco De	1485-1558

Sannazaro, Jacopo	1458-1530	Torres Naharro	
Sanuto, Marino	1466-1533	Bartolome De	1480-1530
Savonarola, Girolamo	1452-1495	Valdes, Juan De	1500-1541
Sceve, Maurice	1500-1564	Vida, Marco, Girolamo	1489-1566
Sepulveda, Juan Gines De	1490-1574	Vincente, Gil	1465-1536
Skelton, John	1460-1529	Virgil, Polydore	1470-1555
Stewart, William	1480-1550	Vives, Juan Luis	1492-1540
Stumpf, Johann	1500-1576	Worcester, William	1415-1482
Tasso, Bernardo	1493-1569	Zwingli, Huldreich	1484-1531

ARTISTS

Albertinelli, Mariotto	1474-1515	Cousin, Jean	1500-1590
Altdorfer, Albrecht	1480-1538	Coxcie, Michael	1499-1592
Antonello Da Messina	1430-1479	Cranach, Lucas	1472-1553
Baccio D'Agnolo	1460-1543	Credi, Lorenzo Di	1457-1537
Bagnacavallo,		Crivelli, Carlo	1433-1493
Bartolommeo	1484-1545	Della Colle, Raffaellino	1490-
Baldovinetti, Alessio	1427-1499	Delle Robbia, Andrea	1435-1525
Bandinelli, Baccio	1493-1560	Della Robbia, Giovanni	1469-1529
Bartolommeo Di Paghlo,		Della Robbia, Girolamo	1488-1566
Fra	1475-1517	Della Robbia, Luca	c. 1400-1482
Bartolommeo, Veneto	1480-1555	Dosso Dossi, Giovanni	1479-1542
Beccafumi, Domenico		Durer, Albrecht	1471-1528
Di Pace	1486-1551	Ferrari, Gaudenzio	1480-1546
Bellini, Gentile	1429-1507	Fiorenzo Di Lorenzo	1445-1525
Bellini, Giovanni	1430-1516	Foppa, Vincenzo	1427-1515
Bianchiferrari,		Fouquet, Jean	1415-1485
Francesco De	1460-1510	Francia	1450-1517
Boltraffio, Giovanni		Franciabigio	1482-1525
Francesco de	1467-1516	Froment, Nicolas	1450-1490
Bordone, Paris	1500-1571	Garofalo	1481-1559
Borgdgnone, Ambrogio	1473-1524	Geertgen, Van Haarlem	1465-1493
Bosch, Hieronymus	1460-1516	Genga, Girolamo	1476-1551
Botticelli, Sandro	1444-1510	Ghirlandajo, Domenico	1449-1494
Bramante, Donato	1444-1514	Ghirlandajo, Ridolfo	1483-1561
Briosca, Andrea	1470-1532	Giocondo, Fra Giovanni	1433-1515
Burgkmair, Hans	1473-1531	Giorgione	1478-1511
Campagnola, Domenico	1484-1563	Guilio, Romano	1499-1546
Caravagio, Polidoro Da	1500-1543	Gozzoli, Benozzo	1420-1497
Carpaccio, Vittorio	1465-1522	Grunewald, Mathias	1480-1528
Caroto, Giovanni		Heemskerk, Marten	
Francesco	1480-1555	Jacobisz	1498-1574
Castagno, Andrea Del	1409-1480	Holbein, Hans The elder	1460-1524
Castello, Giovanni Battista	1500-1569	Holbein, Hans	1497-1543
Catena, Vincenzo Di		Joos Van Cleve	1480-1540
Biagio	1470-1531	Krafft, Adam	1455-1509
Cavazzola, Paolo Morando	1486-1522	Leonardo Da Vinci	1452-1519
Cellini, Benvenuto	1500-1571	Liberale, Antonio	1445-1526
Cima, Giambattista	1459-1517	Lippi, Fillipine	1458-1504
Civerchio, Vincinzo	1500-	Lotto, Lorenzo	1480-1556
Civitali, Matteo	1435-1501	Lucas, Van Leyden	1494-1533
Cleve, Van Joos		Luini, Barnardino	1475-1532
Van Der Beke	1480-1540	Mabuse, Jan	1472-1534
Clouet, Jean	1485-1541	Mantegna, Andrea	1431-1506
Cornelisz, Lucas	1495-1552	Manuel, Nikolaus	1484-1550
Corregio	1494-1534	Marmion, Simon	1425-1489
Cossa, Francesco Del	1435-1477	Matsys, Quentin	1466-1530
Costa, Lorenzo	1460-1535	Melozzo Da Forli	1438-1494

Memlinc, Hans	1430-1494	Roberti, Ercole De	1455-1496
Michelangelo	1475-1564	Rossellino, Antonio	1427-1479
Mino Da Fiesola	1430-1484	Rossi, Giovanni	
Montagna, Bartolomeo	1450-1523	Battista De	1494-1541
Moretto Il	1494-1554	Sanmichele, Michele	1484-1559
Morone, Domenico	1442-1517	Sansovino, Andrea	
Morone, Francesco	1471-1529	Contucci Del Monte	1460-1529
Moulins, Master of	1460-1529	Sansovino, Jacopo	1486-1570
Orley, Bernard Van	1490-1540	Sarto, Andrea del	1486-1531
Pacchia, Girolamo Del	1477-1535	Schongauer, Martin	1445-1491
Pacher, Michael	1465-1498	Signorelli, Luca	1450-1523
Palma, Jacopo	1480-1528	Sodoma, Il	1477-1549
Patinir, Joachim De	1475-1524	Solaria, Andrea Da	1460-1520
Perino Del Vaga	1500-1547	Stoss, Veit	1438-1533
Peruzzi, Baldassare	1481-1536	Suardi, Bartolommeo	1455-1536
Perugino, Pietro	1450-1524	Titian	1477-1576
Piero Della Francesca	1420-1492	Torrigiano, Pietro	1472-1522
Piero Di Cosimo	1462-1521	Tura, Cosimo	1430-1498
Pinturicchio	1454-1513	Van Der Goes, Hugo	1440-1482
Piombo, Sebastian Del	1485-1547	Verrocchio, Andrea Del	1435-1488
Pontormo, Jacopo Da	1494-1552	Vivarini, Antonio	1440-1476
Pordenone, Il	1483-1539	Vivarini, Bartolommeo	1450-1499
Raphael, Sanzio	1483-1520	Vivarini, Luigi	1457-1503
Riemenschneider, Tilman	1460-1531	Wohlgemuth, Michael	1434-1519

COMPOSERS

Animuccia, Giovanni	1490-1571	Jimenez De Quesada	
Cornyshe, William	1465-1523	Gonzalo	1500-1579
Despres, Josquin	1450-1521	Obrecht, Jakob	1430-1500
Festa, Constanzo	1495-1545	Okhegem, Johannes	1430-1495
		Taverner, John	1495-1545

1500 Portuguese discover Brazil.
1506 Building of St. Peters, Rome.
1513 Battle of Flodden.
1519 Cortes conquers Mexico.
1521 Luther. Diet of Worms.

PROMINENT PEOPLE

Borgia, Cesare	1476-1507	Luther, Martin	1483-1546
Borgia, Lucrece	1480-1519	More, Sir Thomas	1478-1535
Cabot, Sebastian	1474-1557	Nostradamus	1503-1566
Calvin, John	1509-1564	Pizarro, Francesco	1471-1541
Colombus, Christopher	1446-1506	Vasco De Gama	1460-1524
Copernicus, Nicolaus	1473-1543	Wolsey, Thomas, Cardinal	1471-1530
Cortes, Hernando	1485-1547		

EMPERORS OF CHINA

Hsiao Tsung	1487-1505	Shih Tsung	1521-1566
Wu Tsung	1505-1521		

POPES

Alexander VI	1492-1503	Leo X	1513-1521
Pius III	1503	Adrian VI	1522-1523
Julius II	1503-1513	Clement VII	1523-1534

FRANCE. HEADS OF STATE

Louis XII	1498-1515	Francis I	1515-1547

HOLY ROMAN EMPERORS

Maximilian I	1493-1519	Charles V	1519-1558

ENGLAND. SOVEREIGNS

Henry VII	1485-1509	Henry VIII	1509-1547

SWEDEN. KINGS

John II	1497-1501	Regency under Sten Sture	
Regency under Sten Sture		The Younger	1512-1520
The Elder	1501-1503	Christian II	1520-1523
Regency under		Gustavius	1523-1560
Svante Sture	1504-1512		

PORTUGAL. KINGS

Manoel I	1495-1521	John III	1521-1557

SCOTLAND. KINGS

James IV	1488-1513	James V	1513-1542

ELECTORS OF BRANDENBURG

Joachim, I	1499-1535

Isabella	d. 1504	Charles V	1516-1556
Ferdinand	d. 1516		

RUSSIA. TSARS

Ivan III, The Great	1462-1505	Vassili III	1505-1533

WRITERS

Abarbanel, Isaac Ben Jehudah	1437-1508	Cavendish, George	1500-1562	
Accolti, Bernardo	1465-1536	Cecchi, Giammaria	1518-1587	
Accorso, Mariangelo	1490-1544	Celtes, Konrad	1459-1508	
Achillini, Alessandro	1463-1512	Cetina, Gutierre De	1518-1572	
Aconzio, Jacopo	1500-1566	Chaloner, Sir Thomas	1521-1565	
Adams, Clement	1519-1587	Churchyard, Thomas	1520-1604	
Adriani, Giovanni Baptista	1513-1579	Cieza De Leon, Pedro De	1519-1560	
Agrippa Von Nettesheim, Henry Cornelius	1486-1535	Colonna, Vittoria	1490-1547	
		Comines, Phillipe De	c. 1445-1509	
Agricola (Magister Islebius) Johann	1492-1566	Cooper, Thomas	1517-1594	
		Copernicus, Nicolas	1473-1543	
Alamanni, Luigi	1495-1556	Costanzo, Angelo Di	1507-1591	
Alberus, Erasmus	1500-1553	Coverdale, Miles (trans. bible)	1488-1569	
Alunno, Niccolo	1430-1502	Cranmer, Thomas	1489-1556	
Amyot, Jacques	1513-1593	Daurat, Jean	1508-1588	
Arason, Jon	1484-1551	Della Casa, Giovanni	1503-1556	
Aretino, Pietro	1492-1556	Des Periers, Bonaventure	1500-1544	
Ariosto, Lodovico	1474-1533	Diaz Del Castillo, Bernal	1492-1581	
Ascham, Roger	1515-1568	Dolce, Lodovico	1508-1568	
Auvergne, Martial d'	1430-1508	Douglas, Gavin	1474-1522	
Aventius	1477-1534	Du Bellay, Joachim	1522-1560	
Avila, Juan de	1500-1569	Dunbar, William	1460-1520	
Avila Y Zuniga, Luis	1490-1560	Edwards, Richard	1523-1566	
Baldung, Grun Hans	1476-1545	Elyot, Sir Thomas	1490-1546	
Bale, John	1495-1563	Encina, Juan Del	1468-1529	
Bandello, Matteo	1480-1562	Erasmus, Desiderius	1466-1536	
Bandinelli, Baccio	1493-1560	Fabricius, Georg	1516-1571	
Barclay, Alexander	1476-1552	Fabyan, Robert	d. 1513	
Barros, Joao De	1496-1570	Falcao, Christovam	1512-1553	
Bellay, Joachim Du	1522-1560	Firenzuola, Agnolo	1493-1545	
Bembo, Pietro	1470-1547	Fleuranges, Robert de la Marck	1491-1537	
Berni, Francesco	1497-1536	Folengo, Theofil	1491-1544	
Blois, Louis De	1506-1566	Foxe, John	1516-1587	
Boone, Andrew	1490-1549	Gesner, Konrad Von	1516-1565	
Boscan-Almogaver, Juan	1490-1542	Giraldi, Giovanni Battista	1504-1573	
Boyce, Hector	1465-1536	Giraldi, Giglio Gregorio	1479-1552	
Bradshaw, Henry	1450-1513	Grazzini, Antonio Francesco	1503-1583	
Brant, Sebastian	1457-1521	Grimald, Nicholas	1519-1562	
Buchanan, George	1506-1582	Gringoire, Pierre	1475-1539	
Busbecq, Ogier Ghislain De	1522-1592	Guevara, Antonio De	1490-1545	
Calvin, John	1509-1564	Guicciardini, Francesco	1483-1540	
Camoens, Louis De	1524-1580	Guidiccioni, Giovanni	1480-1541	
Caro, Annibale	1507-1566	Hall, Edward	1499-1547	
Casa, Giovanni Della	1503-1556	Hawes, Stephen	1502-1521	
Castellesi, Adriano	1460-1521	Hessus, Helius Eobanus	1488-1540	
Castiglioni, Baldassare	1478-1529	Heywood, John	1497-1580	
Castillejo, Cristobal De	1490-1550	Hughes, Thomas	1500-	

Jewell, John	1522-1571	Reuchlin, Johann	1455-1522
Jovius, Paulus	1483-1552	Ribeiro, Bernardim	1482-1552
Kennedy, Walter	1460-1508	Ronsard, Pierre De	1524-1585
Knox, John	1513-1572	Ruccelai, Giovanni	1475-1525
Krantz, Albert	1450-1517	Rueda, Lope De	1510-1565
Languet, Hubert	1518-1581	Ruzzante	1502-1542
Latimer, Hugh	c. 1485-1555	Sachs, Hans	1494-1576
Leland, John	1506-1552	Sa De Miranda,	
Le Maire De Belges, Jean	1473-1525	Francisco De	1485-1558
Lemnius	1505-1550	Sannazaro, Jacopo	1458-1530
Lopez De Gomara,		Sanuto, Marino	1466-1533
Francisco	1511-1557	Sceve, Maurice	1500-1564
Loyala, Ignatius de	1491-1556	Sepulveda, Juan Gines De	1490-1574
Luther, Martin	1483-1546	Skelton, John	1460-1529
Lyndsay, Sir David	1490-1555	Sleidanus, Johannes	1506-1556
Machiavelli, Niccolo	1469-1527	Stewart, William	1480-1550
Magnus	1490-1558	Stow, John	1525-1605
Maitland, Sir Richard	1496-1586	Surrey, Henry Howard,	
Major, John	1470-1550	Earl of	c. 1517-1547
Marguerite of Navarre	1492-1549	Tasso, Bernardo	1493-1569
Marot, Clement	1496-1544	Taverner, Richard	1505-1575
Medwall, Henry	1462-1505	Telesio, Bernardio	1509-1588
Melanchthon, Philip	1497-1560	Theresa (St.)	1515-1582
Mendoza, Diego Hurtado		Torres Naharro, Bartolome	
De	1503-1575	De	1480-1530
Molinet, Jean	1433-1507	Tschudi, Giles	1505-1572
Montemor, Jorge	1520-1561	Tusser, Thomas	1524-1580
More, Sir Thomas	1478-1535	Tyard, Pontus De	1521-1605
Murner, Thomas	1475-1537	Udal, Nicholas	1504-1556
Nardi, Jacopo	1476-	Valdes, Juan De	1500-1541
Nifo, Agostino	1473-1538	Varthema, Ludovico Di	1502-1510
Ovideo Y Valdes,		Vaux of Harrowdene,	
Gonzales Fernandez De	1478-1557	Thomas Vaux	1510-1556
Paracelsus	1493-1541	Vega, Garcilaso De La	1503-1536
Pedersen, Christiern	1480-1554	Vida, Marco Girolamo	1489-1566
Peter Martyr Anglerius	1459-1525	Vincente, Gil	1465-1536
Pontanus, Jovianus	1426-1503	Virgil, Polydore	1470-1555
Porta, Guglielmo Della	1516-1577	Vives, Juan Luis	1492-1540
Rabelais, Francois	1495-1553	Winzet, Ninian	1518-1592
Rastell, John	1475-1536	Wyatt, Sir Thomas	1503-1542
Resende, Garcia De	1470-1536	Zwingli, Huldreich	1484-1531

ARTISTS

Aartsen, Pieter	1507-1573	Bartolommeo, Veneto	1480-1555
Abatti, Niccolo	1512-1571	Bassano, Giacomo Da	
Albertinelli, Mariotto	1474-1515	Ponte	1510-1592
Aldegraf, Heinrich	1502-1558	Beccafumi, Domenico Di	
Alessi, Galeazzo	1512-1572	Pace	1486-1551
Altdorfer, Albrecht	1480-1538	Bellini, Gentile	1429-1507
Amalteo, Pomponio	1505-1584	Bellini, Giovanni	1430-1516
Ammanati, Bartolomeo	1511-1592	Bianchiferrari, Francesco	
Baccio D'Agnolo	1460-1543	De	1460-1510
Bagnacavallo,		Bologna, Giovanni Da	1524-1608
Bartolommeo	1484-1545	Boltraffio, Giovanni	
Bandinelli, Baccio	1493-1560	Antonio	1467-1516
Barocchio, Giacomo	1507-1573	Bordone, Paris	1500-1571
Bartolommeo Di Paghlo,		Borgdgnone, Ambrogio	1473-1524
Fra	1475-1517	Bosch, Hieronymous	1460-1516

Botticelli, Sandro	1444-1510	Heemskerk, Marten	
Bramante, Douato	1444-1514	Jacobsz	1498-1574
Briosco, Andrea	1470-1532	Holbein, Hans, The elder	1460-1524
Bronzino, Il	1503-1572	Holbein, Hans	1497-1543
Brueghel, Pieter	1525-1569	Joos Van Cleve	1480-1540
Burgkmair, Hans	1473-1531	Krafft, Adam	1455-1509
Campagnola, Domenico	1484-c. 1563	Kempener, Peter De	1505-1580
Campi, Giulio	1502-1572	Leonardo Da Vinci	1452-1519
Caravaggio, Polidoro Da	1500-1543	Leoni, Leone	1509-1590
Carpaccio, Vittorio	1465-1522	Leopardi, Alessandro	1512
Caroto, Giovanni		Lescot, Pierre	1510-1578
Francesco	1480-1555	Liberale, Antonio	1445-1526
Castello, Giovanni		Limousin, Leonard	1505-1577
Battista	1500-1569	Lippi, Filippino	1457-1504
Catena, Vincenzo Di		Lotto, Lorenzo	1480-1556
Biagio	1470-1531	Lucas Van Leyden	1494-1533
Cattaneo, Danese Di		Luini, Barnardino	1475-1532
Michele	1509-1573	Mabuse, Jan	1472-1534
Cavazzola, Paolo, Morando	1486-1522	Mantegna, Andrea	1431-1506
Cellini, Benvenuto	1500-1571	Manuel, Hans Rudolf	1525-1571
Cima, Giambattista	1459-1517	Manuel, Nikolaus	1484-1550
Civerchio, Vincinzo	1500-	Matsys, Quentin	1466-1530
Civitali, Matteo	1435-1501	Michelangelo	1475-1564
Cleve, Van Cornelis	1520-1567	Montagna, Bartolomeo	1450-1523
Cleve, Van Joos Van Der		Morales, Luis D	1509-1586
Beke	1480-1540	Moretto, Il	1494-1554
Clouet, Jean	1485-1541	Moro, Antonio	1512-1575
Cockx, Hieronymus	1510-1570	Morone, Domenico	1442-1517
Coello, Alonso Sanchez	1515-1590	Morone, Francesco	1471-1529
Cornelisz, Lucas	1495-1552	Moroni, Giambattista	1525-1578
Corregio	1492-1534	Moulins, Master of	1460-1529
Costa, Lorenzo	1460-1535	Orley, Bernard Van	1490-1540
Cousin, Jean	1500-1590	Pacchia, Girolamo Del	1477-1535
Coxcie, Michael	1499-1592	Palissy, Bernard	1510-1589
Cranach, Lucas	1472-1553	(Potter)	
Credi, Lorenzo Di	1457-1537	Palladio, Andrea	1518-1580
David, Gerard	-1523	Palma, Jacopo	1480-1528
Della Colle, Raffaellino	1490-	Parmigiano	1504-1540
Delle Robbia, Andrea	1435-1525	Patinir, Joachim De	1475-1524
Della Robbia, Giovanni	1469-1529	Perino Del Vaga	1500-1547
Della Robbia, Girolamo	1488-1566	Peruzzi, Baldassare	1481-1536
De L'Orme, Philibert	1510-1570	Perugino, Pietro	1450-1524
Dosso Dossi, Giovanni	1479-1542	Piero Di Cosimo	1462-1521
Durer, Albrecht	1471-1528	Pinturicchio	1454-1513
Farinato, Paolo	1524-1606	Piombo, Sebastian Del	1485-1547
Ferrari, Gaudenzio	1480-1546	Pontormo, Jacopo Da	1494-1552
Fiorenzo Di Lorenzo	1445-1525	Pordenone, Il	1483-1539
Fontana, Prospero	1512-1597	Primaticcio, Francesco	1504-1570
Foppa, Vincenzo	1427-1515	Procaccini, Ercole	1520-1591
Francia	1450-1517	Raphael, Sanzio	1483-1520
Franciabigio	1482-1525	Riemenschneider, Tilman	1460-1531
Garofalo	1481-1559	Rossi, Giovanni	
Genga, Giralamo	1476-1551	Battista De	1494-1541
Ghirlandajo, Ridolfo	1483-1501	Sanmichele, Michele	1484-1559
Giocondo, Fra Giovanni	1433-1515	Sansovino, Andrea	
Giorgione	1478-1511	Contucci	1460-1529
Giulio, Romano	1499-1546	Sansovino, Jacopo	1486-1570
Goujon, Jean	1520-1566	Sarto, Andrea del	1486-1531
Grunewald, Mathias	1500-1530	Signorelli, Luca	1450-1523
H		Sodoma, Il	1477-1549

Solario, Andrea Da	1460-1520	Vasari, Giorgio	1511-1574
Stoss, Veit	1483-1533	Vignola, Giacomo	
Suardi, Bartolommeo	1455-1536	Barozzi Da	1507-1573
Titian	1477-1576	Vivarini, Luigi	fl. 1417-1503
Tintoretto, Jacopo Robusti	1518-1594	Volterra, Daniele Da	1509-1566
Torrigiano, Pietro	1472-1522	Wohlgemuth, Michael	1434-1519

COMPOSERS

Animuccia, Giovanni	1490-1571	Gabrieli, Andrea	1510-1586
Arcadelt, Jakob	1514-1575	Goudimel, Claude	1510-1572
Cabezon, Antonio De	1510-1566	Jimenez De Queseda,	
Cornyshe, William	1465-1523	Gonzalo	1500-1579
Des Pres, Josquin	1450-1521	Tallis, Thomas	1515-1585
Festa, Constanzo	1495-1545	Taverner, John	1495-1545

1526	Tyndale's New Testament published.
1528	Conquest of Peru.
1529	Fall of Wolsey.
1534	Papal power abolished in England. Act of Supremacy.
1535	More executed. First English Bible published.
	Loyola founds Jesuits.
1536	Catherine of Aragon dies. Anne Boleyn executed.
	Henry VIII marries Jane Seymore.
1537	Death of Jane Seymore.
	Mount Etna in eruption.
1538	Henry VIII Excommunicated.
	Parish registers established in England.
1539	Revolt of Ghent.
1540	Henry VIII marries Anne of Cleves.
	Henry VIII marries Catherine Howard.
1544	Henry VIII invades France.
1545	Needles first produced in England.
1549	Act of Uniformity.

PROMINENT PEOPLE

Cabot, Sebastian	1474-1557	More, Sir Thomas	1478-1535
Calvin, John	1509-1564	Nostradamus	1503-1566
Copernicus, Nicolaus	1473-1543	Pizarro, Francesco	1471-1541
Cortes, Hernando	1485-1547	Tyndale, William	1492-1536
Loyola, St. Ignatius	1491-1556	Wolsey, Thomas, Cardinal	1471-1530
Luther, Martin	1483-1546		

EMPERORS OF CHINA (MING DYNASTY)

Shih Tsung	1521-1566

POPES

Clement VII	1523-1534	Julius III	1550-1555
Paul III	1534-1549		

FRANCE. HEADS OF STATE

Francis I	1515-1547	Henry II	1547-1559

HOLY ROMAN EMPERORS

Charles V	1519-1558

ENGLAND. SOVEREIGNS

Henry VIII	1509-1547	Edward VI	1547-1553

SWEDEN. KINGS

Gustavius I	1523-1560

PORTUGAL. KINGS

John III	1521-1557

James V   1513-1542   Mary   1542-1567

ELECTORS OF BRANDENBURG

Joachim I   1499-1535   Joachim II   1535-1571

RUSSIA. TSARS

Vasili II   1505-1533   Ivan IV, The Terrible   1533-1584

SPAIN. SOVEREIGNS

Charles V   1516-1556

WRITERS

Accolti, Bernardo	1465-1536	Berni, Francesco	1497-1536
Accorso, Mariangelo	1490-1544	Blois, Louis De	1506-1566
Aconzio, Jacopo	1500-1566	Bodin, Jean	1530-1596
Acosta, Jose De	1539-1600	Boone, Andrew	1490-1549
Adams, Clement	1519-1587	Boscan-Almogaver, Juan	1490-1542
Adriani, Giovanni		Boyce, Hector	1465-1536
Baptista	1513-1579	Brantome, Pierre De	
Aemilius, Paulus	-1529	Bourdeilles	1530-1614
Agrippa Von Nettesheim,		Breton, Nicholas	1545-1626
Henry Cornelius	1486-1535	Bruno, Giordano	1548-1600
Agricola (Magister Islebius)		Bryskett, Lodowyck	1545-1612
Johann	1492-1566	Buchanan, George	1506-1582
Alamanni, Luigi	1495-1556	Busbecq, Ogier Ghislain	
Alberus, Erasmus	1500-1553	De	1522-1592
Alcazar, B. Del	1530-1606	Calvin, John	1509-1564
Aleman, Mateo	1547-1609	Camoens, Louis De	1524-1580
Allori, Alessandro	1535-1607	Caro, Annibale	1507-1566
Alvarez Do Oriente,		Casa, Giovanni Della	1503-1556
Fernao	1540-1595	Castiglioni, Baldassare	1478-1529
Ammirato, Scipione	1531-1601	Castillejo, Cristobal De	1490-1550
Amyot, Jacques	1513-1593	Cavendish, George	1500-1562
Arason, Jon	1484-1551	Cecchi, Giammaria	1518-1587
Aretino, Pietro	1492-1556	Cervantes, Saavedra,	
Ariosto, Lodovico	1474-1533	Miguel De	1547-1616
Ascham, Roger	1515-1568	Cetina, Gutierre De	1518-1572
Aventus	1477-1534	Chaloner, Sir Thomas	1521-1565
Avila, Juan de	1500-1569	Charron, Pierre	1541-1603
Avila Y Zuniga, Luis	1490-1560	Chrestien, Florent	1541-1596
Baif, Jean Antoine De	1532-1589	Churchyard, Thomas	1520-1604
Baldung, Grun Hans	1476-1545	Cieza De Leon, Pedro De	1510-1560
Bale, John	1495-1563	Colonna, Vittoria	1490-1547
Balfour, Robert	1550-1625	Cooper, Thomas	1517-1594
Bandello, Matteo	1480-1562	Copernicus, Nicolas	1473-1543
Bandinelli, Baccio	1493-1560	Corte-Real, Jeronymo	1533-1588
Barohona De Soto, Luis	1548-1595	Costanzo, Angelo Di	1507-1591
Barclay, Alexander	1476-1552	Coverdale, Miles	1488-1569
Baronius, Caeser	1538-1607	(trans bible)	
Barros, Joao De	1496-1570	Craig, Sir Thomas	1530-1608
Bellay, Joachim Du	1522-1560	Cranmer, Thomas	1489-1556
Belleau, Remy	1528-1577	Cueva, Juan De La	1550-1610
Bellenden, John	1533-1587	Daurat, Jean	1508-1588
Bembo, Pietro	1470-1547	Dee, John	1527-1608

Della Casa, Giovanni	1503-1556	Knox, John	1513-1572
Deloney, Thomas	1550-1600	Kochanowski, Jan	1530-1589
Des Periers, Bonaventure	1500-1544	Languet, Hubert	1518-1581
Desportes, Phillipe	1546-1606	Larivey, Pierre	1550-1612
Diaz Del Castillo, Bernal	1492-1581	La Taille, Jean De	1540-1608
Dolce, Lodovico	1508-1568	Latimer, Hugh	c. 1485-1555
Dorleans, Louis	1544-1629	Leland, John	1506-1552
Du Bartas, Guillaume		Leon, Luis Ponce De	1527-1591
De Salluste	1544-1590	Lindesay, Robert	1530-1590
Du Bellay, Joachim	1522-1560	Lopez De Gomara	
Edwards, Richard	1523-1566	Francisco	1511-1557
Elyot, Sir Thomas	1490-1546	Loyala, Ignatius de	1491-1556
Encina, Juan Del	1468-1529	Luther, Martin	1483-1546
Erasmus, Desiderius	1466-1536	Lyndsay, Sir David	1490-1555
Ercilla Y Zuniga,		Machiavelli, Niccolo	1469-1527
Alonso De	1533-1594	Magnus	1490-1558
Espinel, Vincente Martinez	1550-1624	Maitland, Sir Richard	1496-1586
Fabricius, Georg	1516-1571	Major, John	1470-1550
Falcao, Christovam	1512-1553	Manzolli, Pier Angelo	1543
Fenton, Sir Geoffrey	1539-1608	Marguerite of Navarre	1492-1549
Ferreira, Antonio	1528-1569	Mariana, Juan De	1536-1624
Figueroa, Francisco De	1536-1617	Marot, Clement	1496-1544
Firenzuola, Agnolo	1493-1545	Mazzonni, Giacomo	1548-1598
Fischart, Johann	1545-1591	Medwall, Henry	1490-
Fletcher, Giles	1548-1611	Melanchthon, Philip	1497-1560
Fleuranges, Robert		Mendoza, Diego Hurtado	
De La Marck	1491-1537	De	1503-1575
Folengo, Theofilo	1491-1544	Molina, Luis	1535-1600
Foxe, John	1516-1587	Montaigne, Michel De	1533-1592
Francheville, Pierre	1548-1616	Montemor, Jorge	1520-1561
Frischlin, Philipp		Montgomerie, Alexander	1550-1610
Nikodemus	1547-1590	More, Sir Thomas	1478-1535
Garnier, Robert	1534-1590	Murner, Thomas	1475-1537
Gascoigne, George	1535-1577	Nardi, Jacopo	1476-
Gesner, Konrad Von	1516-1565	Nifo, Agostino	1473-1538
Gil Polo, Gaspar	1530-1591	Norton, Thomas	1532-1584
Giraldi, Giovanni Battista	1504-1573	Oviedo Y Valdes, Gonzales	
Giraldi, Giglio Gregorio	1479-1552	Fernandez De	1478-1557
Googe, Barnabe	1540-1594	Paracelsus	1493-1541
Grazzini, Antonio		Pasquier, Etienne	1529-1615
Francesco	1503-1583	Passerat, Jean	1534-1602
Grevin, Jacques	1539-1570	Patrizzi, Francesco	1529-1597
Grimald, Nicholas	1519-1562	Paynter, William	1540-1594
Gringoire, Pierre	1475-1539	Pedersen, Christiern	1480-1554
Guarini, Giovanni Battista	1538-1612	Perez De Hita, Gines	1544-1619
Guevara, Antonio De	1490-1545	Pibrac, Guy De Faur	1529-1584
Guicciardini, Francesco	1483-1540	Rabelais, Francois	1495-1553
Guidiccioni, Giovanni	1480-1541	Rastell, John	1475-1536
Hall, Edward	1499-1547	Resende, Garcia De	1470-1536
Harvey, Gabriel	1545-1630	Ribeiro, Bernadim	1482-1552
Herrera, Antoine De	1549-1625	Rich, Barnabe	1540-1617
Herrera, Fernando De	1534-1597	Ronsard, Pierre De	1524-1585
Hessus, Helius Eobanus	1488-1540	Rueda, Lope De	1510-1565
Heywood, John	1497-1580	Ruzzante	1502-1542
Hughes, Thomas	1500-	Sachs, Hans	1494-1576
Hurtardo, Luis	1530-1598	Sackville, Thomas	1530-1608
Jewell, John	1522-1571	Sa De Miranda,	
Jodelle, Etienne	1532-1573	Francisco De	1485-1558
Jovius, Paulus	1483-1552	Sanders, Nicholas	1530-1581
Knolles, Richard	1545-1610	Sannazaro, Jacopo	1458-1530

Sanuto, Marino	,466-1533	Turberville George	1540-1610
Sceve, Maurice	1500-1564	Tusser, Thomas	1524-1580
Scot, Reginald	1538-1599	Tyard, Pontus De	1521-1605
Scott, Alexander	1550-	Tyndale, William	-1536
Sepuvelda, Juan Gines de	1490-1574	Udal, Nicholas	1504-1556
Skelton, John	1460-1529	Valdes, Juan De	1500-1541
Sleidanus, Johannes	1506-1556	Vauquelin De La Fresnaye,	
Stewart, William	1480-1550	Jean	1536-1608
Stow, John	1525-1605	Vaux of Harrowdene,	
Stumpf, Johann	1500-1576	Thomas, Vaux	1510-1556
Surrey, Henry Howard,		Vega, Garcilaso De La	1503-1536
Earl of	c. 1517-1547	Vega, Garcilaso, De La	
Tasso, Bernardo	1493-1569	El Inca	1535-1611
Tasso, Torqueto	1544-1595	Victoria, Thomas Luis De	
Taverner, Richard	1505-1575	Vida, Marco Girolamo	1489-1566
Telesio, Bernardio	1509-1588	Vincente, Gil	1465-1536
Theresa (St.)	1515-1582	Virgil, Polydore	1470-1555
Torres Naharro,		Vives, Juan Luis	1492-1540
Bartolome, de	1480-1530	Winzet, Ninian	1518-1592
Tschudi, Giles	1505-1572	Zwingli Huldreich	1484-1531
Tulsi, Das	1532-1623	Wyatt, Sir Thomas	1503-1542

ARTISTS

Aartsen, Pieter	1507-1573	Cattaneo, Danese	
Abati, Niccolo	1512-1571	Di Michele	1509-1573
Aldegraf, Heinrich	1502-1558	Cellini, Benvenuto	1500-1571
Alessi, Galeazzo	1512-1572	Cespedes, Pablo de	1536-1608
Altdorfer, Albrecht	1480-1538	Civerchio, Vincinzo	1500-
Amalteo, Pomponio	1505-1584	Clouet, Jean	1485-1541
Amman, Jost	1539-1591	Cockx, Hieronymus	1510-1570
Ammanati, Bartolomeo	1511-1592	Coello, Alonso Sanchez	1515-1590
Baccio D'Agnolo	1460-1543	Colins, Alexandre	1526-1612
Bagnacavallo, Bartolommeo	1484-1545	Coninxloo, Gillis Van	1544-1605
Bandinelli, Bartolommeo	1493-1560	Cornelisz, Jakob	fl. 1530
Barocci, Federigo	1528-1612	Cornelisz, Lucas	1495-1552
Barrocchio, Giacomo	1507-1573	Correggio	1494-1534
Bartolommeo, Veneto	1480-1555	Costa, Lorenzo	1460-1535
Bassano, Giacomo DaPonte	1510-1592	Cousin, Jean	1500-1590
Beccafumi, Domenico		Coxcie, Michael	1499-1592
Di Pace	1486-1551	Cleve, Van Cornelis	1520-1567
Bologna, Giovanni Da	1524-1608	Cleve, Van Joos	
Bordone, Paris	1500-1571	Van Der Beke	1480-1540
Brill, Mattys	1550-1584	Cranach, Lucas	1472-1553
Briosco, Andrea	1470-1532	Credi, Lorenzo Di	1457-1537
Bronzino, Il	1503-1572	Della Colle, Raffaellino	1490-
Brueghel, Pieter	1525-1569	Della Robbia, Giovanni	1469-1529
Burgkmair, Hans	1473-1531	Della Robbia, Girolamo	1488-1566
Calvart, Denis	1540-1619	De L'Orme, Philibert	1510-1570
Cambiasi, Luca	1527-1585	Dosso Dossi, Giovanni	1479-1542
Campagna, Gerolamo	1549-1626	Durer, Albrecht	1471-1528
Campagnola, Domenico	1484-c. 1563	Farinato, Paolo	1524-1606
Campi, Giulio	1502-1572	Ferrari, Gaudenzio	1480-1546
Campi, Vincenzo	1536-1591	Fontana, Prospero	1512-1597
Caracci, Annibale	1540-1609	Fontana, Domenico	1543-1607
Caroto, Giovanni Francesco	1480-1555	Garofalo	1481-1559
Castello, Giovanni Battista	1500-1569	Genga, Girolamo	1476-1551
Catena, Vincenzo		Giulio, Romano	1499-1546
Di Biagio	1470-1531	Goujon, Jean	1520-1566

Grunewald, Mathias	1500-1530	Perino Del Vaga	1500-1547
Heemskerk, Marten Jacobz	1498-1574	Peruzzi, Baldassare	1481-1536
Hilliard, Nicholas	1537-1619	Pilon, Germain	1537-1590
Hoefnagel, Joris	1542-1600	Piombo, Sebastian Del	1485-1547
Holbein, Hans	1497-1543	Pontormo, Jacopo Da	1494-1552
Kempener, Peter De	1505-1580	Pordenone, Il	1483-1539
Leoni, Leone	1509-1590	Porta, Giacomo Della	1541-1604
Leopardi, Alessandro	1512-	Primaticcio, Francesco	1504-1570
Lescot, Pierre	1510-1578	Procaccini, Camilio	1546-1629
Liberale, Antonio	1445-1526	Procaccini, Ercole	1520-1591
Limousin, Leonard	1505-1577	Ribalta, Francisco De	1550-1628
Lucas Van Leyden	1494-1533	Riemenschneider, Tilman	1460-1531
Luini, Barnardino	1475-1532	Rossi, Giovanni Battista De	1494-1541
Mabuse, Jan	1472-1534	Sanmichele, Michele	1484-1559
Mander, Carel Van	1548-1606	Sansovino, Andrea Contucci	1460-1529
Manuel, Hans Rudolf	1525-1571	Sansovino, Jacopo	1486-1570
Manuel, Nikolaus	1484-1530	Sarto, Andrea del	1486-1531
Matsys, Quentin	1466-1530	Sebastiano, Del Piombo	1485-1547
Michelangelo	1475-1564	Sodoma, Il	1477-1549
Morales, Luis De	1509-1586	Steenwijk, Hendrik Van	c. 1550-1603
Moretto, Il	1494-1554	Stoss, Veit	1483-1533
Moro. Antonio	1512-1575	Suardi, Bartolommeo	1455-1536
Morone, Francesco	1471-1529	Theotocopouli, Domenico	
Moroni, Giambattista	1525-1578	(El Greco)	1542-1614
Moulins, Master of	1460-1529	Titian	1477-1576
Muziano, Girolamo	1528-1592	Tintoretto, Jacopo Robusti	1517-1594
Navarrette, Juan		Vasari, Giorgio	1511-1574
Fernandez De	1526-1579	Veronese, Paolo	1528-1588
Orley, Bernard Van	1490-1540	Vignola, Giacomo	
Pacchia, Girolamo Del	1477-1535	Barozzi Da	1507-1573
Palladio, Andrea	1518-1580	Volterra, Daniele Da	1509-1566
Palma, Jacopo	1480-1528	Wyatt, Sir Thomas	1503-1542
Palissy, Bernard	1510-1589	Zuccaro, Frederico	1539-1609
(Potter)		Zuccaro, Tadeo	1529-1566
Parmigiano	1504-1540		

COMPOSERS

Animuccia, Giovanni	1490-1571	Guerrero, Francisco	1528-1599
Arcadelt, Jakob	1514-1575	Handl, Jacob	1550-1591
Artusi, Giovanni Maria	1540-1613	Jimenez De Quesada,	
Byrd, William	1543-1623	Gonzalo	1500-1579
Cabezon, Antonio De	1510-1566	Lasso, Orlando	1530-1594
Cavalieri, Emilio De	1550-1599	Palestrina, Giovanni	
Festa, Constanzo	1495-1545	Pierluigi Da	1526-1594
Gabrieli, Andrea	1510-1586	Tallis, Thomas	1515-1585
Goudimel, Claude	1510-1572	Taverner, John	1495-1545

1554 Lady Jane Grey Executed.
1555 Diet of Augsburg.
1557 Battle of St. Quentin.
1560 Reformation established in Scotland.
1568 Revolt of Moors in Spain.
1569 Battle of Jarnac.
1572 St. Bartholomew massacre.
1573 Siege of La Rochelle.

PROMINENT PEOPLE

Cabot, Sebastian	1474-1557	Loyola, St. Ignatius	1491-1556
Calvin, John	1509-1564	Nostradamus	1503-1566
Knox, John	1505-1572	Catherine De Medici	1519-1589

EMPERORS OF CHINA (Ming Dynasty)

Mu Tsung	1566-1572	Shen Tsung	1572-1620

POPES

Julius III	1550-1555	Pius IV	1559-1565
Marcellus II	1555-	St. Pius V	1566-1572
Paul IV	1555-1559	Gregory XIII	1572-1585

FRANCE. HEADS OF STATE

Henry II	1547-1559	Charles IX	1560-1574
Francis II	1559-1560	Henry III	1574-1589

HOLY ROMAN EMPERORS

Charles V	1519-1558	Maximilian II	1564-1576
Ferdinand I	1558-1564		

ENGLAND. SOVEREIGNS

Edward VI	1547-1553	Elizabeth I	1558-1603
Mary I	1553-1558		

SWEDEN. KINGS

Gustavius I	1523-1560	John III	1568-1592
Eric XIV	1560-1568		

PORTUGAL. KINGS

John III	1521-1557	Sebastian	1557-1578

SCOTLAND. KINGS

Mary (Abdicated)	1542-1567	James VI	1567-1603

ELECTORS OF BRANDENBURG

Joachim II	1535-1571	John George	1571-1598

Ivan IV, The Terrible　　　1533-1584

SPAIN. SOVEREIGNS

Charles V　　　　　　1516-1556　　Philip II　　　　　　1556-1598

WRITERS

Aconzio, Jacopo	1500-1566	Bodin, Jean	1530-1596
Acosta, Jose De	1539-1600	Bracciolini, Francesco	1566-1645
Adams, Clement	1519-1587	Brantome, Pierre De	
Adriani, Giovanni		Bourdeilles	1530-1614
Baptista	1513-1579	Breton, Nicholas	1545-1626
Agricola (Magister		Broke, Arthur	-1563
Islebius) Johann	1492-1566	Brosse, Salomon De	1565-1626
Alabaster, William	1567-1640	Bruno, Giordano	1548-1600
Alamanni, Luigi	1495-1556	Bryskett, Lodowyck	1545-1612
Alberus, Erasmus	1500-1553	Buchanan, George	1506-1582
Alcazar, D. Del	1530-1606	Busbecq, Ogier	
Aleman, Mateo	1547-1609	Ghislain De	1522-1592
Allori, Alessandro	1535-1607	Calderwood, David	1575-1650
Alvarez Do Oriente,		Calvin, John	1509-1564
Fernao	1540-1595	Camden, William	1551-1623
Ammirato, Scipione	1531-1601	Camoens, Louis De	1524-1580
Amyot, Jacques	1513-1593	Campanella, Tommaso	1568-1639
Andrews, Lancelot	1555-1626	Campion, Thomas	1567-1620
Arason, Jon	1484-1551	Carew, Richard	1555-1620
Aretino, Pietro	1492-1556	Caro, Annibale	1507-1566
Argensola, Lupercio		Casa, Giovanni Della	1503-1556
Leonardo De	1559-1613	Castro Y Bellvis,	
Arminius, Jacobus	1560-1609	Guillen De	1569-1631
Arquijo, Juan De	1564-1623	Cavendish, George	1500-1562
Ascham, Roger	1515-1568	Cecchi, Giammaria	1518-1587
Aubigne, Theodore		Cervantes Saavedra,	
Agrippa De	1552-1630	Maguel De	1547-1616
Avila Juan De	1500-1569	Cetina, Gutierre De	1518-1572
Avila, Y Zuniga, Louis	1490-1560	Chaloner, Sir Thomas	1521-1565
Ayton, Sir Robert	1570-1638	Chapman, George	1559-1634
Bacon, Francis	1561-1626	Charron, Pierre	1541-1603
Baif, Jean Antoine De	1532-1589	Chettle, Henry	1560-1607
Baker, Sir Richard	1568-1645	Chiabrera, Gabriello	1552-1638
Balassa, Balint	1551-1594	Chrestien, Florent	1541-1596
Balbuena, Bernardo De	1568-1627	Churchyard, Thomas	1520-1604
Baldi, Bernardino	1553-1617	Cieza De Leon, Pedro De	1519-1560
Bale, John	1495-1563	Constable, Henry	1562-1613
Balfour, Robert	1550-1625	Cooper, Thomas	1517-1594
Bandello, Matteo	1480-1562	Corte-Real, Jeronymo	1533-1588
Bandinelli, Baccio	1493-1560	Costanzo, Angelo Di	1507-1591
Barahona De Soto, Luis	1548-1595	Coverdale, Miles	1488-1569
Barclay, Alexander	1476-1552	(trans bible)	
Baronius, Caesar	1538-1607	Craig, Sir Thomas	1530-1608
Barnfield, Richard	1574-1627	Cranmer, Thomas	1489-1556
Barros, Joao De	1496-1570	Cueva, Juan De La	1550-1610
Bellay, Joachim Du	1522-1560	Daniel, Samuel	1562-1619
Belleau, Remy	1528-1577	Daurat, Jean	1508-1588
Bellenden, John	1533-1587	Davies, John	1565-1618
Bellenden, William	1555-1633	Davies, Sir John	1569-1626
Blois, Louis De	1506-1566	Day, John	1574-1640
Boccalini, Trajano	1556-1613	Dee, John	1527-1608

Montchretien, Antoine De	1575-1621
Montemor, Jorge	1520-1561
Montgomerie, Alexander	1550-1610
Moryson, Fynes	1566-1630
Munday, Anthony	1553-1633
Nashe, Thomas	1567-1601
Norton, Thomas	1532-1584
Oviedo Y Valdes,	
Gonzales Fernandez De	1478-1557
Pasquier, Etienne	1529-1615
Passerat, Jean	1534-1602
Patrizzi, Francesco	1529-1597
Paynter, William	1540-1594
Pedersen, Christiern	1480-1554
Peele, George	1558-1597
Perez De Hita, Gines	1544-1619
Pibrac, Guy De Faur	1529-1584
Rabelais, Francois	1495-1553
Regnier, Mathurin	1573-1613
Ribeiro, Bernadim	1482-1552
Rich, Barnabe	1540-1617
Rinuccini, Attavio	1562-1621
Rolland, John	1560-
Ronsard, Pierre De	1524-1585
Rueda, Lope De	1510-1565
Sachs, Hans	1494-1576
Sackville, Thomas	1530-1608
Sa De Miranda,	
Francisco De	1485-1558
Sanders, Nicholas	1530-1581
Sceve, Maurice	1500-1564
Scot, Reginald	1538-1599
Scott, Alexander	1550-
Sepuvelda, Juan Gines De	1490-1574
Shakespeare, William	1564-1616
Sidney, Sir Philip	1554-1586
Sleidanus, Johannes	1506-1556
Sousa, Luiz De	1555-1632
Southwell, Robert	1561-1595
Speed, John	1552-1629

Spenser, Edmund	1552-1599
Stevenson, William	-1575
Stirling, William	
Alexander	1567-1640
Stow, John	1525-1605
Straparola, Giovan	
Francesco	-1557
Stumpf, Johann	1500-1576
Sylvester, Joshua	1563-1618
Tasso, Bernardo	1493-1569
Taverner, Richard	1505-1575
Telesio, Bernardio	1509-1588
Theresa (St.)	1515-1582
Thou, Jacques Auguste De	1553-1617
Tirso De Molina	1571-1648
Totnes, George Carew	1555-1629
Tourneur, Cyril	1575-1626
Tschudi, Giles	1505-1572
Tulsi, Das	1532-1623
Turberville, George	1540-1610
Tusser, Thomas	1524-1580
Tyard, Pontus De	1521-1605
Udal, Nicholas	1504-1556
Urfe, Honore D'	1568-1625
Vauquelin De La	
Fresnaye, Jean	1536-1608
Vaux of Harrowdene,	
Thomas Vaux	1510-1556
Vega Carpio, Lope	
Felix De	1562-1635
Vega, Garcilaso	
De La El Inca	1535-1616
Victoria, Tomas Luis De	1535-1611
Vida, Marco Girolamo	1489-1566
Virgil, Polydore	1470-1555
Watson, Thomas	1557-1592
Whetstone, George	1551-1587
Winzet, Ninian	1518-1592
Wotton, Sir Henry	1568-1639

ARTISTS

Aartsen, Pieter	1507-1573
Abati, Niccolo	1512-1571
Aldegraf, Heinrich	1502-1558
Alessi, Galeazzo	1512-1572
Amalteao, Pomponio	1505-1584
Amman, Jost	1539-1591
Ammanati, Bartolomeo	1511-1592
Anna, Baldasarre	1560-1639
Balen, Henry Van	1560-1632
Bandinelli, Bartolommeo	1493-1560
Barocci, Federigo	1528-1612
Barocchio, Giacomo	1507-1573
Bartolommeo, Veneto	1480-1555
Bassano, Giacomo Da	
Ponte	1510-1592

Beccafumi, Domenico Di	
Pace	1486-1551
Bloemart, Abraham	1564-1651
Bologna, Giovanni Da	1524-1608
Bordone, Paris	1500-1571
Brill, Mattys	1550-1584
Brill, Paul	1554-1626
Brozino, Il	1503-1572
Brueghel, Pieter	1525-1569
Caluart, Denis	1540-1619
Cambiasi, Luca	1527-1585
Campagna, Gerolamo	1549-1626
Campagnola, Domenico	c. 1484-1563
Campi, Giulio	1502-1572
Campi, Vincenzo	1536-1591
Caracci, Agostino	1557-1602

Caracci, Annibale	1540-1609	Jones, Inigo	1573-1651
Caracci, Ludovico	1555-1619	Kempener, Peter De	1505-1580
Caravaggio, Michel Angelo	1573-1610	Keyser, Hendrik De	1565-1621
Carducci, Bartolommeo	1568-1610	Leoni, Leone	1509-1590
Caroto, Giovanni		Leopardi, Alessandro	1512-
Francesco	1480-1555	Lescot, Pierre	1510-1578
Castello, Bernado	1557-1629	Limousin, Leonard	1505-1577
Castello, Giovanni		Mander, Carel Van	1548-1606
Battista	1500-1569	Manuel, Hans Rudolf	1525-1571
Cattaneo, Danese Di		Michelangelo	1475-1564
Michele	1509-1573	Mierevelt, Michiel	
Cellini, Benvenuto	1500-1571	Jansz Van	1567-1641
Cesari, Giuseppe	1568-1640	Moretto, Il	1494-1554
Cespedes, Pablo De	1536-1608	Morales, Luis De	1509-1586
Civerchio, Vincinzo	1500-	Moro, Antonio	1512-1575
Cigoli, Lodovico Cardi Da	1559-1613	Moroni, Giambattista	1525-1578
Cleve, Van Cornelis	1520-1567	Muziano, Girolamo	1528-1592
Clouet, Francois	-1572	Navarrete, Juan	
Cockx, Hieronymus	1510-1570	Fernandez De	1526-1579
Coello, Alonso Sanchez	1515-1590	Pacheco, Francisco	1571-1654
Colins, Alexandre	1526-1612	Palladio, Andrea	1518-1580
Coninxloo, Gillis Van	1544-1605	Palissy, Bernard	1510-1589
Corenzio, Belisario	1558-1643	(Potter)	
Cornelisz, Cornelisz	1562-1638	Pilon, Germain	1537-1590
Cornelisz, Lucas	1495-1552	Pontormo, Jacopo Da	1495-1552
Cousin, Jean	1500-1590	Porta, Giacomo Della	1541-1604
Coxcie, Michael	1499-1592	Procaccini, Camilio	1546-1629
Cranach, Lucas	1472-1553	Procaccini, Ercole	1520-1591
Crespi, Giovanni Battista	1557-1633	Primaticcio, Francesco	1504-1570
Della Robbia, Girolamo	1488-1566	Reni, Guido	1575-1642
De L'Orme, Philibert	1510-1570	Ribalta, Francesco de	1550-1628
Farinato, Paolo	1524-1606	Sanmichele, Michele	1484-1559
Fontana, Domenico	1543-1607	Sansovino, Jacopo	1486-1570
Fontana, Lavinia	1552-1614	Steenwijk, Hendrik Van	c. 1550-1603
Fontana, Prospero	1512-1597	Theotocopouli, Domenico	
Garofalo	1481-1559	(El Greco)	1542-1614
Genga, Girolamo	1476-1551	Titian	1477-1576
Gentileschi, Orazio De	1562-1647	Tintoretto, Jacopo Robusti	1518-1594
Gheeraerts, Marcus	1561-1635	Van Veen, Otto	1556-1634
Goujon, Jean	1520-1566	Vasari, Giorgio	1511-1574
Heemskerk, Marten		Veronese, Paolo	1528-1588
Jacobsz	1498-1574	Vignola, Giacomo	
Hilliard, Nicholas	1537-1619	Barozzi Da	1507-1573
Hoefnagel, Joris	1542-1600	Volterra, Daniele Da	1509-1566
Janssens, Van Nuyssen		Zuccaro, Frederigo	1539-1609
Abraham	1575-1632	Zuccaro, Taddep	1529-1566

COMPOSERS

Aichinger, Gregor	1565-1628	Carlton, Richard	1560-1638
Animuccia, Giovanni	1490-1571	Cavalieri, Emilio De	1550-1599
Arcadelt, Jacob	1514-1575	Cooper, John	1570-1627
Artusi, Giovanni Maria	1540-1613	Dowland, John	1563-1626
Basile, Giambattista	1575-1632	Eccard, Johann	1553-1611
Bateson, Thomas	1570-1630	Farmer, John	1565-1605
Bull, John	1562-1628	Farnaby, Giles	c. 1560-1600
Byrd, William	1543-1623	Gabrieli, Andrea	1510-1586
Cabezon, Antonio De	1510-1566	Gesualdo, Don Carlos	1560-1613
Caccini, Guilio	1558-1615	Goudimel, Claude	1510-1572

Guerrero, Francisco	1528-1599	Palestrina, Giovanni	
Handl, Jacob	1550-1591	Pierluigi Da	1526-1594
Hassler, Hans Leo	1564-1612	Peri, Jacopo	1561-1633
Jimenez De Quesada,		Praetorius, Michael	1571-1621
Gonzalo	1500-1579	Sweelinck, Jan Pieter	1562-1621
Lasso, Orlando	1530-1594	Tallis, Thomas	1515-1585
Marenzio, Luca	1560-1599	Tomkins, Thomas	1572-1656
Monteverdi, Claudio	1567-1643	Wilbye, John	1574-1638
Morley, Thomas	1558-1603		

1577   Drake's first voyage round the world.
1586   Battle of Zutphen.
1588   Defeat of the Spanish Armada.
1590   Battle of Ivry.
1595   Tyrone rebellion.
1600   English East India Company formed.

PROMINENT PEOPLE

Catherine De Medici	1519-1589	Richelieu, Jean Du Plessis	
Drake, Sir Francis	1540-1596	Cardinal Duc De	1585-1642

EMPERORS OF CHINA

Shen Tsung   1572-1620

POPES

Gregory XIII	1572-1585	Gregory XIV	1590-1591
Sixtus V	1585-1590	Innocent IX	1591
Urban VII	1590	Clement VIII	1592-1605

FRANCE. HEADS OF STATE

Henry III	1574-1589	Henry IV	1589-1610

HOLY ROMAN EMPERORS

Maximilian II	1564-1576	Rudolf II	1576-1612

ENGLAND, SOVEREIGNS

Elizabeth I   1558-1603

PORTUGAL. KINGS

Sebastian	1557-1578	Under Spanish Suzerainty	1581-1640
Henry	1578-1580		

SCOTLAND. KINGS

James VI   1567-1603

ELECTORS OF BRANDENBURG

John George	1571-1598	Joachim III Frederick	1598-1608

RUSSIA. TSARS

Ivan IV, The Terrible	1533-1584	Boris	1598-1605
Theodore I	1584-1598		

SPAIN. SOVEREIGNS

Philip II	1556-1598	Philip III	1598-1621

John III	1568-1592	Charles IX	1600-1611
Sigismund	1592-1599		

WRITERS

Acosta, Jose De	1539-1600	Brathwait, Richard	1588-1673
Adams, Clement	1519-1587	Breton, Nicholas	1545-1626
Adriani, Giovani Baptista	1513-1579	Brosse, Salomon De	1565-1626
Aitzema, Lieuwe Van	1600-1669	Browne, William	1591-1643
Alabaster, William	1567-1640	Bruno, Giordano	1548-1600
Alarcon Y Mendoza,		Bryskett, Lodowyck	1545-1612
Jean Ruiz de	1580-1639	Buchanan, George	1506-1582
Alcazar, B. Del	1530-1606	Burton, Robert	1577-1640
Aleman, Mateo	1547-1609	Busbecq, Ogier Ghislain	
Allori, Allesandro	1535-1607	De	1522-1592
Alvarez Do Oriente,		Calderon, De La Barca	
Fernao	1540-1595	Pedro	1600-1681
Ammirato, Scipione	1531-1601	Calderwood, David	1575-1650
Amyot, Jacques	1513-1593	Camden, William	1551-1623
Andrewes, Lancelot	1555-1626	Camoens, Louis De	1524-1580
Argensola, Lupercio		Campanella, Tommaso	1568-1639
Leonardo De	1559-1613	Campion, Thomas	1567-1620
Arminius, Jacobus	1560-1609	Carew, Richard	1555-1620
Arrebo, Anders		Carew, Thomas	1595-1638
Christiensen	1587-1637	Caro, Annibale	1507-1566
Arquijo, Juan De	1564-1623	Castillo, Solorzano,	
Aubigne, Theodore		Alonso De	1584-1647
Agrippa De	1552-1630	Castro Y Bellvis,	
Avercamp, Hendrik	1585-1634	Guillen De	1569-1631
Avila, Gil Gonzalez De	1577-1658	Cats, Jakob	1577-1660
Ayton, Sir Robert	1570-1638	Cecchi, Giammaria	1518-1587
Bacon, Francis	1561-1626	Cervantes Saavedra,	
Baif, Jean Antoine De	1532-1589	Miguel De	1547-1616
Baillie, Robert	1599-1662	Cespedes Y Meneses,	
Baker, Sir Richard	1568-1645	Gonzalo De	1585-1638
Balassa, Balint	1551-1594	Chapman, George	1559-1634
Balbuena, Bernardo De	1568-1627	Chapelaine, Jean	1595-1674
Baldi, Bernardino	1553-1617	Charron, Pierre	1541-1603
Balfour, Robert	1550-1625	Chettle, Henry	1560-1607
Balzac, Jean Louis		Chiabrera, Gabriello	1552-1638
Guez De	1594-1654	Chrestien, Florent	1541-1596
Barahona De Soto, Luis	1548-1595	Churchyard, Thomas	1520-1604
Baronus, Caesar	1538-1607	Cluwer, Philip	1580-1623
Barnfield, Richard	1574-1627	Comenius, Johann Amos	1592-1670
Bassompiere, Francois De	1579-1646	Constable, Henry	1562-1613
Baudier, Michel	1589-1645	Constanzo, Angelo D.	1507-1591
Beaumont, Francis	1584-1616	Cooper, Thomas	1517-1594
Beaumont, Sir John	1583-1627	Corbet, Richard	1582-1635
Belleau, Remy	1528-1577	Corte-Real, Jeronymo	1533-1588
Bellenden, John	1533-1587	Coryate, Thomas	1577-1617
Bellenden, William	1555-1633	Cotton, John	1584-1652
Boccalini, Trajano	1556-1613	Craig, Sir Thomas	1530-1608
Bodin, Jean	1530-1596	Cueva, Juan De La	1550-1610
Boisrobert, Francois Le		Daniel, Samuel	1562-1619
Metel De	1592-1662	Daurat, Jean	1508-1588
Bracciolini, Francesco	1566-1645	Davies, John	1565-1618
Bradford, William	1590-1657	Davies, Sir John	1569-1626
Brantome, Pierre De		Davila, Enrico Caterino	1576-1613
Bourdeille	c. 1540-1640		

Day, John	1574-1640	Grotius, Hugo	1583-1645
Dee, John	1527-1608	Guarini, Giovanni	
Dekker, Thomas	1570-1641	Battista	1538-1612
Delmedigo, Joseph		Guevara, Luis De Velez	1570-1644
Soloman	1591-1655	Gundulic, Ivan	1588-1638
Deloney, Thomas	1550-1600	Hajji, Khalifa	c. 1599-1658
Dempster, Thomas	1570-1625	Hake, Edward	1579
Descartes, Rene	1596-1650	Hakluyt, Richard	1552-1616
Desmarets, Jean	1595-1676	Hall, Joseph	1574-1656
Desportes, Philippe	1546-1606	Hardy, Alexandre	1569-1631
Diaz Del Castillo, Bernal	1492-1581	Harington, Sir John	1561-1612
Donne, John	1573-1631	Harlib, Samuel	1599-1670
Dorleans, Louis	1544-1629	Harvey, Gabriel	c. 1545-1630
Drayton, Michael	1563-1631	Harvey, William	1578-1657
Drummond, William	1585-1649	Haughton, William	1598
Du Bartas, Guillaume		Hayward, Sir John	1560-1627
De Salluste	1544-1590	Heemskerk, Johan Van	1597-1656
Duchesne, Andre	1584-1640	Herbert, George	1593-1633
Du Vair, Guillaume	1556-1621	Herbert of Cherbury	1583-1648
Ercilla Y Zuniga,		Herrera, Antoine De	1549-1625
Alonso De	1533-1594	Herrera, Fernando De	1534-1597
Espinel, Vincente Martinez	1550-1624	Herrick, Robert	1591-1674
Fairfax, Edward	1580-1635	Heylyn, Peter	1600-1662
Faria Y Sousa, Manuel De	1590-1649	Heywood, Thomas	1574-1641
Fenton, Sir Geoffrey	1539-1608	Hobbes, Thomas	1588-1679
Ferishta, Mohammed		Holinshed, Raphael	d. c. 1580
Kasim	1570-1611	Holles, Denzil Holles	1599-1680
Field, Nathan	1587-1619	Hooft, Pieter Cornelissen	1581-1647
Figueroa, Francisco De	1536-1617	Hooker, Richard	1553-1600
Filmer, Sir Robert	1590-1653	Howell, James	1594-1666
Fischart, Johann	1545-1591	Hume, Alexander	1557-1609
Flecknoe, Richard	1600-1678	Hunnis, William	-1597
Fletcher, Giles	1548-1611	Hortado, Luis	1530-1598
Fletcher, Giles	1584-1623	Huygens, Sir Constantijn	1596-1687
Fletcher, John	1579-1625	Jansen, Cornelius	1585-1638
Fletcher, Phineas	1582-1650	Jauregui, Juan De	1583-1641
Florio, John	c. 1553-1625	Johnson, Richard	1573-1659
Fludd, Robert	1575-1637	Jonson, Ben	1573-1637
Ford, John	1586-1640	Knolles, Richard	1545-1610
Fowler, William	1560-1614	Kochanowski, Jan	1530-1584
Foxe, John	1516-1587	Kyrke, Edward	1553-1613
Francheville, Pierre	1548-1616	Kydd, Thomas	1558-1594
Francis of Sales	1567-1622	La Mothe Le Vayer,	
Fraunce, Abraham	1558-1663	Francois De	1588-1672
Frischlin, Philipp		Languet, Hubert	1518-1581
Nikodemus	1547-1590	Larivey, Pierre	1550-1612
Galilei, Galileo	1564-1642	La Taille, Jean De	1540-1608
Garnier, Robert	1534-1590	Laud, William (Archbishop	
Gascoigne, George	1535-1577	of Canterbury)	1573-1645
Gassendi, Pierre	1592-1655	Leon, Luis Ponce De	1527-1591
Gil Polo, Gaspar	1530-1591	Lindesay, Robert	1530-1590
Godwin, Francis	1562-1633	Lobo, Francisco	
Gongora Y Argote,		Rodriguez	1580-1622
Luis De	1561-1627	Lodge, Thomas	1558-1625
Googe, Barnabe	1540-1594	Lyly, John	1553-1606
Gasson, Stephen	1554-1624	Maitland, Sir Richard	1496-1586
Grazzini, Antonio		Makkari, Ahmed El	1585-1631
Francesco	1503-1583	Malherbe, Francois De	1555-1628
Greene, Robert	1558-1592	Manzolli, Pier Angelo	1543-
Greville, Sir Fulke	1554-1628	Marca, Pierre De	1594-1662

Mariana, Juan De	1536-1624	Scot, Reginald	1538-1599
Marini, Giovanni Battista	1569-1625	Scott, Alexander	1550-
Markham, Gervase	1568-1637	Selden, John	1584-1654
Marlowe, Christopher	1564-1593	Shakespeare, William	1564-1616
Marston, John	1575-1634	Shirley, James	1596-1666
Massinger, Philip	1583-1640	Sidney, Sir Philip	1554-1586
May, Thomas	1595-1650	Smith, John	1580-1631
Mazzoni, Giacomo	1548-1598	Sorel, Charles	1597-1674
Meres, Francis	1565-1647	Sousa, Luiz De	1555-1632
Middleton, Thomas	1570-1627	Southwell, Robert	1561-1595
Mira De Amescua,		Spenser, Edmund	1552-1599
Antonio	1578-1644	Speed, John	1552-1629
Molina, Luis	1535-1600	St. Jernhjelm, Georg	1598-1672
Montainge, Michel De	1533-1592	Stirling, William	
Montchretien, Antoine De	1575-1621	Alexander	1567-1640
Montgomerie, Alexander	1550-1610	Stow, John	1525-1605
Moryson, Fynes	1566-1630	Stumpf, Johann	1500-1576
Munday, Anthony	1553-1633	Sylvester, Joshua	1563-1618
Mure, Sir William	1594-1657	Tasso, Torqueto	1544-1595
Mytens, Daniel	1590-1642	Taylor, John	1580-1653
Najara, Israel Ben Moses	1587-	Telesio, Bernardio	1509-1588
Nashe, Thomas	1567-1601	Theresa (St.)	1515-1582
Norton, Thomas	1532-1584	Thou, Jacques Auguste De	1553-1617
Ogilby, John	1600-1676	Tirso De Molina	1571-1648
Opitz, Von Boberfeld,		Totnes, George Carew	1555-1629
Martin	1597-1639	Tourneur, Cyril	1575-1626
Overbury, Sir Thomas	1581-1613	Tulsi, Das	1532-1623
Parker, Martin	1600-1656	Turberville, George	1540-1610
Pasquier, Etienne	1529-1615	Tusser, Thomas	1524-1580
Passerat, Jean	1534-1602	Tyard, Pontus De	1521-1605
Patrizzi, Francesco	1529-1597	Urfe, Honore D'	1568-1625
Paynter, William	1540-1594	Vaugelas, Claude Faure	1596-1650
Peacham, Henry	1576-1643	Vaughan, William	1577-1641
Peele, George	1558-1597	Vauquelin De La	
Perez De Hita, Gines	1544-1619	Fresnaye, Jean	1536-1608
Pibrac, Guy De Faur	1529-1584	Vega Carpio, Lope	
Purchas, Samuel	1577-1626	Felix De	1562-1635
Puttenham, George	-1590	Vega, Garcilaso De La	
Quarles, Francis	1592-1644	(El Inca)	1535-1616
Quevedo Y Villegas,		Velez De Guevara, Luis	1579-1644
Francisco Gomez De	1580-1645	Viau, Theophile de	1590-1626
Racan, Honore De Bueil	1589-1670	Victoria, Tomas Luis de	1535-1611
Regnier, Mathurin	1573-1613	Villamediana Count De	1580-1622
Rich, Barnabe	1540-1617	Voiture, Vincent	1598-1648
Rinuccini, Ottavio	1562-1621	Vondel, Joost Van Den	1587-1679
Rolland, John	1560-	Walton, Izaak	1593-1683
Ronsard, Pierre De	1524-1585	Watson, Thomas	1557-1692
Rowley, William	1585-1642	Whetstone, George	1551-1587
Sachs, Hans	1494-1576	Wilson, Robert	-1600
Sackville, Thomas	1530-1608	Winslow, Edward	1595-1655
Saint-Amant, Marc		Winthrop, John	1588-1649
Antoine De Gerard	1594-1661	Winzet, Ninian	1518-1592
Sanders, Nicholas	1530-1581	Wither, George	1588-1667
Sandys, George	1578-1644	Wotton, Sir Henry	1568-1639

ARTISTS

Albani, Francesco	1578-1660	Amalteo, Pomponio	1505-1584
Allori, Christofand	1577-1621	Amman, Jost	1539-1591

I

Ammanati, Bartolomeo	1511-1592
Anna, Baldasarre	1560-1639
Badalocchio, Sisto	1581-1647
Balen, Henry Van	1560-1632
Barbieri, Giovanni	
Francesco	1591-1666
Barocci, Federigo	1528-1612
Bassano, Giacomo	
Da Ponte	1510-1592
Bernini, Giovanni Lorenzo	1598-1680
Bloemart, Abraham	1564-1651
Bologna, Giovanni Da	1524-1608
Borromini, Francesco	1599-1667
Brill, Mattys	1550-1584
Brill, Paul	1554-1626
Caluart, Denis	1540-1619
Callot, Jacques	c. 1594-1635
Cambiasi, Luca	1527-1585
Camp, Huysen Dirk	
Rafelsz	1586-1627
Campi, Vincenzo	1536-1591
Caravaggio, Michel	
Angelo	1573-1610
Carducci, Bartolommeo	1568-1610
Carracci, Agostino	1557-1602
Carracci, Annibale	1540-1609
Carracci, Lodovico	1555-1619
Castello, Bernado	1557-1629
Cavedone, Jacopo	1577-1660
Cesari, Giuseppe	1568-1640
Cespedes, Pablo De	1536-1608
Cigoli, Lodovico	
Cardi Da	1559-1613
Claude-Lorraine	1600-1682
Codde, Pieter	1599-1678
Coello, Alonso Sanchez	1515-1590
Colins, Alexandre	1526-1612
Coninxloo, Gillis Van	1544-1605
Corenzio, Belisario	1558-1643
Cornelisz, Cornelis	1562-1638
Cousin, Jean	1500-1590
Cortona, Pietro	
Berrettini Da	1596-1669
Coxcie, Michael	1499-1592
Crayer, Gaspard De	1584-1669
Crespi, Daniele	1590-1630
Crespi, Giovanni Battista	1557-1633
De Keyser, Thomas	1596-1667
Diaz, Diego Valentin	1585-1660
Diepenbeek, Abraham Van	1596-1675
Domenichino, Zampieri	1581-1641
Duck, Jacob	1600-1660
Elsheimer, Adam	1579-1620
Elstracke, Renold	c. 1590-1630
Falcone, Aniello	1600-1656
Farinato, Paolo	1524-1606
Fontana, Domenico	1543-1607
Fontana, Lavinia	1552-1614
Fontana, Prospero	1512-1597
Gentileschi, Artemisia	1597-1651

Gentileschi, Orazio De	1562-1647
Gheeraerts, Marcus	1561-1635
Goyen, Jan Josephszoon	
Van	1596-1656
Guercino	1590-1666
Hals, Frans	1580-1666
Heem, Jan Davidz Van	1600-1683
Hernandes, Gregorio	1576-1636
Hilliard, Nicholas	1537-1619
Hoefnagel, Joris	1542-1600
Honthorst, Gerard, Van	1590-1656
Iwasa, Matahei	1578-1650
Jameson, John	1588-1644
Janssen, Cornelis	1593-1664
Janssens, Van Nuyssen	
Abraham	1575-1632
Jones, Inigo	1573-1651
Jonson, Cornelis	
Van Ceulen	1593-1662
Jordaens, Jacob	1593-1678
Kempener, Peter De	1505-1580
Keyser, Hendrik De	1565-1621
Laar, Pieter Van	1590-1658
Lanfranco, Giovanni	1581-1647
Leoni, Leone	1509-1590
Lescot, Pierre	1510-1578
Limousin, Leonard	1505-1577
Mander, Carel Van	1548-1606
Mansart, Francois	1598-1666
Mierevelt, Michiel Jansz	
Van	1567-1641
Montanes, Juan Martinez	1580-1649
Morales, Luis De	1509-1586
Moroni, Giambatista	1525-1578
Muziano, Girolamo	1528-1592
Navarrete, Juan	
Fernandez De	1526-1579
Pacheco, Francisco	1571-1654
Palladio, Andrea	1518-1580
Palissy, Bernard	1510-1589
(potter)	
Pilon, Germain	1537-1590
Porta, Giacomo Della	1541-1604
Poussin, Nicolas	1594-1665
Procaccini, Camillo	1546-1629
Procaccini, Ercole	1520-1591
Procaccini, Ercole the	
younger	1596-1676
Quesnoy, Francois Du	1594-1646
Reni, Guido	1575-1642
Ribalta, Francisco De	1550-1628
Ribera, Josepe De	1588-1656
Rubens, Peter Paul	1577-1640
Sacchi, Andrea	1600-1661
Sarrazin, Jacques	1588-1660
Snyders, Frans	1579-1657
Steenwijk, Hendrik Van	c. 1550-1603
Stone, Nicholas	1587-1647
Teniers, David the elder	1582-1649
Terbrugghen, Hendrik	1588-1629

Theotocopouli, Domenico		Velasquez, Diego	
(El Greco)	1542-1614	Rodriguez	1599-1660
Titian	1477-1576	Veronese, Paolo	1528-1588
Tintoretto, Jacopo Rubusti	1518-1594	Vos, Cornelis De	1585-1651
Van De Velde, Jan	1593-1641	Vouet, Simon	1590-1649
Van Dyck, Anthony Sir	1599-1641	Zuccaro, Frederigo	1539-1609
Van Veen, Otto	1556-1634	Zurbaran, Francisco De	1598-1669

COMPOSERS

Aichinger, Gregor	1565-1628	Guerrero, Francisco	1528-1599
Allegri, Gregorio	1582-1652	Handl, Jacob	1550-1591
Artusi, Giovanni Maria	1540-1613	Hassler, Hans Leo	1564-1612
Basile, Giambattista	1575-1632	Jenkins, John	1592-1678
Bateson, Thomas	1570-1630	Jimenes De Quesada,	
Bull, John	1562-1628	Gonzalo	1500-1579
Byrd, William	1543-1623	Lasso, Orlando	1530-1594
Caccini, Guilio	1558-1615	Lawes, Henry	1596-1662
Carlton, Richard	1560-1638	Marenzio, Luca	1560-1599
Cavalieri, Emilio De	1550-1599	Monteverdi, Claudio	1567-1643
Cooper, John	1570-1627	Morley, Thomas	1558-1603
Cruger, Johann	1598-1662	Palestrina, Giovanni	
Dowland, John	1563-1626	Pierluigi Da	1526-1594
East, Michael	1580-1648	Peri, Jacopo	1561-1633
Eccard, Johann	1553-1611	Praetorius, Michael	1571-1621
Farmer, John	1565-1605	Ravencroft, Thomas	1590-1633
Farrant, Richard	d. 1580	Schutz, Heinrich	1585-1672
Ford, Thomas	1580-1648	Sweelinck, Jan Pieter	1562-1621
Frescobaldi, Girolmo	1583-1644	Tallis, Thomas	1515-1585
Gabrieli, Andrea	1510-1586	Tomkins, Thomas	1572-1656
Gabrieli, Giovani	1557-1612	Wilbye, John	1574-1638
Gesualdo, Don Carlos	1560-1613	Wilson, John	1595-1674
Gibbons, Orlando	1583-1625		

1603   England and Scotland united.
1605   Gunpowder plot.
1607   Dutch destroy Spanish fleet at Gibraltar.
1618   Thirty years war begins. Sir Walter Raleigh executed.
1620   Treaty of Ulm. Pilgrim Fathers land in New England.
1624   Barbadoes colonised by English.
1625   Parliament dissolved by Charles I.

PROMINENT PEOPLE

Cromwell, Oliver	1599-1658	Richelieu, Armand Jean	
Raleigh, Sir Walter	1552-1618	Du Plessis Cardinal	
		Duc De	1585-1642

EMPERORS OF CHINA
(Ming Dynasty)

Shen Tsung	1572-1620	Hsi Bung	1620-1627
Kuang Tsung	1620		

POPES

Clement VIII	1592-1605	Gregory XV	1621-1623
Leo XI	1605	Urban VIII	1623-1644
Paul V	1605-1621		

FRANCE. HEADS OF STATE

Henry IV	1589-1610	Louis XIII	1610-1643

HOLY ROMAN EMPERORS

Rudolf II	1576-1612	Ferdinand II	1619-1637
Matthias	1612-1619		

ENGLAND. SOVEREIGNS

Elizabeth I	1558-1603	Charles I	1625-1649
James I	1603-1625		

SWEDEN. KINGS

Charles IX	1600-1611	Gustavius II	1611-1632

PORTUGAL. KINGS

Under Spanish Suzerainty   1581-1640

SCOTLAND. KINGS

James VI	1567-1603

ELECTORS OF BRANDENBURG

Joachim III Frederick	1598-1608	George William	1619-1640
John Sigismund	1608-1619		

Boris	1598-1605	Michael	1613-1645
Theodore II	1605	Alexis	1645-1676
Interregnum	1605-1613		

SPAIN. SOVEREIGNS

| Philip III | 1598-1621 | Philip IV | 1621-1665 |

WRITERS

Aitzema, Lieuwe Van	1600-1669	Boccalini, Trajano	1556-1613
Alabaster, William	1567-1640	Boisrobert, Francois Le	
Alarcon Y Mendoza,		Metel De	1592-1662
Jean Ruiz De	1580-1639	Bracciolini, Francesco	1566-1645
Alcazar, B. Del	1530-1606	Bradford, William	1590-1657
Aleman, Mateo	1547-1609	Bradstreet, Ann	1612-1672
Allori, Allesandro	1535-1607	Brantome, Pierre De	
Ammirato, Scipione	1531-1601	Bourdeille	c. 1540-1640
Angelus, Silecius	1624-1677	Brathwaite, Richard	1588-1673
Andrewes, Lancelot	1555-1626	Breton, Nicholas	1545-1626
Argensola, Lupercio		Brome, Alexander	1620-1666
Leonardo De	1559-1613	Brosse, Salomon De	1565-1626
Arminius, Jacobus	1560-1609	Browne, Sir Thomas	1605-1682
Arnault, Antoine	1612-1694	Browne, William	1591-1643
Arrebo, Anders		Bryskett, Lodowyck	1545-1612
Christiensen	1587-1637	Bulstrode, Sir Richard	1610-1711
Arquijo, Juan De	1564-1623	Burton, Robert	1577-1640
Ashmole, Elias	1617-1692	Bussy, Roger de Rabutin	1618-1693
Aubignac, Francois		Butler, Samuel	1612-1680
Hedelin Abbe De	1604-1676	Calderon, De La Barca	
Aubigne, Theodore		Pedro	1600-1681
Agrippa De	1562-1630	Calderwood, David	1575-1650
Avercamp, Hendrik	1585-1634	Calprenede, Gautier Des	
Avila, Gil Gonzales De	1577-1658	Costes De La	1610-1663
Ayrer, Jakob	-1605	Camden, William	1551-1623
Ayton, Sir Robert	1570-1638	Campanella, Tommaso	1568-1639
Bacon, Francis	1561-1626	Campion, Thomas	1567-1620
Baillie, Robert	1599-1662	Carew, Richard	1555-1620
Baker, Sir Richard	1568-1645	Carew, Thomas	1595-1638
Balbuena, Bernardo De	1568-1627	Cartwright, William	1611-1643
Baldinucci, Filippo	1624-1696	Castillo Solorzano,	
Balfour, Robert	1550-1625	Alonso De	1584-1647
Baldi, Bernardino	1553-1617	Castro Y Bellvis,	
Balzac, Jean Louis		Guillen De	1569-1631
Guez De	1594-1654	Cats, Jakob	1577-1660
Barclay, Robert	1648-1690	Cervantes Saavedra,	
Baronius, Caesar	1538-1607	Miguel De	1547-1616
Barnfield, Richard	1574-1627	Cespedes Y Menses,	
Bartoli, Danielle	1608-1685	Gonzalo De	1585-1638
Bassompiere, Francois De	1579-1646	Chamberlayne, William	1619-1679
Baudier, Michel	1589-1645	Chapman, George	1559-1634
Beaumont, Francis	1584-1616	Chapelaine, Jean	1595-1674
Beaumont, Sir John	1583-1627	Charron, Pierre	1541-1603
Beaumont, Joseph	1616-1699	Chettle, Henry	1560-1607
Bellenden, William	1555-1633	Chiabreka, Gabriello	1552-1638
Benlowes, Edward	1603-1676	Churchyard, Thomas	1520-1640
Benserade, Isaac De	1613-1691	Clarendon, Edward Hyde	
Bergerac, Cyrano,		(1st Earl)	1609-1674
Savinien De	1619-1655	Clauberg, Johann	1622-1665

Cleveland, John	1613-1658	Fleming, Paul	1609-1640
Cluwer, Philip	1580-1623	Fletcher, Giles	1548-1611
Coello, Antonio	1611-1652	Fletcher, Giles	1584-1623
Cokain, Sir Aston	1608-1684	Fletcher, John	1579-1625
Comenius, Johann Amos	1592-1670	Fletcher, Phineas	1582-1650
Constable, Henry	1562-1613	Florio, John	c. 1553-1625
Corbet, Richard	1582-1635	Fludd, Robert	1575-1637
Corneille, Pierre	1606-1684	Ford, John	1586-1640
Corneille, Thomas	1625-1709	Fowler, William	1560-1614
Coryate, Thomas	1577-1617	Fox, George	1624-1691
Cotton, John	1584-1652	Francheville, Piere	1548-1616
Cowley, Abraham	1618-1667	Francis of Sales	1567-1622
Craig, Sir Thomas	1530-1608	Fraunce, Abraham	1558-1663
Crashaw, Richard	1613-1649	Froberger, Johann Jakob	1616-1667
Cudworth, Ralph	1617-1688	Fuller, Thomas	1608-1661
Cueva, Juan De La	1550-1610	Furetiere, Antoine	1619-1688
Culpeper, Nicholas	1616-1654	Galilei, Galileo	1564-1642
Dach, Simon	1605-1659	Garcilaso De La Vega,	
Daniel, Samuel	1562-1619	El Inca	1540-1616
Davenant, Sir William	1606-1668	Gassendi, Pierre	1592-1655
Davenport, Robert	1623-1639	Gauden, John	1605-1662
Davies, John	1565-1618	Gerhardt, Paul	1607-1676
Davies, Sir John	1569-1626	Geulincx, Arnold	1624-1669
Davila, Enrico Caterino	1576-1631	Godwin, Francis	1562-1633
Day, John	1574-1640	Gongora Y Argote,	
Dee, John	1527-1608	Luis De	1561-1627
Dekker, Thomas	1570-1641	Gosson, Stephen	1554-1624
Delmedigo, Joseph		Gracian Y Morales,	
Soloman	1591-1655	Baltasar	1601-1658
Dempster, Thomas	1570-1625	Greville, Sir Fulke	1554-1628
Denham, Sir John	1615-1669	Grimmelshausen, Hans	
Descartes, Rene	1596-1650	Jakob Christof Fel Von	1625-1676
Desmarets, Jean	1595-1676	Grotius, Hugo	1583-1645
Desportes, Phillippe	1546-1606	Gryphius, Andreas	1616-1664
Digby, Sir Kenelm	1603-1665	Guarini, Giovanni Battista	1538-1612
Donne, John	1573-1631	Guericke, Otto Von	1602-1686
Dorleans, Louis	1544-1629	Guevara, Luis Velez De	1570-1644
Drayton, Michael	1563-1631	Gundulic, Ivan	1588-1638
Drummond, William	1585-1649	Gyongyosi, Istvan	1620-1704
Duchesne, Andre	1584-1640	Habingdon, William	1605-1654
Dugdale, Sir William	1605-1686	Hajji, Khalifa	c. 1599-1658
Du Ryer, Pierre	1606-1658	Hake, Edward	1579-
Du Vair, Guillaume	1556-1621	Hakluyt, Richard	1552-1616
Enriquez, Gomes Antonio	1602-1662	Hall, Joseph	1574-1656
Espinel, Vincente Martinez	1550-1624	Hardy, Alexandre	1569-1631
Evelyn, John	1620-1706	Harington, Sir John	1561-1612
Fairfax, Edward	1580-1635	Harlib, Samuel	1599-1670
Falkland, Lucius Cary		Harrington, James	1611-1677
Viscount	1610-1643	Harsdorffer, Georg Philipp	1607-1658
Fanshawe, Sir Richard	1608-1666	Harvey, Gabriel	c. 1545-1630
Faria Y Sousa, Manuel De	1590-1649	Harvey, William	1578-1657
Felltham, Owen	1602-1668	Haughton, William	1598-
Fenton, Sir Geoffrey	1539-1608	Hayward, Sir John	1560-1627
Ferishta, Mohammed		Heemskerk, Johan Van	1597-1656
Kasim	1570-1611	Herbert, George	1593-1633
Field, Nathan	1587-1619	Herbert of Cherbury	1583-1648
Figueroa, Francisco De	1536-1617	Herbert, Sir Thomas	1608-1682
Filmer, Sir Robert	1590-1653	Herrera, Antoine De	1549-1625
Flecknoe, Richard	1600-1678	Herrick, Robert	1591-1674

Heylyn, Peter	1600-1662
Heywood, Thomas	1574-1641
Hobbes, Thomas	1588-1679
Holles, Denzil Holles	1599-1680
Hooft, Pieter Cornelissen	1581-1647
Howell, James	1594-1666
Hume, Alexander	1557-1609
Huygens, Sir Constantijn	1596-1687
Jansen, Cornelius	1585-1638
Janssen, Geraert	fl. 1616
Jauregui, Juan De	1583-1641
Johnson, Richard	1573-1659
Jonson, Ben	1573-1637
Jordan, Thomas	1612-1685
Killigrew, Thomas	1612-1683
Killigrew, Sir William	1606-1695
Kirke, Edward	1553-1613
Knolles, Richard	1545-1610
La Calprenede, Gauthier De Costes	1610-1663
La Fontaine, Jean De	1621-1695
La Mothe Le Vayer, Francois De	1588-1672
Larivey, Pierre	1550-1612
La Rochefoucauld, Francois De	1613-1680
La Taille, Jean De	1540-1608
La Tour, Georges de	1593-1652
Laud, William (Archbishop of Canterbury)	1573-1645
L'Estrange, Sir Roger	1616-1704
Lobo, Francisco Rodrigues	1580-1622
Lodge, Thomas	1558-1625
Lovelace, Richard	1618-1658
Lyly, John	1553-1606
Maimbourg, Louis	1610-1686
Mairet, Jean De	1604-1686
Makkari, Ahmed El	1585-1631
Malherbe, Francois De	1555-1628
Manuel De Mello, Don Francisco	1608-1666
Marca, Pierre De	1594-1662
Mariana, Juan De	1536-1624
Marini, Giovanni Battista	1569-1625
Markham, Gervase	1568-1637
Marston, John	1575-1634
Marvell, Andrew	1621-1678
Massinger, Philip	1583-1640
Matos, Fragoso, Juan De	1608-1689
May, Thomas	1595-1650
Melo, Francisco Manuel De	1608-1666
Meres, Francis	1565-1647
Middleton, Thomas	1570-1627
Milton, John	1608-1674
Mira De Amescua, Antonio	1578-1644
Moliere, (Jean Baptiste Poquelin)	1622-1673
Montchretien, Antoine De	1575-1621

Montgomerie, Alexander	1550-1610
More, Henry	1613-1687
Moreto Y Cavana, Agustin	1618-1669
Moryson, Fynes	1566-1630
Moscherrosch, Johann Michael	1601-1669
Motteville, Francoise Bertraut De	1621-1689
Munday, Anthony	1553-1633
Mure, Sir William	1594-1657
Mytens, Daniel	1590-1642
Najara, Israel Ben Moses	1587-
Nashe, Thomas	1567-1601
Ogilby, John	1600-1676
O'Higgin, Tadhg, Dall	-1616
Opitz Von Boberfield, Martin	1597-1639
Overbury, Sir Thomas	1581-1613
Pallavicino, Ferrante	1618-1644
Pallavicino, Pietro Sforza	1607-1667
Parker, Martin	1600-1656
Pascal, Blaise	1623-1662
Pasquier, Etienne	1529-1615
Passerat, Jean	1534-1602
Peacham, Henry	1576-1643
Perez, De Hita, Gines	1544-1619
Purchas, Samuel	1577-1626
Quarles, Francis	1592-1644
Quevedo Y Villegas, Francisco Gomez De	1580-1645
Racan, Honore De Bueil	1589-1670
Randolph, Thomas	1605-1635
Regnier, Mathurin	1573-1613
Retz, Cardinal de	1614-1679
Rich, Barnabe	1540-1617
Rich, Richard	1610-
Rinuccini, Ottavio	1562-1621
Rolland, John	1560-
Rotrou, Jean De	1609-1650
Rowley, William	1585-1642
Rushworth, John	1612-1690
Sackville, Thomas	1530-1608
Saint-Amant, Marc Antoine De Gerard	1594-1661
Saint Evremond, Charles Marquetel De Saint Denis-Segnieur De	1610-1703
Sandys, George	1578-1644
Sarasin, Jean Francois	1614-1654
Scarron, Paul	1610-1660
Scudery, Georges De	1601-1667
Scudery, Madeleine De	1607-1701
Selden, John	1584-1654
Shakespeare, William	1564-1616
Shirley, James	1596-1666
Smith, John	1580-1631
Solis Y Ribadeneyra, Antonio De	1610-1686
Sorel, Charles	1597-1674
Sousa, Louiz De	1555-1632

Speed, John	1552-1629	Vaughan, Henry	1622-1695
St. Jernhjelm, George	1598-1672	Vaughan, William	1577-1641
Stanley, Thomas	1625-1678	Vauquelin, De La Fresnaye	
Stow, John	1525-1605	Jean	1536-1608
Strode, William	1602-1645	Vega Carpio, Lope	
Sturling, William Alexander	1567-1640	Felix De	1562-1635
Suckling, Sir John	1609-1642	Vega, Garcilaso De La	
Sylvester, Joshua	1563-1618	(El Inca)	1535-1616
Tallemant, Gedeon Sieur		Velez De Guevara, Luis	1579-1644
Des Reaux	1619-1692	Viau, Theophile de	1590-1626
Taylor, Jeremy	1613-1667	Victoria, Tomas Luis De	1553-1611
Taylor, John	1580-1653	Vieira, Antonio	1608-1697
Thomas, Nabbes	1605-	Villamediana Count De	1580-1622
Thou, Jacques, Auguste De	1553-1617	Voiture, Vincent	1598-1648
Tirso De Molina	1571-1648	Vondel, Joost Van Den	1587-1679
Totnes, George Carew	1555-1629	Waller, Edmund	1606-1687
Tourneur, Cyril	1575-1626	Walton, Izaak	1593-1683
Tulsi Das	1532-1623	Webster, John	1602-1624
Turberville, George	1540-1610	Whichcote, Benjamin	1609-1683
Tyard, Pontus De	1521-1605	Williams, Roger	c.1600-1683
Urfe, Honore D'	1568-1625	Winslow, Edward	1595-1655
Urquhart, Sir Thomas	1611-1660	Winthrop, John	1588-1649
Vane, Sir Henry	1613-1662	Wither, George	1588-1667
Vaugelas, Claude Faure	1596-1650	Wotton, Sir Henry	1568-1639

ARTISTS

Algardi, Alessandro	1602-1654	Castello, Bernado	1557-1629
Allori, Christofand	1577-1621	Castello, Valerio	1625-1659
Albani, Francesco	1578-1660	Cavedone, Jacopo	1577-1660
Anguier, Francois	1604-1669	Cesari	1568-1640
Anguier, Michel	1612-1686	Cespedes, Pablo de	1536-1608
Anna, Baldasarre	1560-1639	Champaign, Phillipe De	1602-1674
Badalocchio, Sisto	1581-1647	Cigoli, Lodovico, Cardi Da	1559-1613
Balen, Henry Van	1560-1632	Claude Lorrain	1600-1682
Barbieri, Giovanni		Codde, Pieter	1599-1678
Francesco	1591-1666	Colin, Alexandre	1526-1612
Barocci, Federigo	1528-1612	Coninxloo Gillis Van	1544-1605
Berchem, Nicolaes	1620-1683	Cooper, Samuel	1609-1672
Bernini, Giovanni Lorenzo	1598-1680	Coques, Gonzales	1614-1684
Bloemart, Abraham	1564-1651	Corenzio, Belisario	1558-1643
Bolagna, Giovanni Da	1524-1608	Cornelisz, Cornelis	1562-1638
Borromini, Francesco	1599-1667	Cortona, Pietro Berrettini	
Both, Jan	1618-1652	Da	1596-1669
Brill, Paul	1554-1626	Courtois, Jacques	1621-1676
Brouwer, Adrian	1606-1638	Crayer, Gaspard De	1584-1669
Callot, Jacques	c. 1594-1635	Crespi, Daniele	1590-1630
Caluart, Denis	1540-1619	Crespi, Giovanni Batista	1557-1633
Camphuysen, Dirk Rafelsz	1586-1627	De Keyser, Thomas	1596-1667
Cano, Alonzo	1601-1667	Dobson, William	1610-1646
Cantarini, Simone	1612-1648	Dolci, Carlo	1616-1686
Cappelle, Jan Van Der	1624-1679	Domenichino, Zampieri	1581-1641
Caracci, Agostino	1557-1602	Douw, Gerrit	1613-1675
Caracci, Annibale	1540-1609	Duck, Jacob	1600-1660
Caracci, Ludovico	1555-1619	Eekhout, Gerbrand	
Caravaggio, Michel Angelo	1573-1610	Van Den	1621-1674
Carducci, Bartolommeo	1568-1610	Elsheimer, Adam	1579-1620
Carreno De Miranda,		Elstracke, Renold	c. 1590-1630
Juan	1614-1685	Everdingen, Allart Van	1621-1675

Fabritius, Carel	1624-1654	Mignard, Pierre	1610-1695
Faithorne, William	1616-1691	Montanes, Juan Martinez	1580-1649
Falcone, Aniello	1600-1656	Murillo, Bartolome	
Farinato, Paolo	1524-1606	Esteban	1617-1682
Felibien, Andre	1619-1695	Oliver, Isaac Peter	d. 1617
Flemal, Bertholet	1614-1675	Ostade, Adriaan Van	1610-1685
Flinck, Govert	1615-1660	Pacheco, Francisco	1564-1654
Fontana, Domenico	1543-1607	Paolini, Pietro	1603-1682
Fontana, Lavinia	1552-1614	Pareja, Juan De	1606-1670
Franceschini, Baldassare	1611-1689	Petitot, Jean	1608-1691
Fresnoy, Charles		Porta, Giacomo Della	1541-1604
Alphonse Du	1611-1665	Post, Pieter	1608-1669
Fyt, Jan	1609-1661	Potter, Paul	1625-1654
Gentileschi, Artemisia	1597-1651	Poussin, Gaspar	1613-1675
Gentileschi, Orazio De	1562-1647	Poussin, Nicolas	1594-1665
Gheeraerts, Marcus	1561-1635	Procaccini, Camillo	1546-1629
Goyen, Jan Josephzoon Van	1596-1656	Procaccini, Ercole the	
Grimaldi, Giovanni		younger	1596-1676
Francesco	1606-1680	Puget, Pierre	1622-1694
Guercino	1590-1666	Quesnoy, Francois du	1594-1646
Hals, Franz	1580-1666	Rembrandt, Harmensz	
Heem, Jan Davidz Van	1600-1683	Van Rijn	1606-1669
Helst, Bartholomaens		Reni, Guido	1575-1642
Van Der	1613-1670	Ribalta, Francisco de	1550-1628
Hernandes, Gregorio	1576-1636	Ribera, Jusepe de	1588-1656
Herrera, Francisco		Rosa, Salvator	1615-1673
"El Mozo"	1622-1685	Rubens, Peter Paul	1577-1640
Hilliard, Nicholas	1537-1619	Sacchi, Andrea	1600-1661
Hollar, Wenceslaus	1607-1677	Sandrart, Joachim Van	1606-1688
Honthorst, Gerard Van	1590-1656	Sarrazin, Jacques	1588-1660
I Wasa, Matahei	1578-1650	Sassoferato	1605-1685
Jamesone, John	1588-1644	Snyders, Frans	1579-1657
Janssen, Cornelis	1593-1664	Steenwijk, Hendrik Van c.	1550-1603
Janssens, Van Nuyssen		Stone, Nicholas	1587-1647
Abraham	1675-1632	Teniers, David the Elder	1582-1649
Jones, Inigo	1573-1651	Teniers, David the	
Jonson, Cornelis Van		Younger	1610-1690
Ceulen	1593-1662	Ter Borch, Gerard	1617-1681
Jordaens, Jacob	1593-1678	Terbrugghen, Hendrik	1588-1629
Keyser, Hendrik De	1565-1621	Theotocopouli, Domenico	
Koninck, Philips	1619-1688	(El Greco)	1542-1614
Laar, Pieter Van	1590-1658	Van De Velde, Jan	1593-1641
Lahire, Laurent De	1606-1656	Van De Velde, William	1611-1693
Lanfranco, Giovanni	1581-1647	Van Dyck, Sir Anthony	1599-1641
Le Brun, Charles	1619-1690	Van Veen, Otto	1556-1634
Lely, Sir Peter	1618-1680	Velasquez, Diego	
Le Sueur, Eustache	1616-1655	Rodriguez	1599-1660
Lievensz, Jan	1607-1674	Vos Cornelis De	1585-1651
Lorenzo, Lippi	1606-1664	Vovet, Simon	1590-1649
Mander, Carel Van	1548-1606	Weenix, Jan Baptist	1621-1660
Mansart, Francois	1598-1666	Wouwerman, Philip	1619-1668
Maratta, Carlo	1625-1713	Zuccaro, Frederigo	1539-1609
Mierevelt, Micheil		Zurbaran, Francisco De	1598-1669
Jansz Van	1567-1641		

COMPOSERS

Aichinger, Gregor	1565-1628	Allegri, Gregorio	1582-1652
Albert, Heinrich	1604-1651	Artusi, Giovanni Maria	1540-1613

Basile, Giambattista	1575-1632	Gibbons, Orlando	1583-1625
Bateson, Thomas	1570-1630	Hassler, Hans Leo	1564-1612
Bull, John	1562-1628	Holborn, Anthony	died c. 1602
Byrd, William	1543-1623	Jenkins, John	1592-1678
Caccini, Guilio	1558-1615	Lawes, Henry	1596-1662
Carissimi, Giacomo	1604-1674	Legrenzi, Giovanni	1625-1690
Carlton, Richard	1560-1638	Monteverdi, Claudio	1567-1643
Cavalli, Francesco	1602-1676	Morley, Thomas	1558-1603
Cesti, Marc'Antonio	1618-1669	Peri, Jacopo	1561-1633
Cooper, John	1570-1627	Praetorius, Michael	1571-1621
Cruger, Johann	1598-1662	Ravencroft, Thomas	1590-1633
Dowland, John	1563-1626	Schmelzer, Johann	
East, Michael	1586-1648	Heinrick	1623-1680
Eccard, Johann	1553-1611	Schutz, Heinrich	1585-1672
Farmer, John	1565-1605	Sweelinck, Jan Pieter	1562-1621
Ford, Thomas	1580-1648	Tomkins, Thomas	1572-1656
Frescobaldi, Girolamo	1583-1644	Weelkes, Thomas	d. 1623
Gabrieli, Giovanni	1557-1612	Wilbye, John	1574-1638
Gesualdo, Don Carlos	1560-1613	Wilson, John	1595-1674

1631 Battle of Leipsic.
1632 Battle of Lutzen.
1641 Coffee first drunk in England.
1642 New Zealand and Tasmania discovered.   Battle of Worcester.
     Battle of Edge Hill.
1643 Battle of Newbury.
1644 Battle of Marston Moor   2nd Battle of Newbury.
1645 Battle of Naseby.
1648 Battle of Preston.   Rump Parliament elected.
1649 Charles I executed.

PROMINENT PEOPLE

Cromwell, Oliver	1599-1658	Newton, Sir Isaac	1642-1727
Jeffrey, George (Judge)	1648-1689	Richelieu, Armand Jean Du	
Kidd, Captain William	1645-1701	Plessis, Cardinal Duc De	1585-1642

EMPERORS OF CHINA

Hsi Tsung		Shih Tsu [Manchu	
(Ming Dynasty)	1620-1627	(Ching) Dynasty]	1644-1661
Ssu Tsung			
(Ming Dynasty)	1627-1644		

POPES

Urban VIII	1623-1644	Innocent X	1644-1655

FRANCE. HEADS OF STATE

Louis XIII	1610-1643	Louis, XIV	1643-1715

HOLY ROMAN EMPERORS

Ferdinand II	1619-1637	Ferdinand III	1637-1657

ENGLAND. SOVEREIGNS

Charles I	1625-1649	Commonwealth &	
		Protectorate	1649-1660

SWEDEN. KINGS

Gustavius II	1611-1632	Christina	1632-1654

PORTUGAL. KINGS

Under Spanish Suzerainty	1581-1640	John IV	1640-1656

ELECTORS OF BRANDENBURG

George, William	1619-1640	Frederick William	1640-1688

RUSSIA. TSARS

Michael	1613-1645	Alexis	1645-1676

SPAIN. SOVEREIGNS

Philip IV	1621-1665

Acosta, Uriel	d. 1647	Brathwaite, Richard	1588-1673
Aitzema, Lieuwe Van	1600-1669	Breton, Nicholas	1545-1626
Alabaster, William	1567-1640	Broekhuizew, Jan Van	1649-1707
Alarcon Y Mendoza,		Brome, Alexander	1620-1666
Jean Ruiz de	1580-1639	Brosse, Salemon de	1565-1626
Alcoforado, Marianna	1640-1723	Browne, Sir Thomas	1605-1682
Alleine, Joseph	1634-1668	Browne, William	1591-1643
Amelot de la Houssaey,		Bulstrode, Sir Richard	1610-1711
Abraham Nicolas	1634-1706	Bunyan, John	1628-1688
Angelus, Silecius	1624-1677	Burnet, Gilbert	1643-1715
Arnault, Antoine	1612-1694	Burnet, Thomas	1635-1715
Arrebo, Anders		Burton, Robert	1577-1640
Christiensen	1587-1637	Butler, Samuel	1612-1680
Ashmole, Elias	1617-1692	Bussy, Roger de Rabutin	1618-1693
Aubignac, Francois		Calderon, De La Barca	
Hedelin Abbe de	1604-1676	Pedro	1600-1681
Aubigne, Theodore		Calderwood, David	1575-1650
Agrippa De	1562-1630	Calprenede, Gautier Des	
Aubrey, John	1626-1697	Costes De La	1610-1663
Aulnoy, Marie Catherine		Campanella, Tommaso	1568-1639
le Jumel de Barneuille		Castillo Solorzano,	
de la Motte	1650-1705	Alonso De	1584-1647
Auton, Sir Robert	1570-1638	Castro Y Bellvis,	
Avercamp, Hendrik	1585-1634	Guillen De	1569-1631
Avila Gil Gonzales De	1577-1658	Carew, Thomas	1595-1638
Bacon, Francis	1561-1626	Cartwright, William	1611-1643
Baillie, Robert	1599-1662	Cats, Jakob	1577-1660
Baker, Sir Richard	1568-1645	Cespedes Y Meneses,	
Balbuena, Bernardo De	1568-1627	Gonsalo De	1585-1638
Baldinucci, Filippo	1624-1696	Chamberlayne, William	1619-1679
Balzac, Jean Louis		Chapelaine, Jean	1595-1674
Guez De	1594-1654	Chapman, George	1559-1634
Barclay, Robert	1648-1690	Chaulieu, Guillaume	
Barnfield, Richard	1574-1627	Amfrye De	1639-1720
Bartoli, Danielle	1608-1685	Chiabreka, Gabriello	1552-1638
Bartoli, Pietro Santo	1635-1700	Choisy, Francois	
Bassompiere, Francois De	1579-1646	Timoleon Abbe De	1644-1724
Baudier, Michel	1589-1645	Clarendon, Edward Hyde	
Bayle, Pierre	1647-1706	1st Earl of	1609-1674
Beaumont, Sir John	1583-1627	Clauberg, Johann	1622-1665
Beaumont, Joseph	1616-1699	Cleveland, John	1613-1658
Behn, Aphra	1640-1689	Cocker, Edward	1631-1675
Bellenden, William	1555-1633	Coello, Antonio	1611-1652
Benlowes, Edward	1603-1676	Cokain, Sir Aston	1608-1684
Benserade, Isaac De	1613-1691	Comenius, Johann Amos	1592-1670
Bergerac, Cyrano de	1619-1655	Corbet, Richard	1582-1635
Blackmore, Sir Richard	1650-1729	Corneille, Pierre	1606-1684
Blount, Sir Thomas Pope	1649-1687	Corneille, Thomas	1625-1709
Boileau-Despreaux,		Cotton, Charles	1630-1687
Nicolas	1636-1711	Cowley, Abraham	1618-1667
Boirobert, Francois		Crashaw, Richard	1613-1649
Le Metel De	1592-1662	Crowne, John	1640-1703
Bossuet, Jacques Benigne	1627-1704	Cudworth, Ralph	1617-1688
Boursault, Edme	1638-1701	Culpeper, Nicholas	1616-1654
Boyle, Robert	1627-1691	Cumberland, Richard	1631-1718
Bracciolini, Francesco	1566-1645	Dach, Simon	1605-1659
Bradford, William	1590-1657	Dalgarno, George	1626-1687
Bradstreet, Ann	1612-1672	Daniel, Gabriel	1649-1728
Brantome, Pierre De		Dass, Petter	1647-1708
Bourdeille	1540-c. 1640	Davenant, Sir William	1606-1668

Davenport, Robert	1623-1639	Guericke, Otto Von	1602-1686
Davies, Sir John	1569-1626	Guevara, Luis Velez De	1570-1644
Davila, Enrico Caterino	1576-1631	Guidi, Carlo Alessandro	1650-1712
Day, John	1574-1640	Gundulic, Ivan	1588-1638
Dekker, Thomas	c. 1570-1641	Guyon, Jeanne Marie	
Delmedigo, Joseph Soloman	1591-1655	Bouvier de la Mothe	1648-1717
Denham, Sir John	1615-1669	Gyongyosi, Istvan	1620-1704
Descartes, Rene	1596-1650	Habingdon, William	1605-1654
Deshoulieres, Antoinette	1638-1694	Hajji Khalifa	1599-c. 1658
Desmarets, Jean	1595-1676	Hake, Edward	1579-
Digby, Sir Kennelm	1603-1665	Hall, Joseph	1574-1656
Dodwell, Henry	1641-1711	Hamilton, Anthony	1645-1720
Donne, John	1573-1631	Hardy, Alexander	1569-1631
Dorleans, Louis	1544-1629	Harlib, Samuel	1599-1670
Drayton, Michael	1563-1631	Harrington, James	1611-1677
Drummond, William	1585-1649	Harsdorffer, Georg Philipp	1607-1658
Dryden, John	1631-1700	Harvey, Gabriel	1545-c. 1630
Duchesne, Andre	1584-1640	Harvey, William	1578-1657
Dugdale, Sir William	1605-1686	Haughton, William	1598-
Du Ryer, Pierre	1606-1658	Hayward, Sir John	1560-1627
Ellwood, Thomas	1639-1714	Heemskerk, Johan Van	1597-1656
Enriquez, Gomez Antonio	1602-1662	Herbert, George	1593-1633
Etherege, Sir George	1635-1691	Herbert of Cherbury	1583-1648
Evelyn, John	1620-1706	Herbert, Sir Thomas	1608-1682
Fairfax, Edward	1580-1635	Herrick, Robert	1591-1674
Falkland, Lucius Cary		Heylyn, Peter	1600-1662
Viscount	1610-1643	Heywood, Thomas	1580-1641
Fanshawe, Sir Richard	1608-1666	Hobbes, Thomas	1588-1679
Faria Y Sousa, Manuel De	1590-1649	Holles, Denzil Holles	1599-1680
Felltham, Owen	1602-1668	Hooft, Pieter Cornelissen	1581-1647
Filicaia, Vincenzo da	1642-1707	Howard, Sir Robert	1626-1698
Filmer, Sir Robert	1590-1653	Howell, James	1594-1666
Flecknoe, Richard	1600-1678	Hoz Y Mota, Juan	
Fleming, Paul	1609-1640	Claudio De La	1630-1714
Fletcher, Phineas	1582-1650	Huygens, Sir Constantijn	1596-1687
Fleury, Claude	1640-1723	Jansen, Cornelius	1585-1638
Fludd, Robert	1575-1637	Jauregui, Juan De	1583-1641
Ford, John	1586-1640	Johnson, Richard	1573-1659
Fox, George	1624-1691	Jonson, Ben	1573-1637
Fraunce, Abraham	1558-1663	Jordan, Thomas	1612-1685
Froberger, Johann Jakob	1616-1667	Killigrew, Thomas	1612-1683
Fuller, Thomas	1608-1661	Killigrew, Sir William	1606-1695
Furetiere, Antoine	1619-1688	Kingo, Thomas Hansen	1634-1703
Galilei, Galileo	1564-1642	Kirk, Robert	1641-1692
Gassendi, Pierre	1592-1655	La Bruyere, Jean De	1645-1696
Gauden, John	1605-1662	La Calprenede, Gauthier	
Gerhardt, Paul	1607-1676	De Costes	1610-1663
Geulincx, Arnold	1624-1669	La Fayette, Marie	
Glanville, Joseph	1636-1680	Madeleine	1634-1693
Glapthorne, Henry	1635-1642	La Fontaine, Jean De	1621-1695
Godwin, Francis	1562-1633	Lairesse, Gerard De	1641-1711
Gongora Y Argote,		La Mothe Le Vayer,	
Luis De	1561-1627	Francois De	1588-1672
Gracian Y Morales,		La Rochefoucauld,	
Baltasar	1601-1658	Francois De	1613-1680
Greville, Sir Fulke	1554-1628	Latour, Georges de	1593-1652
Grimmelshausen, Hans		Laud, William (Archbishop	
Jacob Christof Felvon	1625-1676	of Canterbury)	1573-1645
Grotius, Hugo	1583-1645	Leibniz, Gottfried	
Gryphius, Andreas	1616-1664	Wilhelm	1646-1716

L'Estrange, Sir Roger	1616-1704	Quinault, Phillipe	1635-1688
Locke, John	1632-1704	Racan, Honore De Bueill	1589-1670
Lovelace, Richard	1618-1658	Racine, Jean	1639-1699
Maimbourg, Louis	1610-1686	Randolph, Thomas	1605-1635
Mairet, Jean De	1604-1686	Retz, Cardinal de	1614-1679
Makkari, Ahmed el	1585-1631	Rochester, John Wilmot	1647-1680
Malebranche, Nicolas	1638-1715	Roscommon, Wentworth	
Maleherbe, Francois De	1555-1628	Dillon	1630-1685
Manuel De Mello,		Rotrou, Jean De	1609-1650
Don Francisco	1608-1666	Rowley, William	1585-1642
Marca, Pierre De	1594-1662	Rushworth, John	1612-1690
Markham, Gervase	1568-1637	Rymer, Thomas	1641-1713
Marston, John	1575-1634	Saint Amant, Marc	
Marvell, Andrew	1621-1678	Antoine De Gerard	1594-1661
Massinger, Philip	1583-1640	Saint Evremond, Charles	
Mather, Increase	1639-1723	Marquetel de Saint	
Matos, Fragoso, Juan De	1608-1689	Denis Seigneur de	1610-1703
May, Thomas	1595-1650	Saint Real, Cesar Vichard	
Melo, Francisco		Abbé de	1631-1692
Manuel de	1608-1666	Sandys, George	1578-1644
Meres, Francis	1565-1647	Sarasin, Jean Francois	1614-1654
Middleton, Thomas	1570-1627	Scarron, Paul	1610-1660
Mira De Amescua,		Scudery, Georges De	1601-1667
Antonio	1578-1644	Scudery, Madeleine De	1607-1701
Milton, John	1608-1674	Sedley, Sir Charles	1639-1701
Moliere, (Jean Baptiste		Selden, John	1584-1654
Poquelin)	1622-1673	Settle, Elkanam	1648-1724
More, Henry	1614-1687	Sevigne, Marie De	
Moreto Y Cavana, Agustin	1618-1669	Rabutin-Chantal	1626-1696
Moryson, Fynes	1566-1630	Shadwell, Thomas	1642-1692
Moscherosch, Johann		Sherlock, William	1641-1707
Michael	1601-1669	Shirley, James	1596-1666
Motteville, Francoise		Smith, John	1580-1631
Bertaut De	1621-1689	Solis Y Ribadeneyra,	
Munday, Anthony	1553-1633	Antonio de	1610-1686
Mure, Sir William	1594-1657	Sorel, Charles	1597-1674
Mytens, Daniel	1590-1642	Sousa, Luiz De	1555-1632
Najara, Israel Ben Moses	1587-	Speed, John	1552-1629
Newton, Sir Isaac	1642-1727	Spinoza, Benedictus De	1632-1677
Ogilby, John	1600-1676	St. Jernhjelm, Georg	1598-1672
Opitz Von Boberfeld,		Stanley, Thomas	1625-1678
Martin	1597-1639	Stillingfleet, Edward	1635-1699
Pallavicino, Ferrante	1618-1644	Stirling, William	
Pallavicino, Pietro, Sforza	1607-1667	Alexander	1567-1640
Parker, Martin	1600-1656	Strode, William	1602-1645
Pascal, Blaise	1623-1662	Strype, John	1643-1737
Peacham, Henry	1576-1643	Suckling, Sir John	1609-1642
Penn, William	1644-1718	Tallemant, Gedeon	
Pepys, Samuel	1633-1703	Sieur Des Reaux	1619-1692
Perrault, Charles	1628-1703	Taylor, Jeremy	1613-1667
Philips, Katharine	1631-1664	Taylor, John	1580-1653
Phillips, Edward	1630-1696	Temple, Sir William	1628-1699
Phillips, John	1631-1706	Thomas, Nabbes	1605-
Pozzo, Andrea	1642-1709	Tillemont, Sebastian Le	
Puffendorf, Samuel		Nain De	1637-1698
Freiherr Von	1632-1694	Tirso De Molina	1571-1648
Quarles, Francis	1592-1644	Totnes, George Carew	1555-1629
Quesnel, Pasquier	1634-1719	Traherne, Thomas	1637-1674
Quevedo Y Villegas,		Tourneur, Cyril	1575-1626
Francisco Gomez De	1580-1645		

Urquhart, Sir Thomas	1611-1660	Waller, Edmund	1606-1687
Vane, Sir Henry	1613-1662	Walton, Izaak	1593-1683
Vaugelas, Claude Faure	1596-1650	Whichcote, Benjamin	1609-1683
Vaughan, Henry	1622-1695	Wigglesworth, Michael	1631-1705
Vaughan, William	1577-1641	Williams, Roger	c. 1600-1683
Vega Carpio, Lope		Winslow, Edward	1595-1655
Felix De	1562-1635	Winthrop, John	1588-1649
Velez De Guevara, Luis	1579-1644	Wither, George	1588-1667
Viau, Theophile De	1590-1626	Wood, Anthony	1632-1695
Vieira, Antonio	1608-1697	Wotton, Sir Henry	1568-1639
Voiture, Vincent	1598-1648	Wyncherley, William	1640-1716
Vodel, Joost Van Den	1587-1679	Young, Edward	1638-1765

ARTISTS

Algardi, Alessandro	1602-1654	Corenzio, Belisario	1558-1643
Albani, Francesco	1578-1660	Cortona, Pietro	
Anguier, Francois	1604-1669	Berrettini Da	1596-1669
Anguier, Michel	1612-1686	Cotton, John	1584-1652
Anna, Baldasarre	1560-1639	Courtois, Guillaume	1628-1679
Backhuysen, Ludolf	1631-1708	Courtois, Jacques	1621-1676
Badalocchio, Sisto	1581-1647	Coypel, Noel	1628-1707
Balen, Henry Van	1560-1632	Coysevox, Charles Antoine	1640-1720
Barbieri, Giovanni		Crayer, Gaspard De	1584-1669
Francesco	1591-1666	Crespi, Daniele	1590-1630
Beck, David	1621-1656	Crespi, Giovanni Battista	1557-1633
Berchem, Nicolaes	1620-1683	De Keyser, Thomas	1596-1667
Bernini, Giovanni		Dobson, William	1610-1646
Lorenzo	1598-1680	Dolci, Carlo	1616-1686
Bloemart, Abraham	1564-1651	Domenichino, Zampieri	1581-1641
Borromini, Francesco	1599-1667	Douw, Gerrit	1613-1675
Both, Jan	1618-1652	Duck, Jacob	1600-1660
Boulle, Andre Charles	1642-1732	Eeckhout, Gerbrand	
(cabinet maker)		Van Den	1621-1674
Bourse, Esaias	1630-1673	Elstracke, Renold	c. 1590-1630
Brill, Paul	1554-1626	Everdingen, Allart Van	1621-1675
Brouwer, Adrian	1606-1638	Fabritius, Carel	1624-1654
Callot, Jacques	c. 1594-1635	Faed, John	died 1626
Camphuysen, Dirk Rofelsz	1586-1627	Faithorne, William	1616-1691
Cano, Alonzo	1601-1667	Falcone, Aniello	1600-1656
Cantarini, Simone	1612-1648	Felibien, Andre	1619-1695
Cappelle, Jan Van Der	1624-1679	Ferri, Ciro	1634-1689
Carreno De Miranda,		Flatman, Thomas	1637-1688
Juan	1614-1685	Flemal, Bertholet	1614-1675
Castello, Bernado	1557-1629	Flinck, Govert	1615-1660
Castello, Valerio	1625-1659	Fontana, Carlo	1638-1714
Cavedone, Jacopo	1577-1660	Franceschini, Baldassare	1611-1689
Cesari, Giuseppe	1568-1640	Franceschini, Marco	
Champaign, Phillipe De	1602-1674	Antonio	1648-1729
Churriguera, Don José	1650-1725	Fresnoy, Charles Alphonse	1611-1665
Cibber, Caius Gabriel	1630-1700	Fruytiers, Philip	1627-1666
Cignani, Carlo	1628-1719	Fyt, Jan	1609-1661
Claude, Lorrain	1600-1682	Gentileschi, Artemisia	1597-1651
Cleve, Van Jan	1646-1716	Gentileschi, Orazioi De	1562-1647
Codde, Pieter	1599-1678	Gheeraerts, Marcus	1561-1635
Coello, Claudio	1630-1693	Gibbons, Grinling	1648-1721
Cooper, Samuel	1609-1672	Giordano, Luca	1632-1705
Coques, Gonzales	1614-1684	Girardon, Francois	1628-1715
Cornelisz, Cornelis	1562-1638		

Goyen, Jan Josephzoon		Montanes, Juan Martinez	1580-1649
Van	1596-1656	Murillo, Bartolome	
Grimaldi, Giovanni		Esteban	1617-1682
Francesco	1606-1680	Netscher, Gaspar	1639-1684
Guernico	1590-1666	Ostade, Adriaan Van	1610-1685
Hals, Franz	1580-1666	Pacheco, Francisco	1564-1654
Heem, Jan Davidz Van	1600-1683	Paolini, Pietro	1603-1682
Helst, Bartholomaeus,		Pareja, Juan De	1606-1670
Van Der	1613-1670	Petitot, Geacomo Della	1541-1604
Hernandes, Gregorio	1576-1636	Post, Pieter	1608-1669
Herrera, Francisco		Potter, Paul	1625-1654
"El Mozo"	1622-1685	Poussin, Gaspar	1613-1675
Heyden, Jan Van Der	1637-1712	Prieur, Pierre	1626-1676
Hilliard, Lawrence	-1640	Procaccini, Camillo	1546-1629
Hobbema, Meyndert	1638-1709	Procaccini, Ercole the	
Hollar, Wenceslaus	1607-1677	younger	1596-1676
Hondecoeter, Melchior D'	1636-1695	Poussin, Nicolas	1594-1665
Honthorst, Gerard, Van	1590-1656	Puget, Pierre	1622-1694
Hooch, Pieter De	1629-1683	Quesnoy, Francois du	1594-1646
Hoogstraten, Samuel		Rembrandt, Harmensz	
Dirksz Van	1627-1678	Van Rijn	1606-1669
Huchtenburg, John Van	1647-1733	Reni, Guiedo	1575-1642
Huysmans, Cornelius	1648-1727	Ribalta, Francisco de	1550-1628
Huysmans, Jacob	1633-1696	Ribera, Jusepe de	1588-1656
I Wasa Matahei	1578-1650	Rosa, Salvatore	1615-1673
Jamesone, John	1588-1644	Rubens, Peter Paul	1577-1640
Janssen, Cornelis	1593-1664	Ruysdael, Jacob Van	1628-1682
Janssens, Van Nuyssen		Sacchi, Andrea	1600-1661
Abraham	1575-1632	Sandrart, Joachim Van	1606-1688
Jones, Inigo	1573-1651	Sarrazin, Jacques	1588-1660
Jonson, Cornelius Van		Sassoferato	1605-1685
Ceulen	1593-1662	Snyders, Frans	1579-1657
Jordaens, Jacob	1593-1678	Steen, Jan Havicksz	1626-1679
Jouvenet, Jean	1644-1717	Stone, Nicholas	1587-1647
Kneller, Sir Godfrey	1648-1723	Stradivari, Antonio	1644-1737
Koninck, Philips	1619-1688	(Violin maker)	
Laar, Pieter Van	1590-1658	Teniers, David the elder	1582-1649
Lafosse, Charles De	1640-1716	Teniers, David the	
Lahire, Laurent De	1606-1656	younger	1610-1690
Lanfranco, Giovanni	1581-1647	Ter Borch, Gerard	1617-1681
Le Brun, Charles	1619-1690	Ter Brugghen, Hendrik	1588-1629
Lely, Sir Peter	1618-1680	Van De Velde, Adrian	1636-1672
Le Sueur, Eustache	1616-1655	Van De Velde, Jan	1593-1641
Lievensz, Jan	1607-1674	Van De Velde, the younger	1633-1707
Lorenzo, Lippi	1606-1664	Van Dyck, Sir Anthony	1599-1641
Maes, Nicholas	1632-1693	Van Veen, Otto	1556-1634
Mansard, Joels Hardouin	1646-1708	Velasquez, Diego	
Mansart, Francois	1598-1666	Rodriguez	1599-1660
Maratta, Carlo	1625-1713	Vermeer, Jan Van	
Metsu, Gabriel	1630-1667	Der Meer	1632-1675
Meulen, Adam Frans		Verrio, Antonio	1639-1707
Van Der	1632-1690	Vos, Cornelis de	1585-1651
Mierevelt, Michiel Jansz		Vouet, Simon	1590-1649
Van	1567-1641	Weenix, Jan Baptist	1621-1660
Mieris, Frans Van	1635-1681	Wouwerman, Philip	1619-1668
Mignard, Pierre	1610-1695	Wren, Sir Christopher	1632-1723
Mignon, Abraham	1640-1697	Zurbaran, Francisco De	1598-1669
Mile, Jean Francois	1642-1679		

Aichinger, Gregor	1565-1628	Eccles, John	1650-1735
Albert, Heinrich	1604-1651	Ferrabosco, Alfonso	d. 1628
Alegri, Gregorio	1582-1652	Ford, Thomas	1580-1648
Basile, Giambattista	1575-1632	Frescobaldi, Girolamo	1583-1644
Bateson, Thomas	1570-1630	Jenkins, John	1592-1678
Biber, Heinrich Johann		Lawes, Henry	1596-1662
Franz Von	1644-1704	Legrenzi, Giovanni	1625-1690
Blow, John	1648-1708	Locke, Matthew	1630-1677
Bononcini, Giovanni		Lully, Jean-Baptiste	1639-1687
Maria	1642-1678	Monteverdi, Claudio	1567-1643
Bull, John	1562-1628	Peri, Jacopo	1561-1633
Cambert, Robert	1628-1677	Pilkington, Francis	1638-
Carissimi, Giacomo	1604-1674	Ravencroft, Thomas	1590-1633
Carlton, Richard	1560-1638	Schmeltzer, Johann	
Cavalli, Francesco	1602-1676	Heinrich	1623-1680
Cesti, Marc'Antoni	1618-1669	Schütz, Heinrich	1585-1672
Cooper, John	1570-1627	Stradella, Allessandro	1645-1682
Couperin, Charles	1638-1679	Tomkins, Thomas	1572-1656
Cruger, Johann	1598-1662	Wilbye, John	1574-1638
East, Michael	1580-1648	Wilson, John	1595-1674

K

1652   England at War with the Dutch.
1654   England and Holland at Peace.
1658   Richard Cromwell made protector.
1660   Charles II proclaimed.
1664   England and Holland at War.
1665   Great Plague in London.   London Gazette first published.
1666   France declares war on England.   Great Fire of London.
1668   Triple Alliance. England, Holland and Sweden.
1670   Hudson Bay Co. formed.
1672   England and France form treaty. Join forces against Dutch.
1674   England and Holland at Peace.

PROMINENT PEOPLE

Cromwell, Oliver	1599-1658	**Marlborough,** John	
Cromwell, Richard	1626-1712	Churchill 1st Duke	1650-1722
Kidd, Captain William	1645-1701	**Newton,** Sir Isaac	1642-1727

EMPERORS OF CHINA
[Manchu (Ch-ing) Dynasty]

Shih Tsu	1644-1661	**Kang Tsi**	1662-1722

POPES

Innocent X	1644-1655	**Clement IX**	1667-1669
Alexander VII	1655-1667	**Clement X**	1670-1676

FRANCE. HEADS OF STATE

Louis XIV	1643-1715

HOLY ROMAN EMPERORS

Ferdinand III	1637-1657	**Leopold I**	1658-1705

ENGLAND. SOVEREIGNS

Commonwealth &		**Charles II**	1660-1685
Protectorate	1649-1660		

SWEDEN. KINGS

Christina	1632-1654	**Charles XI**	1660-1697
Charles X	1654-1660		

PORTUGAL. KINGS

John IV	1640-1656	**Alphonso VI**	1656-1683

ELECTORS OF BRANDENBURG

Frederick William	1640-1688

RUSSIA. TSARS

Alexis	1645-1676

WRITERS

Addison, Joseph	1672-1719	Burnet, Gilbert	1643-1715
Aguesseau, Henri		Burnet, Thomas	1635-1715
François d'	1668-1751	Butler, Samuel	1612-1680
Ainsworth, Robert	1660-1743	Bussy, Roger de Rabutin	1618-1693
Aitzema, Lieuwe Van	1600-1669	Byrd, William	1674-1744
Alcoforado, Marianna	1640-1723	Calderon De La Barca,	
Alleine, Joseph	1634-1668	Pedro	1600-1681
Amelot de la Houssaey,		Calprenede, Gautier Des	
Abraham Nicolas	1634-1706	Costes De La	1610-1633
Angelus, Silecius	1624-1677	Campistron, Jean	
Arbuthnot, John	1667-1735	Galbert De	1656-1723
Arnault, Antoine	1612-1694	Cats, Jakob	1577-1660
Asgill, John	1659-1738	Centlivre, Susanna	1667-1723
Ashmole, Elias	1617-1692	Chamberlayne, William	1619-1679
Astell, Mary	1668-1731	Chapelaine, Jean	1595-1674
Atterbury, Francis	1663-1732	Chaulieu, Guillaume	
Aubignac, Francois		Amerye De	1639-1720
Hedelin Abbe De	1604-1676	Coisy, Francois Timoleon	
Aubrey, John	1626-1697	Abbe de	1644-1724
Aulnoy, Marie Cathrine	1650-1705	Cibber, Colley	1671-1757
Baillie, Lady Grizel	1665-1746	Clarendon, Edward Hyde	
Baillie, Robert	1599-1662	(1st Earl of)	1609-1674
Baldinucci, Filippo	1624-1696	Clarke, Samuel	1675-1729
Balzac, Jean-Louis		Clauberg, Johann	1622-1665
Guez De	1594-1654	Cleland, William	1661-1689
Barclay, Robert	1648-1690	Cleveland, John	1613-1658
Bartoli, Danielle	1608-1685	Cocker, Edward	1631-1675
Bartoli, Pietro Santo	1635-1700	Coello, Antonio	1611-1652
Bayle, Pierre	1647-1706	Cokain, Sir Aston	1608-1684
Beaumont, Joseph	1616-1699	Comenius, Johann Amos	1592-1670
Behn, Aphra	1640-1689	Congreve, William	1670-1729
Benlowes, Edward	1603-1676	Corneille, Pierre	1606-1684
Benserade, Isaac De	1613-1691	Corneille, Thomas	1625-1709
Bentley, Richard	1662-1742	Cotton, John	1584-1652
Bergerac, Cyrano de	1619-1655	Cotton, Charles	1630-1687
Blackmore, Sir Richard	1650-1729	Cowley, Abraham	1618-1667
Blount, Sir Thomas Pope	1649-1697	Crebillon, Prosper Jolyot	
Boileau-Despreaux		De	1674-1762
Nicolas	1636-1711	Crescimbeni, Giovanni	
Boisrobert, Francois Le		Mario	1663-1728
Metel De	1592-1662	Crousaz, Jean Pierre	1663-1748
Bossuet, Jacques Benigne	1627-1704	Crowne, John	1640-1703
Boulainvilliers, Henri	1658-1722	Cudworth, Ralph	1617-1688
Boursault, Edme	1638-1701	Culpeper, Nicholas	1616-1654
Boyle, Robert	1627-1691	Cumberland, Richard	1631-1718
Bradford, William	1590-1657	Cutts of Gowran,	
Bradstreet, Ann	1612-1672	John Cutts	1661-1707
Brady, Nicholas	1659-1726	Dach, Simon	1605-1659
Brathwait, Richard	1588-1673	Dahlstjerna, Gunno	1661-1709
Broekhuizen, Jan Van	1649-1707	Dalgarno, George	1626-1687
Brome, Alexander	1620-1666	Dampier, William	1652-1715
Brome, Richard	-1652	Dancourt, Florent Carton	1661-1725
Browne, Sir Thomas	1605-1682	Daniel, Gabriel	1649-1728
Bulstrode, Sir Richard	1610-1711	Dass, Petter	1647-1708
Bunyan, John	1628-1688	Davenant, Sir William	1606-1668

Defoe, Daniel	1659-1731	Helyot, Pierre	1660-1716
Delmedigo, Joseph		Herbert, Sir Thomas	1608-1682
Soloman	1591-1655	Herrick, Robert	1591-1674
Denman, Sir John	1615-1669	Heylyn, Peter	1600-1662
Dennis, John	1657-1734	Hobbes, Thomas	1588-1679
Deshoulieres, Antoinette	1638-1694	Holles, Denzil Holles	1599-1680
Desmartes, Jean	1595-1676	Howard, Sir Robert	1626-1698
Digby, Sir Kenelm	1603-1665	Howell, James	1594-1666
Dodwell, Henry	1641-1711	Hoz Y Mota, Juan	
Dryden, John	1631-1700	Claudio De La	1630-1714
Dugdale, Sir William	1605-1686	Huygens, Sir Constantijn	1596-1687
Dupin, Louis Ellies	1657-1719	Johnson, Richard	1573-1659
D'Urfey, Thomas	1654-1723	Jordan, Thomas	1612-1685
Du Ryer, Pierre	1606-1658	Killigrew, Thomas	1612-1683
Ellwood, Thomas	1639-1714	King, William	1663-1712
Enriquez, Gomez Antonio	1602-1662	Kingo, Thomas Hansen	1634-1703
Etherege, Sir George	1635-1691	Kirk, Robert	1641-1692
Evelyn, John	1620-1706	La Bruyere, Jean De	1645-1696
Fanshawe, Sir Richard	1608-1666	La Calprenede, Gauthier	
Felltham, Owen	1602-1668	De Costes	1610-1663
Fénelon, François de		La Fayette, Marie-	
Salignac de la Mothe	1651-1715	Madeleine	1634-1693
Filicaia, Vincenzo da	1642-1702	La Fontaine, Jean De	1621-1695
Filmer, Sir Robert	1590-1653	Lairesse, Gerard De	1641-1711
Flacknoe, Richard	1600-1678	La Mothe Le Vayer,	
Fleury, Claude	1640-1723	Francois De	1588-1672
Folard, Jean Charles	1669-1752	La Motte, Antoine	
Fontenelle, Bernard Le		Houder De	1672-1731
Bovier De	1657-1757	La Rochefoucauld,	
Fortiguerra, Nicolo	1674-1735	Francois De	1613-1680
Fox, George	1624-1691	La Tour, Georges De	1593-1652
Fraunce, Abraham	1558-1663	Lee, Nathaniel	1653-1692
Froberger, Johann Jakob	1616-1667	Leibniz, Gottfried	
Gassendi, Pierre	1592-1655	Wilhelm	1646-1716
Gauden, John	1605-1662	Le Sage, Alain Rene	1668-1747
Gerhardt, Paul	1607-1676	L'Estrange, Sir Roger	1616-1704
Geulincx, Arnold	1624-1669	Locke, John	1632-1704
Glanville, Joseph	1636-1680	Lockhart, George	1673-1731
Gracian Y Morales,		Lovelace, Richard	1618-1658
Baltasar	1601-1658	Maffei, Francesco	
Grimmelshausen, Hans		Scipione	1675-1755
Jakob Christof Flevon	1625-1676	Magnusson, Arni	1663-1730
Gryphius, Andreas	1616-1664	Maimbourg, Louis	1610-1686
Guericke, Otto Von	1602-1686	Mairet, Jean De	1604-1686
Guidi, Carlo Alessandro	1650-1712	Malebranche, Nicholas	1638-1715
Guyon, Jeanne Marie		Mandeville, Bernard De	1670-1733
Bouvier De La Mothe	1640-1717	Manley, Mary	
Gyongyosi, Istvan	1620-1704	De La Riviere	1663-1724
Habingdon, William	1605-1654	Manuel De Mello, Don	
Hajji Khalifa	1599-c. 1658	Francisco	1608-1666
Hake, Edward	1579-	Marais, Marin	1656-1728
Halifax, Charles Montague	1661-1715	Marca, Pierre De	1594-1662
Hall, Joseph	1574-1656	Marsigli, Luigi	
Hamilton, Anthony	1645-1720	Ferdinando	1658-1730
Harlib, Samuel	1599-1670	Marvell, Andrew	1621-1678
Harvey, William	1578-1657	Mather, Cotton	1663-1728
Harrington, James	1611-1677	Mather, Increase	1639-1723
Harris, John	1666-1719	Matos, Fragoso, Juan De	1608-1689
Harsdorffer, Georg Philipp	1607-1658	Melo, Francisco	
Heemskerk, Johan Van	1597-1656	Manuel de	1608-1666

Milton, John	1608-1674	Saint Evremond, Charles	
Moliere, (Jean Baptiste,		Marquetel de Saint	
Poquelin)	1622-1673	Denis Seigneur de	1610-1703
More, Henry	1614-1687	Saint, Pierre, Charles	
Moreto Y Cavana,		Irenee Castel	1658-1743
Agustin	1618-1669	Saint Real, Cesar, Vichard	
Moscherosch, Johann		Abbé De	1631-1692
Michael	1601-1669	Saint-Simon, Louis De	
Motteux, Pierre Antoine	1663-1718	Rouvroy	1675-1755
Motteville, Francois		Scarron, Paul	1610-1660
Bertaut De	1621-1689	Scudery, Georges De	1601-1667
Muratori, Ludovico		Scudery, Madeleine De	1607-1701
Antonio	1672-1750	Sedley, Sir Charles	1639-1701
Mure, William (Sir)	1594-1657	Selden, John	1584-1654
Najara, Israel Ben Moses	1587-	Settle, Elkanah	1648-1724
Newton, Sir Isaac	1642-1727	Sevigne, Marie De	
Norris, John	1657-1711	Rabutin Chantal	1626-1696
North, Roger	1653-1734	Sewall, Samuel	1652-1730
O'Carolan, Turlogh	1670-1738	Shadwell, Thomas	1642-1692
Ogilby, John	1600-1676	Shaftesbury, Anthony	
Oldham, John	1653-1683	Ashley Cooper 3rd Earl	1671-1713
Oldmixon, John	1673-1742	Sherlock, William	1641-1707
Otway, Thomas	1652-1685	Shirley, James	1596-1666
Pallavicino, Pietro Sforza	1607-1667	Solis Y Ribadeneyra	
Parker, Martin	1600-1656	Antonio De	1610-1686
Pascal, Blaise	1623-1662	Somerville, William	1675-1742
Paterson, William	1658-1719	Sorel, Charles	1597-1674
Penn, William	1644-1718	Southerne, Thomas	1660-1746
Pepusch, Johann		Speke, Hugh	1656-1724
Christoph	1667-1752	Spinoza, Benedictus De	1632-1677
Perrault, Charles	1628-1703	St. Jernhjelm, Georg	1598-1672
Philips, Ambrose	1675-1749	Stanley, Thomas	1625-1678
Philips, Katharine	1631-1664	Steel, Sir Richard	1672-1729
Phillips, Edward	1630-1696	Stillingfleet, Edward	1635-1699
Phillips, John	1631-1706	Strype, John	1643-1737
Pitcairn, Archibald	1652-1713	Tallemant, Gedeon Sieur	
Pomfret, John	1667-1702	Des Reaux	1619-1692
Pozzo, Andrea	1642-1709	Tate, Nahum	1652-1715
Prior	1664-1721	Taylor, Jeremy	1613-1667
Puffendorf, Samuel		Taylor, John	1580-1653
Freiherr Von	1632-1694	Temple, Sir William	1628-1699
Quesnel, Pasquier	1634-1719	Thomas, Nabbes	1605-
Quinault, Phillipe	1635-1688	Thomasius, Christian	1655-1728
Racan, Honore De Beuil	1589-1670	Tillemont, Sebastian	
Racine, Jean	1639-1699	Le Nain De	1637-1698
Rapin, Paul De	1661-1725	Tindal, Matthew	1656-1733
Regnard, Jean Francois	1655-1709	Traherne, Thomas	1637-1674
Retz, Cardinal de	1614-1679	Urquhart, Sir Thomas	1611-1660
Rochester, John Wilmot	1647-1680	Vanbrugh, Sir John	1664-1726
Rollin, Charles	1661-1741	Vane, Sir Henry	1613-1662
Roscommon, Wentworth		Vaughan, Henry	1622-1695
Dillon	1630-1685	Vico, Giovanni Battista	1668-1744
Rousseau, Jean Baptiste	1671-1741	Vieira, Antonio	1608-1697
Rowe, Nicholas	1674-1718	Vondel, Joost Van Den	1587-1679
Rushworth, John	1612-1690	Waller, Edmund	1606-1687
Rymer, Thomas	1641-1713	Walton, Izaak	1593-1683
Saint Amant, Marc		Watts, Isaac	1674-1748
Antoine Gerard	1594-1661	Wharton, Henry	1664-1695
		Whichcote, Benjamin	1609-1683
		Wigglesworth, Michael	1631-1705

Williams, Roger	c. 1600-1683	Woolaston, William	1654-1724
Winchelsea, Anne Finch	1661-1720	Wood, Anthony	1632-1695
Winslow, Edward	1595-1655	Wyncherley, William	1640-1716
Wither, George	1588-1667	Young, Edward	1638-1765

ARTISTS

Albani, Francesco	1578-1660	Dolci, Carlo	1616-1686
Algardi, Alessandro	1602-1654	Douw, Gerrit	1613-1675
Allou, Gilles	1670-1751	Duck, Jacob	1600-1660
Anguier, Francois	1604-1669	Dusart, Cornelis	1660-1704
Anguier, Michel	1612-1686	Eekhout, Gerbrand Van	
Archer, Thomas	1668-1743	Den	1621-1674
Backhuysen, Ludolf	1631-1708	Everingen, Allart Van	1621-1675
Barbieri, Giovanni		Fabritius, Carel	1624-1654
Francesco	1591-1666	Faithorne, William	1616-1691
Beck, David	1621-1556	Falcone, Aniello	1600-1656
Berchem, Nicholaes	1620-1683	Felibien, Andre	1619-1695
Bernini, Giovanni Lorenzo	1598-1680	Ferri, Ciro	1634-1689
Bloeman, Jan Frans Van	1662-1740	Fischer, Johann Berhard	1656-1723
Bloemart, Abraham	1564-1651	Flatman, Thomas	1637-1688
Borromini, Francesco	1599-1667	Flemal, Bertholet	1614-1675
Both, Jan	1618-1652	Flinck, Govert	1615-1660
Bouchardon, Edme	1698-1762	Fontana, Carlo	1638-1714
Boulle, Andre Charles	1642-1732	Franceschini, Baldassare	1611-1689
(cabinet maker)		Franceschini, Marco	
Bourse, Esaias	1630-1673	Antonio	1648-1729
Cano, Alonzo	1601-1667	Fresnoy, Charles	
Cappelle, Jan Van Der	1624-1679	Alphonse Du	1611-1665
Carreno De Miranda, Juan	1614-1685	Fruytiers, Philip	1627-1666
Carriera, Rosalba	1675-1757	Fyt, Jan	1609-1661
Cassana, Niccolo	1659-1714	Gentileschi, Artemisia	1597-1651
Castello, Valerio	1625-1659	Gibbons, Grinling	1648-1721
Cavedone, Jacopo	1577-1660	Gillot, Claude	1673-1722
Champaign, Phillipe De	1602-1674	Giordano, Luca	1632-1705
Churriguera, Don Jose	1650-1725	Girardon, Francois	1628-1715
Cibber, Caius Gabriel	1630-1700	Goven, Jan Josephzoon	
Cignani, Carlo	1628-1719	Van	1596-1656
Claude, Lorrain	1600-1682	Grimaldi, Giovanni	
Cleve, Van Jan	1646-1716	Francesco	1606-1680
Closterman, John	1656-1713	Guercino	1590-1666
Codde, Pieter	1599-1678	Hals, Frans	1580-1666
Coello, Claudio	1630-1693	Hawksmoor, Nicholas	1661-1736
Cooper, Alexander	-1660	Heem, Jan Davidz Van	1600-1683
Cooper, Samuel	1609-1672	Herrera, Francisco	
Coques, Gonzales	1614-1684	"El Mozo"	1622-1685
Cornelisz, Cornelis	1562-1638	Helst, Batholomaens	
Cortona, Pietro		Van Der	1613-1670
Berrettini Da	1596-1669	Heyden, Jan Van Der	1637-1712
Courtois, Guillaume	1628-1679	Hobbema, Meyndert	1638-1709
Courtois, Jacques	1621-1676	Hollar, Wenceslaus	1607-1677
Coustou, Nicolas	1658-1733	Hondecoeter, Melchior De	1636-1695
Coypel, Antoine	1661-1722	Honthorst, Gerard Van	1590-1656
Coypel, Noel	1628-1707	Hooch, Pieter De	1629-1683
Coysevoy, Charles Antoine	1640-1720	Hoogstraten, Samuel	
Craver, Gaspard De	1584-1769	Dirksz Van	1627-1678
Crespi, Giuseppi, Maria	1665-1747	Houbraken, Arnold	1660-1719
Dahl, Michael	1656-1743	Huchtenburg, John Van	1647-1733
De Keyser, Thomas	1596-1667	Huysmans, Jacob	1633-1696

Huysmans, Jan Baptist	1654-1716	Pareja, Juan De	1606-1670
Huysmans, Cornelius	1648-1727	Petitot, Jean	1608-1691
Janssen, Cornelis	1593-1664	Post, Pieter	1608-1669
Janssens, Victor Honorius	1658-1736	Potter, Paul	1625-1654
Jones, Inigo	1573-1651	Poussin, Gaspar	1613-1675
Jonson, Cornelis		Prieur, Pierre	1626-1676
Van Ceulen	1593-1662	Procaccini, Ercole the	
Jordaens, Jacob	1593-1678	younger	1596-1676
Jouvenet, Jean	1644-1717	Poussin, Nicholas	1594-1665
Kneller, Sir William	1648-1723	Puget, Pierre	1622-1694
Koninck, Philips	1619-1688	Rembrandt, Harmensz	
Laar, Pieter Van	1590-1658	Van Rijn	1606-1669
Lafosse, Charles De	1640-1716	Ribera, Jusepe De	1588-1656
Laguerre, Louis	1663-1721	Rigaud, Hyacinthe	1659-1743
Lahire, Laurent De	1606-1656	Rosa, Salvator	1615-1673
Largilliere, Nicolas	1656-1746	Ruysdael, Jacob Van	1628-1682
Le Brun, Charles	1619-1690	Sacchi, Andrea	1600-1661
Legros, Pierre	1656-1719	Sandrart, Joachim Van	1606-1688
Lely, Sir Peter	1618-1680	Sarrazin, Jacques	1588-1660
Le Sueur, Eustache	1616-1655	Sassoferato	1605-1685
Lievensz, Jan	1607-1674	Smybert, John	1584-1651
Lorenzo, Lippi	1606-1664	Snyders, Frans	1579-1657
Maes, Nicholas	1632-1693	Steen, Jan Havicksz	1626-1679
Magnasco, Alessandro	1667-1749	Stradivari, Antonio	1644-1737
Mansard, Jules Hardouin	1646-1708	(violin maker)	
Mansart, Francois	1598-1666	Ter Borch, Gerard	1617-1681
Maratta, Carlo	1625-1713	Teniers, David the	
Marot, Daniel	1661-1712	younger	1610-1690
Metsu, Gabriel	1630-1667	Vanbrugh, Sir John	1664-1726
Meulen, Adam Frans		Van De Velde, Adrian	1636-1672
Van Der	1632-1690	Van Der Velde,	
Mieris, Frans Van	1635-1681	William the younger	1633-1707
Mignard, Pierre	1610-1695	Velasquez, Diego	
Mignon, Abraham	1640-1697	Rodriguez	1599-1660
Mile, Jean Francois	1642-1679	Vermeer, Jan Van Der	
Murillo, Bartolome		Meer	1632-1675
Esteban	1617-1682	Verrio, Antonio	1639-1707
Nash, Richard	1674-1762	Vos, Cornelis De	1585-1651
Netscher, Gaspar	1639-1684	Walker, Robert	-1658
Ostade, Adriaan Van	1610-1685	Weenix, Jan Baptist	1621-1660
Pacheco, Francisco	1564-1654	Wouwerman, Philip	1619-1668
Palomino De Castro,		Wren, Sir Christopher	1632-1723
Antonio	1653-1726	Zurbaran, Francisco De	1598-1669
Paolini, Pietro	1603-1682		

COMPOSERS

Albert, Heinrich	1604-1651	Campra, Anore	1660-1744
Albinoni, Tommaso	1674-1745	Carissimi, Giacomo	1604-1674
Allegri, Gregorio	1582-1652	Cavalli, Francesco	1602-1676
Ariosti, Attilio	1660-	Cesti, Marc'Antonio	1618-1669
Blow, John	1648-1708	Clari, Giovanni Carlo	
Bononcini, Giovanni		Maria	1669-1745
Battista	1670-1755	Clarke, Jeremiah	1659-1707
Bononcini, Giovanni		Corelli, Arcangelo	1653-1713
Maria	1642-1678	Couperin, Charles	1638-1679
Bononcini, Marc Antonio	1675-1726	Couperin, Francois	1668-1733
Caldara, Antonio	1670-1736	Cruger, Johann	1598-1662
Cambert, Robert	1628-1677	Eccles, John	1650-1735

Garth, Sir Samuel	1661-1719	Pachelbel, Johan	1653-1706
Innes, Thomas	1663-1744	Purcell, Henry	1659-1695
Jenkins, John	1592-1678	Scarlatti, Alessandro	1659-1725
Keiser, Reinhold	1673-1739	Schmelzer, Johann	
Lawes, Henry	1596-1662	Heinrich	1623-1680
Legrenzi, Giovanni	1625-1690	Steffani, Agostino	1653-1728
Locke, Matthew	1630-1677	Stradella, Alessandro	1645-1682
Lotti, Antonio	1667-1740	Tomkins, Thomas	1572-1656
Lully, Jean-Baptiste	1639-1687	Wilson, John	1595-1674

1678   English and Dutch Alliance.
1679   Habeas Corpus Act.
1685   Battle of Sedgemoor.
       Bloody Assizes.
1688   Smyrna destroyed by earthquake.
1689   Battle of Killiecrankie.
       Bill of Rights passed.
1690   Battle of the Boyne.
       Siege of Limerick.
1692   Massacre of Glencoe.
       Battle of La Hogue.
       Battle of Steinkirk.
1694   Bank of England incorporated.

PROMINENT PEOPLE

Cromwell, Richard	1626-1712	**Marlborough,** John	
Fahrenheit, Gabriel Daniel	1686-1736	Churchill, 1st Duke	1650-1722
Kidd, Captain William	1645-1701	Newton, Sir Isaac	1642-1727
		Penn, William	1644-1718

EMPERORS OF CHINA
[Manchu (Ching) Dynasty]

Kang Tsi   1662-1722

POPES

Clement X	1670-1676	**Alexander VIII**	1689-1691
Innocent XI	1676-1689	**Innocent XII**	1691-1700

FRANCE. HEADS OF STATE

Louis XIV   1643-1715

HOLY ROMAN EMPERORS

Leopold I   1658-1705

ENGLAND. SOVEREIGNS

Charles II	1660-1685	**William III & Mary**	1689-1694
James II	1685-1688	**William III**	1694-1702

SWEDEN. KINGS

Charles XI	1660-1697	**Charles XII**	1697-1718

PORTUGAL. KINGS

Alphonso VI	1656-1683	**Pedro II**	1683-1706

ELECTORS OF BRANDENBURG

Frederick William	1640-1688	**Frederick III**	1688-1713

RUSSIA. TSARS

Alexis	1645-1676	**Ivan II**	1682-1689
Theodore III	1676-1682	**Peter the Great** 1	1682-1725

Charles II   1665-1700

WRITERS

Abauzit, Firmin	1679-1767	Bulstrode, Sir Richard	1610-1711
Addison, Joseph	1672-1719	Bunyan, John	1628-1688
Aguesseau, Henry		Burnet, Gilbert	1643-1715
François d'	1668-1751	Burnet, Thomas	1635-1715
Ainsworth, Robert	1660-1743	Butler, Samuel	1612-1680
Alcoforado, Marianna	1640-1723	Bussy, Roger de Rabutin	1618-1693
Amelot de la Houssaey,		Byrd, William	1674-1744
Abraham Nicolas	1634-1706	Byrom, John	1692-1763
Ames, Joseph	1689-1759	Calderon De La Barca,	
Amhurst, Nicholas	1697-1742	Pedro	1600-1681
Amory, Thomas	1691-1788	Campistron, Jean	
Arbuthnot, John	1667-1735	Galbert De	1656-1723
Arnault, Antoine	1612-1694	Canizares, Jose De	1676-1750
Asgill, John	1659-1738	Carey, Henry	1690-1743
Ashmole, Elias	1617-1692	Carte, Thomas	1686-1754
Astell, Mary	1688-1731	Centlivre, Susanna	1667-1723
Atterbury, Francis	1663-1732	Challoner, Richard	1691-1781
Aubignac, Francois		Chamberlayne, William	1619-1679
Hedelin Abbe De	1604-1676	Chaulieu, Guillaume	
Aubrey, John	1626-1697	Amfrye De	1639-1720
Aulnoy, Marie Cathrine		Chesterfield, Philip	
Le Jumel	1650-1705	Dormer Stanhope	
Bachaumont, Louis		(4th Earl of)	1694-1773
Petit De	1690-1771	Choisy, Francois	
Baillie, Lady Grizel	1665-1746	Timoleon, Abbe De	1644-1724
Baldinucci, Filippo	1624-1696	Cibber, Colley	1671-1757
Barclay, Robert	1608-1685	Clarke, Samuel	1675-1729
Bartoli, Danielle	1608-1685	Cleland, William	1661-1689
Bartoli, Pietro Santo	1635-1700	Cokain, Sir Aston	1608-1684
Bayle, Pierre	1647-1706	Colden, Cadwallader	1688-1776
Beaumont, Joseph	1616-1699	Collier, Arthur	1680-1732
Behn, Aphra	1640-1689	Congreve, William	1670-1729
Benserade, Isaac De	1613-1691	Corneille, Pierre	1606-1684
Bentley, Richard	1662-1742	Cornielle, Thomas	1635-1709
Berkeley, George	1685-1753	Cotton, Charles	1630-1687
Bilfinger, George		Crebillon, Prosper	
Bernhard	1693-1750	Jolyot De	1674-1762
Blackmore, Sir Richard	1650-1729	Crescimbeni, Giovanni	
Blair, Robert	1699-1746	Mario	1663-1728
Blount, Sir Thomas Pope	1649-1697	Crousaz, Jean Pierre	1663-1748
Bodmer, Johann Jakob	1698-1783	Crowne, John	1640-1703
Boileau-Despreaux,		Cudworth, Ralph	1617-1688
Nicolas	1636-1711	Cumberland, Richard	1631-1718
Bolingbroke, Henry St. John	1678-1751	Cutts of Gowran, John	
Bossuet, Jacques Benigne	1627-1704	Cutts	1661-1707
Boston, Thomas	1677-1732	Dahlstjerna, Gunno	1661-1709
Boulainvilliers, Henri	1658-1722	Dalgarno, George	1626-1687
Boursault, Edme	1638-1701	Dampier, William	1652-1715
Boyle, Robert	1627-1691	Dancourt, Florent Carton	1661-1725
Brady, Nicholas	1659-1726	Daniel, Gabriel	1649-1728
Brockes, Barthold Heinrich	1680-1747	Dass, Petter	1647-1708
Broekhuizen, Jan Van	1649-1707	Defoe, Daniel	1659-1731
Brorson, Hans Adolf	1694-1764	Dennis, John	1657-1734
Browne, Sir Thomas	1605-1682	Deshoulieres, Antoinette	1638-1694
Brucker, Johann Jakob	1696-1770	Desmartes, Jean	1595-1676

Destouches, Phillipe	1680-1754
Dodwell, Henry	1641-1711
Dryden, John	1631-1700
Dupin, Louis Ellies	1657-1719
D'Urfey, Thomas	1653-1723
Dyer, John	1699-1757
Ellwood, Thomas	1639-1714
Etherege, Sir George	1635-1691
Eusden, Laurence	1688-1730
Evelyn, John	1620-1706
Farquhar, George	1677-1707
Fénelon, François de Salignac	
de la Mothe	1651-1715
Fenton, Elijah	1683-1730
Filicaia, Vincenzo Da	1642-1707
Flecknoe, Richard	1600-1678
Fleury, Claude	1640-1723
Folard, Jean Charles	1669-1752
Fontenelle, Bernard	
Le Bovier De	1657-1757
Fortiguerra, Nicolo	1674-1735
Fox, George	1624-1691
Frugoni, Carlo Innocenzo	
Maria	1692-1768
Gay, John	1685-1732
Gerhardt, Paul	1607-1676
Giannone, Pietro	1676-1748
Glanville, Joseph	1636-1680
Gottsched, Johann	
Churtaph	1700-1766
Green, Matthew	1696-1737
Grimmelshausen, Hans Jakob	
Christof Felvon	1625-1676
Guericke, Otto Von	1602-1686
Guidi, Carlo Alessandro	1650-1712
Gunther, Johann Christian	1695-1723
Guyon, Jeanne Marie	1648-1717
Gyongyosi, Istvan	1620-1704
Hake, Edward	1579-
Halifax, Charles Montague	1661-1715
Hamilton, Anthony	1645-1720
Harrington, James	1611-1677
Harris, John	1666-1719
Haywood, Eliza	1693-1756
Hearne, Thomas	1678-1735
Heylot, Pierre	1660-1716
Henault, Charles Dean	
Francois	1685-1770
Herbert, Sir Thomas	1608-1682
Hervey of Ickworth, John	
Hervey	1696-1743
Hill, Aaron	1685-1750
Hobbes, Thomas	1588-1679
Holberg, Ludvig Holberg	1684-1754
Holles, Denzil Holles	1599-1680
Howard, Sir Robert	1626-1698
Hoz Y Mota, Juan Claudio	
De La	1630-1714
Hughes, John	1677-1720
Hutcheson, Francis	1694-1746

Huygens, Sir Constantijn	1596-1687
Jordan, Thomas	1612-1685
Kames, Henry Home	1696-1782
Killigrew, Thomas	1612-1683
King, William	1663-1712
Kingo, Thomas Hansen	1634-1703
Kirk, Robert	1641-1692
La Bruyere, Jean De	1645-1696
La Chaussee, Pierre Claude	
Nivelle De	1692-1754
La Fayette, Marie	
Madeleine	1634-1693
La Fontaine, Jean De	1621-1695
Lagrange-Chancel, François	
Joseph	1677-1758
Lairesse, Gerard De	1641-1711
Lamotte, Antoine Houdar	
De	1672-1731
La Rochefoucauld,	
Francois De	1613-1680
Law, William	1686-1761
Lee, Nathaniel	1653-1692
Leibniz, Gottfried	
Wilhelm	1646-1716
Le Sage, Alain Rene	1668-1747
L'Estrange, Sir Roger	1616-1704
Lillo, George	1693-1739
Locke, John	1632-1704
Lockhart, George	1673-1731
Macklin, Charles	1697-1797
Maffei, Francesco	
Scipione	1675-1755
Magnusson, Arni	1663-1730
Maimbourg, Louis	1610-1686
Mairet, Jean De	1604-1686
Malebranchie, Nicholas	1638-1715
Mandeville, Bernard De	1670-1733
Manley, Mary De La	
Riviere	1663-1724
Marais, Marin	1656-1728
Marivaux, Pierre,	
Carlet De Chamlain De	1688-1763
Marsigli, Luigi Fernando	1658-1730
Marvell, Andrew	1621-1678
Mather, Cotton	1663-1728
Mather, Increase	1639-1723
Matos, Fragoso, Juan De	1608-1689
Metastasio	1698-1782
Montagu, Lady Mary	
Wortley	1689-1762
Montesquieu, Charles Louis	
De Secondat	1689-1755
More, Henry	1614-1687
Motteux, Pierre Antoine	1663-1718
Motteville, Francoise	
Bertaut De	1621-1689
Muratori, Ludovico	
Antonio	1672-1750
Neal, Daniel	1678-1743
Newton, Sir Isaac	1642-1727

Norris, John	1657-1711	Settle, Elkanah	1648-1724
North, Roger	1653-1734	Sevigne, Marie de	
O'Carolan, Turlough	1670-1738	Rabutin-Chantal	1626-1696
Ogilby, John	1600-1776	Sewall, Samuel	1652-1730
Oldham, John	1653-1683	Shadwell, Thomas	1642-1692
Oldmixon, John	1673-1742	Shaftesbury, Anthony	
Orrery, Charles Boyle	1676-1731	Ashley Cooper, 3rd Earl	1671-1713
Ottway, Thomas	1652-1685	Sherlock, William	1641-1707
Patlock, Robert	1697-1767	Solis Y Ribadeneyra,	
Parnell, Thomas	1679-1718	Antonio De	1610-1686
Paterson, William	1658-1719	Somervile, William	1675-1742
Pellisson, Paul	1624-1693	Southern, Thomas	1660-1746
Penn, William	1644-1718	Speke, Hugh	1656-1724
Pepusch, Johann Christolph	1667-1752	Spence, Joseph	1699-1768
Pepys, Samuel	1633-1703	Spinoza, Benedictus De	1632-1677
Perrault, Charles	1628-1703	Staal, Marguerite Jeanne	
Philips, Ambrose	1675-1749	Cordier De Launay	1684-1750
Philips, John	1676-1708	Steele, Sir Richard	1672-1729
Phillips, Edward	1630-1696	Stillingfleet, Edward	1635-1699
Phillips, John	1631-1706	Strype, John	1643-1737
Piron, Alexis	1689-1773	Swedenborg, Emanuel	1688-1772
Pitcairn, Archibald	1652-1713	Swift, Jonathan	1676-1745
Pomfret, John	1667-1702	Tallemant, Gedeon	
Pontoppidan, Erik	1698-1764	Sieur Des Reaux	1619-1692
Pope, Alexander	1688-1744	Tate, Nahum	1652-1715
Pozzo, Andrea	1642-1709	Temple, Sir William	1628-1699
Prevost, Antoine Francois	1697-1763	Tencin, Claudine	
Prior, Matthew	1664-1721	Alexandrine Guerin De	1681-1749
Puffendorf, Samuel Frieherr		Theobald, Lewis	1688-1744
Von	1632-1694	Thomasius, Christian	1655-1728
Quesnel, Pasquier	1634-1719	Thomson, James	1700-1748
Quinault, Phillipe	1635-1688	Tickell, Thomas	1686-1740
Racine, Jean	1639-1699	Tillemont, Sebastian le	
Racine, Louis	1692-1763	Nain De	1637-1698
Ramsay, Allan	1686-1758	Tindal, Matthew	1656-1733
Ramsay, Andrew Michael	1686-1743	Torres Y Villaroel,	
Rapin, Paul de	1661-1725	Diego De	1696-1759
Regnard, Jean Francois	1655-1709	Vanbrugh, Sir John	1664-1726
Reimarus, Hermann Samuel	1694-1768	Vaughan, Henry	1622-1695
Retz, Cardinel de	1614-1679	Vilo, Giovanni Battista	1668-1744
Richardson, Samuel	1689-1761	Vieira, Antonio	1608-1697
Rochester, John Wilmot	1647-1680	Voltaire, Francois Marie	
Rollin, Charles	1661-1741	Arouet De	1694-1788
Roscommon, Wentworth		Vondel, Joost Van Den	1587-1679
Dillon	1630-1685	Waller, Edmund	1606-1687
Rousseau, Jean Baptiste	1671-1741	Walton, Izaak	1593-1683
Rowe, Nicholas	1674-1718	Watts, Isaac	1674-1748
Rushworth, John	1612-1690	Wharton, Henry	1664-1695
Rymer, Thomas	1641-1713	Whichcote, Benjamin	1609-1683
Saint Evremond, Charles		Wigglesworth, Michael	1631-1705
Marquetel de Saint Denis		Williams, Roger	c. 1600-1683
Seigneur de	1610-1703	Winchelsea, Anne Finch	1661-1720
Saint-Pierre, Charles		Wodrow, Robert	1619-1734
Irenee Castel	1658-1743	Wollaston, William	1659-1724
Saint Real, Cesar Vichard		Wolff, Christian	1679-1754
Abbé de	1631-1692	Wood, Anthony	1632-1695
Saint-Simon, Louis de		Wyncherley, William	1640-1716
Rouvroy	1675-1755	Young, Edward	1638-1765
Savage, Richard	1697-1743	Zinzendorf, Nicolaus	
Sedley, Sir Charles	1639-1701	Ludwig Grafron	1700-1760

Allou, Gilles	1670-1751	Franceschini, Marco	
Anguier, Michael	1612-1686	Antonio	1648-1729
Archer, Thomas	1668-1743	Gabriel, Jacques Ange	1698-1782
Backhuysen, Ludolf	1631-1708	Gibbons, Grinling	1648-1721
Berchem, Nicolaes	1620-1683	Gibbs, James	1682-1754
Bernini, Giovanni Lorenzo	1598-1680	Gillot, Claude	1673-1722
Bloeman, Jan Frans Van	1662-1740	Giordano, Luca	1632-1705
Bouchardon, Edme	1698-1762	Girardon, Francois	1628-1715
Boulle, Andre Charles	1642-1732	Grimaldi, Giovanni	
(Cabinet maker)		Francesco	1606-1680
Bredael, Jan Frans Van	1683-1750	Hawksmoor, Nicholas	1661-1736
Briseux, Charles Etienne	1680-1754	Heem, Jan Davidz Van	1600-1683
Burlington, Richard Boyle		Herrera, Francisco	
3rd Earl of	1695-1753	"El Moso"	1622-1685
Caffieri, Jacques	1678-1755	Heyden, Jan Van Der	1637-1712
Canaletto	1697-1768	Highmore, Joseph	1692-1780
Cappelle, Jan Van Der	1624-1679	Hobbema, Meyndert	1638-1709
Carreno De Miranda, Juan	1614-1685	Hogarth, William	1697-1764
Carriera, Rosalba	1675-1757	Hollar, Wenceslaus	1607-1677
Cassana, Niccolo	1659-1714	Hondecoetter, Melchoir D'	1636-1695
Chardin, Jean Baptiste		Hooch, Pieter, De	1629-1683
Simeon	1699-1779	Hoogstraten, Samuel	
Churriguera, Don Jose	1650-1725	Dirksz Van	1627-1678
Cibber, Caius Gabriel	1630-1700	Houbraken, Arnold	1660-1719
Cignani, Carlo	1628-1719	Huchtenburg, John Van	1647-1733
Claude, Lorrain	1600-1682	Huysmans, Cornelius	1648-1727
Cleve, Van Jan	1646-1716	Huysmans, Jacob	1633-1696
Closterman, John	1656-1713	Huysmans, Jan Baptist	1654-1716
Codde, Pieter	1599-1678	Huysum, Jan Van	1682-1749
Coello, Claudio	1630-1693	Janssens, Victor Honorius	1658-1736
Coques, Gonzales	1614-1684	Jordaens, Jacob	1593-1678
Cortona, Pietro Benettini da	1596-1669	Jouvenet, Jean	1644-1717
Courtois, Guillaume	1628-1679	Kent, William	1685-1748
Courtois, Jacques	1621-1676	Kneller, Sir Godfrey	1648-1723
Coustou, Guillaume	1678-1746	Koninck, Philips	1619-1688
Coustou, Nicholas	1658-1733	Lafosse, Charles De	1640-1716
Coypel, Antoine	1661-1722	Laguerre, Louis	1663-1721
Coypel, Charles Antoine	1694-1752	Lancret, Nicholas	1690-1743
Coypel, Noel	1628-1707	Largilliere, Nicolas	1656-1746
Coypel, Noel Nicholas	1692-1734	Le Brun, Charles	1619-1690
Coysevoy, Charles Antoine	1640-1720	Le Gros, Pierre	1656-1719
Crespi, Giuseppe Maria	1665-1747	Lely, Sir Peter	1618-1680
Cressent, Charles	1685-1768	Lemoine, Francois	1688-1737
Cuvilles, Francois De	1698-1767	Limborch, Hendrick Van	1680-1758
Dahl, Michael	1656-1743	Maes, Nicholas	1632-1693
Diaz, Diego Valentin	1685-1660	Magnasco, Alessandro	1667-1749
Diepenbeek, Abraham Van	1596-1675	Mansard, Jules Hardouin	1646-1708
Dolci, Carlo	1616-1686	Maratta, Carlo	1625-1713
Donner, Raphael George	1693-1741	Marot, Daniel	1661-1712
Dusart, Cornelis	1660-1704	Meissonier, Juste Aurele	1693-1750
Faithorne, William	1616-1691	Mena, Pedro De	1693-
Falens, Karel Van	1683-1733	Meulen, Adam Frans Van	
Felibien, Andre	1619-1695	Der	1632-1690
Ferri, Ciro	1634-1689	Mieris, Frans Van	1635-1681
Fischer, Johann Bernard		Mignard, Pierre	1610-1695
Von Erlach	1656-1723	Mignon, Abraham	1640-1697
Flatman, Thomas	1637-1688	Mile, Jean Francois	1642-1679
Flitcroft, Henry	1679-1769	Murillo, Bartolome Esteban	1617-1682
Fontana, Carlo	1638-1714	Nash, Richard	1674-1762
Frenceschini, Baldassare	1611-1689	Nattier, Jean Marc	1685-1766

Netscher, Gaspar	1639-1684	Scheemakers, Pieter	1691-1770
Neumann, Balthasar	1687-1753	Steen, Jan Havicksz	1626-1679
Ostade, Adriaan Van	1610-1685	Stradivari, Antonio	1644-1737
Palomino De Castro,		(Violin maker)	
Antonio	1653-1726	Subleyras, Pierre	1699-1749
Paolini, Pietro	1603-1682	Teniers,	
Pater, Jean Baptiste Joseph	1695-1736	David the younger	1610-1690
Pergolesi, Michael Angelo	1700-1736	Ter Borch, Gerard	1617-1681
Petitot, Jean	1608-1691	Thornhill, Sir James	1676-1734
Prieur, Pierre	1626-1676	Tiepolo, Giovanni Battista	1692-1769
Procaccini,		Vanbrugh, Sir John	1664-1726
Ercole the younger	1596-1676	Van Der Velde,	
Puget, Pierre	1622-1694	Willem the Younger	1633-1707
Rigaud, Hyacinthe	1659-1743	Van Goyen, Jan Josephzem	1696-1756
Roubillac, Louis Francois	1695-1762	Van Loo, Jean Baptiste	1684-1745
Ruysdael, Jacob Van	1628-1682	Verrio, Antonio	1639-1707
Rysbrack, Michael	1693-1770	Watteau, Antoine	1684-1721
Sandrart, Joachim Van	1606-1688	Wren, Sir Christopher	1632-1723
Sassoferato	1605-1685		

COMPOSERS

Albinoni, Tommaso	1674-1745	Jenkins, John	1592-1678
Astorga, Emanuele	1680-1755	Keiser, Reinhold	1673-1739
Bach, Johan Sebastian	1685-1750	Lawes, Henry	1596-1662
Barsanti, Francesco	1690-1775	Leclair, Jean Marie	1697-1764
Blow, John	1648-1708	Legrenzi, Giovanni	1625-1690
Bononcini, Giovanni		Leo, Leonardo	1694-1744
Baptista	1670-1755	Locke, Matthew	1630-1677
Bononcini, Giovanni Maria	1642-1678	Logroscino, Nicola	1700-1763
Bononcini, Marc Antonio	1675-1726	Lotti, Antonio	1667-1740
Caldara, Antonio	1670-1736	Lully, Jean-Baptiste	1639-1687
Cambert, Robert	1628-1677	Marcello, Benedetto	1686-1739
Campra, Anore	1660-1744	Mattheson, Johann	1681-1764
Cavalli, Francesco	1602-1676	Pachebel, Johann	1653-1706
Clari, Giovanni Carlo		Porpora, Niccola Antonio	1686-1767
Maria	1669-1745	Purcell, Henry	1659-1695
Clarke, Jeremiah	1659-1707	Quantz, Johann Joachim	1697-1773
Corelli, Arcangelo	1653-1713	Rameau, Jean Philippe	1683-1764
Croft, William	1678-1727	Roman, Johan Helmich	1694-1758
Couperin, Charles	1638-1679	Scarlatti, Alessandro	1659-1725
Couperin, Francois	1668-1733	Scarlatti, Guiseppe	
Daquin, Louis Claude	1694-1772	Domenico	1685-1757
Durante, Francesco	1684-1755	Schmeltzer, Johann	
Fasch, Johann Friedrich	1688-1758	Heinrich	1623-1680
Finger, Godfrey	1685-1717	Schütz, Heinrich	1585-1672
Garth, Sir Samuel	1661-1719	Steffani, Agostino	1653-1728
Greene, Maurice	1695-1755	Stradella, Alessandro	1645-1682
Handel, George Frederick	1685-1759	Tartini, Giuseppe	1692-1770
Hasse, Johann Adolph	1699-1783	Telemann, Georg Philip	1681-1767
Heinicken, Johann David	1683-1729	Vivaldi, Antonio	1678-1741
Innes, Thomas	1663-1744		

1701   War of the Spanish succession.
1702   England declares war on France and Spain.
1703   Battle of Pultusk.
1704   Battle of Blenheim.
1705   Battle of Cassano.
1706   Battle of Ramillies.
1707   First Parliament of Great Britain.
1708   Battle of Oudenarde.
1709   Battle of Malplaquet.
1710   Battle of Saragossa.
1713   Peace of Utrecht.
1715   Riot Act passed.
        Battle of Sheriffmuir.
        Battle of Preston.
1717   Triple Alliance. England, France and Holland.
1718   Quadruple Alliance. Great Britain, France, Holland and the Emperor.
        England declares war against Spain.
1719   France declares war against Spain.
1720   Spain joins Quadruple Alliance.
        South Sea Bubble bursts.

PROMINENT PEOPLE

Clive, Lord Robert	1725-1774	Marlborough, John	
Cromwell, Richard	1626-1712	Churchill, 1st Duke	1650-1722
Fahrenheit, Gabriel Daniel	1686-1736	Newton, Sir Isaak	1642-1727
Kidd, Captain William	1645-1701	Penn, William	1644-1718
		Turpin, Dick	1705-1739

EMPERORS OF CHINA (MANCHU (Ch'ing) DYNASTY)

Kang Tsi	1662-1722	Yung Cheng	1723-1735

POPES

Clement XI	1701-1721	Benedict XIII	1724-1730
Innocent XIII	1721-1724		

FRANCE. HEADS OF STATE

Louis XIV	1643-1715	Louis XV	1715-1774

HOLY ROMAN EMPERORS

Leopold I	1658-1705	Charles VI	1711-1740
Joseph I	1705-1711		

ENGLAND. SOVEREIGNS

William III	1694-1702	George I	1714-1727
Anne	1702-1714		

SWEDEN. KINGS

Charles XII	1697-1718	Frederick I	1720-1751
Ulrica Eleanora	1718-1720		

PORTUGAL. KINGS

Pedro II	1683-1706	John V	1706-1750

Frederick I (Frederick III   Frederick William I   1713-1740
  Elector of Brandenburg) 1701-1713

RUSSIA. TSARS
Peter the Great I   1682-1725   Catherine I   1725-1727

SPAIN. SOVEREIGNS
Philip V   1700-1724   Philip V   1724-1746
Luis   1724

WRITERS

Abauzit, Firmin	1679-1767	Blomefield, Francis	1705-1752
Abel, Karl Friedrich	1725-1787	Boccage, Marie Anne	
Adam, Jean	1710-1765	Fiquet du	1710-1802
Addison, Joseph	1672-1719	Bodmer, Johann Jakob	1698-1783
Aepinus, Franz Ulrich		Boileau-Despreaux, Nicolas	1636-1711
Theodor	1724-1802	Bolingbroke, Henry	
Aguesseau, Henri		St. John	1678-1751
François d'	1668-1751	Bossuet, Jacques Benigne	1627-1704
Ainsworth, Robert	1660-1743	Boston Thomas	1677-1732
Akenside, Mark	1721-1770	Boulainvilliers, Henri	
Alcoforado, Marianna	1640-1723	Compte de	1658-1722
Alembert, Jean Le Rond D'	1717-1783	Boursault, Edme	1638-1701
Algarotti, Francesco,		Brady, Nicholas	1659-1726
Count	1712-1764	Brockes, Barthold	
Amelot de la Houssaey,		Heinrich	1680-1747
Abraham Nicholas	1634-1706	Broekhuizen, Jan Van	1649-1707
Ames, Joseph	1689-1759	Brooke, Henry	1703-1783
Amhurst, Nicholas	1697-1742	Brorson, Hans Adolf	1694-1764
Amory, Thomas	1691-1788	Brosses, Charles de	1709-1777
Anquetil, Louis Pierre	1723-1808	Brown, John	1715-1766
Anstey, Christopher	1724-1805	Browne, Isaac Hawkins	1705-1760
Arbuthnot, John	1667-1735	Brucker, Johann Jakob	1696-1770
Argens, Jean Baptiste		Bryant, Jacob	1715-1804
de Boyer, Marquis de	1704-1771	Bulstrode, Sir Richard	1610-1711
Armstrong, John	1709-1779	Buonafede, Appiano	1716-1793
Asgill, John	1659-1738	Burnet, Gilbert	1643-1715
Astell, Mary	1668-1731	Burnet, Thomas	1635-1715
Atterbury, Francis	1663-1732	Byrd, William	1674-1744
Aubrey, John	1626-1697	Byrom, John	1692-1763
Aulnoy, Marie Cathrine	1650-1705	Cambridge, Richard	
Bachaumont, Louis		Owen	1717-1802
Petit de	1690-1771	Campistron, Jean	
Baillie, Grizel, Lady	1665-1746	Galbert De	1656-1723
Barthelemy, Jean Jakob	1716-1795	Canizares, Jose De	1676-1750
Baumgarten, Alexander		Carey, Henry	1690-1743
Gottlieb	1714-1762	Carte, Thomas	1686-1754
Bayle, Pierre	1647-1706	Carter, Elizabeth	1717-1806
Bentley, Richard	1662-1742	Casanova De Seingalt,	
Berkeley, George	1685-1753	Giovanni Jacopo	1725-1798
Bilfinger, George		Casti, Giovanni Battista	1724-1803
Bernhard	1693-1750	Cazotte, Jacques	1719-1792
Birch, Thomas	1705-1766	Centlivre, Susanna	1667-1723
Blacklock, Thomas	1721-1791	Challoner, Richard	1691-1781
Blackmore, Sir Richard	1650-1729	Chaulieu, Guillaume	
Blair, Robert	1699-1746	Amfrye De	1639-1720

Chesterfield, Philip Dormer	
Stanhope (4th Earl of)	1694-1713
Choisy, Francois	
Timoleon Abbe De	1644-1724
Cibber, Colley	1671-1757
Cibber, Theophilus	1703-1758
Clarke, Samuel	1675-1729
Clement, Francois	1714-1793
Cockburn, Alicia	1713-1794
Colden, Cadwallader	1688-1776
Colle, Charles	1709-1783
Collier, Arthur	1680-1732
Collier, John	1708-1786
Collins, William	1721-1759
Condillac, Etienne	
Bonnot De	1715-1780
Congreve, William	1670-1729
Cooke, Thomas	1703-1756
Cornielle, Thomas	1625-1709
Correa Garcao, Pedro	
Antonio Joaquim	1724-1772
Crebillon, Prosper	
Jolyot De	1674-1762
Crescimbeni, Giovanni	
Mario	1663-1728
Crousaz, Jean Pierre	1663-1748
Crowne, John	1640-1703
Cruden, Alexander	1701-1770
Crusius, Christian August	1715-1775
Cumberland, Richard	1631-1718
Cutts of Gowran,	
John Cutts	1661-1707
Dahlstjerna, Gunno	1661-1709
Dalin, Olof Von	1708-1763
Dampier, William	1652-1715
Dancourt, Florent Carton	1661-1725
Daniel, Gabriel	1649-1728
Dass, Petter	1647-1708
Defoe, Daniel	1659-1731
Dennis, John	1657-1734
Destouches, Phillipe	1680-1754
Diderot, Denis	1713-1784
Dodsley, Robert	1703-1764
Dodwell, Henry	1641-1711
Dupin, Louis Ellies	1657-1719
D'Urfey, Thomas	1653-1723
Dyer, John	1699-1757
Edwards, Jonathan	1703-1758
Ekhof, Konrad	1720-1778
Ellwood, Thomas	1639-1714
Eusden, Laurence	1688-1730
Evelyn, John	1620-1706
Farquhar, George	1677-1707
Farvart, Charles Simon	1710-1792
Fénelon, François de	
Salignac de la Mothe	1651-1715
Fenton, Elijah	1683-1730
Ferguson, Adam	1723-1816
Fielding, Henry	1707-1754
Filicaia, Vincenzo da	1642-1707
Fleury, Claude	1640-1723

Folard, Jean Charles	1669-1752
Fontenelle, Bernard Le	
Bovier De	1657-1757
Foote, Samuel	1720-1777
Fortiguera, Nicolo	1674-1735
Franklin, Benjamin	1706-1790
Frugoni, Carlo Innocenzo	
Maria	1692-1768
Gay, John	1685-1732
Gellert, Christian	
Furchtegott	1715-1769
Genovesi, Antonio	1712-1769
Giannone, Pietro	1676-1748
Gleim, Johann Wilhelm	
Ludwig	1719-1803
Glover, Richard	1712-1785
Goldoni, Carlo	1707-1793
Gottsched, Johann	
Christoph	1700-1766
Gotz, Johann Nikolaus	1721-1781
Gozzi, Carlo	1720-1806
Graves, Richard	1715-1804
Gray, Thomas	1716-1771
Green, Matthew	1696-1737
Gresset, Jean Baptiste	
Louis	1709-1777
Grimm, Friedrich	
Melchior	1723-1807
Guidi, Carlo Alessandro	1650-1712
Gunther, Johann	
Christian	1695-1723
Guyon, Jeanne Marie	
Bouvier De La Mothe	1648-1717
Gyongyosi, Istvan	1620-1704
Hagedorn, Friedrich Von	1708-1754
Halifax, Charles Montague	1661-1715
Hamilton, Anthony	1645-1720
Hamilton, William	1704-1754
Hanbury, Williams,	
Sir Charles	1708-1759
Harris, John	1666-1719
Hartley, David	1705-1757
Hawkesworth, John	1715-1773
Hawkins, Sir John	1719-1789
Haywood, Eliza	1693-1756
Hearne, Thomas	1678-1735
Helvetius, Claude Adrien	1715-1771
Helyot, Pierre	1660-1716
Hemsterhuis, Francois	1721-1790
Henault, Charles Jean	
Francois	1685-1770
Hervey of Ickworth,	
John Hervey	1696-1743
Hill, Aaron	1685-1750
Hill, John	1716-1775
Holbach, Paul Heinrich	
Dietrich	1723-1789
Holberg, Ludvig Holberg	1684-1754
Home, John	1722-1808
Hontheim, Johann	
Nikolaus Von	1701-1790

L

Hoz Y Mota, Juan		Mather, Increase	1639-1723	
Claudio De La	1630-1714	Metastasio	1698-1782	
Hughes, John	1677-1720	Michell, John	1724-1793	
Hume, David	1711-1776	Mirabeau, Victor Riqueti	1715-1789	
Hurd, Richard	1720-1808	Montagu, Elizabeth	1720-1800	
Hutcheson, Francis	1694-1746	Montagu, Lady Mary		
Isla, Jose Francisco De	1703-1781	Wortley	1689-1762	
Jenyns, Soame	1704-1787	Montesquieu, Charles Louis		
Johnson, Samuel	1709-1784	De Secondat	1689-1755	
Kames, Henry Home	1696-1782	Moore, Edward	1712-1757	
Kant, Immanuel	1724-1804	Motteux, Pierre Antoine	1663-1718	
King, William	1663-1712	Muratori, Ludovico		
Kingo, Thomas Hansen	1634-1703	Antonio	1672-1750	
Kleist, Ewald Christian		Neal, Daniel	1678-1743	
Von	1715-1759	Newton, Sir Isaac	1642-1727	
Klopstock, Friedrich		Norris, John	1657-1711	
Gottlieb	1724-1803	North, Roger	1653-1734	
La Chaussee, Pierre		O'Carolan, Turlogh	1670-1738	
Claude Nivelle De	1692-1754	Oldmixon, John	1673-1742	
La Grange-Chancel,		Orrery, Charles Boyle	1676-1731	
Francois Joseph	1677-1758	Paltock, Robert	1697-1767	
Lairesse, Gerard De	1641-1711	Parnell, Thomas	1679-1718	
Lamettrie, Julien		Paterson, William	1658-1719	
Offray De	1709-1751	Payne, Henry Neville	died c. 1710	
La Motte, Antoine		Penn, William	1644-1718	
Houdar De	1672-1731	Pepusch, Johann		
Law, William	1686-1761	Christoph	1667-1752	
Leibnitz, Gottfried		Pepys, Samuel	1633-1703	
Wilhelm	1646-1716	Perrault, Charles	1628-1703	
Lennox, Charlotte	1720-1804	Philips, Ambrose	1675-1749	
Le Sage, Alain Rene	1668-1747	Philips, John	1676-1708	
L'Estrange, Sir Roger	1616-1704	Phillips, John	1631-1706	
Lillo, George	1693-1739	Piranesi, Giambattista	1720-1778	
Linnaeus, Carl	1707-1778	Piron, Alexis	1689-1773	
Locke, John	1632-1704	Pitcairn, Archibald	1652-1713	
Lockhart, George	1673-1731	Pomfret, John	1667-1702	
Lomonosov, Mikhail		Pontoppidan, Erik	1698-1764	
Vasilievich	1711-1765	Pope, Alexander	1688-1744	
Luzan Claramunt, De		Pozzo, Andrea	1642-1709	
Suelves Y Guerea		Prevost, Antoine Francois	1697-1763	
Ignaccio	1702-1754	Price, Richard	1723-1791	
Luzzatto, Moses Hayim	1707-1747	Prior, Matthew	1664-1721	
Lyttelton, George,		Quesnel, Pasquier	1634-1718	
1st Baron	1709-1773	Racine, Louis	1692-1763	
Macklin, Charles	1697-1797	Ramsay, Allan	1686-1758	
Mably, Gabriel Bonnot De	1709-1785	Ramsay, Andrew Michael	1686-1743	
Maffei, Francesco		Rapin, Paul De	1661-1725	
Scipione	1675-1755	Raynal, Guillaume		
Magnusson, Arni	1663-1730	Thomas Francois	1713-1796	
Malebranche, Nicolas	1638-1715	Regnard, Jean Francois	1655-1709	
Mallet, David	1705-1765	Reid, Thomas	1710-1796	
Mandeville, Bernard De	1670-1733	Reimarus, Hermann		
Manley, Mary De La		Samuel	1694-1768	
Riviere	1663-1724	Richardson, Samuel	1689-1761	
Marais, Marin	1656-1728	Robertson, William	1721-1793	
Marivaux, Pierre Carlet		Rollin, Charles	1661-1741	
De Chamblain De	1688-1763	Rousseau, Jean Baptiste	1671-1741	
Marmontel, Jean Francois	1723-1799	Rousseau, Jean Jacques	1712-1778	
Marsigli, Luigi Ferdinando	1658-1730	Rowe, Nicholas	1674-1718	
Mason, William	1725-1797	Rymer, Thomas	1641-1713	
Mather, Cotton	1663-1728			

Saint Evremond, Charles Marquetul de Saint Denis Seigneur de	1610-1703	Strype, John	1643-1737
		Swedenborg, Emanuel	1688-1772
Saint-Lambert, Jean Francois De	1716-1803	Swift, Jonathan	1676-1745
		Tate, Nahum	1652-1715
Saint-Pierre, Charles Irenee Castel	1658-1743	Tencin, Claudine Alexandrine Guerin De	1681-1749
Saint-Simon, Louis De Rouvroy	1675-1755	Theobald, Lewis	1688-1744
		Tickell, Thomas	1686-1740
Savage, Richard	1697-1743	Tindal, Matthew	1656-1733
Sedaine, Michel Jean	1719-1797	Thomasius, Christian	1655-1728
Sedley, Sir Charles	1639-1701	Thomson, James	1700-1748
Semler, Johann Salomo	1725-1791	Torres Y Villaroel, Diego De	1696-1759
Settle, Elkanan	1648-1724	Uz, Johann Peter	1720-1796
Sewall, Samuel	1672-1730	Vanbrugh, Sir John	1664-1726
Shaftesbury, Anthony Ashley Cooper, 3rd Earl of	1671-1713	Vilo, Giovanni Battista	1668-1744
		Voltaire, Francois Marie Arouet De	1694-1778
Shenstone, William	1714-1763	Walpole, Horace	1717-1797
Sheridan, Thomas	1719-1788	Warton, Joseph	1722-1800
Sherlock, William	1641-1707	Watts, Isaak	1674-1748
Silva, Antonio Jose Da	1705-1739	Wesley, John	1703-1791
Smart, Christopher	1722-1771	White, Gilbert	1720-1793
Smith, Adam	1723-1790	Whitehead, Paul	1710-1774
Smollet, Tobias George	1721-1771	Whitehead, William	1715-1785
Somerville, William	1675-1742	Wigglesworth, Michael	1631-1705
Southerne, Thomas	1660-1746	Winchelsea, Anne Finch	1661-1720
Speke, Hugh	1656-1724	Wodrow, Robert	1679-1734
Spence, Joseph	1699-1768	Wolff, Christian	1679-1754
Staal, Marguerite Jeanne Cordier De Launay	1684-1750	Wollaston, William	1659-1724
		Wyncherley, William	1640-1716
Steele, Sir Richard	1672-1729	Young, Edward	1638-1765
Sterne, Laurence	1713-1768	Zinzendorf, Nicolaus Ludwig, Graf von	1700-1760
Stillingfleet, Benjamin	1702-1771		

ARTISTS

Allou, Gilles	1670-1751	Cassana, Niccolo	1659-1714
Archer, Thomas	1668-1743	Chardin, Jean Baptiste Simeon	1699-1779
Backhuysen, Ludolf	1631-1708	Chippendale, Thomas (cabinet maker)	1718-1779
Batoni, Pompeo Grolamo	1708-1787		
Blondel, Jacques Francois	1705-1774	Churriguera, Don Josi	1650-1725
Bouchardon, Edme	1698-1762	Cignani, Carlo	1628-1719
Boucher, Francois	1703-1770	Closterman, John	1656-1713
Boulle, Andre Charles (cabinet maker)	1642-1732	Coustou, Guillaume I	1678-1746
		Coustou, Guillaume II	1716-1777
Boydell, John	1719-1804	Coustou, Nicolas	1658-1733
Bredael, Jan Frans Van	1683-1750	Coypel, Antoine	1661-1722
Briseux, Charles Etienne	1680-1754	Coypel, Charles Antoine	1694-1752
Brown, Lancelot (" Capability ") (landscape gardener)	1715-1783	Coypel, Noel	1628-1707
		Coypel, Noel Nicholas	1692-1734
Burlington, Richard Boyle, 3rd Earl of	1695-1753	Coysevoy, Charles Antoine	1640-1720
		Crespi, Giuseppi Maria	1665-1747
Caffieri, Jacques	1678-1755	Cressent, Charles	1685-1768
Camus De Mezieres, Nicolas Le	1721-1789	Cuvilles, Francois De	1698-1767
		Dahl, Michael	1656-1743
Canaletto	1697-1768	Dietrich, Christian Wilhelm Ernst	1712-1774
Canaletto, Bernardo Beleto	1720-1780		
Carriera, Rosalba	1675-1757	Donner, Raphael Georg	1693-1741

Dusart, Cornelis	1660-1704	Longhi, Petro	1702-1785
Falconet, Ettienne		Magnasco, Alessandro	1667-1749
Maurice	1716-1791	Mansard, Jules, Hardouin	1646-1708
Falens, Karel Van	1683-1733	Maratta, Carlo	1625-1713
Fischer, Johann Bernard	1656-1723	Marot, Daniel	1661-
Flitcroft, Henry	1679-1769	Meissonier, Juste Aurele	1693-1750
Fontana, Carlo	1638-1714	Mena, Pedro De	1693-
Franceschini, Marco		Nash, Richard	1674-1762
Antonio	1648-1729	Nattier, Jean Marc	1685-1766
Gabriel, Jacques Ange	1698-1782	Neumann, Balthasar	1687-1753
Gibbons, Grinling	1648-1721	Palomino De Castro,	
Gibbs, James	1682-1754	Antonio	1653-1726
Gillot, Claude	1673-1722	Pater, Jean Baptiste	
Giordano, Luca	1632-1705	Joseph	1695-1736
Girardon, Francois	1628-1715	Pergolesi, Michael Angelo	1700-
Greuze, Jean Baptiste	1725-1805	Pigalle, Jean Baptiste	1714-1785
Guardi, Francesco	1712-1793	Ramsay, Allan	1713-1784
Hawksmoor, Nicholas	1661-1736	Reynolds, Sir Joshua	1723-1792
Heyden, Jan Van Der	1637-1712	Rigaud, Hyacinthe	1659-1743
Highmore, Joseph	1692-1780	Roubillac, Louis Francois	1695-1762
Hobbema, Meyndert	1638-1709	Rysbrack, Michael	1693-1770
Hogarth, William	1697-1764	Sandby, Paul	1725-1809
Houbraken, Arnold	1660-1719	Scheemakers, Pieter	1691-1770
Huchtenburg, John Van	1647-1733	Stradivari, Antonio	1644-1737
Huysmans, Cornelius	1648-1727	(violin maker)	
Huysmans, Jan Baptist	1654-1716	Soufflot, Jacques Germain	1709-1780
Huysum, Jan Van	1682-1749	Stuart, James	1713-1788
Janssens, Victor Honorius	1658-1736	Subleyras, Pierre	1699-1749
Jouvenet, Jean	1644-1717	Thornhill, Sir James	1676-1734
Kent, William	1685-1748	Tiepolo, Giovanni Battista	1692-1769
Kneller, Sir Godfrey	1648-1723	Vanbrugh, Sir John	1664-1726
Lafosse, Charles De	1640-1716	Van Der Velde, Willem	
Laguerre, Louis	1663-1721	the younger	1633-1707
La Grenee, Jean Louis		Van Goyen, Jan Josephzoon	1696-1756
Francois	1724-1805	Van Loo, Charles Andre	1705-1765
Lancret, Nicolas	1690-1743	Van Loo, Jean Baptiste	1684-1745
Largilliere, Nicolas	1656-1746	Vernet, Claude Joseph	1714-1789
La Tour, Maurice		Verrio, Antonio	1639-1707
Quentin De	1704-1788	Watteau, Antoine	1684-1721
Legros, Pierre	1656-1719	Wilson, Richard	1714-1782
Lemoine, Francois	1688-1737	Wood, John	1705-1754
Lemoyne, Jean Baptiste	1704-1778	Wren, Sir Christopher	1632-1723
Limborch, Hendrick Van	1680-1758	Zuccarelli, Francesco	1702-1788
Liotard, Jean Etienne	1702-1789		

COMPOSERS

Alberti, Domenico	1710-1740	Bononcini, Giovanni	
Albinoni, Tommaso	1674-1745	Battista	1670-1755
Arne, Thomas Augustine	1710-1778	Bononcini, Marc Antonio	1675-1726
Astorga, Emanuele		Boyce, William	1710-1779
Gioacchino	1680-1755	Caldara, Antonio	1670-1736
Bach Johann Sebastian	1685-1750	Campra, Anore	1660-1744
Bach, Karl Philipp		Clari, Giovanni Carlo	
Emanuel	1714-1788	Maria	1669-1745
Bach, Wilhelm Friedmann	1710-1784	Clarke, Jeremiah	1659-1707
Barsanti, Francesco	1690-1775	Corelli, Arcangelo	1653-1713
Benda, Georg	1722-1795	Croft, William	1678-1727
Blow, John	1648-1708	Couperin, Francois	1668-1733
		Daquin, Louis Claude	1694-1772

Durante, Francesco	1684-1755	Mattheson, Johann	1681-1764
Eberlin, Johann Ernst	1702-1762	Nardini, Pietro	1722-1793
Fasch, Johann Friedrich	1688-1758	Nares, James	1715-1783
Finger, Godfrey	1685-1717	Pachebel, Johan	1653-1706
Galuppi, Baldassare	1706-1785	Pergolesi, Giovanni	
Garth, Sir Samuel	1661-1719	Battista	1710-1736
Gluck, Christoph Willibald	1714-1787	Porpora, Niccola Antonio	1686-1767
Graun, Karl Heinrich	1701-1759	Quantz, Johann Joachim	1697-1773
Greene, Maurice	1695-1755	Rameau, Jean	1683-1764
Handel, George Frederick	1685-1759	Roman, Johan Helmich	1694-1758
Hasse, Johann Adolph	1699-1783	Scarlatti, Alessandro	1659-1725
Heinichen, Johann David	1683-1729	Scarlatti, Guiseppe	
Innes, Thomas	1663-1744	Domenico	1685-1757
Jommelli, Niccolo	1714-1774	Schobert, Johann	1720-1767
Keiser, Reinhold	1673-1739	Stamitz, Johann	1717-1757
Leclair, Jean Marie	1697-1764	Stanley, John	1713-1786
Leo, Leonardo	1694-1744	Steffan, Agostino	1653-1728
Logroscino, Nicola	1700-1763	Tartini, Giuseppe	1692-1770
Lotti, Antonio	1667-1740	Telemann, George Philipp	1681-1767
Marcello, Benedetto	1686-1739	Vivaldi, Antonio	1678-1741

1729   Peace between Britain, France and Spain.
1734   Siege of Dantzig.
1738   Lorraine ceded to France.
1739   England goes to war with Spain.
1742   France declares war against Maria Theresa of Austria, England and
       Holland.
1745   Battle of Fontenoy.
       Battle of Prestonpans.
1746   Battle of Falkirk.
       Battle of Culloden.
1748   Peace concluded at Aix la Chapelle.

PROMINENT PEOPLE

Clive, Lord Robert	1725-1774	Newton, Sir Isaac	1642-1727
Cook, Captain James	1728-1770	Turpin, Dick	1705-1739
Fahrenheit, Gabrielle		Wilkes, John	1727-1797
Daniel	1686-1736	Wolfe, General James	1727-1759
Hastings, Warren	1732-1818		

EMPERORS OF CHINA (MANCHU (Ch'ing) DYNASTY)

Yung Cheng	1723-1735	Kao Tsung	1735-1795

POPES

Benedict XIII	1724-1730	Benedict XIV	1740-1758
Clement XII	1730-1740		

FRANCE. HEADS OF STATE

Louis XV	1715-1774

HOLY ROMAN EMPERORS

Charles VI	1711-1740	Francis I of Lorraine	1745-1765
Charles VII of Bavaria	1742-1745		

ENGLAND. SOVEREIGNS

George I	1714-1727	George II	1727-1760

SWEDEN. KINGS

Frederick I	1720-1751

PORTUGAL. KINGS

John V	1706-1750	Joseph	1750-1777

PRUSSIA. KINGS

Frederick William I	1713-1740	Frederick II	1740-1786

RUSSIA. TSARS

Catherine I	1725-1727	Ivan VI	1740-1741
Peter II	1727-1730	Elizabeth	1741-1762
Anne	1730-1740		

WRITERS

Abauzit, Firmin	1679-1767	Bickerstaffe, Isaac	1735-1812
Abel, Karl Friedrich	1725-1787	Bilfinger, George Bernhard	1693-1750
Adam, Alexander	1741-1809	Birch, Thomas	1705-1766
Adam, Jean	1710-1765	Blacklock, Thomas	1721-1791
Adams, John	1735-1826	Blackmore, Sir Richard	1650-1729
Adanson, Michel	1727-1806	Blair, Robert	1699-1746
Aepinus, Franz Ulrich		Blamire, Susanna	1747-1794
Theodor	1724-1802	Blomefield, Francis	1705-1752
Aguesseau, Henri		Boccage, Marie Anne	
Francois d'	1668-1751	Fiquet De	1710-1802
Aikin, John	1747-1822	Bodmer, Johann Jakob	1698-1783
Ainsworth, Robert	1660-1743	Boie, Heinrich Christian	1744-1806
Akenside, Mark	1721-1770	Bolingbroke, Henry	
Alembert, Jean Le		St. John	1678-1751
Rond D'	1717-1783	Bolyai, Wolfgang	1775-1856
Alfireri, Vittorio, Count	1749-1803	Bonstetten, Charles	
Algarotti, Francesco,		Victor De	1745-1832
Count	1712-1764	Boston, Thomas	1677-1732
Ames, Joseph	1689-1759	Boswell, James	1740-1795
Amhurst, Nicholas	1697-1742	Brady, Nicholas	1659-1726
Amory, Thomas	1691-1788	Brockes, Barthold Heinrich	1680-1747
Anderson, John	1726-1796	Brooke, Henry	1703-1783
Anderson, Robert	1750-1830	Brorson, Hans Adolf	1694-1764
Andrews, James Pettit	1737-1797	Brosses, Charles de	1709-1777
Anquetil, Louis Pierre	1723-1808	Brown, John	1715-1766
Anspach, Elizabeth,		Browne, Isaac Hawkins	1705-1760
Margravine of	1750-1828	Bruce, Micheal	1746-1767
Anstey, Christopher	1724-1805	Brucker, Johann Jakob	1696-1770
Arbuthnot, John	1667-1735	Bryant, Jacob	1715-1804
Archenholz, Johann		Buonafede, Appiano	1716-1793
Wilhelm Von	1743-1812	Burger, Gottfried August	1747-1794
Argens, Jean Baptiste		Burke, Edmund	1729-1797
De Boyer, Marquis D'	1704-1771	Byrd, William	1674-1744
Armstrong, John	1709-1779	Byrom, John	1692-1763
Asgill, John	1659-1738	Cadalso, Vasquez Jose	1741-1782
Astell, Mary	1668-1731	Cambridge, Richard	
Atterbury, Francis	1663-1732	Owen	1717-1802
Bachaumont, Louis		Canizares, Jose De	1676-1750
Petit De	1690-1771	Carey, Henry	1690-1743
Baillie, Lady Grizel	1665-1746	Carte, Thomas	1686-1754
Barbauld, Anna Letitia	1743-1825	Carter, Elizabeth	1717-1806
Barnard, Lady Anne	1750-1825	Casanova De Seingalt,	
Barthelemy, Jean-Jacques	1716-1795	Giovanni Jacopo	1725-1798
Baumgarten, Alexander		Casti, Giovanni Battista	1724-1803
Gottlieb	1714-1762	Cazotte, Jacques	1719-1792
Beattie, James	1735-1803	Cerutti, Giuseppe	1728-1792
Beaumarchais, Pierre		Cesarotti, Melchiore	1730-1808
Augustin Caron De	1732-1799	Challoner, Richard	1697-1781
Beccaria, Cesare		Chamfort, Sebastien Roch	
Marchese De	1738-1794	Nicolas	1741-1794
Bekker, Elizabeth	1738-1804	Chapone, Hester	1727-1801
Bellman, Karl Mikael	1740-1795	Charriere, Isabelle De	1740-1805
Belloy, Dormont De	1727-1775	Churchill, Charles	1731-1764
Bentham, Jeremy	1748-1832	Cibber, Colley	1671-1757
Bentley	1662-1742	Cibber, Theophilus	1703-1758
Berkeley, George	1685-1753	Clarke, Samuel	1675-1729

Claudius, Matthias	1740-1815		Dutens, Louis	1730-1812
Clement, Francois	1714-1793		Dyer, John	1699-1757
Cockburn, Alicia	1713-1794		Eberhard, Johann	
Colden, Cadwallader	1688-1776		Augustus	1739-1809
Coleman, George	1732-1794		Edgeworth, Richard Lovell	1744-1817
Collé, Charles	1709-1783		Edwards, Bryan	1743-1800
Collier, Arthur	1680-1732		Edwards, Jonathan	1703-1758
Collier, John	1708-1786		Ekhof, Konrad	1720-1778
Collins, William	1721-1759		Elliot, Jean	1727-1805
Colman, George the Elder	1732-1794		Engel, Johann Jakob	1741-1802
Combe, William	1741-1823		Epinay, Louise Florence	
Condorcet, Marie Jean			Petronille Tardieu	
Antoine, Marquis De	1743-1794		d'esclavelles D'	1726-1783
Condillac, Etienne			Erskine, Henry	1746-1817
Bonnot De	1715-1780		Eschenburg, Johann	
Congreve, William	1670-1729		Joachim	1743-1820
Cooke, Thomas	1703-1756		Eusden, Laurence	1688-1730
Correa, Garcao, Pedro			Ewald, Johannes	1743-1781
Antonio Joaquim	1724-1772		Fabroni, Angelo	1732-1803
Cowley, Hannah	1743-1809		Falconer, William	1732-1769
Cowper, William	1731-1800		Farvart, Charles Simon	1710-1792
Coxe, William	1747-1828		Fawkes, Francis	1720-1777
Crauford, Quintin	1743-1819		Fenton, Elijah	1683-1730
Crebillon, Prosper			Ferguson, Adam	1723-1816
Jolyot De	1674-1762		Fergusson, Robert	1750-1774
Crescimbeni, Giovanni			Fielding, Henry	1707-1754
Mario	1663-1728		Folard, Jean Charles	1669-1752
Crousaz, Jean Pierre	1663-1748		Fontenelle, Bernard Le	
Cruden, Alexander	1701-1770		Bovier De	1657-1757
Crusius, Christian August	1715-1775		Fortiguera, Niccolo	1674-1735
Cruz E Silva, Antonio			Foote, Samuel	1720-1777
Diniz Da	1731-1799		Francois De Neufchateau,	
Cruz, Raymon De La	1731-1794		Nicolas Louis	1750-1828
Cumberland, Richard	1732-1811		Franklin, Benjamin	1706-1790
Dalin, Olof Von	1708-1763		Frugoni, Carlo Innocenzo	
Daniel, Gabriel	1649-1728		Maria	1692-1768
Da Ponté, Lorenzo	1749-1838		Garat, Dominique Joseph	1749-1833
Darwin, Erasmus	1731-1802		Garcia De La Huerta,	
Dashkova, Catherina			Vincente Antonio	1734-1787
Romanovna	1744-1810		Gay, John	1685-1732
Day, Thomas	1748-1789		Gellert, Christian	
Defoe, Daniel	1659-1731		Furchtegott	1715-1769
Delille, Jacques	1738-1813		Genlis, Stephanie Felicite	
Delolme, Jean Louis	1740-1806		Ducrest De St. Aubin	1746-1830
Denina, Carlo Giovanni			Genovesi, Antonio	1712-1769
Maria	1731-1813		Gerard, Alexander	1728-1795
Dennis, John	1657-1734		Gerstenberg, Heinrich	
Denis, Michael	1729-1800		Wilhelm Von	1737-1823
Derzhavin, Gavrila			Giannone, Pietro	1676-1748
Romanovich	1743-1816		Gibbon, Edward	1737-1794
Desforges, Pierre Jean			Gillies, John	1747-1836
Baptiste Choudard	1746-1806		Ginguenne, Pierre Louis	1748-1815
Destouches, Phillipe	1680-1754		Gleim, Johann Wilhelm	
Diderot, Denis	1713-1784		Ludwig	1719-1803
Diniz Da Cruz E Silva,			Glover, Richard	1712-1785
Antonio	1731-1799		Goethe, Johann Wolfgang	
Dodsley, Robert	1703-1764		Von	1749-1832
Dorat, Claude Joseph	1743-1780		Goldoni, Carlo	1707-1793
Ducis, Jean Francois	1733-1816		Goldsmith, Oliver	1728-1774
Dupuis, Charles Francois	1742-1809		Gottsched, Johann	
Durao, Jose De Santa Rita	1737-1784		Christoph	1700-1766

Gotter, Friedrich Wilhelm	1746-1797	Jovellanos, Gaspar	
Gotz, Johann Nikolaus	1721-1781	Melchor De	1744-1811
Gozzi, Carlo	1720-1806	Kames, Henry Home	1696-1782
Graves, Richard	1715-1804	Kant, Immanuel	1724-1804
Gray, Thomas	1716-1771	Kelly, Hugh	1739-1777
Green, Matthew	1696-1737	King, Thomas	1730-1805
Gresset, Jean Baptiste		Kleist, Ewald Christian	
Louis	1709-1777	Von	1715-1759
Grimm, Friedrich		Klopstock, Friedrich	
Melchior	1723-1807	Gottlieb	1724-1803
Hagedorn, Friedrich Von	1708-1754	Knebel, Karl Ludwig Von	1744-1834
Hamann, Johann Georg	1730-1788	La Chaussee, Pierre	
Hamilton, William	1704-1754	Claude Nivelle De	1692-1754
Hanbury, Williams, Sir		Laclos, Pierre Amboise	
Charles	1708-1759	Francois	1741-1803
Hartley, David	1705-1757	Lagrange-Chancel,	
Hasted, Edward	1732-1812	Francois Joseph	1677-1758
Hawkesworth, John	1715-1773	Lamarck, Jean Chevalier	
Hawkins, Sir John	1719-1789	de	1744-1829
Hayley, William	1745-1820	Lamettrie, Julien Offray	
Haywood, Eliza	1693-1756	De	1709-1751
Hearne, Thomas	1678-1735	La Motte, Antoine	
Heinse, Johann, Jakob		Houdar De	1672-1731
Wilhelm	1749-1803	Langhorne, John	1735-1779
Helvetius, Claude Adrien	1715-1771	Lavater, Johann Kaspar	1741-1801
Hemstehuis, Francois	1721-1790	Law, William	1686-1761
Henault, Charles Jean		Lee, Sophia	1750-1824
Francois	1685-1770	Lemierre, Antoine Marin	1733-1793
Herder, Johann Gottfried		Lennox, Charlotte	1720-1804
Von	1744-1803	Le Sage, Alain Rene	1668-1747
Hervey of Ickworth, John		Lespinasse, Julie De	1732-1776
Hervey	1696-1743	Lessing, Gotthold Ephraim	1729-1781
Hill, Aaron	1685-1750	Lichtenberg, Georg	
Hill, John	1716-1775	Christoph	1742-1799
Hippel, Theodor Gottlieb		Ligne, Charles Joseph	1735-1814
Von	1741-1796	Lillo, George	1693-1739
Holbach, Paul Heinrich		Linnaeus, Carl	1707-1778
Dietrich	1723-1789	Lockhart, George	1673-1731
Holberg, Ludvig Holberg	1684-1754	Logan, John	1748-1788
Holcroft, Thomas	1745-1809	Lomonosov, Mikhail	
Holland, Henry	1746-1806	Vasilievich	1711-1765
Holty, Ludwig Heinrich		Luzan Claramunt, De	
Cristoph	1748-1776	Suelves Y Gurrea	
Home, John	1722-1808	Ignacio	1702-1754
Hontheim, Johann		Luzzatto, Moses Hayim	1707-1747
Nikolaus Von	1701-1790	Lyttelton, George,	
Hook, James	1746-1827	1st Baron	1709-1773
Hopkinson, Francis	1737-1791	Mably, Gabriel Bennet De	1709-1785
Huerta, Vincente		Mackenzie, Henry	1745-1831
Garcia de la	1730-1787	Macklin, Charles	1697-1797
Hume, David	1711-1776	Macpherson, James	1736-1796
Hurd, Richard	1720-1808	Madan, Martin	1726-1790
Hutcheson, Francis	1694-1746	Maffei, Francesco Scipione	1675-1755
Iriarte, Tomas De	1750-1791	Magnusson, Arni	1663-1730
Isla, Jose Francisco De	1703-1781	Mallet, David	1705-1765
Jacobi, Friedrich Heinrich	1743-1819	Mandeville, Bernard De	1670-1733
Jacobi, Johann Georg	1740-1814	Marais, Marin	1656-1728
Jefferson, Thomas	1743-1826	Marivaux, Pierre Carlet	
Jenyns, Soame	1704-1787	De Chamblain De	1688-1763
Jephson, Robert	1736-1803	Marmontel, Jean Francois	1723-1799
Johnson, Samuel	1709-1784	Marsigli, Luigi Ferdinando	1658-1730

Masdeu, Juan Francisco De	1744-1817	Raynal, Guillaume Thomas Francois	1713-1796
Mason, William	1725-1797	Reeve, Clara	1729-1807
Mather, Cotton	1663-1728	Reid, Thomas	1710-1796
Mendelsshon, Moses	1729-1786	Reimarus, Hermann Samuel	1694-1768
Mercier, Sebastien	1740-1814	Restif, Nicolas Edme	1734-1806
Merck, Johann Heinrich	1741-1791	Richardson, Samuel	1689-1761
Metastasio	1698-1782	Robertson, William	1721-1793
Michell, John	1724-1793	Rollin, Charles	1661-1741
Mickle, William Julius	1735-1788	Rousseau, Jean Baptiste	1671-1741
Mirabeau, Victor Riqueti	1715-1789	Rousseau, Jean Jacques	1712-1778
Mitford, William	1744-1827	Rulhiere, Claude Carloman De	1735-1791
Montagu, Elizabeth	1720-1800	Sade, Donatien Alphonse Francois, Marquis De	1740-1814
Montagu, Lady Mary Wortley	1689-1762	Saint-Lambert, Jean Francois De	1716-1803
Montesquieu, Charles Louis De Secondat	1689-1755	Saint-Martin, Louis Claude De	1743-1803
Moore, Edward	1712-1757	Saint-Pierre, Bernardin De	1737-1814
Moore, John	1729-1802	Saint-Pierre, Charles Irenee Castel	1658-1743
More, Hannah	1745-1833	Saint-Simon, Louis De Rouvroy	1675-1755
Morellet, Andre	1727-1819	Salomon, Johann Peter	1745-1815
Muller, Friedrich	1749-1825	Savage, Richard	1697-1743
Muratori, Ludovico Antonio	1672-1750	Schlozer, August Ludwig Von	1735-1809
Murphy, Arthur	1727-1805	Schubart, Christian Friedrich Daniel	1739-1791
Musaus, Johann Karl August	1735-1787	Sedaine, Michel Jean	1719-1797
Nascimento, Francisco Manoel De	1734-1819	Semler, Johann Salomo	1725-1791
Neal, Daniel	1678-1743	Senac De Meilhan, Gabriel	1736-1803
Newton, Sir Isaac	1642-1727	Sewall, Samuel	1652-1730
Nichols, John	1745-1826	Seward, Anna	1747-1809
Nicolai, Christoph Friedrich	1733-1811	Shenstone, William	1714-1763
North, Roger	1653-1734	Sheridan, Thomas	1719-1788
O'Carolan, Turlogh	1670-1738	Silva, Antonio Jose Da	1705-1739
Oldmixon, John	1673-1742	Smart, Christopher	1722-1771
Orme, Robert	1728-1801	Smith, Adam	1723-1790
Orrery, Charles Boyle	1676-1731	Smith, Charlotte	1749-1806
Paine, Thomas	1737-1809	Smith, John Stafford	1750-1836
Paley, William	1743-1805	Smollett, Tobias George	1721-1771
Paltock, Robert	1697-1767	Somervile, William	1675-1742
Parini, Giuseppe	1729-1799	Southerne, Thomas	1660-1746
Pepusch, Johann Christoph	1667-1752	Spence, Joseph	1699-1768
Percy, Thomas	1729-1811	Staal, Marguerite Jeanne Cordier De Launay	1684-1750
Philips, Ambrose	1675-1749	Steele, Sir Richard	1672-1729
Piozzi, Hester Lynch	1741-1821	Sterne, Laurence	1713-1768
Piranesi, Giambattista	1720-1778	Stilling, Heinrich	1740-1817
Piron, Alexis	1689-1773	Stillingfleet, Benjamin	1702-1771
Pontoppidan, Erik	1698-1764	Stolberg, Friedrich Leopold	1750-1819
Pope, Alexander	1688-1744	Struensee, Johan Frederick	1737-1772
Prevost, Antoine Francois	1697-1763	Strutt, Joseph	1742-1802
Price, Richard	1723-1791	Strype, John	1643-1737
Priestly, Joseph	1733-1804	Swedenborg, Emanuel	1688-1772
Prior, Matthew	1664-1721	Swift, Jonathan	1676-1745
Proud, Robert	1728-1813		
Pye, Henry James	1745-1813		
Racine, Louis	1692-1763		
Ramsay, Allan	1686-1758		
Ramsay, Andrew Michael	1686-1743		
Raspe, Rudolf Erich	1737-1794		

Tencin, Claudine	
Alexandrine Guerin De	1681-1749
Theobald, Lewis	1688-1744
Thomasius, Christian	1655-1728
Thomson, James	1700-1748
Tickell, Thomas	1686-1740
Tindal, Matthew	1656-1733
Torres Y Villaroel,	
Diego De	1696-1759
Trumbull, John	1750-1831
Uz, Johann Peter	1720-1796
Vanbrugh, Sir John	1664-1726
Vico, Giovanni Battista	1668-1744
Voltaire, Francois Marie	
Arouet De	1694-1778
Walker, John	1732-1807
Walpole, Horace	1717-1797
Warton, Joseph	1722-1800
Warton, Thomas	1728-1790

Washington, George	1732-1799
Watts, Isaac	1674-1748
Wesley, John	1703-1791
West, Benjamin	1738-1820
White, Gilbert	1720-1793
Wieland, Christoph	
Martin	1733-1813
Whitehead, Paul	1710-1774
Whitehead, William	1715-1785
Wodrow, Robert	1679-1734
Wolcot, John	
(Peter Pindar)	1738-1819
Wolff, Christian	1679-1754
Young, Arthur	1741-1820
Young, Edward	1638-1765
Zimmermann, Johan Georg,	
Ritter Van	1728-1795
Zinzendorf, Nicolaus	
Ludwig, Graf von	1700-1760

ARTISTS

Abilgaard, Nicolaj	
Abraham	1744-1809
Adam, James	1730-1794
Adam, Robert	1728-1792
Allan, David	1744-1796
Allou, Gilles	1670-1751
Alvarez, Don Manuel	1727-1797
Archer, Thomas	1668-1743
Bacon, John	1740-1799
Banks, Thomas	1735-1805
Barker, Robert	1739-1806
Barry, James	1741-1806
Bartolozzi, Francesco	1727-1815
Batoni, Pompeo Girolamo	1708-1787
Blondel, Jacques Francois	1705-1774
Bonomi, Giuseppe	1739-1808
Bouchardon, Edme	1698-1762
Boucher, Francois	1703-1770
Boulle, Andre Charles	
(cabinet maker)	1642-1732
Boydell, John	1719-1804
Bredael, Jan Frans Van	1683-1750
Briseux, Charles Etienne	1680-1754
Brown, Lancelot	
(" Capability ")	
(landscape gardener)	1715-1783
Burlington, Richard Boyle,	
3rd Earl of	1695-1753
Burney, Charles	1726-1814
Caffieri, Jacques	1678-1755
Camus, De Mezieres	
Nicolas Le	1721-1789
Canaletto	1697-1768
Canaletto, Bernardo Belleto	1720-1780
Carriera, Rosalba	1675-1757
Casanova De Seingalt,	
Francesco	1727-1805

Casanova De Seingalt,	
Giovanni Batista	1728-1795
Chambers, Sir William	1726-1796
Chardin, Jean Simeon	1699-1779
Chippendale, Thomas	
(cabinet maker)	1718-1779
Chodowiecki, Daniel	
Nicolas	1726-1801
Cipriani, Giovanni Batista	1727-1785
Cleveland, John	1747-1786
Cleveland, Robert	1747-1809
Copley, John Singleton	1737-1815
Coustou, Guillaume I	1678-1746
Coustou, Guillaume II	1716-1777
Coustou, Nicolas	1658-1733
Cosway, Richard	1742-1821
Coypel, Charles Antoine	1694-1752
Coypel, Noel Nicholas	1692-1734
Crespi, Giuseppi Maria	1665-1747
Cressent, Charles	1685-1768
Cuvilles, Francois De	1698-1767
Dahl, Michael	1656-1743
Damer, Anne Seymour	1749-1828
Dance, George	1741-1825
Daniell, Thomas	1749-1840
David, Jacques Louis	1748-1825
De Loutherbourg, Philip	
James	1740-1812
Denon, Dominique Vivant	1747-1825
Dietrich, Christian	
Wilhelm Ernts	1712-1774
Donner, Raphael Georg	1693-1741
Downman, John	1750-1824
Doyen, Gabriel Francois	1726-1806
Earlom, Richard	1743-1822
Falconet, Ettienne Maurice	1716-1791
Falens, Karel Van	1683-1733
Farington, Joseph	1747-1821

Fiorillo, Johann Dominicus	1748-1821	Northcote, James	1746-1831
Flitcroft, Henry	1679-1769	Pajou, Augustin	1730-1809
Fragonard, Jean Honore	1732-1806	Palomino Decastro,	
Franceschini, Marco		Antonio	1653-1726
Antonio	1648-1729	Pater, Jean Baptiste	
Fuseli, Henry	1741-1835	Joseph	1695-1736
Gabriel, Jacques Ange	1698-1782	Peale, Charles Willson	1741-1827
Gainsborough, Thomas	1727-1788	Pergolesi, Michael Angelo	1700-1736
Gessner, Salomon	1730-1788	Pigalle, Jean Baptiste	1714-1785
Gibbs, James	1682-1754	Pine, Robert Edge	1730-1788
Goya Y Lucientes,		Ramsay, Allan	1713-1784
Francisco	1746-1828	Reynolds, Sir Joshua	1723-1792
Greuze, Jean Baptiste	1725-1805	Rigaud, Hyacinthe	1659-1743
Guardi, Francesco	1712-1793	Robert, Hubert	1733-1808
Hawksmoor, Nicholas	1661-1736	Romney, George	1734-1802
Highmore, Joseph	1692-1780	Rousseau, De La Rottiere	
Hogarth, William	1697-1764	Jean Simeon	1747-
Houdon, Jean Antoine	1740-1828	Roubillac, Louis Francois	1695-1762
Huchtenburg, John Van	1647-1733	Rysbrack, Michael	1693-1770
Humphrey, Ozias	1742-1810	Sandby, Paul	1725-1809
Huysmans, Cornelius	1648-1727	Scheemakers, Pieter	1691-1770
Huysum, Jan Van	1682-1749	Smart, John	1740-1811
Janssens, Victor Honorius	1658-1736	Soufflot, Jacques Germain	1709-1780
Kauffmann, Angelica	1741-1807	Stradivari, Antonio	
Kent, William	1685-1748	(violin maker)	1644-1737
La Grenee, Jean Louis		Stuart, James	1713-1788
Francois	1724-1805	Subleyras, Pierre	1699-1749
Lancret, Nicolas	1690-1743	Thornhill, Sir James	1676-1734
Largilliere, Nicolas	1656-1746	Tiepolo, Giovanni Battista	1692-1769
La Tour, Maurice		Towne, Francis	1739-1816
Quentin De	1704-1788	Vanbrugh, Sir John	1664-1726
Lemoine, Francois	1688-1737	Van Goyen, Jan	
Lemoyne, Jean Baptiste	1704-1778	Josephzoon	1696-1756
Limborch, Hendrick Van	1680-1758	Van Loo, Charles Andrew	1705-1765
Liotard, Jean Etienne	1702-1789	Van Loo, Jean Baptiste	1684-1745
Longhi, Pietro	1702-1785	Vernet, Claude Joseph	1714-1789
Magnasco, Alessandro	1667-1749	Wedgewood, Josiah	
Meissonier, Juste Aurele	1693-1750	(potter)	1730-1795
Mena, Pedro de	1693-	Wilson, Richard	1714-1782
Mengs, Antony Raphael	1728-1779	Wood, John	1705-1754
Michel, Claude	1738-1814	Wright, Joseph	1734-1797
Nash, Richard	1674-1762	Wyatt, James	1746-1813
Nattier, Jean Marc	1685-1766	Zuccarelli, Francesco	1702-1788
Neumann, Balthazar	1687-1753	Zoffany, Johann	1733-1810
Nollekens, Joseph	1737-1823	Zucchi, Antonio Pietro	1726-1795

COMPOSERS

Albrechtberger, Johann		Bach, Karl Philip	
Gregory	1736-1809	Emanuel	1714-1788
Alberti, Domenico	1710-1740	Barsanti, Francesco	1690-1775
Albinoni, Tommaso	1674-1745	Batishill, Jonathan	1738-1801
Arne, Thomas Augustine	1710-1778	Benda, Georg	1722-1795
Arnold, Samuel	1740-1802	Boccherini, Luigi	1743-1805
Astorga, Emanuele		Bononcini, Giovanni	
Giocchino	1680-1755	Battista	1670-1755
Avison, Charles	1710-1770	Boyce, William	1710-1779
Bach, Johann Christian	1735-1782	Caldara, Antonio	1670-1736
Bach, Johann Sebastian	1685-1750	Cambini, Giovanni	
Bach, Wilhelm Friedmann	1710-1784	Giuseppe	1746-1825

Campra, Anore	1660-1744	Leo, Leonardo	1694-1744
Cannabich, Christian	1731-1798	Linley, Thomas	1732-1795
Cimarosa, Domenico	1749-1801	Logroscino, Nicola	1700-1763
Clari, Giovanni Carlo		Lotti, Antonio	1667-1740
Maria	1669-1745	Lucchesi, Andrea	1741-1800
Corri, Domenico	1746-1825	Marcello, Benedetto	1686-1739
Couperin, Francois	1668-1733	Mattheson, Johann	1681-1764
Croft, William	1678-1727	Monsigny, Pierre	
Daquin, Louis Claude	1694-1772	Alexandre	1729-1817
Dibdin, Charles	1745-1814	Nardini, Pietro	1722-1793
Dittersdorf, Karl		Nares, James	1715-1783
Ditters Von	1739-1799	Paisiello, Giovanni	1741-1816
Durante, Francesco	1684-1755	Pergolesi, Giovanni	
Eberlin, Johann Ernst	1702-1762	Battista	1710-1736
Fasch, Friedrich	1688-1758	Philidor, Francois Andre	
Galuppi, Baldassare	1706-1785	Danican	1726-1795
Gazzaniga, Giuseppe	1743-1818	Piccinni, Niccola	1728-1800
Giordani, Giuseppe	1744-1798	Porpora, Niccola Antonio	1686-1767
Gluck, Christoph		Quantz, Johann Joachim	1697-1773
Willibald	1714-1787	Rameau, Jean Phillipe	1683-1764
Gossec, Francois Joseph	1734-1829	Roman, Johan Helmich	1694-1758
Gow, Niel	1727-1807	Sacchini, Antonio Maria	
Graun, Karl Heinrich	1701-1759	Gaspare	1734-1786
Greene, Maurice	1695-1755	Salieri, Antonio	1750-1825
Gretry, Andre Ernest		Sarti, Giuseppe	1729-1802
Modeste	1741-1813	Scarlatti, Guiseppe	
Handel, George Frederick	1685-1759	Domenico	1685-1757
Hasse, Johann Adolph	1699-1783	Schobert, Johann	1720-1767
Haydn, Franz Joseph	1732-1809	Shield, William	1748-1829
Haydn, Michael	1737-1806	Stamitz, Carl Philipp	1745-1801
Heinichen, Johann David	1683-1729	Stamitz, Johann	1717-1757
Hiller, Johann Adam	1728-1804	Stanley, John	1713-1786
Innes, Thomas	1663-1744	Tartini, Giuseppe	1692-1770
Jommelli, Niccolo	1714-1774	Telemann, Georg Philipp	1681-1767
Jackson, Wilhelm	1730-1803	Vivaldi, Antonio	1678-1741
Keiser, Reinhold	1673-1739	Vogler, George Joseph	1749-1814
Leclair, Jean Marie	1697-1764		

1752   Great Britain adopts new style calendar.
1755   Lisbon earthquake.
       Etna erupts.
1756   Great Britain declares war against France.
       Seven Years' War begins.
       Black Hole of Calcutta atrocity.
1759   Battle of Minden.
       Battle of Quebec.
1762   Great Britain declares war against Spain.
1763   Treaty of Peace between Great Britain, France, Spain and Portugal.
1770   Discovery of New South Wales.
1772   Treaty for partition of Poland between Austria, Prussia and Russia.
1773   Boston tea party.
1775   Battle of Lexington.
       Battle of Bunker's Hill.

PROMINENT PEOPLE

Clive, Robert, Lord	1725-1774	Marat, Jean Paul	1743-1793
Cook, Captain James	1728-1770	Marie Antoinette	1755-1793
Danton, Georges Jacques	1759-1794	Mirabeau, Gabriel,	
Hastings, Warren	1732-1818	Comte de	1749-1791
Hood, Samuel, Admiral,		Nelson, Horatio ,Viscount	1758-1805
1st Viscount	1724-1816	Wellington, Duke of	1769-1852
Jenner, Edward	1749-1823	Wilkes, John	1727-1797
Josephine, Empress	1763-1814	Wolfe, General James	1727-1759

EMPERORS OF CHINA (MANCHU (Ch'ing) DYNASTY)

Kao Tsung   1735-1795

POPES

Benedict XIV	1740-1758	Clement XIV	1769-1774
Clement XIII	1758-1769	Pius VI	1775-1799

FRANCE. HEADS OF STATE

Louis XV   1715-1774   Louis XVI   1774-1793

HOLY ROMAN EMPERORS

Francis I of Lorraine   1745-1765   Joseph II   1765-1790

ENGLAND. SOVEREIGNS

George II   1727-1760   George III   1760-1820

SWEDEN. KINGS

Frederick I	1720-1751	Gustavius III	1771-1792
Adolphus Frederick	1751-1771		

PORTUGAL. KINGS

Joseph   1750-1777

PRUSSIA. KINGS

Frederick II   1740-1786

| Elizabeth | 1741-1762 | Catherine the Great II | 1762-1796 |
| Peter III | 1762- | | |

SPAIN. SOVEREIGNS

| Ferdinand VI | 1746-1759 | Charles III | 1759-1788 |

WRITERS

Abauzit, Firmin	1679-1767	Barrington, George	
Abel, Karl Friedrich	1725-1787	(Waldren)	1755-1804
Abernethy, John	1764-1831	Barthelemy, Jean-Jacques	1716-1795
Adam, Alexander	1741-1809	Baumgarten, Alexander	
Adam, Jean	1710-1765	Gottlieb	1714-1762
Adams, Hannah	1755-1831	Beattie, James	1735-1803
Adams, John	1735-1826	Beauchamp, Alphonse De	1767-1832
Adams, John Quincy	1767-1848	Beaumarchais, Pierre	
Adanson, Michel	1725-1806	Augustin Caron De	1732-1799
Aepinus, Franz Ulrich		Beaumont, Sir George	
Theodor	1724-1802	Howland	1753-1827
Adolphus, John	1768-1845	Beccaria, Cesare,	
Aikin, John	1747-1822	Marchese De	1738-1794
Akenside, Mark	1721-1770	Beck, Christian Daniel	1757-1832
Alembert, Jean Le		Beck, Jakob Sigismund	1761-1840
Rond D'	1717-1783	Beckford, William	1760-1844
Alfireri, Vittorio, Count	1749-1803	Beechey, Sir William	1753-1839
Algarotti, Francesco,		Beffroy De Reigny, Louis	
Count	1712-1764	Abel	1757-1811
Ames, Joseph	1689-1759	Bekker, Elizabeth	1738-1804
Amory, Thomas	1691-1788	Bellman, Karl Mikael	1740-1795
Ancillon, Johann Peter		Belloy, Dormont De	1727-1775
Friedrich	1766-1836	Bentham, Jeremy	1748-1832
Anderson, John	1726-1796	Berkeley, George	1685-1753
Anderson, Robert	1750-1830	Berry, Mary	1763-1852
Andrews, James Pettit	1737-1797	Bickerstaffe, Isaac	1735-1812
Andrieux, Francois		Bignon, Louis Pierre	
Guillaume Jean		Edouard	1771-1841
Stanislas	1759-1833	Bilderijk, Willem	1756-1831
Anquetil, Louis Pierre	1723-1808	Birch, Thomas	1705-1766
Anstey, Christopher	1724-1805	Blacklock, Thomas	1721-1791
Archenholz, Johann		Blake, William	1757-1827
Wilhelm Von	1743-1812	Blamire, Susanna	1747-1794
Argens, Jean Baptiste de		Blomefield, Francis	1705-1752
Boyer, Marquis d'	1704-1771	Bloomfield, Robert	1766-1823
Armstrong, John	1709-1779	Bocage, Manvel Maria	
Arnault, Antoine Vincent	1766-1834	Barbosa De	1765-1805
Arndt, Ernst Moritz	1769-1860	Boccage, Marie Anne	
Anspach, Elizabeth		Fiquet De	1710-1802
Maravine of	1750-1828	Bodmer, Johann Jakob	1698-1783
Austen, Jane	1775-1817	Boie, Heinrich Christian	1744-1806
Azais, Pierre Hyacinthe	1766-1845	Bolingbroke, Henry	
Bachaumont, Louis Petit		St. John	1678-1751
De	1690-1771	Bolyai, Wolfgang	1775-1856
Bacsanyi, Janos	1763-1845	Bonald, Louis Gabriel	
Baggesen, Jens Immanuel	1764-1826	Ambrose	1754-1840
Baillie, Joanna	1762-1851	Bonneville, Nicholas De	1760-1828
Barbauld, Anna Letitia	1743-1825	Bonstetten, Charles	
Barker, Thomas of Bath	1769-1847	Victor De	1745-1832
Barlow, Joel	1754-1812	Boswell, James	1740-1795
Barnard, Lady Anne	1750-1825		

Botta, Carlo Guiseppe		Chesterfield, Philip Dormer	
Guglielmo	1766-1837	Stanhope (4th Earl of)	1694-1773
Bouilly, Jean-Nicolas	1763-1842	Churchill, Charles	1731-1764
Bouterwek, Friedrich	1765-1828	Cibber, Colley	1671-1757
Bowdler, Thomas		Cibber, Theophilus	1703-1758
(editor)	1754-1825	Clarke, Edward Daniel	1769-1822
Bowles, William Lisle	1762-1850	Claudius, Matthias	1740-1815
Bree, Mathias Ignatius		Clement, Francois	1714-1793
Van	1773-1839	Cobbett, William	1763-1835
Brillat-Savarin, Anthelme	1755-1826	Cockburn, Alicia	1713-1794
Brissot de Warville,		Colden, Cadwallader	1688-1776
Jacques Pierre	1754-1793	Coleman, George	1732-1794
Brooke, Henry	1703-1783	Coleridge, Samuel Taylor	1772-1834
Brorson, Hans Adolf	1694-1764	Collé, Charles	1709-1783
Brosses, Charles de	1709-1777	Collier, John	1708-1786
Brown, Charles Brockden	1771-1810	Collin, Heinrich Joseph	
Brown, John	1715-1766	Von	1771-1811
Browne, Isaac Hawkins	1705-1760	Collin D'Harleville, Jean	
Bruce, Micheal	1746-1767	Francois	1755-1806
Brucker, Johann Jakob	1696-1770	Collins, William	1721-1759
Bryant, Jacob	1715-1804	Colma, George the Elder	1732-1794
Brydges, Sir Samuel		Colman, George	1762-1836
Egerton	1762-1837	Combe, William	1741-1823
Buonafede, Appiano	1716-1793	Condorcet, Marie Jean	
Burger, Gottfried		Antoine Nicolas Caritat	
August	1747-1794	Marquis De	1743-1794
Burke, Edmund	1729-1797	Condillac, Etienne Bonnot	
Burney, Charles	1726-1814	De	1715-1780
Burney, Fanny (Madame		Constant De Rebecque,	
D'Arblay)	1752-1840	Henri Benjamin	1767-1830
Burns, Robert	1759-1796	Cooke, Thomas	1704-1756
Bury, Lady Charlotte		Correa Garcao, Pedro	
Susan Maria	1775-1861	Antonio Joaquim	1724-1772
Byrom, John	1692-1763	Cottin, Marie	1770-1807
Cadalso, Vasquez Jose	1741-1782	Courier, Paul Louis	1773-1825
Cambridge, Richard Owen	1717-1802	Cowley, Hannah	1743-1809
Campan, Jeanne Louise		Cowper, William	1731-1800
Henriette	1752-1822	Coxe, William	1747-1828
Campbell, Thomas	1777-1844	Crabbe, George	1754-1832
Carte, Thomas	1686-1754	Craufurd, Quintin	1743-1819
Carter, Elizabeth	1717-1806	Crebillon, Prosper Jolyot	
Casanova De Seingalt,		De	1674-1762
Giovanni Jacopo	1725-1798	Creevey, Thomas	1768-1838
Casti, Giovanni Battista	1724-1803	Creuzer, George Friedrich	1771-1858
Cazotte, Jacques	1719-1792	Crocker, Hannah Mather	1752-1829
Cerutti, Giuseppe	1738-1792	Croft, Sir Herbert	1751-1816
Cesarotti, Melchiore	1730-1808	Cruden, Alexander	1701-1770
Challoner, Richard	1691-1781	Crusius, Christian August	1715-1775
Chalmers, Alexander	1759-1834	Cruz E Silva, Antonio	
Chamfort, Sebastien Roch		Diniz Da	1731-1799
Nicolas	1741-1794	Cruz, Raymon De La	1731-1794
Chapone, Hester	1727-1801	Csokonai, Mihaly Vitez	1773-1805
Charriere, Isabelle De	1740-1805	Cumberland, Richard	1732-1811
Chateaubriand, Francois		Cuvier, Georges (Leopold)	1769-1832
Rene	1768-1848	Dalin, Olof Von	1708-1763
Chatterton, Thomas	1752-1770	Da Ponte, Lorenzo	1749-1838
Chenedolle, Charles Julien		Daru, Piere Antoine	
Lioult De	1769-1833	Comte	1767-1829
Chenier, Marie Andre De	1762-1794	Darwin, Erasmus	1731-1802
Chenier, Marie-Joseph		Dashkova, Catherina	
Blaise De	1764-1811	Romanovna	1744-1810

Daunov, Pierre Claude		Fabre D'Eglantine,	
Francois	1761-1840	Philippe Francois	
Day, Thomas	1748-1789	Nazaire	1755-1794
Delarue, Gervais	1751-1835	Fabroni, Angelo	1732-1803
Delille, Jacques	1738-1813	Falconer, William	1732-1769
Delolme, Jean Louis	1740-1806	Falk, Johann Daniel	1768-1826
Denina, Carlo Giovanni		Farvart, Charles Simon	1710-1792
Maria	1731-1813	Fawkes, Francis	1720-1777
Denis, Michael	1729-1800	Feith, Rhijnvis	1753-1824
Derzhavin, Gavrila		Fejer, Gyorgy	1766-1852
Romanovich	1743-1816	Ferguson, Adam	1723-1816
Desagiers, Marc Antoine		Fergusson, Robert	1750-1774
Madeleine	1772-1827	Feuerbach, Paul Johann	
Desforges, Pierre Jean		Anselm	1775-1833
Baptiste Choudard	1746-1806	Fichte, Johann Gottlieb	1762-1814
Destouches, Phillipe	1680-1754	Florian, Jean Pierre	
Dibdin, Thomas John	1771-1841	Claris De	1755-1794
Diderot, Denis	1713-1784	Fontanes, Louis	1757-1821
Diniz Da Cruz E Silva	1731-1799	Fontenelle, Bernard Le	
D'Israeli, Isaac	1766-1848	Bovier De	1657-1757
Dmitriev, Ivan Ivanovich	1760-1837	Foote, Samuel	1720-1777
Dodsley, Robert	1703-1764	Forner, Juan Pablo	1756-1797
Dorat, Claude Joseph	1734-1780	Forster, Johann George	
Drake, Nathan	1766-1836	Adam	1754-1794
Drinkwater, Betthune		Foster, John	1770-1843
John	1762-1844	Fourier, Francois Marie	
Droz, Francois-Xavier	1773-1850	Charles	1772-1837
Ducis, Jean Francois	1733-1816	Frampton, Mary	1773-1846
Dumont, Pierre Etienne		Francois De Neufchateau,	
Louis	1759-1829	Nicolas Louis	1750-1828
Dunlap, William	1766-1839	Franklin, Benjamin	1706-1790
Dupuis, Charles Francois	1742-1809	Franzen, Frans Michael	1772-1847
Durao, Jose De Santa Rita	1737-1784	Freneau, Philip Morin	1752-1832
Dutens, Louis	1730-1812	Frere, John Hookham	1769-1846
Duval, Alexandre Vincent		Fries, Jakob Friedrich	1773-1843
Pineux	1767-1842	Frugoni, Carlo Innicenzo	
Dwight, Timothy	1752-1817	Maria	1692-1768
Dyer, John	1699-1757	Gagern, Hans Christoph	
Eberhard, Christian August		Ernst	1766-1852
Gottlob	1769-1845	Galluppi, Pasquale	1770-1846
Eberhard, Johann		Garat, Dominique Joseph	1749-1833
Augustus	1739-1809	Garcia De La Huerta,	
Edgeworth, Maria	1767-1849	Vincente Antonio	1734-1787
Edgeworth, Richard Lovell	1744-1817	Gellert, Christian	
Edwards, Bryan	1743-1800	Furchtegott	1715-1769
Edwards, Jonathan	1703-1758	Genlis, Stephanie Felicité	
Egan, Pierce	1772-1849	Ducrest De St. Aubin	1746-1830
Ekhof, Konrad	1720-1778	Genovesi, Antonio	1712-1769
Elliot, Jean	1727-1805	Gerard, Alexander	1728-1795
Ellis, George	1753-1815	Gerstenberg, Heinrich	
Engel, Johann Jakob	1741-1802	Wilhelm Von	1737-1823
Epinay, Louise Florence		Gibbon, Edward	1737-1794
Petronille Tardieu		Gifford, William	1756-1826
d'esclavelles D'	1726-1783	Gilbert, Nicolas Joseph	
Erskine, Henry	1746-1817	Laurent	1751-1780
Eschenburg, Johann		Gillies, John	1747-1836
Joachim	1743-1820	Ginguene, Pierre Louis	1748-1815
Eschenmayer, Adam Karl		Gioja, Melchiorre	1767-1829
August Von	1768-1852	Giordani, Pietro	1774-1848
Escoquiz, Juan	1762-1820	Gleim, Johann Wilhelm	
Ewald, Johannes	1743-1781	Ludwig	1719-1803

M

Glover, Richard 1712-1785
Godwin, Mary
  Wollstonecraft 1759-1797
Godwin, William 1756-1836
Goethe, Johann Wolfgang
  Von 1749-1832
Goldoni, Carlo 1707-1793
Goldsmith, Oliver 1728-1774
Good, John Mason 1764-1827
Gotter, Friedrich Wilhelm 1746-1797
Gottsched, Johann
  Christoph 1700-1766
Gotz, Johann Nikolaus 1721-1781
Gozzi, Carlo 1720-1806
Grant, Anne 1755-1838
Graves, Richard 1715-1804
Gray, Thomas 1716-1771
Gresset, Jean Baptiste
  Louis 1709-1777
Grimm, Friedrich
  Melchior 1723-1807
Gyllembourg-Ehrensvard,
  Thomasine Christine 1773-1856
Hamilton, Elizabeth 1758-1816
Hagedorn, Friedrich Von 1708-1754
Hamann, Johann Georg 1730-1788
Hamilton, William 1704-1754
Hanbury, Williams,
  Sir Charles 1708-1759
Hartley, David 1705-1757
Hasted, Edward 1732-1812
Hawkesworth, John 1715-1773
Hawkins, Sir John 1719-1789
Hayley, William 1745-1820
Haywood, Eliza 1693-1756
Heeren, Arnold Hermann
  Ludwig 1760-1842
Hegel, Georg Wilhelm
  Friedrich 1770-1831
Heinse, Johann Jakob
  Wilhelm 1749-1803
Helmers, Jan Frederick 1767-1813
Helvetius, Claude Adrien 1715-1771
Hemsterhuis, Francois 1721-1790
Henault, Charles Jean
  Francois 1685-1770
Herder, Johann Gotfried
  Von 1744-1803
Hill, John 1716-1775
Hippel, Theodor Gottlieb
  Von 1741-1796
Hogg, James 1770-1835
Holbach, Paul Heinrich
  Dietrich 1723-1789
Holberg, Ludvig Holberg 1684-1754
Holcroft, Thomas 1745-1809
Holderlin, Johann
  Christian Friedrich 1770-1843
Holland, Henry 1746-1806
Holty, Ludwig Heinrich
  Cristoph 1748-1776

Home, John 1722-1808
Hontheim, Johann
  Nikolaus Von 1701-1790
Hook, James 1746-1827
Hopkinson, Francis 1737-1791
Huerta, Vincente
  Garcia de la 1730-1787
Humboldt, Friedrich
  (Baron Von) 1769-1859
Humboldt, Karl Wilhelm
  Von 1767-1835
Hume, David 1711-1776
Hurd, Richard 1720-1808
Iffland, August Wilhelm 1759-1814
Inchbald, Elizabeth 1753-1821
Iriarte, Tomas De 1750-1791
Isla, Jose Francisco De 1703-1781
Jacobi, Friedrich Heinrich 1743-1819
Jacobi, Johann Georg 1740-1814
Jakob, Ludwig Heinrich
  Von 1759-1827
Jefferson, Thomas 1743-1826
Jenyns, Soame 1704-1787
Jephson, Robert 1736-1803
Johnson, Samuel 1709-1784
Joubert, Joseph 1754-1824
Jouy, Victor Joseph
  Etienne De 1764-1846
Jovellanos, Gaspar
  Melchor De 1744-1811
Kames, Henry Home 1696-1782
Kant, Immanuel 1724-1804
Karamzin, Nicolai
  Mikhailovich 1765-1826
Karman, Jozsef 1769-1795
Kazinczy, Ferencz 1759-1831
Kellgren, Johan Henrik 1751-1795
Kelly, Hugh 1739-1777
King, Thomas 1730-1805
Kisfaludy, Sandor 1772-1844
Kleist, Ewald Christian
  Von 1715-1759
Klinger, Friedrich
  Maximilian Von 1752-1831
Klopstock, Friedrich
  Gottlieb 1724-1803
Knebel, Karl Ludwig Von 1744-1834
Knigge, Adolf Franz
  Friedrich 1752-1796
Kotzebue, August Friedrich
  Ferdinand Von 1761-1819
Krug, Wilhelm Traugott 1770-1842
Krylov, Ivan Andreevich 1768-1844
Lacepede, Bernard De
Laville, Compte De 1756-1825
La Chaussee, Pierre Claude
  Nivelle De 1692-1754
Laclos, Piere Amboise
  Francois 1741-1803
Lacretelle, Jean Charles
  Dominique de 1766-1855

Lagrange-Chancel, Francois		Maistre, Joseph De	1754-1821
Joseph	1677-1758	Maistre, Xavier De	1763-1852
La Harpe, Frederic Cesare	1754-1838	Mallet, David	1705-1765
Laing, Malcolm	1762-1818	Malthus, Thomas Robert	1766-1834
Lamarck, Jean Chevalier		Manuel, Louis Pierre	1751-1793
de	1744-1829	Marivaux, Pierre Carlet	
Lamb, Charles	1775-1834	De Chamblain De	1688-1763
Lamettrie, Julien Offray		Marmontel, Jean Francois	1723-1799
De	1709-1751	Martin, Francois Xavier	1762-1846
Landor, Walter Savage	1775-1864	Masdeu, Jean Francisco	
Langhorne, John	1735-1779	De	1744-1817
Laromiguiere, Pierre	1756-1837	Mason, William	1725-1797
Las Cases, Emmanuel		Matthisson, Friedrich Von	1761-1831
Diendonné, Compte de	1766-1842	Melendez Valdes, Juan	1754-1817
Lavater, Johann Kaspar	1741-1801	Mendelssohn, Moses	1729-1786
Law, William	1686-1761	Mercier, Sebastien	1740-1814
Laya, Jean Louis	1761-1833	Merck, Johann Heinrich	1741-1791
Lee, Harriet	1757-1851	Metastasio	1698-1782
Lee, Sophia	1750-1824	Michaud, Joseph Francois	1767-1839
Lemercier, Nepomucene	1771-1840	Michell, John	1724-1793
Lemierre, Antoine Marin	1733-1793	Mickle, William Julius	1735-1788
Lennox, Charlotte	1720-1804	Mill, James	1773-1836
Lenz, Jakob Michael		Mirabeau, Victor Riqueti	1715-1789
Reinhold	1751-1792	Mitford, William	1744-1827
Les Pinasse, Lulie De	1732-1776	Montagu, Elizabeth	1720-1800
Lessing, Gotthold Ephraim	1729-1781	Montagu, Lady Mary	
Lewis, Matthew Gregory	1775-1818	Wortley	1689-1762
Leyden, John	1775-1811	Montefiore, Joshua	1762-1843
Lichtenberg, Georg		Montesquieu, Charles	
Christoph	1742-1799	Louis De Secondat	1689-1755
Ligne, Charles Joseph	1735-1814	Montgomery, James	1771-1854
Lingard, John	1771-1851	Monti, Vincenzo	1754-1828
Linnaeus, Carl	1707-1778	Moore, Edward	1712-1757
Lista y Aragon, Alberto	1775-1848	Moore, John	1729-1802
Lodge, Edmund	1756-1839	Moratin, Leandro	
Lofft, Capel	1751-1824	Fernandez De	1760-1820
Logan, John	1748-1788	More, Hannah	1745-1833
Lomonosov, Mikhail		Morellet, Andre	1727-1819
Vasilievich	1711-1765	Moritz, Karl Philipp	1757-1793
Louvet De Couvrai, Jean		Morton, Thomas	1764-1838
Baptiste	1760-1797	Muller, Friedrich	1749-1825
Luttrel, Henry	1765-1851	Muller, Johannes Von	1752-1809
Luzan, Claramunt de		Murphy, Arthur	1727-1805
Suelves Y Gurrea		Musaus, Johann Karl	
Ignacio	1702-1754	August	1735-1787
Lyttelton, George,		Nascimento, Francisco	
1st Baron	1709-1773	Manoel De	1734-1819
Mably, Gabriel Bennet De	1709-1785	Nicholas, John	1745-1826
Macedo, Jose Agostinho		Nicholson, William	1753-1815
De	1761-1831	Nicolai, Christoph	
Mackenzie, Henry	1745-1831	Friedrich	1733-1811
Mackintosh, Sir James	1765-1832	Opie, Amelia	1769-1853
Macklin, Charles	1697-1797	Orme, Robert	1728-1801
Macpherson, James	1736-1796	Paine, Thomas	1737-1809
M'crie, Thomas	1772-1835	Paley, William	1743-1805
Madan, Martin	1726-1790	Paltock, Robert	1697-1767
Maffei, Francesco		Parini, Giuseppe	1729-1799
Scipione	1675-1755	Pepusch, Johann	
Maimon, Salomon	1754-1800	Christoph	1667-1752
Maine De Biran, Francois		Percy, Thomas	1729-1811
Pierre Gonthier	1766-1824	Pindemonte, Ippolito	1753-1828

Piozzi, Hester Lynch	1741-1821	Schlozer, August Ludwig	
Piranezi, Giambattista	1720-1778	Von	1735-1809
Piron, Alexis	1689-1773	Schubart, Christian	
Pontoppidan, Erik	1698-1764	Friedrich Daniel	1739-1791
Prevost, Antoine Francois	1697-1763	Scott, Sir Walter	1771-1832
Price, Richard	1723-1791	Sedaine, Michel Jean	1719-1797
Priestley, Joseph	1733-1804	Seguier, William	1771-1843
Proud, Robert	1728-1813	Semler, Johann Salomo	1725-1791
Pye, Henry James	1745-1813	Senac De Meilhan, Gabriel	1736-1803
Pyne, William Henry	1769-1843	Senancour, Etienne Pivert	
Quincy, Josiah	1772-1864	De	1770-1846
Quintana, Manuel José	1772-1857	Seward, Anna	1747-1809
Racine, Louis	1692-1763	Shenstone, William	1714-1763
Radcliffe, Ann	1764-1823	Sheridan, Richard	
Ramsay, Allan	1686-1758	Brinsley Butler	1751-1816
Raspe, Rudolf Erich	1737-1794	Sheridan, Thomas	1719-1788
Raynal, Guillaume		Sherwood, Mary Martha	1775-1851
Thomas Francois	1713-1796	Shiels, Robert	-1753
Raynouard, Francois		Sismondi, Jean Charles	
Juste Marie	1761-1836	Leonard Simonde	1773-1842
Reeve, Clara	1729-1807	Smart, Christopher	1722-1771
Reid, Thomas	1710-1796	Smith, Adam	1723-1790
Reimarus, Hermann		Smith, Charlotte	1749-1806
Samuel	1694-1768	Smith, James	1775-1839
Restif, Nicolas Edme	1734-1806	Smith, John Stafford	1750-1836
Richardson, Samuel	1689-1761	Smith, Sidney	1771-1845
Richmond, Legh	1772-1827	Smollett, Tobias George	1721-1771
Richter, Johann Paul		Southey, Robert	1774-1843
Friedrich	1763-1825	Souza-Botelho, Adelaide	
Rivarol, Antoine De	1753-1801	Filleul	1761-1836
Robertson, William	1721-1793	Spence, Joseph	1699-1768
Rogers, Samuel	1763-1855	Stael, Madame De	1766-1817
Roscoe, William	1753-1831	Steffens, Henrik	1773-1845
Rouget De Lisle, Claude		Sterne, Laurence	1713-1768
Joseph	1760-1836	Stewart, Dugald	1753-1828
Rousseau, Jean Jacques	1712-1778	Stilling, Heinrich	1740-1817
Royer-Collard, Pierre		Stillingfleet, Benjamin	1702-1771
Paul	1763-1845	Stolberg, Friedrich	
Rulhiere, Claude		Leopold	1750-1819
Carloman De	1735-1791	Struensee, Johan	1737-1772
Russell, Thomas	1762-1788	Strutt, Joseph	1742-1802
Sade, Donatien Alphonse		Swedenborg, Emanuel	1688-1772
Francois, Marquis De	1740-1814	Tannahill, Robert	1774-1810
Saint-Lambert, Jean		Taylor, William	1765-1836
Francois De	1716-1803	Tieck, Johann Ludwig	1773-1853
Saint-Mattin, Louis		Torres Y Villaroel,	
Claude De	1743-1803	Diego De	1696-1759
Saint-Pierre, Bernardin De	1737-1814	Trumbull, John	1750-1831
Saint-Simon, Louis De		Turner, Sharon	1768-1847
Rouvroy	1675-1755	Uz, Johann Peter	1720-1796
Salomon, Johann Peter	1745-1815	Volney, Constantin	
Savage, Richard	1743-	Francois Chasseboeuf	
Schelling, Friedrich		Compte de	1757-1820
Wilhelm Joseph Von	1775-1854	Voltaire, Francois Marie	
Schiller, Johann Cristoph		Arouet De	1694-1778
Friedrich Von	1759-1805	Voss, Johann Heinrich	1751-1826
Schlegel, August		Wackenroder, Wilhelm	
Wilhelm Von	1767-1845	Heinrich	1773-1798
Schlegel, Friedrich Von	1772-1829	Walker, John	1732-1807
Schleiermacher, Friedrich		Walpole, Horace	1717-1797
Daniel Ernst	1768-1834	Warton, Joseph	1722-1800

Warton, Thomas	1728-1790	Wolcott, John	
Washington, George	1732-1799	(Peter Pinder)	1738-1819
Webster, Noah	1758-1843	Wollaston, William Hyde	1766-1828
Werner, Zacharias	1768-1823	Wordsworth, Dorothy	1771-1855
Wesley, John	1703-1791	Wordsworth, William	1770-1850
West, Benjamin	1738-1820	Wraxall, Sir Nathaniel	
White, Gilbert	1720-1793	William	1751-1831
Whitehead, Paul	1710-1774	Young, Arthur	1741-1820
Whitehead, William	1715-1785	Young, Edward	1683-1765
Wieland, Christoph		Zimmerman, Johan Georg	
Martin	1733-1813	Ritter Van	1728-1795
Wilberforce, William	1759-1833	Zinzendorf, Nicolaus	
Wilson, Alexander	1766-1813	Ludwig Graf Von	1700-1760
Wirt, William	1772-1834	Zschokke, Johann	
		Heinrich Daniel	1771-1848

ARTISTS

Abilgaard, Nicolaj		Canaletto, Bernardo	
Abraham	1744-1809	Balleto	1720-1780
Adam, James	1730-1794	Canova, Antonio	1757-1822
Adam, Robert	1728-1792	Carriera, Rosalba	1675-1757
Allan, David	1744-1796	Carstens, Armus Jacob	1754-1798
Allou, Gilles	1670-1751	Casanova De Seingalt,	
Alvarez, Don Emanuel	1727-1797	Francois	1727-1805
Alvarez, Don Jose	1768-1827	Casanova De Seingalt,	
Appiani, Andrea	1754-1817	Giovanni Battista	1728-1795
Bacon, John	1740-1799	Catlin, George	1796-1872
Baltard, Louis Pierre	1764-1846	Chambers, Sir William	1726-1796
Banks, Thomas	1735-1805	Chardin, Jean Baptiste	
Barker, Robert	1739-1806	Simeon	1699-1779
Baroni, Pompeo		Chippendale, Thomas	
Girolamo	1708-1787	(cabinet maker)	1718-1779
Barry, James	1741-1806	Chodowiecki, Daniel	
Bartolini, Lorenzo	1777-1850	Nicolas	1726-1801
Bartolozzi, Francesco	1727-1815	Cipriani, Giovanni Batista	1727-1785
Bewick, Thomas	1753-1828	Cleveland, John	1747-1786
Bird, Edward	1772-1819	Cleveland, Robert	1747-1809
Blondel, Jacques Francois	1705-1774	Copley, John Singleton	1737-1815
Bone, Henry	1755-1834	Corbould, Richard	1757-1831
Bonomi, Giuseppe	1739-1808	Cosway, Richard	1742-1821
Bosio, Francois Joseph		Coypel, Charles Antoine	1694-1752
Baron	1769-1845	Cozens, John Robert	1752-1797
Bouchardon, Edme	1698-1762	Cressent, Charles	1685-1768
Boucher, Francois	1703-1770	Crome, John	1768-1821
Boydell, John	1719-1809	Cuvilles, Francois De	1698-1767
Briseux, Charles Etienne	1680-1754	Damer, Anne Seymour	1749-1828
Brown, Lancelot		Dance, George	1741-1825
("Capability")		Daniell, Samuel	1775-1811
landscape gardener	1715-1783	Daniell, Thomas	1749-1840
Bulfinch, Charles	1763-1844	Daniell, William	1769-1837
Burlington, Richard		Dannecker, Johann	
Boyle, 3rd Earl of	1695-1753	Heinrich Von	1758-1841
Caffieri, Jacques	1678-1755	David, Jacques Louis	1748-1825
Cagnola, Luigi	1762-1833	De Loutherbourg, Philip	
Camuccini, Vincenzo	1773-1844	James	1740-1812
Camus De Mesieres,		Denon, Dominique Vivant	1747-1825
Nicolas De	1721-1789	Desmoulins, Camille	1760-1794
Canaletto	1697-1768	Dietrich, Christian	
		Wilhelm Ernst	1712-1774

Downman, John	1750-1824	Liotard, Jean Etienne	1702-1789
Doyen, Gabriel Francois	1726-1806	Longhi, Pietro	1702-1785
Drouais, Jean Germain	1763-1788	Manwaring, Robert	
Dumont, Francois	1751-1831	(cabinet maker)	1760-
Earlom, Richard	1743-1822	Mena, Pedro De	1693-
Engleheart, George	1752-1829	Mengs, Antony Raphael	1728-1779
Exshaw, Charles	-1771	Michel, Claude	1738-1814
Falconet, Ettienne		Morland, George	1763-1804
Maurice	1716-1791	Motte, William de la	1775-1863
Farington, Joseph	1747-1821	Nash, John	1752-1835
Fiorillo, Johann		Nash, Richard	1674-1762
Dominicus	1748-1821	Nasmyth, Alexander	1758-1840
Flaxman, John	1755-1826	Nattier, Jean Marc	1685-1766
Flitcroft, Henry	1679-1769	Neumann, Balthazar	1687-1753
Fontaine, Pierre Francois		Nollekens, Joseph	1737-1823
Leonard	1762-1853	Northcote, James	1746-1831
Fragonard, Jean Honore	1732-1806	Opie, John	1761-1807
Friedrich, Caspar David	1774-1840	Pajou, Augustin	1730-1809
Fuseli, Henry	1741-1825	Peale, Charles Willson	1741-1837
Gabriel, Jacques Ange	1698-1782	Percier, Charles	1764-1838
Gainsborough, Thomas	1727-1788	Pergolesi, Michael Angelo	1700-
Gerard, Francois	1770-1837	Pigalle, Jean Baptiste	1714-1785
Gessner, Salomon	1730-1788	Pine, Robert Edge	1730-1788
Gibbs, James	1682-1754	Plimer, Andrew	1763-1837
Gillray, James	1757-1815	Porter, Robert Ker	1775-1842
Girodet De Roussy, Anne		Prud'hon, Pierre	1758-1823
Louis	1767-1824	Raeburn, Sir Henry	1756-1823
Girtin, Thomas	1775-1802	Ramsay, Allan	1713-1784
Goya Y Lucientes,		Reynolds, Sir Joshua	1723-1792
Francisco	1746-1828	Robert, Hubert	1733-1808
Granet, Francois Marius	1775-1849	Romney, George	1734-1802
Greuze, Jean Baptiste	1725-1805	Rousseau, De La Rottiere	
Gros, Antoine Jean	1771-1835	Jean Simeon	1747-
Guardi, Francesco	1712-1793	Roubillac, Louis Francois	1695-1762
Guerin, Pierre Narcisse	1774-1833	Rowlandson, Thomas	1756-1827
Hansen, Christian		Rysbrack, Michael	1693-1770
Frederik	1756-1845	Sandby, Paul	1725-1809
Heaphy, Thomas	1775-1835	Schadow, Johann Gottfried	1764-1850
Hepplewhite, George		Scheemakers, Pieter	1691-1770
(cabinet maker)	-1786	Shee, Sir Martin Archer	1769-1850
Highmore, Joseph	1692-1780	Sheraton, Thomas (cabinet	
Hogarth, William	1697-1764	maker)	1751-1806
Hokusai, Katsushika	1760-1849	Smart, John	1740-1811
Hoppner, John	1758-1810	Smith, John Raphael	1752-1812
Houdon, Jean Antoine	1740-1828	Soane, Sir John	1753-1837
Humphrey, Ozias	1742-1810	Soufflot, Jacques Germain	1709-1780
Ince, William (cabinet		Sowerby, James	1757-1822
maker)	1762-	Stothard, Thomas	1755-1834
Isabey, Jean Baptiste	1767-1855	Stuart, Gilbert	1755-1828
Kauffmann, Angelica	1741-1807	Stuart, James	1713-1788
La Grenee, Jean Louis		Thorvaldsen, Bertol	1770-1844
Francois	1742-1805	Tiepolo, Giovanni Battista	1692-1769
La Tour, Maurice		Towne, Francis	1739-1816
Quentin De	1704-1788	Trumbull, John	1756-1843
Lawrence, Sir Thomas	1769-1830	Turner, Joseph Mallord	
Le Brun, Marie Elizabeth		William	1775-1851
Louise	1755-1842	Utamaro	1754-1806
Lejeune, Louis Francois	1775-1848	Vangoyen, Jan Josephzoon	1696-1756
Lemoyne, Jean Baptiste	1704-1778	Vanloo, Charles Andrew	1705-1765
L'Enfant, Pierre Charles	1754-1835	Vernet, Antoine Charles	
Limborch, Hendrick Van	1680-1758	Horace	1758-1835

Vernet, Claude Joseph	1714-1789	Wood, John	1705-1754
Vigee-Lebrun, Marie		Wright, Joseph	1734-1797
Anne Elizabeth	1755-1842	Wyatt, James	1746-1813
Wedgewood, Josiah		Zoffany, Johann	1733-1810
(potter)	1730-1795	Zuccarelli, Francesco	1702-1786
Westmacott, Sir Richard	1775-1856	Zucchi, Antonio Pietro	1726-1795
Wilson, Richard	1714-1782		

COMPOSERS

Albrechtberger, Johann		Gluck, Christoph	
Gregory	1736-1809	Willibald	1714-1787
Arne, Thomas Augustine	1710-1778	Gossec, Francois Joseph	1734-1829
Arnold, Samuel	1740-1802	Gow, Niel	1727-1807
Asioli, Bonifacio	1769-1832	Graun, Karl Heinrich	1701-1759
Astorga, Emannuele		Greene, Maurice	1695-1755
Gioacchino	1680-1755	Gretry, Andre Ernest	
Attwood, Thomas	1765-1838	Modeste	1741-1813
Avison, Charles	1710-1770	Handel, George Frederick	1685-1759
Bach, Johann Christian	1735-1782	Hasse, Johann Adolph	1699-1783
Bach, Karl Philipp		Haydn, Franz Joseph	1732-1809
Emanuel	1714-1788	Haydn, Michael	1737-1806
Bach, Wilhelm		Hiller, Johann Adam	1728-1804
Friedemann	1710-1784	Himmel, Frederick Henry	1765-1814
Baini, Guiseppe	1775-1844	Jackson, Wilhelm	1730-1803
Barsanti, Francesco	1690-1775	Jommelli, Niccolo	1714-1774
Batishill, Jonathan	1738-1801	Kelly, Michael	1762-1826
Beethoven, Ludwig Van	1770-1827	Leclair, Jean Marie	1697-1764
Benda, Georg	1722-1795	Lesueur, Jean Francois	1760-1837
Boccherini, Luigi	1743-1805	Linley, Thomas	1732-1795
Boieldieu, Francois		Logroscino, Nicola	1700-1763
Adrien	1775-1834	Lucchesi, Andrea	1741-1800
Bononcini, Giovanni		Mattheson, Johann	1681-1764
Baptista	1670-1755	Mehul, Etienne Nicolas	1763-1817
Boyce, William	1710-1779	Monsigny, Pierre	
Callcott, John Wall	1766-1821	Alexandre	1729-1817
Cambini, Giovanni		Mozart, Wolfgang	
Giuseppe	1746-1825	Amadeus	1756-1791
Campenhout, Francois		Nardini, Pietro	1722-1793
Von	1779-1849	Nares, James	1715-1783
Cannabich, Christian	1731-1798	Paer, Ferdinando	1771-1839
Cherubini, Maria Luigi	1760-1842	Paisiello, Giovanni	1741-1816
Cimarosa, Domenico	1749-1801	Philidor, Francois Andre	
Clementi, Muzio	1752-1832	Danican	1726-1795
Corri, Domenico	1746-1825	Piccinni, Niccola	1728-1800
Crotch, William	1775-1847	Pleyel, Ignaz Joseph	1757-1831
Daquin, Louis Claude	1694-1772	Porpora, Niccola Antonio	1686-1767
Dibdin, Charles	1745-1814	Quantz, Johann Joachim	1697-1773
Dittersdorf, Karl Ditters		Rameau, Jean Philippe	1683-1764
Von	1739-1799	Roman, Johan Helmich	1694-1758
Durante, Francesco	1684-1755	Sacchini, Antonio Maria	1734-1786
Dussek, Jan Ladislav	1761-1812	Salieri, Antonio	1750-1825
Eberlin, Johann Ernst	1702-1762	Sarti, Giuseppe	1729-1802
Eberwein, Traugott		Scarlatti, Guiseppe	
Maximilian	1775-1831	Domenico	1685-1757
Fasch, Johann Friedrich	1688-1758	Schobert, Johann	1720-1767
Galuppi, Baldassare	1706-1785	Shield, William	1748-1829
Garcia, Manoel	1775-1832	Spontini, Gasparo Luigi	1774-1851
Gazzaniga, Giuseppe	1743-1818	Stamitz, Carl Philipp	1745-1801
Giordanni, Giuseppe	1744-1798	Stamitz, Johann	1717-1757

Stanley, John	1713-1786	Viotti, Giovanni Battista	1753-1824
Steibelt, Daniel	1764-1823	Vogler, Georg Joseph	1749-1814
Storace, Stephen	1763-1796	Wesley, Samuel	1766-1837
Tartini, Giuseppe	1692-1770	Zingarelli, Niccolo	1752-1837
Telemann, Georg Philipp	1681-1767		

1776　Declaration of American Independence.
　　　Battle of Trenton.
1777　Battle of Brandy Wine.
　　　Battle or Germantown.
1778　France declares war against Great Britain.
1779　Spain declares war against England.
1780　Gordon riots in London.
1783　Peace established between England and U.S.
　　　France and Spain agree on terms of peace.
1788　" Times " first published.
1789　Mutiny of the Bounty.
　　　French revolution begins. Bastille destroyed.
1791　New French constitution adopted by National Assembly.
1793　Reign of terror starts in France.　　Marat assassinated.
　　　Marie Antoinette executed.
1794　Danton executed. End of reign of terror.
1796　Battle of Lodi.
　　　Spain declares war on England.
　　　Battle of Arcola.
1797　Battle of Rivoli.
　　　Vaccination introduced.
1798　Battle of the Pyramids.
　　　Battle of the Nile.
　　　Rebellion in Ireland.
1799　Battle of Aboukir.
　　　Income Tax.
1800　Battle of Marengo.
　　　Battle of Hohenlinden.

PROMINENT PEOPLE

Beau Brummell, George Bryan	1778-1840	Josephine, Empress	1763-1814
Danton, Georges Jacques	1759-1794	Marat, Jean Paul	1743-1793
Emmett, Robert	1778-1803	Marie Antoinette	1755-1793
Faraday, Michael	1791-1867	Mirabeau, Gabriel, Comte de	1749-1791
Hastings, Warren	1732-1818	Nelson, Horatio, Viscount	1758-1805
Hood, Samuel, 1st Viscount, Admiral	1724-1816	Paganini, Nicolo	1782-1840
Jenner, Edward	1749-1823	Wellington, Duke of	1769-1852

EMPERORS OF CHINA (MANCHU (Ch'ing) DYNASTY)

Kao Tsung	1735-1795	Jen Tsung	1795-1820

POPES

Pius VI	1775-1799	Pius VII	1800-1823

FRANCE. HEADS OF STATE

Louis XVI	1774-1793	The Directors	1795-1799
Robespierre	1792-1794	The Consulate	1799-1804

HOLY ROMAN EMPERORS

Joseph II	1765-1790	Francis II	1792-1806
Leopold II	1790-1792		

George III	1760-1820		

SWEDEN. KINGS

Gustavius III	1771-1792	Gustavius IV	1792-1809

PORTUGAL. KINGS

Joseph	1750-1777	Maria I	1777-1816
Pedro III	1777-1786		

PRUSSIA. KINGS

Frederick II	1740-1786	Frederick William III	1797-1840
Frederick William II	1786-1797		

RUSSIA. TSARS

Catherine the Great II	1762-1796	Paul	1796-1801

SPAIN. SOVEREIGNS

Charles III	1759-1788	Charles IV	1788-1808

U.S.A. PRESIDENTS

George Washington	1789-1797	John Adam	1797-1801

WRITERS

Abel, Karl Friedrich	1725-1787
Abernethy, John	1764-1831
Adam, Alexander	1741-1809
Adams, Hannah	1755-1831
Adams, John	1735-1826
Adams, John Quincy	1767-1848
Adanson, Michel	1727-1806
Adolphus, John	1768-1845
Adolphus, John Leycester	1795-1862
Aepinus, Franz Ulrich Theodor	1724-1802
Afzelius, Aruid August	1785-1871
Aikin, John	1747-1822
Aikin, Lucy	1781-1864
Ainslie, Hew	1792-1878
Aksakov, Sergei Timofeyevich	1791-1859
Alaman, Lucas	1792-1853
Alcott, Amos Bronson	1799-1888
Alembert, Jean Le Rond D'	1717-1783
Alexis, Willibald	1798-1871
Alfireri, Vittorio, Count	1749-1803
Alison, Sir Archibald	1792-1867
Almeida-Garrett, Joao Battista da	1799-1854
Almqvist, Karl Jonas Ludwig	1793-1866
Amory, Thomas	1691-1788

Ancelot, Jacques Arsene Francois Polycarpe	1794-1854
Ancillon, Johann Peter Friedrich	1766-1836
Anderson, John	1726-1796
Anderson, Robert	1750-1830
Andrews, James Pettit	1737-1797
Andrieux, Francois Guillaume Jean Stanislas	1759-1833
Anspach, Elizabeth, Margravine of	1750-1828
Anquetil, Louis Pierre	1723-1808
Anstey, Christopher	1724-1805
Apperley, Charles James (Nimrod)	1777-1843
Arago, Jacques Etienne Victor	1790-1855
Archenholz, Johann Wilhelm Von	1743-1812
Argens, Jean Baptiste De Boyer, Marquis D'	1704-1771
Aribau, Bonaventura Carles	1795-1862
Armstrong, John	1709-1779
Arnault, Antoine-Vincent	1766-1834
Arndt, Ernst Moritz	1769-1860
Arnim, Elizabeth (Bettina) Von	1785-1859

Arnim, Ludwig Achim Von	1781-1831
Arnold, Thomas	1795-1842
Atkinson, Thomas Witlam	1799-1861
Austen, Jane	1775-1817
Austin, Sarah	1793-1867
Azais, Pierre Hyacinthe	1766-1845
Azeglio, Massimo Taparelli, Marquis D'	1798-1866
Bacsanyi, Janos	1763-1845
Baggesen, Jens Immanuel	1764-1826
Bahr, Johann Christian Felix	1798-1872
Bailey, Samuel	1791-1870
Ballanche, Pierre Simon	1776-1847
Baillie, Joanna	1762-1851
Balbo, Cesare, Count	1789-1853
Balzac, Honore De	1799-1850
Banim, John	1798-1842
Barante, Amable Guillaume Propser Brugiere	1782-1866
Barker, Thomas of Bath	1769-1847
Barlow, Joel	1754-1812
Barlow, Peter	1776-1862
Barnard, Lady Anne	1750-1825
Barnes, William	1800-1886
Barrington, George (Waldren)	1755-1804
Barthelemy, Auguste Marseille	1796-1867
Barthelemy, Jean-Jacques	1716-1795
Barton, Bernard	1784-1849
Basevi, George	1794-1845
Baudissin, Wolf Heinrich	1789-1878
Batyushkov, Konstantin Nikolaievitch	1787-1855
Baumgarten, Alexander Gottlieb	1714-1762
Bautain, Louis Eugene Marie	1796-1867
Bayly, Thomas Haynes	1797-1839
Beattie, James	1735-1803
Beauchamp, Alphonse De	1767-1832
Beaufort, Louis De	-1795
Beaumarchais, Pierre Augustin Caron De	1732-1799
Beaumont, Sir George Howland	1753-1827
Beccaria, Cesare, Marchese De	1738-1794
Beck, Christian Daniel	1757-1832
Beck, Jakob Sigismund	1761-1840
Beckford, William	1760-1844
Beechey, Sir William	1753-1839
Beffroy, De Reigny Louis Abel	1757-1811
Bekker, Elizabeth	1738-1804
Belli, Giuseppe Gioachino	1791-1863
Bellman, Karl Mikael	1740-1795
Beneke, Friedrich Edouard	1798-1856
Bentham, Jeremy	1748-1832

Beranger, Pierre Jean De	1780-1857
Berard, Joseph Frederic	1789-1828
Berchet, Giovanni	1783-1851
Berry, Mary	1763-1852
Berzsenyi, Daniel	1776-1836
Beskow, Bernhard Von	1796-1868
Bibaud, Michel	1782-1857
Bickerstaffe, Isaac	1735-1812
Bignon, Louis Pierre Edouard	1771-1841
Bilderdijk, Willem	1756-1831
Bissen, Herman Vilhelm	1798-1868
Bitzius, Albrecht	1797-1854
Blacklock, Thomas	1721-1791
Blake, William	1757-1827
Blamire, Susanna	1747-1794
Blessington, Marguerite	1789-1849
Blicher, Steen Steensen	1782-1848
Bloomfield, Robert	1766-1823
Blore, Edward	1787-1879
Bocage, Manuel Maria Barbosa De	1765-1805
Boccage, Marie Anne Fiquet de	1710-1802
Bodmer, Johann Jakob	1698-1783
Boerne, Karl Ludwig	1786-1837
Boie, Heinrich Christian	1744-1806
Bolyai, Wolfgang	1775-1856
Bonald, Louis Gabriel Ambroise	1754-1840
Bonneville, Nicholas de	1760-1828
Bonstetten, Charles Victor De	1745-1832
Borne, Ludwig	1786-1837
Bostrom, Christoffer Jacob	1797-1866
Boswell, James	1740-1795
Botta, Carlo Guiseppe Guglielmo	1766-1837
Bouilly, Jean-Nicolas	1763-1842
Bouterwek, Friedrich	1765-1828
Bowdich, Thomas Edward	1790-1824
Bowdler, Thomas (editor)	1754-1825
Bowles, William Lisle	1762-1850
Bree, Matthias Ignatius Van	1773-1839
Brentano, Clemens	1778-1842
Breton, de Los Herreros, Manuel	1796-1873
Brillat-Savarin, Anthelme	1755-1826
Brissot de Warville, Jacques Pierre	1754-1793
Brooke, Henry	1703-1783
Brosses, Charles de	1709-1777
Broughton, John Cam Hobhouse	1786-1869
Brown, Charles Brockden	1771-1810
Brown, Thomas	1778-1820
Browne, James	1793-1841
Brunton, Mary	1778-1818

Bryant, Jacob	1715-1804	Claudius, Matthias	1740-1815
Bryant, William Cullen	1794-1878	Clausewitz, Karl Von	1780-1831
Brydges, Sir Samuel		Clement, Francois	1714-1793
Egerton	1762-1837	Cobbett, William	1763-1835
Buchez, Philippe Benjamin		Cockburn, Alicia	1713-1794
Joseph	1796-1865	Colden, Cadwallader	1688-1776
Buckingham, James Silk	1786-1855	Coleman, George	1732-1794
Bulgarin, Thaddeus	1789-1859	Coleridge, Hartley	1796-1849
Buonafede, Appiano	1716-1793	Coleridge, Samuel-Taylor	1772-1834
Burger, Gottfried August	1747-1794	Colle, Charles	1709-1783
Burke, Edmund	1729-1797	Collier, John	1708-1786
Burney, Charles	1726-1814	Collier, John Payne	1789-1883
Burney, Fanny		Collin, Heinrich Joseph	
(Madame D'Arblay)	1752-1840	Von	1771-1811
Burns, Robert	1759-1796	Collin D'Harleville, Jean	
Bury, Lady Charlotte		Francois	1755-1806
Susan Maria	1775-1861	Collins, William	1788-1847
Byron, George Gordon		Colma, George the Elder	1732-1794
Byron	1788-1824	Colman, George	1762-1836
Caballero, Fernan	1796-1877	Combe, William	1741-1823
Cadalso, Vasquez Jose	1741-1782	Comte, Auguste	1798-1857
Cambridge, Richard Owen	1717-1802	Condorcet, Marie Jean	
Campan, Jeanne Louise		Antoine Nicolas Caritat,	
Henriette	1752-1822	Marquis De	1743-1794
Campbell, Thomas	1777-1844	Condillac, Etienne Bonnot	
Canina, Luigi	1795-1856	De	1715-1780
Carleton, William	1794-1869	Constant De Rebecque,	
Carlyle, Thomas	1795-1881	Henri Benjamin	1767-1830
Carter, Elizabeth	1717-1806	Cooper, James Fenimore	1789-1851
Casanova De Seingalt,		Costello, Louisa Stuart	1799-1870
Giovanni Jacopo	1725-1798	Cottin, Marie	1770-1807
Castelli, Ignaz Franz	1781-1862	Courier, Paul Louis	1773-1825
Casti, Giovanni Battista	1724-1803	Cousin, Victor	1792-1867
Cazotte, Jacques	1719-1792	Cowley, Hannah	1743-1809
Cerutti, Giuseppe	1738-1792	Cowper, William	1731-1800
Cesarotti, Melchiore	1730-1808	Coxe, William	1747-1828
Challoner, Richard	1691-1781	Cozens, Alexander	died 1782
Chalmers, Alexander	1759-1834	Crabbe, George	1754-1832
Chalybaus, Heinrich		Craufurd, Quintin	1743-1819
Moritz	1796-1862	Creevey, Thomas	1768-1838
Chamfort, Sebastien Roch		Creuzer, George Friedrich	1771-1858
Nicolas	1741-1794	Crocker, Hannah Mather	1752-1829
Chamier, Fredrick	1796-1870	Croft, Sir Herbert	1751-1816
Chamisso, Adelbert Von	1781-1838	Croker, John Wilson	1780-1857
Channing, William		Croker, Thomas Crofton	1798-1854
Ellery	1780-1842	Crusenstolpe, Magnus	
Chapone, Hester	1727-1801	Jakob	1795-1865
Charriere, Isabelle De	1740-1805	Cruz E Silva, Antonio	
Chasles, Philarete	1798-1873	Diniz Da	1731-1799
Chateaubriand, Francois		Cruz, Raymon De La	1731-1794
Rene	1768-1848	Csokonai, Mihaly Vitez	1773-1805
Chatterton, Thomas	1752-1770	Cumberland, Richard	1732-1811
Chenedolle, Charles		Cunningham, Allan	1784-1842
Julien Lioult De	1769-1833	Cunninghame-Graham,	
Chenier, Marie Andre de	1762-1794	Robert	-1797
Chenier, Marie Joseph		Cuvier, Georges	
Blaise De	1764-1811	(Leopold)	1769-1832
Christopoulos, Athanasios	1772-1847	Da Costa, Isaak	1798-1860
Clare, John	1793-1864	Dahlgren, Karl Frederik	1791-1844
Clarke, Charles Cowden	1787-1877	Dahlmann, Friedrich	
Clarke, Edward Daniel	1769-1822	Christoph	1785-1860

Da Ponte, Lorenzo	1749-1838	Eberhard, Johann	
Darley, George	1795-1846	Augustus	1739-1809
Daru, Pierre Antoine,		Eckermann, Johann Peter	1792-1864
Comte	1767-1829	Edgeworth, Maria	1767-1849
Darwin, Erasmus	1731-1802	Edgeworth, Richard	
Dashkova, Catherina		Lovell	1744-1817
Romanovna	1744-1810	Edwards, Bryan	1743-1800
D'Aubigné, Jean Henri		Egan, Pierce	1772-1849
Merle	1794-1872	Eichendorff, Joseph	
Daunov, Pierre Claude		Freiherr Von	1788-1857
Francois	1761-1840	Ekhof, Konrad	1720-1778
David, Pierre Jean	1789-1856	Elliot, Jean	1727-1805
Day, Thomas	1748-1789	Elliott, Ebenezer	1781-1849
Delarue, Gervais	1751-1835	Ellis, George	1753-1815
Delavigne, Jean Francois		Elphinstone, Mountstuart	1779-1859
Casimir	1793-1843	Engel, Johann Carl	
Delille, Jacques	1738-1813	Ludwig	1778-1840
Delolme, Jean Louis	1740-1806	Engel, Johann Jakob	1741-1802
Delvig, Anton Antonovich,		Ennemoser, Joseph	1787-1855
Baron Von	1798-1831	Epinay, Louise Florence	
Denina, Carlo Giovanni		Petronille Tardieu	
Maria	1731-1813	D'Esclavelles D'	1726-1783
Denis, Michael	1729-1800	Erskine, Henry	1746-1817
De Quincey, Thomas	1785-1859	Erskine, Thomas	1788-1870
Derzhavin, Gavrila		Eschenburg, Johann	
Romanovich	1743-1816	Joachim	1743-1820
Desagiers, Marc Antoine		Eschenmayer, Adam Karl	
Madeleine	1772-1827	August Von	1768-1852
Desforges, Pierre Jean		Escoquiz, Juan	1762-1820
Baptiste Choudard	1746-1806	Estebanez, Caldren	
Deschamps, Emile	1791-1871	Serafin	1799-1867
Dibdin, Thomas John	1771-1841	Etienne, Charles	
Diderot, Dennis	1713-1784	Guillaume	1777-1845
Diniz Da Cruz E Silva,		Everett, Alexander Hill	1790-1847
Antonio	1731-1799	Ewald, Johannes	1743-1781
D'Israeli, Isaac	1766-1848	Fabre D'Eglantine,	
Dmitriev, Ivan Ivanovich	1760-1837	Philippe Francois	
Dollinger, Johann Joseph		Nazaire	1755-1794
Ignaz Von	1799-1890	Fabriani, Severino	1792-1849
Dorat, Claude Joseph	1734-1780	Fabroni, Angelo	1732-1803
Drake, Nathan	1766-1836	Fahlcrantz, Christian	
Drinkwater, Betthune		Erik	1790-1866
John	1762-1844	Fain, Agathon Jean	
Droste-Hulshoff, Annette		Francois	1778-1837
Elizabeth	1797-1848	Falk, Johann Daniel	1768-1826
Droz, Francois-Xavier	1773-1850	Fallmerayer, Jakob Phillip	1790-1861
Ducange, Victor Henri		Farvart, Charles Simon	1710-1792
Joseph Brahain	1783-1833	Fauriel, Claude Charles	1782-1844
Ducis, Jean Francois	1733-1816	Fawkes, Francis	1720-1777
Dumont, Pierre Etienne		Fay, Andreas	1786-1864
Louis	1759-1829	Feith, Rhijnvis	1753-1824
Dunlap, William	1766-1839	Fejer, Gyorgy	1766-1852
Dupuis, Charles Francois	1742-1809	Ferguson, Adam	1723-1816
Durao, Jose De Santa		Fergusson, Robert	1750-1774
Rita	1737-1784	Ferrier, Susan Edmonstone	1782-1854
Dutens, Louis	1730-1812	Feuerbach, Paul Johann	
Duval, Alexandre		Anselm	1775-1833
Vincent Pineux	1767-1842	Fichte, Immanuel	
Dwight, Timothy	1752-1817	Hermann Von	1796-1879
Eberhard, Christian		Fichte, Johann Gottlieb	1762-1814
August Gottlob	1769-1845		

Fielding, Anthony Van Dyke Copley	1787-1855	Gilbert, Nicolas Joseph Laurent	1751-1780
Finlay, George	1799-1875	Gillies, John	1747-1836
Fitzball, Edward	1792-1873	Ginguene, Pierre Louis	1748-1815
Florian, Jean Pierre Claris De	1755-1794	Gioja, Melchiorre	1767-1829
Foa, Eugene Rodriguez-Gradis	1798-1853	Giordani, Pietro	1774-1848
		Giraud, Giovanni	1776-1834
Follen, Adolf Ludwig	1794-1855	Gleig, George Robert	1796-1888
Follen, Karl	1795-1840	Gleim, Johann Wilhelm Ludwig	1719-1803
Fontanes, Louis	1757-1821	Glen, William	1789-1826
Foote, Samuel	1720-1777	Glinka, Fedor Nikolayevich	1788-1880
Ford, Richard	1796-1858	Glover, Richard	1712-1785
Forner, Juan Pablo	1756-1797	Godwin, Mary Wollstonecraft	1759-1797
Forster, Friedrich Christoph	1791-1868	Godwin, William	1756-1836
Forster, Johann Georg Adam	1754-1794	Goethe, Johann Wolfgang Von	1749-1832
Foscolo, Ugo	1778-1827	Goldoni, Carlo	1707-1793
Foster, John	1770-1843	Good, John Mason	1764-1827
Fouque, Friedrich Heinrich Karl De La Motte	1777-1843	Goodrich, Samuel Griswold	1793-1860
Fourier, Francois Marie Charles	1772-1837	Gore, Catherine Grace Frances	1799-1861
Frampton, Mary	1773-1846	Gorres, Joseph Von	1776-1848
Francois De Neufchateau, Nicolas Louis	1750-1828	Gotter, Friedrich Wilhelm	1746-1797
Franklin, Bejamin	1706-1790	Gotz, Johann Nikolaus	1721-1781
Franzen, Frans Michael	1772-1847	Gozzi, Carlo	1720-1806
Fraser, James Baillie	1783-1856	Grant, Anne	1755-1838
Freneau, Philip Morin	1752-1832	Graves, Richard	1715-1804
Frere, John Hookham	1769-1846	Gresset, Jean Baptiste Louis	1709-1777
Fries, Jakob Friedrich	1773-1843	Greville, Charles Cavendish Fulke	1794-1865
Froebel, Friedrich Wilhelm August	1782-1852	Griboyedov, Alexander Sergeyevich	1795-1829
Frohlich, Abraham Emanuel	1796-1865	Grimm, Friedrich Melchior	1723-1807
Frugoni, Carlo Innocenzo Maria	1692-1768	Grimm, Jacob Ludwig Carl	1785-1863
Fryxell, Anders	1795-1881	Grimm, Wilhelm Carl	1786-1859
Gagern, Hans Christoph Ernst	1766-1852	Grossi, Tommaso	1791-1853
Galluppi, Pasquale	1770-1846	Grote, George	1794-1871
Galt, John	1779-1839	Grundtvig, Nikolai Frederik Severin	1783-1872
Garat, Dominique Joseph	1749-1833	Guizot, Francois Pierre Guillaume	1787-1874
Garcia De La Huerta, Vincente Antonio	1734-1787	Gyllembourg-Eh Rensvard, Thomasine Christine	1773-1856
Garrett, Joao Baptista Da Silva Leitao De Almeida	1799-1854	Hale, Sarah Josepha	1788-1879
Geiser, Eric Gustav	1783-1877	Haliburton, Thomas Chandler	1796-1865
Genlis, Stephanie Felicite Ducrest De St. Aubin	1746-1830	Hall, Basil	1788-1844
Gerard, Alexander	1728-1795	Hallam, Henry	1777-1859
Gerstenberg, Heinrich Wilhelm Von	1737-1823	Halleck, Fitz-Green	1790-1867
Gesenius, Friedrich Heinrich Wilhelm	1786-1842	Hamilton, Elizabeth	1758-1816
Gibbon, Edward	1737-1794	Hamilton, Thomas	1789-1842
Gieseler, Johan Karl Ludwig	1792-1854	Hamilton, Sir William	1788-1856
Gifford, William	1756-1826	Hamann, Johann Georg	1730-1788
		Hardwyck, Philip	1792-1870

Haring, George Wilhelm Heinrich	1798-1871
Hasted, Edward	1732-1812
Hawkins, Sir John	1719-1789
Hazlitt, William	1778-1830
Hayley, William	1745-1820
Heeren, Arnold Hermann Ludwig	1760-1842
Hegel, Georg Wilhelm Friedrich	1770-1831
Heiberg, Johan Ludvig	1791-1860
Heine, Heinrich	1797-1856
Heinse, Johann Jakob Wilhelm	1749-1803
Helmers, Jan Frederik	1767-1813
Hemans, Dorothea Felicia	1793-1835
Hemsterhuis, Francois	1721-1790
Herbart, Johann Friedrich	1776-1841
Herder, Johann Gottfried Von	1744-1803
Hertz, Henrik	1797-1870
Hinrichs, Hermann Friedrich Wilhelm	1794-1861
Hippel, Theodor Gottlieb Von	1741-1796
Hoffman, August Heinrich	1798-1874
Hoffman, Ernst Theodor Wilhelm	1776-1822
Hogg, James	1770-1835
Hogg, Thomas Jefferson	1792-1862
Holbach, Paul Heinrich Dietrich	1723-1789
Holcroft, Thomas	1745-1809
Holderlin, Johann Christian Friedrich	1770-1843
Holland, Henry	1746-1806
Holland, Sir Henry	1788-1873
Holtei, Karl Eduard Von	1798-1880
Holty, Ludwig Heinrich Christoph	1748-1776
Home, John	1722-1808
Hone, William	1780-1842
Hontheim, Johann Nikolaus Von	1701-1790
Hood, Thomas	1799-1845
Hook, James	1746-1827
Hook, Theodore Edward	1788-1841
Hopkinson, Francis	1737-1791
Hormayr, Joseph Frerherr Von	1782-1848
Howitt, Mary	1799-1888
Howitt, William	1792-1879
Huerta, Vincente Garcia de la	1730-1787
Humboldt, Friedrich (Baron Von)	1769-1839
Humboldt, Karl Wilhelm Von	1767-1835
Hume, David	1711-1776
Hunt, James Henry Leigh	1784-1859
Hunter, Joseph	1783-1861
Hurd, Richard	1720-1808
Hyslop, James	1798-1827
Iffland, August Wilhelm	1759-1814
Immermann, Karl Leberecht	1796-1840
Inchbald, Elizabeth	1753-1821
Ingemann, Bernhard Severin	1789-1862
Ingoldsby, Thomas	1788-1845
Innes, Cosmo	1798-1874
Iriarte, Tomas De	1750-1791
Irving, Washington	1783-1859
Isla, Jose Francisco De	1703-1781
Jacobi, Friedrich Heinrich	1743-1819
Jacobi, Johann, Georg	1740-1814
Jakob, Ludwig Heinrich Von	1759-1827
James, George Payne Rainsford	1799-1860
Jameson, Anna Brownell	1794-1860
Jasmin, Jacques	1798-1864
Jefferson, Thomas	1743-1826
Jenyns, Soame	1704-1787
Jephson, Robert	1736-1803
Jesse, Edward	1780-1868
Johnson, Samuel	1709-1784
Josika, Miklos	1794-1865
Joubert, Joseph	1754-1824
Jouffroy, Theodore Simon	1796-1842
Jouy, Victor Joseph Etienne De	1764-1846
Jovellanos, Gaspar Mechor De	1744-1811
Kames, Henry Home	1696-1782
Kant, Immanuel	1724-1804
Karadzic, Viek Stefanovic	1787-1864
Karamzin, Nicolai Mikhailovich	1765-1826
Karman, Jozsef	1769-1795
Kazinczy, Ferencz	1759-1831
Keats, John	1795-1821
Keble, John	1792-1866
Keightley, Thomas	1789-1872
Kellgren, Johan Henrik	1751-1795
Kelly, Hugh	1739-1777
Kenney, James	1780-1849
Kerner, Justinus Andreas Christian	1786-1862
Key, Francis Scott	1779-1843
King, Thomas	1730-1805
Kisfaludy, Karoly	1788-1830
Kisfaludy, Sandor	1772-1844
Kleist, Heinrich Wilhelm Von	1777-1811
Klinger, Friedrich Maximilian Von	1752-1831
Klopstock, Friedrich Gottlieb	1724-1803
Knebel, Karl Ludwig Von	1744-1834

Knigge, Adolf Franz	
Friedrich	1752-1796
Knight, Charles	1791-1873
Knowles, James Sheridan	1784-1862
Kock, Charles Paul De	1793-1871
Kolcsey, Ferencz	1790-1888
Kopisch, August	1799-1853
Korner, Karl Theodor	1791-1813
Kotzebue, August Friedrich	
Ferdinand Von	1761-1819
Krause, Karl Christian	
Friedrich	1781-1832
Krug, Wilhelm Traugott	1770-1842
Kuhlau, Friedrich	1786-1832
Krylou, Ivan Andreevich	1768-1844
Lacepede, Bernard De	
Laville, Compte De	1756-1825
Laclos, Rene Amboise	
Francois	1741-1803
Laharpe, Frederic Cesar	1754-1838
Laing, Malcolm	1762-1818
Lacretelle, Jean Charles	
Dominique de	1766-1855
Lamarck, Jean Chevalier	
de	1744-1829
Lamartine, Alphonse De	1790-1869
Lamb, Charles	1775-1834
Lamennais, Hugues	
Felicite Robert De	1782-1854
Landor, Walter Savage	1775-1864
Langhorne, John	1735-1779
Lappenberg, Johann	
Martin	1794-1865
Laromibuiere, Pierre	1756-1837
Las Cases, Emmanuel	
Dieudonné, Compte de	1766-1842
Lauder, Sir Thomas Dick	1784-1848
Lavater, Johann Kaspar	1741-1801
Laya, Jean Louis	1761-1833
Lee, Harriet	1757-1851
Lee, Sophia	1750-1824
Le Mercier, Nepomuvene	1771-1840
Lemierre, Antoine Marin	1733-1793
Lennoz, Charlotte	1720-1804
Lenz, Jakob Michael	
Reinhold	1751-1792
Leo, Heinrich	1799-1878
Leopardi, Giacomo	1798-1837
Leroux, Pierre	1798-1871
Lespinasse, Julie De	1732-1776
Lessing, Gotthold Ephraim	1729-1781
Lewis, Matthew Gregory	1775-1818
Leyden, John	1775-1811
Lichtenberg, Georg	
Christoph	1742-1799
Ligne, Charles Joseph	1735-1814
Lingard, John	1771-1851
Linnieus, Carl	1707-1778
Lista Y Aragon, Alberto	1775-1848
Lyttleton, George,	
1st Baron	1709-1773

Lockhart, John Gibson	1794-1854
Lodge, Edmund	1756-1839
Lofft, Capel	1751-1824
Logan, John	1748-1788
Louvet De Couvrai, Jean	
Baptiste	1760-1797
Lover, Samuel	1797-1868
Luttrell, Henry	1765-1851
Mably, Gabriel Bennet De	1709-1785
Macedo, Jose Agostinho De	1761-1831
Mackenzie, Henry	1745-1831
Mackintosh, Sir James	1765-1832
Maclaren, Charles	1782-1866
Macpherson, James	1736-1796
Madan, Martin	1726-1790
M'Crie, Thomas	1772-1835
Maggin, William	1793-1842
Magny, Claude Drigon	1797-1879
Maine De Biran, Francois-	
Pierre Gonthier	1766-1824
Maistre, Joseph De	1754-1821
Maistre, Xavier De	1763-1852
Majlath, Janos	1786-1855
Malthus, Thomas Robert	1766-1834
Manuel, Louis Pierre	1751-1793
Manzoni, Alessandro	1785-1873
Markham, Mrs.	1780-1837
Marmontel, Jean Francois	1723-1799
Marryat, Frederick	1792-1848
Martin, Francois Xavier	1762-1846
Martin, Martin	fl.1790
Martinez De La Rosa,	
Francisco De Paula	1787-1862
Masdeu, Juan Francisco	
De	1744-1817
Mason, William	1725-1797
Matthisson, Friedrich Von	1761-1831
Maturin, Charles Robert	1782-1824
Maurer, Georg Ludwig	
Von	1790-1872
Melendez Valdes, Juan	1754-1817
Mendelsshon, Moses	1729-1786
Menzel, Wolfgang	1798-1873
Mercier, Sebastien	1740-1814
Merck, Johann Heinrich	1741-1791
Metastasio	1698-1782
Michaud, Joseph Francois	1767-1839
Michelet, Jules	1798-1874
Michell, John	1724-1793
Mickiewicz, Adam	1798-1855
Mickle, William Julius	1735-1788
Mignet, Francois Auguste	
Marie	1796-1884
Mill, James	1773-1836
Milman, Henry Hart	1791-1868
Mirabeau, Victor Riqueti	1715-1789
Mitford, John	1781-1859
Mitford, Mary Russell	1787-1855
Mitford, William	1744-1827
Moir, David Macbeth	1798-1851
Moller, Poul Martin	1794-1838

Montagu, Elizabeth	1720-1800	Prescott, William Hickling	1796-1859
Montefiore, Joshua	1762-1843	Price, Richard	1723-1791
Montgomery, James	1771-1854	Priestley, Joseph	1733-1809
Monti, Vincenzo	1754-1828	Pringle, Thomas	1789-1834
Moore, John	1729-1802	Procter, Bryan Waller	1787-1874
Moore, Thomas	1779-1852	Proud, Robert	1728-1813
Moratin, Leandro		Pushkin, Alexander	1799-1837
Fernandez De	1760-1828	Pye, Henry James	1745-1813
More, Hannah	1745-1833	Pyne, William Henry	1769-1843
Morellet, Andre	1727-1819	Quincy, Josiah	1772-1864
Morgan, Lady Sydney	1783-1859	Quintana, Manuel Jose	1772-1857
Morier, James	1780-1849	Radcliffe, Ann	1764-1823
Moritz, Karl Philipp	1757-1793	Ranke, Leopold Von	1795-1886
Morton, Thomas	1764-1838	Raspe, Rudolf Erich	1737-1794
Motherwell, William	1797-1835	Rauch, Christian Daniel	1777-1875
Muller, Friedrich	1749-1825	Raumer, Friedrich Ludwig	
Muller, Johannes Von	1752-1809	George Van	1781-1873
Muller, Wilhelm	1794-1827	Raynal, Guillaume Thomas	
Murphy, Arthur	1727-1805	Francois	1713-1796
Musaus, Johann Karl		Raynouard, Francois Juste	
August	1735-1787	Marie	1761-1836
Nairne, Carolina Oliphant	1766-1845	Reeve, Clara	1729-1807
Nascimento, Francisco		Reid, Thomas	1710-1796
Manoel De	1734-1819	Remusat, Charles Francois	
Nasmyth, Patrick	1787-1831	Marie	1797-1875
Neal, John	1793-1876	Restif, Nicolas Edme	1734-1806
Neander, Johann	1789-1850	Richmond, Legh	1772-1827
Nichols, John	1745-1826	Richter, Johann Paul	
Nicholson, William	1753-1815	Freidrich	1763-1825
Nicolai, Christoph		Ritter, Heinrich	1791-1869
Friedrich	1733-1811	Rivarol, Antoine De	1753-1801
Niebuhr, Barthold Georg	1776-1831	Rivas, Angel De Saavedra	1791-1865
Nitzsch, Karl Immanuel	1787-1868	Robertson, William	1721-1793
Nodier, Charles	1780-1844	Rogers, Samuel	1763-1855
Normanby, Constantine		Roscoe, William	1753-1831
Henry Phipps	1797-1863	Rosmini-Serbati, Antonio	1797-1855
Ohlenschlager, Adam		Rossetti, Gabriele	1783-1854
Gottlob	1779-1850	Rouget De Lisle, Claude	
Olmedo, Jose Joaquin De	1780-1847	Joseph	1760-1836
Opie, Amelia	1769-1853	Rousseau, Jean Jacques	1712-1778
Orme, Robert	1728-1801	Royer-Collard, Pierre Paul	1763-1845
Paine, Thomas	1737-1809	Rückert, Freidrich	1788-1866
Palacky, Frantisek	1798-1876	Rulhiere, Claude	
Paley, William	1743-1805	Carloman De	1735-1791
Palfrey, John Gorham	1796-1881	Russell, Thomas	1762-1788
Palgrave, Sir Francis	1788-1861	Sade, Donatien Alphonse	
Parini, Giuseppe	1729-1799	Francois, Marquis De	1740-1814
Paulding, James Kirke	1778-1860	Safarik, Pavel Joseph	1795-1861
Payne, John Howard	1791-1852	Saintine, Joseph Xavier	1798-1865
Peacock, Thomas Love	1785-1866	Saint-Lambert, Jean	
Pellico, Silvio	1788-1854	Francois De	1716-1803
Percival, James Gates	1795-1856	Saint-Martin, Louis	
Percy, Thomas	1729-1811	Claude De	1743-1803
Pertz, Georg Heinrich	1795-1876	Saint-Pierre, Bernadin De	1737-1814
Picken, Andrew	1788-1833	Salomon, Johann Peter	1745-1815
Pindemonte, Ippolito	1753-1828	Schelling, Friedrich	
Piozzi, Hester Lynch	1741-1821	Wilhelm Joseph Von	1775-1854
Piranesi, Giambattista	1720-1778	Schiller, Johann Cristoph	
Planche, James Robinson	1796-1880	Friedrich Von	1759-1805
Porter, Anna Maria	1780-1832	Schimmelpenninck, Mary	
Porter, Jane	1776-1850	Ann	1778-1856

N

Schlegel, August Wilhelm Von	1767-1845
Schlegel, Friedrich Von	1772-1829
Schleiermacher, Friedrich Daniel Ernst	1768-1834
Schlozer, August Ludwig Von	1735-1809
Schopenhaur, Arthur	1788-1860
Schubart, Christian Friedrich Daniel	1739-1791
Scott, Sir Walter	1771-1832
Scribe, Eugene	1791-1861
Sedaine, Michel Jean	1719-1797
Seguir, William	1771-1843
Segur, Philippe Paul, Comte De	1780-1873
Semler, Johann, Salomo	1725-1791
Senac De Meilhan, Gabriel	1736-1803
Senancour, Etienne Pivert De	1770-1846
Seward, Anna	1747-1809
Sheil, Richard Lalor	1791-1851
Shelley, Mary Wollstonecraft	1797-1851
Shelley, Percy Bysshe	1792-1822
Sheridan, Richard Brinsley Butler	1751-1816
Sheridan, Thomas	1719-1788
Sherwood, Mary Martha	1775-1851
Sigourney, Lydia Huntley	1791-1865
Sismondi, Jean Charles Leonard Simonde	1773-1842
Smith, Adam	1723-1790
Smith, Charlotte	1749-1806
Smith, Horace	1779-1849
Smith, James	1775-1839
Smith, John Stafford	1750-1836
Smith, Sydney	1771-1845
Southey, Robert	1774-1843
Souza-Botelo, Adelaide Filleul	1761-1836
Sparks, Jared	1789-1866
Stael, Madame De	1766-1817
Steffens, Henrik	1773-1845
Stendhal, Marie Henry Beyle	1783-1842
Stewart, Dugald	1753-1828
Stilling, Heinrich	1740-1817
Stolberg, Friedrich Leopold	1750-1819
Struensee, Johan Frederick	1737-1772
Strutt, Joseph	1742-1802
Swetchine, Madame	1782-1857
Talfourd, Sir Thomas Noon	1795-1854
Tannahill, Robert	1774-1810
Taylor, Ann	1782-1866
Taylor, Isaak	1787-1865
Taylor, Jane	1783-1824
Taylor, William	1765-1836
Tegner, Essaias	1782-1846
Tennant, William	1784-1848

Thierry, Jacques Nicolas Augustin	1795-1856
Thiers, Louis Adolph	1797-1877
Thirlwall, Connop	1797-1875
Thompson, William c.	1785-1833
Ticknor, George	1791-1871
Tieck, Johann Ludwig	1773-1853
Topffer, Rodolphe	1799-1846
Toreno, Jose Maria Queipo De Llano	1786-1843
Trelawny, Edward John	1792-1881
Trollope, Frances	1780-1863
Trumbull, John	1750-1831
Turner, Sharon	1768-1847
Uhland, Johann Ludwig	1787-1862
Uz, Johann Peter	1720-1796
Varnhagen Von Ense, Karl August	1785-1858
Verplanck, Gulian Crommelin	1786-1870
Vigny, Alfred De	1797-1863
Villemain, Abel Francois	1790-1870
Volney, Constantin Francois Chasseboeuf, Compte De	1757-1820
Voltaire, Francois Marie Arouet De	1694-1778
Voss, Johann Heinrich	1751-1826
Waagen, Gustav Friedrich	1794-1868
Wackenroder, Wilhelm Heinrich	1773-1798
Walker, John	1732-1807
Walker, Thomas	1784-1836
Walpole, Horace	1717-1797
Warton, Joseph	1722-1800
Warton, Thomas	1728-1790
Washington, George	1732-1799
Webster, Noah	1758-1843
Wells, Charles Jeremiah	1798-1879
Werner, Zacharias	1768-1823
Wesley, John	1703-1791
West, Benjamin	1738-1820
Whately, Richard	1787-1863
Whewell, William	1794-1866
White, Gilbert	1720-1793
White, Henry Kirke	1785-1806
Whitehead, Paul	1710-1774
Whitehead, William	1715-1785
Wieland, Christoph Martin	1733-1813
Wilberforce, William	1759-1833
Wilson, Alexander	1766-1813
Wilson, John	1785-1854
Winther, Christian	1796-1876
Wirt, William	1772-1834
Wolcot, John (Peter Pindar)	1738-1819
Wolfe, Charles	1791-1823
Wollaston, William Hyde	1766-1828
Wordsworth, Dorothy	1771-1855
Wordsworth, William	1770-1850
Wraxall, Sir Nathaniel William	1751-1831

Wyss, Johann	1781-1830	Zimmermann, Johan Georg	
Young, Arthur	1741-1820	Ritter Von	1728-1795
Zhukovsky, Vasili		Zschokke, Johann Heinrick	
Andreyevich	1783-1852	Daniel	1771-1848

ARTISTS

Abildgaard, Nicolaj		Chambers, Sir William	1726-1796
Abraham	1744-1809	Chantrey, Sir Francis	
Adam, James	1730-1794	Legatt	1781-1841
Adam, Robert	1728-1792	Chardin, Jean Baptiste	
Allan, David	1744-1796	Simeon	1699-1779
Allan, Sir William	1782-1850	Charlet, Nicolas Toussaint	1792-1845
Allston, Washington	1779-1843	Chippendale, Thomas	
Alvarez, Don Jose	1768-1827	(cabinet maker)	1718-1779
Alvarez, Don Manuel	1727-1797	Chisholm, Alexander	1792-1847
Appiani, Andrea	1754-1817	Chodowiecki, Daniel	
Audubon, John James	1785-1851	Nicolas	1726-1801
Bacon, John	1740-1799	Cipriani, Giovanni Bastista	1727-1785
Baily, Edward Hodges	1788-1867	Cleveland, John	1747-1786
Baltard, Louis Pierre	1764-1846	Cleveland, Robert	1747-1809
Banks, Thomas	1735-1805	Cockerell, Charles Robert	1788-1863
Barker, Robert	1739-1806	Constable, John	1776-1837
Barry, Sir Charles	1795-1860	Cooper, Abraham	1787-1868
Barry, James	1741-1806	Corbould, Richard	1757-1831
Bartolini, Lorenzo	1777-1850	Cornelius, Peter Von	1783-1867
Bartolozzi, Francesco	1727-1815	Corot, Jean-Baptiste	
Barye, Antoine Louis	1796-1875	Camille	1796-1875
Batoni, Pompeo Girolamo	1708-1787	Cosway, Richard	1742-1821
Begas, Karl	1794-1854	Cotman, John Sell	1782-1842
Bewick, Thomas	1753-1828	Cox, David	1783-1859
Bird, Edward	1772-1819	Cozens, Alexander	d. 1782
Bone, Henry	1755-1834	Cozens, John Robert	1752-1797
Bonomi, Giuseppe	1739-1808	Crome, John	1768-1821
Bosio, Francois Joseph,		Cruikshank, George	1792-1878
Baron	1769-1845	Daguerre, Louis Jacques	
Bossi, Giuseppe	1777-1816	Mande	1789-1851
Boydell, John	1719-1804	Dahl, Johann Kristen	
Brown, Lancelot		Clausen	1788-1857
(" Capability ") (land-		Damer, Anne Seymour	1749-1828
scape gardener)	1715-1783	Danby, Francis	1793-1861
Bulfinch, Charles	1763-1844	Dance, George	1741-1825
Burn, William	1789-1870	Daniell, Samuel	1775-1811
Bystrom, Johan Niklas	1783-1848	Daniell, Thomas	1749-1840
Cagnola, Luigi	1762-1833	Daniell, William	1769-1837
Callcott, Sir Augustus Wall	1779-1844	Dannecker, Johann	
Calvert, Charles	1785-1852	Heinrich Von	1758-1841
Calvert, Edward	1799-1883	Dantan, Antoine Laurent	1798-1878
Camuccini, Vincenzo	1773-1844	Darly, Matthew	-1781
Camus De Mezieres,		David, Jacques Louis	1748-1825
Nicolas Le	1721-1789	Delacroix, Ferdinand	
Canaletto, Bernardo		Victor Eugene	1798-1863
Belleto	1720-1780	Delaroche, Hippolyte	1797-1856
Canova, Antonio	1757-1822	De Loutherbourg, Philip	
Carstens, Armus Jacob	1754-1798	James	1740-1812
Casanova De Seingalt,		Denon, Dominique Vivant,	
Francesco	1727-1805	Baron de	1747-1825
Casanova De Seingalt,		Des Moulins, Camillo	1760-1794
Giovanni Battista	1728-1795	Downman, John	1750-1824
Cattermole, George	1800-1868	Doyen, Gabriel Francois	1726-1806

Drouais, Jean Germain	1763-1788	Kauffmann, Angelica	1741-1807
Dumont, Francois	1751-1831	Kirkup, Seymour Stocker	1788-1880
Durand, Asher Brown	1796-1886	La Grenee, Jean Louis	
Earlom, Richard	1743-1822	Francois	1724-1805
Eastlake, Sir Charles Lock	1793-1865	La Tour, Maurice	
Eckersberg, Kristoffer	1783-1853	Quentin De	1704-1788
Engleheart, George	1752-1829	Lawrence, Sir Thomas	1769-1830
Etty, William	1787-1849	Le Brun, Marie Elizabeth	
Falconet, Ettienne		Louise	1755-1842
Maurice	1716-1791	Lejeune, Louis Francois	1775-1848
Farington, Joseph	1747-1821	Lemaire, Philippe Honoré	1798-1880
Fielding, Copley	1787-1855	Lemoyne, Jean Baptiste	1704-1778
Fiorillo, Johann Dominicus	1748-1821	L'Enfant, Pierre Charles	1754-1825
Flaxman, John	1755-1826	Leslie, Charles Robert	1794-1859
Fogelberg, Benedict Erland	1786-1854	Linnell, John	1792-1882
Fontaine, Pierre Francois		Liotard, Jean Etienne	1702-1789
Leonard	1762-1853	Longhi, Pietro	1702-1785
Fowler, Charles	1792-1867	Martin, John	1789-1854
Fragonard, Jean Honore	1732-1806	Mengs, Antony Raphael	1728-1779
Friedrich, Caspar David	1774-1840	Michel, Claude	1738-1814
Fuseli, Henry	1741-1825	Moore, William	1790-1851
Gabriel, Jacques Ange	1698-1782	Morland, George	1763-1804
Gainsborough, Thomas	1727-1788	Morse, Samuel Finley	
Gerard, Francois	1770-1837	Breese	1791-1872
Gericault, Theodore	1791-1824	Motte, William De La	1775-1863
Gessner, Salomon	1730-1788	Mulready, William	1786-1863
Gibson, John	1790-1866	Nash, John	1752-1835
Gillray, James	1757-1815	Nasmyth, Alexander	1758-1840
Girodet De Roussy, Anne		Nollekens, Joseph	1737-1823
Louis	1767-1824	Northcote, James	1746-1831
Gordon, Sir John Watson	1788-1864	Opie, John	1761-1807
Girtin, Thomas	1775-1802	Overbeck, Johann	
Goya Y Lucientes,		Friedrich	1789-1869
Francisco	1746-1828	Pajou, Augustin	1730-1809
Granet, Francois Marius	1775-1849	Peale, Charles Willson	1741-1827
Greuze, Jean Baptiste	1725-1805	Peale, Rembrandt	1778-1860
Gros, Antoine Jean	1771-1835	Percier, Charles	1764-1838
Guardi, Francesco	1712-1793	Pigalle, Jean Baptiste	1714-1785
Guerin, Pierre Narcisse	1774-1833	Pine, Robert Edge	1730-1788
Gwilt, Joseph	1784-1863	Pinelli, Bartolomeo	1781-1834
Hansen, Christian		Playfair, William Henry	1789-1857
Frederick	1756-1845	Plimer, Andrew	1763-1837
Harding, Chester	1792-1866	Porta, Carlo	1776-1821
Harlow, George Henry	1787-1819	Porter, Robert Ker	1775-1842
Haydon, Benjamin Robert	1786-1846	Prout, Samuel	1783-1852
Hayter, Sir George	1792-1871	Prud'Hon, Pierre	1758-1823
Heaphy, Thomas	1775-1835	Raeburn, Sir Henry	1756-1823
Hepplewhite, George		Ramsay, Allan	1713-1784
(cabinet maker)	-1786	Reynolds, Sir Joshua	1723-1792
Highmore, Joseph	1692-1780	Rickman, Thomas	1776-1841
Hilton, William	1786-1839	Robert, Hubert	1733-1808
Hiroshige, Audo	1797-1858	Roberts, David	1796-1864
Hittorff, Jacques Ignace	1792-1867	Romney, George	1734-1802
Hokusai, Katsushika	1760-1849	Rousseau De La Rottiere,	
Hoppner, John	1758-1810	Jean Simeon	1747-
Houdon, Jean Antoine	1740-1828	Rowlandson, Thomas	1756-1827
Humphry, Ozias	1742-1810	Rude, Francois	1784-1855
Hunt, William Henry	1790-1864	Sandby, Paul	1725-1809
Ingres, Jean Auguste		Schadow, Friedrick	
Dominique	1780-1867	Wilhelm	1798-1862
Isabey, Jean Baptiste	1767-1855	Schadow, Johann Gottlieb	1764-1850

Schadow, Rudolf	1786-1822	Utamaro	1754-1806
Scheffer, Ary	1795-1858	Vanderlyn, John	1776-1852
Schnorr Von Karolsfeld,		Varley, John	1778-1842
Julius	1794-1872	Veit, Philipp	1793-1877
Severn, Joseph	1793-1879	Verboeckhoven, Eugen	
Shee, Sir Marin Archer	1769-1850	Joseph	1798-1881
Sheraton, Thomas		Vernet, Antoine Charles	
(cabinet maker)	1751-1806	Horace	1758-1835
Smart, John	1740-1811	Vernet, Claude Joseph	1714-1789
Smirke, Sir Robert	1781-1867	Vernet, Emile Jean	
Smith, John Raphael	1752-1812	Horace	1789-1863
Soane, Sir John	1753-1837	Vigee-Lebrun, Marie-Anne	
Soufflot, Jacques Germain	1709-1780	Elizabeth	1755-1842
Sowerby, James	1757-1822	Wainewright, Thomas	
Stanfield, William		Griffiths	1794-1852
Clarkson	1794-1867	Waldo, Samuel Lovett	1783-1861
Stark, James	1794-1859	Wedgewood, Josiah	
Stothard, Thomas	1755-1834	(potter)	1730-1795
Stuart, Gilbert	1755-1828	Westmacott, Sir Richard	1775-1856
Stuart, James	1713-1788	Wilkie, Sir David	1785-1841
Sully, Thomas	1783-1872	Wilson, Richard	1714-1782
Thorvaldsen, Bertel	1770-1844	Wint, Peter De	1784-1849
Tite, Sir William	1798-1873	Wright, Joseph	1734-1797
Trumbull, John	1756-1843	Wyatt, James	1746-1813
Towne, Francis	1739-1816	Zoffany, Johann	1733-1810
Turner, Joseph Mallord		Zuccarelli, Francesco	1702-1788
William	1775-1851	Zucchi, Antonio Pietro	1726-1795

COMPOSERS

Albrechtberger, Johann		Corri, Domenico	1746-1825
Gregory	1736-1809	Crotch, William	1775-1847
Arne, Thomas Augustine	1710-1778	Czerny, Karl	1791-1857
Arnold, Samuel	1740-1802	Diabelli, Anton Antonio	1781-1858
Asioli, Bonifacio	1769-1832	Dibdin, Charles	1745-1814
Attwood, Thomas	1765-1838	Dittersdorf, Karl Ditters	
Auber, Daniel Francois		Von	1739-1799
Eprit	1782-1871	Donizetti, Gaetano	1797-1848
Bach, Johann Christian	1735-1782	Dussek, Jan Ladislav	1761-1812
Bach, Karl Philipp		Eberwein, Traugott	
Emanuel	1714-1788	Maximilian	1775-1831
Bach, Wilhelm Friedmann	1710-1784	Fetis, Francois Joseph	1784-1871
Baini, Guiseppe	1775-1844	Field, John	1782-1837
Batishill, Jonathan	1738-1801	Galuppi, Baldassare	1706-1785
Beethoven, Ludwig Van	1770-1827	Gansbacher, Johann	
Benda, Georg	1722-1795	Baptist	1778-1844
Bishop, Sir Henry Rowley	1786-1855	Garcia, Manoel	1775-1832
Boccherini, Luigi	1743-1805	Gazzaniga, Giuseppe	1743-1818
Boieldieu, Francois Adrien	1775-1834	Geddes, Andrew	1783-1844
Boyce, William	1710-1779	Giordani, Guiseppe	1744-1798
Callcott, John Wall	1766-1821	Gluck, Christoph	
Cambini, Giovanni		Willibald	1714-1787
Giuseppe	1746-1825	Gossec, Francois Joseph	1734-1829
Cannabich, Christian	1731-1798	Gow, Niel	1727-1807
Cherubini, Maria Luigi	1760-1842	Gretry, Andre Ernest	1741-1813
Cimarosa, Domenico	1749-1801	Halevy, Jacques Francois	1799-1862
Campenhout, Francois		Hasse, Johann Adolph	1699-1783
Von	1779-1849	Hauptmann, Moritz	1792-1868
Clementi, Muzio	1752-1832	Haydn, Franz Joseph	1732-1809
Corbould, Henry	1787-1844	Haydn, Michael	1737-1806

Herold, Louis Joseph	1791-1833
Hiller, Johann Adam	1728-1804
Himmel, Fredrick Henry	1765-1814
Horn, Charles Edward	1786-1849
Hummel, Johann	
Nepomuk	1778-1837
Jackson, Wilhelm	1730-1803
Kelly, Michael	1762-1826
Kreutzer, Konradin	1780-1849
Lesueur, Jean Francois	1760-1837
Linley, Thomas	1732-1795
Loewe, Johann Karl	
Gottfried	1796-1869
Lucchesi, Andrea	1741-1800
Marschner, Heinrich	
August	1795-1861
Mehul, Etienne Nicolas	1763-1817
Meyebeer, Giacomo	1791-1864
Monsigny, Pierre	
Alexandre	1729-1817
Mozart, Wolfgang	
Amadeus	1756-1791
Nardini, Pietro	1722-1793
Nares, James	1715-1783
Nathan, Isaac	1791-1864
Paer, Ferdinando	1771-1839
Paisiello, Giovanni	1741-1816
Pearsall, Robert Lucas De	1795-1856

Philidor, Francois Andre	
Danican	1726-1795
Piccinni, Niccola	1728-1800
Pleyel, Ignaz Joseph	1757-1831
Retzsch, Friedrich August	
Moritz	1779-1857
Rossini, Gioachino	
Antonio	1792-1868
Salieri, Antonio	1750-1825
Sarti, Giuseppe	1729-1802
Sacchini, Antonio Maria	
Gaspare	1734-1786
Schinkel, Karl Friedrich	1781-1841
Schubert, Franz Peter	1797-1828
Shield, William	1748-1829
Spohr, Ludwig	1784-1859
Spontini, Gasparo Luigi	
Pacifico	1774-1851
Stamitz, Carl Philipp	1745-1801
Stanley, John	1713-1786
Steibelt, Daniel	1764-1823
Storace, Stephen	1763-1796
Viotti, Giovanni Battista	1753-1824
Vogler, Georg Joseph	1749-1814
Weber, Carl Maria	1786-1826
Wesley, Samuel	1766-1837
Zingarelli, Niccolo	1752-1837

1801 Battle of Alexandria.
      Treaty of Peace between Great Britain and France.
1803 Napoleon sells Louisiana to U.S.
      Britain declares war on France.
1804 Code Napoleon published.
      Napoleon and Josephine crowned.
      Spain declares war on Britain.
1805 Battle of Trafalgar.
      Battle of Austerlitz.
1806 Battle of Jena.
1807 Battle of Eylau.
      Battle of Friedland.
1808 Battle of Vimiera.
1809 Battle of Corunna.
      Napoleon excommunicated.
      France and Austria sign peace treaty.
1811 Battle of Fuentes d'Onore.
      Battle of Albuera.
      Luddite riots.
1812 United States declare war on Great Britain.
      Napoleon declares war on Russia.
      Battle of Salamanca.
      Battle of Borodino. Burning of Moscow.
1813 Execution of Luddites.
      Battle of Lutzen.
      Battle of Vittorio.
      Battle of the Pyrenees.
      Battle of Leipsic.
1814 Battle of Orthez.
      Napoleon deposed, banished to Elba.
      Peace between Great Britain and U.S.
1815 Battle of New Orleans.
      Napoleon escapes from Elba. Declares new constitution.
      Battle of Ligny.
      Battle of Quatre Bras.
      Battle of Waterloo.
      Napoleon sent to St. Helena.
1817 Riots at Manchester.
      Battle of Mehudpore.
1819 Florida ceded to U.S. by Spain.
      " Peterloo."
1822 Massacre by Turks at Scio.

PROMINENT PEOPLE

Brown, John	1800-1859	Lessep, Vicomte		
Brummell, 'Beau,' George		Ferdinande de	1805-1894	
Bryan	1778-1840	Livingstone, Dr. David	1813-1873	
Emmett, Robert	1778-1803	Manning, Henry Edward,		
Faraday, Michael	1791-1863	Cardinal	1808-1892	
Hastings, Warren	1732-1818	Nelson, Horatio, Viscount	1758-1805	
Hood, Samuel, 1st Viscount,		Paganini, Nicolo	1782-1840	
Admiral	1724-1816	Smith, Joseph	1805-1844	
Jenner, Edward	1749-1823	Wellington, Duke of	1769-1852	
Josephine, Empress	1763-1814			

EMPERORS OF CHINA (MANCHU (Ch'ing) DYNASTY)

Jen Tsung	1795-1820	Hsuan Tsung	1820-1850

POPES 1801-1825

Pius VII	1800-1823	Leo XII	1823-1829

FRANCE. HEADS OF STATE

The Consulate	1799-1804	Louis XVIII	1814-1824
Napoleon I	1804-1814	Charles X	1824-1830

HOLY ROMAN EMPERORS

Francis II (abdicated)	1792-1806

ENGLAND. SOVEREIGNS

George III	1760-1820	George IV	1820-1830

SWEDEN. KINGS

Gustavius IV	1792-1809	Charles XIV (Bernadotte)	1818-1844
Charles XIII	1809-1818		

PORTUGAL. KINGS

Maria I	1777-1816	John VI	1816-1826

PRUSSIA. KINGS

Frederick William III	1797-1840

RUSSIA. TSARS

Paul	1796-1801	Nicholas I	1825-1855
Alexander I	1801-1825		

SPAIN. SOVEREIGNS

Ferdinand VII	1808	Ferdinand VII	1813-1833
Joseph Bonaparte	1808-1812		

U.S.A. PRESIDENTS

John Adams	1797-1801	James Monroe	1817-1825
Thomas Jefferson	1801-1809	John Quincy Adams	1825-1829
James Maddison	1809-1817		

AUSTRIA. EMPERORS

Franz I	1804-1835

NETHERLANDS. SOVEREIGNS

William I	1815-1840

WRITERS

Aarestrup, Emil	1800-1856	Abbot, Jacob	1803-1879
Aasen, Ivar	1813-1896	A'Beckett, Gilbert, Abbot	1811-1856

Abernethy, John	1764-1831	Anspach, Elizabeth,	
Ackermann, Louise		Magravine of	1750-1828
Victorine Choquet	1813-1890	Anstey, Christopher	1724-1805
Adam, Alexander	1741-1809	Apperley, Charles James	
Adams, Hannah	1755-1831	(Nimrod)	1777-1843
Adams, John	1735-1826	Arago, Jacques Etienne	
Adams, John Quincy	1767-1848	Victor	1790-1855
Adams, Sarah Flower	1805-1848	Arany, Janos	1817-1882
Adams, William Taylor	1822-1897	Archenholz, Johann	
Adanson, Michel	1727-1806	Wilhelm Von	1743-1812
Adolphus, John	1768-1845	Aribau, Bonaventura	
Adolphus, John Leycester	1795-1862	Carles	1798-1862
Aepinus, Franz Ulrich		Armitage, Edward	1817-1896
Theodor	1724-1802	Arnason, Jon	1819-1888
Afzelius, Aruid August	1785-1871	Arnault, Antoine Vincent	1766-1834
Agassiz, Jean Louis		Arndt, Ernst Moritz	1769-1860
Rodolphe	1807-1873	Arneth, Alfred	1819-1897
Aikin, John	1747-1822	Arnim, Elizabeth	
Aikin, Lucy	1781-1864	(Bettina) Von	1785-1859
Aimard, Gustave	1818-1883	Arnim, Ludwig Achim	
Ainslie, Hew	1792-1872	Von	1781-1831
Ainsworth, William		Arnold, Matthew	1822-1888
Harrison	1805-1882	Arnold, Thomas	1795-1842
Aird, Thomas	1802-1876	Arthur, Timothy Shay	1809-1885
Agoult, Marie Catherine		Asbjornsen, Peter Christian	1812-1885
Sophie, Countess de		Atkinson, Thomas Witlam	1799-1861
Flavigny		Auerbach, Berthold	1812-1882
(Daniel Stern)	1805-1876	Auersperg, Anton	
Aguilar, Grace	1816-1847	Alexander	1806-1876
Aguilo Y Fuster, Marian	1825-1897	Augier, Guillaume Victor	
Akers, Benjamin Paul	1825-1861	Emile	1820-1889
Aksakov, Sergei		Austen, Jane	1775-1817
Timofeyevich	1719-1859	Austin, Sarah	1793-1867
Aksakov, Ivan Sergeyevich	1823-1886	Autran, Joseph	1813-1877
Aksakov, Konstantin	1817-1860	Avellanida, Gertrudis	
Alaman, Lucas	1792-1853	Gomez D'	1814-1873
Alcott, Amos Bronson	1799-1888	Aytoun, William	
Alden, Joseph	1807-1885	Edmonstoun	1813-1865
Aleardi, Aleardo	1812-1878	Azais, Pierre Hyacinthe	1766-1845
Alecsandri, Vasile	1821-1890	Azeglio, Massimo	
Alexander, Cecil Francis	1818-1895	Taparelli, Marquis D'	1798-1866
Alexis, Willibald	1798-1871	Bacon, Delia Salter	1811-1859
Alfireri, Vittorio, Count	1749-1803	Bacon, Leonard	1802-1881
Alison, Sir Archibald	1792-1867	Bacsanyi, Janos	1763-1845
Allibone, Samuel Austin	1816-1889	Baedeker, Karl	1801-1859
Allingham, William	1824-1889	Baggesen, Jens Immanuel	1764-1826
Allmers, Hermann	1821-1902	Bahr, Johann Christian	
Almeida-Garrett, Joao		Felix	1798-1872
Baptista Da	1799-1854	Bailey, Philip James	1816-1902
Almqvist, Karl Jonas		Bailey, Samuel	1791-1870
Ludwig	1793-1866	Baillie, Joanna	1762-1851
Ampere, Jean Jacques	1800-1864	Bain, Alexander	1818-1903
Ancelot, Jacques Arsene		Balaguer y Cirera, Victor	1824-1901
Francois Polycarpe	1794-1854	Balbo, Cesare, Count	1789-1853
Ancillon, Johann Peter		Balfe, Michael Willen	1808-1870
Friedrich	1766-1836	Ballanche, Pierre Simon	1776-1847
Andersen, Hans Christian	1805-1875	Ballantine, James	1808-1877
Anderson, Robert	1750-1830	Ballantyne, Robert	
Andrieux, Francois		Michael	1825-1894
Guillaume Jean Stanislas	1759-1833	Balmes, Jaime Luciano	1810-1848
Anquetil, Louis Pierre	1723-1808	Balzac, Honore De	1799-1850

Bancroft, George	1800-1891	Bernard, Charles De	1804-1850
Banim, John	1798-1842	Berry, Mary	1763-1852
Banville, Theodore		Bertrand, Jacques Louis	
Faullain De	1823-1891	Napoleon	1807-1841
Barante, Amable Guillaume		Berzsenyi, Daniel	1776-1836
Prosper Brugiere	1782-1866	Beskow, Bernhard Von	1796-1868
Baratynski, Yevgeniy		Bibaud, Michel	1782-1857
Abramovich	1800-1844	Bickerstaffe, Isaac	1735-1812
Barbauld, Anna Letitia	1743-1825	Biedermann, Friedrich Karl	1812-1901
Barbey D'Aurevilly,		Bignon, Louis Pierre	
Jules Amedee	1808-1889	Edouard	1771-1841
Barbier, Henri Auguste	1805-1882	Bilderdijk, Willem	1756-1831
Barbier, Paul Jules	1825-1901	Billings, Robert William	1813-1874
Barker, Thomas, of Bath	1769-1847	Bissen, Herman Vilhelm	1798-1868
Barker, Thomas Jones		Bitzius, Albrecht	1797-1854
Barker	1815-1882	Blackie, John Stuart	1809-1895
Barlow, Joel	1754-1812	Blackmore, Richard	
Barlow, Peter	1776-1862	Doddridge	1825-1900
Barnard, Lady Anne	1750-1825	Blake, William	1757-1827
Barnes, William	1800-1886	Blanc, Jean Joseph	
Barrington, George		Charles Louis	1811-1882
(Waldron)	1755-1804	Blanchard, Samuel Laman	1804-1845
Barthelemy, Auguste		Blessington, Marguerite	1789-1849
Marseille	1796-1867	Blicher, Steen Steensen	1782-1848
Barthelemy, Saint Hilaire		Bloomfield, Robert	1766-1823
Jules	1805-1895	Blore, Edward	1787-1879
Barton, Bernard	1784-1849	Bocage, Manuel Maria	
Basevi, George	1794-1845	Barbosa De	1765-1805
Batyushkov, Konstantin		Boccage, Marie Anne	
Nikolaievitch	1787-1855	Fiquet De	1710-1802
Baudelaire, Charles Pierre	1821-1867	Bodenstedt, Friedrich	
Baudissin, Wolf Heinrich	1789-1878	Martin Von	1819-1892
Bauer, Bruno	1809-1882	Boerne, Karl Ludwig	1786-1837
Bauernfeld, Eduard Von	1802-1890	Boie, Heinrich Christian	1744-1806
Bautain, Louis Eugene		Boisgobey, Fortune	
Marie	1796-1867	Abraham Du	1824-1891
Bayly, Thomas Haynes	1797-1839	Boker, George Henry	1823-1890
Beattie, James	1735-1803	Bonald, Louis Gabriel	
Beauchamp, Alphonse De	1767-1832	Ambroise	1754-1840
Beaumont, Sir George		Bonneville, Nicholas De	1760-1828
Howland	1753-1827	Bonstetten, Charles	
Beauvoir, Roger De	1809-1866	Victor De	1745-1832
Beck, Christian Daniel	1757-1832	Borel, Petrus	1809-1859
Beck, Jakob Sigismund	1761-1840	Borne, Ludwig	1786-1837
Beckford, William Thomas	1760-1844	Bornier, Henri	1825-1901
Beddoes, Thomas Lovell	1803-1849	Borrow, George Henry	1803-1881
Beecher, Henry Ward	1813-1887	Bosboom-Toussaint, Anna	
Beechey, Sir William	1753-1839	Louisa Geertruida	1812-1886
Beets, Nikolaas	1814-1903	Bostrom, Christoffer Jacob	1797-1866
Beffroy De Reigny, Louis		Botta, Carlo Guiseppe	
Abel	1757-1811	Guglielmo	1766-1837
Bekker, Elizabeth	1738-1804	Boucicault, Dion	1822-1890
Bell, Henry Glassford	1803-1874	Bouilhet, Louis Hyacinthe	1822-1869
Bell, Robert	1800-1867	Bouilly, Jean-Nicolas	1763-1842
Belli, Giuseppe Gioachino	1791-1863	Bouterwek, Friedrich	1765-1828
Benedix, Julius Roderich	1811-1873	Bowdich, Thomas Edward	1790-1824
Beneke, Friedrich Edward	1798-1856	Bowdler, Thomas (editor)	1754-1825
Bentham, Jeremy	1748-1832	Bowen, Francis	1811-1890
Beranger, Pierre Jean De	1780-1857	Bowles, William Lisle	1762-1850
Berard, Joseph Frederic	1789-1828	Boyd, Andrew Kennedy	
Berchet, Giovanni	1783-1851	Hutchinson	1825-1899

Boylai, Wolfgang	1775-1856	Campoamor Y Campoosorio,	
Bree, Matthias Ignatius		Raymon De	1819-1901
Van	1773-1839	Canina, Luigi	1795-1856
Bremer, Fredrika	1801-1865	Cannon, Charles James	1800-1860
Brentano, Clemens	1778-1842	Cantu, Cesare	1804-1895
Breton de Los Herreros,		Capefigue, Jean-Baptiste	
Manuel	1796-1873	Honore Raymond	1801-1872
Brierley, Benjamin	1825-1896	Capern, Edward	1819-1894
Brillat-Savarin, Anthelme	1755-1826	Carlen, Emilia Smith	
Brizeux, Julien Auguste		Flygare	1807-1892
Pelage	1803-1858	Carleton, William	1794-1869
Bronte, Anne	1820-1849	Carlyle, Thomas	1795-1881
Bronte, Charlotte	1816-1855	Carrer, Luigi	1801-1850
Bronte, Emily	1818-1848	Carriere, Moritz	1817-1895
Brooks, Charles William		Carter, Elizabeth	1717-1806
Shirley	1816-1874	Cary, Alice	1820-1871
Broughton, John Cam		Castelli, Ignaz Franz	1781-1862
Hobhouse	1786-1869	Castello, Branco Camillo	1825-1890
Brown, Charles Brockden	1771-1810	Casti, Giovanni Battista	1724-1803
Brown, Samuel Morison	1817-1856	Cattaneo, Carlo	1801-1869
Brown, Thomas	1778-1820	Cavalcaselle, Giovanni	
Browne, James	1793-1841	Battista	1820-1897
Browning, Elizabeth		Cesarotti, Melchiore	1730-1808
Barrett	1806-1861	Chalmers, Alexander	1759-1834
Browning, Robert	1812-1889	Chalybaus, Heinrich	
Brownson, Orestes		Moritz	1796-1862
Augustus	1803-1876	Chambers, Robert	1802-1871
Brunton, Mary	1778-1818	Chamier, Frederick	1796-1870
Bryant, Jacob	1715-1804	Chamisso, Adelbert Von	1781-1838
Bryant, William Cullen	1794-1878	Champfleury	1821-1889
Brydges, Sir Samuel		Channing, William Ellery	1780-1842
Egerton	1762-1837	Chapone, Hester	1727-1801
Buchez, Philippe Benjamin		Charriere, Isabelle De	1740-1805
Joseph	1796-1865	Chasles, Philarete	1798-1873
Buchner, Ludwig	1824-1899	Chateaubriand, Francois	
Buckhardt, Jakob	1818-1897	Rene	1768-1848
Buckingham, James Silk	1786-1855	Chenedolle, Charles Julien	
Buckle, Henry Thomas	1821-1862	Lioult De	1769-1833
Buckstone, John Baldwin	1802-1879	Chenier, Marie-Joseph	
Bulgarin, Thaddeus	1789-1859	Blaise De	1764-1811
Bulwer, Henry Lytton	1801-1872	Cheruel, Pierre Adolphe	1809-1891
Burney, Charles	1726-1814	Child, Francis James	1825-1896
Burney, Fanny		Child, Lydia Maria	1802-1874
(Madame D'Arblay)	1752-1840	Christopoulos, Athanasios	1772-1847
Burrows, Montagu	1819-1905	Cibrario, Luigi, Count	1802-1870
Burton, John Hill	1809-1881	Clare, John	1793-1864
Burton, Sir Richard		Clark, William George	1821-1878
Francis	1821-1890	Clarke, Charles Cowden	1787-1877
Burton, William Evans	1804-1860	Clarke, Edward Daniel	1769-1822
Bury, Lady Charlotte		Claudius, Matthias	1740-1815
Susan Maria	1775-1861	Clausewitz, Karl Von	1780-1831
Byron, George Gordon	1788-1824	Clive, Caroline	1801-1873
Caballero, Fernan	1796-1877	Clough, Arthur Hugh	1819-1861
Caird, John	1820-1898	Cobbe, Frances, Power	1822-1904
Cairns, John Elliot	1823-1875	Cobbett, William	1763-1835
Calvert, George Henry	1803-1889	Cockton, Henry	1807-1853
Calvo, Carlos	1824-1906	Cole, Sir Henry	1808-1882
Cambridge, Richard Owen	1717-1802	Coleridge, Hartley	1796-1849
Campan, Jeanne Louise		Coleridge, Samuel Taylor	1772-1834
Henriette	1752-1822	Coleridge, Sara	1802-1852
Campbell, Thomas	1777-1844	Colet, Louise	1810-1876

Collett, Jacobine Camilla	1813-1895	Darwin, Erasmus	1731-1802
Collier, John Payne	1789-1883	Dashkova, Catherina	
Collin, Heinrich Joseph		Romanovna	1744-1810
Von	1771-1811	D'Aubigné, Jean Henri	
Collin D'Harleville, Jean		Merle	1794-1872
Francois	1755-1806	Daumer, Georg Friedrich	1800-1875
Collins, William	1788-1847	Daunov, Pierre Claude	
Collins, William Wilkie	1824-1889	Francois	1761-1840
Colman, George	1762-1836	David, Pierre Jean	1789-1856
Combe, William	1741-1823	Davis, Thomas Osborne	1814-1845
Comte, Auguste	1798-1857	De Geer, Louis Gerhard,	
Conscience, Hendrik	1812-1883	Baron	1818-1896
Constant De Rebecque,		Dekker, Edward Douwes	1820-1887
Henri Benjamin	1767-1830	Delarue, Gervais	1751-1835
Cooper, James Fenimore	1789-1851	Delavigne, Jean Francois	
Coppee, Henry	1821-1895	Casimir	1793-1843
Costello, Louisa Stuart	1799-1870	Delille, Jacques	1738-1813
Cottin, Marie	1770-1807	Delolme, Jean Louis	1740-1806
Courier, Paul Louis	1773-1825	Delvig, Anton Antonovich,	
Cousin, Victor	1792-1867	Baron Von	1798-1831
Cowley, Hannah	1743-1809	Demogeot, Jacques Claude	1808-1894
Coxe, William	1747-1828	Denina, Carlo Giovanni	
Craven, Pauline	1808-1891	Maria	1731-1813
Crabbe, George	1754-1832	Dennery, Adolphe Philippe	1811-1899
Craufurd, Quintin	1743-1819	De Quincey, Thomas	1785-1859
Creasy, Sir Edward		Derzhavin, Gavrila	
Shepherd	1812-1878	Romanovich	1743-1816
Creevey, Thomas	1768-1838	Desagiers, Marc Antoine	
Cremazie, Octave	1822-1879	Madeleine	1772-1827
Creuzer, George Friedrich	1771-1858	Desforges, Pierre Jean	
Crocker, Hannah Mather	1752-1829	Baptiste Choudard	1746-1806
Croft, Sir Herbert	1751-1816	Deschamps, Emile	1791-1871
Crocker, John Wilson	1780-1857	De Vere, Aubrey Thomas	1814-1902
Croker, Thomas Crofton	1798-1854	Dexter, Henry Martyn	1821-1890
Crowe, Catherine	1800-1870	Dibdin, Thomas John	1771-1841
Crusenstolpe, Magnus		Dickens, Charles John	
Jakob	1795-1865	Huffam	1812-1870
Csengery, Antal	1822-1880	Digby, Kenelm Henry	1800-1880
Csokonai, Mihaly Vitez	1773-1805	Dingelstedt, Franz Von	1814-1881
Cullum, George Washington	1809-1892	Disraeli, Benjamin	1804-1881
Cumberland, Richard	1732-1811	D'Israeli, Isaac	1766-1848
Cunningham, Allan	1784-1842	Dixon, William Hepworth	1821-1879
Curtis, George William	1824-1892	Dmitriev, Ivan Ivanovich	1760-1837
Curtius, Ernst	1814-1896	Dobell, Sydney Thompson	1824-1874
Curtius, Georg	1820-1885	Dollinger, Johann Joseph	
Cuvier, Georges (Léopold)	1769-1832	Ignaz Von	1799-1890
Da Costa, Isaak	1798-1860	Domett, Alfred	1811-1887
Dahlgren, Karl Fredrik	1791-1844	Donoso, Cortez Juan	1809-1853
Dahlmann, Friedrich		Doran, John	1807-1878
Christoph	1785-1860	Dostoievsky, Fyodor	
Dalling and Bulwer,		Mikhaylovich	1821-1881
Baron	1801-1872	Douglas, Sir William Fettes	1822-1891
Dall'Ongaro, Francesco	1808-1873	Doyle, Sir Francis	
Dana, Richard Henry	1815-1882	Hastings Charles	1810-1888
Da Ponte, Lorenzo	1749-1838	Drake, Friedrich	1805-1882
Dareste De La Chavanne,		Drake, Nathan	1766-1836
Cleophas	1820-1882	Draper, William	1811-1882
Darley, George	1795-1846	Drinkwater, Bethune John	1762-1844
Daru, Pierre Antoine		Drobisch, Moritz Wilhelm	1802-1896
Comte	1767-1829	Droste-Hulshoff, Annette	
Darwin, Charles Robert	1809-1882	Elizabeth	1797-1848

Droysen, Johann Gustav	1808-1884	Escoiquiz, Juan	1762-1820
Droz, Francois Xavier	1773-1850	Espronceda, Jose De	1808-1842
Du Camp, Maxime	1822-1894	Esquiros, Henri Francois	
Ducange, Victor Henri		Alphonse	1812-1876
Joseph Brahain	1783-1833	Estebanez Caldren, Serafin	1799-1867
Ducasse, Pierre Emmanuel		Etienne, Charles	
Albert	1813-1893	Guillaume	1777-1845
Ducis, Jean Francois	1733-1816	Everett, Alexander Hill	1790-1847
Dumas, Alexandre	1802-1870	Fabriani, Severino	1792-1849
Dumas, Alexandre (fils)	1824-1895	Fabroni, Angelo	1732-1803
Dumont, Augustin		Fahlcrantz, Christian Erik	1790-1866
Alexandre	1801-1884	Fain, Agathon Jean	
Dumont, Pierre Etienne		Francois	1778-1837
Louis	1759-1829	Falk, Johann Daniel	1768-1826
Duncker, Maximilian		Falke, Johann Friedrich	
Wolfgang	1811-1886	Gottlieb	1823-1876
Dunlap, William	1766-1839	Fallmerayer, Jakob Phillip	1790-1861
Dupuis, Charles Francois	1742-1809	Falloux, Frederic Alfred	
Dupont, Pierre	1821-1870	Pierre	1811-1886
Duruy, Jean Victor	1811-1894	Farini, Luigi Carlo	1812-1866
Dutens, Louis	1730-1812	Fauriel, Claude Charles	1782-1844
Dutt, Michael Madhu		Fay, Andreas	1786-1864
Sudan	1824-1873	Fechner, Gustav Theodor	1801-1887
Duval, Alexandre Vincent		Feith, Rhijnvis	1753-1824
Pineux	1767-1842	Fejer, Gyorgy	1766-1852
Dwight, Timothy	1752-1817	Ferguson, Adam	1723-1816
Eberhard, Christian		Ferguson, Sir Samuel	1810-1886
August Gottlob	1769-1845	Fergusson, James	1808-1886
Eberhard, Johann		Ferrari, Giuseppe	1812-1876
Augustus	1739-1809	Ferrari, Paolo	1822-1889
Eckermann, Johann Peter	1792-1864	Ferrier, Susan Edmonstone	1782-1854
Eddy, Mary Baker Glover	1821-1910	Feuchtersleben, Ernst	1806-1849
Edgeworth, Maria	1767-1849	Feuerbach, Ludwig	
Edgeworth, Richard Lovell	1744-1817	Andreas	1804-1872
Egan, Pierce	1772-1849	Feuerbach, Paul Johann	
Eichendorff, Joseph		Anselm	1775-1833
Freiherr Von	1788-1857	Feuillet, Octave	1821-1890
Eliot, George		Feval, Paul Henri	
(Marian Evans)	1819-1880	Corentin	1817-1887
Elliot, Jean	1727-1805	Feydeau, Ernest Aime	1821-1873
Elliott, Ebenezer	1781-1849	Fichte, Immanuel	
Ellis, Alexander John	1814-1890	Hermann Von	1796-1879
Ellis, George	1753-1815	Fichte, Johann Gottlieb	1762-1814
Elphinstone, Mountstuart	1779-1859	Fielding, Anthony Vandyke	
Emerson, Ralph Waldo	1803-1882	Copley	1787-1855
Engel, Johann Carl		Fields, James Thomas	1817-1881
Ludwig	1778-1840	Figuier, Louis	1819-1894
Engel, Johann Jakob	1741-1802	Finlay, George	1799-1875
Engels, Friedrich	1820-1895	Fisher, Ernst Kuno	
English, Thomas Dunn	1819-1902	Berthold	1824-1907
Ennemoser, Joseph	1787-1855	Fitzball, Edward	1792-1873
Eotvos, Jossef, Baron	1813-1871	Fitzgerald, Edward	1809-1883
Erckmann, Emile	1822-1899	Flaubert, Gustave	1821-1880
Erdelyi, Janos	1814-1868	Foa, Eugenie Rodriguez	
Erdmann, Johann Eduard	1805-1892	Gradis	1798-1853
Erskine, Henry	1746-1817	Follen, Adolf Ludwig	1794-1855
Erskine, Thomas	1788-1870	Follen, Karl	1795-1840
Eschenburg, Johann		Fontan, Louis Marie	1801-1839
Joachim	1743-1820	Fontane, Theodor	1819-1898
Eschenmayer, Adam Karl		Fontanes, Louis	1757-1821
August Von	1768-1852	Ford, Richard	1796-1858

Forster, Friedrich Christoph	1791-1868	Gfrorer, August Friedrich	1803-1861
Forster, John	1812-1876	Giacometti, Paolo	1816-1882
Fortlage, Karl	1806-1881	Giesebrecht, Wilhelm Von	1814-1889
Foscolo, Ugo	1778-1827	Gifford, William	1756-1826
Foster, John	1770-1843	Gilbert, William	1804-1889
Fouque, Friedrich Heinrich Karl De La Motte	1777-1843	Gillies, John	1747-1836
		Gilchrist, Alexander	1828-1861
Fourier, Francois Marie Charles	1772-1837	Gilchrist, Anne	1828-1885
		Ginguene, Pierre Louis	1748-1815
Frampton, Mary	1773-1846	Gioberti, Vincenzo	1801-1852
Francois De Neufchateau, Nicolas Louis	1750-1828	Gioja, Melchiorre	1767-1829
		Giordani, Pietro	1774-1848
Frankl, Ludwig August	1810-1894	Girardin, Delphine De	1804-1855
Franzen, Frans Michael	1772-1847	Giraud, Giovanni	1776-1834
Fraser, Alexander Campbell	1819-1914	Gieseler, Johann Karl Ludwig	1792-1854
		Giudici, Paolo Emiliano	1812-1872
Fraser, James Baillie	1783-1856	Giusti, Guiseppi	1809-1850
Freeman, Edward Augustus	1823-1892	Glassbrenner, Adolf	1810-1876
		Gleig, George Robert	1796-1888
Freiligrath, Ferdinand	1810-1876	Gleim, Johann Wilhelm Ludwig	1719-1803
Freneau, Philip Morin	1752-1832		
Frere, John Hookham	1769-1846	Glen, William	1789-1826
Freytag, Gustav	1816-1895	Glinka, Fedor Nikolayevich	1788-1880
Fries, Jakob Friedrich	1773-1843	Godwin, William	1756-1836
Froebel, Friedrich Wilhelm August	1782-1852	Goethe, Johann Wolfgang Von	1749-1832
		Gogol, Nikolai Vasilievich	1809-1852
Frohlich, Abraham Emanuel	1796-1865	Goldschmidt, Aaron Meier	1819-1887
		Goltz, Bogumil	1801-1870
Frohschammer, Jakob	1821-1893	Goncalves Dias, Antonio	1823-1864
Frothingham, Octavius Brooks	1822-1895	Goncharov, Ivan Alexandrovich	1812-1891
Froude, James Anthony	1818-1894	Goncourt De, Edmond Louis Antoine Huot	1822-1896
Fryxell, Anders	1795-1881		
Fuller, Margaret	1810-1850	Good, John Mason	1764-1827
Fullerton, Lady Georgiana Charlotte	1812-1885	Goodrich, Samuel Griswold	1793-1860
Gachard, Louis Prosper	1800-1885	Gore, Catherine Grace Frances	1799-1861
Gagern, Hans Christoph Ernst	1766-1852	Gorres, Joseph Von	1776-1848
		Gottschall, Rudolf Von	1823-1908
Galluppi, Pasquale	1770-1846	Gould, John	1804-1881
Galt, John	1779-1839	Gozlan, Leon	1803-1866
Garat, Dominique Joseph	1749-1833	Gozzi, Carlo	1720-1806
Garay, Janos	1812-1853	Grabbe, Christian Dietrich	1801-1836
Gareau, Francois Xavier	1806-1866	Grant, Anne	1755-1838
Garrett, Joao Baptista Da Silva Leita De Almeida	1799-1854	Grant, James	1822-1887
		Graves, Richard	1715-1804
Gaskell, (Mrs.) Elizabeth Cleghorn	1810-1865	Gratz, Heinrich	1817-1891
		Greene, George Washington	1811-1883
Gatty, Margaret	1809-1893	Green, Mary Ann Evrett	1818-1895
Gautier, Theophile	1811-1872	Greg, William Rathbone	1809-1881
Geibel, Emanuel	1815-1884	Gregorovius, Ferdinand	1821-1891
Geiser, Eric Gustav	1783-1877	Greville, Charles Cavendish Fulke	1794-1865
Genlis, Stephanie Felicité Ducrest de St. Aubin	1746-1830		
Gerstacker, Friedrich	1816-1877	Griboyedov, Alexander Sergeyevich	1795-1829
Gerssenberg, Heinrich Wilhelm Von	1737-1823	Griffin, Gerald	1803-1840
Gervinus, Georg Gottfried	1805-1871	Grigorovich, Dmitri Vaslievich	1822-1900
Gesenius, Friedrich Heinrich Wilhelm	1786-1842		

Grimm, Friedrich Melchior	1723-1807
Grimm, Jacob Ludwig Carl	1785-1863
Grimm, Wilhelm Carl	1786-1859
Grossi, Tommaso	1791-1853
Grote, George	1794-1871
Grub, George	1812-1892
Grundtvig, Nikolai Frederik	
Severin	1783-1872
Guerin Du Cayla, Georges	
Maurice De	1810-1839
Guerrazzi, Francesco	
Domenico	1804-1873
Guest, Edwin	1800-1880
Guizot, Francois Pierre	
Guillaume	1787-1874
Gutzkow, Karl Ferdinand	1811-1878
Guys, Constantin	1805-1892
Gyllembourg-Eh Rensvard,	
Thomasine Christine	1773-1856
Hacklander, Friedrich	
Wilhelm Von	1816-1877
Hagenbach, Karl Rudolf	1801-1874
Hahn-Hahn, Ida	1805-1880
Hake, Thomas Gordon	1809-1895
Hale, Edward Everett	1822-1909
Hale, Sarah Josepha	1788-1879
Halevy, Jean	1804-1883
Haliburton, Thomas	
Chandler	1796-1865
Hall, Anna Maria	1800-1881
Hall, Basil	1788-1844
Hall, Samuel Carter	1800-1889
Hallam, Henry	1777-1859
Hallgrimson, Jonas	1807-1845
Hamilton, Elizabeth	1758-1816
Hamilton, Thomas	1789-1842
Hamilton, Sir William	1788-1856
Hamley, Sir Edward Bruce	1824-1893
Hammer, Julius	1810-1862
Hardwick, Philip	1792-1870
Haring, George Wilhelm	
Heinrich	1798-1871
Hartmann, Moritz	1821-1872
Hartzenbusch, Juan	
Eugenio	1806-1880
Hasselt, Andre Henri	
Constant Van	1806-1874
Hasted, Edward	1732-1812
Hauch, Johannes Carsten	1790-1872
Hauff, Wilhelm	1802-1827
Haureau, Barthelemy	1812-1896
Hausser, Ludwig	1818-1867
Hawker, Robert Stephen	1803-1875
Hawthorne, Nathaniel	1804-1864
Hayley, William	1745-1820
Haym, Rudolf	1821-1901
Hayward, Abraham	1801-1884
Hazard, Rowland Gibson	1801-1888
Hazlitt, William	1778-1830
Hebbel, Christian	
Friedrich	1813-1863

Heeren, Arnold Hermann	
Ludwig	1760-1842
Hegel, Georg Wilhelm	
Friedrich	1770-1831
Heiberg, Johan Ludvig	1791-1860
Heine, Heinrich	1797-1856
Heinse, Johann Jakob	
Wilhelm	1749-1803
Hellck, Fitz-Greene	1790-1867
Helmers, Jan Frederik	1767-1813
Helmholtz, Hermann Ludwig	
Ferdinand Von	1821-1894
Hemans, Felicia Dorothea	1793-1835
Helps, Sir Arthur	1813-1875
Herbart, Johann Friedrich	1776-1841
Herculano De Carvalno,	
E Araujo Alexandre	1810-1877
Herder, Johann Gottfried	
Von	1744-1803
Heredia Y Heredia, Jose	
Maria	1803-1839
Hertz, Henrik	1797-1870
Herwegh, Georg	1817-1875
Herzen, Alexander	
Ivanovich	1812-1870
Higginson, Thomas	
Wentworth	1823-1911
Himly, Louis-Auguste	1823-1906
Hinrichs, Hermann	
Friedrich Wilhelm	1794-1861
Hoffman, August Heinrich	1798-1874
Hoffman, Ernst Theodor	
Wilhelm	1776-1822
Hoffmann, Heinrich	1809-1894
Hogg, James	1770-1835
Hogg, Thomas Jefferson	1792-1862
Holbach, Paul Heinrich	
Dietrich	1723-1789
Holcroft, Thomas	1745-1809
Holderlin, Johann	
Christian Friedrich	1770-1843
Holland, Henry	1746-1806
Holland, Sir Henry	1788-1873
Holland, Josiah Gilbert	1819-1881
Holmes, Oliver Wendell	1809-1894
Holtei, Karl Eduard Von	1798-1880
Home, John	1722-1808
Hone, William	1780-1842
Hood, Thomas	1799-1845
Hook, James	1746-1827
Hook, Theodore Edward	1788-1841
Hormayr, Joseph	
Freiherr Von	1782-1848
Horne, Richard Henry	1803-1884
Hostrup, Jens Christion	1818-1894
Hotho, Heinrich Gustav	1802-1873
Houghton, Richard	
Monckton Milnes	1809-1885
Houssaye, Arsene	1815-1896
Howe, Julia Ward	1819-1910
Howitt, Mary	1799-1888

Howitt, William	1792-1879	Kazinczy, Ferencz	1759-1831
Hughes, Thomas	1822-1896	Keats, John	1795-1821
Hugo, Victor Marie	1802-1885	Keble, John	1792-1866
Humboldt, Freidrich,		Keightley, Thomas	1789-1872
Baron Von	1769-1859	Keller, Gottfried	1819-1890
Humboldt, Karl Wilhelm		Kemble, John Mitchell	1807-1857
von	1767-1835	Kenealy, Edward Vaughan	
Hunt, James Henry Leigh	1784-1859	Hyde	1819-1880
Hunter, Joseph	1783-1861	Kenney, James	1780-1849
Hurd, Richard	1720-1808	Kerner, Justinus Andreas	
Huxley, Thomas Henry	1825-1895	Christian	1786-1862
Hyslop, James	1798-1827	Kervyn De Lettenhove,	
Iffland, August Wilhelm	1759-1814	Constantine Bruno	1817-1891
Ihne, Wilhelm	1821-1902	Key, Francis Scott	1779-1843
Immermann, Karl Lebrecht	1796-1840	Kierkegaard, Soren Aaby	1813-1855
Inchbald, Elizabeth	1753-1821	King, Thomas	1730-1805
Ingelby, Clement Manfred	1823-1886	Kinglake, Alexander	
Ingelow, Jean	1820-1897	William	1809-1891
Ingemann, Bernhard		Kingsley, Charles	1819-1875
Severin	1789-1862	Kingston, William Henry	
Ingoldsby, Thomas	1788-1845	Giles	1814-1880
Ingraham, Joseph Holt	1809-1860	Kinkel, Johann Gottfried	1815-1882
Innes, Cosmo	1798-1874	Kisfaludy, Karoly	1788-1830
Irving, Washington	1783-1859	Kisfaludy, Sandor	1772-1844
Jacobi, Freidrich Heinrich	1743-1819	Kitto, John	1804-1854
Jacobi, Johann Georg	1740-1814	Klaczko, Julian	1825-1906
Jahn, Otto	1813-1869	Kleist, Bernd Heinrich	
Jakob, Ludwig Heinrich		Wilhelm Von	1777-1811
Von	1759-1827	Klinger, Friedrich	
James, George Payne		Maximilian Von	1752-1831
Rainsford	1799-1860	Klopstock, Friedrich	
Jameson, Anna Brownell	1794-1860	Gottlieb	1724-1803
Janin, Jules Gabriel	1804-1874	Knebel, Karl Ludwig Von	1744-1834
Jasmin, Jacques	1798-1864	Knight, Charles	1791-1873
Jefferson, Thomas	1743-1826	Knowles, James Sheridan	1784-1862
Jephson, Robert	1736-1803	Kock, Charles Paul De	1793-1871
Jerrold, Douglas William	1803-1857	Kolcsey, Ferencz	1790-1888
Jesse, Edward	1780-1868	Kopisch, August	1799-1853
Jewsbury, Geraldine Endsor	1812-1880	Korner, Karl Theodor	1791-1813
Joinville, Francois Fernand		Kotzebue, August Friedrich	
D'Orleans	1818-1900	Ferdinand Von	1761-1819
Jokai, Maurus	1825-1904	Krasinski, Zygmunt, Count	1812-1859
Jones, Ebenezer	1820-1860	Kraszweski, Joseph	
Jones, Ernest	1819-1869	Ignatius	1812-1887
Jordan, Wilhelm	1819-1904	Krause, Karl Christian	
Josika, Miklos	1794-1865	Friedrich	1781-1832
Joubert, Joseph	1754-1824	Krug, Wilhelm Traugott	1770-1842
Jouffroy, Theodore Simon	1796-1842	Krylov, Ivan Andreevich	1768-1844
Jouy, Victor Joseph		Kuhlau, Friedrich	1786-1832
Etienne De	1764-1846	Kurz, Hermann	1813-1873
Jovellanos, Gaspar		Labiche, Eugene Marin	1815-1888
Melchor De	1744-1811	Lacaita, Sir James	1813-1895
Judson, Edward Zane		Lacepede, Bernard De	
Carroll	1823-1886	Laville, Compte De	1756-1825
Kant, Immanuel	1724-1804	Laclos, Pierre Amboise	
Karadzil, Viek Stefanovich	1787-1864	Francois	1741-1803
Karamzin, Nicolai		Lacretelle, Jean Charles	
Mikhailovich	1765-1826	Dominique de	1766-1855
Karr, Alphonse	1808-1890	La Farina, Giuseppe	1815-1863
Kate, Jan Jacob		La Harpe, Frederic	
Lodewijk Ten	1819-1889	Cesare	1754-1838

Laing, Malcolm	1762-1818	Lippincott, Sara Jane	
Laing, Samuel	1810-1897	Clarke	1823-1904
Lamarck, Jean Chevalier		Lista Y Aragon, Alberto	1775-1848
de	1744-1829	Lister, Thomas Henry	1800-1842
Lamartine, Alphonse De	1790-1869	Littre, Maximilien Paul	
Lamb, Charles	1775-1834	Emile	1801-1881
Lamennais Felicite		Livingstone, David	1813-1873
Robert De	1782-1854	Ljunggren, Gustaf Kaken	
Landon, Letitia Elizabeth	1802-1838	Jordan	1823-1905
Landor, Walter Savage	1775-1864	Locker-Lampson, Frederick	1821-1895
Lane, Edward William	1801-1876	Lockhart, John Gibson	1794-1854
Langhorne, John	1735-1779	Lodge, Edmund	1756-1839
Lappenberg, Johann		Lofft, Capel	1751-1824
Martin	1794-1865	Longfellow, Henry	
Laprade, Pierre Marin		Wadsworth	1807-1882
Victor Richard De	1812-1883	Lönnrot, Elias	1802-1884
Laromiguire, Pierre	1756-1837	Lossing, Benson John	1813-1891
Larousse, Pierre Athanase	1817-1875	Lotze, Rudolf Hermann	1817-1881
Larra, Mariano Jose De	1809-1837	Lover, Samuel	1797-1868
Las Cases, Emmanuel		Lowell, James Russell	1819-1891
Dieudonné Compte De	1766-1842	Ludwig, Otto	1813-1865
Laube, Heinrich	1806-1884	Luttrell, Henry	1765-1851
Lauder, Sir Thomas Dick	1784-1848	Lytton, Edward George	
Laurent, Francois	1810-1887	Lytton Bulwer-Lytton	1803-1873
Lavater, Johann Kaspar	1741-1801	Macaulay, Thomas	
Laya, Jean Louis	1761-1833	Babington Macaulay	1800-1859
Layard, Sir Austen Henry	1817-1894	Macedo, Jose Agostinho	
Lazarus, Moritz	1824-1903	De	1761-1831
Lea, Henry Charles	1825-1909	MacCarthy, Denis Florence	1817-1882
Leconte De Lisle, Charles		McCord, Louise Sussana	
Marie Rene	1818-1894	Cheves	1810-1879
Lee, Harriet	1757-1851	Macdonald, George	1824-1905
Lee, Sophia	1750-1824	McGee, Thomas D'Arcy	1825-1868
Le Fanu, Joseph Sheridan	1814-1873	Macgregor, John	1825-1892
Legouve, Gabriel Jean		Mackay, Charles	1814-1889
Baptiste Ernest Wilfrid	1807-1903	Mackenzie, Henry	1745-1831
Leland, Charles Godfrey	1824-1903	Mackintosh, Sir James	1765-1832
Lemercier, Nopmucene	1771-1840	Maclaren, Charles	1782-1866
Le Moine, James		M'Cosh, James	1811-1894
MacPherson	1825-1912	M'Crie, Thomas	1772-1835
Lemon, Mark	1809-1870	Madach, Imre	1823-1864
Lenau, Nikolaus	1802-1850	Maginn, William	1793-1842
Lennep, Jacob Van	1802-1868	Magny, Claude Drigon	1797-1879
Lennox, Charlotte	1720-1804	Maine De Biran, Francois-	
Leo, Heinrich	1799-1878	Pierre Gonthier	1766-1824
Leopardi, Giacomo	1798-1837	Maine, Sir Henry James	
Lermontov, Mikhail		Sumner	1822-1888
Yurevich	1814-1841	Maistre, Joseph De	1754-1821
Leroux, Pierre	1798-1871	Maistre, Xavier De	1763-1852
Lever, Charles James	1806-1872	Maitland, Edward	1824-1897
Lewald, Fanny	1811-1889	Majlath, Janos	1786-1855
Lewes, George Henry	1817-1878	Major, Richard Henry	1818-1891
Lewis, Sir George Corwall	1806-1863	Malleson, George Bruce	1825-1898
Lewis, Matthew Gregory	1775-1818	Malthus, Thomas Robert	1766-1834
Leyden, John	1775-1811	Mangan, James Clarence	1803-1849
Lieber, Francis	1800-1872	Maning, Frederick Edward	1812-1883
Liebrecht, Felix	1812-1890	Mansel, Henry Longueville	1820-1871
Ligne, Charles Joseph	1735-1814	Manzoni, Alessandro	1785-1873
Lincoln, Abraham	1809-1865	Mapu, Abraham	1808-1867
Lindo, Mark Prager	1819-1879	Markham, Mrs.	1780-1837
Lingard, John	1771-1851	Marquardt, Joachim	1812-1882

O

Marryat, Frederick	1792-1848
Marston, John Westland	1819-1890
Martin, Francois Xavier	1762-1846
Martin, Henri	1810-1883
Martin, Sir Theodore	1816-1909
Martineau, Harriet	1802-1876
Martineau, James	1805-1900
Martinez De La Rosa,	
Francisco De Paula	1787-1862
Marx, Karl Heinrich	1818-1883
Masdeu, Juan Francisco	
De	1744-1817
Masson, David	1822-1907
Matthisson, Friedrich Von	1761-1831
Maturin, Charles Robert	1782-1824
Maurer, Georg Ludwig	
Von	1790-1872
Mayhew, Henry	1812-1887
Melendez Valdez, Juan	1754-1817
Melville, Herman	1819-1891
Menard, Louis Nicolas	1822-1901
Menzel, Wolfgang	1798-1873
Mercier, Sebastien	1740-1814
Merimee, Prosper	1803-1870
Merivale, Charles	1808-1893
Mesonero-Romanos,	
Ramon De	1803-1882
Meurice, Paul	1818-1905
Meyer, Conrad Ferdinand	1825-1898
Michaud, Joseph Francois	1767-1839
Michelet, Jules	1798-1874
Mickiewicz, Adam	1798-1855
Mignet, Francois Auguste	
Marie	1796-1884
Mill, James	1773-1836
Mill, John Stuart	1806-1873
Miller, Hugh	1802-1856
Milman, Henry Hart	1791-1868
Mitchell, Donald Grant	1822-1908
Mitford, John	1781-1859
Mitford, Mary Russell	1787-1855
Mitford, William	1744-1827
Moir, David Macbeth	1798-1851
Molesworth, William	
Nassau	1816-1890
Moller, Paul Martin	1794-1838
Mommsen, Theodor	1817-1903
Montalembert, Charles	
Forbes Rene De	1810-1870
Montanelli, Giuseppe	1813-1862
Montefiore, Joshua	1762-1843
Montgomery, James	1771-1854
Montgomery, Robert	1807-1855
Monti, Vincenzo	1754-1828
Monticelli, Adolphe	
Joseph Thomas	1824-1886
Montufar, Lorenzo	1823-1898
Moore, John	1729-1802
Moore, Thomas	1779-1852
Moratin, Leandro	
Fernandez De	1760-1828

More, Hannah	1745-1833
Moreau, Hegesippe	1810-1838
Morellet, Andre	1727-1819
Morgan, Lady Sydney	1783-1859
Morier, James	1780-1849
Morike, Eduard Friedrich	1804-1875
Morley, Henry	1822-1894
Morton, John Maddison	1811-1891
Morton, Thomas	1764-1838
Mosen, Julius	1803-1867
Motherwell, William	1797-1835
Motley, John Lothrop	1814-1877
Muller, Friedrich	1749-1825
Muller, Johannes Von	1752-1809
Muller, Wilhelm	1794-1827
Munch-Bellinghausen,	
Eligius Franz Joseph	1806-1871
Murger, Henry	1822-1861
Murphy, Arthur	1727-1805
Musset, Alfred De	1810-1857
Nairne, Carolina Oliphant	1766-1845
Nascimento, Francisco	
Manoel De	1734-1819
Nasmyth, Patrick	1787-1831
Neal, John	1793-1876
Neander, Johann	1789-1850
Nekrasov, Nikolai	
Alexeyevich	1821-1877
Nerval, Gerard de	1808-1855
Nestroy, Johann	1801-1862
Newman, Francis William	1805-1897
Newman, John Henry	
(Cardinal)	1801-1890
Nicholas, John	1745-1826
Nicholson, William	1753-1815
Nicolai, Christoph	
Friedrich	1733-1811
Nicoll, Robert	1814-1837
Niebuhr, Barthold Georg	1776-1831
Nitzsch, Karl Immanuel	1787-1868
Nitzsch, Karl Wilhelm	1818-1880
Noailles, Paul, Duke de	1802-1885
Nodier, Charles	1780-1844
Normanby, Constantine	
Henry Phipps	1797-1863
Norton, Caroline Elizabeth	
Sarah	1808-1877
Ohlenschlager, Adam	
Gottlob	1779-1850
Olmedo, Jose Joaquin De	1780-1847
Opie, Amelia	1769-1853
Opzoomer, Cornelius	
William	1821-1892
Orme, Robert	1728-1801
Ostrovsky, Alexander	
Nikolaevich	1823-1886
Ozanam, Antoine Frederic	1813-1853
Paine, Thomas	1737-1809
Palacky, Frantisek	1798-1876
Paley, William	1743-1805
Palfrey, John Gorham	1796-1881

Palgrave, Sir Francis	1788-1861	Raugh, Christian Daniel	1777-1875
Palgrave, Francis Turner	1824-1897	Raumer, Friedrick Ludwig	
Paludan-Muller, Frederick	1809-1876	George Van	1781-1873
Parker, Theodore	1810-1860	Ravaison-Mollien, Jean	
Parkman, Francis	1823-1893	Gaspard Felix	1813-1900
Parton, James	1822-1891	Rawlinson, George	1812-1902
Patmore, Coventry Kersey		Raynouard, Francois Juste	
Dighton	1823-1896	Marie	1761-1836
Pattison, Mark	1813-1884	Reade, Charles	1814-1884
Paulding, James Kirke	1778-1860	Redgrave, Richard	1804-1888
Pauli, Reinhold	1823-1882	Reeve, Clara	1729-1807
Payne, John Howard	1791-1852	Reid, Thomas Mayne	1818-1883
Paz Soldan, Mariano		Remusat, Charles Francois	
Felipe	1821-1886	Marie	1797-1875
Peabody, Andrew Preston	1811-1893	Renan, Ernest	1823-1892
Peacock, Thomas Love	1785-1866	Renouvier, Charles	
Peesemsky, Alexey		Bernard	1815-1903
Feofilactovich	1820-1881	Restif, Nicolas Edme	1734-1806
Pellico, Silvio	1788-1854	Reuter, Fritz	1810-1874
Percival, James Gates	1795-1856	Richmond, Legh	1772-1827
Percy, Thomas	1729-1811	Richter, Johann Paul	
Pertz, Georg Heinrich	1795-1876	Friedrich	1763-1825
Petofi, Alexander	1823-1849	Ritter, Heinrich	1791-1869
Picken, Andrew	1788-1833	Rivarol, Antoine De	1753-1801
Pindemonte, Ippolito	1753-1828	Rivas, Angel De Saavedra	1791-1865
Piozzi, Hester Lynch	1741-1821	Rogers, Randolph	1825-1892
Planche, James Robinson	1796-1880	Rogers, Samuel	1763-1855
Poe, Edgar Allan	1809-1849	Roscoe, William	1753-1831
Poerico, Alessandro	1802-1848	Rosenkranz, Karl	1805-1879
Ponsard, Francois	1814-1867	Rosmini-Serbatil, Antonio	1797-1855
Poole, William Frederick	1821-1894	Rossetti, Gabriele	1783-1854
Porter, Anna Maria	1780-1832	Rouget de Lisle, Claude	
Porter, Jane	1776-1850	Joseph	1760-1836
Porter, Noah	1811-1892	Roumanile, Joseph	1818-1891
Potgieter, Everhardes		Royer-Collard, Pierre Paul	1763-1845
Johannes	1808-1875	Rückert, Friedrich	1788-1866
Potthast, August	1824-1898	Ruffini, Giovanni	
Praed, Winthrop		Domenico	1807-1881
Mackworth	1802-1839	Ruge, Arnold	1802-1880
Prantl, Karl Von	1820-1888	Runeberg, Johan Ludvig	1804-1877
Prati, Giovanni	1815-1884	Ruskin, John	1819-1900
Prescott, William Hickling	1796-1859	Sade, Donatien Alphonse	
Priestley, Joseph	1733-1804	Francois (Marquis De)	1740-1814
Pringle, Thomas	1789-1834	Safarik, Pavel Josef	1795-1861
Procter, Adelaide Anne	1825-1864	Sainte-Beuve, Charles	
Procter, Bryan Waller	1787-1874	Augustin	1804-1869
Proud, Robert	1728-1813	Saintine, Joseph Xavier	1798-1865
Proudhon, Pierre Joseph	1809-1865	Saint-Lambert, Jean	
Pusey, Edward Bouverie	1800-1882	Francois De	1716-1803
Pushkin, Alexander	1799-1837	Saint-Marc, Girardin	1801-1873
Pye, Henry James	1745-1813	Saint-Martin, Louis Claude	
Pyne, William Henry	1769-1843	De	1743-1803
Quicherat, Jules Etienne		Saint-Pierre, Bernardin De	1737-1814
Joseph	1814-1882	Salomon, Johann Peter	1745-1815
Quincy, Josiah	1772-1864	Sand, George (Dudevant)	1804-1876
Quinet, Edgar	1803-1875	Sandeau, Leonard Sylvain	
Quintana, Manuel Josè	1772-1857	Julien	1811-1883
Radcliffe, Ann	1764-1823	Sant, James	1820-1916
Ragabe, Alexandros-Rizos	1810-1892	Sarmiento, Domingo	
Rands, William Brighty	1823-1882	Faustino	1811-1888
Ranke, Leopold Von	1795-1886	Saxe, John Godfrey	1816-1887

Schelling, Friedrich
Wilhelm Joseph Von 1775-1854
Schiller, Johann Cristoph
Friedrich Von 1759-1805
Schimmelpenninck, Mary
Ann 1778-1856
Schlegel, August Wilhelm
Von 1767-1845
Schlegel, Friedrich Von 1772-1829
Schleiermacher, Friedrich
Daniel Ernst 1768-1834
Schlozer, August Ludwig
Von 1735-1809
Schopenhauer, Arthur 1788-1860
Scott, Sir Walter 1771-1832
Scribe, Eugene 1791-1861
Seguier, William 1771-1843
Segur, Philippe Paul,
Comte de 1780-1873
Sellar, William Young 1825-1890
Senac de Meilhan, Gabriel 1736-1803
Senancour, Etienne Pivert
De 1770-1846
Settembrini, Luigi 1813-1877
Seward, Anna 1747-1809
Sewell, Anna 1820-1878
Shairp, John Campbell 1819-1885
Shaw, Henry Wheeler 1818-1885
Sheil, Richard Lalor 1791-1851
Shelley, Mary
Wollstonecraft 1797-1851
Shelley, Percy Bysshe 1792-1822
Sheridan, Richard Brinsley
Butler 1751-1816
Sherwood, Mary Martha 1775-1851
Shevchenko, Taras 1814-1861
Sigourney, Lydia Huntley 1791-1865
Simms, William Gilmore 1806-1870
Simon, Jules Francois 1814-1896
Simrock, Karl Joseph 1802-1876
Sismondi, Jean Charles
Leonard Simonde 1773-1842
Skene, William Forbes 1809-1892
Slowacki, Juljusz 1809-1849
Smiles, Samuel 1812-1904
Smith, Charlotte 1749-1806
Smith, Goldwin 1823-1910
Smith, Horace 1779-1849
Smith, James 1775-1839
Smith, John Stafford 1750-1836
Smith, Sidney 1771-1845
Smith, Walter Chalmers 1824-1908
Smith, Sir William 1813-1893
Soloviev, Sergei
Mikhailovich 1820-1879
Southey, Robert 1774-1843
Souza-Botelmo, Adelaide
Filleul 1761-1836
Sparks, Jared 1789-1866
Spencer, Herbert 1820-1903
Stael, Madame De 1766-1817

Stahl, Frierich Julius 1802-1861
Stanhope, Philip Henry
Stanhope 1805-1875
Stanley, Arthur Penrhyn 1815-1881
Steffens, Henrik 1773-1845
Stendhal, (Marie Henry
Beyle) 1783-1842
Sterling, John 1806-1844
Stern, Daniel (Agoult) 1805-1876
Stewart, Dugald 1753-1828
Stifter, Adalbert 1805-1868
Stilling, Heinrich 1740-1817
Stirling, James Hutchinson 1820-1909
Stirling-Maxwell, Sir
William Bart 1818-1878
Stirner, Max 1806-1856
Stoddard, Richard Henry 1825-1903
Stolberg, Friedrich Leopold 1750-1819
Storm, Theodor Wolsden 1817-1888
Stowe, Harriet Elizabeth
Beecher 1811-1896
Strachwitz, Moritz Karl
Wilhelm Anton 1822-1847
Strauss, David Friedrich 1808-1874
Street, Alfred Billings 1811-1881
Strickland, Agnes 1806-1874
Strutt, Joseph 1742-1802
Stubbs, William 1825-1901
Sue, Eugene 1804-1857
Surtees, Robert Smith 1803-1864
Swanwick, Anna 1813-1899
Swetchine, Madame 1782-1857
Sybel, Heinrich Von 1817-1895
Talfourd, Sir Thomas
Noon 1795-1854
Tannahill, Robert 1774-1810
Taylor, Ann 1782-1866
Taylor, Bayard 1825-1878
Taylor, Sir Henry 1800-1886
Taylor, Isaac 1787-1865
Taylor, Isaak 1829-1901
Taylor, Jane 1783-1824
Taylor, Tom 1817-1880
Taylor, William 1765-1836
Tegner, Esaias 1782-1846
Tennant, William 1784-1848
Tennyson, Alfred
Tennyson 1809-1892
Thackeray, William
Makepeace 1811-1863
Thierry, Jacques Nicolas
Augustin 1795-1856
Thiers, Louis Adolph 1797-1877
Thirlwall, Connop 1797-1875
Thompson, William c. 1785-1833
Thoreau, Henry David 1817-1862
Ticknor, George 1791-1871
Tieck, Johann Ludwig 1773-1853
Tischendorf, Lobegott 1815-1874
Tocqueville, Alexis Charles
Henri Clérel 1805-1859

Tolstoy, Alexei		Walker, John	1732-1807
Konstantinovich	1817-1875	Walker, Thomas	1784-1836
Tommaseo, Niccolo	1802-1874	Wallace, Alfred Russel	1823-1913
Tompa, Mihaly	1817-1868	Wallon, Henri Alexandre	1812-1904
Topelius, Zachris	1818-1898	Warburton, Eliot	1810-1852
Topffer, Rodolphe	1799-1846	Warner, Susan Bogert	1819-1895
Toreno, Jose Maria		Warren, Samuel	1807-1877
Queipo De Llano	1786-1843	Waugh, Edwin	1817-1890
Trelawny, Edward John	1792-1881	Webster, Noah	1758-1843
Trench, Richard Chevenix	1807-1886	Welhaven, Johann Sebastian	
Trendelenburg, Friedrich		Cammermeyer	1807-1873
Adolf	1802-1872	Wells, Charles Jeremiah	1798-1879
Trollope, Anthony	1815-1882	Wennerberg, Gunnar	1817-1901
Trollope, Frances	1780-1863	Wergeland, Henrik Arnold	1808-1845
Trollope, Thomas		Werner, Zacharias	1768-1823
Adolphus	1810-1892	West, Benjamin	1738-1820
Trumbull, John	1750-1831	Whately, Richard	1787-1863
Tucker, Charlotte Marie	1821-1893	Whewell, William	1794-1866
Tupper, Martin Farquhar	1810-1889	White, Henry Kirke	1785-1806
Turgenev, Ivan		White, Richard Grant	1821-1885
Sereyevich	1818-1883	Whitehead, Charles	1804-1862
Turner, Charles Tennyson	1808-1879	Whitman, Walt	1819-1892
Turner, Sharon	1768-1847	Whittier, John Greenleaf	1807-1892
Tyndall, John	1820-1893	Wieland, Christoph	
Tyuchev, Fydor Ivanovich	1803-1873	Martin	1733-1813
Uhland, Johann Ludwig	1787-1862	Wilberforce, William	1759-1833
Vacherot, Etienne	1809-1897	Willis, Nathaniel Parker	1806-1867
Valera Y Alcala, Galiano		Wilson, Alexander	1766-1813
Juan	1824-1905	Wilson, John	1785-1854
Van Beers, Jan	1821-1888	Winther, Christian	1796-1876
Vaperau, Louis Gustave	1819-1906	Wirt, William	1772-1834
Varnhagen, Francisco		Wolcot, John (Peter	
Adolpho De	1816-1878	Pinder)	1738-1819
Varnhagen, Von Ense		Wolfe, Charles	1791-1823
Karl August	1785-1858	Wollaston, William Hyde	1766-1828
Verplanck, Gulian		Wood, Mrs. Henry	1814-1887
Crommelin	1786-1870	Wordsworth, Dorothy	1771-1855
Vidyasagar, Iswar		Wordsworth, William	1770-1850
Chandra	1820-1891	Wraxall, Sir Nathaniel	
Vigny, Alfred De	1797-1863	William	1751-1831
Villemain, Abel Francois	1790-1870	Wright, Thomas	1810-1887
Vinje, Aasmund Olavson	1816-1870	Wyatt, Sir Matthew Digby	1820-1877
Vischer, Friedrich		Wyss, Johann	1781-1830
Theodor	1807-1887	Yonge, Charlotte Mary	1823-1901
Volney, Constantin		Young, Arthur	1741-1820
Francois Chasseboeuf,		Zeller, Eduard	1814-1908
Compte de	1757-1820	Zhukovsky, Vasili	
Voss, Johann Heinrich	1751-1826	Andreyevich	1783-1852
Waagen, Gustav Friedrich	1794-1868	Zorrilla, Jose	1817-1893
Wackenroder, Wilhelm		Zschokke, Johann	
Heinrich	1773-1798	Heinrick Daniel	1771-1848

ARTISTS

Achenbach, Andreas	1815-1910	Ansdell, Richard	1815-1885
Ainmuller, Maximilian		Appiani, Andrea	1754-1817
Emmanuel	1807-1870	Armitage, Edward	1817-1896
Allan, Sir William	1782-1850	Audubon, John James	1785-1851
Allston, Washington	1779-1843	Baily, Edward Hodges	1788-1867
Alvarez, Don Jose	1768-1827	Ball, Thomas	1819-1911

Baltard, Louis Pierre	1764-1846	Chasseriau, Theodore	1819-1856
Bandel, Ernst Von	1800-1876	Chisholm, Alexander	1792-1847
Banks, Thomas	1735-1805	Chodowiecki, Daniel	
Barker, Robert	1739-1806	Nicolas	1726-1801
Barry, Sir Charles	1795-1860	Clays, Paul Jean	1819-1900
Barry, James	1741-1806	Cockerell, Charles Robert	1788-1863
Bartolini, Lorenzo	1777-1850	Cole, Thomas	1801-1848
Bartolozzi, Francesco	1727-1815	Constable, John	1776-1837
Barye, Antoine Louis	1796-1875	Cooper, Abraham	1787-1868
Begas, Karl	1794-1854	Cooper, Thomas Sidney	1803-1902
Bell, John	1811-1895	Cope, Charles West	1811-1890
Beverley, William Roxby	1814-1889	Copley, John Singleton	1737-1815
Bewick, Thomas	1753-1828	Corbould, Edward Henry	1815-1905
Birch, Samuel	1813-1885	Corbould, Henry	1787-1844
Bird, Edward	1772-1819	Corbould, Richard	1757-1831
Bone, Henry	1755-1834	Cornelius, Peter Von	1783-1867
Bonomi, Giuseppe	1739-1808	Corot, Jean-Baptiste	
Bonheur, Rosa	1822-1899	Camille	1796-1875
Bonington, Richard		Cosway, Richard	1742-1821
Parkes	1801-1828	Cotman, John Sell	1782-1842
Bosio, Francois Joseph,		Courbet, Gustav	1819-1877
Baron	1769-1845	Couture, Thomas	1815-1879
Bossi, Giuseppe	1777-1816	Crane, Thomas	1808-1859
Boudin, Louis Eugene	1824-1898	Cox, David	1783-1859
Bough, Samuel	1822-1878	Cox, David, the younger	1809-1885
Bouguereau, Adolphe		Crome, John	1768-1821
William	1825-1905	Crawford, Thomas	1814-1857
Boydell, John	1719-1804	Creswick, Thomas	1811-1869
Brascassat, Jacques		Cruikshank, George	1792-1878
Raymond	1804-1867	Daguerre, Louis Jacques	
Brierly, Sir Oswald		Mande	1789-1851
Walters	1817-1894	Dahl, Johann, Kristen	
Bright, Henry	1814-1873	Clausen	1788-1857
Brodie, William	1815-1881	Damer, Anne Seymour	1749-1828
Brown, Ford Madox	1821-1893	Danby, Francis	1793-1861
Brown, George Loring	1814-1889	Dance, George	1741-1825
Brown, Henry Kirke	1814-1886	Daniell, Samuel	1775-1811
Browne, Hablot Knight	1815-1882	Daniell, Thomas	1749-1840
Bulfinch, Charles	1763-1844	Daniell, William	1769-1837
Burn, William	1789-1870	Dannecker, Johann	
Burton, Decimus	1800-1881	Heinrich Von	1758-1841
Butterfield, William	1814-1900	Dantan, Antoine Laurent	1798-1878
Bystrom, Johan Niklas	1783-1848	Dantan, Jean Pierre	1800-1869
Cabanel, Alexandre	1823-1889	Darley, Felix Octavius	
Cagnola, Luigi	1762-1833	Carr	**1822-1888**
Calame, Alexandre	1810-1864	Daubigny, Charles	
Callcott, Sir Augustus		Francois	1817-1878
Wall	1779-1844	Daumier, Honore	1808-1879
Calvert, Charles	1785-1852	David, Jacques Louis	1748-1825
Calvert, Edward	1799-1883	Dawson, Henry	1811-1878
Camphausen, Wilhelm	1818-1885	Decamps, Alexandra	
Camuccini, Vincenzo	1773-1844	Gabriel	1803-1860
Canova, Antonio	1757-1822	Delacroix, Ferdinand	
Capronnier, Jean Baptiste	1814-1891	Victor Eugene	1798-1863
Casanova de Seingalt,		Delaroche, Hippolyte	1797-1856
Francesco	1727-1805	De Loutherbourg,	
Catlin, George	1796-1872	Philip James	1740-1812
Cattermole, George	1800-1868	Denon, Dominique Vivant	1747-1825
Chantrey, Sir Charles		Diaz, Narcisse Virgile	1809-1876
Legatt	1781-1841	Dobson, William Charles	
Charlet, Nicolas Toussaint	1792-1845	Thomas	1817-1898

Doyle, Richard	1824-1883	Goya Y Lucientes,	
Duncan, Thomas	1807-1845	Francisco	1746-1828
Dupre, Giovanni	1817-1882	Granet, Francois Marius	1775-1849
Dupre, Jules	1811-1889	Grant, Sir Francis	1803-1878
Dyce, William	1806-1864	Greenough, Horatio	1805-1852
Downman, John	1750-1824	Greuze, Jean Baptiste	1725-1805
Doyen, Gabriel Francois	1726-1806	Gros, Antoine Jean	1771-1835
Dumont, Francois	1751-1831	Gudin, Theodore	1802-1880
Durand, Asher Brown	1796-1886	Guerin, Pierre Narcisse	1774-1833
Earlom, Richard	1743-1822	Guillaume, Jean Baptiste	
Eastlake, Sir Charles Lock	1793-1865	Claude	1822-1905
Eberz, Josef	1801-1882	Gwilt, Joseph	1784-1863
Eckersberg, Kristoffer	1783-1853	Haag, Carl	1820-1915
Egg, Augustus Leopold	1816-1863	Hamon, Jean Louis	1821-1874
Engleheart, George	1752-1829	Hansen, Christian Frederik	1756-1845
Elliott, Charles Loring	1812-1868	Hansom, Joseph Aloysius	1803-1882
Etex, Antoine	1808-1888	Harding, Chester	1792-1866
Etty, William	1787-1849	Harlow, George Henry	1787-1819
Farington, Joseph	1747-1821	Harpignies, Henri	1819-1916
Fielding, Copley	1787-1855	Harvey, Sir George	1806-1876
Fiorillo, Johann		Haydon, Benjamin Robert	1786-1846
Dominicus	1748-1821	Hayter, Sir George	1792-1871
Flandrin, Jean Hippolyte	1809-1864	Heaphy, Thomas	1775-1835
Flaxman, John	1755-1826	Herbert, John Rogers	1810-1900
Fogelberg, Benedict		Hilderbrandt, Eduard	1818-1869
Erland	1786-1854	Hilton, William	1786-1839
Foley, John Henry	1818-1874	Hiroshege, Ando	1797-1858
Fontaine, Pierre Francois		Hittorff, Jacques Ignace	1792-1867
Leonard	1762-1853	Hokusai, Katsushika	1760-1849
Forster, Ernst	1800-1885	Hook, James Clarke	1819-1907
Foster, Myles Birkett	1825-1899	Hoppner, John	1758-1810
Fowler, Charles	1792-1867	Horsley, John Calcott	1817-1903
Fragonard, Jean Honore	1732-1806	Houdon, Jean Antoine	1740-1828
Francais, Francois Louis	1814-1897	Hubner, Julius	1806-1882
Fremiet, Emmanuel	1824-1910	Huet, Paul	1804-1869
Friedrich, Caspar David	1774-1840	Humphry, Ozias	1742-1810
Fripp, Alfred Downing	1822-1895	Hunt, William Henry	1790-1864
Fripp, George Arthur	1814-1896	Hunt, William Morris	1824-1879
Fuseli, Henry	1741-1825	Huntingdon, Daniel	1816-1906
Frith, William Powell	1819-1909	Hurlstone, Frederick	
Fromentin, Eugene	1820-1876	Yeates	1800-1869
Frost, William Edward	1810-1877	Ingres, Jean Auguste	
Fuhrich, Joseph Von	1800-1876	Dominique	1780-1867
Fuller, George	1822-1884	Inman, Henry	1801-1846
Gallait, Louis	1810-1887	Innes, George	1825-1894
Garnier, Jean Louis Charles	1825-1898	Isabey, Jean Baptiste	1767-1855
Gavarni, Paul	1801-1866	Israel, Josef	1824-1911
Geddes, Andrew	1783-1844	Jacques, Charles	1813-1894
Gericault, Theodore	1791-1824	Jalabert, Charles Francois	1819-1901
Gerome, Jean Leon	1824-1904	Johnson, Eastman	1824-1906
Gerrard, Francois	1770-1837	Jonkind, Johann Barthold	1819-1891
Gibson, John	1790-1866	Jordan, Rudolf	1810-1887
Gilbert, Sir John	1817-1897	Kauffmann, Angelica	1741-1807
Gillray, James	1757-1815	Kaulbach, Wilhelm Von	1805-1874
Girodet De Roussy, Anne		Keene, Charles Samuel	1823-1891
Louis	1767-1824	Kensett, John Frederick	1818-1872
Girtin, Thomas	1775-1802	Kirkup, Seymour Stocker	1788-1880
Gleyre, Charles	1806-1874	La Grenée, Jean Louis	
Goldschmidt, Hermann	1802-1866	Francois	1724-1805
Goodall, Frederick	1822-1904	Landseer, Sir Edwin	
Gordon, Sir John Watson	1788-1864	Henry	1802-1873

Lauder, Robert Scott	1803-1869	Poole, Paul Falconer	1807-1879
Lawrence, Sir Thomas	1769-1830	Porta, Carlo	1776-1821
Lear, Edward	1812-1888	Portaels, Jean Francois	1818-1895
Le Brun, Marie Elizabeth		Porter, Robert Ker	1775-1842
Louise	1755-1842	Powers, Hiram	1805-1873
Leech, John	1817-1864	Prout, Samuel	1783-1852
Lehman, Rudolf	1819-1905	Prud'hon, Pierre	1758-1823
Lejeune, Louis Francois	1775-1848	Pugin, Augustus Welby	
Lemaire, Philippe Honoré	1798-1880	Northmore	1812-1852
L'Enfant, Pierre Charles	1754-1825	Puvis, De Chavannes Pierre	
Leslie, Charles Robert	1794-1859	Cecile	1824-1898
Leutze, Emanuel	1816-1868	Raeburn, Sir Henry	1756-1823
Leys, Hendrik	1815-1869	Renwick, James	1818-1895
Lindsay, Sir Coutts	1824-1913	Rethel, Alfred	1816-1859
Linnell, John	1792-1882	Retzsch, Friedrich August	
Macculoch, Horatio	1805-1867	Moritz	1779-1857
Maclise, Daniel	1806-1870	Richmond, George	1809-1896
MacNee, Sir Daniel	1806-1882	Rickman, Thomas	1776-1841
Madrazo Y Kunt, Don		Rietschel, Ernst	1804-1861
Federico, De	1815-1894	Robert, Hubert	1733-1808
Manes, Josef	1820-1871	Roberts, David	1796-1864
Marochetti, Carlo	1805-1867	Romney, George	1734-1802
Marshall, William Calder	1813-1894	Rousseau, Pierre Etienne	
Martin, John	1789-1854	Theodore	1812-1867
Meissonier, Jean Louis		Rowlandson, Thomas	1756-1827
Ernst	1815-1891	Rude, Francois	1784-1855
Menzel, Adolph Friedrich		Sandby, Paul	1725-1809
Erdmann Von	1815-1905	Schadow, Friedrich	
Michel, Claude	1738-1814	Wilhelm	1798-1862
Millet, Jean Francois	1814-1875	Schadow, Johann Gottfried	1764-1850
Moore, William	1790-1851	Schadow, Rudolf	1786-1822
Morel La Deuil, Leonard	1820-1888	Scheffer, Ary	1795-1858
Morland, George	1763-1804	Schinkel, Karl Friedrich	1781-1841
Morse, Samuel Finley		Schnorr Von Karolsfeld,	
Breese	1791-1872	Julius	1794-1872
Motte, William De La	1775-1863	Schwanthaler, Ludwig	
Mount, William Sidney	1807-1868	Michael	1802-1848
Muller, William James	1812-1845	Schwind, Moritz Von	1804-1871
Mulready, William	1786-1863	Scott, David	1806-1849
Nash, John	1752-1835	Scott, Sir George Gilbert	1811-1878
Nasmyth, Alexander	1758-1840	Semper, Gottfried	1803-1873
Nicol, Erskine	1825-1904	Severn, Joseph	1793-1879
Nollekens, Joseph	1737-1823	Shee, Sir Martin Archer	1769-1850
Northcote, James	1746-1831	Sheraton, Thomas	
Ondine, Eugene Andre	1810-1887	(cabinet maker)	1751-1806
Opie, John	1761-1807	Simson, William	1800-1847
Overbeck, Johann		Smart, John	1740-1811
Friedrich	1789-1869	Smillie, James David	1833-1909
Page, William	1811-1885	Smirke, Sir Robert	1781-1867
Pajou, Augustin	1730-1809	Smith, John Raphael	1752-1812
Palmer, Samuel	1805-1881	Soane, Sir John	1753-1837
Paton, Sir Joseph Noel	1821-1901	Sowerby, James	1757-1822
Paxton, Sir Joseph	1801-1865	Stanfield, William	
Peace, Charles Willson	1741-1827	Clarkson	1794-1867
Peale, Rembrandt	1778-1860	Stark, James	1794-1859
Pearson, John		Steell, Sir John	1804-1891
Loughborough	1817-1897	Steinle, Eduard	1810-1886
Percier, Charles	1764-1838	Story, William Wetmore	1819-1895
Pinelli, Bartolomeo	1781-1834	Stothard, Thomas	1755-1834
Playfair, William Henry	1789-1857	Street, George Edmund	1824-1881
Plimer, Andrew	1763-1837	Stuart, Gilbert	1755-1828

Sully, Thomas	1783-1872	Vigee Lebrun, Marie Anne	
Tenniel, Sir John	1820-1914	Elizabeth	1755-1842
Thorvaldsen, Bertel	1770-1844	Violet Le Duc, Eugen	
Tite, Sir William	1798-1873	Emmanuel	1814-1879
Towne, Francis	1739-1816	Vorosmarty, Mihaly	1800-1855
Travies De Villiers,		Wainewright, Thomas	
Charles Joseph	1804-1859	Griffiths	1794-1852
Troyon, Constant	1810-1865	Waldo, Samuel Lovett	1783-1861
Trumbull, John	1756-1843	Ward, George Frederic	1817-1904
Turner, Joseph Mallord		Weir, Robert Walter	1803-1889
William	1775-1851	Westmacott, Sir Richard	1775-1856
Uta Maro	1754-1806	Wiertz, Anton Joseph	1806-1865
Vanderlyn, John	1776-1852	Wilkie, Sir David	1785-1841
Varley, John	1778-1842	Willems, Florent Joseph	
Veit, Philipp	1793-1877	Marie	1823-1905
Verboeckhoven, Eugene		Wint, Peter De	1784-1849
Joseph	1798-1881	Winter Halter, Franz	
Vernet, Antoine Charles		Xavier	1806-1873
Horace	1758-1835	Wyatt, Johann	1746-1813
Vernet, Emile Jean		Ziem, Felix Francois	
Horace	1789-1863	George	1821-1911
		Zoffany, Johann	1733-1810

COMPOSERS

Abt, Franz	1819-1885	Cimarosa, Domenico	1749-1801
Adam, Adolphe Charles	1803-1856	Chopin, Frederic Francois	1810-1849
Albrechtberger, Johann		Clementi, Muzio	1752-1832
Gregory	1736-1809	Cornelius, Carl August	
Arditi, Luigi	1822-1903	Peter	1824-1874
Arnold, Samuel	1740-1802	Corri, Domenico	1746-1825
Arriaga, Juan	1806-1826	Costa, Sir Michael	1810-1884
Asioli, Bonifacio	1769-1832	Crotch, William	1775-1847
Attwood, Thomas	1765-1838	Czerny, Karl	1791-1857
Auber, Daniel Francois		Dargomijsky, Alexander	
Eprit	1782-1871	Sergeivich	1813-1869
Baini, Guiseppe	1775-1844	David, Felicien	1810-1876
Batishill, Jonathan	1738-1801	Diabelli, Anton Antonio	1781-1858
Barnett, John	1802-1890	Dibdin, Charles	1745-1814
Beethoven, Ludwig Van	1770-1827	Donizetti, Gaetano	1797-1848
Bellini, Vincenzo	1801-1835	Doppler, Albert Franz	1821-1883
Benedict, Sir Julius	1804-1885	Dreyschock, Alexander	1818-1869
Bennett, Sir William		Dussek, Jan Ladislav	1761-1812
Sterndale	1816-1875	Dykes, John Bacchus	1823-1876
Beriot, Charles Auguste		Eberwein, Traugott	
De	1802-1870	Maximilian	1775-1831
Berlioz, Hector	1803-1869	Elvey, Sir George Job	1816-1893
Bishop, Sir Henry Rowley	1786-1855	Ernst, Heinrich Wilhelm	1814-1865
Boccherini, Luigi	1743-1805	Fetis, Francois Joseph	1784-1871
Boieldieu, Francois Adrien	1775-1834	Field, John	1782-1837
Bottesini, Giovanni	1822-1889	Flotow, Friedrich Freiherr	1812-1883
Brabazon, Hercules		Franck, Cesar	1822-1890
Brabazon	1821-1906	Franz, Robert	1815-1892
Bruckner, Anton	1824-1896	Gade, Niels Vilhelm	1817-1890
Callcott, John Wall	1766-1821	Gansbacher, Johann	
Cambini, Giovanni		Baptist	1778-1844
Giuseppe	1746-1825	Garcia, Manoel	1775-1832
Campenhout, Francois		Gazzaniga, Giuseppe	1743-1818
Von	1779-1849	Glinka, Michael Ivanovich	1803-1857
Cherubini, Marcia Luigi	1760-1842	Goss, Sir John	1800-1880

Gossec, Francois Joseph	1734-1829	Nathan, Isaac	1791-1864
Gounod, Charles Francois	1818-1893	Nicolai, Otto	1810-1849
Gow, Niel	1727-1807	Offenbach, Jacques	1819-1880
Gretry, Andre Ernest		Ouseley, Sir Frederick	
Modeste	1741-1813	Arthur Gore	1825-1889
Gung'l, Josef	1810-1889	Paer, Ferdinando	1771-1839
Halevy, Jacques Francois	1799-1862	Paisiello, Giovanni	1741-1816
Hatton, John Liptrot	1809-1886	Pearsall, Robert Lucas De	1795-1856
Hauptmann, Moritz	1792-1868	Pierson, Henry Hugo	1815-1873
Haydn, Franz Joseph	1732-1809	Pleyel, Ignaz-Joseph	1757-1831
Haydn, Michael	1737-1806	Raff, Joseph Joachim	1822-1882
Heller, Stephen	1815-1888	Reineck, Carl Heinrich	1824-1910
Henselt, Adolf Von	1814-1889	Rockstro, William Smith	1823-1895
Herold, Louis Joseph	1791-1833	Rossini, Gioachino	
Herve, Florimond Rounger	1825-1892	Antonio	1792-1868
Herz, Henri	1806-1888	Salieri, Antonio	1750-1825
Hiller, Ferdinand	1811-1885	Sarti, Giuseppe	1729-1802
Hiller, Johann Adam	1728-1804	Schubert, Franz	1808-1878
Himmel, Frederick Henry	1765-1814	Schubert, Franz Peter	1797-1828
Horn, Charles Edward	1786-1849	Schumann, Clara	
Hullah, John Pyke	1812-1884	Josephine	1819-1896
Hummel, Johann		Schumann, Robert	
Nepomuk	1778-1837	Alexander	1810-1856
Jackson, Wilhelm	1730-1803	Shield, William	1748-1829
Kelly, Michael	1762-1826	Smetana, Bedrich	1824-1884
Kjeruf, Halfdan	1815-1868	Spontini, Gasparo Luigi	1774-1851
Kreutzer, Konradin	1780-1849	Spohr, Ludwig	1784-1859
Lacombe, Louis Trouillon	1818-1884	Spottiswoode, Alicia Anne,	
Lado, Edouard	1823-1892	Lady John	1811-1900
Lemmens, Nicolas Jacques	1823-1881	Stamitz, Carl Philipp	1745-1801
Lesueur, Jean Francois	1760-1837	Steibelt, Daniel	1764-1823
Liszt, Franz	1811-1886	Strauss, Johann	1804-1849
Loewe, Johann Karl		Strauss, Johann the	
Gottfried	1796-1869	younger	1825-1899
Lortzing, Albert	1801-1851	Suppe, Franz Von	1820-1895
MacFarren, Sir George		Thomas, Ambroise	1811-1896
Alexander	1813-1887	Verdi, Giuseppe Fortunino	1813-1901
Marschner, Heinrich		Viotti, Giovanni Battista	1753-1824
August	1795-1861	Vogler, George Joseph	1749-1814
Mehul, Etienne Nicolas	1763-1817	Wagner, Wilhelm Richard	1813-1883
Mendelssohn, Bartholdi		Wallace, William Vincent	1812-1865
Jakob Ludwig Felix	1809-1847	Weber, Carl Maria	
Meyebeer, Giacomo	1791-1864	Friedrich	1786-1826
Monk, William Henry	1823-1889	Wesley, Samuel Sebastian	1810-1876
Monsigny, Pierre		Wesley, Samuel	1766-1837
Alexandre	1729-1817	Zingarelli, Niccolo	1752-1837

1827	Kingdom of Greece founded.
	Battle of Navarino.
1830	Warsaw uprising.
1831	First epidemic of Asiatic cholera in England.
1833	Slavery abolished in British colonies.
	First Government grant aid to English schools.
1834	Faraday discovers electrical self-induction.
1837	Morse alphabet adopted.
1838	National Gallery opened.
1839	Gold discovered in Australia.
1840	Penny postage instituted.
1842	Khyber Pass incident.
1843	Battle of Meeanee.
	Battle of Maharajpore.
1845	Battle of Moodkee.
	Battle of Ferozeshah.
1846	Battle of Aliwal.
	Repeal of the Corn Laws.
1847	British Museum opened.
1848	Gold discovered in California.
1849	Hugary invaded by Russia.
1850	Submarine telegraph between England-France.

PROMINENT PEOPLE

Brown, John	1800-1859	Lessepes, Vicomte	
Bismarck, Prince Otto		Ferdinand de	1805-1894
Eduard Leopold Von	1815-1898	Lister, Lord	1827-1912
Booth, General William	1829-1912	Livingstone, Dr. David	1813-1873
Braille, Louis	1809-1852	Manning, Henry Edward,	
Brummell, 'Beau', George		Cardinal	1808-1892
Bryan	1778-1840	Paganini, Nicolo	1782-1840
Edison, Thomas Alva	1847-1931	Pasteur, Louis	1822-1895
Faraday, Michael	1791-1867	Rontgen, Prof. Welhelm	
Garibaldi, Giuseppe	1807-1882	Konrad	1845-1923
Kitchener of Khartoum	1850-1916	Smith, Joseph	1805-1844
		Wellington, Duke of	1769-1852

EMPERORS OF CHINA (MANCHU (Ch'ing) DYNASTY)

Hsuan Tsung   1820-1850

POPES

Leo XII	1823-1829	Pius IX	1830-1878
Pius VIII	1829-1830		

FRANCE. HEADS OF STATE

Charles X	1824-1830	Louis Napoleon Bonaparte	1848-1852
Louis Philippe	1830-1848		

ENGLAND. SOVEREIGNS

George IV	1820-1830	Victoria	1837-1901
William IV	1830-1837		

SWEDEN. KINGS

Charles XIV (Bernadotte)	1818-1844	Oscar I	1844-1859

PORTUGAL. KINGS 1826-1850

John VI	1816-1826	Miguel	1828-1834
Pedro IV	1826-	Maria II (again)	1834-1853
Maria II	1826-1828		

RUSSIA. TSARS

Nicholas I	1825-1855

SPAIN. SOVEREIGNS

Ferdinand VII	1813-1833	Isabella II	1833-1868

U.S.A. PRESIDENTS

John Quincy Adams	1825-1829	J. Knox Polk	1845-1849
Andrew Jackson	1829-1837	Zachary Taylor	1849-1850
Martin Van Buren	1837-1841	Millard Fillimore	
W. H. Harrison	1841-	(Vice P.)	1850-1853
John Tyler (Vice P.)	1841-1845		

PRUSSIA. KINGS

Frederick William III	1797-1840	Frederick William IV	1840-1861

AUSTRIA. EMPERORS

Franz I	1804-1835	Franz Josef	1848-1916
Ferdinand I	1835-1848		

NETHERLANDS. SOVEREIGNS

William I	1815-1840	William III	1849-1890
William II	1840-1849		

BELGIUM. KINGS

Leopold I	1831-1865

WRITERS

Aarestrup, Emil	1800-1856	Adams, Hannah	1755-1831
Aasen, Ivar	1813-1896	Adams, Henry Brooks	1838-1918
Abbott, Edwin Abbott	1838-1926	Adams, John Quincy	1767-1848
Abbott, Evelyn	1843-1901	Adams, Sarah Flower	1805-1848
Abbott, Jacob	1803-1879	Adams, William Taylor	1822-1897
Abbott, Lyman	1835-1922	Adolphus, John	1768-1845
A'Beckett, Gilbert Abbott	1811-1856	Adolphus, John Leycester	1795-1862
Abernethy, John	1764-1831	Afanasiev, Alexander	
Aberigh Mackay, George		Nikolaievitch	1826-1871
Robert	1848-1881	Afzelius, Aruid August	1785-1871
About, Edmond Francois		Agassiz, Jean Louis	
Valentin	1828-1885	Rodolphe	1807-1873
Ackermann, Louise		Agoult, Marie Catherine	
Victorine Choquet	1813-1890	Sophie de Flavigny,	
Acton, John Emrich		Countess de (Daniel	
Edward Dolbey	1834-1902	Stern)	1805-1876
Adam, Juliette	1836-1936	Aguilar, Grace	1816-1847
Adams, Charles Follen	1842-1918	Aguilo I Fuster, Marian	1825-1897

Aicard, Jean Francois
  Victor — 1848-1921
Aide, Hamilton — 1830-1906
Aimard, Gustave — 1818-1883
Ainger, Alfred — 1837-1904
Ainslie, Hew — 1792-1878
Ainsworth, William
  Harrison — 1805-1882
Aird, Thomas — 1802-1876
Akers, Benjamin Paul — 1825-1861
Aksakov, Ivan Sergeyevich — 1823-1886
Aksakov, Konstantin — 1817-1860
Aksakov, Sergei,
  Timofeyevich — 1791-1859
Alaman, Lucas — 1792-1853
Alarcon, Pedro Antonio — 1833-1891
Alcott, Amos Bronson — 1799-1888
Alcott, Louisa May — 1832-1888
Alden, Isabella — 1841-1930
Alden, Joseph — 1807-1885
Aldrich, Thomas Bailey — 1836-1907
Aleardi, Aleardo — 1812-1878
Alecsandri, Vasile — 1821-1890
Alexander, Cecil Francis — 1818-1895
Alexander, William — 1826-1894
Alexis, Willibald — 1798-1871
Alger, Horatio — 1834-1899
Alin, Oscar Josef — 1846-1900
Alison, Sir Archibald — 1792-1867
Allen, Charles Grant
  Blairfindie — 1848-1899
Allen, James Lane — 1849-1925
Allibone, Samuel Austin — 1816-1889
Allingham, William — 1824-1889
Alma-Tadema, Sir
  Lawrence — 1836-1912
Allmers, Hermann — 1821-1902
Almeida-Garrett, Joao
  Baptista Da — 1799-1854
Almqvist, Karl Jonas
  Ludwig — 1793-1866
Amicis, Edmondo De — 1846-1908
Amiel, Henri Frederic — 1821-1881
Ampere, Jean Jacques — 1800-1864
Ancelot, Jacques Arsene
  Francois Polycarpe — 1794-1854
Ancillon, Johann Peter
  Friedrich — 1766-1836
Ancona, Alessandro — 1835-1914
Andersen, Hans
  Christian — 1805-1875
Anderson, Robert — 1750-1830
Andrieux, Francois
  Guillaume Jean
  Stanislas — 1759-1833
Angelier, Auguste Jean — 1848-1911
Anspach, Elizabeth
  Margravine — 1750-1828
Antokolski Mark
  Matreevich — 1843-1902

Anzengruber, Ludwig — 1839-1889
Apperley, Charles James
  (Nimrod) — 1777-1843
Arago, Jacques Etienne
  Victor — 1790-1855
Arany, Janos — 1817-1882
Arbois de Jubainville,
  Marie Henri d' — 1827-1910
Arcault, Antoine-Vincent — 1766-1834
Aribau, Bonaventura
  Carlos — 1798-1862
Armitage, Edward — 1817-1896
Arnason, Jon — 1819-1888
Arndt, Ernst Moritz — 1769-1860
Arneth, Alfred — 1819-1897
Arnim, Elizabeth
  (Bettina) Von — 1785-1859
Arnim, Ludwig Achim
  Von — 1781-1831
Arnold, Sir Edwin — 1832-1904
Arnold, Matthew — 1822-1888
Arnold, Thomas — 1795-1842
Arthur, Timothy Shay — 1809-1885
Asbjornsen, Peter
  Christian — 1812-1885
Ashe, Thomas — 1836-1889
Asnyk, Adam — 1838-1897
Atkinson, Thomas
  Witlam — 1799-1861
Aubanel, Theodore — 1829-1886
Augier, Guillaume Victor
  Emile — 1820-1889
Aulard, Francois Victor
  Alphonse — 1849-1928
Austin, Alfred — 1835-1913
Austin, Sarah — 1793-1867
Autran, Joseph — 1813-1877
Avellanida, Gertrudis
  Gomez d' — 1814-1873
Avenarius, Richard
  Heinrich Ludwig — 1843-1896
Averbach, Berthold — 1812-1882
Aversperg, Anton
  Alexander — 1806-1876
Axelrod, Pavel
  Borriasovich — 1850-1928
Ayala Y Herrera, Adelardo
  Lopez d' — 1828-1879
Aytoun, William
  Edmonstoun — 1813-1865
Azais, Pierre Hyacinthe — 1766-1845
Azeglio, Massimo
  Taparelli, Marquis d' — 1798-1866
Bacon, Delia Salter — 1811-1859
Bacon, Leonard — 1802-1881
Bacsanyi, Janos — 1763-1845
Baedeker, Karl — 1801-1859
Bagehot, Walter — 1826-1877
Baggesen, Jens Immanuel — 1764-1826

Bahr, Johann Christian	
Felix	1798-1872
Bailey, Samuel	1791-1870
Bailey, Philip James	1816-1902
Baillie, Joanna	1762-1851
Bain, Alexander	1818-1903
Baird, Henry Martin	1832-1906
Balaguer, Victor	1824-1901
Balbo, Cesare, Count	1789-1853
Balfe, Michael William	1808-1870
Ballanche, Pierre Simon	1776-1847
Ballantine, James	1808-1877
Ballantyne, Robert	
Michael	1825-1894
Balmes, Jaime Luciano	1810-1848
Balzac, Honore De	1799-1850
Bancroft, George	1800-1891
Bancroft, Hubert Howe	1832-1918
Banim, John	1798-1842
Banville, Theodore	
Faullain De	1823-1891
Barante, Amable Guillaume	
Prosper Brugiere	1782-1866
Baratynski, Yvegeniy	
Abramovich	1800-1844
Barbey D' Aurevilly, Jules	
Amedee	1808-1889
Barbier, Henri Auguste	1805-1882
Barbier, Paul Jules	1825-1901
Baring-Gould, Sabine	1834-1924
Barker, Thomas of Bath	1769-1847
Barker, Thomas James	
Barker	1815-1852
Barlow, Peter	1776-1862
Barnes, William	1800-1886
Barr, Amelia Edith	1831-1919
Barriere, Theodore	1823-1877
Barrili, Antonio Giulio	1836-1908
Barthelemy, Auguste	
Marseille	1796-1867
Barthelemy, Saint	
Hilaire Jules	1805-1895
Barton, Bernard	1784-1849
Bascom, John	1827-1911
Basevi, George	1794-1845
Bates, Arlo	1850-1918
Batyushkov, Konstantin	
Nikolaievitch	1787-1855
Baudelaire, Charles Pierre	1821-1867
Baudissin, Wolf Heinrich	1789-1878
Bauer, Bruno	1809-1882
Bauernfeld, Eduard Von	1802-1890
Baumbach, Rudolf	1840-1905
Bautain, Louis Eugene	
Marie	1796-1867
Bayly, Thomas Haynes	1797-1839
Beauchamp, Alphonse De	1767-1832
Beaumont, Sir George	
Howland	1753-1827
Beauvoir, Roger De	1809-1866
Beck, Christian Daniel	1757-1832

Beck, Jakob Sigismund	1761-1840
Beckford, William	1760-1840
Becque, Henry Francois	1837-1899
Becquer, Gustavo Adolfo	1836-1870
Beddoes, Thomas Lovell	1803-1849
Beecher, Henry Ward	1813-1887
Bede, Cuthbert	1827-1889
Beechey, Sir William	1753-1839
Beeton, Mrs. Isabella	
Mary Mayson	1836-1865
Beets, Nikolaas	1814-1903
Beljame, Alexandre	1842-1906
Bell, Henry Glassford	1803-1874
Bell, Robert	1800-1867
Bellamy, Edward	1850-1898
Belli, Giuseppe	
Gioachino	1791-1863
Benedix, Julius Roderich	1811-1873
Beneke, Friedrich Eduard	1798-1856
Bentham, Jeremy	1748-1832
Bernhardi, Friedrich	
Von	1849-1930
Beranger, Pierre Jean De	1780-1857
Berard, Joseph Frederic	1789-1828
Berchet, Giovanni	1783-1851
Bernard, Charles De	1804-1850
Berry, Mary	1763-1852
Bertrand, Jacques Louis	
Napoleon	1807-1841
Berzsenyi, Daniel	1776-1836
Besant, Annie	1847-1933
Besant, Walter Sir	1836-1901
Beskow, Bernhard Von	1796-1868
Bibaud, Michel	1782-1857
Biedermann, Friedrich	
Karl	1812-1901
Bierce, Ambrose	1842-1916
Bignon, Louis Pierre	
Edouard	1771-1841
Bilderdijk, Willem	1756-1831
Billings, Robert William	1813-1874
Birrell, Augustine	1850-1933
Bishop, Isabella	1831-1904
Bissen, Herman Vilhelm	1798-1868
Bitzius, Albrecht	1797-1854
Bjornson, Bjornstjerne	1832-1910
Black, William	1841-1898
Blackie, John Stuart	1809-1895
Blackmore, Richard	
Doddridge	1825-1900
Blake, William	1757-1827
Blanc, Jean Joseph	
Charles Louis	1811-1882
Blanchard, Samuel Laman	1804-1845
Blavatsky, Helena Petrova	1831-1891
Blessington, Marguerite	1789-1849
Blicher, Steen Steensen	1782-1848
Blind, Mathilde	1841-1896
Bliss, Philip Paul	1838-1876
Blood, Benjamin Paul	1832-1919
Blore, Edward	1787-1879

Blouet, Paul	1848-1903	Brooks, Phillips	1835-1893
Bloy, Leon	1846-1917	Broughton, John Cam	
Blunt, Wilfrid Scawen	1840-1922	Hobhouse	1786-1869
Bodenstedt, Friedrich		Broughton, Rhoda	1840-1920
Martin Von	1819-1892	Brown, Peter Hume	1850-1918
Boerne, Karl Ludwig	1786-1837	Brown, Samuel Morison	1817-1856
Boisgobey, Fortune		Brown, Thomas Edward	1830-1897
Abraham Du	1824-1891	Browne, James	1793-1841
Boker, George Henry	1823-1890	Browning, Elizabeth	
Boldrewood, Rolf	1826-1915	Barrett	1806-1861
Bolyai, Wolfgang	1775-1856	Browning, Oscar	1837-1923
Bonald, Louis Gabriel		Browning, Robert	1812-1889
Ambroise	1754-1840	Brownson, Orestes	
Bonghi, Ruggero	1828-1895	Augustus	1803-1876
Bonneville, Nicholas De	1760-1828	Brugsch, Heinrich Karl	1827-1894
Bonstetten, Charles		Brunner, Henry	1840-1915
Victor De	1745-1832	Bryant, William Cullen	1794-1878
Borel, Petrus	1809-1859	Brydges, Sir Samuel	
Borne, Ludwig	1786-1837	Egerton	1762-1837
Bornier, Henri	1825-1901	Buchanan, Robert	
Borrow, George Henry	1803-1881	Williams	1841-1901
Bosanquet, Bernard	1848-1923	Buchez, Philippe Benjamin	
Bosboom-Toussaint, Anna		Joseph	1796-1865
Louisa Geertruida	1812-1886	Buchner, Ludwig	1824-1899
Bostrom, Christoffer Jacob	1797-1866	Buckingham, James Silk	1786-1855
Botta, Carlo Guiseppe		Buckle, Henry Thomas	1821-1862
Guglielmo	1766-1837	Buckstone, John Baldwin	1802-1879
Boucicault, Dion	1822-1890	Bulgarin, Thaddeus	1789-1859
Bouilhet, Louis Hyacinthe	1822-1869	Bulwer, Henry Lytton	1801-1872
Bouilly, Jean Nicolas	1763-1842	Burckhardt, Jakob	1818-1897
Bouterwek, Friedrich	1765-1828	Burgess, John Bagnold	1830-1897
Bowen, Francis	1811-1890	Burnand, Frederick	
Boweles, William Lisle	1762-1850	Gustavus	1842-1885
Boyd, Andrew Kennedy		Burnett, Frances Eliza	
Hutchinson	1825-1899	Hodgson	1849-1924
Boyesen, Hjalmar	1848-1895	Burney, Fanny	
Braddon, Mary Elizabeth	1837-1915	(Madame D'Arblay)	1752-1840
Bradley, Edward	1827-1889	Burroughs, John	1837-1921
Bradley, Francis Herbert	1846-1924	Burrows, Montagu	1819-1905
Braga, Theophilo	1843-1924	Burton, John Hill	1809-1881
Brandes, Georg Maurice		Burton, Sir Richard	
Cohen	1842-1927	Francis	1821-1890
Bree, Matthias Ignatius		Burton, William Evans	1804-1860
Van	1773-1839	Bury, Lady Charlotte	
Bremer, Fredrika	1801-1865	Susan Maria	1775-1861
Brentano, Clemens	1778-1842	Butler, Samuel	1835-1902
Brentano, Franz	1838-1917	Byron, Henry James	1834-1884
Breton de Los Herreros,		Caballero, Fernan	1796-1877
Manuel	1796-1873	Cable, George	
Bridges, Robert Seymour	1844-1930	Washington	1844-1925
Brierley, Benjamin	1825-1896	Caird, Edward	1835-1908
Brillat-Savarin, Anthelme	1755-1826	Caird, John	1820-1898
Brizeux, Julien Auguste		Calderwood, Henry	1830-1897
Pelage	1803-1858	Calverley, Charles Stuart	1831-1884
Brokmeyer, Henry Conrad	1828-1906	Calvert, George Harris	1803-1889
Bronte, Anne	1820-1849	Calvo, Carlos	1824-1906
Bronte, Charlotte	1816-1855	Cairns, John Elliot	1823-1875
Bronte, Emily	1818-1848	Campbell, Thomas	1777-1844
Brooke, Stopford Augustus	1832-1916	Campoamor Y Campoosorio,	
Brooks, Charles William		Raymon De	1819-1901
Shirley	1816-1874	Canina, Luigi	1795-1856

Cannon, Charles James	1800-1860	Claretie, Jules Arsene	
Canth, Minna	1844-1897	Arnaud	1840-1913
Cantu, Cesare	1804-1895	Clarke, Charles Cowden	1787-1877
Capefigue, Jean Baptiste		Clarke, Marcus Andrew	
Honore Raymond	1801-1872	Hislop	1846-1881
Capern, Edward	1819-1894	Clausewitz, Karl Von	1780-1831
Capuana, Luigi	1839-1915	Clifford, William	
Carducci, Giosue	1835-1907	Kingdon	1845-1879
Carey, Phoebe	1824-1871	Clive, Caroline	1801-1873
Carlen, Emilia Smith		Clough, Arthur Hugh	1819-1861
Flygare	1807-1892	Cobbe, Frances Power	1822-1904
Carleton, Will	1845-1912	Cobbett, William	1763-1835
Carleton, William	1794-1869	Cockton, Henry	1807-1853
Carlyle, Thomas	1795-1881	Cole, Sir Henry	1808-1882
Carmen, Sylva	1843-1916	Coleridge, Hartley	1796-1849
Carnegie, Andrew	1835-1910	Coleridge, Samuel Taylor	1772-1834
Caro, Emile Marie	1826-1887	Coleridge, Sara	1802-1852
Carpenter, Edward	1844-1929	Colet, Louise	1810-1876
Carr, Joseph William		Collett, Jacobine Camilla	1813-1895
Comyns	1849-1916	Collier, John Payne	1789-1883
Carrer, Luigi	1801-1850	Collins, Charles Allston	1828-1873
Carriere, Moritz	1817-1895	Collins, Mortimer	1827-1876
Cary, Alice	1820-1871	Collins, William	1788-1847
Castelli, Ignaz Franz	1781-1862	Collins, William Wilkie	1824-1889
Castello, Branco Camillo	1825-1890	Colman, George	1762-1836
Cattaneo, Carlo	1801-1869	Colomb, Philip Howard	1831-1899
Cavalcaselle, Giovanni		Comte, Auguste	1798-1857
Battista	1820-1897	Conscience, Hendrik	1812-1883
Cazalis, Henri	1840-1909	Constant, Benjamin	
Chalmers, Alexander	1759-1834	Jean Joseph	1845-1902
Chalybaus, Heinrich		Constant De Rebeque,	
Moritz	1796-1862	Henri Benjamin	1767-1830
Chambers, Robert	1802-1871	Conway, Hugh	1847-1885
Chamier, Fredrick	1796-1870	Conway, Moncure Daniel	1832-1907
Chamisso, Adelbert Von	1781-1838	Cook, Edward Dutton	1829-1883
Champfleury	1821-1889	Cooke, John Esten	1830-1886
Channing, William Ellery	1780-1842	Cooke, Rose Terry	1827-1892
Chantavoine, Henri	1850-1918	Coolidge, Susan	1835-1905
Charles, Elizabeth	1828-1896	Cooper, James Fenimore	1789-1851
Chasles, Philarete	1798-1873	Coppee, Francois	1842-1908
Chateaubriand, Francois		Coppee, Henry	1821-1895
Rene	1768-1848	Cossa, Pietro	1830-1881
Chatrian, Alexandre		Costa, Joaquim	1846-1911
(Erckman-Chatrian)	1826-1890	Costello, Louisa Stuart	1799-1870
Chatter Ji, Bankim		Coster, Charles Theodore	
Chandra	1838-1894	Henri De	1827-1879
Chenedolle, Charles		Courthope, William John	1842-1917
Julien Lioult De	1769-1833	Cousin, Victor	1792-1867
Cherbuliez, Charles Victor	1829-1899	Cox, Sir George William	1827-1902
Chernyshevsky, Nikolay		Coxe, William	1747-1828
Gavrilovich	1828-1889	Craddock, Charles Egbert	1850-1922
Cheruel, Pierre Adolphe	1809-1891	Craik, Dinah Maria	1826-1887
Chesney, Charles		Crabbe, George	1754-1832
Cornwallis	1826-1876	Craven, Pauline	1808-1891
Child, Francis James	1825-1896	Creasy, Sir Edward	
Child, Lydia Maria	1802-1874	Shepherd	1812-1878
Christopoulos, Athanasios	1772-1847	Creevey, Thomas	1768-1838
Cibrario, Luigi, Count	1802-1870	Creighton, Mandell	1843-1901
Cladel, Leon	1835-1892	Cremazie, Octave	1822-1879
Clare, John	1793-1864	Cremer, Jakobus Jan	1827-1880
Clark, William George	1821-1878	Creuzer, George Friedrich	1771-1858

Crocker, Hannah Mather	1752-1829	De Morgan, William	
Croker, John Wilson	1780-1857	Trend	1839-1917
Croker, Thomas Crofton	1798-1854	Denifle, Heinrich Seuse	1844-1905
Crowne, Catherine	1800-1870	Dennery, Adolphe	
Crozier, John Beattie	1849-1921	Philippe	1811-1899
Crusenstolpe, Magnus		Dent, John Charles	1841-1887
Jakob	1795-1865	De Quincey, Thomas	1785-1859
Csengery, Antal	1822-1880	Deroulede, Paul	1846-1914
Csiky, Gergoly	1842-1891	Desagiers, Marc Antoine	
Cullum, George		Madeleine	1772-1827
Washington	1809-1892	Deschamps, Emile	1791-1871
Cummins, Maria Suzanna	1827-1866	De Tabley, John Byrne	
Cunningham, Allan	1784-1842	Leicester Warren	1835-1895
Curtis, George William	1824-1892	Deussen, Paul	1845-1919
Curtius, Ernst	1814-1896	De Vere, Aubrey Thomas	1814-1902
Curtius, Georg	1820-1885	Dexter, Henry Martyn	1821-1890
Cuvier, Georges		Dibdin, Thomas John	1771-1841
(Leopold)	1769-1832	Dicey, Edward	1832-1911
Da Costa, Isaak	1798-1860	Dickens, Charles John	
Dahlgreen, Karl Fredrik	1791-1844	Huffam	1812-1870
Dahlmann, Friedrich		Dickinson, Emily	1830-1886
Christoph	1785-1860	Dierx, Leon	1838-1912
Dahn, Julius Sophus		Digby, Kenelm Henry	1800-1880
Felix	1834-1912	Dilthey, Wilhelm	1833-1911
Dalling & Bulwer, Baron	1801-1872	Dingelstedt, Franz Von	1814-1881
Dall 'Ongaro, Francesco	1808-1873	Dionne, Narcisse Eutrope	1848-1917
D'Alviella, Count Goblet	1846-1925	Disreali, Benjamin	1804-1881
Daly, Augustin	1838-1899	D'Israeli, Isaac	1766-1848
Dana, Richard Henry	1815-1882	Dixon, Richard Watson	1833-1900
Da Ponte, Lorenzo	1749-1838	Dixon, William Hepworth	1821-1879
Dareste De La Chavanne,		Dmitriev, Ivan Ivanovich	1760-1837
Cleophas	1820-1882	Dobell, Sydney Thompson	1824-1874
Darley, George	1795-1846	Dobson, Henry Austin	1840-1921
Darmesteter, James	1849-1894	Dodge, Mary	1838-1905
Daru, Pierre Antoine,		Dodge, Theodore Ayrault	1842-1909
Comte	1767-1829	Dollinger, Johann Joseph	
Darwin, Charles Robert	1809-1882	Ignaz Von	1799-1890
D'Aubigné, Jean Henri	1794-1872	Domett, Alfred	1811-1887
Daudet, Alphonse	1840-1897	Donoso, Cortes Juan	1809-1853
Daudet, Ernest	1837-1921	Doran, John	1807-1878
Daumer, Georg Friedrich	1800-1875	Dostoievsky, Fyodor	
Daunou, Pierre Claude		Mikhaylovich	1821-1881
Francois	1761-1840	Doughty, Charles	
David, Pierre Jean	1789-1856	Montagu	1843-1926
Davidson, Thomas	1840-1900	Douglas, Sir William	
Davis, Thomas Osborne	1814-1845	Fettes	1822-1891
Decelles, Alfred Duclos	1843-1925	Dove, Alfred	1844-1916
De Cort, Frans	1834-1878	Dowden, Edward	1843-1913
De Geer, Louis Gerhard,		Doyle, Sir Francis Hastings	
Baron	1818-1896	Charles	1810-1888
Dekker, Edward Douwes	1820-1887	Drachmann, Holger Henrik	
Delarue, Gervais	1751-1835	Herboldt	1846-1908
Delavigne, Jean Francois		Dragomirov, Micheal	
Casimir	1793-1843	Ivanovich	1830-1905
Delbruck, Hans	1848-1929	Drake, Friedrich	1805-1882
Delisle, Leopold Victor	1826-1910	Drake, Nathan	1766-1836
Delvig, Anton Antonovich,		Draper, William	1811-1882
Baron Von	1798-1831	Drinkwater, Bethune	
Demogeot, Jacques		John	1762-1844
Claude	1808-1894	Drobisch, Moritz	
		Wilhelm	1802-1896

P

Fielding, Anthony		Frohschammer, Jakob	1821-1893
Vandyke Copley	1787-1855	Frothingham, Octavius	
Fields, James Thomas	1817-1881	Brooks	1822-1895
Figuier, Louis	1819-1894	Froude, James Anthony	1818-1894
Filon, Augustin	1841-1916	Fryxell, Anders	1795-1881
Finlay, George	1799-1875	Fucini, Renato	1843-1921
Fiske, John	1842-1901	Fuller, Margaret	1810-1850
Fisher, Ernst Kuno		Fullerton, Lady Georgiana	
Berthold	1824-1907	Charlotte	1812-1885
Fitzball, Edward	1792-1873	Fustel De Coulanges,	
Fitzgerald, Edward	1809-1883	Numa Dennis	1830-1889
Fitzgerald, Perry		Fyffe, Charles Alan	1845-1892
Hetherington	1834-1925	Gaboriau, Emile	1835-1873
Flach, Geoffroi Jacques	1846-1919	Gachard, Louis Prosper	1800-1885
Flammarion, Nicolas		Gagern, Hans Christoph	
Camille	1842-1925	Ernst	1766-1852
Flaubert, Gustave	1821-1880	Gairdner, James	1828-1912
Foa, Eugenie		Galluppi, Pasquale	1770-1846
Rodriguez-Gradis	1798-1853	Galt, John	1779-1839
Fogazzaro, Antonio	1842-1911	Garat, Dominique Joseph	1749-1833
Follen, Adolf Ludwig	1794-1855	Garay, Janos	1812-1853
Follen, Karl	1795-1840	Gardiner, Samuel Rawson	1829-1902
Fontan, Louis Marie	1801-1839	Gareau, Francois Xavier	1806-1866
Fontane, Theodor	1819-1898	Garnett, Richard	1835-1906
Ford, Richard	1796-1858	Garrett, Joao Baptista Da	
Forsell, Hans Ludwig	1843-1901	Silva Leitao De	
Forster, Friedrich		Almeida	1799-1854
Christoph	1791-1868	Gaskell, (Mrs.) Elizabeth	
Forster, John	1812-1876	Cleghorn	1810-1865
Fortlage, Karl	1806-1881	Gatty, Margaret	1809-1873
Foscolo, Ugo	1778-1827	Gautier, Leon	1832-1897
Foster, John	1770-1843	Gautier, Theophile	1811-1872
Fouillee, Alfred Jules		Geibel, Emanuel	1815-1884
Emile	1838-1912	Geijer, Eric Gustav	1783-1877
Fouque, Friedrich Heinrich		George, Henry	1839-1897
Karl De La Mote	1777-1843	Genlis, Stephanie Felicité	
Fourier, Francois Marie		Ducrest De Staubin	1746-1830
Charles	1772-1837	Gesenius, Friedrich	
Fowler, Thomas	1832-1904	Heinrich Wilhelm	1786-1842
Frampton, Mary	1773-1846	Gerstacker, Friedrich	1816-1877
France, Anatole	1844-1924	Gervinus, Georg Gottfried	1805-1871
Francois De Neufchateau,		Gezelle, Guido	1830-1899
Nicolas Louis	1750-1828	Gfrorer, August Friedrich	1803-1861
Frankl, Ludwig August	1810-1894	Ghika, Helena	1829-1888
Franzen, Frans Michael	1772-1847	Giacometti, Paolo	1816-1882
Franzos, Karl Emil	1848-1904	Giacosa, Guiseppe	1847-1906
Fraser, Alexander		Gibson, William Hamilton	1850-1896
Campbell	1819-1914	Giesebrecht, Wilhelm	
Fraser, James Baillie	1783-1856	Von	1814-1889
Frechette, Louis Honore	1839-1908	Gifford, William	1756-1826
Freeman, Edward		Gilbert, Sir John Thomas	1829-1898
Augustus	1823-1892	Gilbert, William	1806-1889
Freiligraph, Ferdinand	1810-1876	Gilbert, Sir William	
Freneau, Philip Morin	1752-1832	Schwenk	1836-1911
Frere, John Hookham	1769-1846	Gilchrist, Alexander	1828-1861
Freytag, Gustav	1816-1895	Gilchrist, Anna	1828-1885
Fries, Jakob Friedrich	1773-1843	Gilder, Richard Watson	1844-1909
Froebel, Friedrich		Gillies, John	1747-1836
Wilhelm August	1782-1852	Gindley, Anton	1829-1892
Frohlich, Abraham		Giner De Los Rios,	
Emanuel	1796-1865	Francisco	1840-1915

Gioberti, Vincenzo	1801-1852	Greville, Henry	1842-1902
Gioja, Melchiorre	1769-1829	Griboyedov, Alexander	
Giordani, Pietro	1774-1848	Sergeyevich	1705-1829
Girardin, Delphine De	1804-1855	Griffin, Gerald	1803-1840
Giraud, Giovanni	1776-1834	Grigorovich, Dmitri	
Gieseler, Johann Karl		Vaslievich	1822-1900
Ludwig	1792-1854	Grimm, Jacob Ludwig	
Giudici, Paolo Emiliano	1812-1872	Carl	1785-1863
Giusti, Giuseppi	1809-1850	Grimm, Wilhelm Carl	1786-1859
Glassbrenner, Adolf	1810-1876	Grossi, Tommaso	1791-1853
Glatigny, Joseph Albert		Grossmith, George	1847-1912
Alexandre	1839-1873	Grote, George	1794-1871
Gleig, George Robert	1796-1888	Grub, George	1812-1892
Glen, William	1789-1826	Grundtvig, Nikolai	
Glinka, Fedor		Fredrik Severin	1783-1872
Nikolayevich	1788-1880	Grundy, Sydney	1848-1914
Godwin, William	1756-1836	Gubernatis, Angelo De	1840-1913
Goethe, Johann Wolfgang		Guerin Du Cayla, Georges	
Von	1749-1832	Maurice De	1810-1839
Gogol, Nikolai		Guerrazzi, Francesco	
Vasilievich	1809-1852	Domenico	1804-1873
Goldschmidt, Aaron		Guerrini, Olinda	1845-1916
Meier	1819-1887	Guest, Edwin	1800-1880
Goltz, Bogumil	1801-1870	Guizot, Francois Pierre	
Gomperz, Theodor	1832-1912	Guillaume	1787-1874
Goncalves Dias, Antonio	1823-1864	Gutschmid, Alfred	1835-1887
Goncharov, Ivan		Gutzkow, Karl Ferdinand	1811-1878
Alexandrovich	1812-1891	Guys, Constantin	1805-1892
Goncourt De, Edmond		Gyllembourg Eh Rensvard,	
Louis Antoine Huot	1822-1896	Thomasine Christine	1773-1856
Goncourt De, Jules		Gyp	1849-1932
Alfred Huot	1830-1870	Habberton, John	1842-1921
Good, John Mason	1764-1827	Hacklander, Friedrich	
Goodrich, Samuel		Wilhelm Von	1816-1877
Griswold	1793-1860	Hagenbach, Karl Rudolf	1801-1874
Gordon, Adam Lindsay	1833-1870	Hahn, Ida	1805-1880
Gordon, Leon	1831-1892	Hake, Thomas Gordon	1809-1895
Gore, Catherine Grace		Hale, Edward Everett	1822-1909
Frances	1799-1861	Hale, Sarah Josepha	1788-1879
Gorres, Joseph Von	1776-1848	Halevy, Jean	1804-1883
Gosse, Sir Edmund	1849-1928	Halevy, Ludovic	1834-1908
Gottschall, Rudolf Van	1823-1908	Haliburton, Thomas	
Gould, John	1804-1881	Chandler	1796-1865
Gozlan, Leon	1803-1860	Hall, Anna Maria	1800-1881
Grabbe, Christian		Hall, Basil	1788-1844
Dietrich	1801-1836	Hall, Samuel Carter	1800-1889
Graf, Arturo	1848-1913	Hall, William Edward	1835-1894
Grant, Anne	1755-1838	Hallam, Henry	1777-1859
Grant, James	1822-1887	Halleck, Fitz-Greene	1790-1867
Gratz, Heinrich	1817-1891	Hallgrimson, Jonas	1807-1845
Graves, Alfred Percival	1846-1931	Halliday, Andrew	1830-1877
Gray, David	1838-1861	Hamerton, Philip Gilbert	1834-1894
Green, John Richard	1837-1883	Hamilton, Thomas	1789-1842
Green, Mary Ann Evrett	1818-1895	Hamilton, Sir William	1788-1856
Green, Thomas Hill	1836-1882	Hamley, Sir Edward	
Greene, George		Bruce	1824-1893
Washington	1811-1883	Hammer, Julius	1810-1962
Greg, William Rathbone	1809-1881	Hannay, James	1827-1873
Gregorovius, Ferdinand	1821-1891	Hardwick, Philip	1792-1870
Greville, Charles		Hardy, Thomas	1840-1928
Cavendish Fulke	1794-1865		

Hare, Augustus John Cuthbert	1834-1903
Haring, George Wilhelm Heinrich	1798-1871
Harris, Joel Chandler	1848-1908
Harrison, Frederic	1831-1923
Harte, Francis Bret	1836-1902
Hartmann, Karl Robert Eduard Von	1842-1906
Hartmann, Moritz	1821-1872
Hartzenbach, Juan Eugenio	1806-1880
Hasselt, Andre Henri Constant Van	1806-1874
Hauch, Johannes Carsten	1790-1872
Hauff, Wilhelm	1802-1827
Haureau, Barthelemy	1812-1896
Hausser, Ludwig	1818-1867
Hawker, Robert Stephen	1803-1875
Hawthorne, Nathaniel	1804-1864
Hay, John	1838-1905
Haym, Rudolf	1821-1901
Hayward, Abraham	1801-1884
Hazard, Rowland Gibson	1801-1888
Hazlitt, William	1778-1830
Hebbel, Christian Friedrich	1813-1863
Heeren, Arnold Hermann Ludwig	1760-1842
Hegel, Georg Wilhelm Friedrich	1770-1831
Heiberg, Johan Ludvig	1791-1860
Heine, Heinrich	1797-1856
Helmholtz, Hermann Ludwig Ferdinand Von	1821-1894
Helps, Sir Arthur	1813-1875
Hemans, Felicia Dorothea	1793-1835
Henty, George Alfred	1832-1902
Herbart, Johann Friedrich	1776-1841
Heredia, Jose Maria De	1842-1905
Herculano De Carvalno, E Araujo Alexandre	1810-1877
Heredia Y Heredia, Jose Maria	1803-1839
Hermans, Felicia Dorothea	1793-1835
Hernandez, Jose	1834-1886
Herne, Jame A	1840-1901
Hertz, Henrik	1797-1870
Herwegh, Georg	1817-1875
Herzen, Alexander Ivanovich	1812-1870
Heyse, Paul Johann Ludwig Von	1830-1914
Higginson, Thomas Wentworth	1823-1911
Hill, George Birbeck Norman	1835-1903
Hillebrand, Karl	1829-1884
Himly, Louis-Auguste	1823-1906
Hinrichs, Hermann Friedrich Wilhelm	1794-1861

Hocking, Silas Kitto	1850-1935
Hodgkin, Thomas	1831-1913
Hodgson, John Evan	1831-1895
Hodgson, Shadworth Holloway	1832-1912
Hoffding, Harald	1843-1931
Hoffman, August Heinrich	1798-1874
Hoffman, Heinrich	1809-1894
Hogg, James	1770-1835
Hogg, Thomas Jefferson	1792-1862
Holderlin, Johann Christian Friedrich	1770-1843
Holland, Sir Henry	1788-1873
Holland, Josiah Gilbert	1819-1881
Holmes, Oliver Wendell	1809-1894
Holtei, Karl Eduard Von	1798-1880
Holst, Hermann Eduard Von	1841-1904
Hone, William	1780-1842
Hood, Thomas	1799-1845
Hook, James	1746-1827
Hook, Theodore Edward	1788-1841
Hopfen, Hans Von	1835-1904
Hopkins, Gerard Manley	1844-1889
Hone, Richard Henry	1803-1884
Hormayr, Joseph Freiherr Von	1782-1848
Hosmer, James Kendall	1834-1927
Hostrup, Jens Christion	1818-1892
Hotho, Heinrich Gustav	1802-1873
Houghton, Richard Monckton Milnes	1809-1885
Houssaye, Arsene	1815-1896
Houssaye, Henry	1848-1911
Howe, Julia Ward	1819-1910
Howells, William Dean	1837-1920
Howitt, Mary	1799-1888
Howitt, William	1792-1879
Hudson, William Henry	1841-1922
Hughes, Thomas	1822-1896
Hugo, Victor Marie	1802-1885
Humboldt, Friedrich (Baron Von)	1769-1859
Humboldt, Karl Wilhelm Von	1767-1835
Hunt, James Henry Leigh	1784-1859
Hunter, Joseph	1783-1861
Hutton, Arthur Wollaston	1848-1912
Hutton, Richard Holt	1826-1897
Huxley, Thomas Henry	1825-1895
Huysmans, Joris Karl	1848-1907
Hyslop, James	1798-1827
Ibsen, Henrik Johan	1828-1906
Ihne, Wilhelm	1821-1902
Immermann, Karl Lebrecht	1796-1840
Ingelow, Jean	1820-1897
Ingemann, Bernhard Severin	1789-1862
Ingleby, Clement Manfred	1823-1886

Ingoldsby, Thomas	1788-1845	Kerner, Justinus Andreas	
Ingraham, Joseph Holt	1809-1860	Christian	1786-1862
Ingraham, Prentice	1843-1904	Kervyn De Lettenhove,	
Innes, Cosmo	1798-1874	Constantine Bruno	1817-1891
Irving, Washington	1783-1859	Key, Ellen	1849-1926
Isaacs, Jorge	1837-1895	Key, Francis-Scott	1779-1833
Jackson, Helen Maria	1831-1885	Kielland, Alexander	1849-1906
Jacobsen, Jens Peter	1847-1885	Kierkegaard, Soren Aaby	1813-1855
Jahn, Otto	1813-1869	Kinglake, Alexander	
Jakob, Ludwig Heinrich		William	1809-1891
Von	1759-1827	Kingsley, Charles	1819-1875
James, George Payne		Kingsley, Henry	1830-1876
Rainsford	1799-1860	Kingston, William Henry	
James, Henry	1843-1916	Giles	1814-1880
James, William	1842-1910	Kinkel, Johann Gottfried	1815-1882
Jameson, Anna Brownell	1794-1860	Kisfaludy, Karoly	1788-1830
Janin, Jules Gabriel	1804-1874	Kisfaludy, Sandor	1772-1844
Janssen, Johannes	1829-1891	Kitto, John	1804-1854
Jasmin, Jacques	1798-1864	Kivi, Steuval	1834-1872
Jebb, Sir Richard		Klaczko, Julian	1825-1906
Claverhouse	1841-1905	Klinger, Friedrich	
Jefferies, Richard	1848-1887	Maximilian Von	1752-1831
Jefferson, Thomas	1743-1826	Knebel, Karl Ludwig Von	1744-1834
Jensen, Adolf	1837-1879	Knight, Charles	1791-1873
Jensen, Wilhelm	1837-1911	Knowles, James Sheridan	1784-1862
Jerrold, Douglas William	1803-1857	Kock, Charles Paul De	1793-1871
Jesse, Edward	1780-1868	Kolcsey, Ferencz	1790-1888
Jewett, Sarah Orne	1849-1909	Kopisch, August	1799-1853
Jewsbury, Geraldine		Krasinski, Zygmunt,	
Endsor	1812-1880	Count	1812-1859
Joinville, Francois		Kraszewski, Joseph	
Ferdinand d'Orleans	1818-1900	Ignatius	1812-1887
Jokai, Maurus	1825-1904	Krause, Karl Christian	
Jones, Ebenezer	1820-1860	Friedrich	1781-1832
Jones, Ernest	1819-1869	Kropotkin, Peter	
Jones, Henry	1831-1899	Alexeivich	1842-1921
Jordan, Wilhelm	1819-1904	Krug, Wilhelm Traugott	1770-1842
Josika, Miklos	1794-1865	Krylov, Ivan Andreevich	1768-1844
Jouffroy, Theodore		Kuhlau, Friedrich	1786-1832
Simon	1796-1842	Kurz, Hermann	1813-1873
Jouy, Victor Joseph		Labiche, Eugene Marin	1815-1888
Etienne De	1764-1846	Lacaita, Sir James	1813-1895
Judson, Edward Zane		Lacretelle, Jean Charles	
Carroll	1823-1886	Dominique de	1766-1855
Junqueiro, Abilio Guena	1850-1923	Ladd, George Tumbull	1842-1921
Karadzic, Viek Stefanovic	1787-1864	La Farina, Giuseppe	1815-1863
Karamzin, Nicolai		La Harpe, Frederic Cesare	1754-1838
Mikhailovich	1765-1826	Laing, Samuel	1810-1897
Karr, Alphonse	1808-1890	Lamarck, Jean	
Kate, Jan Jacob		Chevalier de	1744-1829
Lodewyk Ten	1819-1889	Lamartine, Alphonse De	1790-1869
Kazinczy, Ferencz	1759-1831	Lamb, Charles	1775-1834
Keble, John	1792-1866	Lamennais, Hugues	
Keightley, Thomas	1789-1872	Felicite Robert De	1782-1854
Keller, Gottfried	1819-1890	Landon, Letitia Elizabeth	1802-1838
Kemble, John Mitchell	1807-1857	Landor, Walter Savage	1775-1864
Kendall, Henry Clarence	1841-1882	Lane, Edward William	1801-1876
Kenealy, Edward Vaughan		Lanfrey, Pierre	1828-1877
Hyde	1819-1880	Lang, Andrew	1844-1912
Kenney, James	1780-1849	Lange, Friedrich Albert	1828-1875
		Langhorne, John	1735-1779

Lanier, Sidney	1842-1881
Lappenberg, Johann Martin	1794-1865
Laprade, Pierre Marin Victor Richard De	1812-1883
Laromiguiere, Pierre	1756-1837
Larousse, Pierre Athanase	1817-1875
Larra, Mariano Jose De	1809-1837
Las Cases, Emmanuel Dieudonné, Compte de	1766-1842
Laube, Heinrich	1806-1884
Lauder, Sir Thomas Dick	1784-1848
Laurent, Francois	1810-1887
Lavisse, Ernest	1842-1922
Lawless, Emily	1845-1913
Lawrence, George Alfred	1827-1876
Laya, Jean Louis	1716-1833
Layard, Sir Austen Henry	1817-1894
Lazarus, Emma	1849-1887
Lazarus, Moritz	1824-1903
Lea, Henry Charles	1825-1909
Lecky, William Edward Hartpole	1838-1903
Leconte De Lisle, Charles Marie Rene	1818-1894
Lee, Harriet	1757-1851
Le Fanu, Joseph Sheridan	1814-1873
Legouve, Gabriel Jean Baptiste Ernest Wilfrid	1807-1903
Leleand, Charles Godfrey	1824-1903
Le Mercier, Nepomucene	1771-1840
Le Moine, James MacPherson	1825-1912
Lemon, Mark	1809-1870
Lemonnier, Antoine Louis Camille	1844-1913
Lenau, Nikolaus	1802-1850
Lennep, Jakob Van	1802-1868
Leo, Heinrich	1799-1878
Leopardi, Giacomo	1798-1837
Lermontov, Mikhail Yurevich	1814-1841
Leroux, Pierre	1798-1871
Leskov, Nikolai Semenovich	1831-1895
Lever, Charles James	1806-1872
Lewald, Fanny	1811-1889
Lewes, George Henry	1817-1878
Lewis, Sir George Cornwall	1806-1863
Lie, Jonas Lauritz Edemil	1833-1908
Lieber, Francis	1800-1872
Liebrecht, Felix	1812-1890
Liliencron, Detlev Von	1844-1909
Lincoln, Abraham	1809-1865
Lindau, Rudolf	1829-1910
Lindo, Mark Prager	1819-1879
Lingard, John	1771-1851
Lippincott, Sara Jane Clarke	1823-1904

Lista Y Aragon, Alberto	1775-1848
Lister, Thomas Henry	1800-1842
Littre, Maximilien Paul Emile	1801-1881
Livingstone, David	1813-1873
Ljunggren, Gustaf Haken Jordan	1823-1905
Locker-Lampson, Frederick	1821-1895
Lockhart, John Gibson	1794-1854
Lockhart, William Ewart	1846-1900
Lodge, Edmund	1756-1839
Lodge, Henry Cabot	1850-1924
Longfellow, Henry Wadsworth	1807-1882
Lönnrot, Elias	1802-1884
Lossing, Benson John	1813-1891
Loti, Pierre	1850-1923
Lotze, Rudolf Hermann	1817-1881
Lover, Samuel	1797-1868
Lowell, James Russell	1819-1891
Lubke, Wilhelm	1826-1893
Luchaire, Achille	1846-1908
Ludwig, Otto	1813-1865
Lund, Troels Frederik	1840-1921
Luttrell, Henry	1765-1851
Lytton, Edward George Lytton, Bulwer-Lytton	1803-1873
Lytton, Edward Robert Bulwer-Lytton	1831-1891
Macaulay, Thomas Babington Macaulay	1800-1859
MacCarthy, Denis Florence	1817-1882
M'Carthy, Justin	1830-1912
McCord, Louise Susanna Cheves	1810-1879
Macdonald, George	1824-1905
Macedo, Jose Agostinho De	1761-1831
Mach, Ernst	1838-1916
McGee, Thomas D'Arcy	1825-1868
McGonagall, William	1830-
MacGregor, John	1825-1892
Mackay, Charles	1814-1889
Mackaye, Steele	1842-1894
Mackenzie, Henry	1745-1831
Mackintosh, Sir James	1765-1832
Maclaren, Charles	1782-1866
MacNeill, John Gordon Swift	1849-1926
M'Cosh, James	1811-1894
M'Crie, Thomas	1772-1835
Madach, Imre	1823-1864
Maginn, William	1793-1842
Magny, Claude Drigon	1797-1879
Mahan, Alfred Thayer	1840-1914
Maine, Sir Henry James Sumner	1822-1888
Maiste, Xavier De	1763-1852
Maitland, Edward	1824-1897

Maitland, Frederic		Mignet, Francois Auguste	
William	1850-1906	Marie	1796-1884
Majlath, Janos	1786-1855	Mill, James	1773-1836
Major, Richard Henry	1818-1891	Mill, John Stuart	1806-1873
Mallarme, Stephane	1842-1898	Miller, Hugh	1802-1856
Malleson, George Bruce	1825-1898	Miller, Joaquin	1841-1913
Mallock, William Hurrell	1849-1923	Milman, Henry Hart	1791-1868
Malthus, Thomas Robert	1766-1834	Mirbeau, Octave Henri	
Mameli, Goffredo	1827-1849	Marie	1850-1917
Mangan, James Clarence	1803-1849	Mistral, Frederic	1830-1914
Maning, Frederick		Mitchell, Donald Grant	1822-1908
Edward	1812-1883	Mitford, John	1781-1859
Mansel, Henry		Mitford, Mary Russell	1787-1855
Longueville	1820-1871	Mitford, William	1744-1827
Manzoni, Alessandro	1785-1873	Moir, David Macbeth	1798-1851
Mapu, Abraham	1808-1867	Molesworth, Mary Louisa	1839-1921
Maris, Matthys	1839-1917	Molesworth, William	
Maris, Willem	1843-1910	Nassau	1816-1890
Markham, Mrs.	1780-1837	Moller, Poul Martin	1794-1838
Marquardt, Joachim	1812-1882	Mommsen, Theodor	1817-1903
Marryat, Florence	1838-1899	Monkhouse, William	
Marryat, Frederick	1792-1848	Cosmo	1840-1901
Marston, John Westland	1819-1890	Monnier, Marc	1829-1885
Marston, Philip Bourke	1850-1887	Monod, Gabriel	1844-1912
Martin, Francois Xavier	1762-1846	Montalembert, Charles	
Martin, Henri	1810-1883	Forbes Rene De	1810-1870
Martin, Sir Theodore	1816-1909	Montanelli, Giuseppe	1813-1862
Martineau, Harriet	1802-1876	Montefiore, Joshua	1762-1843
Martineau, James	1805-1900	Montgomery, James	1771-1854
Martinez De La Rosa,		Montgomery, Robert	1807-1855
Francisco De Paula	1787-1862	Monti, Vincenzo	1754-1828
Martini, Ferdinando	1841-1928	Monticelli, Adolphe	
Marx, Karl Heinrich	1818-1883	Joseph Thomas	1824-1886
Massey, Gerald	1828-1907	Montufar, Lorenzo	1823-1898
Masson, David	1822-1907	Moore, Thomas	1779-1852
Masson, Frederic	1847-1923	Moratin, Leandro	
Matthisson, Friedrich		Fernandez De	1760-1828
Von	1761-1831	More, Hannah	1745-1833
Maupassant, Henri Rene		Moreau, Hegesippe	1810-1838
Albert Guy De	1850-1893	Morgan, Lady Sydney	1783-1859
Maurer, Georg Ludwig		Morier, James	1780-1849
Von	1790-1872	Morike, Eduard Friedrich	1804-1875
Mayhew, Henry	1812-1887	Morley, Henry	1822-1894
Mehring, Franz	1846-1919	Morley, John Morley	1838-1923
Meilhac, Henri	1831-1897	Morris, Sir Lewis	1833-1907
Melville, Herman	1819-1891	Morris, William	1834-1896
Menard, Louis Nicolas	1822-1901	Morton, John Maddison	1811-1891
Mendes, Catulle	1841-1909	Morton, Thomas	1764-1838
Menzel, Wolfgang	1798-1873	Mosen, Julius	1803-1867
Meredith, George	1828-1909	Motherwell, William	1797-1835
Merimee, Propser	1803-1870	Motley, John Lothrop	1814-1877
Merivale, Charles	1808-1893	Moulton, Louise Chandler	1835-1908
Mesonero Romanos,		Muir, John	1838-1914
Ramon De	1803-1882	Munch-Bellinghausen,	
Meurice, Paul	1818-1905	Eligius Franz Joseph	1806-1871
Meyer, Conrad Ferdinand	1825-1898	Murger, Henry	1822-1861
Meynell, Alice	1849-1922	Musset, Alfred De	1810-1857
Michaud, Joseph Francois	1767-1839	Myers, Frederic William	
Michelet, Jules	1789-1874	Henry	1843-1901
Mickiewicz, Adam	1798-1855	Nairne, Carolina Oliphant	1766-1845
		Nasmyth, Patrick	1787-1831

Neal, John	1793-1876	Pater, Walter Horatio	1839-1894
Neander, Johann	1789-1850	Patmore, Coventry Kersey	
Nekrasov, Nikolai		Dighton	1823-1896
Alexeyevich	1821-1877	Pattison, Mark	1813-1884
Neruda, Jan	1834-1891	Paul, Charles Kegan	1828-1902
Nerval, Gerard De	1808-1855	Pauli, Reinhold	1823-1882
Nestroy, Johann	1801-1862	Paulding, James Kirke	1778-1860
Nettleship, Richard Lewis	1846-1892	Paulsen, Friedrich	1846-1908
Newman, Francis William	1805-1897	Payn, James	1830-1898
Newman, John Henry		Payne, John Howard	1791-1852
(Cardinal)	1801-1890	Paz Soldan, Mariano	
Nichol, John	1833-1894	Felipe	1821-1886
Nichols, John	1745-1826	Peabody, Andrew Preston	1811-1893
Nicoll, Robert	1814-1837	Peacock, Thomas Love	1785-1866
Niebuhr, Barthold Georg	1776-1831	Peesemsky, Alexey	
Nietzsche, Friedrich		Feofilactovich	1820-1881
Wilhelm	1844-1900	Peirce, Charles Sanders	1839-1914
Nitzsch, Karl Immanuel	1787-1868	Pelham, Henry Francis	1846-1907
Nitzsch, Karl Wilhelm	1818-1880	Pellico, Silvio	1788-1854
Noailles, Paul, Duke of	1802-1885	Percival, James Gates	1759-1856
Nodier, Charles	1780-1844	Pereda, Jose Maria De	1833-1906
Noel, Roden Berkeley		Perez Galdos, Benito	1845-1920
Wriothesley	1834-1894	Pertz, Georg Heinrich	1795-1876
Nordau, Max Simon	1848-1923	Petofi, Alexander	1823-1849
Normanby, Constantine		Pfleiderer, Edmund	1842-1902
Henry Phipps	1797-1863	Picken, Andrew	1788-1833
Norris, William Edward	1847-1925	Pindemonte, Ippolito	1753-1828
Norton, Caroline Elizabeth		Planche, James Robinson	1796-1880
Sarah	1808-1877	Poe, Edgar Allan	1809-1849
Norton, Charles Eliot	1827-1908	Poerio, Alessandro	1802-1848
Nunez De Arce, Gaspar	1834-1903	Ponsard, Francois	1814-1867
O'Grady, Standish James	1846-1928	Poole, William Frederick	1821-1894
Ohlenschlager, Adam		Porter, Anna Maria	1780-1832
Gottlob	1779-1850	Porter, Jane	1776-1850
Ohnet, Georges	1848-1918	Porter, Noah	1811-1892
Oliphant, Laurence	1829-1888	Porto-Riche, Georges De	1849-1930
Oliphant, Margaret		Potgieter, Everhardes	
Oliphant	1828-1897	Johannes	1808-1875
Oliveira, Martins Joaquim		Potthast, August	1824-1898
Pedro De	1845-1894	Powell, Frederick York	1850-1903
Olmedo, Jose Joaquin De	1780-1847	Praed, Winthrop	
Opie, Amelia	1769-1853	Mackworth	1802-1839
Opzoomer, Cornelius		Prantl, Karl Von	1820-1888
William	1821-1892	Prati, Giovanni	1815-1884
Orzeszkowa, Eliza	1842-1910	Prel, Karl	1839-1899
O'Shaughnessy, Arthur		Prescott, Harriet	
William Edgar	1844-1880	Elizabeth	1835-1921
Ostrovsky, Alexander		Prescott, William Hickling	1796-1859
Nikolaevich	1823-1886	Pringle, Thomas	1789-1834
Ouida	1839-1908	Procter, Adelaide Anne	1825-1864
Ozanan, Antoine Frederic	1813-1853	Procter, Bryan Waller	1787-1874
Palacky, Frantisek	1798-1876	Proudhon, Pierre Joseph	1809-1865
Palfrey, John Gorham	1796-1881	Prus, Boleslaw	1847-1912
Palgrave, Sir Francis	1788-1861	Prutz, Hans	1843-1929
Palgrave, Francis Turner	1824-1897	Purnell, Thomas	1834-1889
Paludan-Muller, Frederik	1809-1876	Pusey, Edward Bouverie	1800-1882
Paoli, Cesare	1840-1902	Pushkin, Alexander	1799-1837
Paris, Gaston	1839-1903	Pyne, William Henry	1769-1843
Parker, Theodore	1810-1860	Quental, Anthero De	1842-1891
Parkman, Francis	1823-1893	Quicherat, Jules Etienne	
Parton, James	1822-1891	Joseph	1814-1882

Quincy, Josiah	1772-1864	Ruffini, Giovanni	
Quinet, Edgar	1803-1875	Domenico	1807-1881
Quintana, Marnel José	1772-1857	Ruge, Arnold	1802-1880
Raabe, Wilhelm	1831-1910	Runeberg, Johan Ludvig	1804-1877
Ragabe, Alexandros		Ruskin, John	1819-1900
Rizos	1810-1892	Rutherford, Mark	1829-1913
Rambaud, Alfred Nicolas	1842-1905	Rydberg, Abraham Viktor	1828-1895
Ranc, Arthur	1831-1908	Safarik, Pavel Josef	1795-1861
Randall, James Ryder	1839-1908	Sainte-Beuve, Charles	
Rands, William Brighty	1823-1882	Augustin	1804-1869
Ranke, Lepold Von	1795-1886	Saint-Marc, Girardin	1801-1873
Rauch, Christian Daniel	1777-1875	Saintsbury, George	
Raumer, Friedrich Ludwig		Edward Bateman	1845-1933
George Van	1781-1873	Sala, George Augustin	
Ravaisson-Mollien, Jean		Henry	1828-1895
Gaspard Felix	1813-1900	Saltykov, Micheal	
Rawlinson, George	1812-1902	Evgrafovich	1826-1889
Raynouard, Francois Juste		Sand, George (Dudevant)	1804-1876
Marie	1761-1836	Sandeau, Leonard	
Reade, Charles	1814-1884	Sylvain Julien	1811-1883
Realf, Richard	1834-1878	Sanday, William	1843-1920
Reclus, Jean Jacques		Sant, James	1820-1916
Elisée	1830-1905	Santine, Joseph Xavier	1798-1865
Redgrave, Richard	1804-1888	Sardou, Victorien	1831-1908
Reid, Thomas Mayne	1818-1883	Sarmiento, Domingo	
Remusat, Charles Francois		Faustino	1811-1888
Marie	1797-1875	Saxe, John Godfrey	1816-1887
Renan, Ernest	1823-1892	Scheffel, Joseph Viktor	
Renouvier, Charles		Von	1826-1886
Bernard	1815-1903	Schelling, Friedrich	
Reuter, Fritz	1810-1874	Wilhelm Joseph Von	1775-1854
Rice, James	1843-1882	Scherer, Wilhelm	1841-1886
Richepin, Jean	1849-1926	Schimmelpenninck, Mary	
Richmond, Legh	1772-1827	Ann	1778-1856
Riley, James Whitcomb	1849-1916	Schlegel, August Wilhelm	
Ritchie, Anne Isabella,		Von	1767-1845
Lady	1837-1919	Schlegel, Friedrich Von	1772-1829
Ritter, Heinrich	1791-1869	Schleiermacher, Friedrich	
Rivas, Angel De Saavedra	1791-1865	Daniel Ernst	1768-1834
Robertson, Thomas		Schopenhaur, Arthur	1788-1860
William	1829-1871	Schweitzer, Jean Baptista	
Roe, Edward Payson	1838-1888	Von	1833-1875
Rogers, Randolphe	1825-1892	Scott, Sir Walter	1771-1832
Rogers, Samuel	1763-1855	Scribe, Eugene	1791-1861
Roscoe, William	1753-1831	Seebohm, Frederick	1833-1912
Rosegger, Peter	1843-1918	Seeley, Sir John Robert	1834-1895
Rosenkranz, Karl	1805-1879	Seguier, William	1771-1843
Rosmini-Serbati, Antonio	1797-1855	Segur, Philippe Paul,	
Ross, Janet Anne	1842-1927	Comte de	1780-1873
Rossetti, Christina		Sellar, William Young	1825-1890
Georgina	1830-1894	Senancour, Etienne Pivert	
Rossetti, Dante Gabriele	1828-1882	De	1770-1846
Rossetti, Gabriele	1783-1854	Seth, Andrew	1850-1931
Rossetti, William Michael	1829-1919	Settembrini, Luigi	1813-1877
Rouget De Lisle, Claude		Sewell, Anna	1820-1878
Joseph	1760-1836	Shairp, John Campbell	1819-1885
Roumanville, Joseph	1818-1891	Shaw, Henry Wheeler	1818-1885
Royer-Collard, Pierre		Sheil, Richard Lalor	1791-1851
Paul	1763-1845	Shelley, Mary	
Rubinstein, Anton	1824-1894	Wollstonecraft	1795-1851
Rückert, Friedrich	1788-1866	Sherwood, Mary Martha	1775-1851

Shevshenko, Taras	1814-1861	Stoddard, Richard Henry	1825-1903
Shorthouse, Joseph Henry	1834-1903	Stoddard, William Osborn	1835-1925
Sidwick, Henry	1838-1900	Storm, Theodor Wolsden	1817-1888
Sienkiewicz, Henryk	1846-1916	Stowe, Harriet Elizabeth	
Sigourney, Lydia Huntley	1791-1865	Beecher	1811-1896
Sill, Edward Rowland	1841-1887	Strachwitz, Moritz Karl	
Simms, William Gilmore	1806-1870	Wilhelm Anton	1822-1847
Simon, Jules Francois	1814-1896	Strauss, David Friedrich	1808-1874
Simrock, Karl Joseph	1802-1876	Street, Alfred Billings	1811-1881
Sims, George Robert	1847-1922	Strickland, Agnes	1806-1874
Sismondi, Jean Charles		Strindberg, John August	1849-1912
Leonard Simonde	1773-1842	Stubbs, William	1825-1901
Skeat, Walter William	1835-1912	Sue, Eugene	1804-1857
Skene, William Forbes	1809-1892	Sully-Prudhomme, Rene	
Slowacki, Juljusz	1809-1849	Francois Armand	
Smiles, Samuel	1812-1904	Prudhomme	1839-1907
Smith, Alexander	1830-1867	Surtees, Robert Smith	1803-1864
Smith, John Stafford	1750-1836	Suttner, Bertha	1843-1914
Smith, Francis Hopkinson	1838-1915	Swanwick, Anna	1813-1899
Smith, Goldwin	1823-1910	Swetchine, Madame	1782-1857
Smith, Horace	1779-1849	Sybel, Heinrich Von	1817-1895
Smith, James	1775-1839	Swinburne, Algernon	
Smith, Sidney	1771-1845	Charles	1837-1909
Smith, Walter Chalmers	1824-1908	Symonds, John Addington	1840-1893
Smith, Sir William	1813-1893	Tabley, John Byrne	
Snoilsky, Carl Johan		Leicester Warren	1835-1895
Gustaf	1841-1903	Taine, Hippolyte Adolphe	1828-1893
Soloviev, Sergei		Tamayo Y Baus, Manuel	1829-1898
Mikhailovich	1820-1879	Talfourd, Sir Thomas	
Sorel, Albert	1842-1906	Noon	1795-1854
Sorel, Georges	1847-1922	Taylor, Ann	1782-1866
Southey, Robert	1774-1843	Taylor, Bayard	1825-1878
Souza-Botelho, Adelaide		Taylor, Sir Henry	1800-1886
Filleul	1761-1836	Taylor, Isaak	1787-1865
Sparks, Jared	1789-1866	Taylor, Isaak	1829-1901
Spencer, Henry	1820-1903	Taylor, Tom	1817-1880
Spielhagen, Friedrich Von	1829-1911	Taylor, William	1765-1836
Spitteler, Carl	1845-1924	Tedder, Henry Richard	1850-1924
Stahl, Friedrich Julius	1802-1861	Tegner, Esaias	1782-1846
Stanhope, Philip Henry		Tennant, William	1784-1848
Stanhope	1805-1875	Tennyson, Alfred Lord	1809-1892
Stanley, Arthur Penrhyn	1815-1881	Thakaray, William	
Stanley, Sir Henry Morton	1841-1904	Makepeace	1811-1863
Stedman, Edmund		Thaxter, Celia Laighton	1835-1894
Clarence	1833-1908	Theuriet, Claude Adhemar	
Steffens, Henrik	1773-1845	Andre	1833-1907
Stendhal, (Marie Henry		Thierry, Jacques Nicolas	
Beyle)	1783-1842	Augustin	1795-1856
Stephen, Sir Leslie	1832-1904	Thiers, Louis Adolph	1797-1877
Sterling, John	1806-1844	Thirlwall, Connop	1797-1875
Stevenson, Robert Louis		Thomas, Brandon	1849-1914
Balfour	1850-1894	Thompson, William c.	1785-1833
Stewart, Dugald	1753-1828	Thomson, James	1834-1882
Stifter, Adalbert	1805-1868	Thoreau, Henry David	1817-1862
Stirling, James		Ticknor, George	1791-1871
Hutchinson	1820-1909	Tieck, Johann Ludwig	1773-1853
Stirling-Maxwell, Sir		Tischendorf, Lobegatt	1815-1874
William, Bart.	1818-1878	Tocqueville, Alexis	
Stirner, Max	1806-1856	Charles Henri Clarel	1805-1859
Stockton, Francis Richard	1834-1902	Tolstoy, Alexei	
Stoddard, John Lawson	1850-1931	Konstantinovich	1817-1875

Tolstoy, Leo Nikolayevich	1828-1910	Walker, Thomas	1784-1836
Tommaseao, Niccolo	1802-1874	Wallace, Alfred Russel	1823-1913
Tompa, Mihaly	1817-1868	Wallace, Lewis	1827-1905
Topelius, Zachris	1818-1898	Wallace, William	1844-1897
Topffer, Rodolphe	1799-1846	Wallon, Henri Alexandre	1812-1904
Toreno, Jose Maria		Warburton, Eliot	1810-1852
Queipo De Llano	1786-1843	Ward, Artemus	1834-1867
Traill, Henry Duff	1842-1900	Warner, Charles Dudley	1829-1900
Treitschke, Heinrich Von	1834-1896	Warner, Susan Bogert	1819-1895
Trelawny, Edward John	1792-1881	Warren, Samuel	1807-1877
Trench, Richard Chenevix	1807-1886	Watts-Dunton, Walter	
Trendelenburg, Friedrich		Theodore	1832-1914
Adolf	1802-1872	Waugh, Edwin	1817-1890
Trevelyan, Sir George Otto	1838-1928	Webster, Noah	1758-1843
Trollope, Anthony	1815-1882	Welhaven, Johann	
Trollope, Frances	1780-1863	Sebastian Cammermeyer	1807-1873
Trollope, Thomas Adolphus	1810-1892	Wells, Charles Jeremiah	1798-1879
Trumbull, John	1750-1831	Wennerberg, Gunnar	1817-1901
Tucker, Charlotte Marie	1821-1893	Wergeland, Henrik Arnold	1808-1845
Tupper, Martin Farquehar	1810-1889	Whately, Richard	1787-1863
Turgenev, Ivan Sergeyevich	1818-1883	Whewell, William	1794-1866
Turner, Charles Tennyson	1808-1879	White, Richard Grant	1821-1885
Turner, Sharon	1768-1847	White, William Hale	1831-1913
Twain, Mark	1835-1910	Whitehead, Charles	1804-1862
Tyler, Moses Coit	1835-1900	Whitman, Walt	1819-1892
Tyndall, John	1820-1893	Whittier, John Greenleaf	1807-1892
Tyuchev, Fydor Ivanovich	1803-1873	Widmann, Joseph Victor	1842-1911
Uberweg, Friedrich	1826-1871	Wieniawiski, Henri	1835-1880
Uhland, Johann Ludwig	1787-1861	Wilberforce, William	1759-1833
Uspenski, Gleb Ivanovich	1840-1902	Wilde, Lady Jane Francesca	
Valera Y Alcala, Galiano		"Speranza"	1826-1896
Juan	1824-1905	Wildenbruch, Ernst Van	1845-1909
Valles, Jules	1832-1885	Willis, Nathaniel Parker	1806-1867
Vacherot, Etienne	1809-1897	Wills, William Gorman	1828-1891
Van Beers, Jan	1821-1888	Wilson, John	1785-1854
Vapereau, Louis Gustave	1819-1906	Wilcox, Ella	1850-1919
Varnhagen, Francisco		Winsor, Justin	1831-1897
Adolpho De	1816-1878	Winther, Christian	1796-1876
Varnhagen, Von Ense		Wirt, William	1772-1834
Karl August	1785-1858	Wollaston, William Hyde	1766-1828
Vazoff, Ivan	1850-1921	Wood, Mrs. Henry	1814-1887
Veitch, John	1829-1894	Wordsworth, Dorothy	1771-1855
Verdaguer, Mosen Jacinto	1845-1902	Wordsworth, William	1770-1850
Verga, Giovanni	1840-1922	Wraxall, Sir Nathaniel	
Verlaine, Paul	1844-1896	William	1751-1831
Verne, Jules	1828-1905	Wright, Thomas	1810-1887
Verplanck, Gulian		Wright, William Aldis	1836-1914
Crommelin	1786-1870	Wundt, Wilhelm Max	1832-1920
Viaud, Louis Marie Julien	1850-1923	Wyatt, Sir Matthew Digby	1820-1877
Vidyasagar, Isaar Chandra	1820-1891	Wyss, Johann	1781-1830
Vigfusson, Gudbrandr	1828-1889	Yates, Edmund	1831-1894
Vigny, Alfred De	1797-1863	Yonge, Charlotte Mary	1823-1901
Villari, Pasquale	1827-1917	Yriarte, Charles	1832-1898
Villemain, Abel Francois	1790-1870	Zeller, Eduard	1814-1908
Villiers, De L'isle Adam		Zhukovsky, Vasili	
Auguste, Compte De	1838-1889	Andreyevich	1783-1852
Vinje, Aasmund Olavson	1816-1870	Zola, Emile Edouard	
Vischer, Friedrich Theodor	1807-1887	Charles Antoine	1840-1902
Vogue, Eugene Melchior	1848-1910	Zorrilla, Jose	1817-1893
Voss, Johann Heinrich	1751-1826	Zschokke, Johann Heinrich	
Waagen, Gustav Friedrich	1794-1868	Daniel	1771-1848

Achenbach, Andreas	1815-1910
Ainmuller, Maximilian	
Emmanuel	1807-1870
Allan, Sir William	1782-1850
Allston, Washington	1779-1843
Alvarez, Don Jose	1768-1827
Anderson, Sir Robert	
Rowland	1834-1921
Ansdell, Richard	1815-1885
Armitage, Edward	1817-1896
Armstead, Henry Hugh	1828-1905
Audubon, John James	1785-1851
Baily, Edward Hodges	1788-1867
Ball, Thomas	1819-1911
Baltard, Louis Pierre	1764-1846
Bandel, Ernst Von	1800-1876
Barry, Sir Charles	1795-1860
Bartolini, Lorenzo	1777-1850
Bartholdi, Auguste	1834-1904
Bartholome, Paul Albert	1848-1928
Barye, Antoine Louis	1796-1875
Bastien-Lepage, Jules	1848-1884
Bates, Harry	1850-1899
Baudry, Paul Jacques	
Aime	1828-1886
Begas, Karl	1794-1854
Begas, Rheinhold	1831-1911
Bell, John	1811-1895
Bellows, Albert F.	1829-1883
Bentley, John Francis	1839-1902
Besnard, Paul Albert	1849-1934
Beverley, William Roxby	1814-1889
Bewick, Thomas	1753-1828
Bierstadt, Albert	1830-1902
Birch, Samuel	1813-1885
Blakelock, Ralph Albert	1847-1919
Blashfield, Edwin Howland	1848-1936
Blomfield, Sir Arthur	
William	1829-1899
Boehm, Sir Joseph Edgar	1834-1890
Boeklin, Arnold	1827-1901
Bone, Henry	1755-1834
Bonheur, Rosa	1822-1899
Bonington, Richard Parkes	1801-1828
Bonnat, Leon Joseph	
Florentin	1833-1922
Bosio, Francois Joseph	
Baron	1769-1845
Boudin, Louis Eugene	1824-1898
Bough, Samuel	1822-1878
Boughton, George Henry	1833-1905
Bouguereau, Adolphe	
William	1825-1905
Bracquemond, Felix	1833-1914
Bradford, William	1827-1906
Braekeleer, Henri Jean	
Augustin De	1840-1888
Brascassat, Jacques	
Raymon	1804-1867
Breton, Jules Adolphe	
Aime Louis	1827-1906

Bridggman, Frederic	
Arthur	1847-1928
Brierly, Sir Oswald Walters	1817-1894
Bright, Henry	1814-1873
Brock, Sir Thomas	1847-1922
Brodie, William	1815-1881
Brown, George Loring	1814-1889
Brown, Ford Maddox	1821-1893
Brown, Henry Kirke	1814-1886
Brown, John George	1831-1913
Brown, Hablot Knight	1815-1882
Bruce-Joy, Albert	1842-1924
Brunner, Arnold William	1842-1919
Bulfinch, Charles	1763-1844
Burn, William	1789-1870
Burne-Jones, Sir Edward	
Burne	1833-1898
Burnham, Daniel Hudson	1846-1912
Burton, Decimus	1800-1881
Butterfield, William	1814-1900
Bystrom, Johan Niklas	1783-1848
Cabanel, Andreas	1815-1910
Cagnola, Luigi	1762-1833
Calame, Alexander	1810-1864
Caldecott, Randolph	1846-1886
Calderon, Philip	
Hermogenes	1833-1898
Callcott, Sir Augustus	
Wall	1779-1844
Calvert, Charles	1785-1852
Calvert, Edward	1799-1883
Camphausen, Wilhelm	1818-1885
Camuccini, Vincenzo	1773-1844
Capronnier, Jean-Baptiste	1814-1891
Carolus-Duran,	1837-1917
Carpeaux, Jean Baptiste	1827-1875
Carriere, Eugene	1849-1906
Cassatt, Mary	1845-1926
Catlin, George	1796-1872
Cattermole, George	1800-1868
Cazin, Jean Charles	1841-1901
Cezanne, Paul	1839-1906
Chalmers, George Paul	1836-1878
Chantrey, Sir Francis	
Legatt	1781-1841
Chapu, Henri	1833-1891
Charlet, Nicolas Toussaint	1792-1845
Chase, William Merrit	1849-1916
Chasseriau, Theodore	1819-1856
Chisholm, Alexander	1792-1847
Church, Frederick Edwin	1826-1900
Claus, Emile	1849-1924
Clays, Pal Jean	1819-1900
Cockerell, Charles Robert	1788-1863
Cole, Thomas	1801-1848
Cole, Vicat	1833-1893
Collier, Hon. John	1850-1934
Colman, Samuel	1832-1920
Constable, John	1776-1837
Cooper, Abraham	1787-1868
Cooper, Thomas Sidney	1803-1902

Cope, Charles West	1811-1890	Duncan, Thomas	1807-1845
Corbould, Edward Henry	1815-1905	Dupre, Giovanni	1817-1882
Corbould, Henry	1787-1844	Dupre, Jules	1811-1889
Corbould, Richard	1757-1831	Durand, Asher Brown	1796-1886
Corman, John Sell	1782-1842	Duveneck, Frank	1848-1919
Cormon, Fernand	1845-1924	Dyce, William	1806-1864
Cornelius, Peter Von	1783-1867	Eakins, Thomas	1844-1916
Corot, Jean-Baptiste		East, Alfred	1849-1913
Camille	1796-1875	Eastlake, Sir Charles Lock	1793-1865
Costa, Giovanni	1826-1903	Eaton, Wyatt	1849-1896
Courbet, Gustav	1819-1877	Eberlein, Gustav	1847-1926
Couture, Thomas	1815-1879	Ebrz, Josef	1801-1882
Cox, David the Elder	1783-1859	Eckenberg, Kristoffer	1783-1853
Cox, David the Younger	1809-1885	Egg, Augustus Leopold	1816-1863
Crane, Thomas	1808-1859	Elliott, Charles Loring	1812-1868
Crane, Walter	1845-1915	Engleheart, George	1752-1829
Crauck, Gustav	1827-1905	Etex, Antoine	1809-1888
Crawford, Thomas	1814-1857	Etty, William	1787-1849
Creswick, Thomas	1811-1869	Faed, Thomas	1826-1900
Cruickshank, George	1792-1878	Falguiere, Jean Alexandre	
Daguerre, Louis Jacques		Joseph	1831-1900
Mande	1789-1851	Fantin-Latour, Ignace	
Dahl, Johann Kristen		Henri	1836-1904
Clausen	1788-1857	Farquharson, David	1840-1907
Dalou, Jules	1838-1902	Farquharson, Joseph	1846-1935
Damer, Ann Seymour	1749-1828	Feuerbach, Anselm	1829-1880
Danby, Francis	1793-1861	Fielding, Copley	1787-1855
Daniell, Thomas	1749-1840	Fildes, Sir Luke	1844-1927
Daniell, William	1769-1837	Flandrin, Jean	
Dannecker, Johann		Hyppolyte	1809-1864
Heinrich Von	1758-1841	Flaxman, John	1755-1826
Dantan, Antoine Laurent	1798-1878	Fofelberg, Benedict Erland	1786-1854
Dantan, Edward Joseph	1848-1897	Foley, John Henry	1818-1874
Dantan, Jean Pierre	1800-1869	Fontaine, Pierre Francois	
Darley, Felix Octavius		Leonard	1762-1853
Carr	1822-1888	Forster, Ernst	1800-1885
Daubigny, Charles		Fortuny, Mariano Jose	1838-1874
Francois	1817-1878	Foster, Myles Byrkett	1825-1899
Daumet, Pierre Jerome		Fowler, Charles	1792-1867
Honore	1826-1911	Francais, Francois Louis	1814-1897
Daumier, Honore	1808-1879	Fremiet, Emmanuel	1824-1910
Dawson, Henry	1811-1878	French, Daniel Chester	1850-1931
Decamps, Alexandra		Friedrich, Caspar David	1774-1840
Gabriel	1803-1860	Fripp, Alfred Downing	1822-1895
Defregger, Franz Von	1835-1921	Fripp, George Arthur	1814-1896
Degas, Hilaire Germain		Frith, William Powell	1819-1909
Edgar	1834-1917	Fromentin, Eugene	1820-1876
Delacroix, Ferdinand		Frost, William Edward	1810-1877
Victor Eugene	1798-1863	Fuhrich, Joseph Von	1800-1876
Delaroche, Hyppolyte	1797-1856	Fuller, George	1822-1884
Delaunay, Elie	1828-1891	Gallait, Louis	1810-1887
Detaille, Edouard	1848-1912	Garnier, Jean Louis	
Diaz, Narcisse Virgile	1809-1876	Charles	1825-1898
Dielman, Frederick	1847-1935	Gauguin, Paul	1848-1903
Dillens, Julien	1849-1904	Gavarni, Paul	1801-1866
Dobson, William Charles		Gebhardt, Eduard Von	1830-1925
Thomas	1817-1898	Geddes, Andrew	1783-1844
Dore, Paul Gustave	1832-1883	Gerard, Francois	1770-1837
Doyle, Richard	1824-1883	Gerome, Jean Leon	1824-1904
Dubois, Paul	1829-1905	Gibson, John	1790-1866
Dumont, Francois	1751-1831	Gifford, Robert Swain	1840-1905

Gilbert, Sir John	1817-1897	Hunt, William Holman	1827-1910
Gleyre, Charles	1806-1874	Huntingdon, Daniel	1816-1906
Goldschmidt, Hermann	1802-1866	Hurlstone, Frederick Yeates	1800-1869
Goodall, Frederick	1822-1904	Ingres, Jean Auguste	
Gordon, Sir John Watson	1788-1864	Dominique	1780-1867
Goya Y Lucientes,		Inman, Henry	1801-1846
Francisco	1746-1828	Inness, George	1825-1894
Granet, Francois Marius	1775-1849	Isabey, Jean Baptiste	1767-1855
Grant, Sir Francis	1803-1878	Israels, Josef	1824-1911
Greenaway, Kate	1846-1901	Jackson, Sir Thomas	
Gregory, Edward John	1850-1909	Graham	1835-1924
Gros, Antoine Jean	1771-1835	Jalabert, Charles Francois	1819-1901
Gudin, Theodore	1802-1880	Johnson, Eastman	1824-1906
Guerin, Pierre Narcisse	1774-1833	Jonkind, Johann Barthold	1819-1891
Guillamin, Armand	1841-1927	Jordan, Rudolf	1810-1887
Guillaume, Jean Baptiste		Kaulbach, Wilhelm Von	1805-1874
Claude Eugene	1822-1905	Keene, Charles Samuel	1823-1891
Gwilt, Joseph	1784-1863	Keller, Albert Von	1844-1920
Haag Carl	1820-1915	Kensett, John Frederick	1818-1872
Haas, Johannes Hubertus		Kirkup, Seymore Stocker	1788-1880
Leonhardus De	1832-1908	Knaus, Ludwig	1829-1910
Habermann Hugo, Freiherr		Knight, Daniel Ridgway	1845-1924
Von	1849-1929	Knowles, Sir James	1831-1908
Haider, Karl	1846-1912	Kyosai, Sho Fu	1831-1889
Hamon, Jean Louis	1821-1874	La Farge, John	1835-1910
Hansen, Christian		Landseer, Sir Edwin Henry	1802-1873
Frederick	1756-1845	Lathrop, Francis	1849-1909
Hanson, Joseph Acosy,		Lauder, Robert Scott	1803-1869
Aloysius	1803-1882	Laurens, Jean Paul	1838-1921
Harding, Chester	1792-1866	Lawrence, Sir Thomas	1769-1830
Harpignies, Henri	1819-1916	Lear, Edward	1812-1888
Hartley, Jonathan Scott	1845-1912	Le Brun, Marie, Elizabeth	
Harvey, Sir George	1806-1876	Louise	1755-1842
Haydon, Benjamin Robert	1786-1846	Leech, John	1817-1864
Hayter, Sir George	1792-1871	Legros, Alphonse	1837-1911
Hearphy, Thomas	1775-1835	Lehman, Rudolf	1819-1905
Henner, Jean Jacques	1829-1905	Leibl, Wilhelm	1844-1900
Herbert, John Rogers	1810-1900	Leighton, Frederick	
Herkomer, Sir Hubert		Leighton	1830-1896
Von	1849-1914	Lejeune, Louis Francois	1775-1848
Hilderbrand, Adolf	1847-1921	Lemaire, Philippe Honore	1798-1880
Hildersbrand, Eduard	1818-1869	Lenbach, Franz Von	1836-1904
Hilton, William	1786-1839	Leslie, Charles Robert	1794-1859
Hiroshege,	1797-1858	Leutze, Emanuel	1816-1868
Hittorff, Jacques Ignace	1792-1867	Liebermann, Max	1847-1935
Hockert, Johan Frederick	1826-1866	Lindsay, Sir Coutts	1824-1913
Hokusai, Katsushika	1760-1849	Linnell, John	1792-1882
Holiday, Henry	1839-1927	Linton, Sir James	
Holl, Frank	1845-1888	Dromgole	1840-1916
Homer, Winslow	1836-1910	Leys, Hendrik	1815-1869
Hook, James Clarke	1819-1907	Lucas, John Seymour	1849-1923
Horsley, John Callcott	1817-1903	Macbeth, Robert Walker	1848-1910
Hosmer, Harriet Goodhue	1830-1908	Macculoch, Horatio	1805-1867
Houdon, Jean Antoine	1740-1828	McEntee, Jervis	1828-1891
Hovenden, Thomas	1840-1895	McKim, Charles Follen	1847-1909
Hubner, Julius	1806-1882	Maclise, Daniel	1806-1870
Huet, Paul	1804-1869	Macnee, Sir Daniel	1806-1882
Hughes, Arthur	1832-1915	Mactaggart, William	1835-1910
Hunt, Alfred William	1830-1896	Macwhirter, John	1839-1911
Hunt, Richard Morris	1828-1895	Madrazo, Y Kunt Don	
Hunt, William Henry	1790-1864	Fernando De	1815-1894

Makart, Hans	1840-1884	Pearson, John	
Manes, Josef	1820-1871	Loughborough	1817-1897
Manet, Edouard	1832-1883	Percier, Charles	1764-1838
Manson, George	1850-1876	Pettie, John	1839-1893
Marees, Hans Von	1837-1899	Piloty, Karl Von	1826-1886
Maris, Jacob	1837-1899	Pinelli, Bartolomeo	1781-1834
Marochetti, Carlo	1805-1867	Pinwell, George John	1842-1875
Martin, Homer Dodge	1836-1897	Pissaro, Camille	1831-1903
Martin, John	1789-1854	Playfair, William Henry	1789-1857
Matejko, Jan Alois	1838-1893	Plimer, Andrew	1763-1837
Mauve, Anton	1838-1888	Portaels, Jean Francois	1818-1895
Marshall, William Calder	1813-1894	Post, George Browne	1837-1913
Mead, Larkin Goldsmith	1835-1910	Powers, Hiram	1805-1873
Mead, William Rutherford	1846-1928	Poynter, Sir Edward John	1836-1919
Meissonier, Jean Louis		Pradilla, Francisco	1848-1921
Ernest	1815-1891	Prinsep, Valentine	
Menzel, Adolph Fredrich		Cameron	1838-1904
Erdmann Von	1815-1905	Prout, Samuel	1783-1852
Mercie, Marius Jean		Pugin, Augustus Welby	
Antonin	1845-1916	Northmore	1812-1852
Mesdag, Hendrik Willem	1831-1915	Puvis De Chavannes,	
Meunier, Constantin	1831-1905	Pierre Cecil	1824-1898
Millais, Sir John Everett	1829-1896	Redon, Odilon	1840-1916
Millet, Francis Davis	1846-1912	Regnault, Henri	1843-1871
Millet, Jean Francois	1814-1875	Reid, Sir George	1841-1913
Monet, Claude	1840-1926	Renoir, Pierre Auguste	1841-1919
Moore, William	1790-1851	Renwick, James	1818-1895
Moore, Henry	1831-1895	Repin, Ilya Yefimovich	1844-1930
Moran, Edward	1829-1901	Rethel, Alfred	1816-1859
Moreau, Gustave	1826-1898	Retsch, Frederich August	
Morel-Ladeuil, Leonard	1820-1888	Moritz	1779-1857
Morisot, Berthe Marie		Richardson, Henry	
Pauline	1841-1895	Hobson	1838-1886
Morriss, William	1834-1896	Richmond, George	1809-1896
Morse, Samuel Finley		Richmond, Sir William	
Breese	1791-1872	Blake	1842-1921
Mosler, Henry	1841-1920	Rickman, Thomas	1776-1841
Motte, William de la	1775-1863	Rietshel, Ernst	1804-1861
Mount, William Sydney	1807-1868	Riviere, Briton	1840-1920
Muller, William James	1812-1845	Roberts, David	1796-1864
Mulready, William	1786-1863	Rodin, Auguste	1840-1917
Munkacsy, Michael	1846-1900	Rogers, John	1829-1904
Murray, Sir David	1849-1933	Rops, Felicien	1833-1898
Nash, John	1752-1835	Rossetti, Dante Gabriel	1828-1882
Nasmyth, Alexander	1758-1840	Rousseau, Henri	1844-1910
Nesfield, William Eden	1835-1888	Rousseau, Pierre Etienne	
Neuville, Alphonse Marie		Theodore	1812-1867
De	1836-1885	Rowlandson, Thomas	1756-1827
Nicol, Erskine	1825-1904	Rude, Francois	1784-1855
Northcote, James	1746-1831	Ryder, Albert Pinkham	1847-1917
Orchardson, Sir William	1832-1910	Schadow, Friedrich	
Oudine, Eugene Andre	1810-1887	Wilhelm	1798-1862
Overbeck, Johann		Schadow, Johann	
Frederich	1789-1869	Gottfried	1764-1850
Page, William	1811-1885	Scheffer, Ary	1795-1858
Palmer, Samuel	1805-1881	Schilling, Johannes	1828-1910
Parsons, Alfred	1847-1920	Schinkel, Karl Friedrich	1781-1841
Paton, Sir Joseph Noel	1821-1901	Schnorr, Von Karolsfeld	
Paxton, Sir, Joseph	1801-1865	Julius	1794-1873
Peale, Charles Willson	1741-1827	Schreyer, Adolf	1828-1899
Peale, Rembrandt	1778-1860		

Schwanthaler, Ludwig Michael	1802-1848
Schwind, Moritz Von	1804-1871
Scott, David	1806-1849
Scott, Sir George Gilbert	1811-1878
Semper, Gottfried	1803-1873
Shaw, Richard Norman	1831-1912
Shee, Sir Martin Archer	1796-1850
Shields, Frederic James	1833-1911
Simson, William	1800-1847
Sisley, Alfred	1840-1899
Smillie, James David	1833-1909
Smirke, Sir Robert	1781-1867
Soane, Sir John	1753-1837
Somerscales, Thomas Jacques	1842-1928
Stanfield, William Clarkson	1794-1867
Stark, James	1794-1859
Steell, Sir John	1804-1891
Steinle, Eduard	1810-1886
Stevens, Alfred	1818-1875
Stevens, Alfred	1828-1906
Stillman, William James	1828-1901
Story, William Wetmore	1819-1895
Stothard, Thomas	1755-1834
Street, George Edmund	1824-1881
Stuart, Gilbert	1755-1828
Sturgis, Russell	1836-1909
Sully, Thomas	1783-1872
Szynye-Merse, Paul De	1845-1920
Tenniel, Sir John	1820-1914
Thayer, Abbott Handerson	1849-1921
Thoma, Hans	1839-1924
Thompson, Launt	1833-1934
Thornycroft, Sir William Hamo	1850-1925
Thorvaldsen, Berdel	1770-1844
Tiffany, Louis Comfort	1848-1933
Tissot, James Joseph Jacques	1836-1902
Tite, Sir William	1798-1873
Towne, Francis	1739-1816
Travies De Villiers, Charles Joseph	1804-1886
Troyon, Constant	1810-1865
Trumbull, John	1756-1843
Tryon, Dwight William	1849-1925
Turner, Joseph Mallord William	1775-1851
Vanderlyn, John	1776-1852

Van Der Stappen, Charles	1843-1910
Varley, John	1778-1842
Vedder, Elihu	1836-1923
Veit, Philipp	1793-1877
Verboeckhoven, Eugen Joseph	1798-1881
Vereshchagin, Vassili Vassilievich	1842-1904
Vernet, Antoine Charles Horace	1758-1835
Vernet, Emile Jean Horace	1789-1863
Vigee-Lebrun, Marie Anne Elizabeth	1755-1842
Vigne, Paul De	1843-1901
Vinton, Frederic Porter	1846-1911
Viollet Le Duc, Eugene Emmanuel	1814-1879
Volk, Leonard Wells	1828-1895
Vorosmarty, Mihaly	1800-1855
Wainewright, Thomas Griffiths	1794-1852
Waldo, Samuel Lovett	1783-1861
Walker, Frederick	1840-1875
Walker, Henry Oliver	1843-1929
Ward, Edward Matthew	1816-1879
Ward, John Quincy Adams	1830-1910
Waterhouse, Alfred	1830-1905
Waterhouse, John William	1847-1917
Waterlow, Sir Ernst Albert	1850-1919
Watts, George Frederic	1817-1904
Wauters, Emile	1846-1933
Webb, Sir Aston	1849-1930
Webb, Philip Speakman	1831-1915
Weir, Robert Walter	1803-1889
Westmacott, Sir Richard	1775-1856
Weyr, Rudolf Von	1847-1914
Whistler, James Abbott McNeill	1834-1903
Whymper, Edward	1840-1911
Wiertz, Anton Joseph	1806-1865
Wilkie, Sir David	1785-1841
Willems, Florent Joseph Marie	1823-1905
Wint, Peter de	1784-1849
Winter Halter, Franz Xavier	1806-1873
Woolner, Thomas	1826-1892
Wyant, Alexander	1836-1892
Yeams, William Frederick	1835-1918
Ziem, Felix Francois George	1821-1911

COMPOSERS

Abt, Franz	1819-1885
Adam, Adolphe Charles	1803-1856
Arditi, Luigi	1822-1903
Arriaga, Juan	1806-1826
Asioli, Bonifacio	1769-1832

Attwood, Thomas	1765-1838
Auber, Daniel Francois Eprit	1782-1871
Audran, Edmond	1842-1901
Bache, Francis Edward	1833-1858

Q

Baini, Guiseppe	1775-1844
Balakirev, Milly	
Alexeivich	1836-1910
Bargiel, Woldemar	1828-1897
Barnby, Sir Joseph	1838-1896
Barnett, John	1802-1890
Barnett, John Francis	1837-1916
Beethoven, Ludwig Van	1770-1827
Bellini, Vincenzo	1801-1835
Bendl, Karel	1838-1897
Benedict, Sir Julius	1804-1885
Bennett, Sir William	
Sterndale	1816-1875
Benoit, Peter Leonard	
Leopold	1834-1901
Beriot, Charles Auguste De	1802-1870
Berlioz, Hector	1803-1869
Bishop, Sir Henry Rowley	1786-1855
Bizet, Georges	1838-1875
Boieldieu, Francois Adrien	1775-1834
Boito, Arriego	1842-1918
Borodin, Alexander	
Porfyrievich	1834-1887
Bottesini, Giovanni	1822-1889
Brabazon, Hercules	
Brabazon	1821-1906
Brahms, Johannes	1833-1897
Bruch, Max	1838-1920
Bruckner, Anton	1824-1896
Buck, Dudley	1839-1909
Campenhout, Francois Von	1779-1849
Chabrier, Alexis Emmanuel	1841-1894
Cherubini, Maria Luigi	1760-1842
Chopin, Frederic Francois	1810-1849
Clay, Frederic	1838-1889
Clementi, Muzio	1752-1832
Cornelius, Carl August	
Peter	1824-1874
Costa, Sir Michael	1810-1884
Crotch, William	1817-1872
Cui, Cesar Antonovitch	1835-1918
Czerny, Karl	1791-1857
Dargomijsky, Alexander	
Sergeivich	1813-1869
Damrosch, Leopold	1832-1885
David, Felicien	1810-1876
Delibes, Clement Philibert	
Leo	1836-1891
Diabelli, Anton Antonio	1781-1858
Donizetti, Gaetano	1797-1848
Doppler, Albert Franz	1821-1883
Dreyschock, Alexander	1818-1869
Dubois, Francois Clement	1837-1924
Dupark, Henri	1848-1933
Dvorak, Anton	1841-1904
Dykes, John Bacchus	1823-1876
Eberwein, Traugott	
Maximilian	1775-1831
Eitner, Robert	1832-1905
Elvey, Sir George Job	1816-1893
Ernst, Heinrich Wilhelm	1814-1865

Faure, Gabriel	1845-1924
Fetis, Francois Joseph	1784-1871
Fibich, Zdenko	1850-1900
Field, John	1782-1837
Foster, Stephen Collins	1826-1864
Flotow, Friedrich	
Freiherr Von	1812-1883
Franck, Cesar	1822-1890
Franz, Robert	1815-1892
Gade, Niels Vilhelm	1817-1890
Gansbacher, Johann Baptist	1778-1844
Garcia, Manoel	1775-1832
Gazzaniga, Giuseppe	1743-1818
Glinka, Michael Ivanovich	1803-1857
Godard, Benjamin	1849-1895
Goldmark, Karl	1832-1915
Goss, Sir John	1800-1880
Gossec, Francois Joseph	1734-1829
Gounod, Charles Francois	1818-1893
Grieg, Edvard Hagerup	1843-1907
Gung'l, Josef	1810-1889
Halevy, Jacques Francois	1799-1862
Hatton, John Liptrot	1809-1886
Hauptmann, Moritz	1792-1868
Heller, Stephen	1815-1888
Henselt, Adolf Von	1814-1889
Herold, Louis Joseph	1791-1833
Herve, Florimond Rounger	1825-1892
Herz, Henri	1806-1888
Hiller, Ferdinand	1811-1885
Horn, Charles Edward	1786-1849
Hullah, John Pyke	1812-1884
Hummel, Johann Nepomuk	1778-1837
Joachim, Joseph	1831-1907
Joncières, Victorin	1839-1903
Kelly, Michael	1762-1826
Kjerulf, Halfdan	1815-1868
Kreutzer, Konradin	1780-1849
Lacombe, Louis Trouillon	1818-1884
Lalo, Edouard	1823-1892
Lassen, Eduard	1830-1904
Lecocq, Alexandre Charles	1832-1918
Lemmens, Nicolas Jacques	1823-1881
Lesuer, Jean Francois	1760-1837
Lindau, Paul	1839-1919
Liszt, Franz	1811-1886
Loewe, Johann Karl	
Gottfried	1796-1869
Lortzing, Albert	1801-1851
Macfarren, Sir George	
Alexander	1813-1887
Mackenzie, Sir Alexander	
Campbell	1847-1935
Marschner, Heinrich	
August	1795-1861
Massenet, Jules Emile	1842-1912
Mendelssohn, Bartholdi	
Felix	1809-1847
Meyebeer, Giacomo	1791-1864
Monk, William Henry	1823-1889
Mottl, Felix	1856-1911

Moussorgsky, Modest	
Petrovich	1835-1881
Napravnik, Edward	1839-1915
Nathan, Isaac	1791-1864
Nicolai, Otto	1810-1849
Offenbach, Jacques	1819-1880
Ouseley, Sir Frederick	1825-1889
Paer, Ferdinando	1771-1839
Paisiello, Giovanni	1741-1816
Parry, Sir Charles Hubert	1848-1918
Pearsall, Robert Lucas De	1795-1856
Pedrell, Felipe	1841-1922
Pierson, Henry Hugo	1815-1873
Planquette, Robert	1850-1903
Pleyel, Ignaz Joseph	1757-1831
Ponchielli, Amilcare	1834-1886
Raff, Joseph Joachim	1822-1882
Randegger, Alberto	1832-1911
Reineck, Carl Heinrich	1824-1910
Rheinberger, Joseph	
Gabriel	1839-1901
Rimsky-Korsakov, Nicolas	
Andreevich	1844-1908
Rockstro, William Smith	1823-1895
Rossini, Gioachino Antonio	1792-1868
Rubinstein, Anton	1829-1924
Saint-Saens, Charles	
Camille	1835-1921
Scharwenka, Xavier	1850-1924
Schubert, Franz	1808-1878
Schubert, Franz Peter	1797-1828
Schumann, Clara Josephine	1819-1896

Schumann, Robert	
Alexander	1810-1856
Sgambati, Giovanni	1843-1914
Shield, William	1748-1829
Smetana, Bedrich	1824-1884
Soderman, August Johan	1832-1876
Spontini, Gasparo Luigi	
Pacifico	1774-1851
Spohr, Ludwig	1784-1859
Spottiswoode, Alicia Ann,	
Lady Ann	1811-1900
Strauss, Johann	1804-1849
Strauss, Johann, the	
younger	1825-1899
Sullivan, Sir Arthur	
Seymour	1842-1900
Suppe, Franz Von	1820-1895
Svendsen, Johan Severin	1840-1911
Thomas, Ambroise	1811-1896
Thomas, Arthur Goring	1850-1892
Tosti, Sir Francesco Paolo	1846-1916
Tschaikovsky, Peter Ilich	1840-1893
Verdi, Giuseppe Fortunino	
Francesco	1813-1901
Wagner, Wilhelm Richard	1813-1883
Waldteuffel, Emil	1837-1915
Wallace, William Vincent	1812-1865
Weber, Carl Maria	1786-1826
Wesley, Samuel Sebastian	1810-1876
Wesley, Samuel	1766-1837
Widor, Charles Marie	1845-1937
Zingarelli, Niccolo	1752-1837

1854   France declares war on Russia.
        Great Britain declares war on Russia.
        Crystal Palace opened.
        Battle of the Alma.
        Seige of Sebastopol.
        Battle of Balaclava.
        Battle of Inkerman.

1856   Peace treaty signed in Paris.

1857   Indian mutiny.
        Relief of Lucknow.

1858   Atlantic cable.

1859   Battle of Montebello.
        Battle of Magenta.
        Battle of Solferino.

1860   Battle of Volturno.

1862   Battle of Williamsburg.
        Cotton famine in Lancashire.
        2nd Battle of Bull Run.

1863   Slavery abolished in U.S.
        Battle of Chatanooga.

1865   Lincoln assassinated.
        Antiseptic surgery introduced.

1866   Austria declares war on Prussia. Italy.
        Battle of Custozza.
        Battle of Sadowa.
        Battle of Lissa.

1867   Schleswig-Holstein annexed to Prussia.
        Dominion of Canada established.

1869   Suez Canal opened.

1870   France declares war on Prussia.
        Battle of Woerth
        Battle of Gravelotte.
        Battle of Sedan.
        Rome and Papal States annexed to Italy.
        Germany proclaimed a united empire.

1871   Communards destroy Tuileries, set fire to Louvre etc.
        Great fire of Chicago.

1872   The Ballot is introduced in England.

1873   Typewriter invented.

PROMINENT PEOPLE

Bismark, Prince Otto, Eduard Leopold Von	1815-1898
Booth, General William	1829-1912
Braille, Louis	1809-1852
Brown, John	1800-1859
Caruso, Enrico	1873-1921
Curie, Pierre	1859-1906
Curie, Marie	1867-1934
Diaghilev, Sergei Pavlovich	1872-1929
Edison, Thomas Alva	1847-1931
Faraday, Michael	1791-1867
Gandhi, Mahandas Karamchand	1869-1948
Garibaldi, Giuseppe	1807-1882
Kitchener of Khartoum	1850-1916
Lessepes, Vicomte Ferdinande de	1805-1894
Lister, Lord	1827-1912
Livingstone, Dr. David	1813-1873
Lloyd George, David	1863-1945
Manning, Henry Edward Cardinal	1808-1892
Nobel, Alfred	1833-1896
Pankhurst, Emmeline	1858-1928
Pasteur, Louis	1822-1895
Rasputin, Grigori Yefimovich	1871-1916
Rhodes, Cecil	1853-1902
Rontgen, Prof. Wilhelm Konrad	1845-1923

EMPERORS OF CHINA
(MANCHU (Ch'ing) DYNASTY)

Wen Tsung   1850-1861   Mu Tsung   1861-1875

POPES

Piux IX   1846-1878

FRANCE. HEADS OF STATE

Louis Napoleon		President Adolphe Thiers	1871-1873
Bonaparte	1848-1852	President Marshal	
Napoleon III	1852-1870	Macmahon	1873-1879

ENGLAND. SOVEREIGNS

Victoria   1837-1901

SWEDEN. KINGS

Oscar I   1844-1859   Oscar II   1872-1907
Charles XV   1859-1872

PORTUGAL. KINGS

Maria II (Again)   1834-1853   Luiz I   1861-1889
Pedro V   1853-1861

RUSSIA. TSARS

Nicholas I   1825-1855   Alexander II   1855-1881

SPAIN. SOVEREIGNS

Isabella II   1833-1868   Alfonso XII   1874-1885
Interregnum   1868-1874

U.S.A. PRESIDENTS

Millard Fillimore		Abraham Lincoln	1861-1865
(Vice P)	1850-1853	Andrew Johnson	
Franklin Pierce	1853-1857	(Vice P)	1865-1869
James Buchanan	1857-1861	Ulysses Grant	1869-1877

KINGS OF PRUSSIA

Frederick William IV	1840-1861	William I	1861-1888
		became Emperor of	
		Germany 1861	

EMPERORS OF AUSTRIA

Franz Josef   1848-1916

NETHERLANDS. SOVEREIGNS

William III   1849-1890

| Leopold I | 1831-1865 | Leopold II | 1865-1909 |

KING OF ITALY

| Victor Emmanuel II | 1861-1878 |

WRITERS

Aakjaer, Jeppe	1866-1930	Aksakov, Konstantin	1817-1860
Aanrud, Hans	1863-1953	Aksakov, Sergei	
Aansen, Ivar	1813-1896	Timofeyevich	1791-1859
Aarestrup, Emil	1800-1856	Alaman, Lucas	1792-1853
Abbott, Edwin, Abbott	1838-1926	Alarcon, Pedro, Antonio	1833-1891
Abbott, Evelyn	1843-1901	Alas, Leopoldo	1852-1901
Abbott, Jacob	1803-1879	Albert, Eugen Francis	
Abbott, Lyman	1835-1922	Charles d'	1864-1932
Abbott, Wilbur, Cortez	1869-1947	Alcott, Amos Bronson	1799-1888
A Beckett, Gilbert, Abbott	1811-1856	Alcott, Louisa May	1832-1888
Aberigh-Mackay, George		Alcover, Joan	1854-1926
Robert	1848-1881	Alden, Isabella	1841-1930
About, Edmond Francois		Alden, Joseph	1807-1885
Valentin	1828-1885	Aldrich, Thomas Bailey	1836-1907
Ackermann, Louise		Aleardi, Aleardo	1812-1878
Victorine Choquet	1813-1890	Alecsandri, Vasile	1821-1890
Acton, John Emerich		Alexander, Cecil Francis	1818-1895
Edward Dolbey	1834-1902	Alexander, Samuel	1859-1938
Adam, Juliette	1836-1936	Alexander, William	1826-1894
Adam, Paul	1862-1920	Alexis, Willibald	1798-1871
Adams, Andy	1859-1935	Alger, Horatio	1834-1899
Adams, Charles Follen	1842-1918	Alin, Oscar, Josef	1846-1900
Adams, Henry Brooks	1838-1918	Alington, Cyril, Argentine	1872-
Adams, Oscar Fay	1855-1919	Alison, Sir Archibald	1792-1867
Adams, Samuel Hopkins	1871-1958	Allen, Charles Grant	
Adams, William Taylor	1822-1897	Blairfindie	1848-1899
Adamson, Robert	1852-1902	Allen, James Lane	1849-1925
Addams, Jane	1860-1935	Allibone, Samuel, Austin	1816-1889
Ade, George	1866-1944	Allingham, William	1824-1889
Adickes, Erich	1866-1928	Allmers, Hermann	1821-1902
Adolphus, John Leycester	1795-1862	Alma Tadema,	
Adler, Alfred	1870-1937	Sir Laurence	1836-1912
Afzelius, Aruid, August	1785-1871	Almeida-Garrett	
Agassiz, Jean Louis		Joao Baptista da	1799-1854
Rodolphe	1807-1873	Almqvist, Karl Jonas	
Agoult, Marie Catherine		Ludwig	1793-1866
Sophie de Flavigny	1805-1876	Alvarez Quintero,	
Aguilo I Fuster Marian	1825-1897	Joaquin	1873-1944
Aho, Juhani	1861-1921	Alvarez Quintero, Serafin	1871-1938
Aicard, Jean Francois		Amicis, Edmondo de	1846-1908
Victor	1848-1921	Amiel, Henri Frederic	1821-1881
Aide, Hamilton	1830-1906	Ampere, Jean, Jacques	1800-1864
Aimard, Gustave	1818-1883	Ancelot, Jacques Arsene	
Ainger, Alfred	1837-1904	Francois Polycarpe	1794-1854
Ainslie, Hew	1792-1878	Ancona, Alessandro	1835-1914
Ainsworth, William		Andersen, Hans Christian	1805-1875
Harrison	1805-1882	Andrews, Charles	
Aird, Thomas	1802-1876	McLean	1863-1943
Akers, Benjamin Paul	1825-1861	Andreyev, Leonid	
Aksakov, Ivan		Nicolaievich	1871-1919
Sergeyvich	1823-1886	Angell, Sir Norman	1874

Angellier, Auguste Jean	1848-1911	Bacon, Delia Salter	1811-1859
Angus, Marion	1866-1946	Bacon, Leonard	1802-1881
Anker-Larsen, Johannes	1874-1957	Baedeker, Karl	1801-1859
Annunzio, Gabrielle, D'	1863-1938	Bagehot, Walter	1826-1877
Anstey, Francis	1856-1935	Bahr, Hermann	1863-1934
Antokolski, Mark		Bahr, Johann, Christian	
Matveevich	1834-1902	Felix	1798-1872
Anzengruber, Ludwig	1839-1889	Bailey, Philip James	1816-1902
Arago, Jacques Etienne		Bailey, Samuel	1791-1870
Victor	1790-1855	Baillie, Joanna	1762-1851
Arany, Janos	1817-1882	Bain, Alexander	1818-1903
Arbois De Jubainville,		Baird, Henry Martin	1832-1906
Marie Henri d'	1827-1910	Baker, Sir Herbert	1862-1946
Archer, William	1856-1924	Baker, Ray Stannard	1870-1946
Aribau, Bonaventura		Balaguer, Victor	1824-1901
Carles	1798-1862	Balbo, Cesare Count	1789-1853
Arnason, Jon	1819-1888	Baldensperger, Fernand	1871-1958
Arndt, Ernst Moritz	1769-1860	Ballantine, James	1808-1877
Arneth, Alfred	1819-1897	Ballantyne, Robert	
Arnim, Elizabeth (Betinna)		Michael	1825-1894
Von	1785-1859	Balmont, Constantine	1867-1943
Arnold, Sir Edwin	1832-1904	Bancroft, George	1800-1891
Arnold, Matthew	1822-1888	Bancroft, Hubert Howe	1832-1918
Arthur, Timothy Shay	1809-1885	Bang, Hermann Joachim	1858-1912
Asbjornsen, Peter		Banville, Theodore	
Christian	1812-1885	Faullain, De	1823-1891
Ashbee, Charles Robert	1863-1942	Barante, Amable	
Ashe, Thomas	1836-1889	Guillaume Prosper	
Asnyk, Adam	1838-1897	Brugiere	1782-1866
Atherton, Gertrude		Barbey D'aureuilly, Jules	
Franklin	1857-1948	Amedee	1808-1889
Atkinson, Thomas		Barbier, Henri Auguste	1805-1882
Witlam	1799-1861	Barbier, Paul Jules	1825-1901
Aubanel, Theodore	1829-1886	Barbusse, Henri	1873-1935
Auerbach, Berthold	1812-1882	Baring, Maurice	1874-1946
Auersperg, Anton		Baring-Gould, Sabine	1834-1924
Alexander	1806-1876	Barlow, Jane	1860-1917
Augier, Guillaume, Victor		Barlow, Peter	1776-1862
Emile	1820-1889	Barnes, William	1800-1886
Aulard, Francois Victor		Baroja, Pio	1872-1956
Alphonse	1849-1928	Barr, Amelia Edith	1831-1919
Austin, Alfred	1835-1913	Barres, Maurice	1862-1923
Austin, Mary Hunter	1869-1934	Barrie, Sir James	
Austin, Sarah	1793-1867	Matthew	1860-1937
Autran, Joseph	1813-1877	Barriere, Theodore	1823-1877
Avellanida, Gertrudis		Barrili, Antonio Guilio	1836-1908
Gomez D'	1814-1873	Barthelemy, Auguste,	
Avenarius, Richard		Marseille	1796-1867
Heinrich Ludwig	1843-1896	Barthelemy, Saint-Hilaire	
Axelrod, Pavel		Jules	1805-1895
Borriasovich	1850-1928	Bascom, John	1827-1911
Ayala Y Herrera		Bashkirtsev, Marie	1860-1884
Adelardo Lopez d'	1828-1879	Bataille, Felix Henri	1872-1922
Aytoun, William		Bates, Arlo	1850-1918
Edmonstoun	1813-1865	Bates, Katharine Lee	1859-1929
Azeglio, Massimo		Bateson, Mary	1865-1906
Taparelli Marquis d'	1798-1866	Batvushkov, Konstantin	
Azorin, Jose Martinez Ruis	1874-	Nikolaievitch	1787-1855
Babbitt, Irving	1865-1933	Baudelaire, Charles	
Bacheller, Irving Addison	1859-1950	Pierre	1821-1867

Baudissin, Wolf Heinrich	1789-1878	Bibaud, Michel	1782-1857
Bauer, Bruno	1809-1882	Biedermann, Friedrich	
Bauernfeld, Eduard, Von	1802-1890	Karl	1812-1901
Baumbach, Rudolf	1840-1905	Bierce, Ambrose	1842-1916
Bautian, Louis Eugene		Billings, Robert William	1813-1874
Marie	1796-1867	Binding, Rudolf Georg	1867-1938
Bax, Ernest Belfort	1854-1926	Binyon, Laurence	1869-1943
Bazin, Rene	1853-1932	Birrell, Augustine	1850-1933
Beard, Charles Austin	1874-1948	Bishop, Isabella	1831-1904
Beauvoir, Roger De	1809-1866	Bitzius, Albrecht	1797-1854
Becker, Carl L.	1873-1945	Bjornson, Bjornstjerne	1832-1910
Becque, Henry Francois	1837-1899	Black, William	1841-1898
Becquer, Gustavo Adolfo	1836-1870	Blackie, John Stuart	1809-1895
Bede, Cuthbert	1827-1889	Blackmore, Richard	
Bédier, Joseph	1864-1938	Doddridge	1825-1900
Beecher, Henry Ward	1813-1887	Blackwood, Algernon	
Beerbohm, Sir Max	1872-1956	Henry	1869-1951
Beeton (Mrs.) Isabella		Blanc, Jean Joseph	
Mary Mayson	1836-1865	Charles Louis	1811-1882
Beets, Nikolaas	1814-1903	Blavatsky, Helena	
Belasco, David	1854-1931	Petrova	1831-1891
Beljame, Alexandre	1842-1906	Blind, Mathilde	1847-1896
Bell, Henry Glassford	1803-1874	Bliss, Philip Paul	1838-1876
Bell, John Jay	1871-1934	Blok, Petrus Johannes	1855-1932
Bell, Robert, Sir	1800-1867	Blondel, Maurice	1861-1939
Bellamy, Edward	1850-1898	Blood, Benjamin Paul	1832-1919
Belli, Giuseppe		Blouet, Paul	1848-1903
Gioachino	1791-1863	Bloy, Leon	1846-1917
Belloc, Joseph, Hilaire		Blunt, Wilfrid Scawen	1840-1922
Pierre	1870-1953	Boas, Franz	1858-1942
Belloc-Lowndes, Marie		Bodenstedt, Friedrich	
Adelaide	1868-1947	Martin Von	1819-1892
Benavente Y Martinez,		Boisgobey, Fortune	
Jacinto	1866-1954	Abraham Du	1824-1891
Benedix, Julius Roderick	1811-1873	Bojer, Johan	1872-1959
Beneke, Frederich Eduard	1798-1856	Boker, George Henry	1823-1890
Bennett, Enoch Arnold	1867-1931	Boldrewood, Rolf	1826-1915
Benoa, Julien	1867-	Bolyai, Wolfgang	1775-1856
Benson, Arthur		Bonghi, Ruggero	1828-1895
Christopher	1862-1925	Boothby, Guy Newell	1867-1905
Benson, Edward Frederic	1867-1940	Bordeaux, Henri	1870-
Benson, Robert Hugh	1871-1914	Borel, Petrus	1809-1859
Bentley, Edmond		Borrow, George, Henry	1803-1881
Clerihew	1875-1956	Bosanquet, Bernard	1848-1923
Beranger, Pierre		Bosboom Toussaint, Anna	
Jean De	1780-1857	Louisa Geertruida	1812-1886
Berchet, Giovanni	1783-1851	Bostrom, Christoffer	
Berdyaev, Nikolas	1874-1948	Jacob	1797-1866
Berenson, Bernard	1865-1959	Bottomley, Gordon	1874-1948
Beresford, John Davys	1873-1947	Bouchor, Maurice	1855-1929
Bergman, Bo Hjalmar	1869-	Boucicault, Dion	1822-1890
Bergson, Henri	1859-1941	Bouilhet, Louis Hyacinthe	1822-1869
Bernard, Tristan	1866-1947	Bourget, Paul Charles	
Bernhardi, Friedrich Von	1849-1930	Joseph	1852-1935
Berry, Mary	1763-1852	Bowen, Francis	1811-1890
Bertrand, Louis	1866-1941	Boyd, Andrew Kennedy	
Besant, Annie	1847-1933	Hutchinson	1825-1899
Besant, Walter Sir	1836-1901	Boyesen, Hjalmar	1848-1895
Beskow, Bernhard Von	1796-1868	Boylesve, Rene	1867-1926
Bialik, Hayim Nachman	1873-1934	Braddon, Mary Elizabeth	1837-1915

Bradford, Gameliel	1863-1932	Buckstone, John Baldwin	1802-1879
Bradley, Andrew Cecil	1851-1935	Bulgarin, Thaddeus	1789-1859
Bradley, Edward	1827-1889	Bunin, Ivan Alexeyevich	1870-1953
Bradley, Francis Herbert	1846-1924	Bulwer, Henry Lytton	1803-1873
Braga, Theophilo	1843-1924	Burckhardt, Jakob	1818-1897
Brailsford, Henry Noel	1873-1958	Burnand, Frederick	
Bramah, Ernest	1867-1942	Gustavus	1842-1885
Brandes, Gorge Maurice		Burnett, Frances Eliza	
Cohen	1842-1927	Hodgson	1849-1924
Braun, Lily	1865-1916	Burroughs, Edgar Rice	1875-1950
Brazil, Angela	1868-1947	Burroughs, John	1837-1921
Breasted, James Henry	1865-1935	Burrows, Montague	1819-1905
Bremer, Frederika	1801-1865	Burton, John Hill	1809-1881
Bremond, Henri	1865-1933	Burton, Sir Richard	
Brentano, Franz	1838-1917	Evans	1804-1860
Breton de Los Herreros,		Burton, Sir Richard	
Manuel	1796-1873	Francis	1821-1890
Bridges, Robert Seymour	1844-1930	Bury, Lady Charlotte	
Brierly, Benjamin	1825-1896	Susan Maria	1775-1861
Brieux, Eugene	1858-1932	Bury, John Bagnell	1861-1927
Brizeux, Julien Auguste		Butler, Nicholas Murray	1862-1947
Pelage	1803-1858	Butler, Samuel	1835-1902
Brokmeyer, Henry		Buysse, Cyriez	1859-1932
Conrad	1828-1906	Byron, Henry James	1834-1884
Bronte, Charlotte	1816-1855	Caballero, Fernan	1796-1877
Brooke, Stopford		Cable, George Washington	1844-1925
Augustus	1832-1916	Caine, Sir Thomas	
Brooks, Charles William		Henry Hall	1853-1931
Shirley	1816-1874	Caird, Edward	1835-1908
Brooks, Phillips	1835-1893	Caird, John	1820-1898
Broughton, John Cam		Cairns, John Elliot	1823-1875
Hobhouse	1786-1869	Calderon, George	1868-1915
Broughton, Rhoda	1840-1920	Calderwood, Henry	1830-1897
Brown, Alice	1857-1948	Calvert, George Henry	1803-1889
Brown, George Douglas	1869-1902	Calvet, Jean	1874-
Brown, Oliver Maddox	1855-1874	Calvo, Carlos	1824-1906
Brown, Peter Hume	1850-1918	Campoamor Y Campoosorio	
Brown, Samuel Morison	1817-1856	Raymon De	1819-1901
Brown, Thomas, Edward	1830-1897	Canina, Luigi	1795-1856
Browning, Elizabeth		Cannon, Charles James	1800-1860
Barrett	1806-1861	Canth, Minna	1844-1897
Browning, Oscar	1837-1923	Cantu, Cesare	1804-1895
Browning, Robert	1812-1889	Capfigue, Jean Baptiste	
Brownson, Orestes		Honore Raymond	1801-1872
Augustus	1803-1876	Capern, Edward	1819-1894
Brugsch, Hienrick Karl	1827-1894	Capuana, Luigi	1839-1915
Brunner, Henry	1840-1915	Capus, Alfred	1858-1922
Bryant, William Cullen	1794-1878	Caraglia, Joan	1852-1912
Bryce, Lloyd Stephens	1851-1917	Carducci, Giosue	1835-1907
Bryussov, Valery		Carey, Phoebe	1824-1871
Yakovlevich	1873-1924	Carlen, Emilia Smith	
Buchan, John	1875-1940	Flygare	1807-1892
Buchanan, Robert		Carleton, Will	1845-1912
Williams	1841-1901	Carleton, William	1794-1869
Buchez, Philippe		Carlyle, Thomas	1795-1881
Benjamin Joseph	1796-1865	Carman, Bliss	1861-1929
Buchner, Ludwig	1824-1899	Carmen, Sylva	1843-1916
Buckingham, James Silk	1786-1855	Carnegie, Andrew	1835-1918
Buckle, George Earle	1854-1935	Caro, Emile Marie	1826-1887
Buckle, Henry Thomas	1821-1862	Carpenter, Edward	1844-1929

Carr, Joseph William	1849-1916	Cobbe, Frances Power	1822-1904
Carriere, Moritz	1817-1895	Cockton, Henry	1807-1853
Carton, R. C.	1853-1928	Cole, Sir Henry	1808-1882
Cary, Alice	1820-1871	Colerisge, Sara	1802-1852
Cassirer, Ernst	1874-1945	Colet, Louise	1810-1876
Castelli, Ignaz Franz	1781-1862	Colette, Sidonie Gabrielle	1873-1954
Castello, Branco Camillo	1825-1890	Collett, Jacobine Camilla	1813-1895
Castro, Eugenio de	1869-1944	Collier, John Payne	1789-1883
Cattaneo, Carlo	1801-1869	Collins, Charles Allston	1828-1873
Cavalcaselle, Giovanni		Collins, Mortimer	1827-1876
Battista	1820-1897	Collins, William Wilkie	1824-1889
Cazalis, Henri	1840-1909	Colomb, Philip Howard	1831-1899
Chalybaus, Heinrich		Comte, Auguste	1798-1857
Moritz	1796-1862	Conrad, Joseph	1857-1924
Chambers, Robert	1802-1871	Conscience Hendrik	1812-1883
Chamier, Frederick	1796-1870	Conway, Hugh	1847-1885
Champfleury	1821-1889	Conway, Moncure Daniel	1832-1907
Chantavoine, Henri	1850-1918	Cook, Edward Dutton	1829-1883
Chapman, John Jay	1862-1933	Cook, Sir Edward Tyas	1857-1919
Charles, Elizabeth	1828-1896	Cooke, John Esten	1830-1886
Chasles, Philarete	1798-1873	Cooke, Rose Terry	1837-1892
Chatrian, Alexandre		Coolidge, Susan	1835-1905
(Erckman, Chatrian)	1826-1890	Coolus, Romaine	1868-1952
Chatterji, Bankim		Cooper, James Fenimore	1789-1851
Chandra	1838-1894	Coppee, Francois	1842-1908
Chausson, Ernest	1855-1899	Coppee, Henry	1821-1895
Chekhov, Anton Pavlovich	1860-1904	Corelli, Marie	1855-1924
Cherbuliez, Charles		Cossa, Pietro	1830-1881
Victor	1829-1899	Costa, Joaquim	1846-1911
Chernyshevsky, Nikolay		Costello, Louisa Stuart	1799-1877
Gavrilovich	1828-1889	Coster, Charles Theodore	
Cheruel, Pierre Adolphe	1809-1891	Henri, De	1827-1879
Chesney, Charles		Couperus, Louis	1863-1923
Cornwallis	1826-1876	Courteline, Georges	1860-1929
Chesterton, Gilbert Keith	1874-1936	Courthope, William John	1842-1917
Chiesa, Fransesco	1871-	Cousin, Victor	1792-1867
Child, Francis James	1825-1896	Cox, Sir George William	1827-1902
Child, Lydia Maria	1802-1874	Craddock, Charles Egbert	1850-1922
Chopin, Kate	1851-1904	Craig, Edward Gordon	1872-
Churchill, Winston	1871-1947	Craigie, Pearl Mary	
Churchill, Sir Winston		Teresa	1867-1906
Leonard Spencer	1874-1965	Craik, Dinah Maria	1826-1887
Cibrrio, Luigi Count	1802-1870	Crane, Stephen	1871-1900
Cladel, Leon	1835-1892	Craven, Pauline	1808-1891
Clare, John	1793-1864	Crawford, Francis Marion	1854-1909
Claretie, Jules Arsene		Creasy, Sir Edward	
Arnaud	1840-1913	Shepherd	1812-1878
Clarke, Charles Cowden	1787-1877	Creighton, Mandell	1843-1901
Clarke, Marcus Andrew		Cremazie, Octave	1822-1879
Hislop	1846-1881	Cremer, Jakobus Jan	1827-1880
Clark, William George	1821-1878	Creuzer, George Friedrich	1771-1858
Claudel, Paul	1868-1955	Croce, Benedetto	1866-1952
Claussen, Sophus Niels		Crockett, Samuel	
Christen	1865-1931	Rutherford	1860-1914
Clemencau, George	1841-1929	Croker, John Wilson	1780-1857
Clifford, William		Croker, Thomas Crofton	1798-1854
Kingdon	1845-1879	Crowe, Catherine	1800-1870
Clive, Caroline	1801-1873	Crozier, John Beattie	1849-1921
Clough, Arthur Hugh	1819-1861	Crusenstolpe, Magnus	
Clowes, Sir William Laird	1856-1905	Jakob	1795-1865

Csengery, Antal	1822-1880	Dennery, Adolphe		
Csiky, Gregor	1842-1891	Phillippe	1811-1899	
Cullum, George		Dent, John Charles	1841-1887	
Washington	1809-1892	De Quincey, Thomas	1785-1859	
Cummins, Maria Suzanna	1827-1866	Deroulede, Paul	1846-1914	
Cumont, Franz Valery		Deschamps, Emile	1791-1871	
Marie	1868-1947	De Tabley, John Byrne		
Cunninghame, Graham		Leicester Warren	1835-1895	
Robert Bontine	1852-1936	Deussen, Paul	1845-1919	
Curel, Francois		Devere, Aubrey Thomas	1814-1902	
Vicomte, De	1854-1928	Dewey, John	1859-1952	
Curtis, George William	1824-1892	Dexter, Henry Martyn	1821-1890	
Curtius Ernst	1814-1896	Dicey, Edward	1832-1911	
Curtius, Georg	1820-1885	Dickens, Charles John		
Cust, Sir Lionel Henry	1859-1929	Huffam	1812-1870	
Da Costa, Isaak	1798-1860	Dickinson, Emily	1830-1886	
Dahlmann, Friedrich		Dickinson, Goldsworthy		
Christoph	1785-1860	Lowes	1862-1932	
Dahn, Julius Sophus		Dierx, Leon	1838-1912	
Felix	1834-1912	Digby, Kenelm Henry	1800-1880	
Dall'ongaro, Francesco	1808-1873	Dilthey, Wilhelm	1833-1911	
D'Alviella, Count Goblet	1846-1925	Dingelstedt, Franz Von	1814-1881	
Daly, Augustin	1838-1899	Dionne, Narcisse Eutrope	1848-1917	
Dana, Richard Henry	1815-1882	Disreali, Benjamin	1804-1881	
D'Annunzio, Gabriele	1863-1938	Dixon, Richard Watson	1833-1900	
Da Ponte, Lorenzo	1749-1838	Dixon, William Hepworth	1821-1879	
Dareste De La Chavanne,		Dobell, Sydney		
Cleophas	1820-1882	Thompson	1824-1874	
Darmesteter, James	1849-1894	Dobson, Henry Austin	1840-1921	
Darwin, Charles Robert	1809-1882	Dodge, Mary	1838-1905	
D'Aubigné, Sean Henri		Dodge, Theodore Ayault	1842-1909	
Merle	1794-1872	Dodgson, Charles Lutwidge		
Daudet, Alphonse	1840-1897	(Lewis Carroll)	1832-1898	
Daudet, Ernest	1837-1921	Dollinger, Johann Joseph		
Daudet, Leon	1867-1942	Ignaz Von	1799-1890	
Daumer, Georg Friedrich	1800-1875	Domett, Alfred	1811-1887	
Davidson, John	1857-1909	Donnay, Charles Maurice	1859-1945	
Davidson, Thomas	1840-1900	Donoso, Cortez Juan	1809-1853	
Davies, Hubert Henry	1869-1917	Doran, John	1807-1878	
Davies, William Henry	1871-1940	Dostoievsky, Fyodor		
Davis, Henry William		Mikhaylovich	1821-1881	
Carless	1874-1928	Doughty, Sir Arthur		
Davis, Richard Harding	1864-1916	George	1860-1936	
Debosis, Adolfo	1863-1924	Doughty, Charles		
Decelles, Alfred Duclos	1843-1925	Montegu	1843-1926	
De Court, Frans	1834-1878	Douglas, Lord Alfred		
De Geer, Louis Gerhard		Bruce	1870-1945	
Baron	1818-1896	Douglas, Norman	1868-1952	
Dehmel, Richard	1863-1920	Douglas, Sir William		
Dekker, Edward Douwes	1820-1887	Fettes	1822-1891	
De La Mare, Walter John	1873-1956	Dove, Alfred	1844-1916	
Deland, Margaretta		Dowden, Edward	1843-1913	
Wade	1857-1945	Dowson, Ernest	1867-1900	
Delbruck, Hans	1848-1929	Doyle, Sir Arthur Conan	1859-1930	
Deledda, Grazia	1875-1936	Doyle, Sir Francis Hastings		
Delisle, Leopold Victor	1826-1910	Charles	1810-1888	
Demogeot, Jacques Claude	1808-1894	Drachmann, Holger		
De Morgan, William		Henrick Herboldt	1846-1908	
Frend	1839-1917	Dragomirov, Michael		
Denifle, Heinrich Seuse	1844-1905	Ivanovich	1830-1905	

Draper, William	1811-1882	Ellis, Alexander John	1814-1890
Dreiser, Theodore	1871-1945	Ellis, Henry Havelock	1859-1939
Drews, Arthur	1865-1935	Elphinstone, Mountstuart	1779-1859
Driesch, Hans Adolf		Elton, Oliver	1861-1945
Eduard	1867-1941	Emerson, Ralph Waldo	1803-1882
Drobisch, Moritz Wilhelm	1802-1896	Eminescu, Mihail	1849-1889
Droysen, Johann Gustav	1808-1884	Engels Friedrich	1820-1895
Drummond, Henry	1851-1897	English, Thomas Dunn	1819-1902
Duboc, Julius	1829-1903	Ennemoser, Joseph	1787-1855
Dubois, William Edward		Eotvos, Joseph Baron	1813-1871
Burghardt	1868-	Erckmann, Emile	
Du Camp, Maxime	1822-1894	(Erckman-Chatrian)	1822-1899
Ducasse, Pierre Emmanuel		Erdelyi, Janos	1814-1868
Albert	1813-1893	Erdmann, Benno	1851-1921
Duclauz, Agnes Mary		Erdmann, Johann Eduard	1805-1892
Frances	1857-1944	Ernle, Rowland Edmund	
Duff, Sir Mountstuart		Prothero	1851-1937
Elphinstone Grant	1829-1906	Ernst, Paul	1866-1933
Duff-Gordon, Lucie	1829-1869	Erskine, Thomas	1788-1870
Duhring, Eugen Karl	1833-1921	Eschenmayer, Adam Karl	
Dumas, Alexandre	1802-1870	August Von	1768-1852
Dumas, Alexandre (fils)	1824-1895	Esher, Reginald Baliol	
Du Maurier, George Louis		Brett	1852-1930
Palmella Busson	1834-1896	Esquiros, Henri Francois	
Dummler, Ernst Ludwig	1830-1902	Alphonse	1812-1876
Dunbar, Paul Laurence	1872-1906	Estaunie, Edouard	1862-1942
Duncker, Maximilian		Estebanez, Caldren Serafin	1799-1867
Wolgang	1811-1886	Eucken, Rudolf Christoph	1846-1926
Dunne, John William	1875-1949	Evans, George Essex	1863-1909
Dupont, Pierre	1821-1870	Ewing, Juliana Horatia	
Durkheim, Emile	1858-1917	Orr	1841-1885
Duruy, Jean Victor	1811-1894	Fabre, Ferdinand	1830-1898
Dutt, Michael Madhu		Fagan, James Bernard	1873-1933
Sudan	1824-1873	Fagniez, Gustav Charles	1842-1927
Ebers, Georg Moritz	1837-1898	Faguet, Emile	1847-1916
Ebert, Karl Egon	1801-1882	Fahlcrantz, Christian	
Ebner-Eschenbach, Marie	1830-1916	Erik	1790-1866
Eca De Queiroz, Jose Maria	1843-1900	Falke, Gustave	1853-1916
Echegaram Y Eizaguire,		Falke, Johann Friedrich	
José	1833-1916	Gottlieb	1823-1876
Eckermann, Johann Peter	1792-1854	Fallmerayer, Jakob Phillip	1790-1861
Eddy, Mary Baker Glover	1821-1910	Falloux, Frederic Alfred	
Edgren-Lffeler, Anne		Pierre	1811-1886
Charlotte	1849-1892	Farina, Salvatore	1846-1918
Edwards, Amelia	1831-1892	Farini, Luigi Carlo	1812-1866
Eeden, Frederick		Farjeon, Benjamin	
Willem Van	1860-1932	Leopold	1838-1903
Egan, Maurice Francois	1852-1924	Farrar, Frederick	
Egge, Peter Andreas	1869-	William	1831-1903
Eggleston, Edward	1837-1902	Fay, Andreas	1786-1864
Ehrenfels, Christian		Fazy, Henri	1842-1920
Freiherr Von	1859-1932	Fechner, Gustav Theodor	1801-1887
Eichendorff, Joseph		Federer, Heinrich	1866-1928
Freiherr Von	1788-1857	Fejer, Gyorgy	1766-1852
Eisler, Rudolf	1873-1926	Fenn, George Maniville	1831-1909
Eisner, Kurt	1867-1919	Ferguson, Sir Samuel	1810-1886
Eliot, Sir Charles Norton		Fergusson, James	1808-1886
Edgcumbe	1864-1931	Ferrari, Giuseppe	1812-1876
Eliot, George		Ferrari, Paolo	1822-1889
(Marian Evans)	1819-1880	Ferrero, Guglielmo	1871-1942

Ferri, Luigi	1826-1895	Frazer, Sir James George	1854-1941
Ferrier, Paul	1843-1920	Frechette, Louis Honore	1839-1908
Ferrier, Susan		Frederic, Harold	1856-1896
Edmonstone	1782-1854	Freeman, Edward	
Feuerbach, Ludwig		Augustus	1823-1892
Andreas	1804-1872	Freeman, Mary Eleanor	
Feuillet, Octave	1821-1890	Wilkins	1852-1930
Feval, Paul Henri		Freiligrath, Ferdinand	1810-1876
Corentin	1817-1887	Frenssen, Gustav	1863-1945
Feydeau, Ernest-Aime	1821-1873	Freud, Sigmund	1856-1939
Fichte, Immanuel		Frey, Adolf	1855-1920
Hermann, Von	1796-1879	Freytag, Gustav	1816-1895
Field, Eugene	1850-1895	Fried, Alfred Hermann	1864-1921
Fields, James Thomas	1817-1881	Friedjung, Heinrich	1851-1920
Figuier, Louis	1819-1894	Froding, Gustav	1860-1911
Filon, Augustin	1841-1916	Froebel, Friedrich	
Finlay, George	1799-1875	Wilhelm August	1782-1852
Firth, Sir Charles		Frohlich, Abraham	
Harding	1857-1936	Emanuel	1796-1965
Fisher, Ernst Kuno		Frohschammer, Jakob	1821-1893
Berthold	1824-1907	Frost, Robert	1875-
Fisher, Herbert Albert		Frothingham, Octavious	
Laurens	1865-1940	Brooks	1822-1895
Fiske, John	1842-1901	Froude, James Anthony	1818-1894
Fitch, William Clyde	1865-1909	Fryxell, Anders	1795-1881
Fitzball, Edward	1792-1873	Fucini, Renato	1843-1921
Fitzgerald, Edward	1809-1883	Fullerton, Lady Georgiana	
Fitzgerald, Percy		Charlotte	1812-1885
Hetherington	1834-1925	Fustel, De Coulanges	
Flach, Geoffroi Jacques	1846-1919	Numa Denis	1830-1889
Flammarion, Nicolas		Fyffe, Charles Alan	1845-1892
Camille	1842-1925	Gaboriau, Emile	1835-1873
Flaubert, Gustave	1821-1880	Gachard, Louis Prosper	1800-1885
Flers, Robert, De La Motte		Gagern, Hans Christoph	
Ango	1872-1927	Ernst	1766-1852
Foa, Eugenie		Gairdner, James	1828-1912
Rodruguez-Gradis	1789-1853	Gale, Zona	1874-1938
Fogazzaro, Antonio	1842-1911	Galsworthy, John	1867-1933
Follen, Adolf Ludwig	1794-1855	Ganesh Datta Shastri,	
Fontaine, Theodor	1819-1898	Shri Jagadguru	1861-1940
Ford, Paul Leicester	1865-1902	Ganivet, Angel	1865-1898
Ford, Richard	1796-1858	Garay, Janos	1812-1853
Forsell, Hans Ludvig	1843-1901	Garborg, Arne Evensen	1851-1924
Forster, Friedrich		Gardiner, Samuel Rawson	1829-1902
Christoph	1791-1868	Gareau, Francois Xavier	1806-1866
Forster, John	1812-1876	Garland, Hamlin	1860-1940
Fort, Paul	1872-1960	Garnett, Edward	1868-1937
Fortescue, Sir John		Garnett, Richard	1835-1906
William	1859-1933	Garrett, Joao Baptista	
Fortlage, Karl	1806-1881	Da Silva Leitao	
Fouillee, Alfred Jules		De Almeida	1799-1854
Emile	1838-1912	Garshin, Vsevolod	
Fowler, Frank George	1871-1918	Mikhailovich	1855-1888
Fowler, Henry Watson	1858-1933	Gaskell (Mrs.) Elizabeth	
France, Anatole	1844-1924	Cleghorn	1810-1865
Frankl, Ludwig August	1810-1894	Gatty, Margaret	1809-1873
Franzos, Karl Emil	1848-1904	Gautier, Leon	1832-1897
Fraser, Alexander		Gautier, Theophile	1811-1872
Campbell	1819-1914	Geddes, Patrick	1854-1932
Fraser, James Baillie	1783-1856	Geibel, Emanuel	1815-1884

Geijer, Eric Gustav	1783-1877	Gosse, Sir Edmund	1849-1928
Gentile, Giovanni	1875-1944	Gottschall, Rudolf Von	1823-1908
George, Henry	1839-1897	Gould, John	1804-1881
George, Stefan	1868-1933	Gould, Nathaniel	1857-1919
Gerstacker, Friedrich	1816-1877	Gourmont, Remy De	1858-1915
Gervinus, Georg Gottfried	1805-1871	Gozlan, Leon	1803-1866
Gezelle, Guido	1830-1899	Grahame, Kenneth	1859-1922
Gfrorer, August Friedrich	1803-1861	Grand, Sarah	1862-1943
Ghika, Helena	1829-1888	Grant, James	1822-1887
Giacometti, Paolo	1816-1882	Gratz, Heinrich	1817-1891
Giacosa, Guiseppe	1847-1906	Graves, Alfred Percival	1846-1931
Gibson, William		Gray, David	1838-1861
Hamilton	1850-1896	Green, John Richard	1837-1883
Gide, Andre Paul		Green, Mary Ann Everett	1818-1895
Guillaume	1869-1951	Green, Thomas Hill	1836-1882
Giesebrecht, Wilhelm Von	1814-1889	Greene, George	
Gieseler, Johann Karl		Washington	1811-1883
Ludwig	1792-1854	Greg, William Rathbone	1809-1881
Gilbert, Sir John Thomas	1829-1898	Gregorovius, Ferdinand	1821-1891
Gilbert, William	1804-1889	Gregory, Isabella Augusta	1852-1932
Gilbert, Sir William		Greville, Charles Cavendish	
Schwenk	1836-1911	Fulke	1794-1865
Gilder, Richard Watson	1844-1909	Greville, Henry	1842-1902
Gilgik, Iwan	1858-1924	Grey, Zane	1872-1939
Gillette, William Hooker	1853-1937	Grigorovich, Dmitri	
Gindely, Anton	1829-1892	Vaslievich	1822-1900
Giner De Los Rios,		Grillparzer, Franz	1791-1872
Francisco	1840-1915	Grimm, Jacob Ludwig	
Gioberti, Vincenzo	1801-1852	Carl	1785-1863
Girardin, Delphine De	1804-1855	Grimm, Wilhelm Carl	1786-1859
Gissing, George Robert	1857-1903	Groome, Francis Hindes	1851-1902
Giudici, Paolo, Emiliano	1812-1872	Grossi, Tommaso	1791-1853
Gjellerup, Karl	1857-1919	Grossmith, George	1847-1912
Glasgow, Ellen	1874-1945	Grote, George	1794-1871
Glassbrenner, Adolf	1810-1876	Grub, George	1812-1892
Glatigny, Joseph Albert		Grundy, Sydney	1848-1914
Alexandre	1839-1873	Gruntvig, Nikolai Frederick	
Gleig, George Robert	1796-1888	Severin	1783-1872
Glinka, Fedor		Gubernatis, Angelo De	1840-1913
Nikolayevich	1788-1880	Guerin, Charles	1873-1907
Glyn, Elinor	1864-1943	Guerrazzi, Francesco	
Gogol, Nikolai Vasilievich	1809-1852	Domenico	1804-1873
Goldschmidt, Aaron Meier	1819-1887	Guerrini, Olinda	1845-1916
Goltz, Bogumil	1801-1870	Guest, Edwin	1800-1880
Gomperez, Theodor	1832-1912	Guimera, Angel	1849-1924
Goncalves, Dias Antonio	1823-1864	Guizot, Francois Pierre	
Goncharov, Ivan		Guillaume	1787-1874
Alexandrovich	1812-1891	Guthrie, Thomas Anstey	1856-1934
Goncourt De, Edmond	1822-1896	Gutschmid, Alfred	1835-1887
Goncourt De, Jules	1830-1870	Gutzkow, Karl Ferdinand	1811-1878
Gooch, George Peabody	1873-	Guyau, Jean Marie	1854-1888
Goodrich, Samuel		Gyllembourg Eh Rensvard,	
Griswold	1793-1860	Thomasine Christine	1773-1856
Gordon, Adam Lindsay	1833-1870	Gyp	1849-1932
Gordon, Leon	1831-1892	Habberton, John	1842-1921
Gore, Catherine Grace		Hacklander, Friedrich	
Frances	1799-1861	Wilhelm Von	1816-1877
Gorky, Maxim	1868-1936	Hagenbach, Karl Rudolf	1801-1874
Gorst, Harold	1868-1950	Haggard, Sir Henry	
Gorter, Herman	1864-1933	Rider	1856-1925

Hahn-Hahn, Ida	1805-1880	Hawker, Robert Stephen	1803-1875
Hake, Thomas Gordon	1809-1895	Hawthorne, Nathaniel	1804-1864
Haldane Elizabeth		Hay, John	1838-1905
Sanderson	1862-1937	Haym, Rudolf	1821-1901
Haldane, Richard Burdon		Hayward, Abraham	1801-1884
Haldane	1856-1928	Hazard, Rowland Gibson	1801-1888
Hale, Edward Everett	1822-1909	Hebbel, Christian	
Hale, Sarah Josepha	1788-1879	Friedrich	1813-1863
Halevy, Daniel	1872-1962	Heer, Jakob Christoph	1859-1925
Halevy, Elie	1870-1937	Heiberg, Gunnar Edvard	
Halevy, Leon	1802-1883	Rode	1857-1929
Halevy, Ludovic	1834-1908	Heiberg, Johan Ludvig	1791-1860
Haliburton, Thomas		Heidenstam, Verner Von	1859-1940
Chandler	1796-1865	Heijermans, Hermann	1864-1924
Hall, Anna Maria	1800-1881	Heine, Heinrich	1797-1856
Hall, Samuel Carter	1800-1889	Helmholtz, Hermann	
Hall, William Edward	1835-1894	Ludwig Ferdinand Von	1821-1894
Hallam, Henry	1777-1859	Helps, Sir Arthur	1813-1875
Halleck, Fitz-Greene	1790-1867	Henderson, William	
Halliday, Andrew	1830-1877	James	1855-1937
Hamerton, Philip Gilbert	1834-1894	Henley, William Ernest	1849-1903
Hamilton, Sir William	1788-1856	Henry, O.	1862-1910
Hamley, Sir Edward		Henty, George Alfred	1832-1902
Bruce	1824-1893	Herculano De Carvalho	
Hammer, Julius	1810-1862	E. Araujo Alexandre	1810-1877
Hammond, John Lawrence		Herczeg, Ferenc	1863-
Lebreton	1872-1949	Heredia, Jose Maria De	1842-1905
Hamsun, Knut	1859-1952	Hermant, Abel	1862-1950
Handel-Mazzetti, Enrica	1871-1955	Hernandez, Jose	1854-1886
Hannay, James	1827-1873	Herne, Jame A.	1840-1901
Hannay, James Owen	1865-1950	Herrick, Robert	1868-1938
Hanotaux, Albert Auguste		Hervieu, Paul	1857-1915
Gabriel	1853-1944	Hewlett, Maurice Henry	1861-1923
Hansson, Ola	1860-1925	Heyse, Paul Johann	
Hardwick, Philip	1792-1870	Ludwig Von	1830-1914
Hardy, Thomas	1840-1928	Hichens, Robert Smythe	1864-1950
Hare, Augustus John		Higginson, Thomas	
Cuthbert	1834-1903	Wentworth	1823-1911
Haring, Georg Wilhelm		Hill, George Birbeck	
Heinrich	1798-1871	Norman	1835-1903
Harland, Henry	1861-1905	Hillebrand, Karl	1829-1884
Harraden, Beatrice	1864-1936	Himly, Louis-Auguste	1823-1906
Harris, Frank	1856-1931	Hinrichs, Hermann	
Harris, Joel Chandler	1848-1908	Friedrich Wilhelm	1794-1861
Harrison, Frederic	1831-1923	Hippius, Zinaida	1869-1945
Hart, Albert Bushnell	1854-1942	Hobhouse, Leonard	
Harte, Francis Bret	1836-1902	Trelawney	1864-1929
Hartmann, Karl, Robert		Hocking, Silas Kitto	1850-1935
Eduard Von	1842-1906	Hodgkin, Thomas	1831-1913
Hartmann, Moritz	1821-1872	Hodgson, John Evan	1831-1895
Hartzenbusch, Juan		Hodgson, Ralph	1871-
Eugenio	1806-1880	Hodgson, Shadworth	
Hasselt, Andre Henri		Holloway	1832-1912
Constant Van	1806-1874	Hoffding, Harald	1843-1931
Hauch, Johannes Carsten	1790-1872	Hoffman, August	
Hauptmann, Gerhart	1862-1946	Heinrich	1798-1874
Haureau, Barthelemy	1812-1896	Hoffman, Heinrich	1809-1894
Hausser, Ludwig	1818-1867	Hofmannsthal, Hugo Von	1874-1929
Haverfield, Francis John	1860-1919	Holl, Karl	1866-1926
Havet, Julien	1853-1893	Holland, Sir Henry	1788-1873

Holland, Josiah Gilbert	1819-1881	Ivanov, Vyacheslav	
Holmes, Oliver Wendell	1809-1894	Ivanovich	1866-1949
Holtei, Karl Eduard Von	1798-1880	Jacks, Laurence Pearsall	1860-1955
Holst, Hermann, Eduard		Jackson, Frederick John	
Von	1841-1904	Foakes	1855-1941
Holz, Arno	1863-1929	Jackson, Helen Maria	1831-1885
Hope, Anthony	1863-1933	Jacob, Violet	1863-1946
Hopfen, Hans Von	1835-1904	Jacobs, William Wymark	1863-1943
Hopkins, Gerard Manley	1844-1889	Jacobsen, Jens Peter	1847-1885
Horne, Richard Henry	1803-1884	Jahn, Otto	1813-1869
Hornung, Ernest William	1866-1921	James, George Payne	
Hosmer, James Kendall	1834-1927	Rainsford	1799-1860
Hostrup, Jens Christian	1818-1892	James, Henry	1843-1916
Hotho, Heinrich Gustav	1802-1873	James, Montague Rhodes	1862-1936
Houghton, Richard		James, William	1842-1910
Monkton Milnes	1809-1885	Jameson, Anna Brownell	1794-1860
Housman, Alfred Edward	1859-1936	Jammes, Francis	1868-1938
Housman, Laurence	1865-1959	Jane, Frederick Thomas	1870-1916
Houssaye, Arsene	1815-1896	Janin, Jules Gabriel	1804-1874
Houssaye, Henry	1848-1911	Janssen, Johannes	1829-1891
Howe, Julia Ward	1819-1910	Jasmin, Jacques	1798-1864
Howells, William Dean	1837-1920	Jebavy, Vaclav	1868-1929
Howitt, Mary	1799-1888	Jebb, Sir Richard	
Howitt, William	1792-1879	Claverhouse	1841-1905
Hubbard, Elbert	1856-1915	Jefferies, Richard	1848-1887
Huch, Ricarda	1864-1947	Jensen, Johannes Vilhelm	1873-1950
Hudson, William Henry	1841-1922	Jensen, Wilhelm	1837-1911
Huggenberger, Alfred	1867-	Jerome, Jerome Klapka	1859-1927
Hughes, Clovis	1851-1907	Jerrold, Douglas William	1803-1857
Hughes, Thomas	1822-1896	Jesse, Edward	1780-1868
Hugo, Victor Marie	1802-1885	Jewett, Sarah Orne	1849-1909
Humboldt, Friedrich		Jewsbury, Geraldine	
Baron Von	1769-1850	Endsor	1812-1880
Hume, Fergus	1859-1932	Johnson, James Weldon	1871-1938
Hunt, James Henry Leigh	1784-1859	Johnson, Lionel Pigot	1867-1902
Hunter, Joseph	1783-1861	Joinville, Francois	
Hutton, Arthur Wollaston	1848-1912	Ferdinand d'Orlean	1818-1900
Hutton, Richard Holt	1826-1897	Jokai, Maurus	1825-1904
Huxley, Thomas Henry	1825-1895	Jones, Ebenezer	1820-1860
Huysmans, Joris Karl	1848-1907	Jones, Ernest	1819-1869
Hyde, Douglas	1860-1949	Jones, Henry	1831-1899
Hyne, Charles John Cutliffe		Jones, Henry Arthur	1851-1929
Wright	1865-1944	Jordan, Wilhelm	1819-1904
Ibanez, Vincent Blasco	1867-1928	Jorga, Nicolas	1871-1940
Ibsen, Henrik Johan	1828-1906	Jorgensen, Johannes	1866-1951
Ihne, Wilhelm	1821-1902	Josika Miklos	1794-1865
Ilg, Paul	1875-	Judson, Edward Zane	
Inge, William Ralph	1860-1954	Carroll	1823-1886
Ingelow, Jean	1820-1897	Jung, Carl Gustav	1875-1964
Ingemann, Bernhard		Junqueiro, Abilio Guena	1850-1923
Severin	1789-1862	Jusserand, Jean Adrien	
Ingleby, Clement		Antoine Jules	1855-1932
Manfried	1823-1886	Kahn, Gustave	1859-1936
Ingraham, Joseph Holt	1809-1860	Kang Yu-Wei	1857-1927
Ingraham, Prentice	1843-1904	Karadzk, Viek Stefanovic	1787-1864
Innes, Arthur Donald	1863-1938	Karlfeldt, Erik Axel	1864-1931
Innes, Cosmo	1798-1874	Karr, Alphonse	1808-1890
Iqbal, Sir Mohammed	1875-1938	Kate, Jacob Lodewykten	1819-1889
Irving, Washington	1783-1859	Keble, John	1792-1866
Isaacs, Jorge	1837-1895	Keightley, Thomas	1789-1872

Keller, Gottfried	1819-1890	Lane-Poole, Stanley	1854-1931
Kemble, John Mitchell	1807-1857	Lanfrey, Pierre	1828-1877
Kendall, Henry Clarence	1841-1882	Lang, Andrew	1844-1912
Kenealy, Edward Vaughan		Lange, Friedrich Albert	1828-1875
Hyde	1819-1880	Lanier, Sidney	1842-1881
Kerner, Justinus Andreas		Lanson, Gustave	1857-1935
Christian	1786-1862	Lapidoth-Swarth, Helene	1859-1941
Kervyn De Lettenhove,		Lappenberg, Johann	
Joseph	1817-1891	Martin	1794-1865
Key, Ellen	1849-1926	Laprade, Pierre Marin	
Kielland, Alexander	1849-1906	Victor Richard De	1812-1883
Kierkegaard, Soren Aaby	1813-1855	Larousse, Pierre Athanase	1817-1875
Kinck, Hans Ernst	1865-1926	Laube, Heinrich	1806-1884
Kinglake, Alexander		Lauff, Josef	1855-1933
William	1809-1891	Laurent, Francois	1810-1887
Kingsley, Charles	1819-1875	Lavedan, Henri Leon	
Kingsley, Henry	1830-1876	Emile	1859-1940
Kingston, William Henry		Lavisse, Ernest	1842-1922
Giles	1814-1880	Lawless, Emily	1845-1913
Kinkel, Johann Gottfried	1815-1882	Lawrence, George Alfred	1827-1876
Kipling, Rudyard	1865-1936	Lawson, Henry Hertzberg	1867-1922
Kitto, John	1804-1854	Layard, Sir Austen Henry	1817-1894
Kivi, Steuval	1834-1872	Lazarus, Emma	1849-1887
Klaczko, Julian	1825-1906	Lazarus, Moritz	1824-1903
Knight, Charles	1791-1873	Lea, Henry Charles	1825-1909
Knoblock, Edward	1874-1945	Leacock, Stephen Butler	1869-1944
Knowles, James Sheridan	1784-1862	Lecky, William, Edward	
Kock, Charles Paul De	1793-1871	Hartpole	1838-1903
Kolcsey, Ferencz	1790-1888	Leconte De Lisle, Charles	
Korolenko, Vladimir		Marie Rene	1818-1894
Galaktionovich	1853-1921	Lee, Sir Sidney	1859-1926
Kpisch, August	1799-1853	Lee, Vernon,	1856-1935
Krasinski, Zygmunt Count	1812-1859	Le Fanu, Joseph	
Kraszewski, Joseph		Sheridan	1814-1873
Ignatius	1812-1887	Le Gallienne, Richard	1866-1947
Kraus, Karl	1874-1936	Legouve, Gabriel Jean	
Krehbiel, Henry Edward	1854-1923	Baptiste Ernest Wilfred	1807-1903
Kretzer, Marx	1854-1941	Leland, Charles Godfrey	1824-1903
Kropotkin, Peter		Lemaitre, Jules	1853-1914
Alexeivich	1842-1921	Le Moine, James	
Ku Hung-Ming	1856-1928	MacPherson	1825-1912
Kulpe, Oswald	1868-1915	Lemon, Mark	1809-1870
Kuprin, Alexander		Lemonnier, Antoine Louis	
Ivanovich	1870-1938	Camille	1844-1913
Kurz, Hermann	1813-1873	Lenin, Vladimir Ilyich	
Labiche, Euegene Marin	1815-1888	(Ulyonov)	1870-1924
Lacaita, Sir James	1813-1895	Lennep, Jacob Van	1802-1862
Lacretelle, Jean Charles		Leo, Heinrich	1799-1878
Dominique de	1766-1855	Le Queux, William	
Ladd, George Trumbull	1842-1921	Tufnell	1864-1927
La Farina, Giuseppe	1815-1863	Leroux, Pierre	1798-1871
Laforgue, Jules	1860-1887	Leskov, Nikolai	
Lagerlof, Selma	1858-1940	Semenovich	1831-1895
Laing, Samuel	1810-1897	Lever, Charles James	1806-1872
Lamartine, Alphonse, De	1790-1869	Levertin, Oscar Ivan	1862-1906
Lamennais, Hugues		Levy-Bruhl, Lucien	1857-1939
Felicite Robert De	1782-1854	Lewald, Fanny	1811-1889
Landor, Walter Savage	1775-1864	Lewes, George Henry	1817-1878
Lane, Edward William	1801-1876	Lie, Jonas Lauritz Edemil	1833-1908
Lane-Poole, Reginald	1857-1939	Lieber, Francis	1800-1872

R

Liebrecht, Felix	1812-1890	Machar, Jan Svatopluk	1864-1942
Liliencron, Detlev Von	1844-1909	Mackay, Charles	1814-1889
Lincoln, Abraham	1809-1865	Mackaye, Percy	1875-
Lindau, Paul	1839-1919	Mackaye, Steele	1842-1894
Lindau, Rudolf	1829-1910	MacLaren, Charles	1782-1866
Lindo, Mark Prager	1819-1879	Macmaster, John Bach	1852-1932
Lingard, John	1771-1851	MacNeill, John Gordon	
Lippincott, Sara Jane		Swift	1849-1926
Clarke	1823-1904	M'Cosh, James	1811-1894
Lipps, Theodore	1851-1914	M'cTaggart, John	
Littlefiel, Walter	1867-1948	M'cTaggart Ellis	1866-1925
Littre, Maximilien Paul		Madach, Imre	1823-1864
Emile	1801-1881	Maeterlinck, Maurice	1862-1949
Livingstone, David	1813-1873	Magny, Claude Drigon	1797-1879
Ljunggren, Gustaf Haken		Mahan, Alfred Thayer	1840-1914
Jordan	1823-1905	Maine, Sir Henry James	
Locke, William John	1863-1930	Sumner	1822-1888
Locker-Lampson, Frederick	1821-1895	Maironis	1862-1932
Lockhart, John Gibson	1794-1854	Maistre, Xavier De	1763-1852
Lodge, Henry Cabot	1850-1924	Maitland, Edward	1824-1897
Longfellow, Henry		Maitland, Frederic	
Wadsworth	1807-1882	William	1850-1906
Lönnrot, Elias	1802-1884	Majlath, Janos	1786-1855
Lossing, Benson John	1813-1891	Major, Richard Henry	1818-1891
Losski, Nikolai		Malet, Lucas	1852-1931
Onufreivich	1870-	Mallarme, Stephane	1842-1898
Loti, Pierre	1850-1923	Malleson, George Bruce	1825-1898
Lotze, Rudolf Hermann	1817-1881	Mallock, William Hurrell	1849-1923
Louys, Pierre	1870-1925	Maning, Frederick	
Lover, Samuel	1797-1868	Edward	1812-1883
Lowell, Amy	1874-1925	Mann, Heinrich	1871-1950
Lowell, James Russell	1819-1891	Mann, Thomas	1875-1955
Lubke, Wilhelm	1826-1893	Mansel, Henry	
Lucas, Edward Verrall	1868-1938	Longueville	1820-1871
Luchaire, Achille	1846-1908	Manzoni, Alessandro	1785-1873
Ludwig, Emil	1861-1948	Mapu, Abraham	1808-1867
Ludwig, Otto	1813-1865	Marguerite, Paul	1860-1918
Lummis, Charles Fletcher	1859-1928	Marguerite, Victor	1866-1942
Lunacharsky, Anatoly		Markham, Edwin	1852-1940
Vasilievich	1875-1933	Marquardt, Joachim	1812-1882
Lund, Troels Frederick	1840-1921	Marradi, Giovanni	1852-1922
Luttrell, Henry	1765-1851	Marryat, Florence	1838-1899
Lyall, Edna	1857-1903	Marston, John Westland	1819-1890
Lytton, Edward George		Marston, Philip Bourke	1850-1887
Lytton Bulwer-Lytton	1803-1873	Martin, Henri	1810-1883
Lytton, Edward Robert		Martin, Sir Theodore	1816-1909
Bulwer-Lytton	1831-1891	Martin, Violet Florence	1862-1915
Maartens, Maarten	1858-1915	Martineau, Harriet	1802-1876
Macaulay, Thomas		Martineau, James	1805-1900
Babington Macaulay	1800-1859	Martinez De La Rosa	
MacCarthy, Denis		Francisco De Paula	1787-1862
Florence	1817-1882	Martini, Ferdinando	1841-1928
M'Carthy, Justin	1830-1912	Marx, Karl Heinrich	1818-1883
McCord, Louise Susanna		Mason, Alfred Edward	
Cheves	1810-1879	Woodley	1865-1948
MacDonald, George	1824-1905	Mason, Walt	1862-1939
McGee, Thomas D'Arcy	1825-1868	Massey, Gerald	1828-1907
MacGregor, John	1825-1892	Masson, David	1822-1907
Mach, Ernst	1838-1916	Masson, Frederic	1847-1923
Machado, Antonio	1875-1939	Masters, Edgar Lee	1869-1950

Matthews, Brander	1852-1929	Monod, Gabriel	1844-1912
Maugham, William		Monroe, Harriet	1860-1936
Somerset	1874-1965	Montague, Charles	
Maupassant, Henri Rene		Edward	1867-1928
Albert Guy de	1850-1893	Montalembert, Charles	
Maurer, Georg Ludwig		Forbes Rene De	1810-1870
Von	1790-1872	Montanelli, Giuseppe	1813-1862
Maurras, Charles	1868-1952	Montgomery, James	1771-1854
Mayhew, Henry	1812-1887	Montgomery, Robert	1807-1855
Medina, Jose Toribio	1852-1930	Montufar, Lorenzo	1823-1898
Mee, Arthur	1875-1943	Moody, William Vaughan	1869-1910
Mehring, Franz	1846-1919	Moore, George	1852-1933
Meilhac, Henri	1831-1897	Moore, George Edward	1873-1958
Meinong, Alexius Von	1853-1930	Moore, Thomas	1779-1852
Melville, Herman	1819-1891	More, Paul Elmer	1864-1937
Menard, Louis Nicolas	1822-1901	Moreas, Jean	1856-1910
Mendes, Catulle	1841-1909	Morgan, Lady Sydney	1783-1859
Menendez y Pelayo,		Morike, Eduard Friedrich	1804-1875
Marcelino	1856-1912	Morley, Henry	1822-1894
Menzel, Wolfgang	1798-1873	Morley, John Morley	1838-1923
Meredith, George	1828-1909	Morris, Sir Lewis	1833-1907
Merezhkovsky, Dmitri		Morris, William	1834-1896
Sergeievich	1865-1941	Morrison, Arthur	1863-1945
Merimee, Prosper	1803-1870	Morton, John Maddison	1811-1891
Merivale, Charles	1808-1893	Mosen, Julius	1803-1867
Merrick, Leonard	1864-1939	Motley, John Lothrop	1814-1877
Merrill, Stuart	1863-1915	Moulton, Louise Chandler	1835-1908
Merriman, Henry Seton	1862-1903	Muir, John	1838-1914
Mesonero Romanos,		Muirhead, John Henry	1855-1940
Ramon De	1803-1882	Munch-Bellinghausen,	
Meurice, Paul	1818-1905	Eligius Franz Joseph	1806-1871
Mew, Charlotte	1870-1928	Munro, Hector Hugh	
Meyer, Conrad Ferdinand	1825-1898	(Saki)	1870-1916
Meyer, Eduard	1855-1930	Munsterberg, Hugo	1863-1916
Meynell, Alice	1849-1922	Munthe, Axel	1857-1949
Meyrink, Gustav	1868-1932	Murger, Henry	1822-1861
Michelet, Jules	1798-1874	Murray, Gilbert	1866-1957
Mickiewicz, Adam	1798-1855	Musset, Alfred De	1810-1857
Mignet, Francois Auguste		Myers, Frederic William	
Marie	1796-1884	Henry	1843-1901
Mill, John Stuart	1806-1873	Naden, Constance Caroline	
Miller, Hugh	1802-1856	Woodhill	1858-1889
Miller, Joaquin	1841-1913	Neal, John	1793-1876
Milman, Henry Hart	1791-1868	Nekrasov, Nikolai	
Milyukov, Paul		Alexeyeivich	1821-1877
Nikolayevich	1859-1942	Neruda, Jan	1834-1891
Mirbeau, Octave Henri		Nerval, Gerard de	1808-1855
Marie	1850-1917	Nesbit, Edith	1858-1924
Mistral, Frederic	1830-1914	Nestroy, Johann	1801-1862
Mitchell, Donald Grant	1822-1908	Nettleship, Richard Lewis	1846-1892
Mitford, John	1781-1859	Newbolt, Sir Henry John	1862-1938
Mitford, Mary Russell	1787-1855	Newman, Francis William	1805-1897
Moir, David Macbeth	1798-1851	Newman, John Henry	
Molesworth, Mary Louisa	1839-1921	(Cardinal)	1801-1890
Molesworth, William		Nexo, Martin Andersen	1869-1954
Nassau	1816-1890	Nichol, John	1833-1894
Mommsen, Theodor	1817-1903	Nicholson, Meredith	1866-1947
Monkhouse, William		Nietzshe, Friedrich	
Cosmo	1840-1901	Wilhelm	1844-1900
Monnier, Marc	1829-1885	Nitzsch, Karl Immanuel	1787-1868

Nitzsch, Karl Wilhelm	1818-1880	Patmore, Coventry Kersey	
Noailles, Paul Duke of	1802-1885	Dighton	1823-1896
Noel, Roden Berkeley		Pattison, Mark	1813-1884
Wriothesleu	1834-1894	Paul, Charles Kiegan	1828-1902
Nordau, Max Simon	1848-1923	Paulding, James Kirke	1778-1860
Normanby, Constantine		Pauli, Reinhold	1823-1882
Henry Phipps	1797-1863	Paulsen, Friedrich	1846-1908
Norris, Frank	1870-1902	Payn, James	1830-1898
Norris, William Edward	1847-1925	Payne, John Howard	1791-1852
Norton, Caroline Elizabeth		Paz Soldan, Mariano	
Sarah	1808-1877	Felipe	1821-1886
Norton, Charles Eliot	1827-1908	Peabody, Andrew Preston	1811-1893
Nunez De Arce, Gaspar	1834-1903	Peabody, Josephine	
O'Grady, Standish James	1846-1928	Preston	1874-1922
Ohnet, Georges	1848-1918	Peacock, Thomas Love	1785-1866
Oliphant, Laurence	1829-1888	Peesemsky, Alexey	
Oliphant, Margaret		Feofilictovich	1820-1881
Oliphant	1828-1897	Peguy, Charles	1873-1914
Oliveira, Martins Joaquim		Peirce, Charles Sanders	1839-1914
Pedro De	1845-1894	Pelham, Henry Francis	1846-1907
Oman, Sir Charles William		Pellico, Silvio	1788-1854
Chadwick	1860-1946	Pemberton, Sir Max	1863-1950
Opie, Amelia	1769-1853	Percival, James Gates	1795-1856
Oppenheim, Edward		Pereda, Jose Maria De	1833-1906
Phillips	1866-1946	Perez Galdos, Benito	1845-1920
Opzoomer, Cornelius		Perry, Bliss	1860-1945
William	1821-1892	Pertz, Georg Heinrich	1795-1876
Orczy, Baroness Emmuska	1865-1947	Pfleiderer, Edmund	1842-1902
Orzeszkowa, Eliza	1842-1910	Phillips, Stephen	1868-1915
Osbourne, Lloyd	1868-1947	Phillpotts, Eden	1862-1960
O'Shaughnessy, Arthur		Pinero, Sir Arthur Wing	1855-1934
William Edgar	1844-1880	Pirandello, Luigi	1867-1936
Ostrovsky, Alexander		Pirenne, Henry	1862-1935
Nikolaevich	1823-1886	Planche, James Robinson	1796-1880
Ouida	1839-1908	Plekhanov, Georgy	
Ozanam, Antoine Frederic	1813-1853	Valentinovitch	1857-1918
Page, Thomas Nelson	1853-1922	Plieksans, Jan	1865-1929
Page, Walter Hines	1855-1918	Pollard, Alfred Frederick	1869-1948
Pain, Barry Eric Odell	1865-1928	Ponsard, Francois	1814-1867
Palacio Valdes, Armando	1853-1938	Pontoppidan, Henrik	1857-1943
Palacky, Frantisek	1798-1876	Poole, William Frederick	1821-1894
Palamas, Kostes	1859-1943	Porter, Eleanor Hodgman	1868-1920
Paleologue, Maurice		Porter, Gene Stratton	1868-1924
Georges	1859-1944	Porter, Noah	1811-1892
Palfrey, John Gorham	1796-1881	Porto-Riche, Georges De	1849-1930
Palgrave, Francis Turner	1824-1897	Post, Melville Davisson	1871-1930
Paludan-Muller, Frederik	1809-1876	Potgieter, Everhades	
Panzini, Alfredo	1863-1939	Johannes	1808-1875
Paoli, Cesare	1840-1902	Potter, Beatrix	1866-1943
Pardo Bazan, Emilia	1851-1921	Potthast, August	1824-1898
Pares, Sir Bernard	1867-1949	Powell, Frederick York	1850-1904
Paris, Gaston	1839-1903	Powyss, John Cowper	1872-1963
Parker, Sir Gilbert	1862-1932	Powyss, Theodore Francis	1875-1953
Parker, Theodore	1810-1860	Prantl, Karl Von	1820-1888
Parkman, Francis	1823-1893	Prati, Giovanni	1815-1884
Parton, James	1822-1891	Prel, Karl	1839-1899
Pascoli, Giovanni	1855-1912	Prescott, Harriet	
Pater, Walter Horatio	1839-1894	Elizabeth	1835-1921
Paterson, Andrew Barton		Prescott, William	
("Banjo")	1864-1941	Hickling	1796-1859

Prevost, Eugene Marcel	1862-1941	Richardson, Henry	
Pribram, Alfred Francis	1859-1942	Handel	1870-1946
Procter, Adelaide Anne	1825-1864	Richepin, Jean	1849-1926
Procter, Bryan Waller	1787-1874	Ridge, William Pett	1857-1930
Proudhon, Pierre Joseph	1809-1865	Ridgway, Robert	1850-1929
Proust, Marcel	1871-1922	Riley, James Whitcomb	1849-1916
Prus, Boleslaw	1847-1912	Rilke, Rainer Maria	1875-1926
Prutz, Hans	1843-1929	Rimbaud Jean Arthur	1854-1891
Przybyszewski, Stanislaw	1868-1927	Ritchie, Anne Isabella	
Psichari, Ernest	1883-1914	Lady	1837-1919
Purnell, Thomas	1834-1889	Ritter, Heinrich	1791-1869
Pusey, Edward Bouverie	1800-1882	Rivas, Angel De	
Quental, Anthero De	1842-1891	Saavedra	1791-1865
Quicherat, Jules Etienne		Roberts, Sir Charles	
Joseph	1814-1882	George Douglas	1860-1943
Quiller-Couch, Sir Arthur		Roberts, Morley	1857-1942
Thomas	1863-1944	Robertson, Thomas	
Quincy, Josiah	1772-1864	William	1829-1871
Quinet, Edgar	1803-1875	Robinson, Edwin	
Quintana, Manuel José	1772-1857	Arlington	1869-1935
Quintero, Joaquin Alvarez	1873-1944	Robinson, Lennox	1886-1958
Quintero, Serafin Alvarez	1871-1938	Rod, Edouard	1857-1910
Ragabe, Alexandros Rizos	1810-1892	Rodo, Jose Enrique	1872-1917
Raleigh, Sir Walter		Roe, Edward Payson	1838-1888
Alexander	1861-1922	Rogers, Randolph	1825-1892
Rambaud, Alfred Nicolas	1842-1905	Rogers, Samuel	1763-1855
Ranc, Arthur	1831-1908	Rolland, Romain	1866-1944
Randall, James Ryder	1839-1908	Rolleston, Thomas	
Rands, William Brighty	1823-1882	William Hazen	1857-1920
Ranke, Leopold Von	1795-1886	Roosevelt, Theodore	1858-1919
Rashdall, Hastings	1858-1924	Rose, John Holland	1855-1942
Raumer, Fredrich Ludwig		Rosegger, Peter	1843-1918
George Von	1781-1873	Rosenkranz, Karl	1805-1879
Ravaisson-Mollien, Jean		Rosmini-Serbati, Antonio	1797-1855
Gaspard Felix	1813-1900	Rosny, Joseph Henri	1856-1940
Rawlinson, George	1812-1902	Rosny, Seraphin Justin	
Reade, Charles	1814-1884	Francois	1859-1948
Realf, Richard	1834-1878	Ross, Janet Anne	1842-1927
Reclus, Jean Jacques		Rossetti, Dante, Gabriel	1828-1882
Elisée	1830-1905	Rossetti, Christina	
Redgrave, Richard	1804-1888	Georgina	1830-1894
Regnier, Henri Francois		Rossetti, Gabriele	1783-1854
Joseph De	1864-1936	Rossetti, William Michael	1829-1919
Reid, Thomas Mayne	1818-1883	Rostand, Edmond	1869-1918
Reinach, Joseph	1856-1921	Roumanille, Joseph	1818-1891
Remusat, Charles Francois		Royce, Josiah	1855-1916
Marie	1797-1875	Rozanov, Vasili	
Renan, Ernest	1823-1892	Vasilievich	1856-1919
Rennell, James Rennell		Rückert, Friedrich	1788-1866
Rodd 1st Baron	1858-1941	Ruffini, Giovanni	
Renouvier, Charles		Domenico	1807-1881
Bernard	1815-1903	Ruge, Arnold	1802-1880
Reuter, Fritz	1810-1874	Runeberg, Johan Ludvig	1804-1877
Reuter, Gabriel	1859-1941	Ruskin, John	1819-1900
Reymont, Wladyslaw		Russell, Bertrand Arthur	
Stanislaw	1868-1925	William	1872-
Rhys, Ernest Percival	1859-1946	Russell, George William	1867-1935
Rice, James	1843-1882	Rutherford, Mark	1831-1913
Richards, Frank	1875-	Rydberg, Abraham Viktor	1828-1895
Richardson, Dorothy Miller	1873-1957	Sabatier, Paul	1858-1928

Sabatini, Rafael	1875-1950	Sharp, William	1856-1905
Safarik, Pavel Josef	1795-1861	Shaw, George Bernard	1856-1950
Sainte-Beuve, Charles		Shaw, Henry Wheeler	1818-1885
Augustin	1804-1869	Sheil, Richard Lalor	1791-1851
Saint-Marc, Girardin	1801-1873	Shelley, Mary	
Saintsbury, George		Wollenstonecraft	1797-1851
Edward Bateman	1845-1933	Sherwood, Mary Martha	1775-1851
Sala, George Augustin		Shevchenko, Taras	1814-1861
Henry	1828-1895	Shorter, Clement King	1857-1926
Salten, Felix	1869-1945	Shorthouse, Joseph Henry	1834-1903
Saltykov, Michael		Sidgwick, Henry	1838-1900
Evgrafovich	1826-1889	Sienkiewicz, Henryk	1846-1916
Salvemini, Gaetano	1873-	Sigourney, Lydia Huntley	1791-1865
Samain, Albert Victor	1858-1900	Sill, Edward Rowland	1841-1887
Sand, George		Simmel, Georg	1858-1918
(Dudevant)	1804-1876	Simms, William Gilmore	1806-1870
Sanday, William	1843-1920	Simon, Jules Francois	1814-1896
Sandeau, Leonard		Simrock, Karl Joseph	1802-1876
Sylvain Julien	1811-1883	Sims, George Robert	1847-1922
Sant, James	1820-1916	Sinclair, May	1864-1946
Santayana, George	1863-1952	Skeat, Walter William	1835-1912
Santine, Joseph Xavier	1798-1865	Skene, William Forbes	1809-1892
Sardou, Victorien	1831-1908	Smiles, Samuel	1812-1904
Sarmiento, Domingo		Smith, Alexander	1830-1867
Faustino	1811-1888	Smith, Francis	
Saxe, John Godfrey	1816-1887	Hopkinson	1838-1915
Schaffner, Jakob	1875-1944	Smith, Goldwin	1823-1910
Scheffel, Joseph Viktor		Smith, Logan Pearsall	1865-1946
Von	1826-1886	Smith, Norman Kemp	1872-1958
Schelling, Friedrich		Smith, Walter Chalmers	1824-1908
Wilhelm Joseph Von	1775-1854	Smith, Sir William	1813-1893
Scherer, Wilhelm	1841-1886	Snoilsky, Carl Johan	
Schimmelpenninck, Mary		Gustaf	1841-1903
Ann	1778-1856	Sokolov, Nahum	1859-1936
Schlaf, Johannes	1862-1941	Sologub, Fedor	1863-1927
Schnitzler, Arthur	1862-1931	Soloviev, Sergei	
Schonner, Karl	1869-1942	Mikhailovich	1820-1879
Schopenhauer, Arthur	1788-1860	Soloviev, Vladimer	
Shreiner, Olive	1855-1920	Sergeivich	1853-1900
Schweitzer, Albert	1875-1965	Sorabji, Cornelia	1866-1954
Schweitzer, Jean Baptista	1833-1875	Sorel, Albert	1842-1906
Scott, Duncan Campbell	1862-1947	Sorel, Georges	1847-1922
Scott-Moncrieff, Charles		Sparks, Jared	1789-1866
Kenneth Michael	1889-1930	Spence, Lewis	1874-1955
Scribe, Eugene	1791-1861	Spencer, Herbert	1820-1903
Seaman, Sir Owen	1861-1936	Spender, Edward Harold	1864-1926
Sedgwick, Anne Douglas	1873-1935	Spielhagen, Friedrich Von	1829-1911
Seebohm, Frederick	1833-1912	Spitteler, Carl	1845-1924
Seeley, Sir John Robert	1834-1895	Stacpoole, Henry de Vere	1863-1951
Segur, Philippe Paul		Stahl, Frederich Julius	1802-1861
Comte De	1780-1873	Stanley, Arthur Penrhyn	1815-1881
Seignobos Charles	1854-1942	Stanley, Sir Henry Morton	1841-1904
Sellar, William Young	1825-1890	Stedman, Edmund	
Serao, Matilde	1856-1927	Clarence	1833-1908
Sergeyev-Tsensky, Sergey	1875-1958	Steed, Henry Wickham	1871-1956
Service, Robert William	1874-1958	Stein, Gertrude	1874-1946
Seth, Andrew	1850-1931	Steiner, Rudolf	1861-1925
Settembrini, Luigi	1813-1877	Stephen, Sir Leslie	1832-1904
Sewell, Anna	1820-1878	Stepnyak	1852-1895
Sharp, John Campbell	1819-1885	Stern, Daniel (Agoult)	1805-1876

Stevenson, Robert Louis Balfour	1850-1894
Stifter, Adalbert	1805-1868
Stirling, James Hutchinson	1820-1909
Stirling-Maxwell, Sir William Bart	1818-1878
Stirner, Max	1806-1856
Stocker, Helene	1869-
Stockton, Francis Richard	1834-1902
Stoddard, John Lawson	1850-1931
Stoddard, Richard Henry	1825-1903
Stoddard, William Osborn	1835-1925
Storm, Theodor Wolsden	1817-1888
Stout, George Frederick	1860-1944
Stowe, Harriet Elizabeth Beecher	1811-1896
Strauss, David Friedrich	1808-1874
Street, Alfred William	1811-1881
Streuvels, Styn	1871-
Strickland Agnes	1806-1874
Strindberg, Johan August	1849-1912
Stubbs, William	1825-1901
Stuckenberg, Viggo	1863-1905
Sudermann, Hermann	1857-1928
Sue, Eugene	1804-1857
Sully-Prudhomme, Rene Francois Armand	1839-1907
Surtees, Robert Smith	1803-1864
Sutro, Alfred	1863-1933
Suttner, Bertha	1843-1914
Svevo, Italio	1861-1928
Swan, Annie	1860-1943
Swanwick, Anna	1813-1899
Swetchine, Madame	1782-1857
Swinburne, Algernon Charles	1837-1909
Sybel, Heinrich Von	1817-1895
Symonds, John Addington	1840-1893
Symons, Arthur	1865-1945
Synge, John Millington	1871-1909
Tabley, John Byrne Leicester Warren	1835-1895
Tagore, Sir Rabindranath	1861-1941
Taine, Hippolyte, Adolphe	1828-1893
Talfourd, Sir Thomas Noon	1795-1854
Tamayo, Baus Manuel	1829-1898
Tarkington, Newton Booth	1869-1946
Taylor, Alfred Edward	1869-1945
Taylor, Ann	1782-1866
Taylor, Bayard	1825-1878
Taylor, Sir Henry	1800-1886
Taylor, Isaak	1787-1865
Taylor, Isaak	1829-1901
Taylor, Tom	1817-1880
Tedder, Henry Richard	1850-1924
Tennyson, Alfred Lord	1809-1892
Thackeray, William Makepeace	1811-1863

Tharaud, Jerome	1874-1953
Thaxter, Celia Laighton	1835-1894
Thayer, William Roscoe	1859-1923
Theuriet, Claude Adhemar Andre	1833-1907
Thierry, Jacques Nicolas Augustin	1795-1856
Thiers, Louis Adolph	1797-1877
Thirlwall, Connop	1797-1875
Thomas, Augustus	1857-1934
Thomas, Brandon	1849-1914
Thompson, Francis	1859-1907
Thomson, James	1834-1882
Thoreau, Henry David	1817-1862
Thurston, Katherine Cecil	1875-1911
Ticknor, George	1791-1871
Tiek, Johann Ludwig	1773-1853
Tischendorf, Lobegott	1815-1874
Tocqueville, Alexis Charles Henri Clarel	1805-1859
Tolstoy, Alexei, Konstantinovich	1817-1875
Tolstoy, Leo Nokolayevich	1828-1910
Tomlinson, Henry Major	1873-1958
Tommaseo, Niccolo	1802-1874
Tompa, Mihaly	1817-1868
Topelius, Zachris	1818-1898
Toru, Dutt	1856-1877
Tout, Thomas Frederick	1855-1929
Toynbee, Arnold	1852-1883
Traill, Henry Duff	1842-1900
Treitschke, Heinrich Von	1834-1896
Trelawny, Edward John	1792-1881
Trench, Frederick Herbert	1865-1923
Trench, Richard Chevenix	1807-1886
Trendelenburg, Friedrich Adolf	1802-1872
Trevelyan, Sir George Otto	1838-1928
Trevelyan, Robert Calverley	1872-1951
Trollope, Anthony	1815-1882
Trollope, Frances	1780-1863
Trollope, Thomas Adolphus	1810-1892
Tucker, Charlotte Marie	1821-1893
Tupper, Martin Farquhar	1810-1889
Turgenev, Ivan Sergeyevich	1818-1883
Turner, Charles Tennyson	1808-1879
Turner, Frederick Jackson	1861-1932
Twain, Mark	1835-1910
Tyler, Moses Coit	1835-1900
Tynan, Katherine	1863-1931
Tyndall, John	1820-1893
Tyuchev, Fydor Ivanovich	1803-1873
Uberweg, Friedrich	1826-1871
Uhland, Johann Ludwig	1787-1862
Unamuno, Miguel De	1864-1936
Underhill, Evelyn	1875-1941

Uspenski, Gleb Ivanovich 1840-1902
Vachell, Horace Annesley 1861-1955
Vacherot, Etienne 1809-1897
Vaihinger, Hans 1852-1933
Valera Y Alcala,
  Galiano Juan 1824-1905
Valery, Paul 1871-1945
Valle-Inclan, Ramon Del 1869-1936
Valles, Jules 1832-1885
Van, Beers Jan 1821-1888
Van Dyke, Henry 1852-1933
Vaperau, Louis Gustave 1819-1906
Varnhagen, Francesco
  Adolpho De 1816-1878
Varnhagen, Von Ense
  Karl August 1785-1858
Vazoff, Ivan 1850-1921
Veblen, Thornstein B. 1857-1929
Veitch, John 1829-1894
Verdaguer, Mosen Jacinto 1845-1902
Verga, Giovanni 1840-1922
Verhaeren, Emile 1855-1916
Verlaine, Paul 1844-1896
Verne, Jules 1828-1905
Verplanck, Gulian
  Crommelin 1786-1870
Verwey, Albert 1865-1937
Viaud, Louis Marie Julien 1850-1923
Vidyasagar, Iswar,
  Chandra 1820-1891
Viebig, Clara 1860-1952
Viele-Griffen, Francis 1864-1937
Vigfusson, Gudbrandir 1828-1889
Vigny, Alfred De 1797-1863
Villari, Pasquale 1827-1917
Villemain, Abel Francois 1790-1870
Villiers de L'Isle, Auguste
  Compte De 1838-1889
Vinje, Aasmunde Olavson 1816-1870
Vinogradoff, Sir Paul 1854-1925
Vischer, Friedrich
  Theodor 1807-1887
Vogue, Eugene Melchior 1848-1910
Voss, Richard 1851-1918
Vrchlicky, Jasoslav 1853-1912
Vuillard, Jean Edouard 1868-1940
Waagen, Gustav Friedrich 1794-1868
Wallace, Alfred Russel 1823-1913
Wallace, Edgar 1875-1932
Wallace, Lewis 1827-1905
Wallace, William 1844-1897
Wallon, Henri Alexandre 1812-1904
Warburton, Eliot 1810-1852
Ward, Artemus 1834-1867
Ward, Mary Augusta
  (Mrs. Humphrey) 1851-1920
Warner, Charles Dudley 1829-1900
Warner, Susan Bogert 1819-1895
Warren, Samuel 1807-1877

Wasserman, Jakob 1873-1933
Watson, Sir William 1858-1935
Watts-Dunton, Walter
  Theodore 1832-1914
Waugh, Edwin 1817-1890
Webb, Beatrice 1858-1943
Webb, Sidney James 1859-1947
Wedekind, Frank 1864-1918
Welhaven, Johann
  Sebastian Cammermeyer 1807-1873
Wells, Charles Jeremiah 1798-1879
Wells, Herbert George 1866-1946
Wennerberg, Gunnar 1817-1901
Weyman, Stanley John 1855-1928
Wharton, Newbold Edith 1862-1937
White, Richard Grant 1821-1885
White, William Hale 1831-1913
Whitehead, Charles 1804-1862
Whitlock, Brand 1869-1934
Whitman, Walt 1819-1892
Whittier, John Greenleaf 1807-1892
Widmann, Joseph Victor 1842-1911
Wieniawski, Henri 1835-1880
Wiggin, Kate Douglas 1856-1923
Wilcox, Ella 1850-1919
Wilde, Oscar Fingall
  O'Flahertie Wills 1854-1900
Wilde, Speranza Lady 1826-1896
Wildenbruch, Ernst Van 1845-1909
Willis, Nathaniel Parker 1806-1867
Wills, William Gorman 1828-1891
Wilson, John 1785-1854
Winsor, Justin 1831-1897
Winther, Christian 1796-1876
Wister, Owen 1860-1938
Wodsworth, Dorothy 1771-1855
Wolff, Pierre 1865-1944
Wood, Mrs. Henry 1814-1887
Woods, Margaret Louisa 1856-1945
Woolf, Virginia 1882-1941
Wright, Thomas 1810-1887
Wright, William Aldis 1836-1914
Wundt, Wilhelm Max 1832-1920
Wyatt, Sir Matthew
  Digby 1820-1877
Wyndham, George 1863-1913
Yates, Edmund 1831-1894
Yeats, William Butler 1865-1939
Yonge, Charlotte Mary 1823-1901
Yriarte, Charles 1832-1898
Zahn, Ernst 1867-1952
Zangwill, Israel 1864-1926
Zeller, Eduard 1814-1908
Zeromski, Stephen 1864-1925
Zhukovsky, Vasili
  Andreyevich 1783-1852
Zola, Emile Edouard
  Charles Antoine 1840-1902
Zorrilla, Jose 1817-1893

Abbey, Edwin Austin	1852-1911	Boelkin, Arnold	1827-1901
Achenbach, Andreas	1815-1910	Bonheur, Rosa	1822-1899
Adams, Herbert	1858-1945	Bonnard, Pierre	1867-1947
Adamsen, Amandus		Bonnat, Leon Joseph	
Heinrich	1855-1929	Florentin	1833-1922
Ainmuller, Maximilian		Borglum, Gutzon	1871-1941
Emmanuel	1807-1870	Borglum, Solon Hannibal	1868-1922
Alexander, John White	1856-1915	Boudin, Louis Eugene	1824-1898
Anderson, Sir Robert		Bough, Samuel	1822-1878
Rowand	1834-1921	Boughton, George Henry	1833-1905
Ansdell, Richard	1815-1885	Bouguereau, Adolphe	
Armitage, Edward	1817-1896	William	1825-1905
Armstead, Henry Hugh	1828-1905	Bourdelle, Emile Antoine	1861-1929
Auberjonois, Rene	1872-	Boutet de Monvel,	
Audubon, John James	1785-1851	Maurice	1851-1913
Bacon, Henry	1866-1924	Boyle, John	1851-1917
Baer, William Jacob	1860-1941	Bracquemond, Felix	1833-1914
Baily, Edward Hodges	1788-1867	Bradford, William	1827-1892
Bakst, Leon	1866-1924	Braekeleer, Henri Jean	
Ball, Thomas	1819-1911	Augustin De	1840-1888
Balla, Giacomo	1871-1958	Brangwyn, Sir Frank	1867-1956
Bandel, Ernst Von	1800-1876	Brascassat, Jacques	
Barker, Thomas	1815-1882	Raymond	1804-1867
Barnard, George Grey	1863-1938	Breitner, George Hendrik	1857-1923
Bartels, Hans Von	1856-1913	Breton, Jules Adolphe	
Barry, Sir Charles	1795-1860	Aime Louis	1827-1906
Bartholdi, August	1834-1904	Bridgman, Frederic	
Bartholomé, Paul Albert	1848-1928	Arthur	1847-1928
Barye, Antoine Louis	1796-1875	Brierly, Sir Oswald	
Bastien-Lepage, Jules	1848-1884	Walters	1817-1894
Bates, Harry	1850-1899	Bright, Henry	1814-1873
Baudry, Paul Jacques		Brock, Sir Thomas	1847-1922
Aime	1828-1886	Brodie, William	1815-1881
Beardsley, Aubrey Vincent	1872-1898	Brough, Robert	1872-1905
Beaux, Cecilia	1863-1942	Brown, Ford Madox	1821-1893
Beckwith, James Carroll	1852-1917	Brown, George Loring	1814-1889
Begas, Karl	1794-1854	Brown, Henry Kirke	1814-1886
Begas, Reinhold	1831-1911	Brown, John George	1831-1913
Behrens, Peter	1868-1938	Browne, Hablot Knight	1815-1882
Bell, John	1811-1895	Bruce-Joy, Albert	1842-1924
Bellows, Albert F.	1829-1883	Brunner, Arnold William	1857-1925
Benlliure, Y Gil Jose	1855-1937	Brush, George de Forest	1855-1941
Benson, Frank Weston	1862-1951	Brymner, William	1855-1925
Bentley, John Francis	1839-1902	Burgess, John Bagnold	1830-1897
Berlage, Hendrik Petrus	1856-1934	Burn, William	1789-1870
Besnard, Paul Albert	1849-1934	Burne-Jones, Sir Edward	
Beverley, William Roxby	1814-1889	Burne	1833-1898
Bierstadt, Albert	1830-1902	Burne-Jones, Sir Philip	1861-1926
Birch, Samuel	1813-1885	Burnham, Daniel Hudson	1846-1912
Bissen, Herman Vilhelm	1798-1868	Burton, Decimus	1800-1881
Blakelock, Ralph Albert	1847-1919	Butler, Lady Elizabeth	1851-1933
Blanche, Jacques Emile	1862-1942	Butterfield, William	1814-1900
Blashfield, Edwin		Cabanel, Alexandre	1823-1889
Howland	1848-1936	Calame, Alexandre	1810-1864
Blomfield, Sir Arthur		Caldecott, Randolph	1846-1886
William	1829-1899	Calderon, Philip	
Blomfield, Sir Reginald	1856-1942	Hermogenes	1833-1898
Blore, Edward	1787-1879	Calvert, Charles	1785-1852
Blum, Robert Frederick	1857-1903	Calvert, Edward	1799-1883
Boehm, Sir Joseph Edgar	1834-1890	Cameron, Sir David Young	1865-1945

Camphausen, Wilhelm	1818-1885	Dantan, Antoine Laurent	1798-1878
Capronnier, Jean-Baptiste	1814-1891	Dantan, Edward Joseph	1848-1897
Caran D'ache	1858-1909	Dantan, Jean-Pierre	1800-1869
Carolus-Duran	1837-1917	Darley, Felix Octavius	
Carpeaux, Jean Baptiste	1827-1875	Carr	1822-1888
Carrier, Eugene	1849-1906	Daubigny, Charles	
Cassatt, Mary	1845-1926	Francois	1817-1878
Catlin, George	1796-1872	Daumet, Pierre Jerome	
Cattermole, George	1800-1868	Honore	1826-1911
Cazin, Jean Charles	1841-1901	Daumier, Honore	1808-1879
Cezanne, Paul	1839-1906	David, Pierre Jean	1789-1856
Chalmers, George Paul	1836-1878	Davies, Arthur B.	1862-1928
Chapu, Henri	1833-1891	Davis, Charles Harold	1857-1933
Chase, William Merrit	1849-1916	Dawson, Henry	1811-1878
Chasseriau, Theodore	1819-1856	Dawson-Watson, Dawson	1864-1939
Church, Frederick Edwin	1826-1900	Decamps, Alexandre	
Clarke, Thomas Shields	1860-1920	Gabriel	1803-1860
Claus, Emile	1849-1924	Defregger, Franz Von	1835-1921
Clausen, Sir George	1852-1944	Degas, Hilaire Germain	
Clays, Paul Jean	1819-1900	Edgar	1834-1917
Cockerell, Charles Robert	1758-1863	Delacroix, Ferdinand	
Cole, Vicat	1833-1893	Victor Eugene	1798-1863
Collier, Hon Jon	1850-1934	Delaroche, Hippolyte	1797-1856
Colman, Samuel	1832-1920	Delaunay, Elie	1828-1891
Conder, Charles	1868-1909	Denis, Maurice	1870-1943
Constant, Benjamin Jean		Despiau, Charles	1874-1946
Joseph	1845-1902	Detaille, Edouard	1848-1912
Cooper, Abraham	1787-1868	Diaz, Narcisse Virgile	1809-1876
Cooper, Thomas Sidney	1803-1902	Dicksee, Sir Francis	
Cope, Charles West	1811-1890	Bernard	1853-1928
Corbett, Harvey Wiley	1873-1954	Dielman, Frederick	1847-1935
Corbould, Edward Henry	1815-1905	Dillens, Julien	1849-1904
Corinth, Louis	1858-1925	Dobson, William Charles	
Cormon, Fernand	1845-1924	Thomas	1817-1898
Cornelius, Peter Von	1783-1867	Dodge, William de	
Corot, Jean-Baptiste		Leftwich	1867-1935
Camille	1796-1875	Dore, Paul Gustave	1832-1883
Costa, Giovanni	1826-1903	Doyle, Richard	1824-1883
Cottet, Charles	1863-1925	Drake, Friedrich	1805-1882
Courbet, Gustav	1819-1877	Drury, Alfred	1857-1944
Couture. Thomas	1815-1879	Dubois, Paul	1829-1905
Cox, David	1783-1859	Dumont, Augustin	
Cox, David the younger	1809-1885	Alexandre	1801-1884
Cram, Ralph Adams	1863-1942	Dupre, Giovanni	1817-1882
Crane, Thomas	1808-1859	Dupre, Jules	1811-1889
Crane, Walter	1845-1915	Durand, Asher Brown	1796-1886
Crauck, Gustav	1827-1905	Duveneck, Frank	1848-1919
Crawford, Thomas	1814-1857	Dyce, William	1806-1864
Creswick, Thomas	1811-1869	Eakins, Thomas	1844-1916
Cruikshank, George	1792-1878	East, Alfred	1849-1913
Dagnan-Bouveret, Pascal		Eastlake, Sir Charles	
Adolphe Jean	1852-1929	Lock	1793-1865
Daguerre, Louis Jacques		Eaton, Wyatt	1849-1896
Mande	1789-1851	Eberlein, Gustav	1847-1926
Dahl, Johann Kristen	1788-1857	Eberz, Josef	1801-1882
Daingerfield, Elliott	1859-1932	Eckersberg, Kristoffer	1783-1853
Dallin, Cyrus Edwin	1861-1944	Edelfelt, Albert Gunter	1854-1905
Dalou, Jules	1838-1902	Egg, Augustus Leopold	1816-1863
Danby, Francis	1793-1861	Elliott, Charles Loring	1812-1868
Dannat, William T.	1853-1929	Ensor, James	1860-1942

Etex, Antoine	1808-1888	Goldschmidt, Hermann	1802-1866
Faed, Thomas	1826-1900	Goodall, Frederick	1822-1904
Falguiere, Jean Alexandre		Goodhue, Bertram	
Joseph	1831-1900	Grosvenor	1869-1924
Fantin-Latour, Ignace Henri		Gordon, Sir John	
Jean Theodore	1836-1904	Watson	1788-1864
Farquharson, David	1840-1907	Grafly, Charles	1862-1929
Farquharson, Joseph	1846-1935	Grant, Sir Francis	1803-1878
Feininger, Lyonel	1871-1956	Greenough, Horatio	1805-1852
Feuerbach, Anselm	1829-1880	Greenaway, Kate	1846-1901
Fielding, Copley	1787-1855	Gregory, Edward John	1850-1909
Fildes, Sir Luke	1844-1927	Grossmith, Weedon	1853-1919
Finch, Alfred William	1854-1930	Gudin, Theodore	1802-1880
Flagg, Ernest	1857-1947	Guillamin, Armand	1841-1927
Flandrin, Jean Hyppolyte	1809-1864	Guillaume, Jean Baptiste	
Fogelberg, Benedict		Claude Eugene	1822-1905
Erland	1786-1854	Guthrie, Sir James	1859-1930
Foley, John Henry	1818-1874	Guys, Constantin	1805-1892
Fontaine, Pierre Francois		Gwilt, Joseph	1784-1863
Leonard	1762-1853	Haag, Carl	1820-1915
Forain, Jean Louis	1852-1931	Haas, Johannes Hubertus	
Ford, Edward Onslow	1852-1901	Leonhardus De	1832-1908
Forster, Ernst	1800-1885	Habermann, Hugo Freiherr	
Fortuny, Mariano Jose		Von	1849-1929
Maria Bernardo	1838-1874	Hacker, Arthur	1858-1919
Foster, Myles Birket	1825-1899	Haider, Karl	1846-1912
Fowler, Charles	1792-1867	Hamon, Jean Louis	1821-1874
Frampton, Sir George	1860-1928	Hansom, Joseph Aloysius	1803-1882
Francais, Francois Louis	1814-1897	Harding, Chester	1792-1866
Fremiet, Emmanuel	1824-1910	Harpignies, Henri	1819-1916
French, Daniel Chester	1850-1931	Harrison, Thomas	
Fripp, Alfred Downing	1822-1895	Alexander	1853-1930
Fripp, George Anthony	1814-1896	Hartley, Jonathan Scott	1845-1912
Frith, William Powell	1819-1909	Harvey, Sir George	1806-1876
Fromentin, Eugene	1820-1876	Hassall, John	1868-1948
Frost, William Edward	1810-1877	Hayter, Sir George	1792-1871
Fry, Roger Elliot	1866-1934	Henner, Jean Jacques	1829-1905
Fuertes, Louis Agassiz	1874-1927	Henri, Robert	1865-1929
Fuhrich, Joseph Von	1800-1876	Herbert, John Rogers	1810-1900
Fuller, George	1822-1884	Hildebrand, Adolf	1847-1921
Furse, Charles Wellington	1868-1904	Hilderbrandt, Eduard	1818-1869
Gallait, Louis	1810-1887	Hiroshege	1797-1858
Gallen-Kallela, Akseli		Hittorff, Jacques Ignace	1792-1867
Valdemar	1865-1931	Hockert, Johan Frederick	1826-1866
Garnier, Jean Louis		Hodgkins, Francis Mary	1869-1947
Charles	1825-1898	Hodler, Ferdinand	1853-1918
Gauguin, Paul	1848-1903	Hoffman, Josef	1870-
Gaul, Gilbert William	1855-1919	Holiday, Henry	1839-1927
Gavarni, Paul	1801-1866	Holl, Frank	1845-1888
Gay, Walter	1856-1937	Holmes, Sir Charles John	1868-1936
Gebhardt, Eduard Von	1830-1925	Holroyd, Sir Charles	1861-1917
Gerome, Jean Leon	1824-1904	Homer, Winslow	1836-1910
Gervex, Henri	1852-1929	Hook, James Clarke	1819-1907
Gibson, Charles Dana	1867-1944	Horsley, John Callcott	1817-1903
Gibson, John	1790-1866	Hosmer, Harriet	
Gifford, Robert Swain	1840-1905	Goodhue	1830-1908
Gilbert, Sir Alfred	1854-1934	Hovenden, Thomas	1840-1895
Gilbert, Cass	1859-1934	Hubner, Julius	1806-1882
Gilbert, Sir John	1817-1897	Hughes, Arthur	1832-1915
Gleyre, Charles	1806-1874	Hunt, Alfred William	1830-1896

Hunt, Richard Morris	1828-1895	Lemaire, Philip Honore	1798-1880
Hunt, William Henry	1790-1864	Lenbach, Franz Von	1836-1904
Hunt, William Holman	1827-1910	Leslie, Charles Robert	1794-1859
Hunt, William Morris	1824-1879	Lethaby, William Richard	1857-1931
Huntingdon, Daniel	1816-1906	Leutze, Emanuel	1816-1868
Hurlstone, Frederick		Leys, Hendrik	1815-1869
Yeates	1800-1869	Liebermann, Max	1847-1935
Hut, Paul	1804-1869	Lindsay, Sir Coutts	1824-1913
Ingres, Jean Auguste		Linnell, John	1792-1882
Dominique	1780-1867	Linton, Sir James Dromgole	1840-1916
Inness, George	1825-1894	Llewellyn, Sir William	1863-1941
Isabey, Jean Baptiste	1767-1855	Lockhart, William Ewart	1846-1900
Israels, Josef	1824-1911	Lockwood, Wilton	1861-1914
Jackson, Sir Thomas		Lucas, John Seymour	1849-1923
Graham	1835-1924	Lukeman, Henry Augustus	1871-1935
Jacque, Charles	1813-1894	Lutyens, Sir Edwin	
Jalabert, Charles Francois	1819-1901	Landseer	1869-1944
Jawlesky, Alexei Van	1864-1941	Macbeth, Robert Walker	1848-1910
John, Sir William		MacColl, Dugald	
Goscombe	1860-1952	Sutherland	1859-1948
Johnson, Eastman	1824-1906	Macculoch, Horatio	1805-1867
Jonkind, Johann Barthold	1819-1891	McEntee, Jervis	1828-1891
Jonsson Einar	1874-1954	McKim, Charles Follen	1847-1909
Jordan, Rudolf	1810-1887	Mackintosh, Charles	
Kandinsky, Vasily	1866-1944	Rennie	1868-1928
Keene, Charles Samuel	1823-1891	Maclise, Daniel	1806-1870
Keller, Albert Von	1844-1920	MacMannies, Frederick	
Kemp-Welch, Lucy		William	1863-1937
Elizabeth	1869-	MacNee, Sir Daniel	1806-1882
Khnopff, Fernand	1858-1921	MacNeil, Hermon Atkins	1866-1947
Kirkup, Seymore Stocker	1788-1880	MacTaggart, William	1835-1910
Klinger, Max	1857-1920	Macwhirter, John	1839-1911
Knaus, Ludwig	1829-1910	Madrazo Y Kunt, Don	
Knight, Daniel Ridgway	1845-1924	Frederico De	1815-1894
Knight, Harold	1874-1961	Magonigle, Harold Van	
Knowles, Sir James	1831-1908	Buren	1867-1935
Kupka, Frank	1871-1957	Maillol, Aristide Joseph	
Kyosai, Sho-Fu	1831-1889	Bonaventure	1861-1944
La Farge, John	1835-1910	Makart, Hans	1840-1884
Lalique, René	1860-1945	Manes, Josef	1820-1871
Lambeaux, Jef	1852-1908	Manet, Edouard	1832-1883
Lanchester, Henry		Manson, George	1850-1876
Vaughan	1863-1953	Marees, Hans Von	1837-1887
Landseer, Sir Edwin Henry	1802-1873	Marin, John	1870-
Laszlo, Sir Philip	1869-1937	Maris, Jacob	1837-1899
Lathrop, Francis	1849-1909	Maris, Matthiss	1839-1917
La Touche, Gaston	1854-1913	Maris, Willem	1843-1910
Lauder, Robert Scott	1803-1869	Marochetti, Carlo	1805-1867
Laurens, Jean Paul	1838-1921	Marquet, Albert	1875-1947
Lavery, Sir John	1856-1941	Marr, Carl	1859-1936
Lawson, Cecil Gordon	1851-1882	Marshall, William Calder	1813-1894
Lazlo De Lombos, Philip		Martin, Homer Dodge	1836-1897
Alexius	1869-1937	Martin, John	1789-1854
Lear, Edward	1812-1888	Matejko, Jan Alois	1838-1893
Leech, John	1817-1864	Matisse, Henri	1869-1954
Legros, Alphonse	1837-1911	Mauve, Anton	1838-1888
Lehmann, Rudolf	1819-1905	Mead, Larkin Goldsmith	1835-1910
Leibl, Wilhelm	1844-1900	Mead, William Rutherford	1846-1928
Leighton, Frederick		Meissonier, Jean Louis	
Leighton	1830-1896	Ernest	1815-1891

Melchers, Gari	1860-1932	Peale, Rembrandt	1778-1860
Menzel, Adolph Friedrich		Pearce, Charles Sprague	1851-1914
Erdmann-Von	1815-1905	Pearson, John	
Mercie, Marius Jean		Loughborough	1817-1897
Antonin	1845-1916	Pennell, Joseph	1860-1926
Mesdag, Hendrik Willem	1831-1915	Peploe, Samuel John	1871-1935
Meunier, Constantin	1831-1905	Perrett, Auguste	1874-1955
Millais, Sir John Everett	1829-1896	Pettie, John	1839-1893
Millet, Francis Davis	1846-1912	Piloty, Karl Von	1826-1886
Millet, Jean Francois	1814-1875	Pinwell, George John	1842-1875
Mondrian, Pieter Cornelis	1872-1944	Pissaro, Camille	1830-1903
Monet, Claude	1840-1926	Platt, Charles Adams	1861-1933
Monticelli, Adolphe Joseph		Playfair, William Henry	1789-1857
Thomas	1824-1856	Poelzig, Hans	1869-1936
Moore, Albert Joseph	1841-1893	Poole, Paul Falconer	1807-1879
Moore, Henry	1831-1895	Pope, John Russell	1874-1937
Moore, William	1790-1851	Portaels, Jean Francois	1818-1895
Moran, Edward	1829-1901	Post, George Browne	1837-1913
Moreau, Gustave	1826-1898	Powers, Hiram	1805-1873
Morel-Ladeuil, Leonard	1820-1888	Poynter, Sir Edward John	1836-1919
Morisot, Berthe Marie		Pradilla, Francisco	1848-1921
Pauline	1841-1895	Prinsep, Valentine	
Morris, William	1834-1896	Cameron	1838-1904
Morse, Samuel Finley		Proctor, Alexander	
Breese	1791-1872	Phimister	1862-1950
Moses, Anna Mary		Prout, Samuel	1783-1852
(Grandma)	1860-1961	Pugin, Augustus Welby	
Mosler, Henry	1841-1920	Nortmore	1812-1852
Motte, William De La	1775-1863	Purvitis, Vilhelms Karlis	1872-1945
Mount, William Sidney	1807-1868	Puvis De Chavannes	
Mowbray, Harry Siddons	1858-1928	Pierre Cecile	1824-1898
Muenier, Jules A.	1863-1934	Pyle, Howard	1853-1911
Mulready, William	1786-1863	Rackham, Arthur	1867-1939
Munch, Edvard	1863-1944	Raemaekers, Louis	1869-1956
Munkacsy, Michael	1846-1900	Rauch, Christien Daniel	1777-1857
Murphy, John Francis	1853-1921	Raven Hill, Leonard	1867-1942
Murray, Sir David	1849-1933	Redon, Odilon	1840-1916
Nesfield, William Eden	1835-1888	Regnault, Henri	1843-1871
Neuville, Alphonse		Reid, Sir George	1841-1913
Marie De	1836-1885	Reid, Robert	1862-1929
Nicholson, Sir William	1872-1949	Remington, Frederic	1861-1909
Nicol, Erskine	1825-1904	Renoir, Pierre Auguste	1841-1919
Niehaus, Charles Henry	1855-1935	Renwick, James	1818-1895
Nolde, Emil	1867-1956	Repin, Ilya Yefimovich	1844-1930
Ochtmann, Leonard	1854-1934	Rethel, Alfred	1816-1859
Orchardson, Sir William		Retzsch, Friedrich August	
Quiller	1832-1910	Moritz	1779-1857
Oudine, Eugene Andre	1810-1887	Richardson, Henry	
Overbeck, Johann		Hobson	1838-1886
Frederick	1789-1869	Richmond, George	1809-1896
Page, William	1811-1885	Richmond, Sir William	
Palmer, Samuel	1805-1881	Blake	1842-1921
Parsons, Alfred	1847-1920	Ricketts, Charles	1866-1931
Parsons, William Edward	1872-1939	Rietschel, Ernst	1804-1861
Partridge, Sir Bernard	1861-1945	Riviere, Briton	1840-1920
Partridge, William		Roberts, David	1796-1864
Ordway	1861-1930	Robinson, William Heath	1872-1944
Paton, Sir Joseph Noel	1821-1901	Rodin, Auguste	1840-1917
Paul, Bruno	1874-	Roerich, Nikolai	
Paxton, Sir Joseph	1801-1865	Constatinovich	1874-1947

Rogers, John	1829-1904
Rops, Felicien	1833-1898
Rossetti, Dante Gabriel	1828-1882
Rothenstein, Sir William	1872-1945
Rouault, Georges	1871-1958
Rousseau, Henri	1844-1910
Rousseau, Pierre Etienne	
Theodore	1812-1867
Rude, Francois	1784-1855
Ryder, Albert Pinkham	1847-1917
Sargent, John Singer	1856-1925
Salisbury, Frank Owen	1874-1957
Schadow, Friedrich	
Wilhelm	1789-1862
Scheffer, Ary	1795-1858
Schilling, Johannes	1828-1910
Schnorr Von Karolsfeld,	
Julius	1794-1872
Schreyer, Adolf	1828-1899
Schwartze, Teresz	1852-1918
Schwind, Moritz Von	1804-1871
Scott, Sir George Gilbert	1811-1878
Seganti, Giovanni	1858-1899
Semper, Gottfried	1803-1873
Serusier, Paul	1863-1927
Seurat, Georges	1859-1891
Severn, Joseph	1793-1879
Shannon, Charles	
Hazelwood	1863-1937
Shannon, Sir James	
Jebusa	1862-1923
Shaw, Richard Norman	1831-1912
Shields, Frederick James	1833-1911
Short, Sir Frank Job	1857-1945
Sickert, Walter Richard	1860-1942
Signac, Paul	1863-1935
Simmons, Edward	
Emerson	1852-1931
Simpson, Sir John	1858-1933
Sisley, Alfred	1840-1899
Slevogt, Max	1868-1932
Smillie, James David	1833-1909
Smirke, Sir Robert	1781-1867
Somerscales, Thomas	
Jacques	1842-1928
Somov, Konstantin	
Andreevich	1869-
Sorolla Y Bastida, Joaquin	1863-1923
Stanfield, William	
Clarkson	1794-1867
Stark, James	1794-1859
Steell, Sir John	1804-1891
Steer, Philip Wilson	1860-1942
Steinle, Eduard	1810-1886
Steinlen, Theophile	
Alexandre	1859-1923
Stevens, Alfred	1818-1875
Stevens, Alfred	1828-1906
Stillman, William James	1828-1901
Story, William Wetmore	1819-1895

Strachan, Douglas	1875-1950
Strang, William	1859-1921
Street, George Edmund	1824-1881
Sturgis, Russell	1836-1909
Sullivan, Louis Henri	1856-1924
Sully, Thomas	1783-1872
Svabinsky, Max	1873-
Szinye-Merse, Paul De	1845-1920
Taft, Lorado	1860-1936
Tanner, Henry Assawa	1859-1937
Tarbell, Edmond C.	1862-1938
Tenniel, Sir John	1820-1914
Thayer, Abbott Handerson	1849-1921
Thoma, Hans	1839-1924
Thompson, Launt	1833-1934
Thornycroft, Sir William	
Hamo	1850-1925
Tiffany, Louis Comfort	1848-1933
Tissot, James Joseph	
Jacques	1836-1902
Tite, Sir William	1798-1873
Tonks, Henry	1862-1937
Toulouse-Lautrec,	
Henri De	1864-1901
Travies De Villers,	
Charles Joseph	1804-1859
Troubetzkoy, Amelie	
Rives	1863-1945
Troubetzkoy, Pierre	1864-1936
Troyon, Constant	1810-1865
Trubner, Wilhelm	1851-1917
Tryon, Dwight William	1849-1925
Tuke, Henry Scott	1858-1929
Turner, Joseph Mallord	
William	1775-1851
Tweed, John	1869-1933
Valadon, Suzanne	1869-1938
Vallotton, Felix	1865-1929
Vanderlyn, John	1776-1852
Van Der Stappen, Charles	1843-1910
Van De Velde, Henri	1863-1957
Van Gogh, Vincent	1853-1890
Vedder, Elihu	1836-1923
Veit, Philipp	1793-1877
Verboeckhoven, Eugene	
Joseph	1798-1881
Vereshchagin, Vassili	
Vassilievich	1842-1904
Vernet, Emile Jean	
Horace	1789-1863
Vierge, Daniel	1851-1904
Vigeland, Adolf Gustav	1869-1943
Vigne, Paul De	1843-1901
Villon, Jacques	1875-
Vinton, Frederic Porter	1846-1911
Viollet Le Duc, Eugene	
Emmanuel	1814-1879
Vivin, Louis	1861-1936
Volk, Leonard Wells	1828-1895
Vonnoh, Robert William	1858-1933

Vorosmarty, Mihaly	1800-1855	Whistler, James Abbott	
Vuillard, Edward	1868-1940	McNeill	1834-1903
Wainewright, Thomas		White, Stanford	1853-1906
Griffiths	1794-1852	Whymper, Edward	1840-1911
Waldo, Samuel Lovett	1783-1861	Wiertz, Anton Joseph	1806-1865
Walker, Frederick	1840-1875	Willems, Florent Joseph	
Walker, Henry Oliver	1843-1929	Marie	1823-1905
Walker, Horatio	1858-1938	Willette, Leon Adolphe	1857-1926
Ward, Edward Matthew	1816-1879	Willumsen, Jens Ferdinand	1863-1958
Ward, John Quincy		Winterhalter, Franz	
Adams	1830-1910	Xavier	1806-1873
Warren, Whitney	1864-1943	Woolner, Thomas	1826-1892
Waterhouse, Alfred	1830-1905	Wright, Frank Lloyd	1869-1959
Waterhouse, John William	1847-1917	Wyant, Alexander	1836-1892
Waterlow, Sir Ernst		Wyspienski, Stanislaw	1869-1907
Albert	1850-1919	Yeames, William	
Watts, George Frederic	1817-1904	Frederick	1835-1918
Wauters, Emile	1846-1933	Yeats, Jack Butler	1871-1957
Webb, Sir Aston	1849-1930	Ziem, Felix Francois	
Webb, Philip Speakman	1831-1915	George	1821-1911
Weir, Robert Walter	1803-1889	Zorn, Anders	1860-1920
Westmacott, Sir Richard	1775-1856	Zuluago, Ignacio	1870-1945
Weyr, Rudolf Von	1847-1914		

COMPOSERS

Abt, Franz	1819-1885	Boito, Arriego	1842-1918
Adam, Adolphe Charles	1803-1856	Borodin, Alexander	
Albeniz, Isaac	1860-1909	Porfyrievich	1834-1887
Albert, Eugen Francis		Bottesini, Giovanni	1822-1889
Charles D'	1864-1932	Brahms, Johannes	1833-1897
Arditi, Luigi	1822-1903	Bruch, Max	1838-1920
Arensky, Anton		Bruckner, Anton	1824-1896
Stephanovich	1861-1906	Bruneau, Alfred	1857-1934
Auber, Daniel Francois		Buck, Dudley	1839-1909
Eprit	1782-1871	Burleigh, Henry Thaker	1866-1949
Audran, Edmond	1842-1901	Busoni, Ferruccio	1866-1924
Bache, Francis Edward	1833-1858	Chabrier, Alexis	
Balakirev, Milly Aleivich	1836-1910	Emmanuel	1841-1894
Balfe, Michael William	1808-1870	Chaminade, Cecile	1861-1944
Bantock, Sir Granville	1868-1946	Charpentier, Gustave	1860-1956
Bargiel, Woldemar	1828-1897	Chvala, Emanuel	1851-1924
Barnby, Sir Joseph	1838-1896	Clay, Frederick	1838-1889
Barnett, John	1802-1890	Coleridge-Taylor, Samuel	1875-1912
Barnett, John Francis	1837-1916	Cowen, Sir Frederick	
Bemberg, Herman	1861-	Hynam	1852-1935
Bendl, Karel	1838-1897	Cornelius, Carl August	
Benedict, Sir Julius	1804-1885	Peter	1824-1874
Bennett, Sir William		Costa, Sir Michael	1810-1884
Sterndale	1816-1875	Cui, Cesar Antonovitch	1835-1918
Benoit, Pierre Leonard		Czerny, Karl	1791-1857
Leopold	1834-1901	D'Albert, Eugen Francis	
Beriot, Charles Auguste		Charles	1864-1932
De	1802-1870	Damrosch, Leopold	1832-1885
Berlioz, Hector	1803-1869	Dargomijsky, Alexander	
Bishop, Sir Henry Rowley	1786-1855	Sergeivich	1813-1869
Bizet, Georges	1838-1875	David, Felicien	1810-1876
Blumenthal, Jacob	1829-1908	Davies, Sir Henry	
Boelmann, Leon	1862-1897	Walford	1869-1941

Debussy, Claude Achille	1862-1918	Herbert, Victor	1859-1924
De Koven, Reginald	1861-1920	Herve, Florimond Rounger	1825-1892
Delibes, Clement Philbert		Herz, Henri	1806-1888
Leo	1836-1891	Hiller, Ferdinand	1811-1885
Delius, Frederick	1863-1934	Holst, Gustave	1874-1934
Diabelli, Anton Antonio	1781-1858	Hubay, Geno De	1858-1937
D'Indy, Paul Marie		Hullah, John Pyke	1812-1884
Theodore	1851-1931	Humperdinck, Engelbert	1854-1921
Dopper, Cornelis	1870-1939	Jacques-Dalcroze, Emile	1865-1950
Doppler, Albert Franz	1821-1883	Janacek, Leos	1854-1928
Dreyschock, Alexander	1818-1869	Jarnefelt, Edvard Armas	1869-1958
Dubois, Francois Clement	1837-1924	Jensen, Adolf	1837-1897
Dukas, Paul	1865-1935	Joachim, Joseph	1831-1907
Dupark, Henri	1848-1933	Joncieres, Victorin	1839-1903
Dvorak, Antonin	1841-1904	Jongen, Joseph	1873-1953
Dykes, John Bacchus	1823-1876	Kajanus, Robert	1856-1933
Eitner, Robert	1832-1905	Kienzl, Wilhelm	1857-1941
Elgar, Sir Edward	1857-1934	Kjerulf, Holfdan	1815-1868
Elvey, Sir George Job	1816-1893	Kovarovic, Karel	1862-1920
Engel, Karl	1818-1882	Lacomb, Louis Trouvillon	1818-1884
Erlanger, Camille	1863-1919	Lalo, Edouard	1823-1892
Ernst, Heinrich Wilhelm	1814-1865	Lamond, Frederick	1868-1948
Faure, Gabriel	1845-1924	Lassen, Eduard	1830-1904
Fetis, Francois Joseph	1784-1871	Lecocq, Alexandre Charles	1832-1918
Fibich, Zdenko	1850-1900	Lehar, Franz	1870-1948
Finck, Heinrich		Lekeu, Guillaume	1870-1894
Theophilus	1854-1926	Lemmens, Nicolas Jacques	1823-1881
Flotow, Friedrich		Leoncavallo, Ruggiero	1858-1919
Freiherr Von	1812-1883	Liadov, Anatol	1855-1914
Foerster, Josef Bohuslav	1859-	Liszt, Franz	1811-1886
Foote, Arthur William	1853-1937	Loeffler, Charles Martin	1861-1935
Foster, Stephen Collins	1826-1864	Loewe, Johann Karl	
Franck, Cesar	1822-1890	Gottfried	1796-1869
Franz, Robert	1815-1892	Lortzing, Albert	1801-1851
Gade, Niels Vilhelm	1817-1890	Maccun, Hamish	1868-1916
Gatty, Nicholas Comyn	1874-1946	Macdowell, Edward	
German, Sir Edward	1862-1936	Alexander	1861-1908
Glazunov, Alexander		Macfarren, Sir George	
Constantinovich	1865-1936	Alexander	1813-1887
Glinka, Michael Ivanovich	1803-1857	Mackenzie, Sir Alexander	
Godard, Benjamin	1849-1895	Campbell	1847-1935
Godowsky, Leopold	1870-1938	Mahler, Gustav	1860-1911
Goldmark, Karl	1832-1915	Marschner, Heinrich	
Goss, Sir John	1800-1880	August	1795-1861
Gounod, Charles Francois	1818-1893	Mascagni, Pietro	1863-1945
Granados Y Campina,		Mason, Daniel Gregory	1873-1953
Enrique	1867-1916	Massenet, Jules Emile	
Gretchaninov, Alexander		Frederic	1842-1912
Tikhonovich	1864-1956	Mengelberg, Willem	1871-1951
Grieg, Edvard Hagerup	1843-1907	Merikanto, Oskar	1868-1924
Gung'l, Josef	1810-1889	Messager, Andre Charles	
Hadley, Henry Kimball	1871-1937	Prosper	1853-1929
Halevy, Jacques Francois		Meyebeer, Gialomo	1791-1864
Fromental	1799-1862	Monckton, Lionel	1861-1924
Handy, William		Monk, William Henry	1823-1889
Christopher	1873-1958	Moszkowski, Moritz	1854-1925
Hatton, John Liptrot	1809-1886	Mottl, Felix	1856-1911
Hauptmann, Moritz	1792-1868	Moussorgsky, Modest	
Heller, Stephen	1815-1888	Petrovich	1835-1881
Henselt, Adolf Von	1814-1889	Napravnik, Edward	1839-1915

Nathan, Isaac	1791-1864	Scriabin, Alexander	
Nevin, Ethelbert	1862-1901	Nicholaevich	1872-1915
Nielsen, Carl August	1865-1931	Sgambati, Giovanni	1843-1914
Novak, Viteslav	1870-1949	Sibelius, Johan Julius	1865-1958
Offenbach, Jacques	1819-1880	Sinding, Christian	1856-1941
Ouseley, Sir Frederick		Smetana, Bedrich	1824-1884
Arthur	1825-1889	Smyth, Dame Ethel Mary	1858-1944
Paderewski, Ignace Jan	1860-1941	Soderman, August Johan	1832-1876
Parker, Horatio William	1863-1919	Somervell, Sir Arthur	1863-1937
Parry, Sir Charles		Sousa, John Philip	1854-1932
Hubert Hastings	1848-1918	Spohr, Ludwig	1784-1859
Pearsall, Robert Lucas De	1795-1856	Spontini, Gasparo	
Pedrell, Felipe	1841-1922	Luigi Pacifico	1774-1851
Perosi, Lorenzo	1872-1956	Spottiswoode, Alicia Ann	
Pierson, Henry Hugo	1815-1873	Lady John	1811-1900
Planquette, Robert	1850-1903	Stanford, Sir Charles	
Ponchielli, Amilcare	1834-1886	Villiers	1852-1924
Puccini, Giacomo	1858-1924	Straus, Oscar	1870-1954
Rachmaninoff, Sergei		Strauss, Johann the	
Vassilievitch	1873-1943	Younger	1825-1899
Raff, Joseph Joachim	1822-1882	Strauss, Richard	1864-1949
Randegger, Alberto	1832-1911	Suk, Joseph	1875-1935
Ravel, Maurice	1875-1937	Sullivan, Sir Arthur	
Rebikov, Vladimir	1866-1920	Seymour	1842-1900
Reger, Max	1873-1916	Suppe, Franz Von	1820-1895
Reinecke, Carl Heinrich	1824-1910	Svendsen, Johan Severin	1840-1911
Rheinberger, Joseph		Taneiev, Sergius	1856-1915
Gabriel	1839-1901	Tcherepnin, Nicolai	1873-1945
Rimsky-Korsakov,		Thomas, Ambroise	1811-1896
Nikolai Andreivich	1844-1908	Thomas, Arthur Goring	1850-1892
Rockstro, William Smith	1823-1895	Thuille, Ludig	1861-1907
Roger-Ducasse, Jean		Tosti, Sir Francesco	
Jules Aimable	1873-1954	Paolo	1846-1916
Ronald, Sir Landon	1873-1938	Tovey, Sir Donald	
Rossini, Gioachino		Francis	1873-1940
Antonio	1792-1868	Tschaikovsky, Peter Ilyich	1840-1893
Roussel, Albert	1869-1937	Vaughan Williams, Ralph	1872-1958
Rubinstein, Anton	1829-1894	Verdi, Guiseppe Fortunino	
Saint-Saens, Charles		Francesco	1813-1901
Camille	1835-1921	Wagner, Wilhelm	
Satie, Erik Leslie	1866-1925	Richard	1813-1883
Scharwenka, Xavier	1850-1924	Waldteufel, Emil	1837-1915
Schonberg, Arnold	1874-1951	Wallace, William	1860-1940
Schubert, Franz	1808-1878	Wallace, William Vincent	1812-1865
Schumann, Clara		Weingartner, Felix	1863-1942
Josephine	1819-1896	Wesley, Samuel Sebastian	1810-1876
Schumann, Robert		Widor, Charles Marie	1845-1937
Alexander	1810-1856	Wolf, Hugo	1860-1903

S

1876 Bulgarian massacres.
1877 Russia declares war on Turkey.
  Roumania declared independent.
1878 Microphone invented.
1879 Tay Bridge destroyed.
  War in Zululand.
1880 Transvaal declared a republic.
1881 Battle of Majuba Hill.
  Peace arranged with Boers.
1882 Servia declared a kingdom.
1883 Royal College of Music opened.
  Phoenix Park murderers convicted.
1884 Fabian Society founded.
1885 Battle of Abu Klea
  Khartoum captured.
1891 Free education act passed in England.
1894 Japan declares war on China.
  Drevfus convicted of treason.
1896 Discovery of X-Rays.
1897 Turkey declares war on Greece.
1898 Peace between U.S. and Spain.
  Battle of Omdurman.
1899 Battle of Modder River
  Marconi experiments in wireless telegraphy.
1900 Boers attack Ladysmith.
  Relief of Mafeking.

PROMINENT PEOPLE

Baird, John Logie	1888-1946	Hitler, Adolf	1889-1945
Beaverbrook, Lord	1879-1964	Kitchener of Khartoum	1850-1916
Bevin, Ernest	1881-1951	Lessepes, Vicomte	
Bismarck, Leopold Von	1815-1898	Ferdinand de	1805-1894
Booth, General William	1829-1912	Lister, Lord	1827-1912
Caruso, Enrico	1873-1921	Lloyd George, David	1863-1945
Chaliapin, Fedor		Manning, Henry Edward,	
Ivanovich	1873-1938	Cardinal	1808-1892
Curie, Pierre	1859-1906	Marconi, Marchese	
Curie, Marie	1867-1934	Gulielmo	1874-1937
De Gaulle, Charles	1890-	Mussolini, Benito	1883-1945
Diaghilev, Sergei		Nobel, Alfred	1833-1896
Pavlovich	1872-1929	Pankhurst, Emmeline	1858-1928
Edison, Thomas, Alva	1847-1931	Pasteur, Louis	1822-1895
Einstein, Albert	1879-1955	Rasputin, Grigri	
Gandhi, Mahandas		Yefimovich	1871-1916
Karamchand	1869-1948	Rhodes, Cecil	1853-1902
Garibaldi, Giuseppe	1807-1882	Rontgen, Prof. Wilhelm	
		Konrad	1845-1923

EMPERORS OF CHINA (MANCHU (Ch'ing) DYNASTY)

Teh Tsung   1875-1908

POPES

Pius IX   1846-1878   Leo XIII   1878-1903

Macmahon, President, Marshal	1873-1879	Casimir-Perier, President	1894-1895
Grevy, President, Jules	1879-1887	Faure, President, Francois Felix	1895-1899
Carnot, President, Sadi	1887-1894	Loubet, President, Emile	1899-1906

ENGLAND, SOVEREIGNS

Victoria   1837-1901

SWEDEN, KINGS

Oscar II   1872-1907

RUSSIA, TSARS

Alexander II	1855-1881	Nicholas II	1894-1917
Alexander III	1881-1894		

SPAIN, SOVEREIGNS

Alfonso XII	1874-1885	Alfonso XIII	1886-1931

PORTUGAL, KINGS

Luiz I	1861-1889	Carlos I	1889-1908

U.S.A. PRESIDENTS

Grant, Ulysses	1869-1877	Cleveland, Grover	1885-1889
Hayes, Rutherford	1877-1881	Harrison, Benjamin	1889-1893
Garfield, James	1881-	Cleveland, Grover (again)	1893-1897
Arthur, Chester (Vice P)	1881-1885	McKinley, William	1897-1901

PRUSSIA, KINGS

William I   1861-1888
(Became Emperor of
Germany 1871)

AUSTRIA, EMPERORS

Josef, Franz   1848-1916

NETHERLANDS, SOVEREIGNS

William III	1849-1890	Wilhelmina	1890-1948

BELGIUM KINGS

Leopold II   1865-1909

ITALY, KINGS

Emmanuel, Victor	1861-1878	Umberto I	1878-1900

GERMANY, EMPERORS

William I	1871-1888	William II	1888-1918

Aakjaer, Jeppe	1866-1930	Alcott, Louisa May	1832-1888
Aanrud, Hans	1863-1953	Alcover, Joan	1854-1926
Aansen, Ivar	1813-1896	Aldanova, Mark	
Abbott, Edwin Abbott	1838-1926	Alexandrovitch	1889-
Abbott, Evelyn	1843-1901	Alden, Isabella	1841-1930
Abbott, George	1899-	Alden, Joseph	1807-1885
Abbott, Jacob	1803-1879	Aldington, Richard	1892-1962
Abbott, Lyman	1835-1922	Aldrich, Thomas Bailey	1836-1907
Abbott, Wilbur Cortez	1869-1947	Aleardi, Aleardo	1812-1878
Abercrombie, Lascelles	1881-1938	Alecsandri, Vasile	1821-1890
Aberigh-Mackay, George		Alexander, Cecil Francis	1818-1895
Robert	1848-1881	Alexander, Samuel	1859-1938
About, Edmond Francois		Alexander, William	1826-1894
Valentin	1828-1885	Alger, Horatio	1834-1899
Ackerman, Louis		Alin, Oscar Josef	1846-1900
Victorine Choquet	1813-1890	Alington, Cyril Argentine	1872-
Acton, John Emerich		Allen, Charles Grant	
Edward Dolbey	1834-1902	Blairfindie	1848-1899
Adam, Juliette	1836-1936	Allen, James Lane	1849-1925
Adam, Paul	1862-1920	Allen, William Hervey	1889-1949
Adamic, Louis	1899-1951	Allibone, Samuel Austin	1816-1889
Adams, Andy	1859-1935	Allingham, William	1824-1889
Adams, Charles Follen	1842-1918	Allmers, Hermann	1821-1902
Adams, Henry Brooks	1838-1918	Alma Tadema, Sir	
Adams, James Truslow	1879-1949	Laurence	1836-1912
Adams, Oscar Fay	1855-1919	Alonso, Dameso	1898-
Adams, Samuel Hopkins	1871-1958	Alvaro, Corrado	1895-1956
Adams, William Taylor	1822-1897	Alvarez Quintero,	
Adamson, Robert	1852-1902	Joaquin	1873-1944
Addams, Jane	1860-1935	Alvarez Quintero,	
Ade, George	1866-1944	Serafin	1871-1938
Adickes, Erich	1866-1928	Amicis, Edmondo de	1846-1908
Adler, Alfred	1870-1937	Amiel, Henri Frederic	1821-1881
Ady, Endre	1877-1919	Ancona, Alessandro	1835-1914
Agate, James Evershed	1877-1947	Anderson, Maxwell	1888-1959
Agoult, Marie Catherine		Anderson, Sherwood	1876-1941
Sophie de Flavigny	1805-1876	Andrews, Charles	
Aguilo I Fuster, Marian	1825-1897	McLean	1863-1943
Aho Juhani	1861-1921	Andreyev, Leonid	
Aicard, Jean Francois		Nicolaevich	1871-1919
Victor	1848-1921	Andric, Ivo	1892-
Aide, Hamilton	1830-1906	Angell, Sir Norman	1874-
Aiken, Conrad Potter	1889-	Angellier, Auguste Jean	1848-1911
Aimard, Gustave	1818-1883	Angus, Marion	1866-1946
Ainger, Alfred	1837-1904	Anker-Larsen, Johannes	1874-1957
Ainsworth, William		Annunzio, Gabrielle D'	1863-1938
Harrison	1805-1882	Anstey, Francis	1856-1934
Aird, Thomas	1802-1876	Antokolski, Mark	
Aitken, Robert Ingersoll	1878-1949	Matveevich	1843-1902
Akhmatova, Arna		Anzengruber, Ludwig	1839-1889
(Gorenko)	1888-	Apollinnaire, Guillaume	1880-1918
Akins, Zoe	1886-1958	Arany, Janos	1817-1882
Aksakov, Ivan Sergelvich	1823-1886	Arbois De Juainville,	
Alain-Fournier, Henry	1886-1914	Marie Henri d'	1827-1910
Alarcon, Pedro Antonio	1833-1891	Archer, William	1856-1924
Alas, Leopoldo	1852-1901	Arcos, Rene	1881-
Albert, Eugen Francis		Arlen, Michael	1895-1956
Charles d'	1864-1932	Arnason, Jon	1819-1888
Albiker, Karl	1878-	Arneth, Alfred	1819-1897
Alcott, Amos Bronson	1799-1888	Arnold, Sir Edwin	1832-1904

Arnold, Matthew	1822-1888	Barbellion, W.N.P.	1889-1919
Arthur, Timothy Shay	1809-1885	Barbey D'Aurevilly, Jules	
Artzybashev, Mikhail		Amedee	1808-1889
Petrovich	1878-1927	Barbier, Henri Auguste	1805-1882
Asbjornsen, Peter		Barbier, Paul Jules	1825-1901
Christian	1812-1885	Barbusse, Henri	1873-1935
Asch, Sholem	1880-1957	Baring, Maurice	1874-1946
Ashbee, Charles Robert	1863-1942	Baring-Gould, Sabine	1834-1924
Ashe, Thomas	1836-1889	Barlow, Jane	1860-1917
Asnyk, Adam	1838-1897	Barnes, Harry Elmer	1889-
Atherton, Gertrude		Barnes, Margaret Ayer	1886-
Franklin	1857-1948	Barnes, William	1800-1886
Attlee, Clement Richard	1883-	Baroja, Pio	1872-1956
Aubanel, Theodore	1829-1886	Barr, Amelia Edith	1831-1919
Audoux, Marguerite	1880-1937	Barres, Maurice	1862-1923
Auerbach, Berthold	1812-1882	Barrie, Sir James	
Auersperg, Anton		Matthew	1860-1937
Alexander	1806-1876	Barriere, Theodore	1823-1877
Augier, Guillaume		Barrili, Antonio Giulio	1836-1908
Victor Emile	1820-1889	Barry, Philip	1896-1949
Aukrust, Olav Lom	1883-1929	Barthelemy, Saint-Hilaire	
Aulard, Francois Victor		Jules	1805-1895
Alphonse	1849-1928	Bascom, John	1827-1911
Austin, Alfred	1835-1913	Bashkirtsev, Maine	1860-1884
Austin, Mary Hunter	1869-1934	Bataille, Felix Henri	1872-1922
Autran, Joseph	1813-1877	Bates, Arlo	1850-1918
Avenarius, Richare		Bates, Katherine Lee	1859-1929
Heinrich Ludwig	1843-1896	Bateson, Mary	1865-1906
Axelrod, Pavel		Baudissin, Wolf Heinrich	1789-1878
Borriasovich	1850-1928	Bauer, Bruno	1809-1882
Ayala Y Herrera, Adelardo		Bauernfeld, Eduard Von	1802-1890
Lopez d'	1828-1879	Baumbach, Rudolf	1840-1905
Azorin, Jose Martinez		Bax, Ernest Belfort	1854-1926
Ruis	1874-	Bazin, Rene	1853-1932
Babbitt, Irving	1865-1933	Beard, Charles Austin	1874-1948
Babits, Mihaly	1883-1941	Beaverbrook, William	
Bacheller, Irving Addison	1859-1950	Maxwell Aitken	1879-1964
Bachelli, Riccardo	1891-	Becker, Carl L.	1873-1945
Bacon, Leonard	1802-1881	Becque, Henry Francois	1837-1899
Bagehot, Walter	1826-1877	Bede, Cuthbert	1827-1889
Bahr, Hermann	1863-1934	Bédier, Joseph	1864-1938
Bailey, Philip James	1816-1902	Beecher, Henry Ward	1813-1887
Bain, Alexander	1818-1903	Beerbohm, Sir Max	1872-1956
Baird, Henry Martin	1832-1906	Beets, Nikolaas	1814-1903
Baker, Sir Herbert	1862-1946	Behaine, Rene	1889-
Baker, Ray Stannard	1870-1946	Belasco, David	1854-1931
Balaguer, Victor	1824-1901	Beljame, Alexandre	1842-1906
Baldensperger, Fernand	1871-1958	Bell, John Jay	1871-1934
Baldini, Antonio	1889-	Bellamy, Edward	1850-1898
Ballantine, James	1808-1877	Belloc, Joseph Hilaire	
Ballantyne, Robert		Pierre	1870-1953
Michael	1825-1894	Belloc, Lowndes Marie	
Balmont, Constantine	1867-1943	Adelaide	1868-1947
Bancroft, George	1800-1891	Bemis, Samuel Flogg	1891-
Bancroft, Hubert Hoew	1832-1918	Benavente Y Martinez,	
Banerjee, Satyendranath	1897-	Jacinto	1866-1954
Bang, Herman Joachim	1858-1912	Benchley, Robert	1889-1954
Banning, Margaret Culkin	1891-	Benelli, Sem	1877-1949
Banville, Theodore		Benet, Stephen Vincent	1898-1943
Faullain De	1823-1891	Benjamin, Rene	1885-1948

Bennet, Enoch Arnold	1867-1931	Boisgobey, Fortune	
Benoa, Julien	1867-	Abraham, Du	1824-1891
Benson, Arthur		Bojer, Johan	1872-1959
Christopher	1862-1925	Boker, George Henry	1823-1890
Benson, Edward Frederic	1867-1940	Boldrewood, Rolf	1826-1915
Benson, Robert Hugh	1871-1914	Bonghi, Ruggero	1828-1895
Bentley, Edmund		Bonnard, Abel	1883-
Clerihew	1875-1956	Boothby, Guy Newell	1867-1905
Bercovici, Konrad	1881-	Bordeaux, Henri	1870-
Beresford, John Davys	1873-1947	Borrow, George Henry	1803-1881
Bergman, Bo Hjalmar	1869-	Bosanquet, Bernard	1848-1923
Bergman, Hjalmar		Bosboom, Toussaint, Anna	
Frederick Elgerus	1883-1931	Louisa Geertruida	1812-1886
Bergson, Henri	1859-1941	Bottomley, Gordon	1874-1948
Bernanos, Georges	1888-1948	Bouchor, Maurice	1855-1929
Bernard, Jean Jacques	1888-	Boucicault, Dion	1822-1890
Bernard, Tristan	1866-1947	Bourget, Paul Charles	
Barnhardi, Friedrich Von	1849-1930	Joseph	1852-1935
Bernstein, Henry	1876-1953	Bowen, Elizabeth	1889-
Bertrand, Louis	1866-1941	Bowen, Francis	1811-1890
Besant, Annie	1847-1933	Bowers, Claude G.	1878-
Besant, Sir Walter	1836-1901	Boyd, Andrew Kennedy	
Betti, Ugo	1892-1954	Hutchinson	1825-1899
Bialik, Hayim Nachman	1873-1934	Boyd, Ernest	1887-1946
Biedermann, Friedrich		Boyesen, Hjalmar	1848-1895
Karl	1812-1901	Boylesve, Rene	1867-1926
Bierce, Ambrose	1842-1916	Braddon, Mary Elizabeth	1837-1915
Biggers, Earl Derr	1884-1933	Bradford, Gameliel	1863-1932
Billinger, Richard	1893-	Bradley, Andrew Cecil	1851-1935
Binding, Rudolf George	1867-1938	Bradley, Edward	1827-1889
Binyon, Laurence	1869-1943	Bradley, Francis Herbert	1846-1924
Birrell, Augustine	1850-1933	Braithwaite, William	
Bishop, Isabella	1831-1904	Stanley Beaumont	1878-
Biornson, Bjornstjerne	1832-1910	Brailsford, Henry Noel	1873-1958
Black, William	1841-1898	Braga, Theophilo	1843-1924
Blackie, John Stuart	1809-1895	Bramah, Ernest	1867-1942
Blackmore, Richard		Brandes, Gorge Maurice	
Doddridge	1825-1900	Cohen	1842-1927
Blackwood, Algernon		Braun, Lily	1865-1916
Henry	1869-1951	Brazil, Angela	1868-1947
Blanc, Jean Joseph		Breasted, James Henry	1865-1935
Charles Louis	1811-1882	Brecht, Berthold Eugen	
Blavatsky, Helena Petrova	1831-1891	Friedrich	1898-1956
Blind, Mathilde	1847-1896	Bremond, Henri	1865-1933
Blixen, Karen, Baroness	1885-1962	Brentano, Franz	1838-1917
Bloch, Jean Richard	1884-1947	Breton, Andre	1896-
Blok, Alexander	1880-1921	Bridie, James	1888-1951
Blok, Petrus Johannes	1855-1932	Bridges, Robert Seymour	1844-1930
Blondel, Maurice	1861-1939	Brierly, Benjamin	1825-1896
Blood, Benjamin Paul	1832-1919	Brieux, Eugene	1858-1832
Blouet, Paul	1848-1903	Brittain, Vera	1893-
Bloy, Leon	1846-1917	Broad, Charles Dunbar	1887-
Blunck, Hans Friedrich	1888-	Brod, Max	1884-
Blunden, Edmund Charles	1896-	Brokmeyer, Henry	
Blunt, Wilfrid Scawen	1840-1922	Conrad	1828-1906
Boas, Franz	1858-1942	Bromfield, Louis	1896-1956
Bodenheim, Maxwell	1892-1959	Brooke, Rupert Chawner	1887-1915
Bodenstedt, Friedrich		Brooke, Stopford	
Martin, Von	1819-1892	Augustus	1832-1916
		Brooks, Phillips	1835-1894

Brooks, Van Wyek	1886-1963	Calvet, Jean	1874-
Broughton, Rhoda	1840-1920	Calvo, Carlos	1824-1906
Broun, Heywood	1888-1939	Cammaerts, Emile	1878-1953
Brown, Alice	1857-1948	Campoamor Y Campoosorio,	
Brown, George Douglas	1869-1902	Raymon De	1819-1901
Brown, Peter Hume	1850-1918	Canth, Minna	1844-1897
Brown, Thomas Edward	1830-1897	Cantu, Cesare	1804-1895
Browning, Oscar	1837-1923	Capek, Karel	1890-1938
Browning, Robert	1812-1889	Capern, Edward	1819-1894
Brownson, Orestes		Capuana, Luigi	1839-1915
Augustus	1803-1876	Capus, Alfred	1858-1922
Brugsch, Heinrich Karl	1827-1894	Caraglia, Joan	1852-1912
Brunner, Henry	1840-1915	Carco, Francis	1886-1958
Bryant, William Cullen	1794-1878	Carducci, Giosue	1835-1907
Bryce, Lloyd Stephens	1851-1917	Carleton, Will	1845-1912
Bryussov, Valery		Carlen, Emilia Smith	
Yakovlevitch	1873-1924	Flygare	1807-1892
Buber, Martin	1878-	Carman, Bliss	1861-1929
Buchan, John	1875-1940	Carlyle, Thomas	1795-1881
Buchanan, Robert		Carmen, Sylva	1843-1916
Williams	1841-1901	Carnap, Rudolf	1891-
Buchner, Ludwig	1824-1899	Carnegie, Andrew	1835-1918
Bucholtz, Johannes	1882-1940	Caro, Emile Marie	1826-1887
Buck, Pearl Sydenstricker	1892-	Carossa, Hans	1878-1956
Buckle, George Earle	1854-1935	Carpenter, Edward	1844-1929
Buckstone, John Baldwin	1802-1879	Carr, Edward Hallett	1892-
Bull, Olav Jacob Martin		Carr, Joseph William	
Luther	1883-1933	Comyns	1849-1916
Bullett, Gerald	1893-1958	Carriere, Moritz	1817-1895
Bunin, Ivan Alexeyevich	1870-1953	Carton, R. C.	1853-1928
Burckhardt, Jakob	1818-1897	Cary, Joyce	1888-1957
Burgess, John Bagnold	1830-1897	Cassirer, Ernst	1874-1945
Burke, Kenneth	1897-	Castello, Branco Camillo	1825-1890
Burke, Thomas	1886-1945	Castro, Eugenio De	1869-1944
Burnand, Frederick		Cather, Willa Sibert	1876-1947
Gustavus	1842-1885	Cavalcaselle, Giovanni	
Burnett, William Riley	1899-	Battista	1820-1897
Burnett, Frances Eliza		Cazalis, Henri	1840-1909
Hodgson	1849-1924	Cecchi, Emilio	1884-
Burroughs, Edgar Rice	1875-1950	Champfleury	1821-1889
Burroughs, John	1837-1921	Chantavoine, Henri	1850-1918
Burrows, Montague	1819-1905	Chapman, John Jay	1862-1933
Burton, John Hill	1809-1881	Chardonne, Jacques	1884-
Burton, Sir Richard		Charles, Elizabeth	1828-1896
Francis	1821-1890	Chase, Mary Ellen	1887-
Bury, John Bagnell	1861-1927	Chase, Stuart	1888-
Butler, Nicholas Murray	1862-1947	Chatrian, Alexandre	
Butler, Samuel	1835-1902	(Erkman, Chatrian)	1826-1890
Buysse, Cyriez	1859-1932	Chatterji Bankim, Chandra	1838-1894
Byron, Henry James	1834-1884	Chausson, Ernest	1855-1899
Caballero, Fernan	1796-1877	Chekhov, Anton Pavlovich	1860-1904
Cabell, James Branch	1879-1958	Cherbuliez, Charles	
Cable, George Washington	1844-1925	Victor	1829-1899
Caine, Sir Thomas Henry		Chernyshevsky, Nikolay	
Hall	1853-1931	Gavrilovich	1828-1889
Caird, Edward	1835-1908	Cheruel, Pierre Adolphe	1809-1891
Caird, John	1820-1898	Chesney, Charles	
Calderon, George	1868-1915	Cornwallis	1826-1876
Calderwood, Henry	1830-1897	Chesterton, Gilbert Keith	1874-1936
Calvert, George Henry	1803-1889	Chevalier, Gabriel	1895-

Chiarelli, Luigi	1894-1947	Couperus, Louis	1863-1923
Chiesa, Francesco	1871-	Courteline, Georges	1860-1929
Child, Francis James	1825-1896	Courthope, William John	1842-1917
Chopin, Kate	1851-1904	Coward, Noel	1899-
Christie, Agatha Mary		Cox, Sir George William	1827-1902
Clarissa	1891-	Craddock, Charles Egbert	1850-1922
Church, Richard	1893-	Craig, Edward Gordon	1872-
Churchill, Winston	1871-1947	Craigie, Pearl Mary	
Churchill, Sir Winston		Teresa	1867-1906
Spencer	1874-1965	Craik, Dinah Maria	1826-1887
Cibrario, Luigi Count	1802-1870	Crane, Harold Hart	1899-1932
Cladel, Leon	1835-1892	Crane, Stephen	1871-1900
Claretie, Jules Arsene		Craven, Pauline	1808-1891
Arnaud	1840-1913	Crawford, Francis Marion	1854-1909
Clark, William George	1821-1878	Creasy, Sir Edward	
Clarke, Charles Cowden	1787-1877	Shepherd	1812-1878
Clarke, Marcus Andrew		Creighton, Mandell	1843-1901
Hislop	1846-1881	Cremazie, Octave	1822-1879
Claudel, Paul	1868-1955	Cremer, Jakobus Jan	1827-1880
Claussen, Sophus Niels		Cremieux, Benjamin	1888-1944
Christen	1865-1931	Croce, Benedetto	1866-1952
Clemencau, George	1841-1929	Crockett, Samuel	
Clifford, William Kingdon	1845-1879	Rutherford	1860-1914
Clowes, Sir William Laird	1856-1905	Cronin, Archibald Joseph	1896-
Cobb, Irwin Shrewsbury	1876-1944	Crothers, Rachel	1878-
Cobbe, Frances Power	1822-1904	Crozier, John Beattie	1849-1921
Cocteau, Jean	1891-1964	Csengery, Antal	1822-1880
Cohan, George Michael	1878-1942	Csiky, Gregor	1842-1891
Cole, Sir Henry	1808-1882	Cullum, George	
Colet, Louise	1810-1876	Washington	1809-1892
Colette, Sidonie Gabrielle	1873-1954	Cummings, Edward Estlin	1894-
Collett, Jacobine Camilla	1813-1895	Cumont, Franz Valery	
Collier, John Payne	1789-1883	Marie	1868-1947
Collingwood, Robin		Cunninghame, Graham	
George	1899-1943	Robert Bontine	1852-1936
Collins, William Wilkie	1824-1889	Curel, Francois	
Colomb, Philip Howard	1831-1899	Vicomte De	1854-1928
Colum, Padraic	1881-	Curtis, George William	1824-1892
Connelly, Marcus (Marc)		Curtius, Ernst	1814-1896
Cook	1890-	Curtius, Georg	1820-1885
Conscience, Hendrik	1812-1883	Curwood, James Oliver	1878-1927
Conrad, Joseph	1857-1924	Cust, Sir Lionel Henry	1859-1929
Conrad, Noel	1899-	Dahn, Julius Sophus Felix	1834-1912
Conway, Hugh	1847-1885	Dalov, Jules	1838-1902
Conway, Moncure Daniel	1832-1907	D'Alviella, Count Goblet	1846-1925
Cook, Sir Edward Dutton	1829-1883	Daly, Augustin	1838-1899
Cook, Sir Edward Tyas	1857-1919	Dana, Richard Henry	1815-1882
Cooke, John Esten	1830-1886	D'Annunzio, Gabriele	1863-1938
Cooke, Rose Terry	1837-1892	Dantas, Julio	1876-
Coolidge, Susan	1835-1905	Dareste De La Chavanne,	
Coolus, Romaine	1868-1952	Cleophas	1820-1882
Coppee, Francois	1842-1908	Darmesteter, James	1849-1894
Coppee, Henry	1821-1895	Darwin, Charles Robert	1809-1882
Cooper, Alfred Duff		Daubler, Theodore	1876-1934
(1st Viscount Norwich)	1890-1954	Daudet, Alphonse	1840-1897
Corelli, Marie	1855-1924	Daudet, Ernest	1837-1921
Cossa, Pietro	1830-1881	Daudet, Leon	1867-1942
Costa, Joaquim	1846-1911	Davidson, John	1857-1909
Coster, Charles Theodore		Davidson, Thomas	1840-1900
Henri De	1827-1879	Davies, Hubert Henry	1869-1917

Davies, William Henry	1871-1940
Davis, Henry William Carless	1874-1928
Davis, Richard Harding	1864-1916
Debosis, Adolfo	1863-1924
Decelles, Alfred Duclos	1843-1925
De Court, Frans	1834-1878
Deeping, George Warwick	1877-1950
De Gaulle, Charles André Joseph Maurice	1890-
De Geer, Louis Gerhard Baron	1818-1896
Dehmel, Richard	1863-1920
Dekker, Edward Douwes	1820-1887
Delafield, E. M.	1890-1943
De La Mare, Walter John	1873-1956
Deland, Margaretta Wade	1857-1945
De La Roche, Mazo	1885-1961
Delbruck, Hans	1848-1929
Deledda, Grazia	1875-1936
Delisle, Leopold Victor	1826-1910
Dell, Ethel Mary	1881-1939
Demongeot, Jacques Claude	1808-1894
De Morgan, William Frend	1839-1917
Denifle, Heinrich Seuse	1844-1905
Dennery, Adolphe Philippe	1811-1899
Dent, John Charles	1841-1887
De Quincey, Thomas	1785-1859
Dereme, Tristan	1889-1941
Deroulede, Paul	1846-1914
De Tabley, John Byrne Leicester Warren	1835-1895
Deussen, Paul	1845-1919
Devere, Aubrey Thomas	1814-1902
Dewey, John	1859-1952
Dexter, Henry Martyn	1821-1890
Diaz, Daniel Vazquez	1882-
Dicey, Edward	1832-1911
Dickinson, Emily	1830-1886
Dickinson, Goldsworthy Lowes	1862-1932
Dieren, Bernard Van	1884-1936
Dierx, Leon	1838-1912
Digby, Kenelm Henry	1800-1880
Dilthey, Wilhelm	1833-1911
Dimitrov-Maistora, Vladimar	1882-
Dingelstedt, Franz Von	1814-1881
Dionne, Narcisse Eutrope	1848-1917
Disreali, Benjamin	1804-1881
Dixon, Richard Watson	1833-1900
Dixon, William Hepworth	1821-1879
Dobree, Bonamy	1891-
Dobson, Henry Austin	1840-1921
Dodge, Mary	1838-1905
Dodge, Theodore Aynault	1842-1909

Dodgson, Charles Lutwidge (Lewis Carrol)	1832-1898
Dollinger, Johann Joseph Ignaz Von	1799-1890
Domett, Alfred	1811-1887
Donnay, Charles Maurice	1859-1945
Doolittle, Hilda	1886-1961
Doran, John	1807-1878
Dos Passos, John Roderigo	1896-
Dostoievsky, Fyodor Mikhaylovich	1821-1881
Doughty, Sir Arthur George	1860-1936
Doughty, Charles Montegu	1843-1926
Douglas, Lord Alfred	1870-1945
Douglas, Norman	1868-1952
Douglas, Sir William Fettes	1822-1891
Dove, Alfred	1844-1916
Dowden, Edward	1843-1913
Dowson, Ernest	1867-1900
Doyle, Sir Arthur Conan	1859-1930
Dolye, Sir Francis Hastings Charles	1810-1888
Drachmann, Holger Henrik Herboldt	1846-1908
Drake, Friedrich	1805-1882
Dragomirov, Michael Ivanovich	1830-1905
Draper, William	1811-1882
Dreiser, Theodore	1871-1945
Drews, Arthur	1865-1935
Driesch, Hans Adolf Eduard	1867-1943
Drinkwater, John	1882-1937
Drobisch, Moritz Wilhelm	1802-1896
Droysen, Johann Gustav	1808-1884
Drummond, Henry	1851-1897
Duboc, Julius	1829-1903
Dubois, William Edward Burghardt	1868-
Du Bos, Charles	1882-1939
Du Camp, Maxine	1822-1894
Ducasse, Pierre Emmanuel Albert	1813-1893
Duclauz, Agnes Mary Frances	1857-1944
Duff, Sir Mountstuart Elphinstone Grant	1829-1906
Duhamel, George	1884-1966
Duhring, Eugen Karl	1833-1921
Dumas, Alexandre (fils)	1824-1895
Du Maurier, George Louis Palmella Busson	1834-1896
Dummler, Ernst Ludwig	1830-1902
Dunbar, Paul Laurence	1872-1906
Duncker, Maximilian Wolfgang	1811-1886
Dunne, John William	1875-1949

Fitzgerald, Percy	
Hetherington	1834-1925
Fitzgerald, Francis Scott	1896-1940
Flach, Geoffroi Jacques	1846-1919
Flammarion, Nicolas	
Camille	1842-1925
Flaubert, Gustave	1821-1880
Flecker, James Elroy	1884-1915
Flers, Robert De La Motte	
Ango	1872-1927
Fletcher, John Gould	1886-1950
Flint, Frank Stewart	1885-
Fogazzaro, Antonio	1842-1911
Fontaine, Theodor	1819-1898
Forbes, Rosita	1893-
Ford, Paul Leicester	1865-1902
Forester, Cecil Scott	1899-
Forsell, Hans Ludvig	1843-1901
Forster, E. M.	
(Edward Morgan)	1879-
Forster, John	1812-1876
Fort, Paul	1872-1960
Fortescue, Sir John	
William	1859-1933
Fortlage, Karl	1806-1881
Fouillee, Alfred Jules	
Emile	1838-1912
Fowler, Frank George	1871-1918
Fowler, Henry Watson	1858-1933
France, Anatole	1844-1924
Frank, Leonhard	1882-
Frank, Waldo David	1889-
Frankau, Gilbert	1884-1953
Frankl, Ludwig August	1810-1894
Franzos, Karl Emil	1848-1904
Fraser, Alexander	
Campbell	1819-1914
Frazer, Sir James George	1854-1941
Frechette, Louis Honore	1839-1908
Frederic, Harold	1856-1896
Freeman, Edward	
Augustus	1823-1892
Freeman, John	1880-1929
Freeman, Mary Eleanor	
Wilkins	1852-1930
Freiligrath, Ferdinand	1810-1876
Frenssen, Gustav	1863-1945
Freud, Sigmund	1856-1939
Frey, Adolf	1855-1920
Freytag, Gustav	1816-1895
Fried, Alfred Hermann	1864-1921
Friedjung, Heinrich	1851-1920
Froding, Gustav	1860-1911
Frohschammer, Jakob	1821-1893
Frost, Robert	1875-1963
Frothingham, Octavius	
Brooks	1822-1895
Froude, James Anthony	1818-1894
Fryxwell, Anders	1795-1881
Fucini, Renato	1843-1921

Fullerton, Lady Georgiana	
Charlotte	1812-1885
Fustel De Coulanges,	
Numa Denis	1830-1889
Fyffe, Charles Alan	1845-1892
Gachard, Louis Prosper	1800-1885
Gairdner, James	1828-1912
Gale, Zona	1874-1938
Galsworthy, John	1867-1933
Ganesh Datta Shastri,	
Shri Jagadguru	1861-1940
Ganivet, Angel	1865-1898
Garborg, Arne Evensen	1851-1924
Gardiner, Samuel Rawson	1829-1902
Garland, Hamlin	1860-1940
Garnett, David	1892-
Garnett, Edward	1868-1937
Garnett, Richard	1835-1906
Garshin, Vsevolod	
Mikhailovich	1855-1888
Gautier, Leon	1832-1897
Geddes, Patrick	1854-1932
Geibel, Emanuel	1815-1884
Geijer, Eric Gustav	1783-1877
Gentile, Giovanni	1875-1944
George, Henry	1839-1897
George Stefan	1868-1933
Gerstacker, Friedrich	1816-1877
Gervinus, George	
Gottfried	1805-1871
Gezelle, Guido	1830-1899
Ghika, Helena	1829-1888
Giacometti, Paolo	1816-1882
Giacosa, Guiseppe	1847-1906
Gibbings, Robert John	1889-1958
Gibbs, Sir Philip	1877-
Gibson, Wilfred Wilson	1878-
Gibson, William Hamilton	1850-1896
Gide, Andre Paul	
Guillaume	1869-1951
Giesebrecht, Wilhelm Von	1814-1889
Gilbert, Sir John Thomas	1829-1898
Gilbert, William	1804-1889
Gilbert, Sir William	
Schwenk	1836-1911
Gilder, Richard Watson	1844-1909
Gilgik, Iwan	1858-1924
Gill, Erik	1882-1940
Gillette, William Hooker	1853-1937
Gillies, William George	1898-
Gilman, Harold	1878-1919
Gilson, Etienne	1884-
Gindely, Anton	1829-1892
Giner De Los Rios,	
Francisco	1840-1915
Giraudoux, Hippolyte	
Jean	1882-1944
Gissing, George Robert	1857-1903
Gjellerup, Karl	1857-1919
Glasgow, Ellen	1874-1945

Glaspell, Susan	1882-1948	Gumilev, Nikolai	
Glassbrenner, Adolf	1810-1876	Stepanovich	1886-1921
Gleig, George Robert	1796-1888	Gunn, Neil Miller	1891-
Glinka, Fedor		Gurdjieff, George	
Nikolayevich	1788-1880	Ivanovitch	1868-1949
Glyn, Elinor	1864-1943	Guthrie, Thomas Anstey	1856-1934
Golding, Louis	1895-1958	Gutschmid, Alfred	1835-1887
Goldschmidt, Aaron Meier	1819-1887	Gutzkow, Karl Ferdinand	1811-1878
Gollancz, Victor	1893-	Guyau, Jean Marie	1854-1888
Gomperez, Theodor	1832-1912	Gyp	1849-1932
Goncharov, Ivan		Habberton, John	1842-1921
Alexandrovich	1812-1891	Hacklander, Friedrich	
Goncourt De, Edmond	1822-1896	Wilhelm Von	1816-1877
Gooch, George Peabody	1873-	Haggard, Sir Henry Rider	1856-1925
Gordon, Leon	1831-1892	Hahn-Hahn, Ida	1805-1880
Gorky, Maxim	1868-1936	Hake, Thomas Gordon	1809-1895
Gorst, Harold	1868-1950	Haldane, Elizabeth	
Gorter, Herman	1864-1933	Sanderson	1862-1937
Gosse, Sir Edmund	1849-1928	Haldane, Richard Burdon	
Gottschall, Rudolf Von	1823-1908	Haldane	1856-1928
Gould, John	1804-1881	Hale, Edward Everett	1822-1909
Gould, Nathaniel	1857-1919	Hale, Sarah Josepha	1788-1879
Gourmont, Remy De	1858-1915	Halevy, Daniel	1872-1962
Grahame, Kenneth	1859-1922	Halevy, Elie	1870-1937
Grand, Sarah	1862-1943	Halevy, Leon	1802-1883
Grant, James	1822-1887	Halevy, Ludovic	1834-1908
Granville-Barker,		Hall, Anna Maria	1800-1881
Harley Granville	1877-1946	Hall, Marguerite	
Gratz, Heinrich	1817-1891	Radclyffe	1886-1943
Graves, Alfred Percival	1846-1931	Hall, Samuel Carter	1800-1889
Graves, Robert Ranke	1895-	Hall, William Edward	1835-1894
Green, John Richard	1837-1883	Halliday, Andrew	1830-1877
Green, Julian	1900-	Hamerton, Philip Gilbert	1834-1894
Green, Mary Ann		Hamley, Sir Edward	
Everett	1818-1895	Bruce	1824-1893
Green, Thomas Hill	1836-1882	Hammerstein, Oscar	1895-1960
Greene, George		Hammond, John	
Washington	1811-1883	Lawrence Lebreton	1872-1949
Greg, William Rathbone	1809-1881	Hamp, Pierre	1876-
Gregorovius, Ferdinand	1821-1891	Hamsun, Knut	1859-1952
Gregory, Isabella Augusta	1852-1832	Handel-Mazzetti, Enrica	1871-1962
Grenfell, Julian	1888-1915	Hannay, James Owen	1865-1950
Greville, Henry	1842-1902	Hanotaux, Albert Auguste	
Grey, Zane	1872-1939	Gabriel	1853-1944
Grigorovich, Dmitri		Hansson, Ola	1860-1925
Vaslievich	1822-1900	Hardy, Thomas	1840-1928
Groome, Francis Hindes	1851-1902	Hare, Augustus John	
Grossmith, George	1847-1912	Cuthbert	1834-1903
Grub, George	1812-1892	Harland, Henry	1861-1905
Grundy, Sydney	1848-1914	Harraden, Beatrice	1864-1936
Grunewald, Isaak	1889-1946	Harris, Frank	1856-1931
Gubernatis, Angelo De	1840-1913	Harris, Joel Chandler	1848-1908
Guedalla, Phillip	1889-1944	Harrison, Frederic	1831-1923
Guerin, Charles	1873-1907	Hart, Albert Bushnell	1854-1942
Guerrini, Olinda	1845-1916	Harte, Francis Bret	1836-1902
Guest, Edgar Albert	1881-1959	Hartley, Leslie Poles	1895-
Guest, Edwin	1800-1880	Hartmann, Karl Robert	
Guimera, Angel	1849-1924	Eduard Von	1842-1906
Guitry, Sacha	1885-1957	Hartmann, Nicolai	1882-1950

Hartzenbusch, Juan		Hodgson, Shadworth	
Eugenio	1806-1880	Holloway	1832-1912
Harvey, Frederick		Hoetzsh, Otto	1876-1946
William	1888-	Hofer, Karl	1878-1955
Hasenclever, Walker	1890-1940	Hoffding, Harald	1843-1931
Hauptmann, Gerhart	1862-1946	Hoffmann, Heinrich	1809-1894
Haureau, Barthelemy	1812-1896	Hofmannsthal, Hugo Von	1874-1929
Haverfield, Francis John	1860-1919	Hogben, Lancelot	1895-
Havet, Julien	1853-1893	Holl, Karl	1866-1926
Hay, Ian	1876-1952	Holland, Josiah Gilbert	1819-1881
Hay, John	1838-1905	Holmes, Oliver Wendell	1809-1894
Haym, Rudolf	1821-1901	Holst, Hermann Eduard	
Hayward, Abraham	1801-1884	Von	1841-1904
Hazard, Rowland Gibson	1801-1888	Holtby, Winifred	1898-1935
Hecht, Ben	1894-	Holtei, Karl Eduard Von	1798-1880
Heckel, Erich	1883-	Holz, Arno	1863-1929
Heer, Jakob Christoph	1859-1925	Hope, Anthony	1863-1933
Heiberg, Gunnar Edward		Hopfen, Hans Von	1835-1904
Rode	1857-1929	Hopkins, Gerard Manley	1844-1889
Heidegger, Martin	1889-	Horne, Richard Henry	1803-1884
Heidenstam, Verner Von	1859-1940	Hornung, Ernest William	1866-1921
Heijermans, Hermann	1864-1924	Hosmer, James Kendall	1834-1927
Helmholtz, Hermann		Hostrup, Jews Christian	1818-1892
Ludwig Ferdinand Von	1821-1894	Houghton, Richard	
Hemingway, Ernest	1898-1961	Monckton Milnes	1809-1885
Henderson, William James	1855-1937	Houghton, William	
Henley, William Ernest	1849-1903	Stanley	1881-1913
Henry, O.	1862-1910	Housman, Alfred Edward	1859-1936
Henty, George Alfred	1832-1902	Housman, Laurence	1865-1959
Herbert, Allan Patrick	1890-	Houssaye, Arsene	1815-1896
Herculano De Carvalho,		Houssaye, Henry	1848-1911
E Araujo Alexandre	1810-1877	Howard, Sidney Coe	1891-1939
Herczeg, Ferenc	1863-	Howe, Julia Ward	1819-1910
Heredia, Jose Maria De	1842-1905	Howells, Herbert	1892-
Hergesheimer, Joseph	1880-1954	Howells, William Dean	1837-1920
Hermant, Abel	1862-1950	Howitt, Mary	1799-1888
Hernandez, Jose	1854-1886	Howitt, William	1792-1879
Herne, Jame A.	1840-1901	Hubbard, Elbert	1856-1915
Herrick, Robert	1868-1938	Huch, Ricarda	1864-1947
Hervieu, Paul	1857-1915	Hudson, William Henry	1841-1922
Hesse, Herman	1877-1962	Huggenberger, Alfred	1867-
Hewlett, Maurice Henry	1861-1923	Hughes, Clovis	1851-1907
Heyse, Paul Johann		Hughes, Thomas	1822-1896
Ludwig Von	1830-1914	Hugo, Victor Marie	1802-1885
Hichens, Robert Smythe	1864-1950	Hulme, Thomas Ernest	1883-1917
Higginson, Thomas		Hume, Fergus	1859-1932
Wentworth	1823-1911	Hutton, Arthur Wollaston	1848-1912
Hill, George Birbeck		Hutton, Richard Holt	1826-1897
Norman	1835-1903	Huxley, Aldous Leonard	1894-1963
Hillebrand, Karl	1829-1884	Huxley, Sir Julien Sorell	1887-
Hilton, James	1900-1954	Huxley, Thomas Henry	1825-1895
Himly, Louis-Auguste	1823-1906	Huysmans, Joris Karl	1848-1907
Hippius, Zinaida	1869-1945	Hyde, Douglas	1860-1949
Hitler, Adolf	1889-1945	Hyne, Charles John	
Hobhouse, Leonard		Cutliffe Wright	1865-1944
Trelawney	1864-1929	Ibanez, Vincent Blasco	1867-1928
Hocking, Silas Kitto	1850-1935	Ibsen, Henrick Johan	1828-1906
Hodgkin, Thomas	1831-1913	Ihne, Wilhelm	1821-1902
Hodgson, John Evan	1831-1895	Ilg, Paul	1876-
Hodgson, Ralph	1871-1962	Inge, William Ralph	1860-1954

Ingelow, Jean	1820-1897	Kahn, Gustave	1859-1936
Ingleby, Clement		Kaiser, Georg	1878-1945
Manfried	1823-1886	Karr, Alphonse	1808-1890
Ingraham, Prentice	1843-1904	Kate, Jaeds Lodewykten	1819-1884
Innes, Arthur Donald	1863-1938	Kastner, Erich	1899-
Iqbal, Sir Mohammed	1875-1938	Kaufman, George Simon	1889-1961
Isaacs, Jorge	1837-1895	Kaye-Smith, Sheila	1887-1956
Ivanov, Vyacheslav		Keightley, Thomas	1789-1872
Ivanovich	1866-1949	Kellermann, Bernhard	1879-1951
Jacks, Laurence Pearsall	1860-1955	Keller, Gottfried	1819-1890
Jackson, Frederick John		Kendall, Henry Clarence	1841-1882
Foakes	1855-1941	Kenealy, Edward Vaughan	
Jackson, Helen Maria	1831-1885	Hyde	1819-1880
Jacob, Naomi Ellington	1889-1964	Kennedy, Margaret	1896-
Jacob, Violet	1863-1946	Kervyn De Lettenhove,	
Jacobs, William Wymark	1863-1943	Joseph	1817-1891
Jacobsen, Jens Peter	1847-1885	Key, Ellen	1849-1926
James, Henry	1843-1916	Keyserling, Hermann	1880-1946
James, Montague Rhodes	1862-1936	Kielland, Alexander	1849-1906
James, William	1842-1910	Kilmer, Joyce	1886-1918
Jameson, Storm	1897-	Kinck, Hans Ernst	1865-1926
Jammes, Francis	1868-1938	Kinglake, Alexander	
Jane, Frederick Thomas	1870-1916	William	1809-1891
Janssen, Johannes	1829-1891	Kingsley, Henry	1830-1876
Jaspers, Karl	1883-	Kingston, William Henry	
Jebavy, Vaclav	1868-1929	Giles	1814-1880
Jebb, Sir Richard		Kinkel, Johann Gottfried	1815-1882
Claverhouse	1841-1905	Kipling, Rudyard	1865-1936
Jefferies, Richard	1848-1887	Klabund	1891-1928
Jeffers, John Robinson	1887-1962	Klaczko, Julian	1825-1906
Jensen, Johannes Vilhelm	1873-1950	Knox, Edmund George	
Jensen, Wilhelm	1837-1911	Valpy	1881-
Jerome, Jerome Klapka	1859-1927	Koch, Ludwig	1881-
Jesse, Fryn Tennyson	1889-1958	Kolcsey, Ferencz	1790-1888
Jewett, Sarah Orne	1849-1909	Korolenko, Vladimir	
Jewsbury, Geraldine		Galaktionovich	1853-1921
Endsor	1812-1880	Korzybski, Alfred Habdank	
Jimenez, Juan Ramon	1881-1958	Skarbek	1879-1950
Joad, Cyril Edwin		Kraszewski, Joseph	
Mitchinson	1891-1953	Ignatius	1812-1887
Johnson, James Weldon	1871-1938	Kraus, Karl	1874-1936
Johnson, Lionel Pigot	1867-1902	Krehbiel, Henry Edward	1854-1923
Joinville, Francois		Kretzer, Marx	1854-1941
Fernand D'Orleans	1818-1900	Kropotkin, Peter	
Jokai, Maurus	1825-1904	Alexeivich	1842-1921
Jones, Henry	1831-1899	Ku, Hung-Ming	1856-1928
Jones, Henry Arthur	1851-1929	Kulpe, Oswald	1868-1915
Jordan, Wilhelm	1819-1904	Kuprin, Alexander	
Jorga, Nicholas	1871-1940	Ivanovich	1870-1938
Jorgensen, Johannes	1866-1951	Labiche, Euegene Marin	1815-1888
Joyce, James	1882-1941	Lacaita, Sir James	1813-1895
Judson, Edward Zane		Ladd, George Trumbull	1842-1921
Carroll	1823-1886	Laforgue, Jules	1860-1887
Jung, Carl Gustav	1875-1964	Lagerlof, Selma	1858-1940
Junqueiro, Abilio Guena	1850-1923	Lagerkvist, Par	1891-
Jusserand, Jean Adrien		Laing, Samuel	1810-1897
Antoine Jules	1855-1932	Laird, John	1887-1946
Kafka, Franz	1883-1924	Lane, Edward William	1801-1876
Kagawa, Toyohiko	1888-1960	Lane-Poole, Reginald	1857-1939
		Lane-Poole, Stanley	1854-1931

Lanfrey, Pierre	1828-1877
Lang, Andrew	1844-1912
Lanier, Sidney	1842-1881
Lapidoth-Swarth, Helene	1859-1941
Laprade, Pierre Marin	
Victor Richard De	1812-1883
Larbaud, Valery	1881-1957
Lardner, Ring W.	1885-1933
Laski, Harold Joseph	1893-1950
Laube, Heinrich	1806-1884
Lauff, Joseph	1855-1933
Laurent, Francios	1810-1887
Lavedan, Henri Leon	
Emile	1859-1940
Laver, James	1899-
Lavissee, Ernest	1842-1922
Lawless, Emily	1845-1913
Lawrence David Herbert	1885-1930
Lawrence, George Alfred	1827-1876
Lawrence, Thomas	
Edward	1888-1935
Layard, Sir Austen	
Henry	1817-1894
Lazarus, Emma	1849-1887
Lazarus, Moritz	1824-1903
Lea, Henry Charles	1825-1909
Leacock, Stephen Butler	1869-1944
Lecky, William Edward	
Hartpole	1838-1903
Leconte De Lisle, Charles	
Marie Rene	1818-1894
Lee, Sir Sidney	1859-1926
Le Gallienne, Richard	1866-1947
Legouve, Gabriel Jean	
Baptist Ernest Wilfred	1807-1903
Leland, Charles Godfrey	1824-1903
Lemaitre, Jules	1853-1914
Le Moine, James	
MacPherson	1825-1912
Lemonnier, Antoine	
Louis Camile	1844-1913
Lenin, Vladimir Iliych	
Ulyanov	1870-1924
Lenormand, Henri-Rene	1882-1951
Leo, Heinrich	1799-1878
Le Queux, William	
Tufnell	1864-1927
Leskov, Nikolai	
Semenovich	1831-1895
Levertin, Oscar Ivan	1862-1906
Levy-Bruhl, Lucien	1857-1939
Lewald, Fanny	1811-1889
Lewes, George Henry	1817-1878
Lewis, Clive Staples	1898-1963
Lewis, Sinclair	1885-1951
Lewis, Wyndham	1884-1957
Lhote, Andre	1885-
Lie, Jonas Lauritz	
Edemil	1833-1908

Liebrecht, Felix	1812-1890
Liliencron, Detlev Von	1844-1909
Lind-Af-Hageby, Emelie	
Augusta Louisa	1878-
Lindau, Paul	1839-1919
Lindau, Rudolf	1829-1910
Lindo, Mark Prager	1819-1879
Lindsay, Nicholas Vachel	1879-1931
Linklater, Eric	1899-
Lin, Yutang	1895-
Lippincott, Sara Jane	
Clarke	1823-1904
Lissauer, Ernst	1882-1937
Littlefiel, Walter	1867-1948
Littre, Maximilien Paul	
Emile	1801-1881
Ljunggren, Gustaf Haken	
Jordan	1823-1905
Locke, William John	1863-1930
Locker-Lampson, Frederick	1821-1895
Lodge, Henry Cabot	1850-1924
London, John Griffith	
(Jack)	1876-1916
Longfellow, Henry	
Wadsworth	1807-1882
Lönnrot, Elias	1802-1884
Lonsdale, Frederick	1881-1954
Lorca, Federige, Garcia	1899-1936
Lossing, Benson John	1813-1891
Losski, Nikolai	
Onufreivich	1870-
Loti, Pierre	1850-1923
Lotze, Rudolf Hermann	1817-1881
Louys, Pierre	1870-1925
Lowell, Amy	1874-1925
Lowell, James Russell	1819-1891
Lubbock, Percy	1879-
Lubke, Wilhelm	1826-1893
Lucas, Edward Verrall	1868-1938
Lucas, Frank Lawrence	1894-
Luchaire, Achille	1846-1908
Lucka, Emil	1877-1941
Ludwig, Emil	1861-1948
Lu Hsun	1881-1936
Lummis, Charles Fletcher	1859-1928
Lunacharsky, Anatoly	
Vasilievich	1875-1933
Lund, Troels Frederick	1840-1921
Lyall, Edna	1857-1903
Lynd, Robert	1879-1949
Lytton, Edward Robert	
Bulwer-Lytton	1831-1891
Maartens, Maarten	1858-1915
Macaulay, Rose	1889-1958
MacCarthy, Denis	
Florence	1817-1882
MacCarthy, Sir Desmond	1878-1952
M'Carthy, Justin	1830-1912
McCord, Louise Susanna	
Cheves	1810-1879

McDiarmid, Hugh	1892-		Martineau, James	1805-1900
MacDonald, George	1824-1905		Martinez, Gregorio	1881-1947
MacGowan, Kenneth	1888-		Martini, Ferdinando	1841-1928
MacGregor, John	1825-1892		Marx, Karl Heinrich	1818-1883
Mach, Ernst	1838-1916		Masefield, John	1878-
Machado, Antonio	1875-1939		Mason, Alfred Edward	
Machar, Jan Svatopluk	1864-1942		Woodley	1865-1948
Mackay, Charles	1814-1889		Mason, Walt	1862-1939
Mackaye, Percy	1875-		Massey, Gerald	1828-1907
Mackaye, Steele	1842-1894		Masson, David	1822-1907
Mackenzie, Edward			Masson, Frederic	1847-1923
Montague Compton	1883-		Masters, Edgar Lee	1869-1950
MacLeish, Archibald	1892-		Matthews, Brander	1852-1929
M'cMaster, John Bach	1852-1932		Maugham, William	
MacNeill, John Gordon			Somerset	1874-1965
Swift	1849-1926		Maupassant, Henri Rene	
M'Cosh, James	1811-1894		Albert Guy de	1850-1893
M'cTaggart, John			Mauriac, Francois	1885-
M'cTaggart Ellis	1866-1925		Maurois, Andre	1885-
Madariaga, Salvador De	1866-		Maurras, Charles	1868-1952
Maeterlinck, Maurice	1862-1949		Mayakovsky, Vladimir	1894-1930
Magny, Claude Drigon	1797-1897		Mayhew, Henry	1812-1887
Mahan, Alfred Thayer	1840-1914		Medina, Jose Toribio	1852-1930
Maine, Sir Henry James			Mee, Arthur	1875-1943
Sumner	1822-1888		Mehring, Franz	1846-1919
Maironis	1862-1932		Meilhac, Henri	1831-1897
Maitland, Edward	1824-1897		Melville, Herman	1819-1891
Maitland, Frederic			Menard, Louis Nicholas	1822-1901
William	1850-1906		Mendes, Catulle	1841-1909
Major, Richard Henry	1818-1891		Menendez y Pelayo,	
Malet, Lucas	1852-1931		Marcelino	1856-1912
Mallarme, Stephane	1842-1898		Merezhkovsky, Dmitri	
Malleson, George Bruce	1825-1898		Sergeievich	1865-1941
Mallock, William Hurrell	1849-1923		Meredith, George	1828-1909
Maning, Frederick			Merivale, Charles	1808-1893
Edward	1812-1883		Merrick, Leonard	1864-1939
Mann, Heinrich	1871-1950		Mesonero Romanos,	
Mann, Thomas	1875-1955		Ramon De	1803-1882
Mansfield, Katharine	1888-1923		Meurice, Paul	1818-1905
Mao-Tun	1896-		Mew, Charlotte	1870-1928
Marcel, Gabriel	1889-		Meyer, Conrad Ferdinand	1825-1898
Marguerite, Paul	1860-1918		Meyer, Eduard	1855-1930
Marguerite, Victor	1866-1942		Meynell, Alice	1849-1922
Marinetti, Filippo			Mignet, Francois Auguste	
Tommaso	1876-1944		Marie	1796-1884
Maritain, Jacques	1882-		Millay, Edna St. Vincent	1892-1950
Markham, Edwin	1852-1940		Miller, Henry	1891-
Marquand, John Phillip	1893-1960		Miller, Joaquin	1841-1913
Marquardt, Joachim	1812-1882		Milne, Alan Alexander	1882-1956
Marquis, Donald Robert			Milyukov, Paul	
Perry	1878-1937		Nikolayevich	1859-1942
Marradi, Giovanni	1852-1922		Mirbeau, Octave Henri	
Marryat, Florence	1838-1899		Marie	1850-1917
Marston, John Westland	1819-1890		Mistral, Frederic	1830-1914
Marston, Philip Bourke	1850-1887		Mitchell, Donald Grant	1822-1908
Martin Du Gard, Roger	1881-		Mitchell, Margaret	1900-1949
Martin, Henri	1810-1883		Mitchison, Naomi	
Martin, Sir Theodore	1816-1909		Margaret	1897-
Martin, Violet Florence	1862-1915		Moeran, Edward James	1895-1950
Martineau, Marriet	1802-1876		Molesworth, Mary Louisa	1839-1921

Molesworth, William			Newton, Eric	1893-
Nassau	1816-1890		Nexo, Martin Anderson	1869-1954
Molnar, Ferenc	1878-1952		Nichol, John	1833-1894
Mommsen, Theodor	1817-1903		Nichols, Robert Malise	
Monkhouse, William			Bowyer	1893-1944
Cosmo	1840-1901		Nicholson, Meredith	1866-1947
Monnier, Marc	1829-1885		Nicoll, Maurice	1884-1953
Monod, Gabriel	1844-1912		Nicolson, Sir Harold	
Monroe, Harriet	1860-1936		George	1886-
Montague, Charles Edward	1867-1928		Nietzshe, Friedrich	
Montherlant, Henri			Wilhelm	1844-1900
Millon de	1896-		Nitzsch, Karl Wilhelm	1818-1880
Montufar, Lorenzo	1823-1898		Noailles, Anna Elizabeth	
Moody, William Vaughan	1869-1910		Comptesse De	1876-1933
Moore, George	1852-1933		Noailles, Paul Duke of	1802-1885
Moore, Marianne Craig	1887-		Noel, Roden Berkeley	
Morand, Paul	1889-		Wriothesleu	1834-1894
More, Paul Elmer	1864-1937		Nordau, Max Simon	1848-1923
Moreas, Jean	1856-1910		Norris, Frank	1870-1902
Morgan, Charles	1894-1958		Norris, Kathleen	1880-
Morley, Christopher			Norris, William Edward	1847-1925
Darlington	1890-1957		Norton, Caroline Elizabeth	
Morley, Henry	1822-1894		Sarah	1808-1877
Morley, John Morley	1838-1923		Norton, Charles Eliot	1827-1908
Morris, Sir Lewis	1833-1907		Nouy, Pierre Lecompte du	1883-1947
Morris, William	1834-1896		Noyes, Alfred	1880-1958
Morrison, Arthur	1863-1945		Nunez De Arce, Gaspar	1834-1903
Morton, Henry Vollam	1892-		O'Casey, Sean	1884-1964
Morton, John Maddison	1811-1891		O'Faolain, Sean	1900-
Motley, John Lothrop	1814-1877		O'Flaherty, Liam	1897-
Mottram, Ralph Hale	1883-		O'Grady Standish James	1846-1928
Moulton, Louise Chandler	1835-1908		Ohnet, Georges	1848-1918
Muir, Edwin	1887-1959		Oliphant, Laurence	1829-1888
Muir, John	1838-1914		Oliphant, Margaret	
Muirhead, John Henry	1855-1940		Oliphant	1828-1897
Munro, Hector Hugh			Oliveira, Martins Joaquim	
(Saki)	1870-1916		Pedro De	1845-1894
Munsterberg, Hugo	1863-1916		Oman, Sir Charles	
Munthe, Axel	1857-1949		William Chadwick	1860-1946
Murray, Gilbert	1866-1957		O'Neill, Eugene Gladstone	1888-1953
Murry, John Middleton	1889-1957		Oppenheim, Edward	
Myers, Frederick William			Phillips	1866-1946
Henry	1843-1901		Opzoomer, Cornelius	
Nabokov, Vladimir	1899-		William	1821-1892
Naden, Constance			Orczy, Baroness Emmuska	1865-1947
Caroline Woodhill	1858-1889		Orzeszkowa, Eliza	1842-1910
Naidu, Sarojini	1879-1949		Osbourne, Lloyd	1868-1947
Namier, Sir Lewis			O'Shaughnessy, Arthur	
Bernstein	1888-1960		William Edgar	1844-1880
Nazor, Vladimir	1876-1949		Ostrovsky, Alexander	
Neal, John	1793-1876		Nikolaevich	1823-1886
Nehru, Jawaharlal	1889-1964		Ouida	1839-1908
Nekrasov, Nikolai			Ouspensky, P. D.	-1947
Alexeyevich	1821-1877		Owen, Wilfred	1893-1918
Neruda, Jan	1834-1891		Page, Thomas Nelson	1853-1922
Nettleship, Richard Lewis	1846-1892		Page, Walter Hines	1855-1918
Newbolt, Sir Henry John	1862-1938		Pain, Barry Eric Odell	1865-1928
Newman, Francis William	1805-1897		Palacio, Valdes Armando	1853-1938
Newman, John Henry			Palacky, Frantisek	1798-1876
(Cardinal)	1801-1890		Palamas, Kostes	1859-1943

T

Paleologue, Maurice	
Georges	1859-1944
Palfrey, John Gorham	1796-1881
Palgrave, Sir Francis	1788-1861
Palgrave, Francis Turner	1824-1897
Paludan-Muller, Frederik	1809-1876
Panzini, Alfredo	1863-1939
Paoli, Cesare	1840-1902
Papini, Giovanni	1881-1956
Pardo Bazan, Emilia	1851-1921
Pares, Sir Bernard	1867-1949
Paris, Gaston	1839-1903
Parker, Dorothy	1893-
Parker, Sir Gilbert	1862-1932
Parkman, Francis	1823-1893
Parton, James	1822-1891
Partridge, Eric	
Honeywood	1894-
Pascoli, Giovanni	1855-1912
Pasternak, Boris	
Leonidovich	1890-1960
Pater, Walter Horatio	1839-1894
Paterson, Andrew Barton	
("Banjo")	1864-1941
Patmore, Coventry Kersey	
Bighton	1823-1896
Pattison, Mark	1813-1884
Paul, Charles Kiegan	1828-1902
Pauli, Reinhold	1823-1882
Paulsen, Friedrich	1846-1908
Payn, James	1830-1898
Paz Soldan, Mariano	
Felipe	1821-1886
Peabody, Andrew Preston	1811-1893
Peabody, Josephine	
Preston	1874-1922
Peacock, Thomas Love	1785-1866
Pearse, Patrick Henry	1879-1916
Pearson, Hesketh	1887-1964
Peesemsky, Alexey	
Feofilactovich	1820-1881
Peguy, Charles	1873-1914
Peirce, Charles Sanders	1839-1914
Pelham, Henry Francis	1846-1907
Pellico, Silvo	1788-1854
Pereda, Jose Maria De	1833-1906
Perez De Ayala, Ramon	1881-1962
Perez Galdos, Benito	1845-1920
Perry, Bliss	1860-1945
Pertz, Georg Heinrich	1795-1876
Petersen, Nis	1897-1943
Pfleiderer, Edmund	1842-1902
Phillips, Stephen	1868-1915
Phillpotts, Eden	1862-1960
Pinero, Sir Arthur Wing	1855-1934
Pilnyak, Boris	1894-1938
Pirandello, Luigi	1867-1936
Pirenne, Henry	1862-1935
Pitter, Ruth	1897-
Planche, James Robinson	1796-1880

Plekhanov, Georgy	
Valentinovich	1857-1918
Plieksans, Jan	1865-1929
Pollard, Alfred Frederick	1869-1948
Pontoppidan, Henrik	1857-1943
Poole, William Frederick	1821-1894
Porter, Gene Stratton	1868-1924
Porter, Katherine Anne	1894-
Porter, Noah	1811-1892
Porto-Riche, Georges De	1849-1930
Post, Melville Davisson	1871-1930
Potter, Beatrix	1866-1943
Potter, Stephen	1900-
Potthast, August	1824-1898
Pound, Ezra	1885-
Powell, Frederick York	1850-1904
Powys, John Cowper	1872-1963
Powys, Llewelyn	1884-1939
Prantl, Karl Von	1820-1888
Prati, Giovanni	1815-1884
Prel, Karl	1839-1899
Prescott, Harriet	
Elizabeth	1835-1921
Prevost, Eugene Marcel	1862-1941
Pribram, Alfred Francis	1859-1942
Priestly, John Boynton	1894-
Proust, Marcel	1871-1922
Prus, Boleslaw	1847-1912
Prutz, Hans	1843-1929
Przybyszewski, Stanislaw	1868-1927
Psichari, Ernest	1883-1914
Purnell, Thomas	1834-1889
Pusey, Edward Bouverie	1800-1882
Quental, Anthero De	1842-1891
Quicherat, Jules Etienne	
Joseph	1814-1882
Quiller-Couch, Sir Arthur	
Thomas	1863-1944
Quintero, Joaquin Alvarez	1873-1944
Quintero, Serafin Alvarez	1871-1938
Radhakrishnan,	
Sir Sarvepalli	1888-
Ragabe, Alexandros Rizos	1810-1892
Raleigh, Sir Walter	1861-1922
Rambaud, Alfred Nicolas	1842-1905
Ramuz, Charles Ferdinand	1878-1947
Ranc, Arthur	1831-1908
Randall, James Ryder	1839-1908
Rands, William Brighty	1823-1882
Ranke, Leopold Von	1795-1886
Ransome, Arthur Mitchell	1884-
Rashdall, Hastings	1858-1924
Rasmussen, Knud Johan	
Victor	1879-1933
Ravaisson-Mollien, Jean	
Gaspard Felix	1813-1900
Rawlinson, George	1812-1902
Read, Sir Herbert	1893-
Reade, Charles	1814-1884
Realf, Richard	1834-1878

Reboux, Paul	1877-1963	Ross, Janet Anne	1842-1927
Reclus, Jean Jacques		Rossetti, Dante Gabriel	1828-1882
Elisée	1830-1905	Rossetti, Christina	
Regnier, Henri Francois		Georgina	1830-1894
Joseph De	1864-1936	Rossetti, William Michael	1829-1919
Reichenbach, Hans	1891-1953	Rostand, Edmond	1869-1918
Reid, Thomas Mayne	1818-1883	Roumanille, Joseph	1818-1891
Reinach, Joseph	1856-1921	Royce, Josiah	1855-1916
Remarque, Erich Maria	1898-	Rozanov, Vasili	
Remizov, Alexei	1877-1957	Vasilievich	1856-1919
Renan, Ernest	1823-1892	Ruffini, Giovanni	
Rennell, James Rennell		Domenico	1807-1881
Rodd, 1st Baron	1858-1941	Ruge, Arnold	1802-1880
Renouvier, Charles		Runeberg, Johan Ludvig	1804-1877
Bernard	1815-1903	Runyon, Damon	1884-1946
Reuter, Gabriele	1859-1941	Ruskin, John	1819-1900
Reymont, Wladyslaw		Russell, Bertrand Arthur	
Stanlislaw	1868-1925	William	1872-
Reynolds, Stephen	1881-1919	Russell, George William	1867-1935
Rice, Elmer	1892-	Rutherford, Mark	1831-1913
Rice, James	1843-1882	Rydberg, Abraham Viktor	1828-1895
Richards, Frank	1875-1961	Ryle, Gilbert	1900-
Richardson, Dorothy		Sabatier, Paul	1858-1928
Miller	1873-1957	Sabatini, Rafael	1875-1950
Richardson, Henry Handel	1870-1946	Sackville-West, Victoria	
Richepin, Jean	1849-1926	Mary	1892-1962
Ridge, William Pett	1857-1930	Sadleir, Michael	1888-1957
Ridgway, Robert	1850-1929	Saint-Exupery,	
Riisager, Knudage	1897-	Antoine De	1900-1944
Riley, James Whitcomb	1849-1916	Saintsbury, George	
Rilke, Rainer Maria	1875-1926	Edward Bateman	1845-1933
Rimbaud, Jean Arthur	1854-1891	Saint-John, Perse	1887-
Ritchie, Anne Isabella		Sala, George Augustin	
Lady	1837-1919	Henry	1828-1895
Rivière, Jacques	1886-1925	Salten, Felix	1869-1945
Roberts, Sir Charles George		Saltykov, Michael	
Douglas	1860-1943	Evgrafovich	1826-1889
Roberts, Morley	1857-1942	Salvemini, Gaetano	1873-
Robinson, Edwin		Samain, Albert Victor	1858-1900
Arlington	1869-1935	Sand, George (Dudevant)	1804-1876
Robinson, Lennox	1886-1958	Sanday, William	1843-1920
Rod, Edouard	1857-1910	Sandburg, Carl	1878-
Rodo, Jose Enrique	1872-1917	Sandeau, Leonard Sylvain	
Roe, Edward Payson	1838-1888	Julien	1811-1883
Rogers, Randolph	1825-1892	Sant, James	1820-1916
Rohmer, Sax	1886-1959	Santayana, George	1863-1952
Rolland, Romain	1866-1944	Sardou, Victorien	1831-1908
Rolleston, Thomas		Sarmiento, Domingo	
William Hazen	1857-1920	Faustino	1811-1888
Rolvaag, Ole Edvart	1876-1931	Sassoon, Siegfried	
Romains, Jules	1885-	Lorraine	1886-
Roosevelt, Anna Eleanor	1884-1962	Saxe, John Godfrey	1816-1887
Roosevelt, Theodore	1858-1919	Sayers, Dorothy L.	1893-1957
Rose, John Holland	1855-1942	Schaffner, Jakob	1875-1944
Rosegger, Peter	1843-1918	Scheffel, Joseph Viktor	
Rosenkranz, Karl	1805-1879	Von	1826-1886
Rosmini-Serbati, Antonio	1797-1855	Scherer, Wilhelm	1841-1886
Rosny, Joseph Henri	1856-1940	Schickele, Rene	1883-1940
Rosny, Séraphin Justin		Schlick, Moritz	1882-1936
François	1859-1948	Schlaf, Johannes	1862-1941

Schnitzler, Arthur	1862-1931	Soloviev, Vladimir	
Scholes, Percy Alfred	1877-1958	Sergeivich	1853-1900
Schonner, Karl	1869-1942	Sorabji, Cornelia	1866-
Schreiner, Olive	1862-1920	Sorel, Albert	1842-1906
Schweitzer, Albert	1875-1965	Sorel, Georges	1847-1922
Scott, Duncan, Campbell	1862-1947	Sorge, Reinhard Johannes	1892-1916
Scwob, Marcel	1876-1905	Soutar, William	1898-1943
Seaman, Sir Owen	1861-1936	Spence, Lewis	1874-1955
Sedgwick, Anne Douglas	1873-1935	Spencer, Herbert	1820-1903
Seebohm, Frederick	1833-1912	Spender, Edward Harold	1864-1926
Seeley, Sir John Robert	1834-1895	Spengler, Oswald	1880-1936
Seignobos, Charles	1854-1942	Spielhagen, Friedrich Von	1829-1911
Sellar, William Young	1825-1890	Spitteler, Carl	1845-1924
Serao, Matilde	1856-1927	Spring, Howard	1889-1965
Sergeyev-Tsensky,		Squire, Sir John Collings	1884-1958
Sergey	1875-1958	Stacpoole, Hendy de Vere	1863-1951
Service, Robert William	1874-1958	Stanley, Arthur Penrhyn	1815-1881
Seth, Andrew	1850-1931	Stanley, Sir Henry	
Seton-Watson, Robert		Morton	1841-1904
William	1879-	Stedman, Edmund	
Settembrini, Luigi	1813-1877	Clarence	1833-1908
Sewell, Anna	1820-1878	Steed, Henry Wickham	1871-1956
Sharp, John Campbell	1819-1885	Stein, Gertrude	1874-1946
Sharp, William	1856-1905	Steiner, Rudolf	1861-1925
Shaw, George, Bernard	1856-1950	Stephen, Sir Leslie	1832-1904
Shaw, Henry Wheeler	1818-1885	Stephens, James	1882-1950
Sherriff, Robert Cedric	1896-	Stepnyak	1852-1895
Sherwood, Robert Emmet	1896-1955	Stern, Daniel (Agoult)	1805-1876
Shorter, Clement King	1857-1926	Stevens, Wallace	1879-1955
Shorthouse, Joseph Henry	1834-1903	Stevenson, Robert Louis	
Shute, Nevil	1899-1960	Balfour	1850-1894
Sidgwick, Henry	1838-1900	Stirling, James	
Sienkiewicz, Henryk	1846-1916	Hutchinson	1820-1909
Sill, Edward Rowland	1841-1887	Stirling-Maxwell,	
Sillani, Tomaso	1888-	Sir William Bart	1818-1878
Sillanpaa, Frans Eemil	1888-	Stocker, Helene	1869-
Simmel, George	1858-1918	Stockton, Francis Howard	
Simon, Jules Francois	1814-1896	Richard	1834-1902
Simonds, Frank Herbert	1878-1936	Stoddard, John Lawson	1850-1931
Simrock, Karl Joseph	1802-1876	Stoddard, Richard Henry	1825-1903
Sims, George Robert	1847-1922	Stoddard, William Osborn	1835-1925
Sinclair, May	1864-1946	Stopes, Marie Carmichael	1880-1958
Sinclair, Upton	1878-	Storm, Theodor Wolsden	1817-1888
Sitwell, Edith	1887-1964	Stout, George Frederich	1860-1944
Sitwell, Sir Osbert	1892-	Stowe, Harriet Elizabeth	
Sitwell, Sacheverell	1897-	Beecher	1811-1896
Skeat, Walter William	1835-1912	Strachey, Lytton	1880-1932
Skene, William Forbes	1809-1892	Street, Alfred William	1811-1881
Smiles, Samuel	1812-1904	Streuvels, Styn	1871-
Smith, Francis Hopkinson	1838-1915	Strindberg, Johan August	1849-1912
Smith, Goldwin	1823-1910	Strobl, Karl Hans	1877-1946
Smith, Norman Kemp	1872-1958	Strong, Leonard Alfred	
Smith, Walter Chalmers	1824-1908	George	1896-1958
Smith, Sir William	1813-1893	Stubbs, William	1825-1901
Snoilsky, Carl Johan		Stuckenberg, Viggo	1863-1905
Gustaf	1841-1903	Sudermann, Hermann	1857-1928
Sokolov, Nahum	1859-1936	Sully-Prudhomme, Rene	
Sologub, Fedor	1863-1927	Francois Armand	1839-1907
Soloviev, Sergei		Supervielle, Jules	1884-1960
Mikhailovich	1820-1879	Sutro, Alfred	1863-1933

Suttner, Bertha	1843-1914	Treitschke, Heinrich Von	1834-1896
Svevo, Italio	1861-1928	Trelawny, Edward John	1792-1881
Swan, Annie	1860-1943	Trench, Frederick Herbert	1865-1923
Swanwick, Anna	1813-1899	Trench, Richard Chevenix	1807-1886
Swinburne, Algernon		Trevelyan, George	
Charles	1837-1909	Macaulay	1876-1962
Sybel, Heinrich Von	1817-1895	Trevelyan, Robert	
Symonds, John Addington	1840-1893	Calverley	1872-1951
Symons, Arthur	1865-1945	Trevelyan, Sir George	
Synge, John Millington	1871-1909	Otto	1838-1928
Tabley, John Byrne		Trollope, Anthony	1815-1882
Leicester Warren	1835-1895	Trollope, Thomas	
Tagore, Sir Rabindranath	1861-1941	Adolphus	1810-1892
Taine, Hippolyte Adolphe	1828-1893	Trotsky, Lev Davidovich	1879-1940
Tamayo, Baus Manuel	1829-1898	Tupper, Martin Farquhar	1810-1889
Tardieu, Andre Pierre		Turgenev, Ivan	
Gabriel Amedee	1876-1945	Sergeyevich	1818-1883
Tarkington, Newton		Turner, Charles Tennyson	1808-1879
Booth	1869-1946	Turner, Frederick Jackson	1861-1932
Tawney, Richard Henry	1880-1962	Turner, Walter James	
Taylor, Alfred Edward	1869-1945	Redfern	1889-1946
Taylor, Bayard	1825-1878	Twain, Mark	1835-1910
Taylor, Sir Henry	1800-1886	Tyler, Moses Coit	1835-1900
Taylor, Isaak	1829-1901	Tynan, Katherine	1863-1931
Taylor, Tom	1817-1880	Tyndall, John	1820-1893
Tedder, Henry Richard	1850-1924	Unamuno, Miguel de	1864-1936
Teilhard De Jardin,		Underhill, Evelyn	1875-1941
Pierre	1881-1955	Undset, Sigrid	1882-1949
Tennyson, Alfred Lord	1809-1892	Ungaretti, Guiseppe	1888-
Tharaud, Jerome	1874-1953	Unger, Rudolf	1876-
Thaxter, Celia Laighton	1835-1894	Unruh, Fritz, Von	1885-
Thayer, William Roscoe	1859-1923	Uspenski, Gleb Ivanovich	1840-1902
Theuriet, Claude Adhemar		Vachell, Horace	
Andre	1833-1907	Annesley	1861-1955
Thiers, Louis Adolph	1797-1877	Vacherot, Etienne	1809-1897
Thomas, Augustus	1857-1934	Vaihinger, Hans	1852-1933
Thomas, Brandon	1849-1914	Valera Y Alcala, Galiano	
Thompson, Francis	1859-1907	Juan	1824-1905
Thomson, James	1834-1882	Valery, Paul	1871-1945
Thurber, James	1894-1961	Valle-Inclan, Ramon Del	1869-1936
Thurston, Ernest Charles		Valles, Jules	1832-1885
Temple	1879-1933	Van Beers, Jan	1821-1888
Thurston, Katherine Cecil	1875-1911	Van Doren, Carl Clinton	1885-1950
Tillich, Paul Johannes	1886-	Van Doren, Mark Albert	1894-
Toland, Hideki	1885-1948	Van Dyke, Henry	1852-1933
Toller, Ernst	1893-1939	Van Loon, Hendrick	
Tolstoy, Count Alexey		Willem	1882-1944
Nikolayevich	1882-1945	Vaperau, Louis Gustave	1819-1906
Tolstoy, Leo Nokolayevich	1828-1910	Varnhagen, Francisco	
Tomlinson, Henry Major	1873-1958	Adolpho de	1816-1878
Tonks, Henry	1862-1937	Vazoff, Ivan	1850-1921
Topelius, Zachris	1818-1898	Veblen, Thornstein B.	1857-1929
Toru, Dutt	1856-1877	Veitch, John	1829-1894
Tout, Thomas Frederick	1855-1929	Verdaguer, Mosen	
Toynbee, Arnold	1852-1883	Jacinto	1845-1902
Toynbee, Arnold Joseph	1889-	Verga, Giovanni	1840-1922
Tozzi, Federigo	1883-1920	Verhaeren, Emile	1855-1916
Traill, Henry Duff	1842-1900	Verlain, Paul	1844-1896
Travers, Ben	1886-	Verne, Jules	1828-1905
Traz, Robert De	1884-	Verwey, Albert	1865-1937

Viaud, Louis Marie Julien	1850-1923	Whitman, Walt	1819-1892
Vidyasagar, Iswar		Whittier, John Greenleaf	1807-1892
Chandra	1820-1891	Widmann, Joseph Victor	1842-1911
Viebig, Clara	1860-1952	Wiechert, Ernst	1887-1950
Viele-Griffin, Francis	1864-1937	Wiggin, Kate Douglas	1856-1923
Vigfusson, Gudbrandir	1828-1889	Wilcox, Ella	1850-1919
Villari, Pasquale	1827-1917	Wilde, Oscar Fingall	
Villiers, De L'islee		O'Flahertie Wills	1854-1900
August Compt de	1838-1889	Wilde, Speranza Lady	1826-1896
Vinogradoff, Sir Paul	1854-1925	Wildenbruch, Ernst Van	1845-1909
Vischer, Friedrich		Wilder, Thorton	1897-
Theodor	1807-1887	Wildgans, Anton	1881-1932
Vogue, Eugene Melchior	1848-1910	Williamson, Henry	1895-
Voss, Richard	1851-1918	Wills, William Gorman	1828-1891
Vrchlicky, Jaroslav	1853-1912	Wilson, Edmund	1895-
Vuillard, Jean Edouard	1868-1940	Wilson, John Dover	1881-
Waddell, Helen	1889-	Winsor, Justin	1831-1897
Wallace, Alfred Russel	1823-1913	Winther, Christian	1796-1876
Wallace, Edgar	1875-1932	Wister, Owen	1860-1938
Wallace, Lewis	1827-1905	Wittgenstein, Ludwig	
Wallace, William	1844-1897	Josef Johannes	1889-1951
Wallon, Henri Alexandre	1812-1904	Wodehouse, Pelham	
Walpole, Sir Hugh		Grenville	1881-
Seymour	1884-1941	Wolfe, Humbert	1885-1940
Ward, Mary Augusta		Wolfe, Thomas Clayton	1900-1938
(Mrs. Humphry)	1851-1920	Wolff, Pierre	1865-1944
Warner, Charles Dudley	1829-1900	Wood, Mrs. Henry	1814-1887
Warner (Susan Bogert)	1819-1895	Woods, Margaret Louisa	1856-1945
Warren, Samuel	1807-1877	Woolf, Virginia	1882-1941
Wasserman, Jakob	1873-1933	Wright, Thomas	1810-1887
Watson, Sir William	1858-1935	Wright, William Aldis	1836-1914
Watts-Dunton, Walter		Wundt, Wilhelm Max	1832-1920
Theodore	1832-1914	Wyatt, Sir Matthew Digby	1820-1877
Waugh, Alec	1898-	Wylie, Elinor Hoyte	1885-1928
Waugh, Edwin	1817-1890	Wyndham, George	1863-1913
Webb, Beatrice	1858-1943	Yates, Dornford	1885-1960
Webb, Mary Gladys	1881-1927	Yates, Edmund	1831-1894
Webb, Sidney James	1859-1947	Yeats, William Butler	1865-1939
Wedekind, Frank	1864-1918	Yonge, Charlotte Mary	1823-1901
Wellesz, Egon Joseph	1885-	Young, Andrew John	1885-
Wells, Charles Jeremiah	1798-1879	Young, Francis Brett	1884-1954
Wells, Herbert George	1866-1946	Yriarte, Charles	1832-1898
Wennerberg, Gunnar	1817-1901	Zahn, Ernst	1867-1952
Werfel, Franz	1890-1945	Zangwill, Israel	1864-1926
West, Rebecca	1892-	Zeller, Eduard	1814-1908
Weyman, Stanley, John	1855-1928	Zeromski, Stephen	1864-1925
Wharton, Newbold Edith	1862-1937	Zola, Emile Edouard	
Wheeler, Sir Robert		Charles Antoine	1840-1902
Mortimer	1890-	Zorrilla, Jose	1817-1893
White, Richard Grant	1821-1885	Zuckmayer, Carl	1896-
White, William Hale	1831-1913	Zweig, Arnold	1887-
Whitlock, Brand	1869-1934	Zweig, Stefan	1881-1942

ARTISTS

Aalto, Alvar	1899-	Abbey, Edwin Austin	1852-1911
Aaltonen, Waino	1894-	Abercrombie, Sir Patrick	1879-1957
Aba-Novak, Vilmos	1894-1941	Achenbach, Andreas	1815-1910

Adams, Herbert	1858-1945	Blomfield, Sir Arthur	
Adamsen, Amandus		William	1829-1899
Heinrich	1855-1929	Blomfield, Sir Reginald	1856-1942
Alexander, John White	1856-1915	Blore, Edward	1787-1879
Alonso, Mateo Silva		Blum, Robert Frederick	1857-1903
Leitao	1878-	Boccioni, Umberto	1882-1916
Anderson, Sir Robert		Boehm, Sir Joseph Edgar	1834-1890
Rowand	1834-1921	Boelkin, Arnold	1827-1901
Ansdell, Richard	1815-1885	Bombois, Camille	1883-
Archipenko, Alexander	1880-	Bone, Sir Muirhead	1876-1953
Armitage, Edward	1817-1896	Bonheur, Rosa	1822-1899
Armstead, Henry Hugh	1828-1905	Bonnard, Pierre	1867-1947
Armstrong, John	1893-	Bonnat, Leon Joseph	
Artzybashev, Boris	1899-	Florentin	1833-1922
Asplund, Erik Gunnar	1885-1940	Borglum, Gutzon	1871-1941
Attwell, Mabel Lucie	1879-	Borglum, Solon Hannibal	1868-1922
Bacon, Henry	1866-1924	Borie, Adolphe	1877-1934
Baer, William Jacob	1860-1941	Boudin, Louis Eugene	1824-1898
Baker, Bryant	1881-	Bough, Samuel	1822-1878
Bakst, Leon	1866-1924	Boughton, George Henry	1833-1905
Ball, Thomas	1819-1911	Bouguereau, Adolphe	
Balla, Gyacomo	1871-1958	William	1825-1905
Bandel, Ernst Von	1800-1876	Bourdelle, Emile Antoine	1861-1929
Barker, Thomas	1815-1882	Boutet De Monvel,	
Barlach, Ernst	1870-1938	Maurice	1851-1913
Barnard, Georges Grey	1863-1938	Boyle, John J.	1851-1917
Bartels, Hans Von	1856-1913	Bracquemond, Felix	1833-1914
Bartholdi, Auguste	1834-1904	Bradford, William	1827-1892
Bartholome, Paul Albert	1848-1884	Braekeleer, Henri Jean	
Bastien-Lepage, Jules	1848-1884	Augustin De	1840-1888
Bates, Harry	1850-1899	Brancusi, Constantin	1876-1957
Baudry, Paul Jacques		Brangwyn, Sir Frank	1867-1956
Aime	1828-1886	Braque, Georges	1882-1963
Baumeister, Willi	1889-1955	Breitner, George Hendrik	1857-1923
Beach, Chester	1881-	Breton, Jules Adolphe	
Beardsley, Aubrey		Aime Louis	1827-1906
Vincent	1872-1898	Bridgman, Frederic	
Beaudin, André	1895-	Arthur	1847-1928
Beaux, Cecilia	1863-1942	Brierly, Sir Oswald	
Beckmann, Max	1884-1950	Walter	1817-1894
Beckwith, James Carrol	1852-1917	Brock, Sir Thomas	1847-1922
Begas, Reinhold	1831-1911	Brodie, William	1815-1881
Behrens, Peter	1868-1938	Brough, Robert	1872-1905
Bell, John	1811-1895	Brown, Ford Madox	1821-1893
Bellows, Albert F.	1829-1883	Brown, George Loring	1814-1889
Bellows, George Wesley	1882-1925	Brown, Henry Kirke	1814-1886
Benlliure Y Gil, Jose	1855-1937	Brown, John George	1831-1913
Benson, Frank Weston	1862-1951	Brown, Hablot Knight	1815-1882
Bentley, John Francis	1839-1902	Bruce-Joy, Albert	1842-1924
Berlage, Hendrik Petrus	1856-1934	Brunner, Arnold William	1857-1925
Besnard, Paul Albert	1849-1934	Brush, George de Forest	1855-1941
Beverley, William Roxby	1814-1889	Brymner, William	1855-1925
Bierstadt, Albert	1830-1902	Burgess, John Bagnold	1830-1897
Bigge, John	1892-	Burne-Jones, Sir Edward	
Birch, Samuel	1813-1885	Burne	1833-1898
Blakelock, Ralph Albert	1847-1919	Burne-Jones, Sir Philip	1861-1926
Blampied, Edmund	1886-	Burnham, Daniel Hudson	1846-1912
Blanche, Jacques Emile	1862-1942	Burton, Decimus	1800-1881
Blashfield, Edin Howland	1848-1936	Butler, Lady Elizabeth	1857-1933
Bloch, Martin	1883-1954	Butterfield, William	1814-1900

Cabanel, Alexandre	1823-1889	Daumet, Pierre Jerome	
Caldecott, Randolph	1846-1886	Honore	1826-1911
Calderon, Philip		Daumier, Honore	1808-1879
Hermongenes	1833-1898	Davies, Arthur B.	1862-1928
Calvert, Edward	1799-1883	Davis, Charles Harold	1857-1933
Cameron, Sir David		Dawson, Henri	1811-1878
Young	1865-1945	Dawson-Watson, Dawson	1864-1939
Camphausen, Wilhelm	1818-1885	Defregger, Franz Von	1835-1921
Capronnier, Jean Baptiste	1814-1891	Degas, Hilaire Germain	
Carand'Ache	1858-1909	Edgar	1834-1917
Carolus-Duran	1837-1917	Delaunay, Elie	1828-1891
Carra, Carlo	1881-	Delaunay, Robert	1885-1941
Carriere, Eugene	1849-1906	Delvaux, Paul	1897-
Casorati, Felice	1886-	Demuth, Charles	1883-1935
Cassatt, Mary	1845-1926	Denis, Maurice	1870-1943
Cazin, Jean Charles	1841-1901	Derain, Andre	1880-
Cezanne, Paul	1839-1906	Despiau, Charles	1874-1946
Chagall, Marc	1887-	Detaille, Edouard	1848-1912
Chalmers, George Paul	1836-1878	Diaz, Narcisse Virgile	1809-1876
Chapu, Henri	1833-1891	Dicksee, Sir Francis	
Chase, William Merrit	1849-1916	Bernard	1853-1928
Chirico, Giorgio De	1888-	Dielman, Frederick	1847-1935
Church, Frederick Edwin	1826-1900	Dillens, Julien	1849-1904
Clarke, Thomas Shields	1860-1920	Dix, Otto	1891-
Claus, Emile	1849-1924	Dobson, Frank	1887-1963
Clausen, Sir George	1852-1944	Dobson, William Charles	
Clays, Paul Jean	1819-1900	Thomas	1817-1898
Coates, Wells Wintemute	1895-1958	Dodge, William de	
Cole, Vicat	1833-1893	Leftwich	1867-1935
Collier, Hon John	1850-1934	Dore, Paul Gustave	1832-1883
Colman, Samuel	1832-1920	Dougherty, Paul	1877-1947
Conder, Charles	1868-1909	Doyle, Richard	1824-1883
Constant, Benjamin Jean		Drake, Friedrich	1805-1882
Joseph	1845-1902	Drury, Alfred	1857-1944
Cooper, Thomas Sidney	1803-1902	Dubois, Paul	1829-1905
Cope, Charles West	1811-1890	Duchamp, Marcel	1887-
Corbett, Harvey Willey	1873-1954	Dufy, Raoul	1877-1953
Corbould, Edward Henry	1815-1905	Dumont, Augustin	
Corbusier Le, Charles		Alexandre	1801-1884
Edouard	1887-1965	Dupre, Giovanni	1817-1882
Corinth, Louis	1858-1925	Dupre, Jules	1811-1889
Cormon, Fernand	1845-1924	Durand, Asher Brown	1796-1886
Costa, Giovanni	1826-1903	Duveneck, Frank	1848-1919
Cottet, Charles	1863-1925	Eakins, Thomas	1844-1916
Courbet, Gustav	1819-1877	East, Alfred	1849-1913
Couture, Thomas	1815-1879	Eaton, Wyatt	1849-1896
Cram, Ralph Adams	1863-1942	Eberlein, Gustav	1847-1926
Crauck, Gustav	1827-1905	Eberz, Josef	1801-1882
Cruikshank, George	1792-1878	Edelfelt, Albert Gunter	1854-1905
Daingerfield, Elliott	1859-1932	Ensor, James	1860-1942
Dallin, Cyrus Edwin	1861-1944	Epstein, Jacob	1880-1959
Dalou, Jules	1838-1902	Ernst, Max	1891-
Dannat, William T.	1853-1929	Etex, Antoine	1808-1888
Dantan, Antoine Laurent	1798-1878	Faed, Thomas	1826-1900
Dantan, Edward Joseph	1848-1897	Faistauer, Anton	1887-1930
Darley, Felix Octavius		Falguiere, Jean Alexandre	
Carr	1822-1888	Joseph	1831-1900
Daubigny, Charles		Fantin-Latour, Ignace	
Francois	1817-1878	Henri Jean Theodore	1836-1904
		Farquharson, David	1840-1907

Farquharson, Joseph	1846-1935
Feininger, Lyonel	1871-1956
Feuerbach, Anselm	1829-1880
Fildes, Sir Luke	1844-1927
Finch, Alfred William	1854-1930
Flagg, Ernest	1857-1947
Flint, Sir William Russell	1880-
Forain, Jean Louis	1852-1931
Ford, Edward Onslow	1852-1901
Forster, Ernst	1800-1885
Foster, Myles Birket	1825-1899
Frampton, Sir George	1860-1928
Francais, Francois Louis	1814-1897
Fraser, Claud Lovat	1890-1921
Fraser, James Earle	1876-1953
Fremiet, Emmanuel	1824-1910
French, Daniel Chester	1850-1931
Fresnaye, Roger De La	1885-1925
Friesz, Emile Othon	1879-1949
Fripp, Alfred Downing	1822-1895
Fripp, George Arthur	1814-1896
Frith, William Powell	1819-1909
Fromentin, Eugene	1820-1876
Frost, William Edward	1810-1877
Fry, Roger Elliot	1866-1934
Fuertes, Louis Agassiz	1874-1927
Fuhrich, Joseph Von	1800-1876
Fuller, George	1822-1884
Furse, Charles Wellington	1868-1904
Gabo, Naum	1890-
Gallait, Louis	1810-1887
Gallen-Kallela, Akseli Valdemar	1865-1931
Garnier, Jean Louis Charles	1825-1898
Gaudier-Brzeska, Henry	1891-1915
Gauguin, Paul	1848-1903
Gaul, Gilbert William	1855-1919
Gay, Walter	1856-1937
Gebhardt, Eduard Von	1830-1925
Geddes, Norman Bel	1893-1958
Gerome, Jean Leon	1824-1904
Gervex, Henri	1852-1929
Gibson, Charles Dana	1867-1944
Gifford, Robert Swain	1840-1905
Gilbert, Sir Alfred	1854-1934
Gilbert, Cass	1859-1939
Gilbert, Sir John	1817-1897
Gleizes, Albert	1881-1953
Gogh, Vincent Van	1853-1890
Goodall, Frederick	1822-1904
Goodhue, Bertram Grosvenor	1869-1924
Grafly, Charles	1862-1929
Grant, Duncan	1885-
Grant, Sir Francis	1803-1878
Greenway, Kate	1846-1901
Gregory, Edward John	1850-1909
Gris, Juan	1887-1927
Gromaire, Marcel	1892-

Gropius, Walter	1883-
Grossmith, Weedon	1853-1919
Grosz, George	1893-1959
Gudin, Theodore	1802-1880
Guillamin, Armand	1841-1927
Guillaume, Jean Baptiste Claude Euegene	1822-1905
Gunn, James	1893-
Guthrie, Sir James	1859-1930
Guys, Constantin	1805-1892
Haag, Carl	1820-1915
Haas, Johannes Hubertus Leonhardus De	1832-1908
Habermann, Hugo Freiherr Von	1849-1929
Hacker, Arthur	1858-1919
Haider, Karl	1846-1912
Hansom, Joseph Aloysius	1803-1882
Harpignies, Henri	1819-1916
Harrison, Thomas Alexander	1853-1930
Hartley, Jonathan Scott	1845-1912
Harvey, Sir George	1806-1876
Hassall, John	1868-1948
Henner, Jean Jacques	1829-1905
Henri, Robert	1865-1929
Herbert, John Rogers	1810-1900
Hilberseimer, Ludwig	1885-
Hildebrand, Adolf	1847-1921
Hodgkins, Frances Mary	1869-1947
Hodler, Ferdinand	1853-1918
Hoffman, Josef	1870-
Hoffman, Malvina	1887-
Holiday, Henry	1839-1927
Holl, Frank	1845-1888
Holmes, Sir Charles John	1868-1936
Holroyd, Sir Charles	1861-1917
Homer, Winslow	1836-1910
Hook, James Clarke	1819-1907
Horsley, John Callcott	1817-1903
Hosmer, Harriet Goodhue	1830-1908
Hovenden, Thomas	1840-1895
Hubner, Julius	1806-1882
Hughes, Arthur	1832-1915
Hunt, Alfred William	1830-1896
Hunt, Richard Morris	1828-1895
Hunt, William Holman	1827-1910
Hunt, William Morris	1824-1879
Huntingdon, Daniel	1816-1906
Hutchison, Sir William Oliphant	1889-
Innes, James Dickson	1887-1914
Inness, George	1825-1894
Israels, Josef	1824-1911
Jackson, Sir Thomas Graham	1835-1924
Jacque, Charles	1813-1894
Jagger, Charles Sargeant	1885-1934
Jalabert, Charles Francois	1819-1901
Jawlesky, Alexei Van	1864-1941

John, Augustus Edwin	1878-1961	Lemaire, Philipp Honoré	1798-1880
John, Sir William		Lenbach, Franz Von	1836-1904
Goscombe	1860-1952	Lethaby, William	
Johnson, Eastman	1824-1906	Richard	1857-1931
Jonkind, Johann Barthold	1819-1891	Liebermann, Max	1847-1935
Jonsson, Einar	1874-1954	Lindsay, Sir Coutts	1824-1913
Jordan, Rudolf	1810-1887	Lindsay, Norman	1879-
Kandinsky, Vasily	1866-1944	Linnell, John	1792-1882
Kauffer, Edward		Linton, Sir James	
McKnight	1890-	Dromgole	1840-1916
Keene, Charles Samuel	1823-1891	Lipchitz, Jacques	1891-
Keller, Albert Von	1844-1920	Llewellyn, Sir William	1863-1941
Kelly, Sir Gerald Festus	1879-	Lockhart, William Ewart	1846-1900
Kemp-Welch, Lucy		Lockwood, Wilton	1861-1914
Elizabeth	1869-	Lowry, Stephen	1887-
Kennington, Eric Henry	1888-1960	Lucas, John Seymour	1849-1923
Kent, Rockwell	1882-	Lukeman, Henry	
Kirchner, Ernst Ludwig	1880-1938	Augustus	1871-1935
Khnopff, Fernand	1858-1921	Lutyens, Sir Edwin	
Kirkup, Seymore Stocker	1788-1880	Landseer	1869-1944
Klee, Paul	1879-1940	Macbeth, Robert Walker	1848-1910
Klerk, Michel De	1884-1923	MacColl, Dugald	
Klinger, Max	1857-1920	Sutherland	1859-1948
Klint, Kaare	1888-	McEntee, Jervis	1828-1891
Knaus, Ludwig	1829-1910	McEvoy, Ambrose	1878-1927
Knight, Dame Laura	1877-	Macke, August	1887-1914
Knight, Daniel Ridgway	1845-1924	McKim, Charles Follen	1847-1909
Knight, Harold	1874-1961	Mackintosh, Charles Rennie	1868-1928
Knowles, Sir James	1831-1908	MacMannies, Frederick	
Kokoshka, Oskar	1886-	William	1863-1937
Koort, Jaan	1883-1935	MacNee, Sir Daniel	1806-1882
Kramer, Pieter Lodewijk	1881-	MacNeil, Hermon Atkins	1866-1947
Kubin, Alfred	1877-1959	MacTaggart, William	1835-1910
Kupka, Frank	1871-1957	Macwhirter, John	1839-1911
Kuznetson, Pavel	1878-	Madrazo Y Kunt,	
Kyosai, Sho-Fu	1831-1889	Don Federico De	1815-1894
La Farge, John	1835-1910	Magonigle, Harold Van	
Lafresnaye, De Roger	1885-1925	Buren	1867-1935
Lalique, René	1860-1945	Magritte, Réne	1898-
Lambeaux, Jef	1852-1908	Maillol, Aristide	
Lanchester, Henry		Joseph Bonaventure	1861-1944
Vaughan	1863-1953	Makart, Hans	1840-1884
Laszlo, Sir Philip	1869-1937	Manet, Edouard	1832-1883
Lathrop, Francis	1849-1909	Manship, Paul	1885-
La Touche, Gaston	1854-1913	Marc, Franz	1880-1916
Laurencin, Marie	1885-1957	Marchand, Jean	1883-1941
Laurens, Henri	1885-1954	Marees, Hans Von	1837-1887
Laurens, Jean Paul	1838-1921	Marin, John	1870-
Lavery, Sir John	1856-1941	Maris, Jacob	1837-1899
Lawson, Cecil Gordon	1851-1882	Maris, Matthiss	1839-1917
Lazlo De Lombos, Philip		Maris, Willem	1843-1910
Alexius	1869-1937	Marquet, Albert	1875-1947
Lear, Edward	1812-1888	Marr, Carl	1859-1936
Leger, Fernand	1881-1955	Marshall, Willam Calder	1813-1894
Legros, Alphonse	1837-1911	Martin, Frank	1890-
Lehmann, Rudolf	1819-1905	Martin, Homer Dodge	1836-1897
Lehmbruck, Wilhelm	1881-1919	Matejko, Jan Alois	1838-1893
Leibl, Wilhelm	1844-1900	Matisse, Henri	1869-1954
Leighton, Frederick		Mauve, Anton	1838-1888
Leighton	1830-1896	Mead, Larkin Goldsmith	1835-1910

Mead, William Rutherford	1846-1928
Meissonier, Jean Louis Ernest	1815-1891
Melchers, Gari	1860-1932
Mendelsohn	1887-1953
Meninsky, Bernard	1891-1950
Menzel, Adolph Friedrich Erdmann Von	1815-1905
Mercie, Marius Jean Antonin	1845-1916
Mesdag, Hendrik Willem	1831-1915
Mestrovic, Ivan	1883-1962
Meunier, Constantin	1831-1905
Mies Van Der Rohe	1886-
Millais, Sir John Everett	1829-1896
Miro, Joan	1893-
Millet, Francis Davis	1846-1912
Modigliani, Amadeo	1884-1920
Mondrian, Pieter Cornelis	1872-1944
Monet, Claude	1840-1936
Moore, Albert Joseph	1841-1893
Moore, Henry	1831-1895
Moore, Henry Spencer	1893-
Moran, Edward	1829-1901
Morandi, Giorgio	1898-
Moreau, Gustave	1826-1898
Morel-Ladeuil, Leonard	1820-1888
Morisot, Berthe Marie Pauline	1841-1895
Morris, William	1834-1896
Moses, Anna Mary (Grandma)	1860-1961
Mosler, Henry	1841-1920
Mowbray, Harry Siddons	1858-1928
Muenier, Jules, A.	1863-1934
Munch, Edvard	1863-1944
Munk, Kaj	1898-1944
Munkacsy, Michael	1846-1900
Munnings, Alfred	1878-1959
Murphy, John Francis	1853-1921
Murray, Sir David	1849-1933
Nash, Paul	1889-1946
Nervi, Pier Luigi	1891-
Nesfield, William Eden	1835-1888
Neuville, Alphonse Marie De	1836-1885
Nevinson, Christophe Richard Wynne	1889-1946
Nicholson, Ben	1894-
Nicholson, Sir William	1872-1949
Nicol, Erskine	1825-1904
Niehaus, Charles Henry	1855-1935
Nolde, Emil	1867-1956
Ochtmann, Leonard	1854-1934
Orchardson, Sir William Quiller	1832-1910
Orpen, Sir William Newenham Montague	1878-1931

Oud, Jacobus Johann Pieter	1890-
Oudine, Eugene Andre	1810-1887
Ozefant	1886-
Page, William	1811-1885
Palmer, Samuel	1805-1881
Parsons, Alfred	1847-1920
Parsons, William Edward	1872-1939
Partridge, Sir Bernard	1861-1945
Partridge, William Ordway	1861-1930
Paton, Sir Joseph Noel	1821-1901
Paul, Bruno	1874-
Pearce, Charles Sprague	1851-1914
Pearson, John Loughborough	1817-1897
Pennell, Joseph	1860-1926
Peploe, Samuel John	1871-1935
Permeke, Constant	1886-1952
Perrett, Auguste	1874-1955
Pettie, John	1839-1893
Picabia, Francis	1878-1953
Picasso, Pablo	1881-
Piloty, Karl Von	1826-1886
Pissarro, Camille	1830-1903
Platt, Charles Adams	1861-1933
Poelzig, Hans	1869-1936
Poole, Paul Falconer	1807-1879
Pope, John Russell	1874-1937
Portaels, Jean Francois	1818-1895
Post, George Browne	1837-1913
Poynter, Sir Edward John	1836-1919
Pradilla, Francisco	1848-1921
Prinsep, Valentine Cameron	1838-1904
Proctor, Alexander Phimister	1862-1950
Purvitis, Vilhelms Karlis	1872-1945
Puvis De Chavannes, Pierre Cecile	1824-1898
Pyle, Howard	1853-1911
Rackham, Arthur	1867-1939
Raemaekers, Louis	1869-1956
Raven-Hill, Leonard	1867-1942
Redon, Odilon	1840-1916
Redpath, Anne	1895-
Reid, Sir George	1841-1913
Reid, Robert	1862-1929
Remington, Frederic	1861-1909
Renoir, Pierre Auguste	1841-1919
Renwick, James	1818-1895
Repin, Ilya Yefimovich	1844-1930
Richardson, Sir Albert Edward	1880-1963
Richardson, Henry Hobson	1838-1886
Richmond, Sir George	1809-1896
Richmond, Sir William Blake	1842-1921
Ricketts, Charles	1866-1931

Rietschel, Ernst	1804-1861	Steinlen, Theophile	
Rivera, Diego	1886-1957	Alexandre	1859-1923
Riviere, Briton	1840-1920	Stevens, Alfred	1828-1906
Roberts, William	1895-	Stillman, William James	1828-1901
Robinson, William Heath	1872-1944	Story, William Wetmore	1819-1895
Rodin, Auguste	1840-1917	Strachan, Douglas	1875-1950
Roerich, Nikolai		Strang, William	1859-1921
Constantinovich	1874-1947	Street, George Edmund	1824-1881
Rogers, John	1829-1904	Strobl De Kisfalud,	
Rops, Felicien	1833-1898	Sigismund	1884-
Rossetti, Dante Gabriel	1828-1882	Sturgis, Russell	1836-1909
Rothenstein, Sir William	1872-1945	Sullivan, Louis Henri	1856-1924
Rouault, Georges	1871-1958	Svabinsky, Max	1873-
Rousseau, Henri	1844-1910	Szinye-Merse, Paul De	1845-1920
Ryder, Albert Pinkham	1847-1917	Szonyi, Stephen	1894-
Salisbury, Frank Owen	1874-1957	Taft, Lorado	1860-1936
Sargent, John Singer	1856-1925	Tamayo, Rufino	1899-
Schilling, Johannes	1828-1910	Tanner, Henry Assawa	1859-1937
Schmidt-Rottluff, Karl	1884-	Tarbell, Edmund C.	1862-1938
Schreyer, Adolf	1828-1899	Taut, Bruno	1880-
Schwartze, Teresa	1852-1918	Tenniel, Sir John	1820-1914
Scott, Sir George Gilbert	1811-1878	Thayer, Abbott	
Scott, Sir Giles Gilbert	1880-	Handerson	1849-1921
Seganti, Giovanni	1858-1899	Thoma, Hans	1839-1924
Segonzac, André		Thompson, Launt	1833-1934
Dunoyer de	1884-	Thornycroft, Sir William	
Serusier, Paul	1863-1927	Hamo	1850-1925
Seurat, Georges	1859-1891	Tiffany, Louis Comfort	1848-1933
Severini, Gino	1883-	Tissot, James Joseph	
Severn, Joseph	1793-1879	Jacques	1836-1902
Shahn, Ben	1898-	Tonks, Henry	1862-1937
Shannon, Charles		Toulouse-Lautrec,	
Hazelwood	1863-1937	Henri De	1864-1901
Shannon, Sir James Jebusa	1862-1923	Troubetzkoy, Amelie Rives	1863-1945
Shaw, Richard Norman	1831-1912	Troubetzkoy, Pierre	1864-1936
Shields, Frederick James	1833-1911	Troyon, Constant	1810-1865
Short, Sir Frank Job	1857-1945	Trubner, Wilhelm	1851-1917
Sickert, Walter Richard	1860-1942	Tryon, Dwight William	1849-1925
Signac, Paul	1863-1935	Tuke, Henry Scott	1858-1929
Simmons, Edward		Tweed, John	1869-1933
Emerson	1852-1931	Utrillo, Maurice	1883-1955
Simpson, Sir John	1858-1933	Valadon, Suzanne	1869-1938
Sisley, Alfred	1840-1899	Valloton, Felix	1865-1929
Slevogt, Max	1868-1932	Van Der Stappen, Charles	1843-1910
Smillie, James David	1833-1909	Van De Velde, Henri	1863-1957
Smith, Sir Matthew		Van Doesburg, Theo	1883-1931
Arnold	1879-1959	Van Gough, Vincent	1853-1890
Soffici, Ardengo	1879-	Van Meegeren, Han	1889-1947
Somerscales, Thomas		Vedder, Elihu	1836-1923
Jacques	1842-1928	Veit, Philipp	1793-1877
Somov, Konstantin		Verboeckhoven, Eugene	
Andreevich	1869-	Joseph	1798-1881
Sorolla Y Bastida, Joaquin	1863-1923	Vereschagin, Vassili	
Spadini, Armando	1883-1925	Vassilievich	1842-1904
Spencer, Gilbert	1892-	Vierge, Daniel	1851-1904
Spencer, Sir Stanley	1891-1959	Vigeland, Adolf Gustav	1869-1943
Steell, Sir John	1804-1891	Vigne, Paul De	1843-1901
Steer, Philip Philip Wilson	1860-1942	Villon, Jacques	1875-1963
Steinle, Eduard	1810-1886	Vinton, Frederic Porter	1846-1911

Viollet Le Duc, Eugene	
Emmanuel	1814-1879
Vivin, Louis	1861-1936
Volk, Leonard Wells	1828-1895
Vonnoh, Robert William	1858-1933
Vuillard, Edward	1868-1940
Wadsworth, Edward	1889-1949
Walker, Henry Oliver	1843-1929
Walker, Horatio	1858-1938
Ward, Edward Matthew	1816-1879
Ward, John Quincy	
Adams	1830-1910
Warren, Whitney	1864-1943
Waterhouse, Alfred	1830-1905
Waterhouse, John William	1847-1917
Waterlow, Sir Ernst	
Albert	1850-1919
Watts, George Frederic	1817-1904
Wauters, Emile	1846-1933
Webb, Sir Aston	1849-1930
Webb, Philip Speakman	1831-1915
Weber, Max	1881-1961
Weir, Robert Walter	1803-1889
Weyr, Rudolf Von	1847-1914

Wheeler, Sir Charles	1892-
Whistler, James Abbott	
McNeill	1834-1903
White, Ethelbert	1891-
White, Stanford	1853-1906
Whymper, Edward	1840-1911
Willems, Florent Joseph	
Marie	1823-1905
Willette, Leon Adolphe	1857-1926
Willumsen, Jen Ferdinand	1863-1958
Woolner, Thomas	1826-1892
Wright, Frank Lloyd	1869-1959
Wyant, Alexander H.	1836-1892
Wyspianski, Stanislaw	1869-1907
Yeames, William Frederick	1835-1918
Yeats, Jack Butler	1871-1957
Young, Mahonri	
Mackintosh	1877-
Zadkine, Ossip	1890-
Ziem, Felix Francois	
George Philibert	1821-1911
Zorn, Anders	1860-1920
Zuloago, Ignacio	1870-1945

COMPOSERS

Abt, Franz	1819-1886
Albeniz, Isaac	1860-1909
Albert, Eugen Francis	
Charles d'	1864-1932
Alfano, Franco	1876-1954
Antheil, George	1900-1959
Arditi, Luigi	1822-1903
Arensky, Anton	
Stephanovich	1861-1906
Auber, Daniel Francois	
Esprit	1782-1871
Audran, Edmond	1842-1901
Auric, Georges	1899-
Balakirev, Milly	
Alexeivich	1836-1910
Bantock, Sir Granville	1868-1946
Bargiel, Woldemar	1828-1897
Barnby, Sir Joseph	1838-1896
Barnett, John	1802-1890
Barnett, John Francis	1837-1916
Bartok, Bela	1881-1945
Bax, Sir Arnold Edward	
Trevor	1883-1953
Beecham, Sir Thomas	1879-1964
Bendl, Karel	1838-1897
Benedict, Sir Julius	1804-1885
Benjamin, Arthur	1893-1960
Benoit, Pierre Leonard	
Leopold	1834-1901
Berg, Alban	1885-1935
Berlin, Irving	1888-

Berners, Gerald Hugh	
Tyrwhitt-Wilson	1883-1950
Bliss, Sir Arthur	1891-
Bloch, Ernest	1880-
Blom, Eric	1888-1959
Blumenthal, Jacob	1829-1908
Boelmann, Leon	1862-1897
Boito, Arriego	1842-1918
Borodin, Alexander	
Porfyrievich	1834-1887
Bottesini, Giovanni	1822-1889
Brahms, Johannes	1833-1897
Bridge, Frank	1879-1941
Bruch, Max	1838-1920
Bruckner, Anton	1824-1896
Bruneau, Alfred	1857-1934
Buck, Dudley	1839-1909
Burleigh, Henry Thaker	1866-1949
Busoni, Ferruccio	1866-1924
Cadman, Charles	
Wakefield	1881-1946
Carpenter, John Alden	1876-1951
Casals, Pablo	1876-
Casella, Alfred	1883-1947
Castelnuovo-Tedesco,	
Mario	1895-
Chabrier, Alexis	
Emmanuel	1841-1894
Chaminade, Cecile	1861-1944
Charpentier, Gustave	1860-1956
Chvala, Emmanuel	1851-1924
Chavez, Carlos	1899-

Clay, Frederic	1838-1889	Gounod, Charles	
Coates, Albert	1882-1953	Francois	1818-1893
Coates, Eric	1886-1958	Grainger, Percy Aldridge	1882-
Coleridge-Taylor, Samuel	1875-1912	Granados Y Campina,	
Costa, Sir Michael	1810-1884	Enrique	1867-1916
Cowell, Henry Dixon	1897-	Gretchaninov, Alexander	
Cowen, Sir Frederick		Tikhonovich	1864-1956
Hymen	1852-1935	Grieg, Edvard Hagerup	1843-1907
Cui, Cesar Antonovich	1835-1918	Grofé, Ferde	1892-
D'Albert, Eugen Francis		Gung'l, Josef	1810-1889
Charles	1864-1932	Haba, Alois	1893-
Damrosch, Leopold	1832-1885	Hadley, Henry Kimball	1871-1937
Davies, Sir Henry Walford	1869-1941	Handy, William	
Debussy, Claude Achille	1862-1918	Christopher	1873-1958
De Koven, Reginald	1861-1920	Hanson, Howard	1896-
Delibes, Clement Philibert		Harris, Roy	1898-
Leo	1836-1891	Harty, Sir Herbert	
Delius, Frederick	1863-1934	Hamilton	1880-1941
D'Indy, Paul Marie		Hatton, John Liptrot	1809-1886
Theodore Vincent	1851-1931	Heller, Stephen	1815-1888
Dohnanyi, Ernst Von	1877-1960	Henschel, Sir George	1850-1934
Dopper, Cornelis	1870-1939	Henselt, Adolf Von	1814-1889
Doppler, Albert Franz	1821-1883	Herbert, Victor	1859-1924
Dubois, Francois Clement		Herve, Florimond Rounger	1825-1892
Theodore	1837-1924	Herz, Henri	1806-1888
Dukas, Paul	1865-1935	Hiller, Ferdinand	1811-1885
Dunhill, Thomas		Hindemith, Paul	1895-1963
Frederick	1877-1946	Hofmann, Josef Casimir	1876-1957
Duparc, Henri	1848-1933	Holbrooke, Josef Charles	1878-1958
Durey, Louis	1888-	Holst, Gustave	1874-1934
Dvorak, Antonin	1841-1904	Honegger, Arthur	1892-1956
Eitner, Robert	1832-1905	Hubay, Geno De	1858-1937
Elgar, Sir Edward	1857-1934	Hullah, John Pyke	1812-1884
Elvey, Sir George Job	1816-1893	Humperdinck, Engelbert	1854-1921
Enesco, George	1881-1955	Ibert, Jacques	1890-
Engel, Carl	1883-1934	Ireland, John	1879-1962
Engel, Karl	1818-1882	Jacques-Dalcroze, Emile	1865-1950
Erlanger, Camille	1863-1919	Janacek, Leos	1854-1928
Falla, Manuel de	1876-1946	Jarnefelt, Edvard Armas	1869-1958
Faure, Gabriel	1845-1924	Jensen, Adolf	1837-1897
Fibich, Zdenko	1850-1900	Joachim, Joseph	1831-1907
Finck, Heinrich		Joncières, Victoria	1839-1903
Theophilus	1854-1926	Jongen, Joseph	1873-1953
Flotow, Friedrich		Kajanus, Robert	1856-1933
Frieherr Von	1812-1883	Karel, Rudolf	1880-
Foerster, Josef Bohuslav	1859-	Kern, Jerome	1885-1945
Foote, Arthur William	1853-1937	Kienzl, Wilhelm	1857-1941
Franck, Cesar	1822-1890	Kodaly, Zoltan	1882-
Franz, Robert	1815-1892	Korngold, Erich Wolfgang	1897-1957
Gade, Niels Vilhelm	1817-1890	Kovarovic, Karel	1862-1920
Gatty, Nicholas Comyn	1874-1946	Krenek, Ernst	1900-
German, Sir Edward	1862-1936	Kubelik, Jan	1880-1940
Gershwin, George	1898-1937	Lacomb, Louis Trouvillon	1818-1884
Glazunov, Alexander		Lalo, Edouard	1823-1892
Constantinovich	1865-1936	Lassen, Eduard	1830-1904
Godard, Benjamin	1849-1895	Lecocq, Alexandre	
Godowsky, Leopold	1870-1938	Charles	1832-1918
Goldmark, Karl	1832-1915	Lehar, Franz	1870-1948
Goosens, Eugene	1893-1962	Lekeu, Guillaume	1870-1894
Goss, Sir John	1800-1880	Lemmens, Nicolas Jacques	1823-1881

Leoncavallo, Ruggiero	1858-1919		Quilter, Roger	1877-1953
Liadov, Anatol	1855-1914		Rachmaninoff, Sergei	
Liszt, Franz	1811-1886		Vassilievitch	1873-1943
Loeffler, Charles Martin			Raff, Joseph Joachim	1822-1882
Tornov	1861-1935		Randegger, Alberto	1832-1911
Loucheur, Raymond	1899-		Rathaus, Kard	1895-1954
Maccun, Hamish	1868-1916		Ravel, Maurice	1875-1937
MacDowell, Edward			Reger, Max	1873-1916
Alexander	1861-1908		Reinecke, Carl Heinrich	
MacFarren, Sir George			Carsten	1824-1910
Alexander	1813-1887		Respighi, Ottorino	1879-1936
Mackenzie, Sir Alexander			Riegger, Wallingford	1885-
Campbell	1847-1935		Rimsky-Korsakov, Nicolai	
Mahler, Gustav	1860-1911		Andreievich	1844-1908
Malipiero G. Francesco	1882-		Rockstro, William Smith	1823-1895
Martinu, Bohuslar	1890-1959		Roger-Ducasse, Jean Jules	
Mascagni, Pietro	1863-1945		Aimable	1873-1954
Mason, Daniel Gregory	1873-1953		Rogers, Bernard	1893-
Massenet, Jules Emile			Ronald, Sir Landon	1873-1938
Frederic	1842-1912		Roussel, Albert	1869-1937
Medtner, Nikolai	1879-1951		Rubinstein, Anton	1829-1894
Mengelberg, Willem	1871-1951		Saint-Saens, Charles	
Merikanto, Oskar	1868-1924		Camille	1835-1921
Messager, Andre Charles			Satie, Erik Leslie	1866-1925
Prosper	1853-1929		Scharwenka, Xavier	1850-1924
Milhaud, Darius	1892-		Schnabel, Arthur	1882-1951
Monckton, Lionel	1861-1924		Schonberg, Arnold	1873-1951
Monk, William Henry	1823-1889		Schubert, Franz	1808-1878
Morris, Reginald Owen	1886-1948		Schumann, Clara	
Moszkowski, Moritz	1854-1925		Josephine	1819-1896
Mottl, Felix	1856-1911		Schumann, Robert	
Moussorgsky, Modest			Alexander	1810-1856
Petrovich	1835-1881		Scott, Cyril Meir	1879-
Napravnik, Edward	1839-1915		Scott, Francis George	1880-1958
Nevin, Ethelbert	1862-1901		Scriabin, Alexander	
Nielsen, Carl August	1865-1931		Nicholaevich	1872-1915
Novak, Viteslar	1870-1949		Sessions, Roger	1896-
Novello, Ivor	1893-1951		Sgambati, Giovanni	1843-1914
Nystrom, Gosta	1890-		Sibelius, Johan Julius	1865-1958
Offenbach, Jacques	1819-1880		Sinding, Christian	1856-1941
Orff, Carl	1895-		Smetana, Bedrich	1824-1884
Ornstein, Leo	1895-		Smyth, Dame Ethel Mary	1858-1944
Ouseley, Sir Frederick			Soderman, August Johan	1832-1876
Arthur	1825-1889		Somervell, Sir Arthur	1863-1937
Paderewski, Ignace Jan	1860-1941		Sousa, John Philip	1854-1932
Palmgren, Selim	1878-		Souza, Leo	1895-
Parker, Horatio William	1863-1919		Sowerby, Leo	1895-
Parry, Sir Charles Hubert			Spottiswoode, Alicia Ann	
Hastings	1848-1918		Lady John	1811-1900
Pedrell, Felipe	1841-1922		Stanford, Sir Charles	
Perosi, Lorenzo	1872-1956		Villiers	1852-1924
Pijper, Willem	1894-1947		Still, William Grant	1893-
Piston, Walter	1894-		Straus, Oscar	1870-1954
Pizzetti, Ildebrando	1880-		Strauss, Johann	
Planquette, Robert	1850-1903		the younger	1825-1899
Ponchielli, Amilcare	1834-1886		Strauss, Richard	1864-1949
Porter, Cole	1892-1963		Stravinsky, Igor	
Poulenc, Francis	1899-1963		Fedorovich	1882-
Prokofiev, Sergei	1891-1953		Suk, Joseph	1875-1935
Puccini, Giacomo	1858-1924		Sullivan, Sir Arthur	1842-1900

Suppé, Franz Von	1820-1895	Villa-Lobos, Heitor	1887-1959
Svendsen, Johan Severin	1840-1911	Vogel, Vladimir	1896-
Szymanowski, Karol	1883-1937	Vycpalek, Ladislav	1882-
Taneiev, Sergius	1856-1915	Wagner, Wilhelm Richard	1813-1883
Tcherepnin, Nicolai	1873-1945	Waldteufel, Emil	1837-1915
Thomas, Ambroise	1811-1896	Wallace, William	1860-1940
Thomas, Arthur Goring	1850-1892	Warlock, Peter	1894-1930
Thompson, Randall	1899-	Webern, Anton Von	1883-1945
Thomson, Virgil	1896-	Weill, Kurt	1900-1950
Thuille, Ludwig	1861-1907	Weinberger, Jaremir	1896-
Tommasini, Viscenzo	1880-	Weiner, Leo	1885-
Tosti, Sir Francesco Paolo	1846-1916	Weingartner, Felix	1863-1942
Tovey, Sir Donald Francis	1873-1940	Wesley, Samuel Sebastian	1810-1876
Tschaikovsky, Peter Ilyich	1840-1893	Widor, Charles Marie	1845-1937
Turina, Joaquin	1882-1949	Wolf, Hugo	1860-1903
Varese, Edgar	1885-	Wolf-Ferrari, Ermanno	1876-1948
Vaughan Williams, Ralph	1872-1958	Wood, Haydn	1882-1959
Verdi, Giuseppe		Zimbalist, Efrem	1889-
Fortunino Francesco	1813-1901		

INDEX

Clari, Giovanni Carlo Maria	1669-1745
Clark, William George	1821-1878
Clarke, Charles Cowden	1787-1877
Clarke, Edward Daniel	1769-1822
Clarke, Jeremiah	1659-1707
Clarke, Marcus Andrew Hislop	1846-1881
Clarke, Samuel	1675-1729
Clarke, Thomas Shields	1860-1920
Clauberg, Johann	1622-1665
Claude-Lorraine Claude Gelee	1600-1682
Claudel, Paul	1868-1955
Claudianus, Claudius	fl. 395
Claudius, Matthias	1740-1815
Claus, Emile	1849-1924
Clausen, Sir George	1852-1944
Claussen, Sophus, Niels Christen	1865-1931
Clausewitz, Karl von	1780-1831
Clay, Frederic	1838-1889
Clays, Paul Jean	1819-1900
Cleanthes	B.C. 301-232
Cleland, William	1661-1689
Clemenceau, George	1841-1929
Clemens, Samuel (see Mark Twain)	
Clement of Alexandria	c. 150
Clement, Francois	1714-1793
Clementi, Muzio	1752-1832
Cleve, Van Cornelis	1520-1567
Cleve, Van Jan	1646-1716
Cleve, Van Joos Van Der Beke	1480-1540
Cleveland, John	1613-1658
Cleveland, John	1747-1786
Cleveland, Robert	1747-1809
Clifford, William Kingdon	1845-1879
Clive, Caroline	1801-1879
Closterman, John	1656-1713
Clouet, François	d. 1572
Clouet, Jean	1485-1541
Clough, Arthur Hugh	1819-1861
Clowes, Sir William Laird	1856-1905
Cluwer, Philip	1580-1623
Coates, Albert	1882-1953
Coates, Eric	1886-1958
Coates, Wells Wintemute	1895-1958
Cobb, Irvin Shrewsbury	1876-1944
Cobbe, Frances Power	1822-1904
Cobbett, William	1763-1835
Cockburn, Alicia	1713-1794
Cocker, Edward	1631-1675
Cockerell, Charles Robert	1788-1863
Cockton, Henry	1807-1853
Cockx, Hieronymus	1510-1570
Cocteau, Jean	1891-1964
Codde, Pieter	1599-1678
Codinus, George	c. 1400

V

Coello, Alonso Sanchez	1515-1590
Coello, Antonio	1611-1652
Coello, Claudio	1630-1693
Cohan, George Michael	1878-1942
Cokain, Sir Aston	1608-1684
Colden, Cadwallader	1688-1776
Cole, Sir Henry	1808-1882
Cole, Thomas	1801-1848
Cole, Vicat	1833-1893
Coleman, George	1732-1794
Coleridge, Hartley	1796-1849
Coleridge, Sara	1802-1852
Coleridge, Samuel Taylor	1772-1834
Coleridge-Taylor, Samuel	1875-1912
Colet, Louise	1810-1876
Colette, Sidonie Gabrielle	1873-1954
Colins, Alexandre	1526-1612
Colle, Charles	1709-1783
Collett, Jacobine Camilla	1813-1895
Collier, Arthur	1680-1732
Collier, John	1708-1786
Collier, Hon. John	1850-1934
Collier, John Payne	1789-1883
Collin, Heinrich Joseph von	1771-1811
Collingwood, Robin George	1889-1943
Collin D'Harleville, Jean Francois	1755-1806
Collins, Charles Allston	1828-1873
Collins, Mortimer	1827-1876
Collins, William	1721-1759
Collins, William	1788-1847
Collins, William Wilkie	1824-1889
Colman, George	1732-1794
Colman, George the younger	1762-1836
Colman, Samuel	1832-1920
Colomb, Philip Howard	1831-1899
Colonna, Vittoria	1490-1547
Colum, Padraic	1881-
Columban	543-615
Combe, William	1741-1823
Comenius, Johann Amos	1592-1670
Comines, Philippe de	c. 1445-1509
Comte, Auguste	1798-1857
Conder, Charles	1868-1909
Condillac, Etienne Bonnot de	1715-1780
Condorcet (marquis de) Marie Jean Antoine	1743-1794
Confucius	B.C. 551-479
Congreve, William	1670-1729
Coninxloo, Gillis Van	1544-1605
Connelly, Marcus (Marc) Cook	1890-
Conrad, Joseph	1857-1924
Conrad, Noel	1899-
Conrad of Wurzburg	d. 1287
Conscience, Hendrik	1812-1883
Constable, Henry	1562-1613
Constable, John	1776-1837

Fabritius, Carel	1624-1654
Fabroni, Angelo	1732-1803
Fabyan, Robert	d. 1513
Faed, Thomas	1826-1900
Faesi, Robert	1883-
Fagan, James Bernard	1873-1933
Fagniez, Gustav Charles	1842-1927
Faguet, Emile	1847-1916
Fahlcrantz, Christian Erik	1790-1866
Fa Hsien	fl. 399-414
Fain, Agathon Jean	
Francois	1778-1837
Fairfax, Edward	1580-1635
Faistauer, Anton	1887-1930
Faithorne, William	1616-1691
Falcao, Cristovam	1512-1553
Falcone, Aniello	1600-1656
Falconer, William	1732-1769
Falconet, Ettienne Maurice	1716-1791
Falens, Karel van	1683-1733
Falguière, Jean Alexandre	
Joseph	1831-1900
Falk, Johann Daniel	1768-1826
Falkland, Lucius Cary	
Viscount	1610-1643
Falkberget, Johann Petter	1879-
Falke, Gustave	1853-1916
Falke, Johann Friedrich	
Gottlieb	1823-1876
Falla, Manuel de	1876-1946
Fallada, Hans	1893-1947
Fallmerayer, Jakob Phillip	1790-1861
Falloux, Frederic Alfred	
Pierre	1811-1886
Falls, Cyril Bentham	1888-
Fanshawe, Sir Richard	1608-1666
Fantin-Latour, Ignace Henri	
Jean Theodore	1836-1904
Farabi	870-950
Farazdaq	641-728
Faria Y Sousa, Manuel de	1590-1649
Farina, Salvatore	1846-1918
Farinato, Paolo	1524-1606
Farid Ud-Din Attar	1119-1229
Farini, Luigi Carlo	1812-1866
Farjeon, Benjamin Leopold	1838-1903
Farjeon, Eleanor	1881-1965
Farjeon, John Jefferson	1883-1958
Farmer, John	1565-1605
Farnaby, Giles	c. 1550-1600
Farnol, John Jeffrey	1878-1952
Farquhar, George	1677-1707
Farquharson, David	1840-1907
Farquharson, Joseph	1846-1935
Farrant, Richard	d. 1580
Farrere, Claude	1876-1957
Farrar, Frederic William	1831-1903
Farson, James Negley	1890-1960
Farvart, Charles Simon	1710-1792
Fasch, Johann Friedrich	1688-1758

Faulkner, William	
Harrison	1897-1962
Faure, Gabriel	1845-1924
Fauriel, Claude Charles	1782-1844
Favart, Charles Simon	1710-1792
Fawkes, Francis	1720-1777
Fazy, Henry	1842-1920
Fay, Andreas	1786-1864
Fechner, Gustav Theodore	1801-1887
Federer, Heinrich	1866-1928
Feininger, Lyonel	1871-1956
Feith, Rhijnvis	1753-1824
Fejer, Gyorgy	1766-1852
Felibien, Andre	1619-1695
Felltham, Owen	1602-1668
Fénelon, François de Salignac	
de la Mothe	1651-1715
Fenestella	B.C. 52-19 A.D.
Fenn, George Manville	1831-1909
Fenton, Elijah	1683-1730
Fenton, Sir Geoffrey	1539-1608
Ferber, Edna	1887-
Ferguson, Adam	1723-1816
Ferguson, Sir Samuel	1810-1886
Fergusson, James	1808-1886
Fergusson, Robert	1750-1774
Ferishta, Mohammed	
Kasim	1570-1611
Ferrabosco, Alfonso	d. 1628
Ferrari, Gaudenzio	1480-1546
Ferrari, Giuseppe	1812-1876
Ferrari, Paolo	1822-1889
Ferreira, Antonio	1528-1569
Ferrero, Guglielmo	1871-1942
Ferri, Ciro	1634-1689
Ferri, Luigi	1826-1895
Ferrier, Paul	1843-1920
Ferrier, Susan Edmonstone	1782-1854
Festa, Constanzo	1495-1545
Fetis, Francois Joseph	1784-1871
Feuchtersleben, Ernst	1806-1849
Feuchtwanger, Lion	1889-1958
Feurbach, Anselm	1829-1880
Feuerbach, Ludwig	
Andreas	1804-1872
Feuerbach, Paul Johann	
Anselm	1775-1833
Feuillet, Octave	1821-1890
Feval, Paul Henri Corentin	1817-1887
Feydeau, Ernest-Aime	1821-1873
Fibich, Zdenko	1850-1900
Fichte, Immanuel Herman	
von	1796-1879
Fichte, Johann Gottlieb	1762-1814
Ficino, Marsilio	1433-1499
Field, Eugene	1850-1895
Field, John	1782-1837
Field, Nathan	1587-1619
Fielding, Copley	1787-1855
Fielding, Henry	1707-1754

Gore, Catherine Grace	
Frances	1799-1861
Gorgias	B.C. 485-380
Gorky, Maxim	1868-1936
Gorres, Joseph von	1776-1848
Gorst, Harold	1868-1950
Gorter, Hermann	1864-1933
Goss, Sir John	1800-1880
Gosse, Sir Edmond	1849-1928
Gossec, Francois Joseph	1734-1829
Gosson, Stephen	1554-1624
Gotter, Friedrich Wilhelm	1746-1797
Gottfried Von Strassburg	fl. 1200
Gottschall, Rudolf Von	1823-1908
Gottsched, Johann	
Christoph	1700-1766
Gotz, Johann Nikolaus	1721-1781
Goudimel, Claude	1510-1572
Goujon, Jean	1520-1566
Gould, John	1804-1881
Gould, Nathaniel	1857-1919
Gounod, Charles Francois	1818-1893
Gourmont, Remy de	1858-1915
Gow, Niel	1727-1807
Gower, John	d. 1408
Goya Y Lucientes,	
Francisco	1746-1828
Goyen, Jan Josephszoon	
van	1596-1656
Gozlan, Leon	1803-1866
Gozzi, Carlo	1720-1806
Gozzoli, Benozzo	1420-1497
Grabbe, Christian Dietrich	1801-1836
Gracian Y Morales,	
Baltazar	1601-1658
Graf, Arturo	1848-1913
Grafly, Charles	1862-1929
Grahame, Kenneth	1859-1922
Grainger, Percy Aldridge	1882-1961
Granados Y Campina,	
Enrique	1867-1916
Grand, Sarah	1862-1943
Granet, Francois Marius	1775-1849
Grant, Anne	1755-1838
Grant, Duncan	1885-
Grant, Sir Francis	1803-1878
Grant, James	1822-1887
Graves, Richard	1715-1804
Granville-Barker, Harley	
Granville	1877-1946
Gratz, Heinrich	1817-1891
Graun, Karl Heinrich	1701-1759
Graves, Alfred Percival	1846-1931
Graves, Richard	1715-1804
Graves, Robert Ranke	1895-
Gray, David	1838-1861
Gray, Thomas	1716-1771
Grazzini, Antonio Francesco	1503-1583
Greco El (see Theotocopouli)	
Green, John Richard	1837-1883

Green, Julian	1900-
Green, Mary Ann Everett	1818-1895
Green, Matthew	1696-1737
Green, Thomas Hill	1836-1882
Greene, Robert	1558-1592
Greene, George Washington	1811-1883
Greene, Maurice	1695-1755
Greenough, Horatio	1805-1852
Greenaway, Kate	1846-1901
Gregoras, Nicephorus	1295-1360
Greg, William Rathbone	1809-1881
Gregorovius, Ferdinand	1821-1891
Gregory, Edward John	1850-1909
Gregory, Isabella Augusta	1852-1932
Gregory, St. of Tours	538-594
Grenfell, Julian	1888-1915
Gresset, Jean Baptiste	
Louis	1709-1777
Gretchaninov, Alexander	
Tikhonovich	1864-1956
Gretry, Andre Ernest	
Modeste	1741-1813
Greuze, Jean Baptiste	1725-1805
Greville, Charles Cavendish	
Fulke	1794-1865
Greville, Sir Fulke	1554-1628
Greville, Henry (Alice	
Durond)	1842-1902
Grevin, Jacques	1539-1570
Grey, Zane	1872-1939
Griboyedov, Alexander	
Sergeyevitch	1795-1829
Grieg, Edvard Hagerup	1843-1907
Griffin, Gerald	1803-1840
Grigorovich, Dmitri	
Vaslievich	1822-1900
Grimald, Nicholas	1519-1562
Grimaldi, Giovanni	
Francesco	1606-1680
Grimm, Friedrich	
Melchior	1723-1807
Grimm, Jacob Ludwig	
Carl	1785-1863
Grimm, Wilhelm Carl	1786-1859
Grimmelshausen, Hans Jakob	
Christoff Felvon	1625-1676
Gringoire, Pierre	1475-1539
Gris, Juan	1887-1927
Grofé, Ferde	1892-
Gromaire, Marcel	1892-
Groome, Francis Hindes	1851-1902
Gropius, Walter	1883-
Gros, Antoine Jean	1771-1835
Grosseteste, Robert	c. 1175-1253
Grossi, Tommaso	1791-1853
Grossmith, George	1847-1912
Grossmith, Weedon	1853-1919
Grosz, George	1893-1959
Grote, George	1794-1871
Grotius, Hugo	1583-1645

Grub, George 1812-1892
Grundtvig, Nikolai
  Frederik Severin 1783-1872
Grundy, Sydney 1848-1914
Grunewald, Isaak 1889-1946
Grunewald, Mathias 1500-1530
Gryphius, Andreas 1616-1664
Guardi, Francesco 1712-1793
Guarini, Giovanni Battista 1538-1612
Gubernatis, Angelo de 1840-1913
Gudin, Theodore 1802-1880
Guedalla, Philip 1889-1944
Guercino 1590-1666
Guericke, Otto Von 1602-1682
Guerin, Charles 1873-1907
Guerin, Pierre Narcisse 1774-1833
Guerin Du Cayla, Georges
  Maurice de 1810-1839
Guerrazzi, Francesco
  Domenico 1804-1873
Guerrero, Francisco 1528-1599
Guerrini, Olindo 1845-1916
Guest, Edgar Albert 1881-1959
Guest, Edwin 1800-1880
Guevara, Antonio de 1490-1545
Guevara, Luis Velez de 1570-1644
Guiart, Guillaume -1316
Guicciardini, Francesco 1483-1540
Guicciardini, Giovanni 1480-1541
Guidi, Carlo Alessandro 1650-1712
Guidiccioni, Giovanni 1480-1541
Guido Aretinus of Arezzo 990-1050
Guido, Reni 1575-1642
Guillamin, Armand 1841-1927
Guillaume, Jean Baptiste
  Claude Eugene 1822-1905
Guillaume, De Lorris c. 1230
Guillaume de Machaut, see Machaut
Guimera, Angel 1849-1924
Gumilev, Nikolai
  Stepanovich 1886-1921
Guitry, Sacha 1885-1957
Guittone D'Arezzo 1230-1294
Guizot, Francois Pierre
  Guillaume 1787-1874
Gundulic, Ivan 1588-1638
Gung'l, Josef 1810-1889
Gunn, James 1893-
Gunn, Neil Miller 1891-
Gunther, Johann Christian 1695-1723
Gurdjieff, George
  Ivanovitch 1868-1949
Guthrie, Sir James 1859-1930
Guthrie, Thomas Anstey 1856-1934
Gutschmid, Alfred 1835-1887
Gutzkow, Karl Ferdinand 1811-1878
Guyau, Jean Marie 1854-1888
Guyon, Jeanne Marie
  Bouvier de la Mothe 1648-1717
Guys, Constantin 1805-1892

Gwilt, Joseph 1784-1863
Gyongyosi, Istvan 1620-1704
Gyllembourg-Ehrensvard,
  Thomasine Christine 1773-1856
Gyp 1849-1932

Haag, Carl 1820-1915
Haas, Johannes Hubertus
  Leonhardus de 1832-1908
Haba, Alois 1893-
Habberton, John 1842-1921
Habermann, Hugo Freiherr
  Von 1849-1929
Habington, William 1605-1654
Hacker, Arthur 1858-1919
Hacklander, Friedrich
  Wilhelm von 1816-1877
Hadley, Henry Kimball 1871-1937
Hafiz fl. 1388
Hagedorn, Friedrich von 1708-1754
Hagenbach, Karl Rudolf 1801-1874
Haggard, Sir Henry Rider 1856-1925
Hahn-Hahn, Ida 1805-1880
Haider, Karl 1846-1912
Hajji, Khalifa c. 1599-1658
Hake, Edward 1579-
Hake, Thomas Gordon 1809-1895
Hakluyt, Richard 1552-1616
Haldane, Elizabeth
  Sanderson 1862-1937
Haldane, Richard Burdon
  Haldane 1856-1928
Hale, Edward Everett 1822-1909
Hale, Sarah Josepha 1788-1879
Hales, John d. 1571
Halevi, Judah Ben
  Samuel c. 1085-1140
Halevy, Daniel 1872-1962
Halevy, Elie 1870-1937
Halevy, Jacques Francois 1799-1862
Halevy, Jean 1804-1883
Halevy, Ludovic 1834-1908
Haliburton, Thomas
  Chandler 1796-1865
Halifax, Charles Montague 1661-1715
Hall, Anna Maria 1800-1881
Hall, Basil 1788-1844
Hall, Edward 1499-1547
Hall, Joseph 1574-1656
Hall, Marguerite Radcliffe 1886-1943
Hall, Samuel Carter 1800-1889
Hall, William Edward 1835-1894
Hallam, Henry 1777-1859
Hallé, Adam De La 1235-1287
Halleck, Fitz-Greene 1790-1867
Hallgrimsson, Jonas 1807-1845
Halliday, Andrew 1830-1877
Hals, Frans 1580-1666

W

Rydberg, Abraham Viktor 1828-1895
Ryder, Albert Pinkham 1847-1917
Ryle, Gilbert 1900-
Rymer, Thomas 1641-1713
Rysbrack, Michael 1693-1770

Sabatier, Paul 1858-1928
Sabatini, Rafael 1875-1950
Sacchetti, Franco 1330-1400
Sacchi, Andrea 1600-1661
Sacchini, Antonio
  Maria Gaspare 1734-1786
Sachs, Hans 1494-1576
Sackville, Thomas
  (1st Earl of Dorset) 1530-1608
Sackville-West, Victoria
  May 1892-1962
Sade (marquis de),
  Donatien Alphonse
  Francois 1740-1814
Sa De Miranda,
  Fransisco de 1485-1558
Sa'di 1184-1291
Sadleir, Michael 1888-1957
Safarik, Pavel Josef 1795-1861
Saint-Amant, Marc
  Antoine de Girard 1594-1661
Sainte-Beuve, Charles
  Augustin 1804-1869
Saint Evremond, Charles
  Marquet de Saint Denis
  Segmieur de 1610-1703
Saint-Exupery, Antoine de 1900-1944
Saintine, Joseph Xavier 1798-1865
Saint-John, Perse 1887-
Saint-Lambert, Jean
  Francois de 1716-1803
Saint-Marc, Girardon 1801-1873
Saint-Martin, Louis
  Claude de 1743-1803
Saint-Pierre, Bernadin de 1737-1814
Saint-Pierre, Charles
  Irenee Castel 1658-1743
Saint-Real, Cesar
  Vichard Abbé de 1631-1692
Saint-Saens, Charles
  Camille 1835-1921
Saintsbury, George
  Edward Bateman 1845-1933
Saint-Simon, Louis de
  Rouvroy 1675-1755
Sala, George Augustin
  Henri 1828-1895
Salieri, Antonio 1750-1825
Salisbury, Frank Owen 1874-1957
Sallust B.C. 86-34
Salomon, Johann Peter 1745-1815
Salten, Felix 1869-1945

Saltykov, Michael
  Evgrafovich 1826-1889
Salvemini, Gaetano 1873-
Samain, Albert Victor 1858-1900
Sand, George (Dudevant) 1804-1876
Sanday, William 1843-1920
Sandburg, Carl 1878-
Sandby, Paul 1725-1809
Sandeau, Leonard
  Sylvain Julien 1811-1883
Sanders, Nicholas 1530-1581
Sandrart, Joachim van 1606-1688
Sandys, George 1578-1644
Sanmichele, Michele 1484-1559
Sannazaro, Pacopo 1458-1530
Sansovino, Andrea
  Contucci del Monte 1460-1529
Sansovino, Jacopo 1486-1570
Sant, James 1820-1916
Santayana, George 1863-1952
Santine, Joseph Xavier 1798-1865
Sanuto, Marino 1466-1533
Sappho c. B.C. 600
Sarasin, Jean Francois 1614-1654
Sardou, Victorien 1831-1908
Sargent, John Singer 1856-1925
Sarmiento, Domingo
  Faustino 1811-1888
Sarrazin, Jacques 1588-1660
Sarti, Giuseppe 1729-1802
Sarto, Andrea del 1486-1531
Sasseta, Stefano Di
  Giovanni 1392-1450
Sassoferato 1605-1685
Sassoon, Siegfried
  Lorraine 1886-
Satie, Erik Leslie 1866-1925
Savage, Richard 1697-1743
Savonarola, Girolamo 1452-1498
Saxe, John Godfrey 1816-1887
Saxo Grammaticus c. 1150-1206
Sayers, Dorothy L. 1893-1957
Scarlatti, Alessandro 1659-1725
Scarlatti, Guiseppe
  Domenico 1685-1757
Scarron, Paul 1610-1660
Sceve, Maurice 1500-1564
Schadow, Friedrich
  Wilhelm 1798-1862
Schadow, Johann
  Gottfried 1764-1850
Schadow, Rudolf 1786-1822
Schaffner, Jakob 1875-1944
Scharwenka, Xavier 1850-1924
Scheemakers, Pieter 1691-1770
Scheffel, Joseph
  Viktor von 1826-1886
Scheffer, Ary 1795-1858
Schelling, Friedrich
  Wilhelm Joseph von 1775-1854

San Jose Bible College
Memorial Library

Presented by
Friends and relatives

In memory of

JOHN PERRY
Santa Rosa